Semantics of Programming Languages

Foundations of Computing

Michael Garey and Albert Meyer, editors

Semantics of Programming Languages
Structures and Techniques

Carl A. Gunter

The MIT Press
Cambridge, Massachusetts
London, England

DEDICATION

to the memory of Charles R. Carter

Library of Congress Cataloging-in-Publication Data

Gunter, Carl A.
    Semantics of programming languages : structures and techniques
  Carl A. Gunter.
        p.   cm. -- (Foundations of computing)
    Includes bibliographical references and index.
    ISBN 0-262-07143-6
    1. Programming languages (Electronic computers)--Semantics.
  I. Title. II. Series.
  QA76.7.G86   1992
  005.13--dc20   92-10172
                                                            CIP

Contents

List of Figures

List of Tables

Series Foreword

Theoretical computer science has now undergone several decades of development. The "classical" topics of automata theory, formal languages, and computational complexity have become firmly established, and their importance to other theoretical work and to practice is widely recognized. Stimulated by technological advances, theoreticians have been rapidly expanding the areas under study, and the time delay between theoretical progress and its practical impact has been decreasing dramatically. Much publicity has been given recently to breakthroughs in cryptography and linear programming, and steady progress is being made on programming language semantics, computational geometry, and efficient data structures. Newer, more speculative, areas of study include relational databases, VLSI theory, and parallel and distributed computation. As this list of topics continues expanding, it is becoming more and more difficult to stay abreast of the progress that is being made and increasingly important that the most significant work be distilled and communicated in a manner that will facilitate further research and application of this work. By publishing comprehensive books and specialized monographs on the theoretical aspects of computer science, the series on Foundations of Computing provides a forum in which important research topics can be presented in their entirety and placed in perspective for researchers, students, and practitioners alike.

Michael R. Garey
Albert R. Meyer

Preface

This book expounds the basic motivations and philosophy underlying the applications of semantic techniques in programming language theory. There is an emphasis on the structures used in semantics and the techniques that have been developed for relating various approaches to the semantics of programming languages, particularly for languages with higher-order functions. Type systems are the central organizational theme of the discussion.

The book is designed as a text for upper-level and graduate-level students from all areas of computer science; it should also be useful to anyone needing an easily accessed description of fundamental results and calculi from the semantics of programming languages. Some of the primary topics covered here include models of types, operational semantics, category theory, domain theory, fixed-point (denotational) semantics, full abstraction and other semantic correspondence criteria, relationships between types and evaluation, type checking and inference, subtypes, and parametric polymorphism.

As a set of general prerequisites for the book I assume familiarity with the basic concepts of programming languages such as variable binding and scope, evaluation, and parsing. Some familiarity with interpreters and compilers is also expected. Ideally, a multi-lingual student should know something about Lisp (or Scheme), Prolog, and an imperative language such as Pascal or C. Knowledge of a language based on the typed λ-calculus such as ML or Haskell would be helpful (especially for Chapter 7) but it is not assumed. The text by Paulson [189] is a representative discussion of ML programming. For computer science students, this book can serve as an introduction to the mathematical techniques used in the study of programming languages. Some mathematical sophistication is essential, but I have limited the prerequisites to what a student should have encountered already in an undergraduate course on logic or abstract algebra. In summary, general familiarity with a representative from each of the following groups of texts forms an ideal background: the texts of Aho, Sethi, and Ullman [8] or Fischer and LeBlanc [80] for compilers and interpreters; the texts of Sethi [232], Kamin [134], or Friedman, Wand, and Haynes [83] for comparative programming languages; the texts by Boolos and Jeffrey [33] or Lewis and Papadimitriou [152] for logic.

The book consists of eleven chapters. The first chapter is an introduction. The second and third chapters are about the simply-typed λ-calculus without recursive definitions from the perspective of environment models and categorical models respectively. The fourth chapter is about the semantics of recursively defined functions. The fifth chapter is an introduction to domain theory, and the sixth applies some of these ideas to the semantics of programming languages. The seventh chapter is about types and their relationship to the evaluation of computer programs. The eighth chapter focuses on universal domains and how they can be used to model types. The ninth discusses subtype polymorphism. The tenth chapter is about more advanced aspects of domain theory and category theory. These ideas are applied to the semantics of polymorphism in the eleventh chapter.

In general, the contents of the book is self-contained with enough information that a diligent reader can derive full proofs of all the results with enough time, pencils, and paper. At the end of each chapter there is a section of notes in which references to work related to the topic of the chapter are given. It is impossible to list all of the relevant literature in these notes, so the citations there should be viewed as a starting point rather than a definitive enumeration of the noteworthy contributions on a topic. I have focused on citing works that can be found in most libraries, especially seminal works, surveys, up-to-date expository treatments, and works with good bibliographies. When a citation to one work is included while another is omitted, this usually reflects an unavoidable arbitrariness rather than a commentary on my part.

Since students learn best when they interact with the material presented, a wide selection of exercises have been provided at the ends of the sections in which the definitions and methods they draw upon are stated. Those which, for some reason, I felt were slightly harder than average for the point at which they appear are marked with an asterisk*. The exercises in this book have drawn on the collective experience of many people who have taught the semantics of programming languages to students.

Most users of this book will not choose to read it by starting on page one and reading each successive page until they reach the end. Teachers will find the amount of the material here is too much to cover in a typical course on the subject, even when teacher and students are especially quick. A sequence that covers a basic core of concepts might include Chapters 1, 2, and all but the last section of 4. A more substantial program might include additional material on relating operational and fixed-point semantics (the first section of Chapter 5 together with Chapter 6) and/or material on the relationship between typing disciplines and evaluation in Chapter 7. For either of these approaches it will be necessary for an instructor to fill in a little background from omitted parts of the book (for example, a nodding acquaintance with cartesian closed categories, as defined in Section 3.1, is needed to understand Section 5.1). My personal preference is to cover most of Chapters 1-6 and then Chapter 7 if time permits. The last two chapters, which discuss domain theory and polymorphism, are more demanding the the first nine chapters.

I have made an effort to see that the work will be useful for general reference as well as teaching. A reader interested only in how the full abstraction is proved for PCF, for example, will find references to full abstraction in the Subject Index, a listing of the typing and operational rules for PCF in the List of Tables, and a guide to the notations used in the proof of full abstraction in the List of Notations. Particular care has been taken to provide a system of tables that can be consulted efficiently while still being distributed through the text in the places where rules are discussed in detail. For example, to find the typing rules for the polymorphic λ-calculus, begin by consulting the table listed for that calculus in the List of Tables; it is Table 11.2 on page 362. On page 362, the text discusses these rules in detail and says that the polymorphic calculus includes the rules in Table 11.2 together with the rules that appear in Table 2.1. These were the rules given for the simply-typed calculus; they can be found on page 38 according to the List of Tables. It is important to understand the 'binding convention' when tables are related in this way: to get the full set of rules for the polymorphic λ-calculus, assume that the rules in Table 11.2 are simply augmented by the text that appears in Table 2.1. The meanings of expressions appearing in the earlier table are to be taken in the context of the later one—like a kind of dynamic binding or macro expansion. This convention for understanding sets of rules for calculi stresses the relationships between different systems while making it possible to avoid tiresome repetitions of rules and indigestible appendices.

Many people contributed to the development of this book. I had suggestions and comments from more colleagues than I could possibly name, so let me just offer my general thanks to those who have contributed. Several people offered me detailed historical notes, suggestions for exercises, and outlines of arguments that would fit my exposition well. I especially thank Jon Riecke and Albert Meyer for their steady assistance on this project. They and other people who used parts of draft copies of **Structures and Techniques** in courses they taught provided valuable assistance through the wisdom obtained from their experience; for this I also thank Felice Cardone and Mario Coppo, Neil Jones, Jean Gallier, Gary Leavens, Dave MacQueen, and Mitch Wand for their feedback. Many people, especially students, have picked through the details of the text and conveyed their experience about what was easy to understand and what was not. I appreciated their facility in locating errors in drafts of the text. While complete freedom from error is probably impossible in a document like this, it is much closer to perfection than it would have been without their aid. Let me especially thank Peter Baumann, Philippe de Groote, Trevor Jim, Achim Jung, Anthony Kosky, Leonid Libkin, Ray McDowell, John Mitchell, Allen Stoughton, Ramesh Subrahmanyam, Myra VanInwegen, and Limsoon Wong. Some of these people also contributed valuable exercises and examples. I also appreciated referee reports from various reviewers who studied a draft of the book while it was being considered for publication and the copy editing of Jenya Weinreb of MIT Press.

Among the acknowledgements appearing in a book one often finds a note about the patience displayed by the spouse of the author over the years during which the book was written. After more than two years of work on **Structures and Techniques** I now appreciate the stress that a work like this can put on the people close to the author. My own spouse, Elsa Gunter, has not only been extremely patient with me, she has also made numerous contributions to the work itself. Several of the arguments, exercises, and examples in text were contributed by her or came from discussions we have had. She also did much of the thorough and objective proof-reading that an author finds difficult to perform. I owe her my deepest thanks for her contribution to this document.

Semantics of Programming Languages

1 Introduction

The word 'semantics' was introduced in a book of Michel Bréal published in 1900; in that work it refers to the study of how words change their meanings. Subsequently 'semantics' has also changed its meaning, and it is now generally defined as the study of the attachment between the words and sentences of a language (written or spoken) and their meanings. The most established lines of investigation of semantics lie in the areas of linguistics and philosophy that study the meanings of sentences of natural language. A second area of study of semantics focuses on the meanings of sentences in the formal languages of mathematical logic, originally designed to serve as a foundation for general mathematics. This book is devoted to a discussion of topics from a third area of semantics that focuses on developing ways to express the semantics of languages used for programming electronic digital computers. We will be especially concerned with the application of ideas from semantics in mathematical logic toward achieving the goals of the semantics of programming languages.

1.1 Semantics

The methods and objectives of semantics of programming languages are different in many ways from those of the semantics of natural language and mathematical logic but borrow a great deal from the work in these areas. Traditionally, computer languages have been viewed as based on imperative sentences for issuing commands. In natural language the analogous sentences are like those that might be found in a recipe book: 'beat the egg whites until they are stiff'. By contrast, the sentences of mathematical logics are intended to assert timeless truths: 'if beaten, egg whites stiffen'. Much of the current research in methods for reasoning about programs seeks to formalize the relationship between examples such as these—after all, the assertion about the beating of egg whites means that the chef obeying the command from the recipe book will see a successful termination to his labors (although nothing is explicitly said about how tired his arm will be at the end). Moreover, a great deal of current research in programming language design aims at blurring the distinction between a program as a set of instructions and a program as an assertion about the desired answer. This idea is embodied in terms like 'declarative programming' and 'executable specification'. For example, the following pair of assertions (clauses) are a definition of a relation in Prolog syntax:

```
gcd(X,0,X).
gcd(X,Y,Gcd) :- mod(X,Y,Z), gcd(Y,Z,Gcd).
```

Given that mod(X,Y,Z) means that Z is the remainder of X divided by Y, the usual semantics of first-order logic provides a meaning for gcd as the unique relation that satisfies these two formulas (for non-negative values of the identifiers). It is an aim of Prolog programming methodology that one think of the program in these terms whenever possible. In this case the evaluator for Prolog makes it possible to use the program above to calculate a binary function on numbers using the relation **gcd**. Thus these clauses are a piece of logic that has an algorithmic content. Unfortunately, it will not be the case that every assertion in first order logic can be given a similar algorithmic interpretation derived by the Prolog interpreter. The explanation of what a program is required to compute does not necessarily provide an algorithm for computing it. In particular, the *greatest common divisor* of x and y is typically defined as the largest number z such that z divides both x and y. It is not hard to show that this definition is meaningful in the sense that there is a unique relation on numbers that satisfies it. However, this definition does not easily admit the efficient algorithmic interpretation that Prolog endows on the definition of **gcd** despite the fact that both describe the same relation. What Prolog offers beyond a syntax for defining a relation is an algorithm for computing values that satisfy it. The semantics of the Prolog clauses as first-order formulas does not always coincide with the results of this algorithm, but when they do coincide, they offer two different views of the meaning of the program, each having its own advantages in how the programmer wants to understand what has been coded.

Other examples of programs that can be dually viewed as commands or assertions arise as recursive definitions of procedures. The following program codes the greatest common divisor function in the Scheme programming language:

```
(define (gcd x y)
  (if (= y 0)
      x
      (gcd y (rem x y))))
```

Rather than two formulas, the definition has the appearance of an equation

$$\gcd(x, y) = \cdots \gcd \cdots$$

in which the defined function appears on the right-hand side as well as the left. Assuming that the arguments are non-negative, this equation has a unique solution; this solution can be viewed as the meaning of **gcd**. The defining equation is special though since it provides a way to calculate the greatest common divisor following an algorithm defined by the Scheme interpreter. This provides two alternate semantics for the program, each describing the same function but in different ways.

It is also possible to view 'imperative' programming language commands as assertions by thinking of them as asserting a relation between the state of the computer before the execution of the command and the state after its execution. For example, the command x := x+1 can be viewed as an order to the machine: 'take the value in the location x and add one to it, then place the resulting value in the location x'. But it may also be viewed as a relation between the contents of memory locations: an input state is related to an output state via the relation defined by this assignment if the value contained in x in the output is one plus the value stored there in the input (and the state is otherwise unaltered). This relational interpretation of program fragments can be generalized by interpreting a command as a relation between *properties* of input and output values.

The languages of mathematical logic and programming languages share the feature that they are 'artificial' languages distinct from the 'natural' language of everyday writing and discourse. This has an effect on the methodology that is employed in these areas. Natural language research draws from the existing body of spoken and written languages; work in natural language semantics seeks to understand how native speakers attach meaning to their sentences—the ear and intuition of the native speaker is the ultimate authority on what is a correct sentence and what the sentence means. Although grammarians can advise on the proper use of words and their arrangement into pleasing and correct sentences, even the *Académie Française* cannot be credited with designing a natural language. By contrast, the formal languages of logic and programming are synthesized by logicians and computer scientists to meet more or less specific design criteria.

Before discussing some of the consequences of this difference, let us first consider how much similarity there is between work on designing artificial languages and work on understanding natural languages. It is reasonable to view the aim of research in logic (at least during the middle of the twentieth century) as an attempt to formalize the language of mathematicians and formulate axioms and rules capturing the methods of proof in mathematics. If the arguments of mathematicians are viewed as a specialized form of the use of natural language, then this provides some analogy with the work of linguists. At this point in time, it is possible to take a proof written by a mathematician in English (say) and formulate *essentially* the same proof in first-order logic, second-order logic, Church's higher-order logic, or some similar language. Moreover, there are successful efforts to design formal languages capable of turning a mathematical textbook into something that looks like a computer program (although this cannot currently be done automatically). Such a translation ignores the motivations and intuitions as well as the jokes (of which there are few in most mathematics texts anyway) but captures a degree of detail that any mathematician would consider to be sufficient for a proof.

Research on the semantics of programming languages has also had its similarities to the study of natural language. Many approaches to the semantics of programming languages have been offered as tools for language design, but rather often these sometimes meritorious and sometimes over-idealistic approaches have been ignored by the committees responsible for language designs. This has often led to post-design analyses of the semantics of programming languages wherein the syntax of the language is treated as given. A semantics is also given, in some more or less reasonable form. The goal then is to understand the semantics of the language in another way or to sort out anomalies, omissions, or defects in the given semantics. Examples of this kind of analysis have occurred for virtually every programming language in widespread use, and a partial list of papers published in pursuit of such endeavors could fill fifty pages of references at the end of this book. As a result, it is sometimes felt that research in semantics has had less impact on language design than it should have had. While there is probably truth in this, it is also the case that no successful language has been designed without some serious consideration of how the meanings of programs will be best described. Every programmer must understand the meanings of the language constructs he uses at *some* level of abstraction and detail. Post-design analysis of the semantics is reasonable and necessary because there are many different forms of semantic description serving different purposes; it is unlikely that any language can be designed that is optimally understandable in terms of all of them, and it is probably infeasible to investigate all of the myriad descriptive techniques in the course of a given language design. Hence work on the semantics of programming languages will often share with that on natural language the characteristics that the language is given and its explanation is the goal of research.

Despite these similarities, the difference between the studies of natural and artificial languages is profound. Perhaps the most basic characteristic of this distinction is the fact that an artificial language can be fully circumscribed and studied in its entirety. Throughout this book there are tables that hold the grammar, rules, and semantics of artificial languages. These tables furnish the bottom line for the definition of the language; assertions about the language must be justified in terms of them. For this reason, many of the proofs that will be given proceed by cases (usually with an inductive hypothesis) demonstrating the truth of some claim about the language as a whole by justifying it for each of the constructions allowed by its rules for legitimate formation of expressions.

A particularly beneficial aspect of the ability to design a language comes from the opportunity to separate concerns in a way that will simplify the analysis of the language. What is lost by such separations is open to debate, but the techniques have been developed through extensive experience. Perhaps the most important example of a simplification of this kind is the separation of the grammar of a programming language from its semantics. In the simplest case, a language is specified as a sequence of characters, and it is specified how such a sequence of characters is to be divided into tokens (basic lexical units). A set of rules is given for how a sequence of tokens is formed into a parse tree (or rejected if the sequence is illegitimate in some way). Then, finally, a semantics is assigned to parse trees built in this way.[1] This all sounds very reasonable to most computer scientists, but it is worthwhile to reflect that one of the real challenges in the parsing of natural language sentences comes from the fact that the meanings of words seem to influence the correct parsing of a sentence. A well-known example illustrating the problem is the following pair of grammatically correct and sensible English sentences:

> Time flies like an arrow.
> Fruit flies like a banana.

In the first sentence, 'flies' is a verb, and the subject of the sentence is 'time' whereas in the second sentence, 'flies' is a noun. In the first sentence 'like an arrow' is an adverbial phrase indicating how time flies whereas 'like' is a verb in the second sentence with 'a banana' as its object. Why do I think this is the right way to parse these sentences? Reversing the way the sentences are parsed brings up semantic questions: what are 'time flies' (some things that like an arrow, I suppose) and what does it mean to fly like a banana? The problem of what is the interaction between syntax and semantics in natural language is an ongoing topic of research. Perhaps the mechanisms whereby natural language combines parsing with semantics could be useful in artificial language design, but for now it seems that logicians and the designers of programming languages are happy to steer clear of this complexity.

Since artificial languages are engineered rather than given, choosing the best constructions from a wide range of possibilities is a central objective. To do this, it is essential to develop ways to compare different languages and explore how one language may serve a given purpose better than another. Work on the parsing of artificial languages has achieved considerable success in understanding the alternatives for syntax. The most useful methods for specifying grammars have been identified, and algorithms for constructing parse trees have been carefully studied. This generality has benefited the engineering side of language design by providing widely-used tools for the construction of quality lexers and parsers automatically from specifications of the tokens and grammar of a language. The semantic side of language design is now the primary challenge. The development of abstractions for describing the range of possibilities for the semantics of languages has been much harder to achieve than the corresponding development for syntax. Many semantic frameworks have been developed, but there is no universal acceptance of any particular approach.

---

[1] This is an approximation of what happens in practice. For example, it may be that only those parse trees that satisfy certain typing rules are considered to have a semantics. Moreover, the situation can be even more complex if the rules for verifying that a program is well-typed are also used in giving the semantics. These subtleties will later be discussed in detail.

What purpose is served by the semantics of a language? For natural language, the answer seems almost too obvious to state except as another question: what use could be made of a sentence without meaning? If I am told, 'turn right at the next light and you'll see a sign on your left', then my subsequent behavior will depend on what object is denoted by the 'next light', what I think the directions 'right' and 'left' are, what the acts of turning and seeing are, and so on. In mathematical logic, meaning is formalized in the notion of a *model*, which is a mathematical entity like the natural numbers, the complexes, or the quaternions. A logic provides a syntax for asserting facts about the model based on an interpretation of the symbols of the syntax in the model. Ordinarily, the model is the primary object of attention, and the syntax is a tool for its study. For example, the first-order theory of *real closed fields* is a set of axioms from which every first-order fact true of the real numbers can be derived using the laws of first-order logic. This theory is decidable, so any assertion about the reals that can be expressed with a first-order sentence could be established or refuted by submitting it to a computer program that can decide, in principle,[2] whether it is a consequence of the real closed field axioms. Another example of an important model is that of the natural numbers, but a theorem of Kurt Gödel has shown that the first-order theorems that are true of this model (in a language that includes basic operations like addition and multiplication) cannot be decided by a computer. This result has had profound implications, but it is counterbalanced by the existence of a first-order set of axioms, called *Peano arithmetic*, from which many facts about the numbers can be derived—indeed, simple examples of truths about the natural numbers that are not provable from the Peano axioms have been uncovered only recently. Unfortunately, there is no computer program that can tell of a proposition ϕ whether or not it follows from the Peano axioms—any algorithm that seeks to do this will provide wrong answers or fail to terminate on some of its inputs. As a slight compensation for this problem, there is another theory, called *Presburger arithmetic*, that can decide certain propositions about addition. Moreover, there are good algorithms for this decision procedure that are used in practice.

The case in which axioms are intended to describe properties of a given model, the *standard* model, is common in mathematical logic, but there are many instances in which the study of a particular theory is the goal, and no standard model is intended. An example of this from abstract algebra is the the theory of *groups*, which are algebras with a constant for a unit and a single binary operation that is associative and has inverses. There is no 'standard group' that these axioms are intended to describe;[3] instead they describe a collection of properties common to many mathematical structures. Now, a

---

[2] The algorithm is hyper-exponential, so its performance in practice is a different matter!

[3] It is worth noting, however, that the group axioms were originally intended to axiomatize permutations, so it could be argued that permutation groups are the standard models of the group axioms.

valid proposition about groups is a proposition that is true for each group. Since the group axioms can be formulated in first-order logic, if a first-order proposition in this language is valid, then by the completeness theorem it is also *provable* in the formal language of first-order logic. However, in a book on group theory, such facts are often proven 'model-theoretically' rather than through something that looks like a formal first-order proof. For example, a proof is likely to begin with something like 'let G be a group and suppose x, y are elements of G'. Of course, the group axioms will surely be used in the proof (if anything interesting about groups is being proved), but they will be treated as facts satisfied by the model. A second characteristic of such proofs is the fact that they are *informal*. This is not to say that the proof is somehow imprecise; it is crucial to distinguish between a rigorous but informal proof and a formal one: *formal* proofs are those formulated in the syntax of a particular logic and using its axioms and rules, whereas *informal* proofs are embedded in a specialized part of natural language spoken in mathematical discussions.[4] For a given logic, it may be that some rigorous, informal, semantic proofs can be easily converted to formal ones, but it is likely that other proofs will not be so easy. The point here is that semantic arguments are the norm in mathematics, even where formal syntactic proof is quite possible.

By contrast, the literature on proving properties about computer programs places a great deal of emphasis on formal axiom systems and formal proofs of properties of programs. There are several explanations that could partially account for this phenomenon. First of all, computer programs are themselves formal objects. A formal axiom system for reasoning about programs can take advantage of this intrinsic characteristic by making programs into parts of the formulas of the language. *Hoare triples,* which are generally written in the form $\phi\{C\}\psi$, are an example of this idea: in such triples, ϕ and ψ are typically propositions about the computer memory, and C is a program fragment. This may have the practical consequence that assertions can be used to annotate actual computer programs, and these assertions can themselves be processed by an analytic program such as the compiler. A second explanation for the emphasis on formal proof arises from the complexity of computer programs. Large portions of typical programs are filled with long and tedious lists of cases. Informal arguments 'by hand' may be unequal to the task of checking that these cases all satisfy the desired conditions. Often, it is not possible to automate the verification of a condition, but when it is, this could free the human certifier of a program's correctness from a very unpleasant and difficult chore. Since complex programs are often not rigorously proved correct (either formally or informally), good programs for automating parts of such a task might lead to more reliable programs. A

---

[4]In fact, formality is often viewed as a relative matter. A careful, step-by-step proof in precise mathematical language is sometimes called a formal proof when compared to a 'hand-waving' proof that has been carried out through convincing pictures and gesticulations.

third reason for emphasis on formal proof is a poor understanding of how the semantics of a program can be used directly for proving properties of programs. The semantics of a programming language can be very subtle; attempts to avoid semantic arguments by resorting to formal systems of axioms (proved sound for the semantics, of course) are a common way to help deal with this subtlety.

One thing offered by the semantics of a language is a theory of *equivalence* between expressions. Everyone uses the idea that there are many different ways to express the same meaning, but providing a theory that explains this intuitive equivalence relation is no easy task for the semantics of natural language. Theories of semantic equivalence are equally important for programming. In the case of computer programs, the theory of equivalence is based on what is often called the *level of abstraction* of the semantic analysis. To see this at work in a concrete example, consider the following mathematical definition of the Fibonacci function:

$$\text{fib}(n) = \begin{cases} 0 & \text{if } n = 0 \\ 1 & \text{if } n = 1 \\ \text{fib}(n-1) + \text{fib}(n-2) & \text{otherwise.} \end{cases}$$

This definition can be coded directly as a recursive procedure declaration in a language like Scheme:

```
(define (fib n) (if (= n 0) 1
                    (if (= n 1) 1
                        (+ (fib (- n 1))
                           (fib (- n 2))))))).
```

Although this clearly implements the desired mathematical function, the computational properties of this way of coding it are disastrous. Indeed the number of calls to the fib routine will be exponential in the size of the argument n. This program does a great deal of redundant calculation, since the value of (fib (- n 2)) will always be needed in calculating (fib (- n 1)), but this value is recalculated in a separate recursive call. A much better way to code the Fibonacci function is to 'remember' the relevant calculation and pass it as a parameter to the recursive call. An auxiliary function can aid in achieving the desired optimization:

```
(define (fib n)
  (define (fib-iter a b count)
    (if (= count 0)
        b
        (fib-iter (+ a b) a (- count 1))))
  (fib-iter 1 0 n)).
```

In this new coding the number of recursive calls is linear in n, a vast improvement over the performance of the previous implementation. It is possible to understand this improvement in terms of a simple rewriting semantics that models the recursive definition through repeated 'unwinding' of the body of the definition. The two programs given previously are equivalent at one level of abstraction, that which considers only the value of the output on a given input, but inequivalent at another level, in which the number of computational steps are considered. Showing that the efficient implementation is 'correct' in the sense that it really does compute the Fibonacci function involves considering its meaning at an abstract level; the justification that it is efficient is based on a more 'low-level' semantics. Given a still lower-level semantics, a programmer may be able to make conclusions about the use of space that programs will make; for example, in a Scheme compiler the second program will require only a constant amount of space.

1.2   Semantics of Programming Languages

What is meant by the 'semantics' of a programming language? Although researchers in mathematical logic have a clear idea of what semantics is for their languages, this level of clarity is not present in the programming languages literature. A crude view is that the semantics of a programming language as defined by a compiler is the mapping that the compiler defines from the program written by a human to the target code executed by the computer. This view is sometimes refined by separating the syntactic analysis done by the compiler from the semantic analysis by classifying syntax as the context-free phase of the compilation, which builds the parse tree for the program, and semantics as the remaining phases, which check types, generate code, perform optimizations, and so on.

If we think of the programming language as something whose semantics we must define and the instruction set for machine architecture as something whose meaning we understand well, then the compiler provides a sort of semantics through translation. The general idea of semantics through translation is an important and pervasive one in the study of programming languages; it will often arise as a theme in later chapters of this book. Nevertheless, it does not work well to specify the semantics of a programming language through a compiler to a specific piece of commercial hardware. There are at least two problems. First of all, such a specification is not good for portability. If the language has been specified by a compiler for machine M and it is to be implemented on another machine M', then either the machine M must be simulated on M' or the compiler must be translated in a 'compatible' way. The use of the word 'compatible' here begs the question of what invariants should be preserved under the translation. That the user should observe no difference in running his programs is not yet a precise condition since it may not be clear what the user can actually observe. A second problem is that a compiler is likely to provide the wrong level of abstraction for a programmer. It may provide useful insights into which commands of the language will run most efficiently (given an understanding of what runs well on the underlying machine), but it is also likely to provide a great deal of arbitrary detail that a programmer does not need and could not really use.

A common approach to resolving this problem is to formulate an abstract machine that can be easily and efficiently simulated on machines with different instruction sets. A compiler for the language for this abstract machine can then be offered as specification of the semantics of the language. The instructions that a program produces for the abstract machine are sometimes called 'intermediate code' since they stand between the program the user wrote and the basic machine instruction set that is the eventual target of the compilation. This may go far in resolving the problem of portability if the abstract machine is chosen well—just abstract enough to be general but low-level enough to be efficient and easy to implement. In short, a good abstract machine for this purpose is the least common denominator for the class of machines over which it is an abstraction. Unfortunately, an abstract machine description of this kind is unlikely to be as useful to a programmer as it is to an implementor of the language, since the compiler for the abstract machine will still include many complexities that the general programmer does not need (or want) to know.

Informal semantics.

The problem with many abstract machines, therefore, is that they may be abstract enough for some but still too low-level for others. Every programmer who uses a higher-level language must understand its semantics at *some* level of abstraction. A compiler for an abstract machine is likely to be hard to understand in detail, even for the clearest language and simplest abstract machine. Hence programmers ordinarily understand the semantics of a language through examples, intuitions about the underlying machine model, and some kind of *informal* semantic description. By way of illustration, an excerpt from one such specification appears in Table 1.1. The example is taken from the ALGOL 60 Revised Report and describes the semantics of the assignment statements in that language. It is not primarily chosen to point out any particular strength or failing of such informal semantic descriptions but merely to give a good example of one.

The ALGOL 60 report uses English sentences to provide such essential information as the order in which expressions are evaluated. For example, it is indicated that the subscript expressions occurring on the left side of the assignment statement are evaluated from left to right, *before* the expression of the assignment is evaluated. The brevity and

Table 1.1
Algol 60 Semantics for Assignments

4.2.2. Examples

$$s \; := \; p[0] \; := \; n \; := \; n + 1 + s$$
$$n \; := \; n + 1$$
$$A \; := \; B/C - v - q \times S$$
$$S[v, k + 2] \; := \; 3 - arctan(s \times zeta)$$
$$V \; := \; Q > Y \wedge Z$$

4.2.3. Semantics

Assignment statements serve for assigning the value of an expression to one or several variables or procedure identifiers. Assignment to a procedure identifier may only occur within the body of a procedure defining the value of a function designator (cf. section 4.4.4). The process will in the general case be understood to take place in three steps as follows:

4.2.3.1 Any subscript expressions occurring in the left part variables are evaluated in sequence from left to right.

4.2.3.2 The expression of the statement is evaluated.

4.2.3.3. The value of the expression is assigned to all the left part variables, with any subscript expressions having values as evaluated in step 4.2.3.1.

---

apparent simplicity of the description is partly based on assumptions about what the reader of the specification already understands. For example, the sentence

> Assignment statements serve for assigning the value of an expression to one
> or several variables or procedure identifiers.

will mean nothing to someone who does not already understand the idea of assigning a value to a variable. Such assumptions can, and have, led to misunderstandings. In the best circumstances, an experienced programmer's intuition about the meanings of the phrases fills in any omissions in the description, and it can be viewed as a simple, succinct, and readable account of the meanings of language constructs. At worst, however, the description can be fatally ambiguous or misleading, and programming errors or compiler implementation errors can result.

Indeed, the original definition of Algol 60 did contain ambiguities, and a revised report was put out in 1963. Work on understanding the ambiguities in the definition continued for some years further; in 1967, Donald Knuth wrote a summary of the known ambiguities and errors in the 1963 Revised Report. He wrote,

Table 1.2
An ALGOL 60 Program

```
begin integer a;
  integer procedure f(x,y);  value y,x;  integer y,x;
    a := f := x + 1;
  integer procedure g(x);  integer x;  x := g := a + 2;
  a := 0; outreal(1, a + (f(a, g(a)) / g(a))) end
```

When ALGOL 60 was first published in 1960, many new features were introduced
into programming languages.... It was quite difficult at first for anyone to grasp the
full significance of each of the linguistic features with respect to other aspects of the
language, and therefore people commonly would discover ALGOL 60 constructions
they had never before realized were possible, each time they reread the Report. Such
constructions often provided counterexamples to many of the usual techniques of
compiler implementation, and in many cases it was possible to construct programs
that could be interpreted in more than one way.

Let us say that a feature of ALGOL 60 is *ambiguous* if at least two implementations
yielding different behaviors are consistent with its definition in the Report. One of the
features that led to questions about ambiguity was the possibility of *side effects,* that is,
changes to variables resulting from the evaluation of an expression for which the variable
is not local. For example, consider the expression $x + f(x)$. Is it interchangeable with
the expression $f(x) + x$? The answer depends on whether the evaluation of f can alter
('side effect') the value of x; if this is possible, then the two expressions may not be
interchangeable. For the language implementor, this question is intimately connected
with the order in which the parts of an expression are to be evaluated. Consider the
program in Table 1.2. This program defines procedures f and g and calculates the value
of the expression

$$a + (f(a, g(a))/g(a)) \tag{1.1}$$

beginning with zero as the initial value of a. For readers not familiar with the syntax of
ALGOL-like languages, it suffices simply to understand that the evaluation of procedures
f and g changes the state by modifying the global integer variable a. As a result of this
modification, the order in which parts of 1.1 are evaluated will have a significant effect on
its value. For example, if it was felt that an optimization could be achieved by evaluating
the denominator of a fraction first, then an implementation might proceed by evaluating

g(a), then f(a, g'(a)), and then a + (f(a, g(a)) / g(a)). If the parameters for the application of f are evaluated in the order a, g(a), then the result of this evaluation is $4\frac{1}{2}$. On the other hand, if the expression is evaluated 'from left to right', then the final result will be $\frac{1}{3}$. The ALGOL 60 definition is therefore ambiguous, since it does not specify a fixed order of evaluation for expressions or rule out the possibility of side effects in programs.

Further questions about order of evaluation arise in innocent places. For example, the clause 4.2.3.2 in Table 1.1 says that the evaluation of subscripts (that is, array indices) should be done from 'left to right'. In the expression

```
A[a + B[f(a)] + g(a)] := C[a] := 0
```

there are three subscripts. Should they be evaluated by doing a + B[f(a)] + g(a) first, followed by f(a) *again*, and finally a?

From the standpoint of mathematical notation, the idea that an expression such as $x + f(x)$ may be unequal to $f(x) + x$ is unsettling, but the consequence of this distinction has ramifications for the efficiency of evaluation as well. For example, the code generated for $x + f(x)$ must save x before evaluating $f(x)$ because of the (probably unlikely) prospect that the evaluation of $f(x)$ will alter the value of x. Although there might be some advantage therefore in requiring that $x + f(x)$ have the same value as $f(x) + x$, such a requirement is less clearly beneficial in some analogous cases. For instance, it would probably not be a boon for efficiency to require that $x = 0 \vee f(x) = 0$ be equivalent to $f(x) = 0 \vee x = 0$ since the evaluation of $f(x)$ might be avoided if x is zero. Moreover, it might be useful to write $x = 0 \vee f(x) = 0$ in instances where $f(0)$ is undefined.

It is now common for language definitions to explicitly allow the same program to yield different results under different implementations. Ideally, the definition describes clearly how such a situation can arise, and programmers must themselves take responsibility for writing code that will behave differently for different implementations. A typical example of this arises in the definition of the Scheme programming language. The informal description of the language indicates that the operator and operands of a procedure application are evaluated *in an indeterminate order*. Hence programmers cannot rely on the portability of their code if it depends on the choice of evaluation order made by a specific Scheme compiler. Presumably this latitude does not leave open the possibility that a given implementation is non-deterministic but does allow the possibility that the order of evaluation for an expression is different for different occurrences of the expression in a given program. Such nuances are difficult to explain rigorously and even more difficult to formalize. Indeed, the formal definition of Scheme is not quite true to its informal explanation. The following passage from the formal definition indicates the compromise in the formalization:

The order of evaluation within a call is unspecified. We mimic that here by applying arbitrary permutations *permute* and *unpermute,* which must be inverses, to the arguments in a call before and after they are evaluated. This still requires that the order of evaluation be constant throughout a program (for any given number of arguments), but it is a closer approximation to the intended semantics than a left-to-right evaluation would be.

There has been a great deal of effort to ensure that language definitions are clear and do not admit unexpected possibilities in their interpretation. Much effort has been devoted to showing that formal methods of definition can help to achieve this. But, as the Scheme example shows, capturing the exact nuance of the intended specification in the formalism is not an easy task. There are many approaches to the formal specification of programming languages. In the rest of this section I will attempt to survey some significant classes of these.

Transition semantics.

An intuitive model of the execution of a program is to think of it in terms of a machine state consisting of a *control* part representing the instructions to be executed and a *data* part consisting of the structures being manipulated by the instructions of the program. This picture is augmented by some idea of the *point of control* indicating the instruction currently being executed. The computation then is a sequence of transitions in which the data is altered and the point of control moves through the instructions of the program. The semantics of a programming language is then described by saying how it is converted into instructions and what transitions are engendered by instructions. To make such an account more abstract, it is helpful to avoid translation into some low-level instruction set and instead work directly in terms of the syntax of the higher-level programming language. Two abstractions can now lead us to a clear and simple approach to explaining the semantics of programming languages. First, we eliminate the need for a point of control by thinking of the transitions as converting the program before the execution of an instruction into a new program to be executed afterwards. Second, we explain how such transitions are defined by following the *structure* of the programs of the language as given by its grammar and providing one or more transitions for each possible form of program.

Let us illustrate this approach by considering a simple imperative programming language. Its syntax is given as a BNF grammar in Table 1.3 where I ranges over a syntax class of *identifiers* and N ranges over a syntax class of *numerals.* The command **skip** is called *skip.* Commands of the form $C_1; C_2$ are called *sequences.* Those having the forms $I := E$ are called *assignments.* Those having the form **if** B **then** C_1 **else** C_2 **fi** are called

Table 1.3
Syntax for the Simple Imperative Programming Language

I ϵ Identifier

N ϵ Numeral

B ::=   **true** | **false** | B **and** B | B **or** B | **not** B |
                $E < E$ | $E = E$

E ::= N | I | $E + E$ | $E * E$ | $E - E$ | $- E$

C ::=   **skip** | $C; C$ | $I := E$ |
                if B **then** C **else** C **fi** | **while** B **do** C **od**

---

conditionals and those of the form **while** B **do** C **od** are called *while loops.*.

The notion of the data part of a machine state will be represented simply as a function assigning integer values to identifiers. More precisely, we define the domain $\mathbb{M}$ of *memories* to be the set of functions $f :$ Identifier $\rightarrow \mathbb{Z}$ from identifiers to the integers $\mathbb{Z}$. To simplify matters, let us assume that semantic functions for arithmetic expressions and boolean expressions are already known, so we can focus our attention on the semantics of commands. It is traditional to write the syntax of a program within 'semantic brackets' $[\![\cdot]\!]$ to separate terms of the object language (that is, the formal language whose semantics is being described) from the surrounding mathematical metalanguage (that is, the possibly informal language being used to explain the semantics of the object language). When it is important to distinguish one semantic function from another, a calligraphic letter is used to indicate the function in question, and we write something like $\mathcal{A}[\![B]\!]$ and $\mathcal{B}[\![B]\!]$ for the $\mathcal{A}$ and $\mathcal{B}$ meaning functions. When only one semantic function is under discussion, it is simplest to drop the distinguishing letter so long as no confusion is likely to arise. So, for the discussion at hand, let us assume we are given the definition of a meaning function $[\![\cdot]\!]$ on booleans and arithmetic expressions:

$$[\![B]\!] : \mathbb{M} \rightarrow \{\text{true, false}\}$$
$$[\![E]\!] : \mathbb{M} \rightarrow \mathbb{Z}$$

(It can be assumed—for the sake of uniformity—that these semantic functions were also defined by a means similar to that being used here for commands.) The meaning $[\![C]\!]$ of a command C will be defined as a partial function from $\mathbb{M}$ (input) to $\mathbb{M}$ (output). To achieve the desired level of abstraction in the description of its semantics, the state

Table 1.4
Transition Semantics for the Simple Imperative Programming Language

$$(I := E, m) \rightarrow m[I \mapsto [\![E]\!]m] \qquad (\textbf{skip},\ m) \rightarrow m$$

$$\frac{(C_1, m) \rightarrow (C_1', m')}{(C_1; C_2, m) \rightarrow (C_1'; C_2, m')} \qquad \frac{(C_1, m) \rightarrow m'}{(C_1; C_2, m) \rightarrow (C_2, m')}$$

$$\frac{[\![B]\!]m = \mathsf{true}}{(\textbf{if } B \textbf{ then } C_1 \textbf{ else } C_2 \textbf{ fi}, m) \rightarrow (C_1, m)} \qquad \frac{[\![B]\!]m = \mathsf{false}}{(\textbf{if } B \textbf{ then } C_1 \textbf{ else } C_2 \textbf{ fi}, m) \rightarrow (C_2, m)}$$

$$\frac{[\![B]\!]m = \mathsf{false}}{(\textbf{while } B \textbf{ do } C \textbf{ od}, m) \rightarrow m} \qquad \frac{[\![B]\!]m = \mathsf{true}}{(\textbf{while } B \textbf{ do } C \textbf{ od}, m) \rightarrow (C; \textbf{while } B \textbf{ do } C \textbf{ od}, m)}$$

of a machine is represented as a pair (C, m) consisting of a program fragment C and a memory m recording the values of identifiers. When the control part of the program is empty (that is, the program has terminated and there are no more instructions to be executed), we simply write m. More precisely, a *configuration* is either

- a pair (C, m) consisting of a command C and a memory m, or

- a memory m.

Rules for evaluating a program of the Simple Imperative Language are given in terms of a binary relation $\rightarrow$ on configurations; this is defined to be the least relation that satisfies the rules in Table 1.4. In the transition rules for assignment, the evaluation of the command results in a new memory in which the value associated with the identifier I is bound to the value of the expression E in memory m. The notation used there is defined as follows for a value $z \in \mathbb{Z}$:

$$m[I \mapsto z](J) = \left\{ \begin{array}{ll} z & \text{if } I \text{ is the same as } J \\ m(J) & \text{otherwise} \end{array} \right. \tag{1.2}$$

Now, let $\rightarrow^+$ be the transitive closure of the relation $\rightarrow$ (that is, $\rightarrow^+$ is the least transitive relation that contains $\rightarrow$). It is possible to prove the following:

1.1 Lemma. *Let γ be a configuration. If $\gamma \rightarrow^+ m$ and $\gamma \rightarrow^+ m'$ for memories m and m', then $m = m'$.* $\qquad\qquad\square$

The meaning of a program C can therefore be defined as follows:

$$[\![C]\!]m \simeq \begin{cases} m' & \text{if } (C, m) \to^+ m' \\ \text{undefined} & \text{otherwise} \end{cases}$$

where the symbol $\simeq$ is being used rather than $=$ to emphasize that $[\![C]\!]$ is a *partial* function, which may be undefined on some memories m. (This is called *Kleene* equality, and it is used in expressing a relationship between partially defined expressions. Given expressions E and E' where one or both may be undefined, writing $E \simeq E'$ means that either E and E' are both defined and equal or they are both undefined.)

This semantic description induces a set of equations between programs if we take C to be equivalent to C' when $[\![C]\!] = [\![C']\!]$. It is a *virtue* of this equivalence that it ignores important aspects of a program such as its efficiency. It is this separation of concerns that makes it possible to develop a theory of program transformations; we could not say when the replacement of one program by another is legitimate without saying what property is to be preserved under such a replacement.

Let me turn to another example of how transition rules can be used to describe the semantics of a familiar kind of programming language construct. To keep matters simple, let us work with a very terse fragment of a language such as Lisp that allows functions to be taken as arguments or returned as values (a feature sometimes referred to as 'functions as first class citizens'). The minimal grammar is given as follows:

$$M ::= x \mid (M \ M) \mid (\textbf{lambda } x \ M)$$

where x is drawn from a primitive syntax class of identifier names.[5] I will use letters x, y, z, and these letters with primes, subscripts, and so on for identifiers. This language is called the *untyped λ-calculus,* and its expressions are called *λ-terms.* I will use letters L, M, and N to range over λ-terms. The expression (**lambda** x M) is called an *abstraction,* and it is to be thought of as a functional procedure in which x is the *formal parameter* and M is the *body* of the procedure. In particular, the scope of the identifier x is the body of the abstraction. The expression $(M \ N)$ is called an *application,* and it should be thought of as the application of the function M to the argument N.

A λ-term is *closed* if each of its identifiers falls within the scope of an abstraction. For example, the λ-term

(**lambda** x (**lambda** y x))

---

[5]It would be tempting to use letters such as I for identifiers here to maintain uniformity with the notation in the Simple Imperative Language. However, some upper case letters are commonly used to denote various constants in the λ-calculus. For example, I is usually used for an expression of the form (**lambda** x x).

is closed, whereas

(lambda z **(lambda** y x**))**

is not closed (because the identifier x does not lie in the scope of any abstraction whose formal parameter is x). We write $[M/x]N$ to denote the result of *substituting* the λ-term M for the identifier x in the λ-term N. Substitution is a tricky business really, but I will delay its precise definition until the beginning of the detailed discussion of the λ-calculus in Chapter 2. For now let us assume we understand the concept of substitution and look at a semantics for closed λ-terms. Two rules suffice to define how such terms can be viewed as programs. The first of these says that if a step of evaluation can be carried out on the operator of an application, then this step can be done as part of the application:

$$\frac{M \to M'}{(M\ N) \to (M'\ N)}$$

The second says that the result of applying an abstraction to an argument is obtained by substituting the operand for the formal parameter in the body of the abstraction:

$$((\textbf{lambda } x\ M)\ N) \to [N/x]M$$

It is not hard to show the analog of Lemma 1.1 for this relation:

1.2 Lemma. *If M is a closed λ-term such that $M \to^+ N$ and $M \to^+ N'$ for abstractions N and N', then N and N' are the same term.* $\qquad\qquad\square$

We define the value (meaning) of a closed λ-term M as follows:

$$[\![M]\!] \simeq \begin{cases} M & \text{if } M \text{ is an abstraction} \\ N & \text{if } M \to^+ N \text{ for some abstraction } N \\ \text{undefined} & \text{otherwise} \end{cases}$$

It is easy to prove that the value of a closed λ-term is always a closed abstraction.

The rules above define a form of semantics for the evaluation of λ-terms called *call-by-name* because the rule for application may result in an unevaluated term being substituted for the formal parameter of the operator in its body. Another common evaluation order—the one used in Lisp and many similar languages—evaluates the operand of the application before it is substituted for the formal parameter. This is known as *call-by-value* since a value is always substituted for the formal parameter of the operator. It is possible to describe this with a transition semantics and an appropriate set of rules. The description is slightly more complex than the one for call-by-name since there are three rules rather than two. The first of these rules is the same as that given before:

$$\frac{M \circ\!\!\to M'}{(M\ N) \circ\!\!\to (M'\ N)}$$

The little circle on the arrow in the rule is meant to distinguish the call-by-value evaluation relation from the call-by-name one. To simplify notation, let us write V for values (that is, abstractions). The difference between the definitions of $\rightarrow$ and $\circ\!\!\rightarrow$ comes from the fact that only a value is substituted into a function body:

$$((\textbf{lambda } x \ M) \ V) \circ\!\!\rightarrow [V/x]M$$

To obtain an operand that is a value, it is necessary to first evaluate the operand:

$$\frac{N \circ\!\!\rightarrow N'}{(V \ N) \circ\!\!\rightarrow (V \ N')}$$

The definition of the meaning of an expression is defined for call-by-value in basically the same way this was done for call-by-name, but with $\circ\!\!\rightarrow$ supplanting $\rightarrow$ in the defining equation. Differences between the semantics of call-by-name and call-by-value will appear frequently in the discussions of semantics in this book. Fortunately, both call mechanisms can be described in a clear and succinct manner using the formalisms at hand.

Natural semantics.

The transition semantics described in the previous section proceeds in two steps. We begin by defining the notion of a transition relation between configurations or λ-terms. This relation is then used to define a partial function from programs to values, which is taken to be the semantics of the language. Could we combine these two steps somehow and define the desired partial function directly? One approach to this is to axiomatize the relation $\rightarrow^+$ itself. This is indeed possible; the rules for doing this appear for the Simple Imperative Language appear in Table 1.5. They define a binary relation $\Downarrow$ between configurations of the form (C, m) on the left of side of the relation symbol and memories on its right side. The following lemma describes the desired property:

1.3 Lemma. *For any program C and memory m,*

$$(C, m) \rightarrow^+ m' \text{ iff } (C, m) \Downarrow m'. \qquad\qquad\qquad \square$$

The proof of the lemma is somewhat tedious but routine. It shows that the rules in Tables 1.4 and 1.5 define essentially the same semantics for the Simple Imperative Language. A semantics described in the manner of Table 1.5 is sometimes called a *natural* or *relational* semantics. In a natural semantics, an evaluation is very much like the search for a proof. Because of the nature of the rules for the relation given in Table 1.5, it is possible to evaluate a program C in a memory m in the following way. First find a rule for which a conclusion of the form $(C, m) \Downarrow m'$ is possible. For some forms of command C—skip, sequence, and assignment—there is only one rule that could

Table 1.5
Natural Semantics for the Simple Imperative Programming Language

$$(\textbf{skip},\ m) \Downarrow m$$

$$\frac{(C_1, m) \Downarrow m' \qquad (C_2, m') \Downarrow m''}{(C_1; C_2, m) \Downarrow m''}$$

$$(I := E, m) \Downarrow m[I \mapsto [\![E]\!]m]$$

$$\frac{[\![B]\!]m = \textsf{true} \qquad (C_1, m) \Downarrow m'}{(\textbf{if } B \textbf{ then } C_1 \textbf{ else } C_2 \textbf{ fi}, m) \Downarrow m'} \qquad \frac{[\![B]\!]m = \textsf{false} \qquad (C_2, m) \Downarrow m'}{(\textbf{if } B \textbf{ then } C_1 \textbf{ else } C_2 \textbf{ fi}, m) \Downarrow m'}$$

$$\frac{[\![B]\!]m = \textsf{false}}{(\textbf{while } B \textbf{ do } C \textbf{ od}, m) \Downarrow m}$$

$$\frac{[\![B]\!]m = \textsf{true} \qquad (C, m) \Downarrow m' \qquad (\textbf{while } B \textbf{ do } C \textbf{ od}, m') \Downarrow m''}{(\textbf{while } B \textbf{ do } C \textbf{ od}, m) \Downarrow m''}$$

possibly apply; for others—conditional and while loop—there are two possibilities. In each of the latter cases, if a conclusion of the form $(C, m) \Downarrow m'$ is indeed possible, then exactly one of these rules could be used to reach this conclusion. Both could not be applicable because of the boolean test, which cannot be both true and false for the same memory. To evaluate a program (C, m), therefore, find a rule that applies and then try to establish hypotheses for it by attempting to evaluate (find a proof for) each of the programs that appear in its hypotheses. If this effort fails because a hypothesis yields the wrong conclusion (for example, false is obtained when true is sought), then attempt the effort again with another applicable rule, if there is one. The search for a proof may, in fact, proceed without end in some cases; this is how non-termination is represented in this system. Evaluation using a natural semantics is very much like running a *logic program*. Indeed, the rules in Table 1.5 could easily be coded in a language such as Prolog. This connection to logic, in the form of natural deduction proof, is part of the reason the term 'natural semantics' is used for this form of specification.

If a relation $(C, m) \Downarrow m'$ can be established, then it can be shown that there is a unique proof of this fact. This property might be different if the language contains other features. For example, if we add a non-deterministic construct C_1 **or** C_2 that evaluates either C_1 or C_2, its semantics could be given through the following pair of rules:

$$\frac{(C_1, m) \Downarrow m'}{(C_1 \textbf{ or } C_2, m) \Downarrow m'} \qquad \frac{(C_2, m) \Downarrow m'}{(C_1 \textbf{ or } C_2, m) \Downarrow m'}$$

Either of the two rules could be used for reaching a conclusion about the result of evaluating an expression, so more than one outcome is possible.

In some ways, the natural semantics of the λ-calculus is simpler to describe than its transition semantics. Abstractions evaluate to themselves (since they are already values):

$$(\textbf{lambda } x \; M) \Downarrow (\textbf{lambda } x \; M)$$

and, for call-by-name, if the value of the operator is established, then the operand is substituted for the formal parameter and the result is evaluated:

$$\frac{M \Downarrow (\textbf{lambda } x \; M') \qquad [N/x]M' \Downarrow V}{(M \; N) \Downarrow V}$$

It can easily be seen from the rules that if $M \Downarrow U$ and $M \Downarrow V$, then U and V are the same. We therefore define the value of M to be the unique V, if there is one, such that $M \Downarrow V$. If there is no such V, then the value of M is undefined. As with the natural semantics for the simple imperative language, this definition is exactly the same as that given using transitions.

The call-by-value evaluation order has an identical rule for abstractions:

$$(\textbf{lambda } x \; M) \Downarrow^\circ (\textbf{lambda } x \; M)$$

but in the rule for application, it is required that the value of the operand be substituted for the formal parameter in the function body:

$$\frac{M \Downarrow^\circ (\textbf{lambda } x \; M') \qquad N \Downarrow^\circ U \qquad [U/x]M' \Downarrow^\circ V}{(M \; N) \Downarrow^\circ V} \qquad (1.3)$$

Compositionality, fixed points, and denotation.

A common way to give the semantics of a language is to define semantic functions that describe how the semantics of an expression of the language can be obtained from the semantics of its syntactic components. The meaning of an expression can then be obtained by composing the semantic functions determined by its syntactic structure. A semantics given in this way is said to be *compositional*. Compositionality is a property common to the forms of semantic description used in most areas of logic. Consider, for example, the way the Tarski's semantics of first-order logic is given. If ϕ and ψ are first-order formulas and ρ is an assignment of meanings (in the universe of the model), then $[\![\phi \wedge \psi]\!]\rho$ is true if, and only if, $[\![\phi]\!]\rho$ and $[\![\psi]\!]\rho$ are both true. For a identifier x, $[\![\forall x.\ \phi]\!]\rho$ is true if, and only if, for every element a of the model, $[\![\phi]\!](\rho[x \mapsto a])$ is true. Other meanings are defined similarly.

By contrast, in both the transition and natural semantics as described above for the Simple Imperative Language, the meanings of programs were not described with such meaning functions. However, at least for some expressions, it seems that such a meaning function would not be hard to obtain. Let us look now at how we might go about giving a compositional description of the semantics of the Simple Imperative Language. As before, the meaning of a command C is a partial function $[\![C]\!]$ on memories. Clearly $[\![\text{skip}]\!]m = m$. Sequencing is interpreted as composition of partial functions, $[\![C_1; C_2]\!]m \simeq [\![C_2]\!]([\![C_1]\!]m)$ and assignment is updating, $[\![I := E]\!]m \simeq m[I \mapsto [\![E]\!]m]$. We interpret branching by

$$[\![\text{if } B \text{ then } C_1 \text{ else } C_2 \text{ fi}]\!]m \simeq \begin{cases} [\![C_1]\!]m & \text{if } [\![B]\!]m = \text{true} \\ [\![C_2]\!]m & \text{if } [\![B]\!]m = \text{false} \end{cases}$$

So far, so good. However, when we write down the straightforward explanation of the meaning of the loop, a problem appears:

$$[\![\text{while } B \text{ do } C \text{ od}]\!]m \simeq \begin{cases} m & \text{if } [\![B]\!]m = \text{false} \\ [\![\text{while } B \text{ do } C \text{ od}]\!]([\![C]\!]m) & \text{if } [\![B]\!]m = \text{true} \end{cases}$$

In particular, the expression **while** B **do** C **od** we are trying to define appears on *both* sides of the equation.

What is such an equation intended to define? One view holds that

$$[\![\text{while } B \text{ do } C \text{ od}]\!]$$

is some form of *canonical fixed point* of an operator defined by the expression on the right-hand side of the equation. In the case above, the loop construct is defined to be such a fixed point of the function $F : [\mathbb{M} \rightsquigarrow \mathbb{M}] \to [\mathbb{M} \rightsquigarrow \mathbb{M}]$ where

$$F(f)(m) = \begin{cases} m & \text{if } [\![B]\!]m = \text{false} \\ f([\![C]\!]m) & \text{if } [\![B]\!]m = \text{true} \end{cases}$$

and $[\mathbb{M} \rightsquigarrow \mathbb{M}]$ is the set of *partial* functions between memories. Now

$$[\![\text{while } B \text{ do } C \text{ od}]\!] = \text{fix}(F)$$

really *is* a compositional description because the definition of F was made in terms of $[\![C]\!]$ and $[\![B]\!]$ only. This raises two questions: How do we know that such a fixed point exists, and, if it does, is there a way to choose it canonically?

There are several theories about how to solve equations in order to provide meanings for recursive definitions. The typical procedure is this. One defines a class of spaces in which programs take their meanings, and basic operators are interpreted as functions between such spaces. A recursive definition determines an operator $F : D \to D$ on such a space D; the term being defined is interpreted as a fixed point of F. In some theories the fixed point is unique; in others, the semantics is based on a choice of canonical fixed point for an operator. A way to choose a value canonically is to specify some property of the desired fixed point that uniquely specifies it. For instance, it may be the least one, the greatest one, the 'optimal' one (for some definition of optimality), or whatever might be appropriate for the purpose that the semantics is intended to serve. Members of the class of spaces over which recursive definitions are interpreted are usually called *domains*. The term originated from the idea that these spaces are the domains of the operators F used to make recursive definitions. The study of structures appropriate for such applications is called *domain theory*.

In this book, the use of domain theory and fixed points to interpret programs compositionally will be called *fixed-point semantics*. The technique goes by other names as well; it is often called a *denotational* semantics. This nomenclature is motivated by the idea that domains provide a realm of abstract values and that some of these values are denoted by programs. The usage is somewhat vague and sometimes misleading, though. For example, the transition and natural semantics of the Simple Imperative Language appear to have this characteristic (programs denote partial functions on memories). However, to appreciate the terminology better, consider the semantics of the λ-calculus. What mathematical object does a λ-term denote? Looking at the natural semantics, one might begin with the idea that V is the denotation of the term M if $M \Downarrow V$. But if this is what is meant by a denotation, then the semantics is a somewhat trivial one—after all, an abstraction denotes itself! This is far from our intuition about the meanings of such terms in which an abstraction is some kind of function. The domain of such a function might be the λ-terms themselves, but this idea is not *a priori* present in the rules for the natural semantics. In short, a further theory is required to provide a serious semantics in which λ-terms denote mathematical objects. To emphasize this distinction, natural semantics and transition semantics are usually said to be forms of *operational* (as opposed to denotational) semantics.

Abstract machines.

This survey of forms of semantic description began with a discussion of the limitations of abstract machines. But how do abstract machines differ from the kinds of semantics described above? For example, the transition semantics for the Simple Imperative Language could be mechanically executed to provide an interpreter for the Simple Im-

perative Language or for the λ-calculus. By an appropriate form of search, the natural
semantics for these languages could also be viewed as an interpreter. It is less clear
that a denotational semantics has computational content, but in many cases the semantic equations of a denotational semantics can be viewed as a program in a functional
language whose execution serves as an interpreter for the language whose semantics it
defines. (For this reason, languages such as Scheme and ML have often been used as notations for denotational specifications.) There are gray areas between the classification
of forms of semantic specification given above. While overstating differences can mask
important relationships, it is important to recognize distinctions in order to understand
how semantic descriptions can serve different purposes.

The term 'machine' ordinarily refers to a physical device that performs a mechanical
function. The term 'abstract' distinguishes a physically existent device from one that
exists in the imagination of its inventor or user. The archetypical abstract machine is the
Turing machine, which is used to explain the foundations of the concept of mechanical
computability. The idea behind the Turing machine is that it is so concrete that it is
evidently possible to execute its actions in a straightforward, mechanical manner while
also being abstract enough that it is simple to prove theorems about it. The next action
of a Turing machine is entirely determined by the value that it is currently examining, its
current state, and the transitions that constitute its program. By contrast, the transition
semantics for the Simple Imperative Language involved an additional idea: that transitions can also be specified by rules having hypotheses that use the transition relation
itself. This use of rules introduces an implicit stack if one is to think of the transition
relation mechanically. To execute one step in the evaluation of $(C_1; C_2, m)$, it is necessary
to find a configuration γ such that $(C_1, m) \rightarrow \gamma$. If C_1 has the form $C_1'; C_1''$, then it will
be necessary to look for a configuration γ' such that $(C_1', m) \rightarrow \gamma'$. If, eventually, the desired hypotheses are all established, then the evaluation of the configuration $(C_1; C_2, m)$
moves to the next appropriate configuration. In the case of a natural semantics, the
details of evaluation can be even more implicit. For example, in seeking a value V in the
conclusion of the call-by-value application rule 1.3, it has not been explicitly indicated
whether the value of M should be sought first, whether this should instead be preceded
by a search for the value of N, or whether these two searches might be carried out in
parallel. Each approach would lead to the same answer in the end, but the semantic rule
is somewhat abstract in omitting details of how the evaluation should be done mechanically. The details of how a fixed-point interpretation is given for the Simple Imperative
Language were not provided, but the choice of a canonical fixed point to solve a recursive
equation does not in itself indicate how the recursively defined term is to be evaluated.
This level of abstraction has been offered as a virtue of fixed-point semantics, but the
view is controversial since the defining semantic equations can sometimes be viewed as

implicitly describing a particular evaluator.

To make this discussion more concrete, I will briefly describe one of the best-known examples of an abstract machine, the *SECD machine* of Landin. The machine carries out call-by-value evaluation of closed terms of the λ-calculus. It is simple enough that its basic instructions can be easily implemented on standard computer architectures; in particular, the operations of the machine explicitly carry out all needed stack manipulations. It can be described in many different ways, but one approach fairly similar to the way I have treated other semantics is to use λ-terms themselves as part of the instruction set of the machine. The acronym SECD stands for the typical names for the four components of the machine configuration, which is a four tuple (S, E, C, D), where S is the *Stack*, E is the *Environment*, C is the *Code*, and D is the *Dump*. The action of the machine is described by a collection of transitions driven by the next instruction in the code C. An *instruction* for the machine is either a λ-term M or a constant **ap**. The code is a list of instructions; let us write $M :: C$ for the list whose head is M and tail is a list C, and **nil** for the empty list. To describe a stack, we must define the notions of closure and environment. Each is defined in terms of the other: an *environment* E is a partial function that assigns closures to identifiers, and a *closure* is a pair (M, E) consisting of a λ-term M and an environment E. There is also a restriction that the environment in a closure is defined on all of the identifiers of M that are not in the scope of an abstraction; this property is implicitly maintained by the transitions of the SECD machine. Let us simply write $E(x)$ for the value of E on x and $E[x \mapsto Cl]$ for the function that is the same as E except for having value Cl on argument x. (This notation is the same as the one used for assignments in Equation 1.2 of the semantics of the Simple Imperative Language.) Now, the component S is a stack of closures, which we can represent as a list where the head of the list serves as the top of the stack. Finally, a dump is either **empty** or it is a four tuple (S', E', C', D'), where S' is a stack, E' an environment, C' a code (instruction list), and D' another dump.

The SECD machine is described by a collection of transitions that cover all of the cases that can arise starting from a tuple $(\textbf{nil}, \emptyset, M, \textbf{empty})$ where M is a closed λ-term. The list of transition rules appears in Table 1.6. Here are some notes on the rules:

- If there are no further instructions in the command component, then the dump is consulted. The end of the evaluation of a term using the machine is reached when the dump is **empty** and there are no further commands to be executed. In this case the final result of the evaluation is the closure on the top of the stack.

- If an identifier is next on the command list, then it is looked up in the environment and placed on the stack. An identifier appearing in this way will always be in the domain of definition of the environment E.

Table 1.6
Transition Rules for the SECD Machine

$(Cl :: S, \ E, \ \textbf{nil}, \ (S', E', C', D')) \xrightarrow{\text{SECD}} (Cl :: S', \ E', \ C', \ D')$

$(S, \ E, \ x :: C, \ D) \xrightarrow{\text{SECD}} (E(x) :: S, \ E, \ C, \ D)$

$(S, \ E, \ (\textbf{lambda} \ x \ M) :: C, \ D) \xrightarrow{\text{SECD}} (((\textbf{lambda} \ x \ M), E) :: S, \ E, \ C, \ D)$

$(((\textbf{lambda} \ x \ M), E') :: Cl :: S, \ E, \ \textbf{ap} :: C, \ D)$
$\qquad \xrightarrow{\text{SECD}} (\textbf{nil}, \ E'[x \mapsto Cl], \ M, \ (S, E, C, D))$

$(S, \ E, \ (M \ N) :: C, \ D) \xrightarrow{\text{SECD}} (S, \ E, \ N :: M :: \textbf{ap} :: C, \ D)$

- If an abstraction is the next command, it is paired with the environment E to form a closure and put on the top of the stack. The invariants of the evaluation relation will ensure that the pair built in this way is indeed a closure.

- If an application is next on the command list, it is broken into three instructions that replace it at the beginning of the command list. The idea is that the operator and operand must be evaluated before the actual application can take place.

The thing to notice about this SECD semantics is that there are no rules with hypotheses, just transitions. The representation of a term includes its own stacks for holding intermediate values during computation. At the opposite extreme, a natural operational semantics suppresses as much detail about this aspect of computation as possible. Instead of using rewriting as the driving force of computation, it uses search for a proof. The transition semantics provides a compromise between computation as rewriting and computation as proof search. If we think of transitions as a 'horizontal' kind of computation (represented as a sequence of arrows from left to right) and search as a 'vertical' kind of computation (represented as a tree), then the difference between abstract machines, transition semantics, and natural semantics can be graphically illustrated as in Figure 1.1.

Exercises.

1.1 Show that various other orders of evaluation for the ALGOL 60 program in Table 1.2 yield other possible results: $\frac{3}{5}$, $\frac{3}{2}$, $\frac{5}{2}$, $\frac{4}{3}$, $3\frac{3}{5}$, $3\frac{1}{3}$, $5\frac{3}{5}$, $3\frac{1}{2}$, and $7\frac{1}{2}$. (Suggestion: represent the expression $a + f(a, g(a))/g(a)$ as a tree and demonstrate the results obtained from various orders in which its nodes could be calculated.)

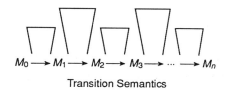

Abstract Machine

Transition Semantics

Natural Semantics

Figure 1.1
Three Forms of Operational Semantics

1.2 Alter the Simple Imperative Language to replace the while command with a command **repeat** C **until** B **end**, which tests the boolean *after* executing the command C rather than *before* as the while command does. For the new command, provide

    a. a careful informal description of its semantics,
    b. a transition semantics,
    c. a natural semantics.

1.3 Augment the λ-calculus with a non-deterministic choice construct. Give a grammar for your language and describe its transition semantics and natural semantics.

1.4 Formulate an analog of Lemma 1.3 for the Simple Imperative Language augmented by a non-deterministic choice construct C_1 **or** C_2.

1.5 Write a non-terminating program in the Simple Imperative Language and study how it runs in a transition or natural semantics. Carry out the same exercise for a non-terminating program in the call-by-value λ-calculus using transition, natural, or SECD semantics.

1.6 Give an example of a program in the Simple Imperative Language augmented by a non-deterministic choice construct C_1 **or** C_2 that has infinitely many possible outcomes. Show that your program can also diverge.

1.7* Formulate and prove a general conjecture about the phenomenon in Exercise 1.6.

1.8 Code the SECD machine in your favorite programming language.

1.9 Modify the definition of the SECD machine so that the evaluation is call-by-value rather than call-by-name.

1.3   Notes

The word 'semantics' was introduced by Micheal Bréal in 1897 and it is the subject of his book [35] on how words change their meanings. It is the most commonly used of a collection of terms derived from the Greek word *sēmainō* for 'to mean'. Some examples are: semiotic, semology, semasiology, and semiology. The last refers to the general subject of the relationship between signs and their meanings, whereas 'semantics' refers primarily to linguistic meaning.

Examples such as the Prolog and Scheme encodings of the gcd function given at the first part of the chapter and the programs for the Fibonacci function given later fill the pages of books that discuss programming methodology for these languages. Books by Sterling and Shapiro [249] and by Abelson and Sussman [2] are well-known examples for Prolog and Scheme respectively. The idea of viewing imperative programs as relations between properties of input and output states has been widely promoted in work of Hoare [116] and Dijkstra [73]. A discussion of the use of such relations together with hosts of references can be found in the survey article by Cousot [61]. Some works that have examined their use in higher-order languages include papers by Tennent [260], by Clarke, German, and Halpern [51; 85], by Goerdt [91], and a doctoral dissertation by O'Hearn [187].

There is a two-volume book by Lyons [153] on the semantics of natural language, and a variety of collections discuss the semantics of natural language and the philosophy of language [67; 135; 214; 248; 273]. There is a substantial literature on semantics in mathematical logic, an area generally known as *model theory*. A comprehensive bibliography is [229]. A standard reference on first-order model theory is the book by Chang and Keisler [50].

Attempts to formalize mathematics have been greatly intensified by the introduction of computers, since formalized proofs can be checked by machine. One successful effort in this direction is the Automath project of de Bruijn *et al.* [69], and another, which focuses on proofs in intuitionistic logic, is Nuprl project of Constable *et al.* [52].

Ever since the introduction of 'formal methods' for proving properties of programs, there has been a heated debate over their usefulness in practice. A well-known argument against formal methods was given in a paper by De Millo, Lipton, and Perlis [70], and a critique of this argument can be found in a paper by D. Scott and Scherlis [219]. A classic discussion of formality in mathematics that has not lost its relevance despite its age is Frege's book on arithmetic [81]; a translation of the work into English is [82].

Gödel's Incompleteness Theorem on the undecidability of truth for arithmetic has been clearly described in many sources. One such account appears in Boolos and Jeffrey [33]. Real closed fields are discussed in a paper by Ben-Or, Kozen, and Reif [23] where it is also possible to find further references.

An article by C. Gunter [98] drawn from this chapter discusses the terminology and history of some of the forms of denotational specification discussed in Section 1.2. The excerpt in Table 1.1 is taken from page 10 of the ALGOL 60 Revised Report [184]. The original report [183] appeared in 1960. The discussion of ALGOL 60 in Section 1.2 draws Exercise 1.1 and most of its examples from the 1967 article [139] of Knuth; his quote in Section 1.2 comes from the introduction of that article (page 611). The definition of the language Scheme [253] appeared first in 1975 followed by a revised report [254] three years later. The discussion of Scheme here is based on a revision to the revision, which is descriptively entitled *The revised*[3] *report on the algorithmic language Scheme* [199]. The quote is taken from the section on formal semantics in that article. A discussion of problems in the specification of the Pascal programming language appears in a paper of Welsh, Sneeringer, and Hoare [271].

Detailed treatments of the various forms of semantics for the Simple Imperative Language and some of its extensions can be found in books by Hennessy [111], Tennent [261], and Hanne and Flemming Nielson [185]. A substantial example of the use of natural semantics in programming language specification is the formal semantics for the Standard ML programming language given by Milner, Tofte, and Harper [173]. A commentary to aid the reader in understanding this definition is [172]. A paper [106] by Hannan and Miller discusses formal relationships between various forms of operational semantics. Fixed-point (denotational) semantics has its origins in the work of D. Scott and Strachey [230; 252]. An influential book on the topic was written by Stoy [252] in the 1970's. A more up-to-date exposition is the book by Schmidt [220]; it focuses on the denotational semantics of programming languages and has a substantial bibliography of further references. There is a handbook article on on denotational semantics by Mosses [179] and one on domain theory by C. Gunter and D. S. Scott [101]. The SECD machine was introduced by Landin [145; 146]. A good treatment of various extensions of the machine in this chapter can be found in the book of Henderson [109]. Some other approaches to specifying the semantics of programming languages include the Vienna Development Method, which is described by Wegner in [270], the evolving algebras of Gurevich [104], and the action semantics of Mosses [180].

The idea of automatically generating a compiler from a formal specification has been an area of active study. Pointers to most of the literature on the subject can be found in the book of Lee [151].

2 The Simply-Typed λ-Calculus

The well-deserved starting point for this discussion of the semantics of programming languages is the simply-typed λ-calculus. The calculus dates back to before the advent of modern higher-order programming languages. It was first studied in the 1930's by Church and others working on the foundations of mathematics. Their results had clear computational significance and were related to the original ideas on which the concept of a computer was based. However, the relevance of the simply-typed calculus (as opposed to the untyped calculus which is discussed later) was not fully appreciated by computer scientists until the 1960's, when its usefulness as the basis of a higher-order language was studied and its potential as a specification language was noted. The calculus can now be found as a fragment of many well-known programming languages, and it is the bedrock of work in the mathematical semantics of programming languages.

The simply-typed λ-calculus is a fundamental and powerful theory of *application and abstraction* governed by a basic theory of *types*. A type can be viewed as a property of an expression that describes how the expression can be used. We say that an expression (program) *M has type $s \to t$* if it can be applied to an expression of type s to yield an expression of type t. As trivial as it sounds, this rule is fundamental to all of our subsequent discussion of types. The expressions of the calculus are also taken to satisfy certain rules. The most important of these is called the *β-rule,* and it says that the application of a function to an argument is equal to the result of substituting the argument for the formal parameters used in defining the function. This sounds much simpler than it really is, and, indeed, the earliest uses of the λ-calculus in programming languages were subject to the problems of clarifying many nuances about what this statement actually means. Note, in particular, that understanding the β-rule involves understanding substitution.

In this chapter we look at the basic syntax and semantics of the simply-typed λ-calculus in an essentially non-computational setting. Its dynamic or operational meaning(s) will be discussed later. In the meantime we touch on several topics that will be fundamental to everything discussed later. After giving the syntax of expressions, the typing rules, and the equational rules for the calculus, the simplest example of a model is given. The *general definition* of a model is then defined rigorously, using the concept of a *type frame,* and other examples of models are given. Using the concept of a *partial homomorphism* between type frames, it is shown that our model using sets and functions is *complete* for the equational rules of the calculus.

2.1 Syntax of λ-Terms

To understand the syntax of the λ-calculus, it is essential to distinguish between three separate notions:

1. the concrete syntax of expressions used to denote term trees,

2. the term trees generated by the context-free grammar, and

3. equivalence classes of term trees modulo renaming of bound variables.

The last of these are the λ-terms, and they are our primary interest. To understand them, it is essential that the parsing conventions that relate concrete syntax to term trees are fully stated and that the equivalence relation on term trees is precisely defined. At one time or another it will be necessary to direct our attention to each of the three levels of description. Let us begin with the context-free grammar for types and terms; it is given in BNF as follows:

$$
\begin{aligned}
x &\in \text{Variable} \\
t &::= \mathbf{o} \mid t \to t \\
M &::= x \mid \lambda x : t.\, M \mid MM
\end{aligned}
$$

where Variable is the primitive syntax class of *variables*.[1] The expressions in the syntax class over which t ranges are called *types,* and those in the class over which M ranges are called *term trees.* In a later chapter, we expand our horizons to admit the possibility that there are variables in the syntax class of types as well as that of term trees; the adjective 'simply-typed' is meant to indicate that our calculus does not include this feature. In general, I use letters from the end of the alphabet such as x, y, z and such letters with subscripts and superscripts as in x', x_1, x_2 to range over variables, but it is also handy to use letters such as f, g for variables in some cases. Types are generally written using letters r, s, and t. Term trees are generally written with letters L, M, N. Such letters with superscripts and subscripts may also be used when convenient.

The type $\mathbf{o}$ is called the *ground* type, and types $s \to t$ are called *higher* types. Term trees of the form $\lambda x : t.\, M$ are called *abstractions,* and those of the form MN are called *applications.* Parentheses are used to indicate how an expression is parsed. For example, without a convention about parsing, the expression $\mathbf{o} \to \mathbf{o} \to \mathbf{o}$ is ambiguous and could be parsed as $(\mathbf{o} \to \mathbf{o}) \to \mathbf{o}$ or $\mathbf{o} \to (\mathbf{o} \to \mathbf{o})$. Similarly, without a convention, $\lambda x : s.\, \lambda y : t.\, xyz$ could be parsed as $(\lambda x : s.\, \lambda y : t.\, x)(yz)$ or $(\lambda x : s.\, \lambda y : t.\, (xy))z$ or as any one of a variety of other term trees. These two term trees are pictured in Figure 2.1

---

[1]Sometimes a distinction is made between a variable and an *identifier.* No such distinction will be made in this book and from now on the term 'variable' will generally be used in place of 'identifier'.

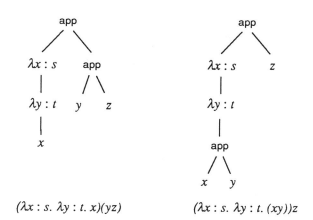

Figure 2.1
Examples of Term Trees

with application nodes labeled by 'appl' and abstraction nodes labeled by the variable and type.

To keep the number of parentheses at a minimum we employ several standard parsing conventions. For types, the *association of the operator* → *is to the right:* thus **o** → **o** → **o** parses as **o** → (**o** → **o**). Dually, *application operations associate to the left:* an application LMN should be parsed as $(LM)N$. So, the expression xyz unambiguously parses as $(xy)z$. If we wish to write the expression that applies x to the result of applying y to z, it is rendered as $x(yz)$. Moreover *application binds more tightly than abstraction:* an expression $\lambda x : t.\ MN$ should be parsed as $\lambda x : t.\ (MN)$. Hence, the expression $\lambda x : s.\ \lambda y : t.\ xyz$ unambiguously parses as $\lambda x : s.\ \lambda y : t.\ ((xy)z)$. Superfluous parentheses can be sprinkled into an expression at will to emphasize grouping. There is no distinction between M and (M), and it is common to surround the operand of an application $M(N)$ with parentheses to mimic the mathematical notation $f(x)$ for a function applied to an argument.[2] It is important to understand the role of meta-variables such as M, N, and t in parsing an expression involving such letters. For example, if M and N are the expressions $\lambda x : \mathbf{o}.\ x$ and y respectively, then the expression MN is $(\lambda x : \mathbf{o}.\ x)y$ and *not* the expression $\lambda x : \mathbf{o}.\ (xy)$, which one might get by concatenating $\lambda x : \mathbf{o}.\ x$ with y and then applying the parsing conventions. A simple strategy for avoiding any error is

---

[2]This is especially worth noting for those familiar with Lisp-like syntax where there is a big difference between f and (f) for an identifier f.

to replace MN by $(M)(N)$ before expanding M and N.

An *occurrence* of a variable in an expression is simply a point in the expression where the variable appears. For example, the underscore indicates:

1. the first occurrence of x in $\lambda \underline{x} : \mathbf{o}.\ (yx)x$

2. the second occurrence of x in $\lambda x : \mathbf{o}.\ (y\underline{x})x$

3. the third occurrence of x in $\lambda x : \mathbf{o}.\ (yx)\underline{x}$

Of course, occurrences can also be described using the tree structure of a term tree by indicating the position of the node in the tree where the variable lies. However, counting occurrences from left to right in the concrete syntax denoting the term tree is a simple approach that is sufficient for our purposes. In an abstraction $\lambda x : t.\ M$, the first occurrence of x is called the *binding occurrence* of the abstraction. The variable x is called the *formal parameter*. The term tree M is called the *body* of the abstraction, and t is the *type tag* of the binding occurrence. A period follows the type tag in the concrete syntax and separates the tag from the body of the abstraction. In an application $M(N)$, the term tree M is the *operator* and N is the *operand* or *argument*.

We may extend the notion of an occurrence to apply to arbitrary term trees as well as variables. For example, there are two occurrences of the term tree $\lambda x : s.\ x$ in the following expression:

$$(\lambda y : t.\ \underbrace{\lambda x : s.\ x}_{\text{first}})(\underbrace{\lambda x : s.\ x}_{\text{second}})$$

Such an occurrence of a term tree within another term tree is called a *subterm*. Care must be taken not to confuse the occurrence of a term tree as a subterm with a *substring* that would denote the term tree in concrete syntax. For example, there is only *one* occurrence of the term tree $\lambda x : s.\ x$ as a subterm of

$$\lambda y : t.\ \lambda x : s.\ x(\underbrace{\lambda x : s.\ x})$$

as indicated by the bracket.

An occurrence of a variable x in a term tree M is *free* if one of the following conditions holds:

- M is x, or

- M has the form $\lambda y : t.\ N$, where y is different from x and the occurrence of x in the subterm N is free, or

- M has the form $L(N)$ and the occurrence of x is free in L or in N.

Let M be a term tree and suppose we are given a binding occurrence of a variable x in M. Suppose, in particular, that the binding occurrence of x in question is in a subterm $\lambda x : t.\ N$ of M. An occurrence of x in M is said to be in the *scope* of this binding if it is free in N. Free occurrences of x in N are said to be *bound* to the binding occurrence of x in the abstraction. The set $\mathrm{Fv}(M)$ of variables having free occurrences in M is defined inductively as follows:

- $\mathrm{Fv}(x) = \{x\}$
- $\mathrm{Fv}(\lambda x : t.\ N) = \mathrm{Fv}(N) - \{x\}$
- $\mathrm{Fv}(L(N)) = \mathrm{Fv}(L) \cup \mathrm{Fv}(N)$

The treatment of bound variables is one of the most subtle points in the study of the λ-calculus or, indeed, in almost any of the areas in computer science and logic where the concept arises. In general, we will want to treat bound variables as 'nameless'. In this chapter, for example, we will not wish to distinguish between the term trees $\lambda x : \mathbf{o}.\ x$ and $\lambda y : \mathbf{o}.\ y$ in which the names of the bound variable are different. However, in a later chapter we will be interested in the idea of substituting a term tree into another term tree in such a way that the names of bound variables *are* essential. For example, if $\lambda x : \mathbf{o}.\ yx$ is viewed as the text of a program, then there is a big difference between putting it in place of the brackets in the expression $\lambda y : \mathbf{o} \to \mathbf{o}.\ y\{\ \}$ versus putting it in place of the brackets in the expression $\lambda x : \mathbf{o} \to \mathbf{o}.\ x\{\ \}$ since the first substitution creates a new binding whereas the second does not. A reasonable theory of program transformations dealing with the substitutability of code fragments should allow for this possibility.

To study this notion further and prepare ourselves for the definitions needed to explicate this dichotomy precisely, we define the *context substitution* $\{M/x\}N$ of a term tree M for a variable x in a term tree N inductively as follows:

- if N is the variable x, then $\{M/x\}N$ is M.
- if N is a variable y different from x, then $\{M/x\}N$ is y.
- if N is an application $N_1(N_2)$, then $\{M/x\}N$ is $(\{M/x\}N_1)(\{M/x\}N_2)$.
- if N is an abstraction $\lambda x : t.\ L$ where the bound variable is x, then $\{M/x\}N$ is N.
- if N is an abstraction $\lambda y : t.\ L$ where the bound variable y is different from x, then $\{M/x\}N$ is $\lambda y : t.\ \{M/x\}L$.

For example, $\{\lambda x : \mathbf{o}.\ yx/z\}\lambda y : \mathbf{o}.\ yz$ is the term tree $\lambda y : \mathbf{o}.\ y(\lambda x : \mathbf{o}.\ yx)$ whereas $\{\lambda x : \mathbf{o}.\ yx/z\}\lambda x : \mathbf{o}.\ xz$ is $\lambda x : \mathbf{o}.\ x(\lambda x : \mathbf{o}.\ yx)$. This notion of substitution *allows* the possibility that an occurrence of a variable that is free in M becomes bound in its occurrence in $\{M/x\}N$.

In most of the literature on the λ-calculus, this capture of free variables under substitution is considered undesirable, and substitution is defined with conditions that avoid the problem. However, the matter has no trivial resolution since it arises from the deep fact that there is a distinction between the textual representation of terms of the λ-calculus, the trees generated by our grammar for such terms, and the underlying structure that generally interests us. In expositions of the λ-calculus, the matter is typically swept under the carpet in one way or another. However, it arises inevitably in any attempt to automate or implement the λ-calculus as a formal system. I will not attempt to discuss the techniques that are used to deal with these implementation problems here since they are not immediately pertinent to the needs of this chapter; instead, I will simply distinguish between the term trees arising from the grammar above and equivalence classes of such terms modulo renaming of bound variables.

Definition: A *relation* is a triple consisting of a pair of sets X, Y called the *domain* and *codomain* (or *range*) of the relation and a set R of pairs (x, y) where $x \in X$ and $y \in Y$. We write $R : X \to Y$ to indicate that R is a relation with domain X and codomain Y. It is common to use an infix notation for relations by writing $x \, R \, y$ if $(x, y) \in R$.

Given a set X, a *binary relation on X* is a relation $R : X \to X$. Such a relation is said to be an *equivalence* if it satisfies the following three properties for any $x, y, z \in X$:

1. Reflexive: $x \, R \, x$;
2. Symmetric: $x \, R \, y$ implies $x \, R \, y$;
3. Transitive: $x \, R \, y$ and $y \, R \, z$ implies $x \, R \, z$. $\qquad\qquad\square$

Definition: The α-*equivalence* of term trees is defined to be the least relation $\equiv$ between term trees such that

- $x \equiv x$
- $MN \equiv M'N'$ if $M \equiv M'$ and $N \equiv N'$
- $\lambda x : t.\ M \equiv \lambda y : t.\ N$ if $\{z/x\}M \equiv \{z/y\}N$ where z is a variable that has no occurrence in M or N. $\qquad\qquad\square$

2.1 Lemma. *The relation $\equiv$ is an equivalence.* $\qquad\qquad\square$

The proof is left as an exercise. Equivalence classes of term trees modulo the relation $\equiv$ are called λ-*terms* or, more simply, *terms*. The equivalence class of term trees determined by a term tree M is called its α-*equivalence class*. In general, the same letters (L, M, N, *etc.*) are used for both λ-terms and term trees, with the understanding that a term is given as the α-equivalence class of a term tree representative. However, for the moment, let us be especially precise and write M^* for the α-equivalence class of M. Substitution on λ-terms is defined to respect these equivalence classes, and our notation for it is similar to the one we used for term trees.

Definition: We define the substitution $[M^*/x]N^*$ of M^* for x in N^* to be the α-equivalence class of $\{M/x\}L$ where $L \equiv N$ and no free variable of M has a binding occurrence in L. ☐

For example, if M is $\lambda x : \mathbf{o}.\ yx$ and N is $\lambda y : \mathbf{o}.\ yz$, then $[M^*/z]N^*$ is $(\lambda u : \mathbf{o}.\ u(\lambda x : \mathbf{o}.\ yx))^*$ where u is some new variable. What if we had chosen another variable besides u? If the new choice is v, say, this would give us a different term tree, but

$$\lambda u : \mathbf{o}.\ u(\lambda x : \mathbf{o}.\ yx) \equiv \lambda v : \mathbf{o}.\ v(\lambda x : \mathbf{o}.\ yx)$$

so this choice makes no difference in determining the equivalence class. To be fully precise we need to prove a lemma that the substitution operation is well-defined on α-equivalence classes. The proof is left for the reader.

In the future we will work with λ-terms as equivalence classes of term trees without explicitly mentioning term trees. To rid our discussion of many tedious repetitions of assumptions about the names of bound variables, it is helpful to use a convention about the choice of the representative of an α-equivalence class.

Notation: (Bound Variable Naming Convention.) When a term tree representative of an α-equivalence class is chosen, the name of the bound variable of the representative is distinct from the names of free variables in other terms being discussed. ☐

When we encounter the need to deal explicitly with the names of bound variables, then term trees will be distinguished from λ-terms explicitly.

Although we are not concerned with the possibility of bound variables at the level of types in this chapter, this will become an issue later. So, in anticipation of this expansion, we write $s \equiv t$ to indicate that the types s and t generated from our grammar for types are the same. For instance, $\mathbf{o} \to \mathbf{o} \to \mathbf{o} \equiv \mathbf{o} \to (\mathbf{o} \to \mathbf{o})$, but $\mathbf{o} \to \mathbf{o} \to \mathbf{o} \not\equiv (\mathbf{o} \to \mathbf{o}) \to \mathbf{o}$.

Exercises.

2.1 Assuming that there are no parsing conventions, list all of the ways in which the expression $\lambda x : s.\ \lambda y : t.\ xyz$ could potentially be parsed. For each possible parsing, indicate the relationship between all binding and bound occurrences of variables.

2.2 Prove that any type t can be written in the form $t_1 \to t_2 \to \cdots \to t_n \to o$ for some $n \geq 0$ and type expressions $t_1, \ldots t_n$.

Table 2.1
Typing Rules for the Simply-Typed λ-Calculus

[Proj]	$H, x : t, H' \vdash x : t$
[Abs]	$\dfrac{H,\ x : s \vdash M : t}{H \vdash \lambda x : s.\ M : s \rightarrow t}$
[Appl]	$\dfrac{H \vdash M : s \rightarrow t \qquad H \vdash N : s}{H \vdash M(N) : t}$

2.2 Rules

There are two systems of rules describing the simply-typed λ-calculus. The first of these determines which of the terms described in the previous section are to be viewed as *well-typed*. These are the terms to which we will assign a meaning in our semantic model. The second set of rules of the calculus forms its *equational theory,* which consists of a set of rules for proving equalities between λ-terms.

Typing rules.

A *type assignment* is a list $H \equiv x_1 : t_1, \ldots, x_n : t_n$ of pairs of variables and types such that the variables x_i are distinct. The empty type assignment $\emptyset$ is the degenerate case in which there are no pairs. I write $x : t \in H$ if x is x_i and t is t_i for some i. In this case it is said that x *occurs* in H, and this may be abbreviated by writing $x \in H$. If $x : t \in H$, then define $H(x)$ to be the type t.

A *typing judgement* is a triple consisting of a type assignment H, a term M, and a type t such that all of the free variables of M appear in H. We will write this relation between H, M, and t in the form $H \vdash M : t$ and read it as 'in the assignment H, the term M has type t'. It is defined to be the least relation satisfying the axiom and two rules in Table 2.1. Here are some comments on the rules:

- The projection rule [Proj] asserts, in effect, that $H \vdash x : H(x)$ provided $x \in H$.

- The application rule [Appl] says that, for a type assignment H, a term of the form $M(N)$ has a type t if there is a type s such that the operand N has type s and the operator M has type $s \rightarrow t$.

- The abstraction rule [Abs] is the most subtle of the typing rules. It says that a term of the form $\lambda x : s.\ M$ has the type $s \rightarrow t$ in type assignment H if M has type t in type assignment $H, x : s$. Note, however, the relationship between the conclusion of the rule, where x represents a bound variable on the right side of the $\vdash$, and its hypothesis, where x is a free variable in M. It is essential that the bound variable in the term tree representative of the conclusion not appear in H since otherwise $H, x : s$ would not be a well-formed type assignment.

A demonstration of $H \vdash M : t$ from these rules is called a *typing derivation*. Such derivations are trees with nodes labeled by typing judgements. As an example, consider how it can be shown that

$$\vdash \lambda x : \mathbf{o}.\ \lambda f : \mathbf{o} \to \mathbf{o}.\ f(x) : \mathbf{o} \to (\mathbf{o} \to \mathbf{o}) \to \mathbf{o}$$

To derive the desired conclusion, begin by noting that the hypotheses of the following instance of the application rule both follow from projection:

$$\frac{x : \mathbf{o}, f : \mathbf{o} \to \mathbf{o} \vdash f : \mathbf{o} \to \mathbf{o} \qquad x : \mathbf{o}, f : \mathbf{o} \to \mathbf{o} \vdash x : \mathbf{o}}{x : \mathbf{o}, f : \mathbf{o} \to \mathbf{o} \vdash f(x) : \mathbf{o}}$$

and two instances of the abstraction rule can be used to complete the proof:

$$\frac{\dfrac{x : \mathbf{o}, f : \mathbf{o} \to \mathbf{o} \vdash f(x) : \mathbf{o}}{x : \mathbf{o} \vdash \lambda f : \mathbf{o} \to \mathbf{o}.\ f(x) : (\mathbf{o} \to \mathbf{o}) \to \mathbf{o}}}{\vdash \lambda x : \mathbf{o}.\ \lambda f : \mathbf{o} \to \mathbf{o}.\ f(x) : \mathbf{o} \to (\mathbf{o} \to \mathbf{o}) \to \mathbf{o}}$$

Large proofs of this kind can become cumbersome to write as a tree on the page; to get a tabular representation that can be written as three columns, one can list the addresses of the nodes of the tree in postfix order with the labeling judgement written next to the address. Here is an example in which the nodes are also labeled with the rule used:

000	$x : \mathbf{o}, f : \mathbf{o} \to \mathbf{o} \vdash f : \mathbf{o} \to \mathbf{o}$	[Proj]
001	$x : \mathbf{o}, f : \mathbf{o} \to \mathbf{o} \vdash x : \mathbf{o}$	[Proj]
00	$x : \mathbf{o}, f : \mathbf{o} \to \mathbf{o} \vdash f(x) : \mathbf{o}$	[Appl]
0	$x : \mathbf{o} \vdash \lambda f : \mathbf{o} \to \mathbf{o}.\ f(x) : (\mathbf{o} \to \mathbf{o}) \to \mathbf{o}$	[Abs]
	$\vdash \lambda x : \mathbf{o}.\ \lambda f : \mathbf{o} \to \mathbf{o}.\ f(x) : \mathbf{o} \to (\mathbf{o} \to \mathbf{o}) \to \mathbf{o}$	[Abs]

In this addressing scheme, if b is any sequence of zeroes and ones, $b0$ and $b1$ are the first and second sons respectively of the node addressed by b. For example, the judgement at node 00 in this proof follows by the application rule from hypotheses 000 and 001. Each of these hypotheses is an instance of the projection axiom. In some cases a rule has only one hypothesis, and in such cases it is addressed as a first son; for instance, 0 follows from 00 by abstraction. The conclusion is addressed by the empty sequence and appears as the last line of the derivation.

To illustrate the care that must be taken in dealing with bound variables in the abstraction rule, let $t \equiv \mathbf{o} \to (\mathbf{o} \to \mathbf{o}) \to \mathbf{o}$ and consider the term

$$M \equiv \lambda x : \mathbf{o}.\; \lambda y : t.\; yx(\lambda x : \mathbf{o}.\; x).$$

This term has type $\mathbf{o} \to t \to \mathbf{o}$. To prove this, it is essential to work with a term tree representative that uses a different name for one of the bound occurrences of x. Here is a derivation:

0000	$x : \mathbf{o},\; y : t \vdash y : t$	[Proj]
0001	$x : \mathbf{o},\; y : t \vdash x : \mathbf{o}$	[Proj]
000	$x : \mathbf{o},\; y : t \vdash yx : (\mathbf{o} \to \mathbf{o}) \to \mathbf{o}$	[Appl]
0010	$x : \mathbf{o},\; y : t,\; z : \mathbf{o} \vdash z : \mathbf{o}$	[Proj]
001	$x : \mathbf{o},\; y : t \vdash \lambda z : \mathbf{o}.\; z : \mathbf{o} \to \mathbf{o}$	[Abs]
00	$x : \mathbf{o},\; y : t \vdash yx(\lambda z : \mathbf{o}.\; z) : \mathbf{o}$	[Appl]
0	$x : \mathbf{o} \vdash \lambda y : t.\; yx(\lambda z : \mathbf{o}.\; z) : t \to \mathbf{o}$	[Abs]
	$\vdash \lambda x : \mathbf{o}.\; \lambda y : t.\; yx(\lambda z : \mathbf{o}.\; z) : \mathbf{o} \to t \to \mathbf{o}$	[Abs]

Since the term tree representative used for the term M above is α-equivalent to the last term in this derivation tree, we conclude that M has type $\mathbf{o}$.

In general, we will only be interested in terms M and type assignments H such that $H \vdash M : t$ for some type t. Arbitrary terms (including terms that do not have a type) are sometimes called 'raw terms' since they are terms that do not satisfy any such relation. For example, $\lambda x : \mathbf{o}.\; x(x)$ fails to have a type in any type assignment. But if a term has a type in a given assignment, then that type is uniquely determined. To prove this, and many other properties of the λ-calculus, one can use a technique known as *structural induction*. Essentially, this is an induction on the height of the parse tree of the term; a property of terms M is proved by first showing that it holds if M is a variable and then showing that the property is satisfied by M if it is satisfied by each of its subterms.

2.2 Lemma. *If $H \vdash M : t$ and x does not appear in H, then x is not free in M.*

Proof: If M is a variable y, then it cannot be x since $H \vdash M : t$ must follow from projection, so $y \in H$. Suppose the lemma is known for subterms of M; that is, suppose that, for any subterm M' of M, if $H' \vdash N : t'$ and x' is a variable that does not appear in H', then x' is not free in M'. Now the goal is to prove that the lemma holds for M itself.

If M is an abstraction, then M must have the form $\lambda y : r.\; M'$ where $H,\; y : r \vdash M' : s$ and $t \equiv r \to s$. If it happens that this y is the same as x, then the desired conclusion is immediate since x is not free in $\lambda x : r.\; M'$. If, on the other hand, y is different from

x, then x does not appear in H, $y : r$ so the fact that the lemma is assumed, by the inductive hypothesis, to hold for subterms of M means that it holds for M'. Hence x is not free in M' and therefore not free in M.

If M is an application, then it has the form $L(N)$. Since the application rule is the only way to prove that this term has a type, we must have $H \vdash L : s \to t$ and $H \vdash N : s$ for some type s. The inductive hypothesis says that the lemma is true for these two subterms of M, so x is free in neither L nor N. Therefore, it is not free in M. □

A similar argument can be used to prove the following:

2.3 Lemma. *If $H \vdash \lambda x : s.\ M : t$, then $H,\ y : s \vdash [y/x]M : t$ for any variable y that does not appear in H.* □

The proof is left as an exercise.

2.4 Lemma. *If $H \vdash M : s$ and $H \vdash M : t$, then $s \equiv t$.*

Proof: The proof is by induction on the structure of M. If $M \equiv x$ for a variable x then $s \equiv H(x) \equiv t$.

If $M \equiv \lambda x : u.\ M'$, then $s \equiv u \to s'$ where $H,\ x : u \vdash M' : s'$ and also $t \equiv u \to t'$ where $H,\ x : u \vdash M' : t'$ (by Lemma 2.3 and a suitable choice of x). Since M' is a subterm of M, we may conclude that it satisfies the lemma and that $s' \equiv t'$. But this immediately implies that $s \equiv t$.

If $M \equiv L(N)$, then $H \vdash L : u \to s$ for some u. Similarly, there is a type v such that $H \vdash L : v \to t$. Since L is a subterm of M, we must have $u \to s \equiv v \to t$ and therefore $s \equiv t$. □

Type tags are placed on bound variables in abstractions just to make Lemma 2.4 true. If we try to simplify our notation by allowing terms of the form $\lambda x.\ M$ and a typing rule of the form

$$[\text{Abs}]^- \qquad \frac{H,\ x : s \vdash M : t}{H \vdash \lambda x.\ M : s \to t},$$

then Lemma 2.4 would *fail*. For example, we would then have

$$\vdash \lambda x.\ x : \mathbf{o} \to \mathbf{o}$$

as well as

$$\vdash \lambda x.\ x : (\mathbf{o} \to \mathbf{o}) \to (\mathbf{o} \to \mathbf{o}).$$

Most of the calculi introduced in this book have a syntax with enough type tags to ensure that an appropriate version of Lemma 2.4 holds.

There are several basic properties of type assignments that can be proved by structural induction.

2.5 Lemma. *If H, $x : r$, $y : s$, $H' \vdash M : t$, then H, $y : s$, $x : r$, $H' \vdash M : t$.*

Proof: The proof proceeds by induction on the structure of the term M. Assume, as the inductive hypothesis, that the lemma holds for any subterm of M. Let $H_0 \equiv H$, $x : r$, $y : s$, H' and $H_1 \equiv H$, $y : s$, $x : r$, H'.

Case $M \equiv x$. Then $r \equiv t$, and the projection axiom applies. A similar argument applies when $M \equiv y$.

Case $M \equiv z$ where $z \not\equiv x$ and $z \not\equiv y$. Then $z : t \in H$ or $z : t \in H'$, and the projection axiom applies.

Case $M \equiv \lambda z : u.\ N$. Then $t \equiv u \to v$ for some type v. Since $H_0 \vdash M : u \to v$, we must have $H_0, z : u \vdash N : v$ so $H_1, z : u \vdash N : v$ follows from the inductive hypothesis. Hence, by the abstraction rule, $H_1 \vdash M : t$ as desired.

Case $M \equiv L(N)$. In this case, there is some type u such that $H_0 \vdash L : u \to t$ and $H_0 \vdash N : u$ since this is the only way $H_0 \vdash M : t$ could have been derived. By the inductive hypothesis, we may conclude that $H_1 \vdash L : u \to t$ and $H_1 \vdash N : u$. By the application rule, we must therefore have $H_1 \vdash M : t$ as desired. $\qquad\square$

The proof of the lemma may equivalently be viewed as a proof by induction on the height of the derivation of the typing judgement $H, x : r, y : s, H' \vdash M : t$ since the structure of that derivation follows the structure of the term. Or, indeed, it may be viewed as an induction simply on the number of symbols appearing in M, since each subterm will have fewer symbols than the term of which it is a part. Here is another example of a proof by structural induction. The lemma will be needed to prove a crucial property of the equational theory of the lambda-calculus.

2.6 Lemma. *If $H, x : s, H' \vdash M : t$ and $H, H' \vdash N : s$, then $H, H' \vdash [N/x]M : t$.*

Proof: The proof is by structural induction on M. If $M \equiv x$, then $s \equiv t$ and the result is immediate. If M is a variable y different from x, then the desired conclusion follows from [Proj]. If M is an application, then the conclusion of the lemma follows from the inductive hypothesis and the definition of the substitution operation. Now, if $M \equiv \lambda y : u.\ L$ and $t \equiv u \to v$, then $H, x : s, H', y : u \vdash L : v$ so $H, H', y : u \vdash [N/x]L : v$ by the inductive hypothesis. Thus $H, H' \vdash [N/x]M : t$ by [Abs] and the definition of substitution. $\qquad\square$

Equational rules.

An *equation* in the simply-typed lambda-calculus is a four-tuple (H, M, N, t) where H is a type assignment, M, N are λ-terms, and t is a type. To make a tuple like this more readable, it is helpful to replace the commas separating the components of the tuple by more suggestive symbols and to write $(H \rhd M = N : t)$. The triangular marker is intended to indicate where the interesting part of the tuple begins. The heart of the tuple is the pair of terms on either side of the of equation symbol; H and t provide typing information about these terms. An *equational theory* T is a set of equations $(H \rhd M = N : t)$ such that $H \vdash M : t$ and $H \vdash N : t$. An equation $(H \rhd M = N : t)$ should be viewed only as a formal symbol. For the judgement that an equation is *provable*, we define the relation $\vdash$ between theories T and equations $(H \rhd M = N : t)$ to be the least relation satisfying the rules in Table 2.2. The assertion $T \vdash (H \rhd M = N : t)$ is called an *equational judgement*. Of course, the turnstile symbol $\vdash$ is also used for typing judgements, but this overloading is never a problem because of the different appearance of the two forms of judgement. The two are related by the fact that if $T \vdash (H \rhd M = N : t)$, then both M and N have type t relative to H. Before proving this fact, let us look at some specific remarks about the equational judgements. For many of the rules, the best way to understand the rule is to think of the theory T, the type assignment H, and the type t as fixed. Then $\vdash$ can be viewed as defining a binary relation between terms M and N. Of course, this is the usual way to think of the equality relationship, but the indirect route taken by defining equations as tuples makes it easier to account for the role that typing judgements play in describing the semantics of terms in our subsequent discussions. An equation $(H \rhd M = N : t)$ is *provable* in theory T just in the case where $T \vdash (H \rhd M = N : t)$. A demonstration of an equational rule is called an *equation derivation*. As with typing derivation, such demonstrations have the structure of a tree labeled with equational judgements. Here are specific comments about the rules.

- The axiom rule {Axiom} asserts that all of the equations in T are provable from T.

- The addition rule {Add} asserts that the type assignment H in an equation can be extended by assignment of a type to a new variable. The drop rule {Drop} asserts that an assignment of a type to a variable can be removed from the type assignment component of an equation if the variable does not have a free occurrence in either of the term components of the equation. By the permutation rule {Permute}, any equation E obtained from an equation E' by permuting the order of variable/type pairs in the assignment component of E' is provable if E' is.

- The reflexivity rule {Refl}, symmetry rule {Sym}, and transitivity rule {Trans} assert that $=$ can be viewed as an equivalence relation on terms relative to a fixed theory and type tags.

- The congruence rule {Cong} and the ξ-rule assert that application and abstraction respectively are congruences relative to the equality relation (relative to a fixed theory and type tags).

Table 2.2
Equational Rules for the Simply-Typed λ-Calculus

{Axiom}
$$\frac{(H \rhd M = N : t) \in T}{T \vdash (H \rhd M = N : t)}$$

{Add}
$$\frac{T \vdash (H \rhd M = N : t) \qquad x \notin H}{T \vdash (H, \ x : s \rhd M = N : t)}$$

{Drop}
$$\frac{T \vdash (H, \ x : s \rhd M = N : t) \qquad x \notin \mathrm{Fv}(M) \cup \mathrm{Fv}(N)}{T \vdash (H \rhd M = N : t)}$$

{Permute}
$$\frac{T \vdash (H, \ x : r, \ y : s, H' \rhd M = N : t)}{T \vdash (H, \ y : s, \ x : r, \ H' \rhd M = N : t)}$$

{Refl}
$$\frac{H \vdash M : t}{T \vdash (H \rhd M = M : t)}$$

{Sym}
$$\frac{T \vdash (H \rhd M = N : t)}{T \vdash (H \rhd N = M : t)}$$

{Trans}
$$\frac{T \vdash (H \rhd L = M : t) \qquad T \vdash (H \rhd M = N : t)}{T \vdash (H \rhd L = N : t)}$$

{Cong}
$$\frac{T \vdash (H \rhd M = M' : s \to t) \qquad T \vdash (H \rhd N = N' : s)}{T \vdash (H \rhd M(N) = M'(N') : t)}$$

{ξ}
$$\frac{T \vdash (H, \ x : s \rhd M = N : t)}{T \vdash (H \rhd \lambda x : s. \ M = \lambda x : s. \ N : s \to t)}$$

{β}
$$\frac{H, x : s \vdash M : t \qquad H \vdash N : s}{T \vdash (H \rhd (\lambda x : s. \ M)(N) = [N/x]M : t)}$$

{η}
$$\frac{H \vdash M : s \to t \qquad x \notin \mathrm{Fv}(M)}{T \vdash (H \rhd \lambda x : s. \ M(x) = M : s \to t)}$$

- The β- and η-rules are the key to the λ-calculus. The β-rule says that the application of an abstraction to an operand is equal to the result of substituting the operand for the bound variable of the abstraction in the body of the abstraction. It is harder to explain the η-rule; it says that if M is a function, then the function that takes an argument x and applies M to it is indistinguishable from M.

- In the η-rule, the variable x cannot have a free occurrence in the term M. It is important to note the parsing in this axiom. For example, if x is not free in M, then $(\lambda x : s.\ M)x = M$ because of the β-rule. But $\lambda x : s.\ (M(x)) = M$ does *not* follow from β.

Properties of theories and equations are often proved by induction on the structure of terms, but there is another form of argument that is very common for such properties: induction on the height of a derivation tree. In general, the *height* of a tree is the length of the longest branch in the tree. To prove a property of a collection of trees by induction on the height involves checking the result for base cases—trees of height 1—and establishing that a tree of height $n + 1$ has the property if any tree of height n does. Derivations of equations in the simply-typed λ-calculus are trees where each node corresponds to an instance of a rule of the equational system given in Table 2.2. A proof by induction on the heights of such derivations can be carried out by verifying that each rule preserves the desired property in the sense that the property is satisfied by the conclusion whenever it is satisfied by its hypotheses. Here is a typical example of a proof by induction on the heights of derivation trees.

2.7 Lemma. *If T is a theory and $T \vdash (H \rhd M = N : t)$, then $H \vdash M : t$ and $H \vdash N : t$.*

Proof: This is proved by induction on the height of the derivation of the judgement $T \vdash (H \rhd M = N : t)$. The idea is to assume that the lemma holds for any equation that appears in the hypothesis of a rule from which this judgement is derived and then prove that it holds for $T \vdash (H \rhd M = N : t)$ as well. Suppose that the rule employed in the last step of the derivation is an instance of {Axiom}. Then $(H \rhd M = N : t) \in T$, and by the definition of a theory it follows that $H \vdash M : t$ and $H \vdash N : t$. Suppose that the last step of the derivation is an instance of {Permute}. In this case, Lemma 2.5 states the desired conclusion. Similar results for {Add} and {Drop} have been left as an exercise. If the last step in the proof is an instance of {Refl}, {Trans}, or {Sym}, then the desired conclusion follows immediately from the inductive hypothesis. If the last step is an instance of {Cong}, then $M \equiv M'(M'')$ and $N \equiv N'(N'')$ where, by the inductive hypothesis,

$$H \vdash M' : s \to t \quad H \vdash M'' : s$$
$$H \vdash N' : s \to t \quad H \vdash N'' : s$$

so $H \vdash M : t$ and $H \vdash N : t$ by [Appl]. Similarly, the case of the ξ-rule follows from [Abs] and the inductive hypothesis. If the η-rule is the last step of the derivation, then $t \equiv u \to v$ for some u, v, and we must show that $H \vdash \lambda x : u. M(x) : v$ given that $H \vdash M : u \to v$. This follows easily if we can show that $H, x : u \vdash M : u \to v$. The proof of this is left as an exercise. Finally, if the last step of the derivation is an instance of the β-rule, then N has the form $[N'/x]M'$ where $H, x : s \vdash M' : t$ and $H \vdash N' : s$. The conclusion for N therefore follows from Lemma 2.6. For M in this case, the desired conclusion follows from [Abs] and [Appl].   □

To prove some basic facts about equations below it is essential to know more about how typing and equational judgements are related. The reader can prove as an exercise this lemma:

2.8 Lemma. *If $H \vdash M : t$ and $H' \vdash M : t$, then $H(x) = H'(x)$ for every $x \in \mathrm{Fv}(M)$.* □

This is needed to prove the following:

2.9 Lemma. *Suppose $H \vdash M : t$ and $H \vdash N : t$. If $T \vdash (H' \rhd M = N : t)$ for any type assignment H', then also $T \vdash (H \rhd M = N : t)$.*

Proof: Let G be the sublist of H' obtained by removing from H' all of the assignments of types to variables that are not in $\mathrm{Fv}(M) \cup \mathrm{Fv}(N)$. By repeated application of the {Permut} and {Drop} rules, it is possible to conclude that $T \vdash (G \rhd M = N : t)$. By Lemma 2.7, $G \vdash M : t$ and $G \vdash N : t$ so, by Lemma 2.8, $G(x) = H(x)$ for each $x \in \mathrm{Fv}(M) \cup \mathrm{Fv}(N)$. By Lemma 2.2, it must be the case that every variable in $\mathrm{Fv}(M) \cup \mathrm{Fv}(N)$ also appears in H. Since every variable in G is in $\mathrm{Fv}(M) \cup \mathrm{Fv}(N)$, it must be the case that G is a permutation of a sublist of H. Let G' be the sublist of H all of whose variables are not in $\mathrm{Fv}(M) cup \mathrm{Fv}(N)$. Then by repeated applications of {Add}, it is possible to conclude that $T \vdash (G, G' \rhd M = N : t)$. Since G, G' is just a permutation of H, it follows from repeated applications of {Permut} that $T \vdash (H \rhd M = N : t)$.   □

Exercises.

2.3 Structural induction is used to prove properties of term trees as well as properties of terms.

   a. Prove that $\equiv$ is an equivalence relation (Lemma 2.1).
   b. Prove that substitution is well-defined on α-equivalence classes. That is, if M, M' and N, N' are term trees such that $M \equiv M'$ and $N \equiv N'$, then $[M/x]N \equiv [N'/x]M'$.

2.4 Prove Lemma 2.3.

2.5 Prove that the term $\lambda x : \mathbf{o}.\ x(x)$ does not have a type.

2.6 Complete the proof of Lemma 2.7 by proving results that apply to the rules {Add} and {Drop}:

    a. Show that if $H \vdash M : t$ and $x \notin H$, then $H, x : t \vdash M : t$.

    b. Show that if $H, x : s \vdash M : t$ and x is not free in M, then $H \vdash M : t$.

2.7 Prove Lemma 2.8.

2.8 For a type assignment $H = x_1 : t_1, \ldots, x_n : t_n$ and a variable x_i' not occurring in H, let $[x_i'/x_i]H$ be the assignment $x_1 : t_1, \ldots, x_i' : t_i, \ldots, x_n : t_n$. Show that if $H \vdash M = N : t$, then $[x_i'/x_i]H \vdash [x_i'/x_i]M = [x_i'/x_i]N : t$. In other words, equality is preserved under a renaming of free variables.

2.9 Note that some of the equational rules for the λ-calculus in Table 2.2 involve typing judgements $H \vdash M : t$ as well as equational judgements $T \vdash (H \rhd M = N : t)$. It is possible to modify the equational rules for the lambda-calculus so that typing judgements are not needed in the equational rules. To do this, replace the three equational rules in which typing judgements appear with the following rules:

$$\{\text{Refl}'\} \qquad \frac{x \in H}{T \vdash (H \rhd x = x : H(x))}$$

$$\{\beta'\} \qquad \frac{T \vdash (H,\ x : s \rhd M = M : t) \qquad T \vdash (H \rhd N = N : s)}{T \vdash (H \rhd (\lambda x : s.\ M)(N) = [N/x]M : t}$$

$$\{\eta'\} \qquad \frac{T \vdash (H \rhd M = M : s \to t) \qquad x \notin H}{T \vdash (H \rhd \lambda x : s.\ M(x) = M : s \to t)}$$

Prove a version of Lemma 2.7 for this new system and conclude that it is equivalent to the official set of rules in Table 2.2. Show that this new formulation makes it possible to give typing judgements as a defined notion rather than providing a separate axiomatization as in Table 2.1.

2.3   Models

There are two ways to view the relationship between an object language calculus and a model. One holds that the model is a means for studying the calculus itself. This is a common way to see things in the semantics of programming languages, since attention is very often focused on syntax. However, under another view, the calculus is a syntax for expressing elements of a distinguished model M. We then think of M as *standard* because the calculus is being judged in terms of the model. This dual view generalizes to a situation in which there is a *class* of models for a calculus where there may or may not be a distinguished standard model. This section discusses these perspectives for the semantics of the simply-typed λ-calculus. We begin with a discussion of what one might view as the standard model, in which types are interpreted as sets of functions, and then look at the definition of a class of models for the λ-calculus. It can be shown that the equational rules of the simply-typed calculus are *sound* for reasoning about the equational properties of the class of models in the sense that each equation is satisfied by all of the models in the class. Moreover, the equational rules are *complete* in the sense that an equation that is true in all of the models can actually be proved from the equational theory. At the end of the section it is shown that something more is true: an equation is provable just in the case where it holds in the standard model.

Sets and functions.

Our starting point for the discussion of models of typed calculi is the 'standard' model of the simply-typed λ-calculus in which sets are types and functions are denoted by terms. Before giving the semantic interpretation, let us pause to state the definition of a function precisely and introduce a notation for the set of functions.

Definition: A *function* (or *map*) is a relation $f : X \to Y$ such that for each $x \in X$, there is a unique $y \in Y$ such that $(x, y) \in f$. For each $x \in X$, the notation $f(x)$ is used for this unique element of Y and we say that f *maps* x to y. The set of all $y \in Y$ such that $f(x) = y$ for some $x \in X$ is called the *image* of f. Given X and Y, the set of all functions with domain X and codomain Y is written Y^X. $\qquad \qquad \Box$

Now, the semantic interpretation of types is relative to a given set X, which serves as the interpretation for the base type. To keep a notational barrier between the types and terms of the λ-calculus on the one hand, and the mathematics that surrounds the semantic description on the other, syntax is ordinarily enclosed between *semantic brackets:* $[\![\cdot]\!]$. The meaning $[\![t]\!]$ of a type t is a set defined inductively as follows:

- $[\![\mathbf{o}]\!] = X$
- $[\![s \to t]\!] = [\![t]\!]^{[\![s]\!]}$.

So, for example, $[\![\mathbf{o} \to (\mathbf{o} \to \mathbf{o})]\!]$ is the set of functions f such that, for each $x \in X$, $f(x)$ is a function from X into X. On the other hand, $[\![(\mathbf{o} \to \mathbf{o}) \to \mathbf{o}]\!]$ is the set of functions F such that, for each function f from X to X, $F(f)$ is an element of X.

Describing the meanings of terms is more difficult than describing the meanings of types, and we require some further vocabulary and notation. While a type assignment associates *types* with variables, an *environment* associates *values* to variables. Environments are classified by type assignments: if H is a type assignment, then an H-*environment* is a function ρ on variables that maps each $x \in H$ to a value $\rho(x) \in [\![H(x)]\!]$. If ρ is an H-environment, $x : t \in H$, and $d \in [\![t]\!]$, then we define

$$\rho[x \mapsto d](y) = \begin{cases} d & \text{if } y \equiv x \\ \rho(y) & \text{otherwise.} \end{cases}$$

This is the 'update' operation. One can read $\rho[x \mapsto d]$ as 'the environment ρ with the value of x updated to d'. The notation is very similar to that used for syntactic substitution, but note that this operation on environments is written as a postfix. So another way to read $\rho[x \mapsto d]$ is 'the environment ρ with d for x.' Note that if $x \notin H$ for an assignment H, then $\rho[x \mapsto d]$ is an $H, x : t$ assignment if $d \notin [\![t]\!]$. Now, the meaning of a term M is described relative to a type assignment H and a type t such that $H \vdash M : t$. We use the notation $[\![H \rhd M : t]\!]$ for the meaning of term M relative to H, t. Here, as in the case of equations earlier, the triangle is intended as a kind of marker or separator between the type assignment H and the term M. We might have written $[\![H \vdash M : t]\!]$ for the meaning, but this confuses the use of $\vdash$ as a relation for typing judgements with its syntactic use as a punctuation in the expression within the semantic brackets. Nevertheless, it is important to remember that $[\![H \rhd M : t]\!]$ only makes sense if $H \vdash M : t$.

The meaning $[\![H \rhd M : t]\!]$ is a function from H-environments to $[\![t]\!]$. The semantics is defined by induction on the typing derivation of $H \vdash M : t$,

- Projection: $[\![H \rhd x : t]\!]\rho = \rho(x)$.

- Abstraction: $[\![H \rhd \lambda x : u.\ M' : u \to v]\!]\rho$ is the function from $[\![u]\!]$ to $[\![v]\!]$ given by $d \mapsto [\![H, x : u \rhd M' : v]\!](\rho[x \mapsto d])$, that is, the function f defined by

$$f(d) = [\![H, x : u \rhd M' : v]\!](\rho[x \mapsto d]).$$

- Application: $[\![H \rhd L(N) : t]\!]\rho$ is the value obtained by applying the function $[\![H \rhd L : s \to t]\!]\rho$ to argument $[\![H \rhd N : s]\!]\rho$ where s is the unique type such that $H \vdash L : s \to t$ and $H \vdash N : s$.

It will save us quite a bit of ink to drop the parentheses that appear as part of expressions such as $[\![H, x : u \rhd M' : v]\!](\rho[x \mapsto d])$ and simply write $[\![H, x : u \rhd M' : v]\!]\rho[x \mapsto d]$. Doing so appears to violate our convention of associating applications to the left, but there is little chance of confusion in the case of expressions such as these. Hence, we will adopt the convention that the postfix update operator binds more tightly than general application.

It must be shown that this assignment of meanings respects our equational rules. This is the *soundness* property of the semantic interpretation:

2.10 Theorem (Soundness). *If* $\vdash (H \rhd M = N : t)$, *then* $[\![H \rhd M : t]\!] = [\![H \rhd N : t]\!]$.   □

To prove this theorem, we must check that each of the rules of the λ-calculus is satisfied. The proof proceeds by induction on the height of the derivation of an equality. The rules {Refl}, {Sym}, {Trans}, and {Cong} are immediate from the corresponding properties for equality of sets. Suppose that a proof ends by an application of the ξ-rule:

$$\frac{\vdash (H, x : s \rhd M = M' : t)}{\vdash (H \rhd \lambda x : s.\ M = \lambda x : s.\ M' : s \to t)}.$$

We apply the definition of our semantic function and the inductive hypothesis to calculate

$$([\![H \rhd \lambda x : s.\ M : s \to t]\!]\rho)(d)$$
$$= [\![H, x : s \rhd M : t]\!]\rho[x \mapsto d]$$
$$= [\![H, x : s \rhd M' : t]\!]\rho[x \mapsto d] \qquad (2.1)$$
$$= ([\![H \rhd \lambda x : s.\ M' : s \to t]\!]\rho)(d)$$

where Equation 2.1 follows from the inductive hypothesis on equational derivations. This shows that

$$[\![H \rhd \lambda x : s.\ M : s \to t]\!] = [\![H \rhd \lambda x : s.\ M' : s \to t]\!]$$

since a function is determined by its action on its arguments—a property known as *extensionality*.

To prove soundness of the η-rule we use the following:

2.11 Lemma. *Suppose M is a term and $H \vdash M : t$. If $x \notin H$ and $d \in [\![s]\!]$, then* $[\![H, x : s \rhd M : t]\!]\rho[x \mapsto d] = [\![H \rhd M : t]\!]\rho$.   □

The proof is left as an exercise. The lemma essentially asserts that the meaning of a term M in a type environment H depends only on the values H assigns to free variables of M. We may therefore calculate

$$[\![H \rhd \lambda x : s.\ M(x) : s \to t]\!]\rho$$
$$= (d \mapsto [\![H, x : s \rhd M(x) : t]\!]\rho[x \mapsto d])$$
$$= (d \mapsto ([\![H, x : s \rhd M : s \to t]\!]\rho[x \mapsto d])(d))$$
$$= (d \mapsto ([\![H \rhd M : s \to t]\!]\rho)(d))$$
$$= [\![H \rhd M : s \to t]\!]\rho$$

where the final equation follows from Lemma 2.11.

To prove soundness of the β-rule, we could begin the calculation as follows:

$$\begin{aligned}
&[\![H \rhd (\lambda x : s.\ M)(N) : t]\!]\rho \\
&= \quad ([\![H \rhd \lambda x : s.\ M : s \to t]\!]\rho)([\![H \rhd N : s]\!]\rho) \\
&= \quad [\![H, x : s \rhd M : t]\!]\rho[x \mapsto ([\![H \rhd N : s]\!]\rho)]
\end{aligned}$$

but we now wish to conclude that this last expression is equal to $[\![H \rhd [N/x]M : t]\!]\rho$. This relationship between substitution and the 'updating' of the environment is the essence of the meaning of the β-rule. We summarize it as the following:

2.12 Lemma (Substitution). *If $H \vdash N : s$ and $H, x : s \vdash M : t$, then*

$$[\![H \rhd [N/x]M : t]\!]\rho = [\![H, x : s \rhd M : t]\!]\rho[x \mapsto ([\![H \rhd N : s]\!]\rho)].$$

Proof: Let $e = [\![H \rhd N : s]\!]\rho$. The proof of the lemma is by induction on the structure of M.

Case $M \equiv y$ where $y \not\equiv x$. Then

$$\begin{aligned}
[\![H \rhd [N/x]y : t]\!]\rho &= [\![H \rhd y : t]\!]\rho \\
&= \rho(y) \\
&= [\![H, x : s \rhd y : t]\!]\rho[x \mapsto e]
\end{aligned}$$

Case $M \equiv x$. In this case, $s \equiv t$. We have

$$\begin{aligned}
[\![H \rhd [N/x]x : t]\!]\rho &= [\![H \rhd N : t]\!]\rho \\
&= \rho[x \mapsto e](x) \\
&= [\![H, x : s \rhd M : t]\!]\rho[x \mapsto e]
\end{aligned}$$

Case $M \equiv \lambda y : u.\ M'$. We have $t \equiv u \to v$. (By the Bound Variable Convention we assume that $y \not\equiv x$ and $y \notin \mathrm{Fv}(N)$.)

$$\begin{aligned}
&[\![H \rhd [N/x]\lambda y : u.\ M' : u \to v]\!]\rho \\
&= \quad [\![H \rhd \lambda y : u.\ [N/x]M' : u \to v]\!]\rho \\
&= \quad (d \mapsto [\![H, y : u \rhd [N/x]M' : u \to v]\!]\rho[y \mapsto d]) \\
&= \quad (d \mapsto [\![H, y : u, x : s \rhd M' : u \to v]\!](\rho[y \mapsto d][x \mapsto e])) \\
&= \quad (d \mapsto [\![H, x : s, y : u \rhd M' : u \to v]\!](\rho[x \mapsto e][y \mapsto d])) \\
&= \quad [\![H, x : s \rhd \lambda y : u.\ M' : u \to v]\!](\rho[x \mapsto e])
\end{aligned}$$

Case $M \equiv M_0(M_1)$. We have

$$[\) : t]\!]\rho$$

$$= (\llbracket H \, \triangleright \, [N/x]M_0 : u \to t \rrbracket \rho)(\llbracket H \, \triangleright \, [N/x]M_1 : u \rrbracket \rho)$$
$$= (\llbracket H, \; x : s \, \triangleright \, M_0 : u \to t \rrbracket \rho[x \mapsto e])(\llbracket H, \; x : s \, \triangleright \, M_1 : u \rrbracket \rho[x \mapsto e])$$
$$= \llbracket H, \; x : s \, \triangleright \, M_0(M_1) : t \rrbracket \rho[x \mapsto e] \qquad\qquad \square$$

As an application of the soundness of our interpretation, consider the following:

2.13 Theorem. *The simply-typed λ-calculus is non-trivial. That is, for any type t and pair of distinct variables x and y, it is not the case that $\vdash (x : t, \; y : t \, \triangleright \, x = y : t)$.*

Proof: Suppose, on the contrary, that $\vdash (x : t, \; y : t \, \triangleright \, x = y : t)$. Let X be any set with more than one element and consider the model of the simply-typed λ-calculus generated by X. It is not hard to see that $\llbracket t \rrbracket$ has at least two distinct elements p and q. Now, let ρ be an $x : t, \; y : t$ environment such that $\rho(x) = p$ and $\rho(y) = q$. Then $\llbracket x : t, \; y : t \, \triangleright \, x : t \rrbracket \rho = \rho(x) = p \neq q = \rho(y) = \llbracket x : t, \; y : t \, \triangleright \, y : t \rrbracket \rho$. But this contradicts the soundness of our interpretation. $\qquad\qquad \square$

It is instructive, as an exercise on the purpose of providing a semantic interpretation for a calculus, to try proving Theorem 2.13 directly from first principles and the rules for the λ-calculus using syntactic means. The soundness result provides us with a simple way of demonstrating properties of the rules of our calculus or, dually, a syntax for proving properties of our model (sets and functions).

Type frames.

Although we have given a way to associate a 'meaning' $\llbracket H \, \triangleright \, M : t \rrbracket$ to a tuple, and demonstrated that our assignment of meaning preserves the required equations, we did not actually provide a rigorous description of the ground rules for saying when such an assignment really is a *model* of the simply-typed λ-calculus. In fact, there is more than one way to do this, depending on what one considers important about the model. The choice of definition may be a matter of style or convenience, but different choices may also reflect significant distinctions. Indeed, many different definitions were presented and studied in the late 1970's, (especially for the *untyped* λ-calculus, which we will discuss later). The definition provided in this section is, perhaps, the simplest and most intuitive one, although not always the easiest to check and not the most general. An 'environment model' is an interpretation that assigns a meaning to a term M with respect to an environment ρ. The model we gave above is an example of a presentation in this form. The notion of an environment is designed to deal with the meaning of an expression that has free variables. Although every model of the λ-calculus must deal with the meanings of free variables, there are other ways to handle them that reflect a different style of description. In particular, another definition of model, based on the idea of a *category*, will be given later.

For the sake of convenience, our first definition of a model of the simply-typed λ-calculus is broken into two parts. Models are called frames; these are defined in terms of a more general structure called a pre-frame.

Definition: A *pre-frame* is a pair of functions $\mathcal{A}[\![\cdot]\!]$ and A on types and pairs of types respectively such that

- $\mathcal{A}[\![t]\!]$ is a non-empty set, which we view as the interpretation of type t, and
- $A^{s,t} : \mathcal{A}[\![s \to t]\!] \times \mathcal{A}[\![s]\!] \to \mathcal{A}[\![t]\!]$ is a function that we view as the interpretation of the application of an element of $\mathcal{A}[\![s \to t]\!]$ to an element of $\mathcal{A}[\![s]\!]$,

and such that the *extensionality property* holds: that is, whenever $f, g \in \mathcal{A}[\![s \to t]\!]$ and $A^{s,t}(f, x) = A^{s,t}(g, x)$ for every $x \in \mathcal{A}[\![s]\!]$, then $f = g$. $\qquad\Box$

To make the notation less cumbersome, we write $(\mathcal{A}, A)$ for a pre-frame and use $\mathcal{A}$ to represent the pair. Pre-frames are very easy to find. For example, we might take $\mathcal{A}[\![s]\!]$ to be the set of natural numbers for every s and define $A^{s,t}(f, x)$ to be the product of f and x. Since $f * 1 = g * 1$ implies $f = g$, the extensionality property is clearly satisfied. Nevertheless, this multiplication pre-frame does not provide any evident interpretation for λ-terms (indeed, there is none satisfying the equational rules—see Exercise 2.12).

A frame is a pre-frame together with a sensible interpretation for λ-terms.

Definition: A *type frame* (or *frame*) is a pre-frame $(\mathcal{A}^{\text{type}}, A)$ together with a function $\mathcal{A}^{\text{term}}$ defined on triples $H \rhd M : t$ such that $H \vdash M : t$. An *H-environment* is a function ρ from variables to meanings such that $\rho(x) \in \mathcal{A}^{\text{type}}[\![H(x)]\!]$ whenever $x \in H$. $\mathcal{A}^{\text{term}}[\![H \rhd M : t]\!]$ is a function from H-environments into $\mathcal{A}^{\text{type}}[\![t]\!]$. The function $\mathcal{A}^{\text{term}}[\![\cdot]\!]$ is required to satisfy the following equations:

1. $\mathcal{A}^{\text{term}}[\![H \rhd x : t]\!]\rho = \rho(x)$
2. $\mathcal{A}^{\text{term}}[\![H \rhd M(N) : t]\!]\rho = A^{s,t}(\mathcal{A}^{\text{term}}[\![H \rhd M : s \to t]\!]\rho,\ \mathcal{A}^{\text{term}}[\![H \rhd N : s]\!]\rho)$
3. $A^{s,t}(\mathcal{A}^{\text{term}}[\![H \rhd \lambda x : s.\ M : s \to t]\!]\rho,\ d) = \mathcal{A}^{\text{term}}[\![H, x : s \rhd M : t]\!]\rho[x \mapsto d]$. $\qquad\Box$

If a pre-frame has an extension to a frame, then the extension is unique.

2.14 Lemma. *Let $(\mathcal{A}^{\text{type}}, A)$ be a pre-frame over which $\mathcal{A}^{\text{term}}[\![\cdot]\!]$ and $\bar{\mathcal{A}}^{\text{term}}[\![\cdot]\!]$ define frames. Then $\mathcal{A}^{\text{term}}[\![H \rhd M : t]\!] = \bar{\mathcal{A}}^{\text{term}}[\![H \rhd M : t]\!]$ whenever $H \vdash M : t$.*

Proof: The proof is by induction on the structure of M. The only non-trivial case occurs when $t \equiv r \to s$ and $M \equiv \lambda x : r . N$. In this case,

$$
\begin{aligned}
A^{r,s}(\mathcal{A}^{\text{term}}[\![H \rhd M : r \to s]\!]\rho, \, d) &= \mathcal{A}^{\text{term}}[\![H, \, x : r \rhd N : s]\!]\rho[x \mapsto d] \\
&= \bar{\mathcal{A}}^{\text{term}}[\![H, \, x : r \rhd N : s]\!]\rho[x \mapsto d] \\
&= A^{r,s}(\bar{\mathcal{A}}^{\text{term}}[\![H \rhd M : r \to s]\!]\rho, \, d)
\end{aligned}
$$

so the desired result follows from the extensionality property for pre-frames. $\square$

In the future I will use the same notation $\mathcal{A}$ for both $\mathcal{A}^{\text{type}}[\![\cdot]\!]$ and $\mathcal{A}^{\text{term}}[\![\cdot]\!]$. The lemma says that the former together with an application operation A determines the latter, so it simplifies matters to write a pair $(\mathcal{A}, A)$ for a frame. When the application operation A is not explicitly mentioned or when it is understood from context, I may simply write $\mathcal{A}$ for the frame itself.

A frame $\mathcal{A}$ should be viewed as a model of the λ-calculus; we write

$$
\mathcal{A} \models (H \rhd M = N : t)
$$

if, and only if, $\mathcal{A}[\![H \rhd M : t]\!]\rho = \mathcal{A}[\![H \rhd N : t]\!]\rho$ for each H-environment ρ. Whenever it will not cause confusion, it helps to drop the type tags and type and write $\mathcal{A} \models M = N$. If T is a set of equations, then

$$
\mathcal{A} \models T
$$

if, and only if, $\mathcal{A} \models (H \rhd M = N : t)$ for each equation $(H \rhd M = N : t)$ in T. Define $T \models M = N$ if $\mathcal{A} \models M = N$ whenever $\mathcal{A} \models T$.

The most basic example of a frame is the interpretation we discussed in the previous section. Given a set X, the *full frame over* X is $\mathcal{F}_X = (\mathcal{F}_X[\![\cdot]\!], F_X)$ where

- $\mathcal{F}_X[\![\mathbf{o}]\!] = X$ and $\mathcal{F}_X[\![s \to t]\!]$ is the set of functions from $\mathcal{F}_X[\![s]\!]$ to $\mathcal{F}_X[\![t]\!]$
- $F_X^{s,t}(f, x) = f(x)$, that is, $F_X^{s,t}$ is ordinary function application,
- on terms, $\mathcal{F}_X[\![\cdot]\!]$ is the function $[\![\cdot]\!]$ defined in the previous section.

It is easy to see that our definition of the semantic function $[\![\cdot]\!]$ corresponds exactly to the three conditions in the definition of a frame. Moreover, these were essentially the properties that made our proof of the soundness property for the interpretation possible. To be precise:

2.15 Theorem (Soundness for Frames). *For any theory T and frame $\mathcal{A}$, if $\mathcal{A} \models T$ and $T \vdash (H \rhd M = N : t)$, then $\mathcal{A} \models (H \rhd M = N : t)$.* $\square$

The proof of the Theorem is left as an exercise; it is very similar to the proof of the soundness of the full type frame. When T is empty, we have the following:

2.16 Corollary. *For any frame $\mathcal{A}$, if $\vdash M = N$, then $\mathcal{A} \models M = N$*   □

Example: A binary relation $\sqsubseteq$ on a set P is said *anti-symmetric* if $x = y$ whenever $x \sqsubseteq y$ and $y \sqsubseteq x$. A *partial order* or *poset* is a set P together with a binary relation $\sqsubseteq$ that is reflexive, transitive, and anti-symmetric. If $(P, \sqsubseteq_P)$ and $(Q, \sqsubseteq_Q)$ are partial orders, a function $f : P \to Q$ is *monotone* if $x \sqsubseteq_P y$ implies $f(x) \sqsubseteq_Q f(y)$. Given posets P and Q, the monotone functions $f : P \to Q$ between P and Q are themselves a poset; the *pointwise ordering* on these functions is defined by taking $f \sqsubseteq g$ iff $f(x) \sqsubseteq_Q g(x)$ for each $x \in P$. Given a poset P, there is a frame $\mathcal{A}$ where $\mathcal{A}[\![o]\!] = P$ and $\mathcal{A}[\![s \to t]\!]$ is the poset of monotone functions from $\mathcal{A}[\![s]\!]$ to $\mathcal{A}[\![t]\!]$ under the pointwise ordering. Application for this frame is the usual function application.   □

Another important class of examples of frames can be formed from equivalence classes of well-typed terms of the simply-typed calculus. To define these frames we need some more notation for type assignments. An *extended* type assignment $\mathcal{H} = x_1 : t_1, \, x_2 : t_2, \ldots$ is an infinite list of pairs such that every finite subset $H \subseteq \mathcal{H}$ is a type assignment and every type appears infinitely often. Note that if $H \vdash M : t$ and $H' \vdash M : s$ where $H, H' \subseteq \mathcal{H}$, then $s \equiv t$. Now, fix an extended type assignment $\mathcal{H}$. Let T be a set of equations of the form $(H \rhd M = N : t)$ where $H \subseteq \mathcal{H}$. If $H \vdash M : t$ for some $H \subseteq \mathcal{H}$, define

$$[M]_T = \{M' \mid T \vdash (H' \rhd M = M' : t) \text{ for some } H' \subseteq \mathcal{H}\}.$$

This defines an equivalence relation on such terms M (the proof is left as an exercise). When T is the empty set, we drop the subscript T. For each type t, define

$$\mathcal{T}_T[\![t]\!] = \{[M]_T \mid H \vdash M : t \text{ for some } H \subseteq \mathcal{H}\}.$$

For each pair of types s, t, define $\text{TermAppl}_T^{s,t} : \mathcal{T}_T[\![s \to t]\!] \times \mathcal{T}_T[\![s]\!] \to \mathcal{T}_T[\![t]\!]$ by

$$\text{TermAppl}_T^{s,t}([M]_T, [N]_T) = [M(N)]_T.$$

This is well-defined because of the congruence rule for application. These operations define what is called the *term* pre-frame:

2.17 Lemma. *The pair $(\mathcal{T}_T, \text{TermAppl}_T)$ is a pre-frame.*

Proof: Suppose $[f]_T, [g]_T \in \mathcal{T}_T[\![s \to t]\!]$ and $[f(M)]_T = [g(M)]_T$ for all M of type s. Let $x : s \in \mathcal{H}$ be a variable that has no free occurrence in f or g. Then $[f(x)]_T = [g(x)]_T$, so $T \vdash (H \rhd f(x) = g(x) : t)$ for some $H \subseteq \mathcal{H}$. By ξ-rule (together with the rules for permuting and adding, to be precise), we have

$$T \vdash (H \rhd \lambda x : s.\ f(x) = \lambda x : s.\ g(x) : s \to t).$$

Hence, by the η-rule, $T \vdash (H \rhd f = g : s \to t)$. Thus $[f]_T = [g]_T$. □

We now show that this pre-frame is a frame, which is called the *term model* over T. To do this we begin by extending our earlier definition of a substitution to permit *simultaneous* substitutions. We write $\sigma = [M_1, \ldots, M_n/x_1, \ldots, x_n]$ for the function that maps the variable x_i to the term M_i for each i and acts as the identity on other variables. It is assumed that $x_1, \ldots, x_n$ are distinct. The *support* of the substitution is the set of variables on which the substitution is not the identity; of course, the support of $[M_1, \ldots, M_n/x_1, \ldots, x_n]$ is a subset of $\{x_1, \ldots, x_n\}$. The substitution $\sigma = [M_1, \ldots, M_n/x_1, \ldots, x_n]$ can be extended to substitution on terms by inductively defining

- $\sigma(M(N)) \equiv (\sigma(M))(\sigma(N))$
- $\sigma(\lambda x : t.\ M) \equiv \lambda x : t.\ \sigma(M)$ where x is not in the support of σ or in $\mathrm{Fv}(\sigma(y))$ for any y in the support of σ.

This generalizes our earlier notation $[M/x]$ which may now be viewed as a substitution with support $\{x\}$. When x is not in the support of σ, we write $\sigma[x \mapsto M]$ or $\sigma[M/x]$ for $[M_1, \ldots, M_n, M/x_1, \ldots, x_n, x]$.

Let ρ be an H-environment for the term pre-frame: that is, $\rho(x) \in \mathcal{T}_T[\![H(x)]\!]$ whenever $x \in H$. Let us say that a substitution σ *represents* ρ over H if, for each x in H, the term $\sigma(x)$ is a representative of the term model equivalence class $\rho(x)$.

2.18 Lemma. *Let* $\mathcal{T}_T[\![H \rhd M : t]\!]\rho = [\sigma(M)]_T$ *where* σ *is a substitution representing* ρ *over* H. *Then* $(\mathcal{T}_T, \mathrm{TermAppl}_T)$ *is a type frame.*

Proof: That $\mathcal{T}_T[\![\cdot]\!]$ is well-defined follows from the congruence of application and abstraction with respect to equality. To prove that we have a frame, the appropriate conditions for variables, applications, and abstractions must be established. I will leave the variable and application cases to the reader and prove the necessary condition for abstractions.

Suppose σ represents ρ over H, then

$$
\begin{aligned}
\mathrm{TermAppl}_T^{s,t}(\mathcal{T}_T[\![H \rhd \lambda x : s.\ M : s \to t]\!]\rho,\ [N]_T) \\
=\quad & \mathrm{TermAppl}_T^{s,t}([\sigma(\lambda x : s.\ M : s \to t)]_T,\ [N]_T) \\
=\quad & \mathrm{TermAppl}_T^{s,t}([\lambda x : s.\ \sigma(M) : s \to t]_T,\ [N]_T) \\
=\quad & [(\lambda x : s.\ \sigma(M))(N)]_T \\
=\quad & [(\sigma[N/x])M]_T \\
=\quad & \mathcal{T}_T[\![H,\ x : s \rhd M : t]\!]\rho[x \mapsto [N]_T]
\end{aligned}
$$

since $\sigma[N/x]$ represents $\rho[x \mapsto [N]_T]$ over H, $x : s$.   □

We are now ready to see the proof of the main result of this section:

2.19 Theorem (Completeness for Frames). *$T \vdash M = N$ if, and only if, $T \models M = N$.*

This follows immediately from Lemma 2.18 and the following:

2.20 Theorem. *$T \vdash (H \rhd M = N : t)$ if, and only if, $\mathcal{T}_T \models (H \rhd M = N : t)$.*

Proof: Necessity ($\Rightarrow$) follows immediately from the Soundness Theorem 2.15 for frames and the fact that the term model is a frame (Lemma 2.18).

To prove sufficiency ($\Leftarrow$), rename the variables in H so that $H \subseteq \mathcal{H}$ (see Exercise 2.8). Choose ρ to be the identity environment $\rho : x \mapsto [x]_T$. The identity substitution $\sigma : x \mapsto x$ represents this over H. Now, $[M]_T = [\sigma(M)]_T = \mathcal{T}_T[\![H \rhd M : t]\!]\rho = \mathcal{T}_T[\![H \rhd N : t]\!]\rho = [\sigma(N)] = [N]_T$ so $T \vdash (H' \rhd M = N : t)$ for some $H' \subseteq \mathcal{H}$. Hence, by Lemma 2.9, $T \vdash (H \rhd M = N : t)$ as well.   □

A particularly important example of a frame in the class of term models is the one induced by the empty theory: $\mathcal{T}_\emptyset$. For this particular term model it is convenient to drop the subscript $\emptyset$. As an instance of Theorem 2.20, we have the following:

2.21 Corollary. *$\vdash M = M'$ if, and only if, $\mathcal{T} \models M = M'$.*   □

Completeness of the full type frame.

Given a collection of mathematical structures, it is usually fruitful to find and study collections of structure-preserving transformations or mappings between them. Homomorphisms of algebras are one such example, and continuous maps on the real numbers another example. What kinds of mappings between type frames should we take to be 'structure-preserving'? The definition we seek for the goal of this section is obtained by following the spirit of homomorphisms between algebras but permitting *partial* structure-preserving mappings and requiring such maps to be surjective. This will provide the concept needed to prove that the full type frame is complete.

Definition: A *partial function* $f : A \rightsquigarrow B$ is a subset of $A \times B$ such that whenever $(x, y), (x, z) \in f$, then $y = z$. The *domain of definition* of f is the set of $x \in A$, such that $(x, y) \in f$ for some $y \in B$. For a partial function f, we write $f(x) = y$ if, and only if, $(x, y) \in f$. A partial function $f : A \rightsquigarrow B$ is a *surjection* if, for any $y \in B$, there is some $x \in A$ such that $(x, y) \in f$. □

Notation: Another common notation used to indicate that a set $f \subseteq A \times B$ is a partial function is to write $f : A \rightharpoonup B$ using a kind of half arrow. This is easier to write than $\rightsquigarrow$ but has the disadvantage of looking too much like $\rightarrow$. A simple notation to write that is almost as pleasing to read as the official one given in the definition above is to put a tilde on top of an arrow to emphasize the possibility of partiality; one writes $f : A \overset{\sim}{\rightarrow} B$. □

Definition: Let $\mathcal{A}$ and $\mathcal{B}$ be frames. A *partial homomorphism* $\Phi : \mathcal{A} \rightarrow \mathcal{B}$ is a family of surjective partial functions $\Phi^s : \mathcal{A}[\![s]\!] \rightsquigarrow \mathcal{B}[\![s]\!]$ such that, for each s, t, and $f \in \mathcal{A}[\![s \rightarrow t]\!]$ either

1. there is some $g \in \mathcal{B}[\![s \rightarrow t]\!]$ such that

$$\Phi^t(A^{s,t}(f, x)) = B^{s,t}(g, \Phi^s(x)) \tag{2.2}$$

   for all x in the domain of definition Φ^s and $\Phi^{s \rightarrow t}(f) = g$, or
2. there is no element $g \in \mathcal{B}[\![s \rightarrow t]\!]$ that satisfies Equation 2.2 and $\Phi^{s \rightarrow t}(f)$ is undefined. □

Suppose that g and h are solutions to Equation 2.2. Then $B^{s,t}(g, y) = B^{s,t}(h, y)$ for each $y \in \mathcal{B}[\![s]\!]$ since Φ^s is a surjection. Extensionality therefore implies that g and h are equal. So, if there is a solution in $\mathcal{B}[\![s \rightarrow t]\!]$ for Equation 2.2, then there is a unique one.

The following is the basic fact about partial homomorphisms:

2.22 Lemma. *Let $\mathcal{A}$ and $\mathcal{B}$ be frames. If $\Phi : \mathcal{A} \rightarrow \mathcal{B}$ is a partial homomorphism and ρ is an H-environment for $\mathcal{A}$ and ρ' is an H-environment for $\mathcal{B}$ such that $\Phi^t(\rho(x)) = \rho'(x)$ for each variable x in H, then*

$$\Phi^t(\mathcal{A}[\![H \triangleright M : t]\!]\rho) = \mathcal{B}[\![H \triangleright M : t]\!]\rho'$$

whenever $H \vdash M : t$.

Proof: The proof proceeds by induction on the structure of M.
    Case $M \equiv x$. Then $\Phi^t(\mathcal{A}[\![H \triangleright x : t]\!]\rho) = \Phi^t(\rho(x)) = \rho'(x) = \mathcal{B}[\![H \triangleright x : t]\!]\rho'$.

Case $M \equiv L(N)$.

$$\Phi^t(\mathcal{A}[\![H \rhd L(N) : t]\!]\rho)$$
$$= \quad \Phi^t(A^{s,t}(\mathcal{A}[\![H \rhd L : s \to t]\!]\rho, \mathcal{A}[\![H \rhd N : s]\!]\rho))$$
$$= \quad B^{s,t}(\Phi^{s \to t}(\mathcal{A}[\![H \rhd L : s \to t]\!]\rho), \Phi^t(\mathcal{A}[\![H \rhd N : s]\!]\rho))$$
$$= \quad B^{s,t}(\mathcal{B}[\![H \rhd L : s \to t]\!]\rho', \mathcal{B}[\![H \rhd N : s]\!]\rho')$$
$$= \quad \mathcal{B}[\![H \rhd L(N) : t]\!]\rho'.$$

Case $M \equiv \lambda x : u. \ M'$ where $t \equiv u \to v$. If d is in the domain of Φ^u, then

$$B^{u,v}(\mathcal{B}[\![H \rhd \lambda x : u. \ M' : u \to v]\!]\rho', \Phi^u(d))$$
$$= \mathcal{B}[\![H, \ x : u \rhd M' : v]\!]\rho'[x \mapsto \Phi^u(d)]$$
$$= \Phi^v(\mathcal{A}[\![H, \ x : u \rhd M' : v]\!]\rho[x \mapsto d])$$
$$= \Phi^v(A^{u,v}(\mathcal{A}[\![H \rhd \lambda x : u. \ M' : u \to v]\!]\rho, \ d)).$$

The conclusion of the lemma therefore follows directly from the condition on $\Phi^{u \to v}$ in the definition of a partial homomorphism.

2.23 Lemma. *If there is a partial homomorphism* $\Phi : \mathcal{A} \to \mathcal{B}$, *then*

$$\mathcal{A} \models (H \rhd M = N : t) \ \text{implies} \ \mathcal{B} \models (H \rhd M = N : t).$$

Proof: Suppose ρ' is an H-environment for $\mathcal{B}$. Choose ρ so that $\rho'(x) = \Phi^t(\rho(x))$ for each x in H. This is possible because Φ^s is a surjection. Then

$$\mathcal{B}[\![H \rhd M : t]\!]\rho' = \Phi^t(\mathcal{A}[\![H \rhd M : t]\!]\rho)$$
$$= \Phi^t(\mathcal{A}[\![H \rhd N : t]\!]\rho)$$
$$= \mathcal{B}[\![H \rhd N : t]\!]\rho'. \qquad \qquad \Box$$

2.24 Lemma. *Let $\mathcal{A}$ be a type frame and suppose there is a surjection from a set X onto $\mathcal{A}[\![o]\!]$. Then there is a partial homomorphism from $\mathcal{F}_X$ (the full type frame over X) to $\mathcal{A}$.*

Proof: Let $\Phi^o : X \to \mathcal{A}[\![o]\!]$ be any surjection. Suppose $\Phi^s : \mathcal{F}_X[\![s]\!] \to \mathcal{A}[\![s]\!]$ and $\Phi^t : \mathcal{F}_X[\![t]\!] \to \mathcal{A}[\![t]\!]$ are partial surjections. We define $\Phi^{s \to t}(f)$ to be the unique element of $\mathcal{A}[\![s \to t]\!]$, if it exists, such that $A^{s,t}(\Phi^{s \to t}(f), \Phi^s(y)) = \Phi^t(f(y))$ for all y in the domain of definition of Φ^s. Proof that this defines a surjection is carried out by induction on structure of types. It holds by assumption for ground types; suppose $g \in \mathcal{A}[\![s \to t]\!]$ and Φ^s, Φ^t are surjections. Choose $g' \in \mathcal{F}_X[\![s \to t]\!] = \mathcal{F}_X[\![s]\!] \to \mathcal{F}_X[\![t]\!]$ such that, for all y in the domain of definition of Φ^s, we have $g'(y) \in (\Phi^t)^{-1}(A^{s,t}(g, \Phi^s(y)))$. This is possible because Φ^t is a surjection. Since $\mathcal{A}$ is a type frame, extensionality implies that $\Phi^{s \to t}(g') = g$. By the definition of Φ^s it is therefore a partial homomorphism. $\qquad \Box$

2.25 Theorem (Completeness for Full Type Frame). *If X is infinite, then*

$$\vdash (H \rhd M = N : t)$$

if, and only if,

$$\mathcal{F}_X \models (H \rhd M = N : t).$$

Proof: We proved soundness ($\Rightarrow$) earlier. To prove sufficiency ($\Leftarrow$), begin by noting that Lemma 2.24 implies that there is a a partial homomorphism from the full type frame, $\mathcal{F}_X$, onto the term model, T. If $\mathcal{F}_X \models (H \rhd M = N : t)$, then $T \models (H \rhd M = N : t)$ by Lemma 2.23. By Theorem 2.20, this means that $\vdash (H \rhd M = N : t)$, the desired conclusion. □

Exercises.

2.10 Prove Lemma 2.11.

2.11 Let $t \equiv \mathbf{o} \to \mathbf{o}$. Show it is not the case that

$$\vdash \lambda f : t. \, \lambda x : \mathbf{o}. \, f(f(x)) = \lambda f : t. \, \lambda x : \mathbf{o}. \, f(x).$$

2.12 Prove that the 'multiplication' pre-frame, which takes $\mathcal{A}[\![s]\!]$ to be the set of natural numbers for every s and $A^{s,t}(m, n) = m * n$, is not a type frame.

2.13 Let $\mathcal{H}$ be an extended assignment and let T be a theory. Given terms M and N, say $M \sim N$ if there is some $H \subseteq \mathcal{H}$ and type t such that $T \vdash (H \rhd M = M' : t)$. Prove that $\sim$ is an equivalence relation on such terms. Note that this equivalence relation determines the equivalence classes $[M]_T$ in the term model.

2.14 Prove the Soundness Theorem for frames, Theorem 2.15.

2.15* Show that Theorem 2.25 fails when X is not infinite.

Definition: Let $\mathcal{A}$ and $\mathcal{B}$ be frames. A family of relations R^s indexed over types s is said to be a *logical relation* between $\mathcal{A}$ and $\mathcal{B}$ if

- $R^s \subseteq \mathcal{A}[\![s]\!] \times \mathcal{B}[\![s]\!]$.
- $f \, R^{s \to t} \, g$ if, and only if, the following condition holds for every x, y: if $x \, R^s \, y$, then $A^{s,t}(f, x) \, R^t \, B^{s,t}(g, y)$. □

2.16 The notion of a partial homomorphism is a special instance of a logical relation. Explain why this is the case and conjecture a version of Lemma 2.22 about partial homomorphisms that would apply to logical relations. Prove your version of the lemma.

2.4   Notes

A basic introduction to the simply-typed λ-calculus can be found in the book of Hindley and Seldin [114]. Much of the material in the last section of this chapter draws on the paper of Friedman [84] in which the Completeness Theorem for the full type frame is proven. The notion of a partial homomorphism comes from that paper, but the generalization of partial homomorphisms called a *logical relation* defined in Exercise 2.16 is a fundamental tool in the study of the simply-typed λ-calculus. Many of the basic properties of logical relations were developed by Tait, Statman, and Howard [118; 244; 245; 246; 247; 255], and they continue to be a topic of interest for applications. A general survey on logical relations is included in a handbook article of Mitchell [175]. A paper by Burn, Hankin, and Abramsky [41] furnishes an example of how logical relations can be applied to the static analysis of programs.

3 Categorical Models of Simple Types

In this chapter we explore an abstract approach to the concept of functions and application, in the context of *category theory*. Category theory originated, in part, as a technique for seeing a collection of similar results from disparate parts of mathematics as instances of a more general theory of mathematical structures and the relationships between structures. To encompass a wide range of results, it was necessary to develop a quite abstract collection of conditions that apply in many instances. As a result, mathematicians sometimes refer to category theory as 'abstract nonsense'—especially when they are taking advantage of its power of generality! Because of this generality, category theory has had a crucial influence on the study of the semantics of programming languages, often guiding or inspiring the discovery of the right concepts, definitions, structures, and theorems. As a tool for studying the semantics of programming languages, the usefulness of category theory goes beyond its position as a well-developed, general theory of mathematical structures. In many instances, the 'categorical viewpoint' matches much better with basic motivations in computer science than the alternative foundational theories.

Category theory is a large subject, and our interest in it is different from that of the researchers who developed it. Hence, this chapter should be taken as a slanted introduction to a small piece of the subject. In later chapters we will need more significant topics from category theory, but rather than digress into a lengthy discussion at this early stage, the treatment will be primarily call-by-need. We begin, therefore, with the most fundamental connection between category theory and its computer science applications, the concepts of *application* and *abstraction,* categorically described in the form of a structure known as a *cartesian closed category.*

3.1   Products and Cartesian Closure

The most basic definition of category theory is, naturally, that of a category. The axioms for categories are quite general and they are very easy to find throughout mathematics and computer science. A *category* $\mathbf{C}$ consists of

1. A collection $\mathrm{Ob}(\mathbf{C})$ of *objects* and a collection $\mathrm{Ar}(\mathbf{C})$ of *arrows*.

2. Operations

   $$\mathrm{dom} : \mathrm{Ar}(\mathbf{C}) \to \mathrm{Ob}(\mathbf{C})$$
   $$\mathrm{codom} : \mathrm{Ar}(\mathbf{C}) \to \mathrm{Ob}(\mathbf{C}).$$

   We write $f : A \to B$ if $\mathrm{dom}(f) = A$ and $\mathrm{codom}(f) = B$ and call A and B the *domain* and *codomain* of the arrow f respectively. We write $\mathbf{C}(A, B)$ for the collection of arrows $f : A \to B$.

3. A *composition operator,* which assigns to arrows f, g such that $\mathrm{dom}(f) = \mathrm{codom}(g)$ an arrow $f \circ g : \mathrm{dom}(g) \to \mathrm{codom}(f)$ such that the associativity axiom holds:

$$(f \circ g) \circ h = f \circ (g \circ h)$$

for any $h : A \to B$, $g : B \to C$, $f : C \to D$.

4. For each object A, an identity arrow $\mathrm{id}_A : A \to A$ such that $\mathrm{id}_B \circ f = f$ and $f \circ \mathrm{id}_A = f$ for every $f : A \to B$.   □

Perhaps it is easiest to get a grip on the abstract definition through a few typical examples. One of the best-known is the category **Set** of sets and (total) functions. This category has sets as its objects and functions between sets as its arrows. Ordinary composition of functions is the binary operator $\circ$: that is, the composition $f \circ g$ is defined by $x \mapsto f(g(x))$. The arrow id_A is the identity map on A. We write **Set** for the category of sets and functions. Another category that has the same objects but different arrows is that of sets and inclusions. An *inclusion* is a function f between sets A and B where $A \subseteq B$ and $f(x) = x$ for each $x \in A$. In this category, there is at most one arrow between any pair of objects.

Recall that a *poset* is a set P together with a binary relation $\sqsubseteq \subseteq P \times P$ that is transitive, reflexive, and anti-symmetric. Given posets $(P, \sqsubseteq_P)$ and $(Q, \sqsubseteq_Q)$, a function $f : P \to Q$ is *monotone* if $f(x) \sqsubseteq_Q f(y)$ whenever $x \sqsubseteq_P y$. Posets and monotone functions form a category **Poset** in which $\circ$ is ordinary function composition.

A *monoid* is a triple $(M, \cdot, e)$ in which M is a set, $\cdot : M \times M \to M$ is an associative binary operation on M, and e is an element of M such that $e \cdot x = x \cdot e = x$. A *homomorphism* f between a monoid $(M, \cdot_M, e_M)$ and a monoid $(N, \cdot_N, e_N)$ is a function from M to N such that $f(x \cdot_M y) = f(x) \cdot_N f(y)$ and $f(e_M) = e_N$. Monoids and homomorphisms of monoids form a category **Monoid**. Given a category **C**, a *subcategory* **D** of **C** is a category whose objects are also objects of **C** and such that for each pair of objects A, B in **D**, $\mathbf{D}(A, B) \subseteq \mathbf{C}(A, B)$. As an example, a monoid $(M, \cdot, e)$ is *commutative* if $x \cdot y = y \cdot x$ for each $x, y \in M$. The commutative monoids form a subcategory of **Monoid**.

Diagrams.

Let **C** be a category. A *diagram* over **C** is a directed graph with its edges labeled by arrows and its vertices labeled by objects. This labeling must be done so that the label of the *source* of an edge is the *domain* of the arrow labeling the edge and the label of the *target* of the edge is the *codomain* of the arrow that labels the edge. For example, the following diagram

$$A \xrightarrow{\ f\ } B \xrightarrow{\ g\ } C$$

has edges labeled by arrows $f : A \to B$ and $g : B \to C$. A diagram is said to *commute* if, for every pair A, B of vertices, and paths $f_1, \ldots, f_n$ and $g_1, \ldots, g_m$ between A and B, we have $f_n \circ \cdots \circ f_2 \circ f_1 = g_m \circ \cdots \circ g_2 \circ g_1$. For example, the diagram

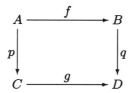

commutes if, and only if, $q \circ f = g \circ p$. It is often helpful to use dotted lines to emphasize the existence of an arrow that makes a diagram commute (or 'completes' the diagram), so we write

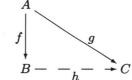

to mean that there is an arrow $h : B \to C$ such that $h \circ f = g$. An exclamation mark is used to emphasize that there is a *unique* arrow completing the diagram. For example, to say that there is a unique arrow that completes the following diagram:

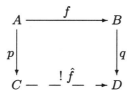

is to say that $q \circ f = g \circ p$ implies $g = \hat{f}$ for any $g : C \to D$. In particular, $\hat{f}$ completes the diagram if, and only if, it makes the diagram commute. We will sometimes wish to infer the commutativity of a diagram from the commutativity of its parts. For example, to show that the following diagram commutes:

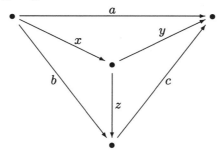

(where the objects associated with the vertices have been suppressed) if each of the three inner triangles commutes, one uses a calculation like the following: $a = y{\circ}x = (c{\circ}z){\circ}x = c \circ (z \circ x) = c \circ b$. Such a calculation is sometimes called a 'diagram chase'.

Binary products.

The primary interest that we have in categories is the basis that they provide for explaining a variety of familiar operators in a general way. One of the most commonly used of these is the product or pairing operator. The product $A \times B$ of sets A and B is the set of ordered pairs (a, b) where $a \in A$ and $b \in B$. Textbooks on set theory often represent ordered pairs in terms of sets by defining (a, b) to be the set $\{\{a\}, \{a, b\}\}$ (the set with two elements tells what are the values in the pair, and the other set tells what is their order). Other representations are possible; the important thing is to find something from which one can obtain the first and second coordinates of the pair such that the pair is uniquely determined by these coordinates. In particular, there are *projections* $\mathsf{fst} : A \times B \to A$ and $\mathsf{snd} : A \times B \to B$ given by $\mathsf{fst} : (a, b) \mapsto a$ and $\mathsf{snd} : (a, b) \mapsto b$. Moreover, a pair is *uniquely* determined by its projections in the sense that, for any $x \in A \times B$, we have $x = (\mathsf{fst}(x), \mathsf{snd}(x))$.

However, the idea of a product of structures is more general than this. The product of *posets* $(P, \sqsubseteq_P)$ and $(Q, \sqsubseteq_Q)$ is the set product $P \times Q$ of the underlying sets P and Q with an ordering $\sqsubseteq_{P \times Q}$ given by $(x, y) \sqsubseteq_{P \times Q} (x', y')$ iff $x \sqsubseteq_P x'$ and $y \sqsubseteq_Q y'$. The projections are defined as they are for sets, and it is easy to see that these are monotone maps. The product of two monoids M and N is the product $M \times N$ of the underlying sets, together with the binary operation on the product defined componentwise, that is,

$$(x, y) \cdot (x', y') = (x \cdot x', y \cdot y').$$

The unit of the product is the pair (e_M, e_N) of units of M and N respectively.

We can use categories as a language for expressing the essential common structure of operators such as the three above. The following definition of a product in a category is a characteristic category-theoretic expression of the definition of a construct. In particular, note that everything is (must be!) defined in terms of the arrows of the category.

Definition: Let $\mathbf{C}$ be a category. A *product* of a pair of objects $A, B \in \mathrm{Ob}(\mathbf{C})$ is an object $A \times B$ and a pair of arrows fst and snd such that, for each pair of arrows $f : C \to A$

and $g : C \to B$, there is a unique arrow such that the following diagram commutes:

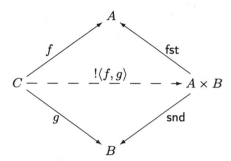

Given arrows $f : A \to B$ and $f' : A' \to B'$, we also define an arrow

$$f \times f' = \langle f \circ \mathsf{fst}, f' \circ \mathsf{snd} \rangle : A \times A' \to B \times B'. \qquad \square$$

When more than one product is present in a calculation, it is essential to distinguish between the projections on different products. For this, it is helpful to use the names fst and snd but with tags indicating the product on which they are projections. Strictly speaking, one needs to know the objects A, B involved in the product and the product object $A \times B$ itself. If, however, the product operation $\times$ is understood (for example, it is defined to be ordered pairs represented in a certain way) and the definition of a projection is also understood (in terms of the definition of $\times$), then one only needs to know the objects A and B. These could be written as subscripts $\mathsf{fst}_{A,B}, \mathsf{snd}_{A,B}$ or omitted if no confusion is likely to arise. Nevertheless, in some calculations, it becomes cumbersome to use lengthy subscripts, and omitting them makes it harder to remember the types of the functions involved. For this reason, it is convenient to write the product name in square brackets on the line, $\mathsf{fst}[A, B], \mathsf{snd}[A, B]$. I will sometimes replace the comma by the product operator symbol, $\mathsf{fst}[A \times B], \mathsf{snd}[A \times B]$ although this is a modest abuse of notation since the object $A \times B$ may not uniquely determine A and B. A similar notation is handy for other arrows; for example, id_A could also be written as $\mathsf{id}[A]$. In the case of the identity, though, there is a very compact abbreviation. Since the object A uniquely determines id_A in the category, and because it is usually easy to tell whether a symbol is an arrow or an object, one may simply write A for id_A. If $f : A \to B$, then the equations for the identity would be written as $B \circ f = f$ and $f \circ A = f$.

As an example of how one proves properties of products and projections, let us consider a proof that for any arrow $h : C \to A \times B$,

$$\langle \mathsf{fst} \circ h, \mathsf{snd} \circ h \rangle = h. \qquad (3.1)$$

To see this, note that h makes this diagram commute:

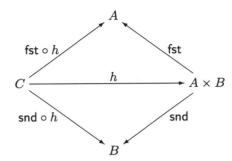

But, by the definition of the product, the unique arrow with this property is $\langle \text{fst} \circ h, \text{snd} \circ h \rangle$. Thus Equation 3.1 must hold. Note that we can obtain from an instance of Equation 3.1 that $\langle \text{fst}, \text{snd} \rangle = \text{id}$.

The notion of 'structural identity' of objects in a category is expressed as follows:

Definition: Let A and B be objects in a category **C**. An arrow $f : A \to B$ is said to be an *isomorphism* if there is an arrow $g : B \to A$ such that $g \circ f = \text{id}_A$ and $f \circ g = \text{id}_B$. In case there is an isomorphism between objects A and B, we say that they are *isomorphic* and we write $A \cong B$.   □

Here is an example of a more complex calculation involving products. As an exercise, the reader may wish to insert the names of the products involved where the projections are used.

3.1 Proposition. *In a category with products, $A \times (B \times C) \cong (A \times B) \times C$.*

Proof: Define

$$\alpha = \langle \langle \text{fst}, \ \text{fst} \circ \text{snd} \rangle, \text{snd} \circ \text{snd} \rangle : A \times (B \times C) \to (A \times B) \times C$$
$$\beta = \langle \text{fst} \circ \text{fst}, \ \langle \text{snd} \circ \text{fst}, \ \text{snd} \rangle \rangle : (A \times B) \times C \to A \times (B \times C)$$

and calculate,

$$
\begin{aligned}
\alpha \circ \beta &= \langle \text{fst} \circ \alpha \circ \beta, \text{snd} \circ \alpha \circ \beta \rangle \\
&= \langle \langle \text{fst}, \ \text{fst} \circ \text{snd} \rangle \circ \beta, \text{snd} \circ \text{snd} \circ \beta \rangle \\
&= \langle \text{fst}, \ \text{snd} \rangle \\
&= \langle \text{fst} \circ \text{id}, \ \text{snd} \circ \text{id} \rangle \\
&= \text{id}
\end{aligned}
\tag{3.2}
$$

To see why 3.2 holds, let $h = \langle \mathsf{fst},\ \mathsf{fst} \circ \mathsf{snd}\rangle \circ \beta$. Then

$$
\begin{aligned}
h &= \langle \mathsf{fst} \circ h,\ \mathsf{snd} \circ h\rangle \\
&= \langle \mathsf{fst} \circ \beta,\ \mathsf{fst} \circ \mathsf{snd} \circ \beta\rangle \\
&= \langle \mathsf{fst} \circ \mathsf{fst},\ \mathsf{snd} \circ \mathsf{fst}\rangle \\
&= \mathsf{fst}
\end{aligned}
$$

Showing that $\beta \circ \alpha = \mathsf{id}$ is left as an exercise for the reader. $\quad\square$

Products themselves are uniquely determined up to isomorphism in the following sense:

3.2 Proposition. *Let* $\mathbf{C}$ *be a category and suppose that* A, B *are objects in* $\mathbf{C}$. *If* $A \times B$ *is a product with projections* $\mathsf{fst}, \mathsf{snd}$ *and* $A \times' B$ *is a product with projections* fst' *and* snd', *then* $A \times B \cong A \times' B$.

Proof: Let $\langle \cdot, \cdot \rangle'$ be the pairing operation associated with the product $A \times' B$. There is a unique arrow $\langle \mathsf{fst}, \mathsf{snd}\rangle' : A \times B \to A' \times B'$ that completes the diagram in the definition of the product. This arrow and the arrow $\langle \mathsf{fst}', \mathsf{snd}'\rangle : A' \times B' \to A \times B$ define the desired isomorphism. $\quad\square$

Tuples.

It is often desirable to form the product of a collection of objects. For this, we generalize from the idea of a product of an ordered *pair* of objects to that of a product of a *list* of objects. This generalization is defined by induction starting with the degenerate case in which we take the product of 0 objects. To be precise:

Definition: A *terminal object* in a category $\mathbf{C}$ is an object 1 such that, for each object A, there is a unique arrow $\mathsf{t}_A : A \to 1$. $\quad\square$

For example, in **Set**, any singleton set $\{x\}$ is a terminal object. Since there are many such sets, evidently not all terminal objects in a category are equal. It is easy to see, however, that a terminal object is unique up to isomorphism. For if 1 and $1'$ are terminal objects, then there are arrows $\mathsf{t} : 1' \to 1$ and $\mathsf{t}' : 1 \to 1'$. Now, $\mathsf{t}' \circ \mathsf{t} : 1 \to 1$ and $\mathsf{t} \circ \mathsf{t}' : 1' \to 1'$ are uniquely determined since these are arrows into terminal objects 1 and $1'$ respectively. But we also have $\mathsf{id}_1 : 1 \to 1$ and $\mathsf{id}_{1'} : 1' \to 1'$. Hence $\mathsf{t} \circ \mathsf{t}' = \mathsf{id}_{1'}$ and $\mathsf{t}' \circ \mathsf{t} = \mathsf{id}_1$ and therefore $1 \cong 1'$.

Although our examples have not suggested it, it is possible to describe categories in which the objects are not sets of points. However, we may recover a general concept of an 'element' of an object A in a category with a terminal object by using arrows $p : 1 \to A$.

Such arrows are called the *points* of the object A. In a category such as **Set**, there is an exact correspondence between the elements of a set A in the usual sense and the points of A in this categorical sense. The only object A for which there is no arrow $f : 1 \to A$ is the empty set. More generally we say that an object A of a category with a terminal object is *non-empty* if there is such an arrow. In a future section we will be using points of non-empty objects to interpret terms of the simply-typed λ-calculus. Moreover, we will make use of the sense in which a terminal object may be viewed as a degenerate case of the product. Let us say that a *category with finite products* is a triple $(\mathbf{C}, \times, 1)$ consisting of a category $\mathbf{C}$, a given terminal object 1 of $\mathbf{C}$, and, for every pair of objects A and B, a product $A \times B$. An example of a category with finite products is $(\mathbf{Set}, \times, 1)$ where $\times$ is the usual product and $1 = \{\emptyset\}$. Although a category with products is really a triple, I will generally refer simply to $\mathbf{C}$ as a category with finite products if the choice of product and terminal object is unimportant or clear from context.

3.3 Proposition. *Suppose $\mathbf{C}$ is a category with finite products. In $\mathbf{C}$, the terminal object 1 is a unit for the product in the sense that $1 \times A \cong A \times 1 \cong A$ for any object A.* $\qquad\square$

In a category with finite products, the object $\times(A_1, \ldots, A_n)$ is defined inductively as follows:

$$\times() = 1$$
$$\times(A) = 1 \times A$$
$$\times(A_1, \ldots, A_n) = (\times(A_1, \ldots, A_{n-1})) \times A_n$$

We define a generalized form of projection $\pi_i^n : \times(A_1, \ldots, A_n) \to A_i$ by setting $\pi_n^n = \mathsf{snd}$ and $\pi_i^n = \pi_i^{n-1} \circ \mathsf{fst}$ when $i < n$. Following the notational convention for binary projections, it will sometimes be convenient to tag a projection with its domain, writing $\pi_i^n[A]$ where $A = \times(A_1, \ldots, A_n)$. Of course there is a generalization of pairing that goes with this:

$$\langle\,\rangle = \mathsf{t}_1 : 1 \to 1$$
$$\langle f \rangle = \langle \mathsf{t}_1, f \rangle : A \to \times(A)$$
$$\langle f_1, \ldots, f_n \rangle = \langle \langle f_1, \ldots, f_{n-1} \rangle \times f_n \rangle : A \to \times(A_1, \ldots, A_n)$$

There is another important class of arrows on products consisting of arrows that permute the coordinates of a product. Consider the products

$$A = \times(A_1, \ldots, A_k, A_{k+1}, \ldots A_n)$$
$$A' = \times(A_1, \ldots, A_{k+1}, A_k, \ldots A_n)$$

where $1 \le k < n$. By induction on n, we define a map $\tau_k^n[A] : A \to A'$ as follows:

$$\tau_k^n = \begin{cases} \langle \langle \mathsf{fst} \circ \mathsf{fst}, \mathsf{snd} \rangle, \mathsf{snd} \circ \mathsf{fst} \rangle & \text{if } k+1 = n \\ \tau_k^{n-1} \times \mathsf{id}_{A_n} & \text{if } k+1 < n \end{cases}$$

In the base case, $n = 2$ and the first clause of the equation above provides the definition (since $k = 1$). The following captures the basic relationship between projections and permutations:

3.4 Lemma. *For each i and k such that $1 < k+1 \leq n$ and i is not equal to k or $k+1$, we have the following equations:*

1. $\pi_k^n[A] = \pi_{k+1}^n[A'] \circ \tau_k^n[A]$
2. $\pi_{k+1}^n[A] = \pi_k^n[A'] \circ \tau_k^n[A]$
3. $\pi_i^n[A] = \pi_i^n[A'] \circ \tau_k^n[A]$

These three equations are not difficult to understand intuitively. Equation 3 says that the i coordinate of the tuple before the permutation is the i coordinate of the tuple after the permutation if the i coordinate is not one of the ones permuted. Equation 1 says that, after permutation, the $k + 1$ coordinate is the same as the k coordinate before permutation. Equation 2 says that, after permutation, the k coordinate is the same as the $k + 1$ coordinate before permutation.

Proof: All three equations are proved simultaneously by induction on n. In the base case, $n = 2$ and Equation 3 does not apply (because of the restriction on i). The proofs for the base cases of the other two equations are straightforward. To prove the inductive step for Equation 1, suppose that the lemma is known for $n - 1$. The argument requires consideration of two cases; assume first that $k + 1 = n$. Then

$$
\begin{aligned}
\pi_{k+1}^n[A'] \circ \tau_k^n[A] &= \mathsf{snd}[A'] \circ \langle \langle \mathsf{fst} \circ \mathsf{fst}, \mathsf{snd} \rangle, \mathsf{snd} \circ \mathsf{fst} \rangle \\
&= \mathsf{snd} \circ \mathsf{fst} \\
&= \pi_{n-1}^n \\
&= \pi_k^n.
\end{aligned}
$$

If, on the other hand, $k + 1 < n$, then

$$
\begin{aligned}
\pi_{k+1}^n[A'] \circ \tau_k^n[A] &= (\pi_{k+1}^{n-1} \circ \mathsf{fst}) \circ (\tau_k^{n-1} \times \mathsf{id}_{A_n}) \\
&= \pi_{k+1}^{n-1} \circ \tau_k^{n-1} \circ \mathsf{fst} \\
&= \pi_k^{n-1} \circ \mathsf{fst} \qquad\qquad\qquad (3.3) \\
&= \pi_k^n
\end{aligned}
$$

where Equation 3.3 follows from the induction hypothesis. This establishes Equation 1 of the lemma. Equation 2 has a similar proof, which is left as an exercise. To prove

Equation 3, it is again necessary to consider several cases. Suppose first that $i < n$. If $k + 1 < n$, then

$$\begin{aligned}
\pi_i^n[A'] \circ \tau_k^n[A] &= \pi_i^{n-1} \circ \mathsf{fst} \circ (\tau_k^{n-1} \times \mathsf{id}_{A_n}) \\
&= \pi_i^{n-1} \circ \tau_k^{n-1} \circ \mathsf{fst} \\
&= \pi_i^{n-1} \circ \mathsf{fst} \\
&= \pi_i^n
\end{aligned}$$

but if $k + 1 = n$, then

$$\begin{aligned}
\pi_i^n[A'] \circ \tau_k^n[A] &= \pi_i^{n-2} \circ \mathsf{fst} \circ \mathsf{fst} \circ \langle \langle \mathsf{fst} \circ \mathsf{fst}, \mathsf{snd} \rangle, \mathsf{snd} \circ \mathsf{fst} \rangle \\
&= \pi_i^{n-2} \circ \mathsf{fst} \circ \mathsf{fst} \\
&= \pi_i^n.
\end{aligned}$$

On the other hand, if $i = n$, then $k + 1 < n$ so

$$\begin{aligned}
\pi_i^n[A'] \circ \tau_k^n[A] &= \mathsf{snd} \circ (\tau_k^{n-1} \times A_n) \\
&= A_n \circ \mathsf{snd} \\
&= \pi_i^n.
\end{aligned}$$

$\square$

Cartesian closed categories.

A categorical construct closely connected with the λ-calculus is the categorical analog of a space of functions. In some categories, the collection of arrows from an object A to an object B can be reflected as itself an object $A \Rightarrow B$ of the category. As an easy example, in the category of sets, the functions from a set A to a set B is itself a set B^A. A slightly more interesting example occurs in the category of posets and monotone functions. There is a natural ordering on monotone functions given by taking $f \sqsubseteq g$ if $f(x) \sqsubseteq g(x)$ for each x in the domain of f. The collection of all monotone functions under this ordering is itself a poset. Now, the categorical characterization of the *product* was identified by finding the basic operators for products (pairing and projections) and their equational properties. In the case of *functions*, what are the analogous basic operators? One of these is *application*. For example, given a function $f : A \to B$ and an element a of A, there is a binary operation between f and a which has as its value the result in B of applying f to a. Such maps were part of the definition of an environment model. This is one of the ideas involved in the categorical definition of the *exponential*. The second idea is more subtle but one with which programmers who have written functional programs are familiar. Given a function $f : A \times B \to C$ of two arguments, there is an induced function f' that takes as an argument an element of A and returns as a result a function from B to C. The function $f'(a)$ for $a \in A$ is the function which, when applied to $b \in B$ yields the value $f(a, b)$. For example, given the addition function plus $: \mathbb{N} \times \mathbb{N} \to \mathbb{N}$, there is a function plus$'$ obtained in this way. For instance plus$'(2)$ is the unary 'add two' function which, when applied to 3, yields 5. This operation appears quite simple, but it has deep mathematical significance. This was recognized and exploited so effectively by the logician Haskell Curry that the operation sometimes bears his name and one says that f' is the result of 'curry-ing' the function f. With this motivation, the rigorous categorical definition of exponentials is given as follows:

Definition: Let **C** be a category with product $\times$. An *exponential* of objects B and C is an object $B \Rightarrow C$ and an arrow, apply, such that, for any object A and arrow $f : A \times B \to C$, there is a unique arrow, curry(f), completing the following diagram:

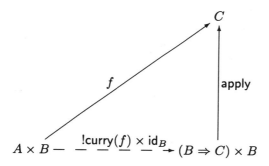

$\square$

As a consequence of the definition, note that

$$h = \mathsf{curry}(\mathsf{apply} \circ (h \times \mathsf{id}_B)) \tag{3.4}$$

for any arrow $h : A \to (B \Rightarrow C)$ since the following diagram evidently commutes,

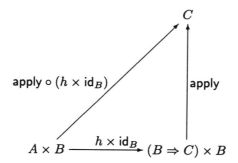

and the arrow h is uniquely determined by the categorical property for the exponential.

A *cartesian closed category (ccc)* is a four-tuple $(\mathbf{C}, \Rightarrow, \times, 1)$ where $(\mathbf{C}, \times, 1)$ is a category with finite products and $\Rightarrow$ is an exponential operator. For example, it is not hard to see that the category with finite products $(\mathbf{Set}, \times, 1)$, together with the exponential $A \Rightarrow B = B^A$ (that is, the set of functions from A to B), is a cartesian closed category. The application function is defined as usual:

$$\mathsf{apply}(f, x) = f(x)$$

and, given a function $f : A \times B \to C$, the arrow $\mathsf{curry}(f)$ is the function

$$\mathsf{curry}(f)(x)(y) = f(x, y).$$

It is straightforward to check that these arrows have the desired properties. Although a cartesian closed category products is a tuple, I will generally refer simply to $\mathbf{C}$ as a ccc if the choice of $\Rightarrow, \times, 1$ is unimportant or clear from context. As with the product and terminal object, it can be shown that the choice of exponential is unique up to isomorphism.

As another example of a calculation involving exponentials, suppose we are given arrows $f : A \to B$ and $g : B \times C \to D$. The following equation holds

$$\mathsf{curry}(g) \circ f = \mathsf{curry}(g \circ (f \times \mathsf{id}_C)). \tag{3.5}$$

To see why, note that each of the inner triangles in the following diagram commutes

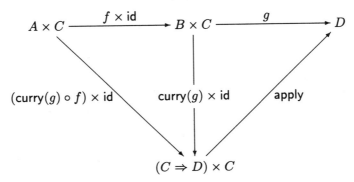

so the outer diagram does too. But the outer diagram must satisfy the uniqueness condition for exponentials, so 3.5 must hold.

Exercises.

3.1 Show that the outer diagram commutes if each of the inner diagrams commutes:

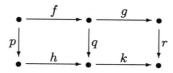

3.2 Prove that the identity arrow id_A is uniquely determined by A. That is, prove that if $i : A \rightarrow A$ has the property that $i \circ f = i$ and $g \circ i = g$ for each f and g such that these compositions make sense, then $i = \mathrm{id}_A$.

3.3 A function f is *injective* if $x = y$ whenever $f(x) = f(y)$. Show that sets and injections form a category. What about sets and surjections?

3.4 Suppose we are given arrows $f : C \rightarrow A$, $g : C \rightarrow B$, and $h : D \rightarrow C$. Show that $\langle f, g \rangle \circ h = \langle f \circ h, g \circ h \rangle$.

3.5 Given arrows $k : C \rightarrow A$, $l : C \rightarrow U$, and $m : C \rightarrow B$, define

$$\tau = \langle \langle \mathsf{fst} \circ \mathsf{fst}, \mathsf{snd} \rangle, \mathsf{snd} \circ \mathsf{fst} \rangle : (A \times U) \times B \rightarrow (A \times B) \times U$$

and show that

$$\tau \circ \langle \langle k, l \rangle, m \rangle = \langle \langle k, m \rangle, l \rangle$$

and, for any arrow $g : A \rightarrow B$,

$$\tau \circ \langle \mathrm{id}_{A \times U,}, g \times \mathsf{fst} \rangle = \langle \mathrm{id}_A, g \rangle \times \mathrm{id}_U.$$

3.6 Show that $\mathrm{id}_A \times \mathrm{id}_B = \mathrm{id}_{A \times B}$ and $(f \times g) \circ (f' \times g') = (f \circ f') \times (g \circ g')$.

3.7 Suppose we are given arrows $f : A \rightarrow B$, $g : B \rightarrow C$, $h : A \rightarrow D$, and $j : D \rightarrow E$. Prove that

$$\langle g \circ f, j \circ h \rangle = (g \times j) \circ \langle f, h \rangle$$

and, in particular,

$$\langle f, h \rangle = (f \times \mathrm{id}) \circ \langle \mathrm{id}, h \rangle = (\mathrm{id} \times h) \circ \langle f, \mathrm{id} \rangle.$$

Definition: A function f is a *bijection* if it is both surjective and injective. □

3.8   a. Show that bijections are the isomorphisms in the category of sets and functions.
   b. Show that monoids M and N are isomorphic if, and only if, there is bijective homomorphism between them.
   c. Is this also true of posets? State and prove a theorem (if it is true) or give a counterexample (if it is not).

3.9 Prove that products are unique up to isomorphism. That is, given objects A and B, demonstrate an isomorphism between any two objects X and Y that each satisfy the conditions for being a product of A and B.

3.10 Show that $A \times B \cong B \times A$.

3.11 Complete the proof of Proposition 3.1 by showing that $\beta \circ \alpha = A \times (B \times C)$.

3.12 Define a reasonable notion of composition on partial homomorphisms and show that type frames and partial homomorphisms form a category.

3.13 Prove Proposition 3.3.

3.14 Give an example of a category that is not well-pointed.

3.15 Prove that exponentials are unique up to isomorphism.

3.16 Prove the second equation in Lemma 3.4.

3.17 Show that the category **Poset** is a cartesian closed category with its usual products and exponentiation defined as monotone functions under the pointwise ordering: $f \sqsubseteq g$ iff $f(x) \sqsubseteq g(x)$.

3.2 λ-Calculus with Constants and Products

In the previous chapter, the simply-typed λ-calculus was presented as a type system with single ground type **o** and no constant symbols. There are many extensions and variations on this basic system, and in this section I present one of these in which the basic system is augmented by constructs for constant symbols and products. The main purpose of the section is to show how this enriched system, which I will call the *simply-typed λ-calculus with products and constants,* can be modeled by a cartesian closed category.

   Let Σ_1 be a collection of type constants and form the *types over* Σ_1 by the syntax

$$t ::= C \mid t \rightarrow t \mid t \times t$$

Table 3.1
Typing Rules for Products and Constants

$$[\text{Constant}] \qquad \frac{c \in \Sigma_0}{H \vdash c : \Sigma_0(c)}$$

$$[\text{Pairing}] \qquad \frac{H \vdash M : s \qquad H \vdash N : t}{H \vdash (M, N) : s \times t}$$

$$[\text{First}] \qquad \frac{H \vdash M : s \times t}{H \vdash \mathbf{fst}(M) : s}$$

$$[\text{Second}] \qquad \frac{H \vdash M : s \times t}{H \vdash \mathbf{snd}(M) : t}$$

---

where $C \in \Sigma_1$. Let Σ_0 be a set of pairs (c, t) where c is a *term constant* and t is a type over Σ_1. We assume that if $(c, t) \in \Sigma_0$ and $(c, t') \in \Sigma_0$, then $t \equiv t'$ (that is, Σ_0 is a function from term constants to types). Form the language of *terms over* Σ_0 by the following syntax:

$$M ::= c \mid x \mid \lambda x : t.\, M \mid MM \mid (M, M) \mid \mathbf{fst}(M) \mid \mathsf{snd}(M).$$

These are the terms of the λ-calculus with products over the *signature* $\Sigma = (\Sigma_0, \Sigma_1)$. Typing rules are those of the simply-typed calculus together with those in Table 3.1. The assignments, terms, and types in the rules for the simply-typed calculus in Table 2.1 are taken to range over those of the calculus with constants and products in this extension. Here are some comments on the new rules.

- In any type assignment, the type of a constant is the type assigned to it in the term part, Σ_0 of the signature. In effect, constants are very much like variables and Σ_0 like an implicit extension of the type assignment H, but because they come from a different syntax class, constants cannot be bound by abstractions whereas variables can be.

- The type of a pair (M, N) is $s \times t$ just in the case where s is the type of M and t is the type of N.

- If a term M has type $s \times t$, then its first coordinate $\mathbf{fst}(M)$ has type s, and its second coordinate $\mathbf{snd}(M)$ has type t.

An equation $(H \rhd M = N : t)$ for the simply-typed λ-calculus with constants and products is essentially the same as for the basic calculus, but the various components are

Table 3.2
Equational Rules for Products

{First}	$$\dfrac{H \vdash M : s \qquad H \vdash N : t}{T \vdash (H \rhd \mathbf{fst}(M, N) = M : s)}$$
{Second}	$$\dfrac{H \vdash M : s \qquad H \vdash N : t}{T \vdash (H \rhd \mathbf{snd}(M, N) = N : t)}$$
{Pairing}	$$\dfrac{H \vdash M : s \times t}{T \vdash (H \rhd (\mathbf{fst}(M),\ \mathbf{snd}(M)) = M : s \times t)}$$

taken from the larger calculus. A *theory* T is a set of equations $(H \rhd M = N : t)$ such that $H \vdash M : t$ and $H \vdash N : t$. Equational rules are those of the simply-typed calculus (as given in Table 2.2, but assuming that assignments, terms, and types are drawn from the larger system) together with those in Table 3.2.

- The first and second coordinates of (M, N) are M and N respectively.
- If a pair is made of the first and second coordinates of M, this pair is equal to M itself.
- If the coordinates of two pairs are equal, then so are the pairs. Actually, this can be derived from the other axioms (see Exercise 3.19).

Ccc models.

A *ccc model* of λ-calculus with signature Σ consists of a cartesian closed category

$$(\mathbf{C},\ \Rightarrow,\ \times,\ 1)$$

together with

- an assignment of a non-empty object $\mathbf{C}[\![C]\!]$ to each type constant $C \in \Sigma_1$ and
- a point $\mathbf{C}[\![c]\!] : 1 \to \mathbf{C}[\![\Sigma_0(c)]\!]$ for each c in the domain of Σ_0 where

$$\mathbf{C}[\![s \to t]\!] = \mathbf{C}[\![s]\!] \Rightarrow \mathbf{C}[\![t]\!]$$
$$\mathbf{C}[\![s \times t]\!] = \mathbf{C}[\![s]\!] \times \mathbf{C}[\![t]\!].$$

To spare notation, assume that Σ and $\mathbf{C}$ are fixed for the rest of our discussion and write $[\![\cdot]\!]$ rather than $\mathbf{C}[\![\cdot]\!]$. Let $H = x_1 : t_1, \ldots, x_n : t_n$ be a type assignment and suppose

$H \vdash M : t$. Let $A = \times(\llbracket t_1 \rrbracket, \ldots, \llbracket t_n \rrbracket)$. The interpretation of $M : t$ in assignment H is an arrow

$$\llbracket H \rhd M : t \rrbracket : A \to \llbracket t \rrbracket.$$

The meaning function on terms is defined inductively as follows:

- Constants: $\llbracket H \rhd c : t \rrbracket = \llbracket c \rrbracket \circ \mathsf{t}_A$ where $t = \Sigma_1(c)$.
- Projection: $\llbracket H \rhd x_i : t_i \rrbracket = \pi_i^n$.
- Abstraction: $\llbracket H \rhd \lambda x : u.\ N : u \to v \rrbracket = \mathsf{curry} \llbracket H,\ x : u \rhd N : v \rrbracket$.
- Application: $\llbracket H \rhd L(N) : s \rrbracket = \mathsf{apply} \circ \langle \llbracket H \rhd L : t \to s \rrbracket,\ \llbracket H \rhd N : t \rrbracket \rangle$.
- Pair: $\llbracket H \rhd (L, N) : s \times t \rrbracket = \langle \llbracket H \rhd L : s \rrbracket,\ \llbracket H \rhd N : t \rrbracket \rangle$.
- First: $\llbracket H \rhd \mathbf{fst}(N) : s \rrbracket = \mathsf{fst} \circ \llbracket H \rhd N : s \times t \rrbracket$.
- Second: $\llbracket H \rhd \mathbf{snd}(N) : t \rrbracket = \mathsf{snd} \circ \llbracket H \rhd N : s \times t \rrbracket$.

Here is an example of how the semantic equations are unwound:

$$
\begin{aligned}
&\llbracket \rhd \lambda x : s.\ \lambda f : s \to t.\ f(x) : s \to (s \to t) \to t \rrbracket \\
=\ &\mathsf{curry} \llbracket x : s \rhd \lambda f : s \to t.\ f(x) : (s \to t) \to t \rrbracket \\
=\ &\mathsf{curry}(\mathsf{curry} \llbracket H \rhd f(x) : t \rrbracket) \\
=\ &\mathsf{curry}(\mathsf{curry}(\mathsf{apply} \circ \langle \llbracket H \rhd f : s \to t \rrbracket,\ \llbracket H \rhd x : s \rrbracket \rangle)) \\
=\ &\mathsf{curry}(\mathsf{curry}(\mathsf{apply} \circ \langle \pi_2^2, \pi_1^2 \rangle))
\end{aligned}
$$

where $H = x : s, f : s \to t$.

We must prove that this interpretation is sound with respect to the equational rules. Assuming that our model satisfies the equations of a theory T, we must show that it satisfies all of the equalities derivable using the equational axioms. The proof is by induction on the height of the derivation of an equality; we proceed by showing that the conclusion of each rule holds for the categorical interpretation under the assumption that its hypotheses do. Because the ccc-model definition explicitly involves the order of the pairs in a type assignment, the proofs of the add, drop, and permute rules are not as straightforward as they were for type frames.

Let us begin with the permutation rule (stated in Table 2.2 on page 44). To prove it, we need a lemma for describing the meaning of a typing judgement after a permutation of its type assignment in terms of the original typing judgement. The lemma uses the permutation combinators τ_i^n described in the previous section.

3.5 Lemma. *Suppose*

$$
\begin{aligned}
H &= x_1 : t_1, \ldots, x_k : t_k,\ x_{k+1} : t_{k+1}, \ldots, x_n : t_n \\
H' &= x_1 : t_1, \ldots, x_k : t_{k+1},\ x_k : t_{k+1}, \ldots, x_n : t_n
\end{aligned}
$$

are type assignments and $H \vdash M : t$. Then

$$[\![H \rhd M : t]\!] = [\![H' \rhd M : t]\!] \circ \tau_k^n.$$

Proof: The proof is by induction on the structure of M. The most complex case is that in which M is a variable x_i. Define

$$A = \times([\![t_1]\!], \ldots, [\![t_k]\!], [\![t_{k+1}]\!], \ldots [\![t_n]\!])$$
$$A' = \times([\![t_1]\!], \ldots, [\![t_{k+1}]\!], [\![t_k]\!], \ldots [\![t_n]\!]).$$

There are three cases depending on i. If i is equal to k, then x_i is the $k + 1$ element in the list H', so $[\![H' \rhd M : t]\!] = \pi_{k+1}^n[A']$. Since $[\![H \rhd M : t]\!] = \pi_k^n[A]$, the desired result follows immediately from Equation 1 of Lemma 3.4. If $i = k+1$, then x_i is the k element of the list H', so $[\![H' \rhd M : t]\!] = \pi_k^n[A']$. But $[\![H \rhd M : t]\!] = \pi_{k+1}^n[A]$, so the desired result follows from Equation 2 of Lemma 3.4. In the remaining case that i is equal to neither k nor $k + 1$, $[\![H' \rhd M : t]\!] = \pi_i^n[A]$ and Equation 3 of Lemma 3.4 provides the desired conclusion. The remaining cases in the structural induction on M are left as an exercise for the reader.   □

3.6 Corollary. *Suppose $H = H_0, x : r, y : s, H_1$ and $H' = H_0, y : s, x : r, H_1$ are assignments, and M, N are terms such that $H \vdash M : t$ and $H \vdash N : t$. If $[\![H \rhd M : t]\!] = [\![H \rhd N : t]\!]$, then $[\![H' \rhd M : t]\!] = [\![H' \rhd N : t]\!]$.*

Proof: If x is the k'th element of H and the length of H is n, then

$$[\![H' \rhd M : t]\!] = [\![H \rhd M : t]\!] \circ \tau_k^n$$
$$= [\![H \rhd N : t]\!] \circ \tau_k^n$$
$$= [\![H' \rhd N : t]\!].$$ □

This proves that the permutation rule ({Permute} in Table 2.2) is satisfied by the interpretation for typing judgements.

Let us now prove the η-rule. Suppose $H \vdash \lambda x : s. M(x) : s \to t$ and say

$$[\![H \rhd \lambda x : s. M(x) : s \to t]\!] : A \to (B \Rightarrow C)$$

where $B = [\![s]\!]$ and $C = [\![t]\!]$.

$$[\![H \rhd \lambda x : s. M(x) : s \to t]\!]$$
$$= \mathsf{curry}(\mathsf{apply} \circ \langle [\![H, x : s \rhd M : s \to t]\!], \mathsf{snd} \rangle)$$
$$= \mathsf{curry}(\mathsf{apply} \circ \langle [\![H \rhd M : s \to t]\!] \circ \mathsf{fst}, \mathsf{snd} \rangle) \qquad (3.6)$$
$$= \mathsf{curry}(\mathsf{apply} \circ ([\![H \rhd M : s \to t]\!] \times \mathsf{id}))$$
$$= [\![H \rhd M : s \to t]\!] \qquad (3.7)$$

where 3.7 follows from Equation 3.4 and the crucial step, Equation 3.6, is summarized by

3.7 Lemma. *If x is not free in M, then $[\![H,\ x:s \rhd M:t]\!] = [\![H \rhd M:t]\!] \circ \mathsf{fst}$.*

Proof: The proof proceeds by induction on the structure of M. Suppose $[\![s]\!] = B$ and $[\![t]\!] = C$ and $[\![H,\ x:s \rhd M:t]\!] : A \times B \to C$.

Case $M \equiv c$. $[\![H,\ x:s \rhd c:s]\!] = [\![c]\!] \circ \mathsf{t}_{A \times B} = [\![c]\!] \circ \mathsf{t}_A \circ \mathsf{fst} = [\![H \rhd c:s]\!] \circ \mathsf{fst}$.

Case $M \equiv x_i \not\equiv x$ where $H = x_1 : t_1, \ldots, x_n : t_n$. Then $[\![H,\ x:s \rhd x_i : t_i]\!] = \pi_i^{n+1} = \pi_i^n \circ \mathsf{fst} = [\![H \rhd x_i : t_i]\!] \circ \mathsf{fst}$.

Case $M \equiv L(N)$.

$$
\begin{aligned}
&[\![H,\ x:s \rhd L(N):t]\!] \\
&\quad = \mathsf{apply} \circ \langle [\![H,\ x:s \rhd L:u \to t]\!],\ [\![H,\ x:s \rhd N:u]\!] \rangle \\
&\quad = \mathsf{apply} \circ \langle [\![H \rhd L:u \to t]\!] \circ \mathsf{fst},\ [\![H \rhd N:u]\!] \circ \mathsf{fst} \rangle \\
&\quad = \mathsf{apply} \circ \langle [\![H \rhd L:u \to t]\!],\ [\![H \rhd N:u]\!] \rangle \circ \mathsf{fst} \\
&\quad = [\![H \rhd M:t]\!] \circ \mathsf{fst}
\end{aligned}
$$

Case $M \equiv \lambda y : u.\ M'$. Then $t \equiv u \to v$ for some v. Let $\tau = \langle \langle \mathsf{fst} \circ \mathsf{fst}, \mathsf{snd} \rangle, \mathsf{snd} \circ \mathsf{fst} \rangle : (A \times B) \times U \to (A \times U) \times B$ where $U = [\![u]\!]$. Now calculate

$$
\begin{aligned}
&[\![H,\ x:s \rhd \lambda y:u.\ M' : u \to v]\!] \\
&\quad = \mathsf{curry}[\![H,\ x:s,\ y:u \rhd M':v]\!] \\
&\quad = \mathsf{curry}([\![H,\ y:u,\ x:s \rhd M':v]\!] \circ \tau) \qquad\qquad (3.8) \\
&\quad = \mathsf{curry}([\![H,\ y:u \rhd M':v]\!] \circ \mathsf{fst} \circ \tau) \\
&\quad = \mathsf{curry}([\![H,\ y:u \rhd M':v]\!] \circ (\mathsf{fst} \times \mathsf{id})) \\
&\quad = (\mathsf{curry}[\![H,\ y:u \rhd M':v]\!]) \circ \mathsf{fst} \qquad\qquad\qquad (3.9) \\
&\quad = [\![H \rhd \lambda y:u.\ M' : u \to v]\!] \circ \mathsf{fst}
\end{aligned}
$$

where 3.8 follows from Lemma 3.5 and 3.9 is an instance of Equation 3.5.

I omit the cases involving the product.   □

The drop rule is an immediate consequence of the following:

3.8 Lemma.   *1. For each type t, the object $[\![t]\!]$ is non-empty.*

2. If $[\![H,\ x:s \rhd M:t]\!] = [\![H,\ x:s \rhd N:t]\!]$ and x is free in neither M nor N, then $[\![H \rhd M:t]\!] = [\![H \rhd N:t]\!]$.

Proof: The proof of the first part is left for the reader. To prove the second, suppose $[\![H, \ x : s \triangleright M : t]\!] : A \times B \to C$. Since $B = [\![s]\!]$ is non-empty, there is an arrow $q : 1 \to [\![s]\!]$. We calculate as follows:

$$
\begin{aligned}
[\![H \triangleright M : t]\!] &= [\![H \triangleright M : t]\!] \circ \mathsf{fst} \circ \langle \mathsf{id}_A, q \circ \mathsf{t}_A \rangle \\
&= [\![H, \ x : s \triangleright M : t]\!] \circ \langle \mathsf{id}_A, q \circ \mathsf{t}_A \rangle && (3.10) \\
&= [\![H, \ x : s \triangleright N : t]\!] \circ \langle \mathsf{id}_A, q \circ \mathsf{t}_A \rangle \\
&= [\![H \triangleright N : t]\!] \circ \mathsf{fst} \circ \langle \mathsf{id}_A, q \circ \mathsf{t}_A \rangle && (3.11) \\
&= [\![H \triangleright N : t]\!]
\end{aligned}
$$

where Equations 3.10 and 3.11 follow from Lemma 3.7. $\qquad\qquad\qquad\qquad$ □

Now we prove the β-rule. Suppose $H \vdash \lambda x : s. \ M : s \to t$ and $H \vdash N : s$. Then

$$
\begin{aligned}
&[\![H \triangleright (\lambda x : s. \ M)(N) : t]\!] \\
&\quad = \mathsf{apply} \circ \langle \mathsf{curry}[\![H, \ x : s \triangleright M : t]\!], \ [\![H \triangleright N : s]\!] \rangle \\
&\quad = \mathsf{apply} \circ (\mathsf{curry}[\![H, \ x : s \triangleright M : t]\!] \times \mathsf{id}) \circ \langle \mathsf{id}, \ [\![H \triangleright N : s]\!] \rangle \\
&\quad = [\![H, \ x : s \triangleright M : t]\!] \circ \langle \mathsf{id}, \ [\![H \triangleright N : s]\!] \rangle \\
&\quad = [\![H \triangleright [N/x]M : t]\!] && (3.12)
\end{aligned}
$$

where Equation 3.12 amounts to the categorical version of the Substitution Lemma:

3.9 Lemma (Substitution). *Let*

$$
\begin{aligned}
f &= [\![H, \ x : s \triangleright M : t]\!] : A \times B \to C \ \text{and} \\
g &= [\![H \triangleright N : s]\!] : A \to B
\end{aligned}
$$

Then $[\![H \triangleright [N/x]M : t]\!] = f \circ \langle \mathsf{id}_A, \ g \rangle : A \to C.$

Proof: The proof is by induction on the structure of M.

Case $M \equiv c$. Then $[\![H \triangleright [N/x]c : t]\!] = [\![H \triangleright c : t]\!] = [\![c]\!] \circ \mathsf{t}_A = [\![c]\!] \circ \mathsf{t}_{A \times B} \circ \langle \mathsf{id}_A, \ g \rangle = f \circ \langle \mathsf{id}_A, \ g \rangle.$

Case $M \equiv x$. Then $s \equiv t$ and $B = C$ and we have $[\![H \triangleright [N/x]x : t]\!] = [\![H \triangleright N : s]\!] = \mathsf{snd} \circ \langle \mathsf{id}, \ g \rangle = [\![H, \ x : s \triangleright M : t]\!] \circ \langle \mathsf{id}, [\![H \triangleright N : s]\!] \rangle = f \circ \langle \mathsf{id}, \ g \rangle.$

Case $M \equiv x_i$ where $H = x_1 : t_1, \ldots, x_n : t_n$ and $x_i \not\equiv x$. Then $[\![H \triangleright [N/x]x_i : t]\!] = [\![H \triangleright x_i : t_i]\!] = \pi_i^n = \pi_i^{n+1} \circ \langle \mathsf{id}, \ g \rangle = f \circ \langle \mathsf{id}, \ g \rangle.$

Case $M \equiv M_0(M_1)$.

$$
\begin{aligned}
&[\![H \triangleright [N/x]M : t]\!] \\
&\quad = \mathsf{apply} \circ \langle [\![H \triangleright [N/x]M_0 : u \to t]\!], \ [\![H \triangleright [N/x]M_1 : u]\!] \rangle
\end{aligned}
$$

$$= \mathsf{apply} \circ \langle \llbracket H,\ x : s \vartriangleright M_0 : u \to t \rrbracket \circ \langle \mathsf{id},\ g \rangle,\ \llbracket H,\ x : s \vartriangleright M_1 : u \rrbracket \circ \langle \mathsf{id},\ g \rangle \rangle$$
$$= (\mathsf{apply} \circ \langle \llbracket H,\ x : s \vartriangleright M_0 : u \to t \rrbracket,\ \llbracket H,\ x : s \vartriangleright M_1 : u \rrbracket \rangle) \circ \langle \mathsf{id},\ g \rangle$$
$$= f \circ \langle \mathsf{id},\ g \rangle$$

Case $M \equiv \lambda y : u.\ M'$ where $t \equiv u \to v$. Let

$$\tau = \langle \langle \mathsf{fst} \circ \mathsf{fst},\ \mathsf{snd} \rangle,\ \mathsf{snd} \circ \mathsf{fst} \rangle : (A \times U) \times B \to (A \times B) \times U$$

and calculate

$$\llbracket H \vartriangleright [N/x] \lambda y : u.\ M' : u \to v \rrbracket$$
$$= \llbracket H \vartriangleright \lambda y : u.\ [N/x] M' : u \to v \rrbracket$$
$$= \mathsf{curry} \llbracket H,\ y : u \vartriangleright [N/x] M' : v \rrbracket$$
$$= \mathsf{curry}(\llbracket H,\ y : u,\ x : s \vartriangleright M' : v \rrbracket \circ \langle \mathsf{id}, \llbracket H,\ y : u \vartriangleright N : s \rrbracket \rangle)$$
$$= \mathsf{curry}(\llbracket H,\ y : u,\ x : s \vartriangleright M' : v \rrbracket \circ \langle \mathsf{id}, g \circ \mathsf{fst} \rangle) \tag{3.13}$$
$$= \mathsf{curry}(\llbracket H,\ x : s,\ y : u \vartriangleright M' : v \rrbracket \circ \tau \circ \langle \mathsf{id}, g \circ \mathsf{fst} \rangle)$$
$$= \mathsf{curry}(\llbracket H,\ x : s,\ y : u \vartriangleright M' : v \rrbracket \circ (\langle \mathsf{id}, g \rangle \times \mathsf{id}))$$
$$= \mathsf{curry}(\llbracket H,\ x : s,\ y : u \vartriangleright M' : v \rrbracket) \circ \langle \mathsf{id}, g \rangle \tag{3.14}$$
$$= f \circ \langle \mathsf{id}, g \rangle$$

where 3.13 follows from Lemma 3.7 and 3.14 is an instance of Equation 3.5.

I omit the cases involving the product.   □

To prove soundness of the first projection rule ({First} in Table 3.2), suppose $H \vdash M : s$ and $H \vdash N : t$. Then

$$\llbracket H \vartriangleright \mathbf{fst}(M, N) \rrbracket = \mathsf{fst} \circ \llbracket H \vartriangleright (M, N) : s \times t \rrbracket$$
$$= \mathsf{fst} \circ \langle \llbracket H \vartriangleright M : s \rrbracket,\ \llbracket H \vartriangleright N : t \rrbracket \rangle$$
$$= \llbracket H \vartriangleright M : s \rrbracket.$$

The second projection rule has a similar proof. The pairing rule is left as an exercise. The rules for equality as an equivalence relation and for congruence (see Table 2.2) follow immediately from facts about equations that hold in ccc's. The ξ-rule follows from the fact that curry is a function. To finish the proof of soundness, this leaves only the add rule, {Add}, which is also left as an exercise. In summary we have the following theorem:

3.10 Theorem (Soundness for CCC-Models). *Let $\mathbf{C}$ be a ccc. If $\vdash (H \vartriangleright M = N : t)$, then $\mathbf{C}\llbracket H \vartriangleright M : t \rrbracket = \mathbf{C}\llbracket H \vartriangleright N : t \rrbracket$.*

Exercises.

3.18 Complete the proof of Lemma 3.5 by doing the remaining steps of the induction.

3.19 Show that a congruence rule for pairs

$$\frac{T \vdash (H \rhd M = M' : s) \qquad T \vdash (H \rhd N = N' : t)}{T \vdash (H \rhd (M, N) = (M', N')) : s \times t}$$

can be derived from the other rules for the simply-typed λ-calculus with products. (Hint: Consider the expression $\lambda x : s. \lambda y : t. (x, y)$ and the congruence rule for application.) Also formulate and prove congruence rules for the projection operators.

3.20 Prove the first part of Lemma 3.8.

3.21 Prove that the pairing rule (Table 3.2) is sound for ccc models.

3.22 Prove that the add rule (from Table 2.2 on page 44) is sound for ccc models.

3.3 The Use of Category Theory

Category theory is a useful tool for the semantics of programming languages. Examples of how it can be used to classify phenomena and how it helps draw attention to essential properties will appear throughout the rest of this book. In this section, I will briefly illustrate this usefulness with three typical applications of categorical concepts. The first discusses the role of category theory as a syntax of fundamental combinators that can be used to eliminate the need for bound variables. The second discusses how certain kinds of cartesian closed categories induce type frames, thus making it possible to demonstrate a type frame by verifying equational properties of currying and application rather than by verifying the frame conditions. The third discusses duality in category theory and illustrates how this notion can be used to see relationships between existing concepts or lead to the discovery of new ones.

Categories and syntax.

Bound variables have often been a troublesome aspect of formal syntax in logic and the semantics of programming languages because of the problems they cause for the definition of substitution. In general, it is not desirable to allow the free variables of a term N to be captured by bindings in an expression M when N is substituted for a variable x in M. If x lies within the scope of a binding in M of a free variable of N, then care must be taken to avoid using a notation that will lead to incorrect bindings. For example, the

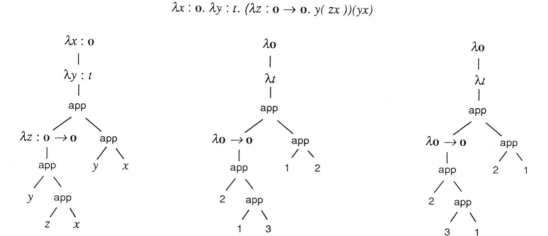

Figure 3.1
Representing Binding in Terms

result of substituting x for y in $\lambda x : t.\ yx$ should *not* be the term denoted by $\lambda x : t.\ xx$. This problem could be blamed on an unfortunate clash between the name of the bound variables and the name of the variable being substituted for y. What is the role served by the bound variable? It is used to indicate the relationship between a leaf in the term tree and the node of the tree to which it is bound. Putting a name (a variable) on these two nodes is not the only way to indicate a relationship between them, however. Another possibility would be to omit the variable name for the binding occurrence and write the 'address' of the binding occurrence in place of the leaves where there are variables bound by this occurrence. Let us consider this using a specific example:

$$\lambda x : \mathbf{o} \to \mathbf{o}.\ \lambda y : t.\ (\lambda z : \mathbf{o} \to \mathbf{o}.\ y(zx))(yx) \tag{3.15}$$

where $t \equiv \mathbf{o} \to (\mathbf{o} \to \mathbf{o})$. The term denoted by this expression has type $\mathbf{o} \to t \to \mathbf{o} \to \mathbf{o}$. The term tree denoted by the expression appears on the left in Figure 3.1. Now, consider the three occurrences of the variable x in the term tree. If the address of the binding occurrence in the term is 0, the leaves where x appears within its scope could be replaced with this address. Following this scheme, the term could be written as follows:

λo. λt. (λo. 00 (0000 0))(00 0)

where the addressing scheme for the nodes of a tree is basically the one used earlier for typing derivations in Section 2.2 (0 for a left son, 1 for a right son, and 0 if there is only one descendent, but here the root node is addressed as 0). If the abstractions are deeply nested, this notation would become very tedious. But there is an easier way to indicate the binding occurrence for a leaf. Given a leaf, there is a unique path leading from the leaf back to the root of the tree. If the leaf is a bound variable, then the binding for the variable must be a node on this path. Rather than indicate the address of this node, it suffices to indicate how many bindings lie between the leaf and the node for the binding occurrence. To find the binding for a leaf, just count back along the path from the leaf. This distance between bound and binding occurrence is called the *de Bruijn* index of the leaf. Since different occurrences of the same bound variable may lie at different distances from the binding occurrence, they may have different indices. For the term tree 3.15 above, the second occurrence of x has index 3 but the third occurrence has index 2. A representation of the term with de Bruijn indices appears in Figure 3.1; it could be written as

λo. λt. (λo. 2(1(3)))(1(2))

With this notation, bound variables do not have names. Returning to our earlier example, the term $\lambda x : t. yx$ would be written as $\lambda t. y1$, and the result of substituting x for y is $\lambda t. x1$. de Bruijn indices eliminate the need to distinguish between term trees and λ-terms, since there are no bound variables to rename.

Now, the syntax used to describe the semantics of a term in a ccc-model is very similar to the de Bruijn index representation of the term tree. For example, recall the calculation given earlier:

$$\mathbf{C}[\![\triangleright \lambda x : s.\ \lambda f : s \to t.\ f(x)]\!] = \mathsf{curry}(\mathsf{curry}(\mathsf{apply} \circ \langle \pi_2^2, \pi_1^2 \rangle))$$

where $H = x : s, f : s \to t$. This example can be used to motivate another notation for λ-terms. Let us just consider the terms that could arise from the semantic equations for ccc-models. It is not hard to see that the notation for the projections contains more information than is really necessary. The superscript on the projection will be determined, in general, by the number of instances of curry that lie above it in the term tree of the ccc term. Thus a shortened notation for the term in the last line of the example might be $\mathsf{curry}(\mathsf{curry}(\mathsf{apply} \circ \langle 2, 1 \rangle))$. Since the apply combinator is always composed with an expression of the form $\langle f, x \rangle$, we could write this in the form $f(x)$ and then the result of our translation above has the shortened form $\mathsf{curry}(\mathsf{curry}(2(1)))$. Replacing curry with λ now gives us an expression very similar to the notation of de Bruijn: $\lambda(\lambda(2(1)))$. This expression could be used in place of the expression with bound variables if tags are placed on the bindings to indicate the types. The tree obtained in this way for the the term 3.15 appears in Figure 3.1.

For closed terms, the notation of de Bruijn and that of cartesian closed categories are similar in spirit but differ in the way bindings are counted to determine the binding occurrence. The ccc semantics yields terms that count down the path to a leaf from the root rather than back along the path from the leaf. Indeed, it is generally the case that the categorical interpretation of a calculus provides a syntax of combinators for expressing the calculus without bound variables. This alternate notation often has useful syntactic properties.

Environments and categories.

What is the relationship between cartesian closed categories and type frames as models of the simply-typed λ-calculus? The two model definitions deal with environments differently, and our definition of a ccc model is for a larger calculus that includes products. However, the big difference between the interpretations has to do with the fact that type frames assumed that terms of higher type are interpreted as *functions* whereas the ccc model interprets a term using a abstract concept of 'point'. This difference is significant, and it turns out that the categorical definition is *more general* than the notion of a type frame as we defined it before. I will not digress on the consequences of this distinction at the moment because my use of categories in the remaining chapters does not require this extra degree of generality. It is possible to specialize categories (to those with 'enough points' to satisfy extensionality) or generalize type frames (by avoiding the extensionality condition) in order to obtain a match between the definitions. However, the direct proof of the soundness of the categorical interpretation would not have been any easier for the less general case, so the more general argument was given.

The primary reason for considering two ways to describe a model of the λ-calculus is that each can play a different role in defining an interpretation. It is appealing to have an environment model for a calculus, but it is convenient to demonstrate a cartesian closed category of types to use for the interpretation. This allows us to avoid demonstrating the substitution property of type frames in favor of checking the diagram expressing the universal property for a cartesian closed category. In effect, we replace a somewhat syntactic condition (whose proof entails a tiresome induction) by a simple equational property. Thus, in general, it is convenient to demonstrate a type frame using a cartesian closed category. As I mentioned, categories are more general than type frames, so we must restrict ourselves to a special kind of category in order to ensure that a type frame can be generated from a category. Recall that *point* of an object A in **C** is an arrow $a : 1 \to A$. Categories in which arrows are uniquely determined by composition with points are said to be 'well-pointed'. More precisely:

Definition: A category with a terminal object 1 is *well-pointed* if, for every pair of arrows $f, g : A \to B$, if $f \circ a = g \circ a$ for every point a of A, then $f = g$.

Suppose **C** is a well-pointed cartesian closed category and A is a non-empty object of **C**. I will show how **C** and A determine a type frame. The simply-typed λ-calculus is a special case of the system with constants where there is only one constant **o** for the ground type. Take $A[\![\mathbf{o}]\!]$ to be the set of points of A and define $A[\![s \to t]\!]$ to be the set of points of $\mathbf{C}[\![s]\!] \Rightarrow \mathbf{C}[\![t]\!]$. Let $U = \mathbf{C}[\![s]\!]$ and $V = \mathbf{C}[\![t]\!]$. Define $A^{s,t} : A[\![s \to t]\!] \times A[\![s]\!] \to A[\![t]\!]$ by taking

$$A^{s,t}(f, d) = \mathsf{apply} \circ \langle f, d \rangle$$

where f is a point of $U \Rightarrow V$ and d is a point of U. To prove that this defines a pre-frame, we must check the extensionality property. Suppose that $f, g \in A[\![s \to t]\!]$ and $A^{s,t}(f, d) = A^{s,t}(g, d)$ for every $d \in A[\![s]\!]$. By definition, this means that

$$\mathsf{apply} \circ \langle f, d \rangle = \mathsf{apply} \circ \langle g, d \rangle$$

for every point d of U. Let $f' = \mathsf{apply} \circ (f \times A)$ and $g' = \mathsf{apply} \circ (g \times A)$ and suppose e is a point of $1 \times U$. Then

$$
\begin{aligned}
f' \circ e &= \mathsf{apply} \circ (f \times U) \circ e \\
&= \mathsf{apply} \circ (f \times U) \circ \langle \mathsf{fst} \circ e, \ \mathsf{snd} \circ e \rangle \\
&= \mathsf{apply} \circ (f \times U) \circ \langle 1, \ \mathsf{snd} \circ e \rangle \\
&= \mathsf{apply} \circ \langle f, e \rangle \\
&= \mathsf{apply} \circ \langle g, e \rangle \\
&= g' \circ e
\end{aligned}
\tag{3.16}
$$

where Equation 3.16 follows from the fact that the only arrow from the terminal object to itself is the identity. Since **C** is well-pointed, it follows that $f' = g'$. But $f = \mathsf{curry}(f')$ and $g = \mathsf{curry}(g')$ by Equation 3.4 so $f = g$ too. It follows therefore that $A[\![\cdot]\!]$ is a pre-frame.

Let $H \equiv x_1 : t_1, \ldots, x_n : t_n$ be an assignment. To extend our pre-frame to a frame, we must define an assignment of points to environments. Let ρ be an H-environment and define

$$\bar{\rho} = \langle \rho(x_1), \ldots, \rho(x_n) \rangle : 1 \to \times(\mathbf{C}[\![t_1]\!], \ldots, \mathbf{C}[\![t_n]\!]).$$

We now define

$$\mathcal{A}[\![H \rhd M : t]\!]\rho = \mathbf{C}[\![H \rhd M : t]\!] \circ \bar{\rho}.$$

To see that this yields a frame, we must check the necessary equations for application and abstraction. Suppose $H \vdash M : s \rightarrow t$ and $H \vdash N : t$, then

$$\mathcal{A}[\![H \rhd M(N) : t]\!]\rho$$
$$= \mathbf{C}[\![H \rhd M(N) : t]\!] \circ \bar{\rho}$$
$$= \mathsf{apply} \circ \langle \mathbf{C}[\![H \rhd M : s \rightarrow t]\!] \circ \bar{\rho}, \mathbf{C}[\![H \rhd N : s]\!] \circ \bar{\rho} \rangle$$
$$= A^{s,t}(\mathbf{C}[\![H \rhd M : s \rightarrow t]\!] \circ \bar{\rho}, \mathbf{C}[\![H \rhd N : s]\!] \circ \bar{\rho})$$
$$= A^{s,t}(\mathcal{A}^{\mathrm{term}}[\![H \rhd M : s \rightarrow t]\!]\rho, \ \mathcal{A}^{\mathrm{term}}[\![H \rhd N : s]\!]\rho).$$

Also, if $H \vdash \lambda x : s. \ M : s \rightarrow t$ and d is a point of $\mathbf{C}[\![s]\!]$, then

$$A^{s,t}(\mathcal{A}[\![H \rhd \lambda x : s. \ M : s \rightarrow t]\!]\rho, d)$$
$$= \mathsf{apply} \circ \langle \mathsf{curry}(\mathbf{C}[\![H, x : s \rhd M : t]\!]) \circ \bar{\rho}, d \rangle$$
$$= \mathsf{apply} \circ (\mathsf{curry}(\mathbf{C}[\![H, x : s \rhd M : t]\!]) \times \mathsf{id}) \circ \langle \bar{\rho}, d \rangle$$
$$= \mathcal{A}[\![H, \ x : s \rhd M : t]\!]\rho[x \mapsto d].$$

These results can be summarized as follows:

3.11 Theorem. *Suppose* $\mathbf{C}$ *is a well-pointed cartesian closed category and* X *is a non-empty object of* $\mathbf{C}$*. Define*

- $\mathcal{A}^{\mathrm{type}}[\![\mathbf{o}]\!] = \mathbf{C}(1, \ X)$,
- $\mathcal{A}^{\mathrm{type}}[\![s \rightarrow t]\!] = \mathbf{C}(1, \ \mathbf{C}[\![s]\!] \Rightarrow \mathbf{C}[\![t]\!])$,
- $A^{s,t}(f, d) = \mathsf{apply} \circ \langle f, d \rangle$ *for each* $f \in \mathcal{A}^{\mathrm{type}}[\![s \rightarrow t]\!]$ *and* $d \in \mathcal{A}^{\mathrm{type}}[\![s]\!]$,
- $\mathcal{A}^{\mathrm{term}}[\![H \rhd M : t]\!]\rho = \mathbf{C}[\![H \rhd M : t]\!] \circ \bar{\rho}$ *where* $H = x_1 : t_1, \ldots, x_n : t_n$ *and* $\bar{\rho} = \langle \rho(x_1), \ldots, \rho(x_n) \rangle$.

Then $(\mathcal{A}^{\mathrm{term}}, \mathcal{A}^{\mathrm{term}}, A)$ *is a type frame.* □

As an example of how the conditions for a ccc can be used to quickly demonstrate type frames, consider the ccc **Poset**. Given a non-empty poset $(P, \sqsubseteq)$, we can form a pre-frame by taking P as the ground type, monotone function spaces for higher types, and application as function application. That this pre-frame has a unique extension to a frame follows immediately from the fact that posets and monotone functions form a well-pointed ccc with monotone function space as exponential and application as function application (see Exercise 3.17).

Duality.

Given a concept of category theory defined using a diagram such as the ones we have seen for products and exponentials, there is a *dual* concept one obtains by the simple subterfuge of reversing all of the arrows in the definition. Through duality, categorical formulations of concepts make it possible to see a rigorous relationship between similar constructs. This technique is so pervasive in category theory that there is a naming convention for dual concepts: the dual of a concept 'foo' is a '*cofoo*'. As an example of the use of duality as a tool for understanding relationships between constructs in programming languages, let us consider a specific example—the dual of the notion of a product:

Definition: Let **C** be a category. A *coproduct* of a pair of objects $A, B \in \text{Ob}(\mathbf{C})$ is an object $A + B$ and a pair of arrows inl and inr called *injections* such that, for each pair of arrows $f : A \to C$ and $g : B \to C$, there is a unique arrow such that the following diagram commutes:

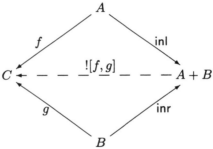

Given arrows $f : A \to B$ and $f' : A' \to B'$, we also define an arrow

$$f + f' = [\text{inl} \circ f, \text{inr} \circ f'] : A + A' \to B + B'. \qquad \Box$$

Let me put off providing a catalog of typical examples of coproducts in mathematics and ask instead how we might expand the λ-calculus to include coproducts. An evident approach is to expand the type system to include + as an operator and include terms for the various arrows whose existence is asserted by the categorical definition. Once the appropriate typing rules are given to ensure that these new terms are built from the right kinds of objects, the equational rules can be based on the equations given by the diagram condition for the definition of the coproduct. So, we could introduce functions **inl** and **inr** for inl and inr respectively and, given terms M and N, we could have a term $[M, N]$. In practice, it is common to modify this approach slightly for convenience and use a syntax that treats **inl** and **inr** distinctly from constants and uses bound variables to make the definition of $[M, N]$ more readable. In programming languages, coproducts are usually called *sums* or *variants*. Here is the grammar for a language including sums based on the simply-typed λ-calculus with constants and products:

$$
\begin{array}{rcl}
t & ::= & C \mid t \to t \mid t \times t \mid t + t \\
M & ::= & c \mid x \mid \lambda x : t.\ M \mid MM \mid \\
& & (M, M) \mid \mathbf{fst}(M) \mid \mathbf{snd}(M) \mid \\
& & \mathbf{inl}[t + t](M) \mid \mathbf{inr}[t + t](M) \mid \\
& & \mathbf{case}\ M\ \mathbf{of}\ \mathbf{inl}(x) \Rightarrow M\ \mathbf{or}\ \mathbf{inr}(x) \Rightarrow M
\end{array}
$$

Note that the injections for the sum in the third line of the grammar for terms are tagged with types; this is needed to ensure the analog of Lemma 2.4 for this system. The case statement involves three parts, the *switch L*, the *first* (or *left*) *branch*, $\mathbf{inl}[t + s](x) \Rightarrow M$, and the *second* (or *right*) branch, $\mathbf{inr}[t + s](y) \Rightarrow N$. Free occurrences of the variable x in M are bound by the occurrence of x on the left of the $\Rightarrow$ in the first branch and free occurrences of y in N are bound by the occurrence of y on the left of the $\Rightarrow$ in the second branch. If we had written the mediating arrow for the coproduct in the form $[M, N]$, then M and N would both need to be functions, so expressions of this kind would often have the appearance

$$
[\lambda x : s.\ M',\ \lambda y : t.\ N'].
$$

This is not really a problem, but it is more common in programming languages to make this structure for the case statement more explicit; the exact analog of the categorical construct $[M, N]$ could, in any case, be given as

$$
\lambda z : s + t.\ \mathbf{case}\ z\ \mathbf{of}\ \mathbf{inl}(x) \Rightarrow M(x)\ \mathbf{or}\ \mathbf{inr}(y) \Rightarrow N(y).
$$

Typing rules for sums are listed in Table 3.3.

- The [Left] and [Right] rules tell how a term of sum type is built. The [Left] rule describes the injection of a term of type s into the left component of the sum $s + t$; the [Right] rule describes the injection of a term of type t into its right component.

- The [Case] rule tells how a term of sum type is to be taken apart. Note that the terms in each branch must have a common type t although the term from the first branch has this type in an assignment with x of type r whereas the second branch has this type in an assignment with y of type s.

Equational rules for sums are given in Table 3.4.

- If the switch of a case is an injection into the left component of the sum type, then the {Left} asserts that the value of the case is equal to the result of substituting the

Table 3.3
Typing Rules for Sums

$$\frac{H \vdash M : s}{H \vdash \mathbf{inl}[s + t](M) : s + t}$$

[Left]

$$\frac{H \vdash M : t}{H \vdash \mathbf{inr}[s + t](M) : s + t}$$

[Right]

$$\frac{H \vdash L : r + s \qquad H, \, x : r \vdash M : t \qquad H, \, y : s \vdash N : t}{H \vdash \mathbf{case} \ L \ \mathbf{of} \ \mathbf{inl}(x) \Rightarrow M \ \mathbf{or} \ \mathbf{inr}(y) \Rightarrow N : t}$$

[Case]

injected value for the bound variable of the first branch in the body of the branch. The {Right} rule has a similar interpretation for right components and the second branch of the case.

- The {Case} rule asserts, in effect, that the elements of the sum type are exactly those values injected from the component types s and t. This equation is derived from the uniqueness condition for the arrow in the definition of the coproduct.

The semantics for our calculus is given for a cartesian closed category $\mathbf{C}$ that has coproducts by adding the following semantic equations to those given earlier:

- $[\ : s + t]\!] = \mathsf{inl}[\![H \rhd M : s]\!]$

- $[\ : s + t]\!] = \mathsf{inr}[\![H \rhd M : t]\!]$

- $[\![H \rhd \mathbf{case} \ L \ \mathbf{of} \ \mathbf{inl}(x) \Rightarrow M \ \mathbf{or} \ \mathbf{inr}(y) \Rightarrow N : t]\!] = \mathsf{apply} \circ \langle [m, n], \, l \rangle$
  where

$$\begin{aligned} l &= [\![H \rhd L : s + t]\!] \\ m &= \mathsf{curry}[\![H, \, x : r \vdash M : t]\!] \\ n &= \mathsf{curry}[\![H, \, y : s \vdash N : t]\!] \end{aligned}$$

Exercises.

Definition: Let $\mathbf{C}$ be a category. Define the *dual* category of $\mathbf{C}^{op}$ as follows. The objects of $\mathbf{C}^{op}$ are the same as the objects of $\mathbf{C}$. For any pair of objects A, B of $\mathbf{C}^{op}$, the arrows in $\mathbf{C}^{op}(A, B)$ are arrows $f \in \mathbf{C}(B, A)$. Given arrows $g \in \mathbf{C}^{op}(A, B)$ and $f \in \mathbf{C}^{op}(B, C)$, the composition $f \circ g$ of f and g in $\mathbf{C}^{op}$ is defined to be the composition $g \circ f$ in $\mathbf{C}$. $\quad\square$

Table 3.4
Equational Rules for Sums

{Left}
$$\frac{H \vdash L : r \qquad H, x : r \vdash M : t \qquad H, y : s \vdash N : t}{T \vdash \left(H \triangleright \left(\begin{array}{ll} \textbf{case} & \textbf{inl}[r,s](L) \\ \textbf{of} & x \Rightarrow M \\ \textbf{or} & y \Rightarrow N \end{array} \right) = [L/x]M : t \right)}$$

{Right}
$$\frac{H \vdash L : s \qquad H, x : r \vdash M : t \qquad H, y : s \vdash N : t}{T \vdash \left(H \triangleright \left(\begin{array}{ll} \textbf{case} & \textbf{inr}[r,s](L) \\ \textbf{of} & x \Rightarrow M \\ \textbf{or} & y \Rightarrow N \end{array} \right) = [L/y]N : t \right)}$$

{Case}
$$\frac{H \vdash M : s + t}{T \vdash \left(H \triangleright M = \left(\begin{array}{ll} \textbf{case} & M \\ \textbf{of} & x \Rightarrow \textbf{inl}[s,t](x) \\ \textbf{or} & y \Rightarrow \textbf{inl}[s,t](y) \end{array} \right) : s + t \right)}$$

3.23 Let $\mathbf{C}$ be a category.

a. Prove that $\mathbf{C}^{op}$ is a category.
b. Show that $\mathbf{C}$ has products if, and only if, $\mathbf{C}^{op}$ has coproducts.

Definition: An object 0 of a category $\mathbf{C}$ is *initial* if, for every other object A of $\mathbf{C}$, there is a unique arrow $i : 0 \rightarrow A$. ☐

3.24 Prove that an initial object is unique up to isomorphism and that $A + 0 \cong A$ in a category $\mathbf{C}$ with initial object 0. What is the dual of this isomorphism?

3.25 Develop the idea of representing terms using de Bruijn notation further:

a. Define a translation from simply-typed λ-calculus (without products or sums, say) to terms in de Bruijn notation.
b. Describe how to recalculate de Bruijn indices for the β-rule.
c. State typing rules for terms in de Bruijn notation and prove that a term has a type t in an assignment H iff the equivalent term in de Bruijn notation does.

3.26 Formulate and prove an analog of Lemma 2.4 for the λ-calculus with constants, products, and sums. Show that this result would fail if tags on the injections were dropped and the [Left] and [Right] rules were given instead by

$$[\text{Left}]^{-} \qquad \frac{H \vdash M : s}{H \vdash \mathbf{inl}(M) : s + t}$$

$$[\text{Right}]^{-} \qquad \frac{H \vdash M : t}{H \vdash \mathbf{inr}(M) : s + t}.$$

To ensure uniqueness of types it is not really necessary to label each injection with *both* components of the sum since only one is really needed. Explain why and suggest a more succinct syntax.

3.27 For the coproduct operator, formulate and prove an analog of the result for products given in Exercise 3.6.

3.28 For the coproduct operator, formulate and prove an analog of the result for products given in Exercise 3.6.

3.29 Prove that if M and N are monoids, then there is a coproduct $M + N$ for them in the category **Monoid.**

3.30 Formulate and prove a dual version of Exercise 3.7.

3.31 Show that the category **Poset** of posets can be made a model of λ-calculus with products and sums by demonstrating a coproduct. $\qquad\qquad\qquad\qquad\qquad\qquad\qquad\qquad$ □

3.4 Notes

Most of the material on category theory in the first section of this chapter could be found in any standard book on the subject such as those of Herrlich and Strecher [113], Mac Lane [148], or Arbib and Manes [14]. Several books on category theory aimed at computer scientists have been written more recently: Pierce [190] provides a succinct introduction; more detailed accounts can be found in Barr and Wells [22] or Asperti and Longo [16]. Another discussion of categories and computation is Rydeheard and Burstall's book [215]. An example of a computational application of categorical combinators is the *categorical abstract machine* described in a paper of Cousineau, Curien, and Mauny [63].The collections [191; 192] provide an overview of the research on category theory in computer science.

The results on the λ-calculus in this chapter are based on research of Lambek [142] and D. S. Scott [225]. For the reader with some background in category theory, the book by Lambek and P. J. Scott [143] is a good source. Calculations similar to the ones given in Section 3.3 for showing that ccc's satisfy the equations of the λ-calculus can be found in research report of Berry [27] where the *untyped* λ-calculus is treated. This report also includes a definition of type frames that does not require extensionality.

4 Recursive Definitions of Functions

From the perspective of programming, the basic simply-typed λ-calculus and the extensions we have described in the last two chapters provide many useful procedures but cannot stand as programming languages on their own. Programming languages do not consist of a syntax and type system alone; they also provide a notion of *evaluation* of a program. Although we provided an equational theory for the λ-calculus, the equations do not immediately imply a particular form of evaluation. Indeed, several approaches to evaluation are possible, each having its own relationship to the equational theory. Given a notion of evaluation, it is essential that a language be rich enough to allow interesting programs to be expressed with respect to this evaluation. For this, one of the most basic of all computational constructs is a mechanism for *recursive definitions*. This chapter focuses on the semantics of recursive definitions. There are several ways to define the semantics, and we investigate how these different methods are related to one another.

Without some constants, it will not be possible to write very many programs. Some construct supporting iteration (such as a while loop) or recursive definitions is essential for universal computing power. Moreover, it is helpful to include more basic types and constants to provide familiar structures such as integers and booleans. Consider, for example, the following program for computing the factorial function

```
val rec f =
    fn n:int => if n = 0 then 1 else n * f(n-1)
```
(4.1)

written in the syntax of the programming language ML.[1] The declaration defines the value of an identifier, f, to be given by the term appearing on the right side of the first occurrence of the equality sign =. In ML, the keyword fn is used in place of the Greek letter, λ and the symbol that follows the binding variable occurrence and type tag is => rather than a period. In 'Lisp notation' (in the language Scheme, to be precise) this definition could take the form

```
(define f (lambda (n)
        (if (= n 0)
            1
        (* n (f (- n 1))))))
```
(4.2)

if we take the liberty of dropping the type tag in the abstraction. From this, it is easy to see how the term (lambda ...) being used to define f can be given in the typed λ-calculus with products and constants as described in the previous chapter:

$$\lambda n : C_{\text{int}}. \ c_{\text{if}}(c_=(n, c_0), \ c_1, \ c_*(n, \ f(c_-(n, \ c_1)))).$$
(4.3)

---

[1]ML stands for *Meta Language*; it is one of the best-known implementations of the typed λ-calculus. The code here is in Standard ML.

If we use constants having 'curried' types, then it is possible to avoid the use of products:

$$\lambda n : C_{\text{int}}.\ c_{\text{if}}(c_{=}(n)(c_0))(c_1)(c_{*}(n)(f(c_{-}(n)(c_1))))$$

If the conditional operator and the binary operators for equality, multiplication, and subtraction were given in this way in Lisp notation, this term would have the following form:

```
(define f (lambda (n)
              (((if ((= n) 0))
               1)
              ((* n) (f ((- n) 1)))))))
```

I expect that some readers join me in the view that this is not very easy to read. The use of 'mix-fix' operators as in the ML-like notation of Program 4.1 or products and prefix as in the Lisp-like notation of Program 4.2 makes it easier to identify the arguments of operators.

Although it is easy enough to see how the term used to define f can be rendered in the λ-calculus with constants, it is less clear how f itself can be defined in this way. After all, f is *recursively* defined since it appears on both sides of the equality in the declaration. In fact, the **val rec** declaration of 4.1 is a binding construct in which the first occurrence of f binds the second occurrence. Since the λ-calculus has only one binding construct, abstraction, this must be used to represent the binding in this program. The trick is to introduce a collection of new constants for recursive definitions. For example, the function defined by Program 4.1 would be rendered with a syntax like the following:

$$\mathbf{Y}\lambda f : \mathbf{num} \to \mathbf{num}.\ \lambda n : \mathbf{num}.\ \mathbf{if}\ n = 0\ \mathbf{then}\ 1\ \mathbf{else}\ n * f(n-1) \qquad (4.4)$$

where $\mathbf{Y}$ is a constant of type

$$((\mathbf{num} \to \mathbf{num}) \to (\mathbf{num} \to \mathbf{num})) \to (\mathbf{num} \to \mathbf{num}).$$

The use of constants and higher-order functions to represent new binding operators is a helpful way to avoid introducing additional syntax. For example, it allows one to use the definition of notions such as substitution for the λ-calculus with constants. Nevertheless, most programming languages do provide new binding operators for recursive definitions since such constructs make programs easier to read.

The syntax used to bind terms to names as in programs 4.1 and 4.2 must be represented in the λ-calculus (as presented so far) through the use of *application*. For example, if M represents the factorial function and one wishes to bind M to the function name f in a program N, then this could be written as the application $(\lambda f.\ N)M$. In some languages, this sort of construct is so common that there is a special syntax for it, and one might write

N **where** $f = M$

or

let $f = M$ **in** N.   (4.5)

but some care must be taken about bindings for variables of M in these expressions. If M is Term 4.4, then there is no question of the bindings for the various occurrences of f. If, however, M is a term such as 4.3, then it is not clear whether occurrences of f in M are bound by the first occurrence of f in 4.5 or not. If the function f is being recursively defined, then one expects that the occurrences of f in M are bound by the defining occurrence of f on the left side of the equality sign. If no recursive definition is intended, then occurrences of f in M are free in the **let** clause. To make a clear distinction between these possibilities, some languages use a special keyword and write

letrec $f = M$ **in** N (4.6)

for the case in which the first occurrence of f binds the occurrences of f in M. This could be viewed as a shorthand for

let $f = \mathbf{Y}\lambda f.\ M$ **in** N.

Most programming languages use some variant of the **letrec** notation 4.6; it is rare to see an explicit use of a recursive definition constant, $\mathbf{Y}$, in a program, and most languages do not provide one as a primitive.

On the other hand, for the theoretical purposes of this chapter, there is a drawback to the **letrec** notation. In Expression 4.6 above it is necessary to include the term N, whereas the notation using $\mathbf{Y}$ makes it possible to ignore N and write a single expression for the recursively defined function. This could be simulated using the **letrec** notation by writing

letrec $f = M$ **in** f,

but this is cumbersome and unnecessary. Rather than introduce a new constant such as $\mathbf{Y}$, it simplifies matters to use instead a refinement of this trivial form of the **letrec** notation obtained by introducing a new binding operator. This works much like the λ-binder but signifies a recursive definition rather than an abstraction. In effect, one replaces the $\mathbf{Y}\lambda$ of Expression 4.4 by the Greek letter μ to obtain

$\mu f : \mathbf{num} \to \mathbf{num}.\ \lambda n : \mathbf{num}.\ \mathbf{if}\ n = 0\ \mathbf{then}\ 1\ \mathbf{else}\ n * f(n - 1)$.

This has an advantage over the **Y** notation in that it distinguishes a recursive definition from an application of a constant. In proofs of properties of programs it is more natural to treat recursive definition as a separate case rather than as a special case of application. It has the advantage of being more flexible than the **letrec** notation, since it represents simply the recursively defined function itself rather than, as in 4.6, a term N with a variable f bound to that recursively defined function. This being said in support of the μ-notation, I think it is fair to say also that each of the three notations would serve well enough for our discussion in the rest of this chapter.

We have now examined several of the alternative forms of *syntax* for recursive definitions, but what is the intended *semantics* for these notations? Recursive definitions are used throughout mathematics without any explicit mention of evaluation. A typical definition of the factorial function might be given by

$$f(n) = \left\{ \begin{array}{ll} 1 & \text{if } n = 0 \\ n * f(n-1) & \text{if } n > 0. \end{array} \right.$$

Despite minor differences in notation, it is easy to see that this is basically the same as the function coded in programs 4.1 and 4.2. The mathematical expression above would typically be taken to denote a particular function from numbers to numbers rather than a prescription for how to perform a calculation. However, the definition clearly describes an algorithm based on the *unwinding* of the recursive definition. For example, to calculate $f(3)$, one unwinds the definition by a step and reduces this task to the calculation of $3 * f(2)$. The next step proceeds by again unwinding the definition of f to reduce the problem to one of calculating $3 * 2 * f(1)$. Two further unwindings produce $3 * 2 * 1 * 1$ and the result, 6, is then obtained by doing the multiplications. How this intuition can be explained formally is the purpose of this chapter. The discussion is based on a simple language, which must now be defined.

4.1   A Programming Language for Computable Functions

The following grammar defines the syntax of *types t* and *terms M* of a simple higher-order **P**rogramming language for **C**omputable **F**unctions known as PCF. We assume a primitive syntax class of variables x; the raw expressions of the calculus are generated by the following grammar:

$$
\begin{array}{lll}
t & ::= & \textbf{num} \mid \textbf{bool} \mid t \rightarrow t \\
M & ::= & \textbf{0} \mid \textbf{true} \mid \textbf{false} \mid \\
& & \textbf{succ}(M) \mid \textbf{pred}(M) \mid \textbf{zero?}(M) \mid \textbf{if } M \textbf{ then } M \textbf{ else } M \mid \\
& & x \mid \lambda x : t.\ M \mid MM \mid \mu x : t.\ M
\end{array}
$$

The syntax of PCF essentially includes the terms of the simply-typed λ-calculus but with two ground types **num** and **bool**. A thorough treatment of PCF syntax would follow along the lines of that given for the λ-calculus in Section 2.1, so I will only sketch the basic points about the syntax of the new language. As was the case for λ-calculus, care must be taken to distinguish between concrete syntax, term trees generated from the grammar, and equivalence classes of term trees modulo renaming of bound variables. The last of these is our primary concern in this chapter; they will be called *PCF terms* or, when the context makes it clear, *terms*. Conventions for naming variables, terms, and so on will remain the same as for the λ-calculus. The parsing conventions for λ-terms remain the same. The new constructs successor, predecessor, and test for zero are written with parentheses to avoid fussing with parsing conventions; this leads to some build-up of parentheses, but the results are not usually difficult to read. PCF also includes one 'mix-fix' operator called the *conditional*. In a conditional, **if** L **then** M **else** N, the term L is called the *condition* or *test*, M is the *first branch,* and N is the *second branch*. There is no ambiguity about L and M in the concrete syntax since these expressions are bracketed by keywords; for N it is assumed that the scope extends as far as possible. For instance, **if** x **then** f **else** gy parses as **if** x **then** f **else** $(g(y))$ rather than (**if** x **then** f **else** $g)(y)$. PCF includes a new binding operator μ for which the definition of α-equivalence and parsing conventions are analogous to those for λ. An expression $\mu x : t.\ M$ is called a *recursion* in which x is the *binding occurrence* and M is the *body*. The occurrence of x after the μ is the binding occurrence for all other occurrences of x that are free in M. Context substitution for term trees is defined accordingly:

- $\{M/x\}\mathbf{0}$ is $\mathbf{0}$, and an analogous definition is used for the boolean constants **true** and **false**.

- $\{M/x\}\mathbf{zero?}(N)$ is $\mathbf{zero?}(\{M/x\}N)$ and an analogous definition is used for the successor and predecessor expressions.

- $\{P/x\}$**if** L **then** M **else** N is   **if** $\{P/x\}L$ **then** $\{P/x\}M$ **else** $\{P/x\}N$.

- If N is an abstraction $\mu x : t.\ L$ where the bound variable is x, then $\{M/x\}N$ is N.

- If N is an abstraction $\mu y : t.\ L$ where the bound variable y is different from x, then $\{M/x\}N$ is $\mu y : t.\ \{M/x\}L$.

Substitution $[M/x]N$ for terms is obtained by renaming the bound variables of the term tree representative N to avoid capturing any of the free variables of the term tree representative M.

Typing rules for PCF are those of the simply-typed λ-calculus (Table 2.1) together with those given in Table 4.1.

Table 4.1
Typing Rules for PCF

[Zero]	$H \vdash \mathbf{0} : \mathbf{num}$
[True]	$H \vdash \mathbf{true} : \mathbf{bool}$
[False]	$H \vdash \mathbf{false} : \mathbf{bool}$
[Pred]	$\dfrac{H \vdash M : \mathbf{num}}{H \vdash \mathbf{pred}(M) : \mathbf{num}}$
[Succ]	$\dfrac{H \vdash M : \mathbf{num}}{H \vdash \mathbf{succ}(M) : \mathbf{num}}$
[IsZero]	$\dfrac{H \vdash M : \mathbf{num}}{H \vdash \mathbf{zero?}(M) : \mathbf{bool}}$
[Cond]	$\dfrac{H \vdash L : \mathbf{bool} \qquad H \vdash M : t \qquad H \vdash N : t}{H \vdash \mathbf{if}\ L\ \mathbf{then}\ M\ \mathbf{else}\ N : t}$
[Rec]	$\dfrac{H,\ x : t \vdash M : t}{H \vdash \mu x : t.\ M : t}$

- **0** has type number. **true** and **false** are of type boolean.

- Given an expression M of type number, $\mathbf{pred}(M)$ and $\mathbf{succ}(M)$ are also of type number but $\mathbf{zero?}(M)$ has type boolean.

- In the conditional expression, the condition L has type boolean and the branches of the conditional M and N must have the *same* type t. This type is also that of the conditional itself.

- If M has type t in a type assignment where x is assigned type t, then $\mu x : t.\ M$ has type t as well.

As an example of a well-typed program in PCF, consider the following expression:

$$\text{Minus} \equiv \mu\, \text{minus} : \mathbf{num} \to \mathbf{num} \to \mathbf{num}.\ \lambda x : \mathbf{num}.\ \lambda y : \mathbf{num}.$$
$$\mathbf{if}\ \mathbf{zero?}(y)\ \mathbf{then}\ x\ \mathbf{else}\ \text{minus}(\mathbf{pred}(x))(\mathbf{pred}(y))$$

The type of Minus is $\mathbf{num} \to \mathbf{num} \to \mathbf{num}$ since the expression

$$\mathbf{if}\ \mathbf{zero?}(x)\ \mathbf{then}\ x\ \mathbf{else}\ \text{minus}(\mathbf{pred}(x))(\mathbf{pred}(y))$$

has type **num** in the assignment

$$\text{minus} : \textbf{num} \to \textbf{num} \to \textbf{num}, \ x : \textbf{num}. \ y : \textbf{num}.$$

To define more complex functions, it is helpful to introduce local definitions. For example, in order to write the function for multiplication, it is convenient to use a local definition for addition:

$$(\lambda \ \text{plus} : \textbf{num} \to \textbf{num} \to \textbf{num}.$$
$$\qquad \mu \ \text{times} : \textbf{num} \to \textbf{num} \to \textbf{num}. \ \lambda x : \textbf{num}. \ \lambda y : \textbf{num}.$$
$$\qquad\qquad \textbf{if zero?}(y) \ \textbf{then 0}$$
$$\qquad\qquad \textbf{else} \ \text{plus}(x)(\text{times}(x)(\textbf{pred}(y)))$$
$$) \ \mu \ \text{plus} : \textbf{num} \to \textbf{num} \to \textbf{num}. \ \lambda x : \textbf{num}. \ \lambda y : \textbf{num}.$$
$$\qquad \textbf{if zero?}(y) \ \textbf{then} \ x$$
$$\qquad \textbf{else} \ \text{plus}(\textbf{succ}(x))(\textbf{pred}(y))$$

Two basic facts about the type system are given by the following:

4.1 Lemma.   *1. If $H \vdash M : s$ and $H \vdash M : t$, then $s \equiv t$.*
2. If $H, x : s \vdash M : t$ and $H \vdash N : s$, then $H \vdash [N/x]M : t$. $\qquad\qquad\qquad$ □

Parts (1) and (2) are the analogs of Lemmas 2.4 (on page 41) and 2.6 (on page 42) respectively; the proofs are left as an exercise.

Although we are able to sketch programs that look like implementations of various arithmetic operations, we are still missing a great deal. Following our development of the simply-typed λ-calculus, let us now consider an equational theory for PCF. In giving the equations, it is helpful to distinguish *numerals* from other expressions. Numerals are of the form

$$\underbrace{\textbf{succ}(\cdots \textbf{succ}(\textbf{0}) \cdots)}_{n \text{ copies}}$$

which is abbreviated as $\underline{n}$. A collection of equational rules for PCF can be obtained by taking the rules that appear in Table 4.2 together with those of the λ-calculus itself as given in Table 2.2.

- The predecessor of the successor of a numeral $\underline{n}$ is $\underline{n}$. The predecessor of zero is zero.

- The test for zero is false on the successor of a numeral and true on zero.

- If the test of a conditional is true, then the conditional is equal to its first branch; if the test is false, then it is equal to the second branch.

Table 4.2
Equational Rules for Call-by-Name PCF

{PredZero} $\vdash (H \rhd \mathbf{pred}(\mathbf{0}) = \mathbf{0} : \mathbf{num})$

{PredSucc} $\vdash (H \rhd \mathbf{pred}(\mathbf{succ}(\underline{n})) = \underline{n} : \mathbf{num})$

{ZeroIsZero} $\vdash (H \rhd \mathbf{zero?}(\mathbf{0}) = \mathbf{true} : \mathbf{num})$

{SuccIsNotZero} $\vdash (H \rhd \mathbf{zero?}(\mathbf{succ}(\underline{n})) = \mathbf{false} : \mathbf{bool})$

{IfTrue}
$$\frac{H \vdash M : t \qquad H \vdash N : t}{\vdash (H \rhd \mathbf{if\ true\ then}\ M\ \mathbf{else}\ N = M : t)}$$

{IfFalse}
$$\frac{H \vdash M : t \qquad H \vdash N : t}{\vdash (H \rhd \mathbf{if\ false\ then}\ M\ \mathbf{else}\ N = N : t)}$$

{μ}
$$\frac{H, x : t \vdash M : t}{\vdash (H \rhd \mu x : t.\ M = [\mu x : t.\ M/x]M : t)}$$

{Cong}

$$\frac{\vdash (H \rhd M = N : \mathbf{num})}{\vdash (H \rhd \mathbf{pred}(M) = \mathbf{pred}(N) : \mathbf{num})} \qquad \frac{\vdash (H \rhd M = N : \mathbf{num})}{\vdash (H \rhd \mathbf{succ}(M) = \mathbf{succ}(N) : \mathbf{num})}$$

$$\frac{\vdash (H \rhd M = N : \mathbf{num})}{\vdash (H \rhd \mathbf{zero?}(M) = \mathbf{zero?}(N) : \mathbf{bool})} \qquad \frac{\vdash (H, x : t \rhd M = N : t)}{\vdash (H \rhd \mu x : t.\ M = \mu x : t.\ N : t)}$$

$$\frac{\vdash (H \rhd L = L' : \mathbf{bool}) \qquad \vdash (H \rhd M = M' : t) \qquad \vdash (H \rhd N = N' : t)}{\vdash (H \rhd \mathbf{if}\ L\ \mathbf{then}\ M\ \mathbf{else}\ N = \mathbf{if}\ L'\ \mathbf{then}\ M'\ \mathbf{else}\ N' : t)}$$

- A recursion $\mu x : t.\ M$ is equal to its *unwinding* obtained by substituting the recursion itself for all free occurrences of x in its body.

- Each construct in the grammar has an associated congruence rule.

These equations are best appreciated in an example. Here is how they could be used to prove that $2 - 1 = 1$ where $\underline{2}$ is **succ(succ(0))** and $\underline{1}$ is **succ(0)**:

$$\mathrm{minus}(\underline{2})(\underline{1}) = \textbf{if zero?}(\underline{1})\ \textbf{then}\ \underline{2} \tag{4.7}$$

$$\textbf{else}\ \mathrm{minus}(\textbf{pred}(\underline{2}))(\textbf{pred}(\underline{1}))$$

$$= \mathrm{minus}(\textbf{pred}(\underline{2}))(\textbf{pred}(\underline{1})) \tag{4.8}$$

$$= \textbf{if zero?}(\textbf{pred}(\underline{1}))\ \textbf{then}\ \textbf{pred}(\underline{2}) \tag{4.9}$$

$$\textbf{else}\ \mathrm{minus}(\textbf{pred}(\textbf{pred}(\underline{2})))(\textbf{pred}((\textbf{pred}(\underline{1}))))$$

$$= \textbf{pred}(\underline{2}) \tag{4.10}$$

$$= \underline{1} \tag{4.11}$$

Taken together with several uses of {Trans} and {Cong}, the steps of this calculation can be justified as follows: Equation 4.7 and Equation 4.9 follow from the μ- and β-rules; Equation 4.8 follows from {SuccIsNotZero} and {IfFalse}; Equation 4.10 follows from {PredSucc}, {ZeroIsZero}, and {IfTrue}; Equation 4.11 follows from {PredSucc}.

But now, do the equational rules tell us all we want to know about PCF *as a programming language?* There is a missing ingredient; although the equations made it possible to deduce that $2 - 1 = 1$, they provided no direct guide to *how* this equation could be derived. Nevertheless, the steps in the calculation deriving the equation seem to follow a certain *strategy* for finding the answer. For example, whenever an application was encountered, the β-rule was employed to obtain an equal expression, which was then manipulated further. Recursions were dealt with by unwinding using the μ-rule. A precise description of a strategy for this rewriting is called an *operational semantics* for the language. One approach to describing such a semantics is to indicate how a term M evaluates to another term M' by defining a relation $M \to M'$ between terms using a set of *evaluation rules*. The goal of such rewriting is to obtain a *value* to which no further rules apply. In order to define precisely how a term is related to a value, we define a binary *transition relation* $\to$ to be the least relation on pairs of PCF terms that satisfies the axioms and rules in Table 4.3. This is called the transition semantics for *call-by-name evaluation* of PCF. The term 'call-by-name' comes from the form of the application rule: an application of an abstraction $\lambda x : t.\ M$ to an argument N evaluates to the result of substituting N for x in the body of the abstraction even though N may not be a value. We will say that a term M evaluates to a value V just in the case $M \to^* V$ where $\to^*$ is

Table 4.3
Transition Rules for Call-by-Name Evaluation of PCF

$$\frac{M \rightarrow N}{\mathbf{pred}(M) \rightarrow \mathbf{pred}(N)} \qquad \mathbf{pred}(0) \rightarrow 0 \qquad \mathbf{pred}(\mathbf{succ}(V)) \rightarrow V$$

$$\frac{M \rightarrow N}{\mathbf{zero?}(M) \rightarrow \mathbf{zero?}(N)} \qquad \mathbf{zero?}(0) \rightarrow \mathbf{true} \qquad \mathbf{zero?}(\mathbf{succ}(V)) \rightarrow \mathbf{false}$$

$$\frac{M \rightarrow N}{\mathbf{succ}(M) \rightarrow \mathbf{succ}(N)}$$

$$\frac{M \rightarrow N}{M(L) \rightarrow N(L)} \qquad (\lambda x : t.\ M)(N) \rightarrow [N/x]M$$

$$\mathbf{if\ true\ then}\ M\ \mathbf{else}\ N \rightarrow M \qquad \mathbf{if\ false\ then}\ M\ \mathbf{else}\ N \rightarrow N$$

$$\frac{L \rightarrow L'}{\mathbf{if}\ L\ \mathbf{then}\ M\ \mathbf{else}\ N \rightarrow \mathbf{if}\ L'\ \mathbf{then}\ M\ \mathbf{else}\ N}$$

$$\mu x : t.\ M \rightarrow [\mu x : t.\ M/x]M$$

the transitive, reflexive closure of the transition relation and a value is a term generated by the following grammar:

$$V ::= 0 \mid \mathbf{true} \mid \mathbf{false} \mid \mathbf{succ}(V) \mid \lambda x : t.\ M \tag{4.12}$$

I will also use the letters U, W to range over values. Note that any value evaluates to itself, and, moreover, the transition relation is deterministic:

4.2 Lemma. *If $M \rightarrow N$ and $M \rightarrow N'$ then $N \equiv N'$.* $\qquad\qquad\qquad\square$

The proof is left as an exercise. Let us write $M \rightarrow_n^* N$ for $n \geq 1$ if there are terms $M_1, \ldots, M_n$ such that $M \rightarrow M_1 \rightarrow M_2 \rightarrow \cdots \rightarrow M_n \equiv N$ and say that the *length* of the evaluation from M to N is n. We write $M \rightarrow_0^* N$ in case $M \equiv N$. The following result provides further insight into the transition relation:

4.3 Lemma. *If $M \rightarrow^* N$, then*

1. $\mathbf{pred}(M) \rightarrow^* \mathbf{pred}(N)$
2. $\mathbf{succ}(M) \rightarrow^* \mathbf{succ}(N)$
3. $\mathbf{zero?}(M) \rightarrow^* \mathbf{zero?}(N)$

4. $M(L) \to^* N(L)$

5. **if** M **then** L_1 **else** $L_2 \to^*$ **if** N **then** L_1 **else** L_2

Proof: The proofs of the parts are very similar, so I will do only the fourth one. The proof is by induction on the length of the evaluation $M \to^* N$. If this length is zero, then there is nothing to prove. Suppose the result is known for evaluations of length less than n and $M \to M' \to^*_{n-1} N$, then $M'(L) \to^* N(L)$ by the inductive hypothesis and $M(L) \to M'(L)$ by the rules defining the transition relation. Thus $M(L) \to^* N(L)$ too.   □

It is helpful to see how these steps are related to our earlier example illustrating the equational theory. The steps in the calculation of $2 - 1$ are related to steps in the transition semantics as follows: 4.7 and 4.9 follow from the transition rules for recursion and application; 4.8 follows from the rules for zero test and conditional; 4.10 follows from the rules for predecessor, zero test, and conditional; 4.11 follows from the rules for predecessor. A precise summary of this relationship is formalized in the following Theorem:

4.4 Theorem. *If* $H \vdash M : t$ *and* $M \to N$, *then* $H \vdash N : t$ *and*

$$\vdash (H \rhd M = N : t).$$

Proof: The proof is by induction on the structure of M. I will write out the proofs for predecessor, application, and recursion.

Suppose that M is a predecessor and consider the rules for which $M \to N$ is a possible conclusion. If it follows from the first of the rules for predecessors in Table 4.3, then $M \equiv \mathbf{pred}(M')$ and $N \equiv \mathbf{pred}(N')$ where $M' \to N'$. By the inductive hypothesis, $H \vdash N' : \mathbf{num}$, so $H \vdash \mathbf{pred}(N') : \mathbf{num}$ too. Moreover, $(H \rhd M' = N' : \mathbf{num})$, and from this it is possible to conclude that $\vdash (H \rhd \mathbf{pred}(M') = \mathbf{pred}(N') : \mathbf{num})$ by the congruence rule for predecessor. If $M \equiv \mathbf{pred}(0)$, then $M \to 0$. Clearly M and 0 both have type $\mathbf{num}$; moreover, $\vdash (H \rhd \mathbf{pred}(0) = 0 : \mathbf{num})$ follows from {PredZero}. If $M \equiv \mathbf{pred}(\mathbf{succ}(V))$, then $M \to V$. Now $H \vdash \mathbf{pred}(\mathbf{succ}(V)) : \mathbf{num}$, so it must be the case that $H \vdash V : \mathbf{num}$ too. Moreover $\vdash (H \rhd M = V : \mathbf{num})$ by {PredSucc}.

Suppose that M is an application. There are two rules that might apply. If $M \equiv L_1(L_2)$ and $L_1 \to L'_1$, then, by the inductive hypothesis, $H \vdash L'_1 : s \to t$ for some type s such that $H \vdash L_2 : s$. By [Appl], we must therefore have $H \vdash L'_1(L_2) : t$. By the inductive hypothesis, we also have $\vdash (H \rhd L_1 = L'_1 : s \to t)$. So, by the congruence rule for application, $\vdash (H \rhd M = N : t)$ too. Suppose now that $M \equiv (\lambda x : s. L_1)(L_2)$ where $H, x : s \vdash L_1 : t$ and $H \vdash L_2 : s$. Now $M \to [L_2/x]L_1$, and, by part (2) of Lemma 4.1, we must have $H \vdash [L_2/x]L_1 : t$. Moreover, by the β-rule, $\vdash (H \rhd M = [L_2/x]L_1 : t)$.

Suppose finally that $M \equiv \mu x : t. \, M'$ is a recursion. Then $M \to [M/x]M'$. By the typing rule for recursion, we know that $H, x : t \vdash M' : t$ so, by part (2) of Lemma 4.1, $H \vdash [M/x]M' : t$ too. Moreover, $\vdash (H \rhd M = [M/x]M' : t)$ follows from the μ-rule. $\square$

Theorem 4.4 really consists of two results. The first of these, which says that $H \vdash M : t$ and $M \to N$ implies $H \vdash N : t$, is known as *Subject Reduction*. The second of these, which concludes that $H \vdash M = N : t$, is the *soundness* of the transition relation $\to$ *relative to the equations.*

As mentioned in Section 1.2 for the Simple Imperative Language, it is sometimes possible to describe the relation $M \to^* V$ more directly using a new set of rules. Such a description is sometimes known as a *natural (operational) semantics*. I now describe such a semantics for PCF. This is done using a binary relation $\Downarrow$ between closed terms of the calculus. The binary relation is defined as the least relation that satisfies the axioms and rules in Table 4.4. In the description of these rules, the terms that appear on the right side have been written using the metavariables U, V, W for values rather than using metavaribles L, M, N for arbitrary terms. To read the rules, assume at first that U, V, W range over all terms. It can then be proved by an induction on the height of a derivation that if $M \Downarrow V$ for any terms M and V, then V is a term generated by the grammar 4.12. In other words, if rules such as

$$\frac{M \Downarrow \mathbf{succ}(V)}{\mathbf{pred}(M) \Downarrow V}$$

were instead written in the form

$$\frac{M \Downarrow \mathbf{succ}(N)}{\mathbf{pred}(M) \Downarrow N},$$

then it would be possible to *prove* that N has the form of a value V. Here are some specific comments on the rules, in the form of a strategy for determining for a term M whether there is a value V such that $M \Downarrow V$:

- Constants evaluate to themselves.

- Two rules describe the evaluation of the predecessor. To evaluate the predecessor of a term, first evaluate the term; if the result of that evaluation is zero, then the predecessor is zero but, if the result is $n + 1$, then the predecessor is n.

- To evaluate the successor of a term, first evaluate the term; if the result of this evaluation is n, then the result of evaluating the successor is $n + 1$.

- Two rules describe the evaluation of a test for zero. To test whether a term is zero, first evaluate the term. If the result of this evaluation is $\mathbf{0}$, then $\mathbf{true}$ is the result of the test. If the result of the evaluation is, instead, a successor, then the result of the test is $\mathbf{false}$.

Table 4.4
Natural Rules for Call-by-Name Evaluation of PCF

$$\mathbf{0} \Downarrow \mathbf{0} \qquad \mathbf{true} \Downarrow \mathbf{true} \qquad \mathbf{false} \Downarrow \mathbf{false}$$

$$\frac{M \Downarrow \mathbf{0}}{\mathbf{pred}(M) \Downarrow \mathbf{0}} \qquad \frac{M \Downarrow \mathbf{succ}(V)}{\mathbf{pred}(M) \Downarrow V} \qquad \frac{M \Downarrow V}{\mathbf{succ}(M) \Downarrow \mathbf{succ}(V)}$$

$$\frac{M \Downarrow \mathbf{0}}{\mathbf{zero?}(M) \Downarrow \mathbf{true}} \qquad \frac{M \Downarrow \mathbf{succ}(V)}{\mathbf{zero?}(M) \Downarrow \mathbf{false}}$$

$$\lambda x : s.\ M \Downarrow \lambda x : s.\ M \qquad \frac{M \Downarrow \lambda x : s.\ M' \quad [N/x]M' \Downarrow V}{M(N) \Downarrow V}$$

$$\frac{M_1 \Downarrow \mathbf{true} \quad M_2 \Downarrow V}{\mathbf{if}\ M_1\ \mathbf{then}\ M_2\ \mathbf{else}\ M_3 \Downarrow V} \qquad \frac{M_1 \Downarrow \mathbf{false} \quad M_3 \Downarrow V}{\mathbf{if}\ M_1\ \mathbf{then}\ M_2\ \mathbf{else}\ M_3 \Downarrow V}$$

$$\frac{[\mu x : t.\ M/x]M \Downarrow V}{\mu x : t.\ M \Downarrow V}$$

- An abstraction evaluates to itself. To evaluate an application of a term M to a term N, begin by evaluating M. If this evaluation yields an abstraction, then evaluate the result of substituting N for the formal parameter of the abstraction in its body. The result (if any) of evaluating this term is the result of the evaluation of the application.

- To evaluate a conditional, begin by evaluating the test. If the test evaluates to **true**, then the result of evaluating the conditional is the result of evaluating the term in the first branch. On the other hand, if the test evaluates to **false**, then the result of evaluating the conditional is the result of evaluating the term in the second branch.

- To evaluate a recursion, substitute the recursion itself for the bound variable of the recursion in its body and evaluate this term. The result (if any) of this evaluation is the result of evaluating the recursion.

This description of the rules appears to say more than the rules themselves, including a number of implicit assumptions about the nature of the $\Downarrow$ relation. One of these is the hint that if $M \Downarrow V$, then V is 'the' result of evaluation. Since the rules were described as a relation rather than a function, it must be shown that this is a legitimate view:

4.5 Lemma. *The relation $\Downarrow$ is a partial function, that is, if $M \Downarrow U$ and $M \Downarrow V$, then $U \equiv V$.*

Proof: The proof proceeds by induction on the length of an evaluation of an expression M, that is, by induction on the height of a proof that $M \Downarrow V$. The desired property certainly holds for the axioms. Suppose that it is known for proofs with height less than n. Suppose, for example, that the last step of a proof of height n is the following instance of the conditional:

$$\frac{L \Downarrow \textbf{true} \qquad M \Downarrow V}{\textbf{if } L \textbf{ then } M \textbf{ else } N \Downarrow V}$$

Suppose **if** L **then** M **else** $N \Downarrow U$ too for some U. By the inductive hypothesis, we know that it is not the case that $L \Downarrow \textbf{false}$, so only one rule could have the conclusion **if** L **then** M **else** $N \Downarrow U$ and this rule has $M \Downarrow U$ as one of its hypotheses. By the inductive hypothesis and the fact that $M \Downarrow V$, we conclude that $U \equiv V$. The proof is similar for all of the other cases. $\qquad\qquad\qquad\qquad\qquad\qquad\qquad\qquad\qquad\qquad\qquad\qquad\Box$

The proof that $\Downarrow$ and $\rightarrow^*$ define the same relationship between PCF terms and values provides an excellent example of the nature of arguments involving each of the two forms of semantic description. We saw in the proof of Theorem 4.4 that basic properties of the relation $\rightarrow$ can be proved by structural induction. This technique works because of the fact that the hypotheses of a rule for the transition semantics as given in Table 4.3 are *structurally inductive* in the sense that the hypothesis of a rule involves only subterms of its conclusion. A transition semantics having such a property is sometimes called a *structural operational semantics* for this reason. Now, to prove properties of $\rightarrow^*$, one typically combines structural induction (for the rules) with induction on the length of an evaluation (for the transitions). This can be understood graphically in terms of the illustration for a transition semantics in Figure 1.1. One of the inductive hypotheses is vertical and the other is horizontal. By contrast, a natural semantics evaluation has no horizontal component (see the illustration in Figure 1.1) so the inductive hypotheses is entirely vertical, proceeding, as in the proof of Lemma 4.5, by induction on the height of the evaluation tree (that is, on the height of the derivation tree in the operational semantics). Although only one inductive hypothesis may be required, facts involving rules in a natural semantics cannot ordinarily be proved by induction on the structure of terms since the terms used in the hypothesis of a rule may not be subterms of those used in its conclusion. For the natural semantics of PCF, the primary fault lies in the rule for recursion:

$$\frac{[\mu x : t. \, M/x]M \Downarrow V}{\mu x : t. \, M \Downarrow V}$$

since the hypothesis explicitly mentions $\mu x : t. \, M$. The natural semantics for the Simple Imperative Language given in Table 1.5 also fails to have this property because of the rule for the evaluation of the while loop. The transition semantics for the Simple Imperative Language given in Table 1.4 does satisfy it, however. In the proof of the theorem below, sufficiency is proved in natural semantics style, by induction on the height of the evaluation; the converse is proved in the style of a structural operational semantics, by induction on the structure of terms and induction on the length of the evaluation sequence.

4.6 Theorem. *$M \Downarrow V$ if, and only if, $M \to^* V$.*

Proof: Proof of ($\Rightarrow$) is by induction *on the height of the derivation* of $M \Downarrow V$. The result is immediate for instances in which this height is 1 since the term M is then a value. Suppose the result is known for shorter proofs; we consider each of the cases for the last step used to derive $M \Downarrow V$. If, for example, M is $\mathbf{pred}(M')$ and $M \Downarrow \mathbf{0}$ because $M' \Downarrow \mathbf{0}$ (the first rule for predecessors in Table 4.4), then $M' \to^* \mathbf{0}$ by the inductive hypothesis. By Lemma 4.3, it follows that $\mathbf{pred}(M') \to^* \mathbf{pred}(\mathbf{0})$. Since $\mathbf{pred}(\mathbf{0}) \to \mathbf{0}$ by the rules for the transition relation, it follows that $M \to^* \mathbf{0}$, the desired conclusion. The argument for other cases involving successor, predecessor, zero test, and application is similar. The only remaining possibility is the rule for recursion. If $M \equiv \mu x : t. \, M'$, then $M \Downarrow V$ follows from $[\mu x : t. \, M'/x]M' \Downarrow V$. Since the inductive hypothesis applies to this latter relationship, we conclude that $[\mu x : t. \, M'/x]M' \to^* V$. But

$$\mu x : t. \, M' \to [\mu x : t. \, M' \, / \, x]M'$$

is the transition rule for recursions, so we must have $M \to^* V$.

The proof of ($\Leftarrow$) involves two inductions: one on the structure of M and another on the length of the evaluation $M \to^* V$. Let us begin by proving *by induction on the structure* of M that if $M \to N \Downarrow V$, then $M \Downarrow V$. Suppose the result is known for subterms of M. Each of the cases for how $M \to N$ could be derived must be considered. If M is a constant, then there is nothing to prove. I will do a few of the non-constant cases and leave others as exercises.

- Suppose $M \equiv \mathbf{pred}(M')$ is a predecessor and $M \to N \Downarrow V$. There are three rules that apply to predecessors.
  First case: $N \equiv \mathbf{pred}(N')$ and $M' \to N'$. Since $\mathbf{pred}(N') \Downarrow V$, it must be the case that $N' \Downarrow \mathbf{succ}(V)$ or $N' \Downarrow \mathbf{0} \equiv V$ since these are the only hypotheses that could derive this relationship. In the first case, we have $M' \to N' \Downarrow \mathbf{succ}(V)$ so we can use the inductive hypothesis to conclude that $M' \Downarrow \mathbf{succ}(V)$ and therefore $M \equiv \mathbf{pred}(M') \Downarrow V$. In the second case $M' \Downarrow \mathbf{0} \equiv V$ so $M \Downarrow V$ too.

Second case: $M \equiv \mathbf{pred}(0) \to 0 \equiv N$. In this case $V \equiv 0$ and $M \Downarrow V$ follows immediately from the rules for $\Downarrow$.

Third case: $M \equiv \mathbf{pred}(\mathbf{succ}(U)) \to U \equiv N$. Then $U \equiv V$ and $M \Downarrow V$ by the appropriate rule for $\Downarrow$.

- Suppose $M \equiv M'(L)$ is an application. There are two rules for applications. First case: $N \equiv N'(L)$ and $M' \to N'$. Since $N'(L) \Downarrow V$, it must be that

$$N' \Downarrow \lambda x : t.\ N'' \text{ and } [L/x]N'' \Downarrow V$$

for some N''. By the inductive hypothesis, $M' \Downarrow \lambda x : t.\ N''$ too so $M \Downarrow V$. Second case: $M' \equiv \lambda x : t.\ M''$ and $N \equiv [L/x]M''$. Now $[L/x]M'' \Downarrow V$ by assumption so, by the rules for $\Downarrow$, we also have $M' \Downarrow \lambda x : t.\ M''$. Thus $M \equiv M'(L) \Downarrow V$.

- Suppose $M \equiv \mu x : t.\ M'$ is a recursion. Then $N \equiv [M/x]M'$, and, by the $\Downarrow$ rule for recursions, $N \Downarrow V$ implies that $M \Downarrow V$ too.

Now, to complete the proof, we proceed by induction *on the length of the evaluation* $M \to^* V$. If the length of the evaluation $M \to^* V$ is zero, then M is a value and therefore $M \Downarrow M \equiv V$. One the other hand, if $M \to_{n+1}^* V$, then there is an N such that $M \to N \to_n^* V$. If we assume that the desired conclusion holds for an evaluation of length n, then $N \Downarrow V$. By the result proved above by induction on the structure of M, we must therefore have $M \Downarrow V$ too. $\qquad\square$

4.7 Corollary. *If $H \vdash M : t$ and $M \Downarrow N$, then $H \vdash N : t$ and*

$$\vdash (H \rhd M = N : t).$$
$\qquad\square$

Exercises.

4.1 Code the factorial program in PCF.

4.2 Demonstrate a PCF program that computes the equality function

$$\text{equal} : \mathbf{num} \to \mathbf{num} \to \mathbf{bool}.$$

4.3 Prove Lemma 4.1.

4.4* The *Fibonacci function* is defined as follows:

$$\text{fibonacci}(x) = \begin{cases} 0 & \text{if } x = 0 \\ 1 & \text{if } x = 1 \\ f(x-1) + f(x-2) & \text{otherwise} \end{cases}$$

It can be coded in PCF as in Table 4.5, but this definition has a very poor computational performance. Explain why and provide another PCF program that implements the Fibonacci function and has better computational properties.

Table 4.5
The Fibonacci Function

$(\lambda$ plus : **num** $\rightarrow$ **num** $\rightarrow$ **num**.
    μ fibonacci : **num** $\rightarrow$ **num**. λx : **num**.
        if zero?(x) **then 0**
        else if zero?$(\textbf{pred}(x))$ **then succ(0)**
        else plus (fibonacci(**pred**(x)))
                  (fibonacci(**pred**(**pred**(x)))))
$)$ μ plus : **num** $\rightarrow$ **num** $\rightarrow$ **num**. λx : **num**. λy : **num**.
    if zero?(y) **then** x
    else plus(**succ**(x))(**pred**(y))

4.5 Prove Lemma 4.2.

4.6 Using your favorite definition of a universal computing machine (*e.g.*, a Turing machine or a universal register machine), show that call-by-name evaluation for PCF provides universal computing power. In other words, show that every partial recursive function from numbers to numbers can be coded in PCF.

4.7 Prove part (1) of Lemma 4.3.

4.8 Let K, L, M be terms such that K : **bool** and L, M : $s_1 \rightarrow s_2 \rightarrow \cdots \rightarrow s_n \rightarrow t$. Given terms N_1 : $s_1, \ldots, N_n$: s_n, prove that if $K \Downarrow$ **true**, then

$$(\textbf{if } K \textbf{ then } L \textbf{ else } M)N_1 \cdots N_n \Downarrow V \quad \text{iff} \quad LN_1 \cdots N_n \Downarrow V,$$

and if $K \Downarrow$ **false**, then

$$(\textbf{if } K \textbf{ then } L \textbf{ else } M)N_1 \cdots N_n \Downarrow V \quad \text{iff} \quad MN_1 \cdots N_n \Downarrow V.$$

4.9 It was suggested in the introduction of the chapter that it is possible to replace the recursion construct $\mu x : t.\ M$ of PCF with a unary operator $\mathbf{Y}$. An alternative grammar for the language might be

$$M \quad ::= \quad \mathbf{0} \mid \textbf{succ}(M) \mid \textbf{pred}(M) \mid \textbf{true} \mid \textbf{false} \mid \textbf{zero?}(M) \mid$$
$$x \mid \lambda x : t.\ M \mid MM \mid \mathbf{Y}(M) \mid \textbf{if } M \textbf{ then } M \textbf{ else } M$$

with a typing rule and operational rule

$$\frac{H \vdash M : t \rightarrow t}{H \vdash \mathbf{Y}(M) : t} \qquad \frac{M(\mathbf{Y}(M)) \Downarrow V}{\mathbf{Y}(M) \Downarrow V}.$$

Formulate and prove a theorem relating this language to the definition of PCF given in this section.

4.2   Fixed Points in Complete Partial Orders

The semantics for PCF given in the previous section was different in some ways from the semantics provided for the λ-calculus in Chapter 2. To have the reference close at hand, recall how the set-theoretic model was defined using the following clauses:

- Projection: $[\![H \triangleright x : t]\!]\rho = \rho(x)$.
- Abstraction: $[\![H \triangleright \lambda x : u.\ M' : u \to v]\!]\rho$ is the function from $[\![u]\!]$ to $[\![v]\!]$ given by $d \mapsto [\![H, x : u \triangleright M' : v]\!](\rho[x \mapsto d])$.
- Application: $[\![H \triangleright L(N) : t]\!]\rho$ is the value obtained by applying the function $[\![H \triangleright L : s \to t]\!]\rho$ to argument $[\![H \triangleright N : s]\!]\rho$ where s is the unique type such that $H \vdash L : s \to t$ and $H \vdash N : s$.

First of all, these meanings are given through the use of *semantic equations* without mentioning a notion of evaluation. But a second point is their similarity to the typing rules for the simply-typed lambda calculus in Table 2.1. For example, the meaning of an application $L(N)$ such that $H \vdash L(N) : t$ is given using the meanings of terms in the hypothesis of the application rule; the typing rule for abstraction has the form

$$\frac{H,\ x : s \vdash M : t}{H \vdash \lambda x : s.\ M : s \to t}.$$

and the meaning of the tuple $H \triangleright \lambda x : s.\ M : s \to t$ is defined in terms of that for $H,\ x : s \triangleright M : t$. In general, the semantics follows the typing judgements for the calculus. Now, if we wish to use this approach for PCF, we should use a similar approach for recursion. Since the typing rule for recursion has the form

$$\frac{H, x : t \vdash M : t}{H \vdash \mu x : t.\ M : t}.$$

we should define $[\![H \vdash \mu x : t.\ M : t]\!]$ in terms of $[\![H, x : t \vdash M : t]\!]$. On the face of it, it is not clear how either of the semantic descriptions used in the previous section would allow us to do this directly. Suppose, on the other hand, we seek to extend the set-theoretic semantics for the λ-calculus. A natural suggestion, based on the equation for recursion,

$$\frac{H, x : t \vdash M : t}{\vdash (H \triangleright \mu x : t.\ M = [\mu x : t.\ M/x]M : t)},$$

is to take a definition such as

- Recursion: $[\![H \rhd \mu x : t.\ M' : t]\!]\rho$ is the element d of $[\![t]\!]$ such that $d = [\![H, x : t \rhd M' : t]\!](\rho[x \mapsto d])$.

But there is a problem. How do we know that there is only *one* element d having the property mentioned above? If there are several, perhaps we could pick one of them, but how this choice is made should be part of the semantic description. More seriously, how do we know that there is *any* element d of $[\![t]\!]$ having the desired property? If there is none, perhaps we want the meaning of the recursion to be 'undefined' in some sense, but how does this fit with the equational theory?

Complete partial orders.

To properly address the question of how to interpret recursions as fixed points, we must develop an appropriate mathematical theory of semantic domains. We begin with the most widely-known theory developed for this purpose. It is based on the idea that types are certain kinds of partial orders. Recall that a *partial order* or *poset* is a set D together with a binary relation $\sqsubseteq$ that is reflexive, anti-symmetric, and transitive. I usually write D for the pair $\langle D, \sqsubseteq \rangle$ when the binary relation is unimportant or clear enough from context. If it is necessary to keep the order relations from more than one poset distinct from one another, the poset name may be attached as a subscript (for example, $\sqsubseteq_D$ and $\sqsubseteq_E$ for the orders on posets D and E). A subset $P \subseteq D$ of a poset D is said to be *bounded (above)* or *consistent* if there is an $x \in D$ such that $y \sqsubseteq x$ for each $y \in P$; in this case x is an *upper bound* of P. The *least upper bound (lub)* of a subset $P \subseteq D$ is an upper bound $\bigsqcup P$ for P such that $x \sqsupseteq \bigsqcup P$ for any other upper bound x of P. If x, y are both lub's for P, then $x \sqsupseteq y$ and $y \sqsupseteq x$, so $x = y$, hence there can be at most one lub for any set. A subset $P \subseteq D$ is *directed* if every finite set $u \subseteq P$ has an upper bound $x \in P$. Note that a directed set P is always non-empty because $\emptyset \subseteq M$ is a finite set that must have a bound in P. A poset D is *complete* (and hence a *cpo*) if every directed subset $P \subseteq D$ has a least upper bound. If a poset D has a least element $\bot_D$, then we say that it is *pointed*.[2] When the pointed cpo D is understood from context, the subscript on $\bot_D$ will usually be dropped.

Many familiar posets are cpo's. For example, it is not hard to see that *any* finite poset is a cpo since the lub of a finite directed set is the largest element of that set. In particular, a poset with a unique element is a (pointed) cpo. This trivial case is very important; let us fix one such single element poset and call it $\mathbb{U}$. Its unique element is its least element as well, so this is denoted $\bot_{\mathbb{U}}$ or, more succinctly, u. Another easy example that comes up later is the poset $\mathbb{O}$, which has two distinct elements $\top$ and $\bot$ with $\bot \sqsubseteq \top$. The *truth value cpo* $\mathbb{T}$ is the poset that has three distinct points, $\bot, \mathsf{true}, \mathsf{false}$, where $\bot \sqsubseteq \mathsf{true}$ and

---

[2]Note that 'pointed' is a property of posets whereas 'well-pointed' is a property of categories.

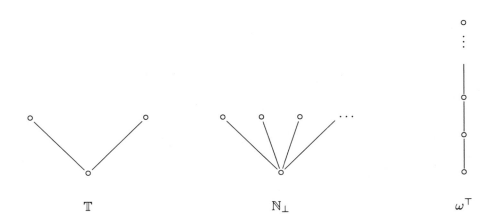

Figure 4.1
Examples of Cpo's

$\bot \sqsubseteq$ false. To create a pictorial representation of a poset, one can use what is known as a *Hasse diagram*. Hasse diagrams use circles to represent elements of the poset and lines to represent the order relation. Larger elements of the poset are drawn above smaller ones and connected by a line. The poset $\mathbb{T}$ is represented by the Hasse diagram on the left in Figure 4.1). The natural numbers (that is, the non-negative integers) are a poset called ω under their usual ordering $\leq$. It is *not* a cpo because it has a directed subset (namely ω itself) that has no least upper bound. To get a cpo, one needs to add a top element, thereby obtaining the cpo $\omega^\top$. Since there are infinitely many elements in this poset, it is clearly impossible to draw its Hasse diagram fully, but a helpful approximation can be had by using elipsis (three dots) as done in the illustration on the right side of Figure 4.1. For a more subtle class of examples of cpo's, let $\mathcal{P}(S)$, the *powerset* of S, be the set of (all) subsets of a set S. Ordered by ordinary set inclusion, $\mathcal{P}(S)$ forms a cpo whose least upper bound operation is just set union. $\mathcal{P}(S)$ is also pointed with $\bot = \emptyset$. The poset $\mathbb{Q}$ of rational numbers with their usual ordering is not a cpo. Of course, $\mathbb{Q}$ lacks a top element, but there is another problem that causes $\mathbb{Q}$ to fail to be a cpo: it lacks, for example, the square root of two! However, the unit interval $[0, 1]$ of real numbers *does* form a cpo.

Any set can be viewed as a cpo under the *discrete order*: $x \sqsubseteq y$ iff $x = y$. Given a set S, the poset, $S_\bot = S \cup \{\bot\}$, obtained by adding a new element, $\bot$, to S and defining

$$x \sqsubseteq y \text{ iff either } x = y \text{ or } x = \bot,$$

yields a cpo called the *lift of S* or the *flat pointed cpo determined by S*. If we write $\mathbb{N}$ for the discretely ordered poset of natural numbers, its lift is the flat cpo illustrated by the Hasse diagram in the center of Figure 4.1. When discussing cpo's I usually refer to $\mathbb{N}_\perp$ simply as the natural numbers (despite the intrusion of $\perp$).

One of the most illustrative examples of a cpo is that of partial functions $[S \rightsquigarrow T]$ between sets S and T. Recall that such partial functions are subsets of $S \times T$; if they are ordered by subset inclusion, the least upper bound is simply set union. This is also a pointed cpo whose least element is the totally undefined function $\emptyset$.

Recall that a function $f : D \to E$ between posets D and E is monotone if $f(x) \sqsubseteq f(y)$ whenever $x \sqsubseteq y$. If f is monotone, and $f(\bigsqcup P) = \bigsqcup \{f(x) \mid x \in P\}$ for every directed P, then f is said to be *continuous*. A function $f : D \to E$ is said to be *strict* if $f(\perp_D) = \perp_E$. I will write $f : D \multimap E$ to indicate that f is strict. If $f, g : D \to E$, then I write $f \sqsubseteq g$ if, and only if, $f(x) \sqsubseteq g(x)$ for every $x \in D$.

To get a few examples of continuous functions, note that when $f : D \to E$ is monotone and D is finite, then f is continuous. In fact, this is true whenever D has no infinite ascending chains. For example, any monotone function $f : \mathbb{N}_\perp \to E$ is continuous. On the other hand, the function $f : \omega^\top \to \mathbb{O}$ that sends the elements of ω to $\perp$ and sends $\top$ to $\top$ is monotone, but it is not continuous. For a more interesting example, let S, T be sets and suppose $f : S \to T$ is a function. The *extension* of f is the function $\mathcal{P}(f) : \mathcal{P}(S) \to \mathcal{P}(T)$ given by taking

$$\mathcal{P}(f)(X) = \{f(x) \mid x \in X\}$$

for each subset $X \subseteq S$. The function $\mathcal{P}(f)$ is monotone and, for any collection X_i of subsets of S, we have

$$\mathcal{P}(f)(\bigcup_i X_i) = \bigcup_i \mathcal{P}(f)(X_i).$$

In particular, $\mathcal{P}(f)$ is continuous.

Let $f : D \to E$ and $g : E \to F$ be continuous functions and suppose $P \subseteq D$ is directed, then

$$(g \circ f)(\bigsqcup P) = \bigsqcup_{x \in P} (g \circ f)(x)$$

because

$$g(f(\bigsqcup P)) = g(\bigsqcup_{x \in P} f(x))$$

by the continuity of f, and this is equal to $\bigsqcup_{x \in P} (g \circ f)(x)$ by the continuity of g. Thus the composition of continuous functions is continuous. Since, moreover, the identity function is continuous and composition of functions is associative, it follows that cpo's with continuous functions form a category **Cpo**.

4.8 Proposition. *If D and E are cpo's, then $D \times E$ is also a cpo under the coordinate-wise order: $(x, y) \sqsubseteq (x', y')$ iff $x \sqsubseteq x$ and $y \sqsubseteq y'$.*

Proof: If $P \subseteq D \times E$ is directed, then $P_1 = \{x \mid (x, y) \in P$ for some $y\}$ and $P_2 = \{y \mid (x, y) \in P$ for some $x\}$ are directed. Moreover, $\bigsqcup P = (\bigsqcup P_1, \bigsqcup P_2)$. $\qquad\square$

A poset P is said to be directed if its universe is directed, that is, the full set of elements of P forms a directed subset of P. The following lemma is extremely useful in arguments involving cpo's and indexed families:

4.9 Lemma (Exchange). *Suppose P and Q are directed posets, D is a cpo, and*

$$f : P \times Q \to D$$

is a monotone function. Then

$$\bigsqcup_{x \in P} \bigsqcup_{y \in Q} f(x, y) = \bigsqcup_{y \in Q} \bigsqcup_{x \in P} f(x, y).$$

Proof: For $\sqsubseteq$, we must show that, for every $x' \in P$, we have

$$\bigsqcup_{y \in Q} f(x', y) \sqsubseteq \bigsqcup_{y \in Q} \bigsqcup_{x \in P} f(x, y).$$

To show this, we must show that, for every $y' \in Q$, we have

$$f(x', y') \sqsubseteq \bigsqcup_{y \in Q} \bigsqcup_{x \in P} f(x, y).$$

But this is obvious. Since x' and y' were chosen arbitrarily, the desired inequation must hold. The proof of $\sqsupseteq$ for the expressions in the lemma is similar. $\qquad\square$

4.10 Proposition. *If D and E are cpo's, then the continuous function space*

$$[D \to E] = \{f : D \to E \mid f \text{ is continuous}\}$$

is a cpo under the pointwise order.

Proof: We show that the least upper bound $\bigsqcup_{f \in P} f$ of a directed set $P \subseteq [D \to E]$ is the function $g : x \mapsto \bigsqcup_{f \in P} f(x)$. This makes sense as a function because the directedness of P means $\{f(x) \mid f \in P\}$ is directed for each x. It is easy to verify that it is monotone. To see that it is continuous, suppose $Q \subseteq D$ is directed. Then

$$g(\bigsqcup_{x \in Q} x) = \bigsqcup_{f \in P} f(\bigsqcup_{x \in Q} x) = \bigsqcup_{f \in P} \bigsqcup_{x \in Q} f(x) = \bigsqcup_{x \in Q} \bigsqcup_{f \in P} f(x) = \bigsqcup_{x \in Q} f(x).$$

where the third equation follows from the Exchange Lemma. Now, clearly $f(x) \sqsubseteq g(x)$ for each $f \in P$. If $g' \sqsupseteq f$ for each $f \in P$, then $g'(x) \sqsupseteq \bigsqcup_{f \in P} f(x)$ for each $x \in D$ so $g' \sqsupseteq g$. $\qquad\square$

The Fixed-Point Theorem.

The key theorem on which much of the discussion of the semantics of programming languages is based says that if $f : D \to D$ is a continuous function, then it has a least fixed point. That is, there is a least $x \in D$ such that $f(x) = x$. The form of the result that we will usually need is the following:

4.11 Theorem (Fixed Point). *If D is a pointed cpo and $f : D \to D$ is continuous, then it has a least fixed point* $\mathsf{fix}(f) \in D$. *That is,*

1. $\mathsf{fix}(f) = f(\mathsf{fix}(f))$, *and*
2. $\mathsf{fix}(f) \sqsubseteq x$ *for any* $x \in D$ *such that* $x = f(x)$. $\qquad\qquad\qquad$ □

This statement can be generalized in many ways, but this simple form will be sufficient for a wide range of basic applications. The proof of the result is delightfully easy; let me give it for a slightly more general result from which Theorem 4.11 follows as a corollary. We require a definition:

Definition: Let D be a partial order. An ω-*chain* $(x_n)_{n \in \omega}$ in D is a set of elements $x_n \in D$ such that $x_n \sqsubseteq x_m$ whenever $n \leq m$. A partial order D is ω-*complete* (and hence an ω-*cpo*) if every ω-chain has a least upper bound. Given ω-cpo's D and E, a monotone function $f : D \to E$ is said to be ω-*continuous* if $f(\bigsqcup_{n \in \omega} x_n) = \bigsqcup_{n \in \omega} f(x_n)$ for any ω-chain $(x_n)_{n \in \omega}$. $\qquad\qquad\qquad$ □

4.12 Theorem (Fixed Points in ω-Cpo's). *Suppose D is an ω-cpo and $f : D \to D$ is ω-continuous. If $x \sqsubseteq f(x)$ for some $x \in D$, then there is a least element $y \in D$ such that*

1. $y = f(y)$, *and*
2. $y \sqsubseteq z$ *for any* $z \in D$ *such that* $z = f(z)$ *and* $x \sqsubseteq z$.

Proof: By an induction on n using the monotonicity of f, it is easy to see that $f^n(x) \sqsubseteq f^{n+1}(x)$ for every n so $(f^n(x))_{n \in \omega}$ is an ω-chain. Set $y = \bigsqcup_{n \in \omega} f^n(x)$. To see property (1), calculate $f(y) = f(\bigsqcup_{n \in \omega} f^n(x)) = \bigsqcup_{n \in \omega} f^{n+1}(x) = \bigsqcup_{n \in \omega} f^n(x) = y$. To verify (2), suppose z is a fixed point of f and $x \sqsubseteq z$. Then, for each n, $f^n(x) \sqsubseteq f^n(z) = z$ so $y = \bigsqcup_{n \in \omega} f^n(x) \sqsubseteq z$. $\qquad\qquad\qquad$ □

To see that the Fixed-Point Theorem is a corollary of Theorem 4.12, note that an ω-chain is a directed set, so a cpo is an ω-cpo and a continuous function is also ω-continuous. Since $\bot \sqsubseteq f(\bot)$, the Fixed-Point Theorem follows immediately.

Let us look at a collection of short examples of how the Fixed-Point Theorem is applied.

Example: *Semantics of the while loop.* Recall the definition provided earlier for the while loop in the Simple Imperative Language:

$$[\![\textbf{while } B \textbf{ do } C \textbf{ od}]\!]m = \begin{cases} m & \text{if } [\![B]\!]m = \textsf{false} \\ [\![\textbf{while } B \textbf{ do } C \textbf{ od}]\!]([\![C]\!]m) & \text{if } [\![B]\!]m = \textsf{true} \end{cases}$$

where $m \in \mathbb{M} = \mathbb{Z}^{\text{Identifier}}$ is a memory. This can be recast as a compositional description by defining the meaning of the while loop as the fixed point of the functional

$$F : [\mathbb{M} \rightsquigarrow \mathbb{M}] \to [\mathbb{M} \rightsquigarrow \mathbb{M}]$$

given by

$$F(f)(m) = \begin{cases} m & \text{if } [\![B]\!]m = \textsf{false} \\ f([\![C]\!]m) & \text{if } [\![B]\!]m = \textsf{true}. \end{cases}$$

Our meaning for the while loop can be taken to be the least fixed point of F. Reasons why we might take the *least* fixed point (could there be others?) will be discussed later, but to see that there *is* a least fixed point of F, we need only show that F is continuous and apply the Fixed-Point Theorem. I will omit the proof that F is monotone and prove continuity assuming monotonicity. Suppose $P \subseteq [\mathbb{M} \rightsquigarrow \mathbb{M}]$ is a directed family of partial functions. If $[\![B]\!]m = \textsf{false}$, then

$$F(\bigsqcup_{f \in P} f)(m) = m = (\bigsqcup_{f \in P} F(f))(m)$$

since $F(f)(m) = m$ for each $f \in P$. If, on the other hand, $[\![B]\!]m = \textsf{true}$, then

$$F(\bigsqcup_{f \in P} f)(m) = (\bigsqcup_{f \in P} f)([\![C]\!]m) = \bigsqcup_{f \in P} f([\![C]\!]m) = (\bigsqcup_{f \in P} F(f))(m).$$

Hence F is continuous and $[\![\textbf{while } B \textbf{ do } C \textbf{ od}]\!] = \textsf{fix}(F)$.   □

Example: *The factorial function.* As a similar illustration of the use of the Fixed-Point Theorem, let us consider how one might define the *factorial function* fact : $\mathbb{N} \to \mathbb{N}$. The usual approach is to say that the factorial function is the unique function that satisfies the following recursive equation for each number n:

$$\text{fact}(n) = \begin{cases} 1 & \text{if } n = 0 \\ n * \text{fact}(n - 1) & \text{if } n > 0. \end{cases}$$

But how do we know that there *is* a function fact that satisfies this equation? One way is to observe that the definition is inductive. But it is also possible to see this using the Fixed-Point Theorem. Let us view the factorial as a partial function $\text{fact} : \mathbb{N} \leadsto \mathbb{N}$. Define a functional

$$F : [\mathbb{N} \leadsto \mathbb{N}] \to [\mathbb{N} \leadsto \mathbb{N}]$$

by setting

$$F(f)(n) = \begin{cases} 1 & \text{if } n = 0 \\ n * f(n-1) & \text{if } n > 0 \end{cases}$$

for each $f : \mathbb{N} \leadsto \mathbb{N}$. The definition of F is *not* recursive (F appears only on the left side of the equation) so F certainly exists. Moreover, it is easy to check that F is continuous. Hence, by the Fixed-Point Theorem, F has a least fixed point $\text{fix}(F)$, and this solution will satisfy the equation for fact. It is illustrative to look briefly at what the approximations to the fixed point given by the proof of the Fixed-Point Theorem turn out to be in this case. Recall that $\text{fix}(F) = \bigsqcup_{n \in \omega} F^n(\perp_{[\mathbb{N} \leadsto \mathbb{N}]})$ where $\perp_{[\mathbb{N} \leadsto \mathbb{N}]}$ is the totally undefined partial function from $\mathbb{N}$ into $\mathbb{N}$. Thus $F^1(\perp)$ is a partial function whose value on 0 is equal to 1 and whose value elsewhere is *undefined*. In essence, it is the function that successfully computes the factorial on the first number but is otherwise undefined. In the case of the n'th approximation $F^n(\perp)$ we have the partial function that successfully provides the factorial of the numbers from 0 up to $n-1$ and diverges on all other arguments. The limit $\bigsqcup_{n \in \omega} F^n(\perp)$ of these 'finite' approximations to the factorial function is the (total) function that successfully calculates the factorial to arbitrary levels of unwinding of its recursive definition. ☐

Example: *Context-Free Grammars.* One familiar kind of recursive equation is a context free grammar. Let Σ be an alphabet. One uses context free grammars to specify subsets of the collection Σ^* of finite sequences of letters from Σ. Here are some easy examples:

1. $E ::= \epsilon \mid Ea$ defines the strings of a's (including the empty string ϵ).
2. $E ::= a \mid bEb$ defines strings consisting either of the letter a alone or a string of n b's followed by an a followed by n more b's.
3. $E ::= \epsilon \mid aa \mid EE$ defines strings of a's of even length.

It is possible to use the Fixed-Point Theorem to provide a precise explanation of the semantics of these grammars. Given subsets $X, Y \subseteq \Sigma$, define the concatenation XY to be the set of strings st such that $s \in X$ and $t \in Y$. It is easy to show that the operations $X \mapsto \{\epsilon\} \cup X\{a\}$, $X \mapsto \{a\} \cup \{b\}X\{b\}$, and $X \mapsto \{\epsilon\} \cup \{a\}\{a\} \cup XX$ are all continuous in the variable X as functions from $\mathcal{P}(\Sigma^*)$ into $\mathcal{P}(\Sigma^*)$, so it follows from the Fixed-Point Theorem that equations such as

1. $X = \{\epsilon\} \cup X\{a\}$

2. $X = \{a\} \cup \{b\} X \{b\}$
3. $X = \{\epsilon\} \cup \{a\}\{a\} \cup XX$

corresponding to the three grammars mentioned above all have least solutions. These solutions are the languages defined by the grammars. Continuity for such operators comes from the observation that the following operators are continuous: constant functions, concatenation, and union. One thing worth noting is that the language specified by a grammar must be the *least* fixed point of the defining operator. □

Example: As a set-theoretic application of the Fixed-Point Theorem let us now look at the proof of a classic result. Given sets X and Y, define $X - Y$ to be the set of elements in X that are not in Y.

4.13 Theorem (Schröder-Bernstein). *Let S and T be sets. If $f : S \to T$ and $g : T \to S$ are injections, then there is a bijection $h : S \to T$.*

Proof: Let $F = \mathcal{P}(f)$ and $G = \mathcal{P}(g)$ be the extensions of f and g respectively. The function $Y \mapsto (T - F(S)) \cup F(G(Y))$ from $\mathcal{P}(T)$ to $\mathcal{P}(T)$ is easily seen to be continuous with respect to the inclusion ordering. Hence, by the Fixed-Point Theorem, there is a subset $Y = (T - F(S)) \cup F(G(Y))$. In particular,

$$
\begin{aligned}
T - Y &= T - ((T - F(S)) \cup F(G(Y))) \\
&= (T - (T - F(S))) \cap (T - (F(G(Y)))) \\
&= F(S) \cap (T - (F(G(Y)))) \\
&= F(S - G(Y)).
\end{aligned}
$$

Now define $h : S \to T$ by

$$
h(x) = \begin{cases} y & \text{if } x = g(y) \text{ for some } y \in Y \\ f(x) & \text{otherwise.} \end{cases}
$$

This makes sense because g is an injection. Moreover, h itself is an injection since f and g are injections. To see that it is a surjection, suppose $y \in T$. If $y \in Y$, then $h(g(y)) = y$. If $y \notin Y$, then $y \in F(S - G(Y))$, so $y = f(x) = h(x)$ for some x. Thus h is a bijection. □

Uniformity.

The question naturally arises why we take the *least* fixed point in order to get the meaning. In most instances there will be other choices. There are several answers to this question. First of all, it seems intuitively reasonable to take the least defined function satisfying a given recursive equation. But more important, taking the least fixed point yields a *canonical* solution. We will show that even more is true: the least fixed-point operator is the *unique* fixed-point operator, which is uniform in a certain sense. To this end, we develop a few more basic facts about cpo's. Given functions $f : E \to F$ and $g : D \to E$, the *composition* $f \circ g$ of f, g is the function from D to F given by $x \mapsto f(g(x))$.

The following fact is quite useful:

4.14 Lemma. *A monotone function* $f : D \times E \to F$ *is continuous if, and only if, it is continuous in each of its arguments, that is,*

$$f(\bigsqcup_{p \in P} p, y) = \bigsqcup_{p \in P} f(p, y) \text{ and } f(x, \bigsqcup_{q \in Q}) = \bigsqcup_{q \in Q} f(x, q)$$

whenever $x \in D, y \in E$ *and* P, Q *are directed subsets of* D *and* E *respectively.* □

Its proof is left as an exercise. It will often be used without being explicitly mentioned.

4.15 Lemma. *The composition function*

$$\circ : [E \to F] \times [D \to E] \to [D \to F]$$

is continuous.

Proof: We need to show that composition is continuous in each of its arguments. Let $P \subseteq [D \to E]$ be a directed set of continuous functions. Then

$$(f \circ (\bigsqcup P))(x) = f(\bigsqcup_{g \in P} g(x)) = (\bigsqcup_{g \in P} f(g(x))) = \bigsqcup_{g \in P}((f \circ g)(x)) = (\bigsqcup_{g \in P}(f \circ g))(x).$$

Continuity in the first argument has a similar proof. □

The following is left as an exercise:

4.16 Lemma (Diagonal). *If* P *is a directed poset and* $f : P \times P \to D$ *is a monotone function into a cpo* D, *then*

$$\bigsqcup_{x \in P} \bigsqcup_{y \in P} f(x, y) = \bigsqcup_{x \in P} f(x, x).$$ □

For $n \geq 0$, define the n'th power f^n of a function $f : D \to D$ by induction on n by taking $f^0 = \mathrm{id}_D$ and $f^{n+1} = f \circ f^n$.

4.17 Lemma. *If* $P \subseteq [D \to D]$ *is a directed set of continuous functions, then*

$$(\bigsqcup_{f \in P} f)^n = \bigsqcup_{f \in P} f^n.$$

Proof: The proof is by induction on n. The case for $n = 0$ is immediate; suppose the result is known for $n - 1$, then

$$\left(\bigsqcup_{f \in P} f\right)^n = \left(\bigsqcup_{g \in P} g\right) \circ \left(\bigsqcup_{f \in P} f\right)^{n-1}$$

$$= \left(\bigsqcup_{g \in P} g\right) \circ \left(\bigsqcup_{f \in P} f^{n-1}\right) \tag{4.13}$$

$$= \bigsqcup_{f \in P} \bigsqcup_{g \in P} (g \circ f^{n-1}) \tag{4.14}$$

$$= \bigsqcup_{f \in P} (f \circ f^{n-1}) \tag{4.15}$$

$$= \bigsqcup_{f \in P} f^n$$

where 4.13 follows from the inductive hypothesis, 4.14 from the continuity of composition (Lemma 4.15), and 4.15 from the Diagonal Lemma. $\quad\square$

Definition: A *fixed-point operator* F is a collection of continuous functions

$$F_D : [D \to D] \to D$$

such that, for each cpo D and continuous function $f : D \to D$,

$$F_D(f) = f(F_D(f)). \qquad\qquad\square$$

Definition: Let us say that a fixed-point operator F is *uniform* if, for any pair of continuous functions $f : D \to D$ and $g : E \to E$ and strict continuous function $h : D \multimap E$ that makes the following diagram commute,

$$
\begin{array}{ccc}
D & \xrightarrow{\quad f \quad} & D \\
{\scriptstyle h}\downarrow & & \downarrow{\scriptstyle h} \\
E & \xrightarrow{\quad g \quad} & E
\end{array}
$$

we have $h(F_D(f)) = F_E(g)$. $\qquad\qquad\square$

4.18 Theorem. fix *is the* unique *uniform fixed-point operator.*

Proof: That $\mathsf{fix}(f) = f(\mathsf{fix}(f))$ for any continuous function $f : [D \to D] \to D$ is a consequence of the Fixed-Point Theorem. We must also show that, given a cpo D, the function

$\text{fix}_D : [D \to D] \to D$ given by $\text{fix}_D(f) = \bigsqcup_n f^n(\bot)$ is actually *continuous* in f. Monotonicity is easily verified. To complete the proof of continuity, suppose $P \subseteq [D \to D]$ is directed. Then

$$\text{fix}_D(\bigsqcup P) = \bigsqcup_{n \in \omega} (\bigsqcup_{f \in P} f)^n(\bot)$$

$$= \bigsqcup_{n \in \omega} \bigsqcup_{f \in P} f^n(\bot) \tag{4.16}$$

$$= \bigsqcup_{f \in P} \bigsqcup_{n \in \omega} f^n(\bot) \tag{4.17}$$

$$= \bigsqcup_{f \in P} \text{fix}_D(f)$$

where 4.16 and 4.17 follow from Lemma 4.17 and the Exchange Lemma respectively. To show that fix is uniform, suppose $f : D \to D$ and $g : E \to E$ are continuous and h is a strict continuous function such that $h \circ f = g \circ h$. Then

$$h(\text{fix}_D(f)) = h(\bigsqcup_{n \in \omega} f^n(\bot)) = \bigsqcup_{n \in \omega} h(f^n(\bot)) = \bigsqcup_{n \in \omega} g^n(h(\bot)) = \bigsqcup_{n \in \omega} g^n(\bot)$$

since h is strict. But this last value is just $\text{fix}_E(g)$ so fix is indeed uniform.

To see why fix is the *unique* uniform fixed-point operator, let D be a cpo and suppose $f : D \to D$ is continuous. Then the set

$$D' = \{x \in D \mid x \sqsubseteq \text{fix}_D(f)\}$$

is a cpo under the order that it inherits from the order on D. In particular, the restriction f' of f to D' has $\text{fix}_D(f)$ as its *unique* fixed point. Moreover, the image of f' is contained in D' because, for any $x \in D'$, we have $f'(x) \sqsubseteq f'(\text{fix}_D(f)) = f(\text{fix}_D(f)) = \text{fix}_D(f)$. Now, if $i : D' \to D$ is the inclusion map, then the following diagram commutes.

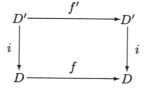

Thus, if F is a uniform fixed-point operator, we must have $F_D(f) = F_{D'}(f')$. But $F_{D'}(f')$ is a fixed point of f' and must therefore be equal to $\text{fix}_D(f)$. $\qquad\square$

Exercises.

4.10 Let P be a poset and suppose $M \subseteq P$ is non-empty. Prove that M is directed if, and only if, for every pair of elements $x, y \in M$, there is some $z \in M$ such that $x, y \sqsubseteq z$.

Definition: A poset is said to have the *ascending chain condition* (the *acc*) if there is no infinite sequence $x_0 \sqsubseteq x_1 \sqsubseteq x_2 \sqsubseteq \cdots$ of distinct elements x_i. □

4.11 Prove that any poset that satisfies the acc is a cpo.

4.12 *Prove or disprove:* Given cpo's D and E, a subset $M \subseteq D \times E$ is directed if, and only if, the sets

$$M_1 = \{x \mid (x, y) \in M \text{ for some } y\}$$
$$M_2 = \{y \mid (x, y) \in M \text{ for some } x\}$$

are directed.

Definition: Given pointed cpo's D and E, define $[D \circ\!\!\rightarrow E]$ to be the poset of strict continuous functions under the pointwise order. □

4.13 Show that if D and E are pointed cpo's, then the poset $[D \circ\!\!\rightarrow E]$ of strict continuous functions forms a pointed cpo under the pointwise order.

4.14 Given sets S and T, show that the cpo of partial functions $[S \rightsquigarrow T]$ is isomorphic to the cpo of strict continuous functions $[S_\perp \circ\!\!\rightarrow T_\perp]$.

Definition: A function $r : S \rightarrow S$ is said to be *idempotent* if $r \circ r = r$. □

4.15 Show that the set of all continuous idempotents on a cpo D forms a cpo.

4.16 Let D be a cpo. Show that the fixed points of a continuous function $f : D \rightarrow D$ form a cpo that is pointed when D is pointed.

4.17 Prove Lemma 4.14.

4.18 Prove the Diagonal Lemma (Lemma 4.16).

Definition: A *lattice* is a poset in which every finite subset has a least upper bound and a greatest lower bound. A poset D is a *complete lattice* if, for every $P \subseteq D$, there is a least upper bound $\bigsqcup P$ of P in D. □

4.19 Prove that every subset of a complete lattice has a greatest lower bound (in particular, a complete lattice is a lattice).

4.20 If D is a complete lattice and $f : D \to D$ is continuous, show that f has a *greatest* fixed point.

4.21 Prove or disprove the following conjecture: If P is a poset (not necessarily directed) and $f : P \times P \to D$ is a monotone function into a complete lattice D, then

$$\bigsqcup_{x \in P} \bigsqcup_{y \in P} f(x, y) = \bigsqcup_{x \in P} f(x, x).$$

Definition: Let X be a set. A set τ of subsets of X is said to be a *topology* on X if

1. $X, \emptyset \in \tau$,
2. τ is closed under finite intersections, and
3. τ is closed under arbitrary unions.

The pair (X, τ) is said to be a *topological space*. The elements of τ are called the *open* subsets of the topological space. Given topologies (X_1, τ_1) and (X_2, τ_2), a function $f : X \to Y$ is said to be *topologically continuous* if, for every open set $U \in \tau_2$, the inverse image $f^{-1}(U) = \{x \in X_1 \mid f(x) \in U\}$ is an element of τ_1. □

Definition: Let D be a cpo. A subset U of D is said to be *Scott open* if

1. whenever $x \in U$ and $x \sqsubseteq y$, then $y \in U$, and
2. whenever $M \subseteq D$ is directed and $\bigsqcup M \in U$, then $M \cap U \neq \emptyset$. □

4.22 Let D and E be cpo's.

a. Show that the Scott open subsets of D form a topology. This is called the *Scott topology* on D.
b. Suppose that $x, y \in D$. Show that $x \sqsubseteq y$ if, and only if, every Scott open subset of D that contains x also contains y.
c. Prove that a function $f : D \to E$ is continuous (that is, $f(\bigsqcup M) = \bigsqcup f(M)$ for each directed $M \subseteq D$) if, and only if, f is topologically continuous.

4.23 (For readers familiar with cardinal and ordinal set theory.) Prove that the Fixed Point Theorem still holds even if the function in the hypothesis is only monotone. That is, prove the following generalization of Theorem 4.11:

Generalized Fixed Point Theorem: If D is a pointed cpo and $f : D \to D$ is monotone, then f has a least fixed point in D. □

Using this result, it can be shown that the basic results of this chapter (including the Adequacy Theorem for an appropriate interpretation of PCF) could have been carried out with monotone functions rather continuous ones. The essential need for continuity does not become clear in computational terms until the domain theory developed in the next chapter is applied in Chapter 6.

4.3   Fixed-Point Semantics of PCF

It is now possible to define the *standard fixed-point model* of PCF using the mathematical machinery developed in the previous section. The ground type expressions **num** and **bool** are interpreted by the flat cpo's $\mathbb{N}_\perp$ and $\mathbb{T}$ respectively. The interpretation $\mathcal{C}[\![s \to t]\!]$ of a higher type is the cpo of continuous functions from $\mathcal{C}[\![s]\!]$ to $\mathcal{C}[\![t]\!]$. We assign meanings to triples H, M, t where $H \vdash M : t$. An H-environment ρ is a partial function that assigns to each variable x such that $x \in H$ a value $\rho(x)$ in $\mathcal{C}[\![H(x)]\!]$. The meaning $\mathcal{C}[\![H \triangleright M : t]\!]$ is a function that assigns to each H-environment ρ a value

$$\mathcal{C}[\![H \triangleright M : t]\!]\rho \in \mathcal{C}[\![t]\!].$$

Our definition of this function will follow the structure of the expression M (or, equivalently, the proof that $H \vdash M : t$). For the simply-typed λ-calculus fragment of PCF, the interpretation, which can be viewed as following the rules in Table 2.1, is basically unchanged:

- Projection: $\mathcal{C}[\![H \triangleright x : t]\!]\rho = \rho(x)$
- Abstraction: $\mathcal{C}[\![H \triangleright \lambda x : s.\ M : s \to t]\!]\rho = (d \mapsto \mathcal{C}[\![H, x : s \triangleright M : t]\!](\rho[x \mapsto d]))$
- Application: $\mathcal{C}[\![H \triangleright M(N) : t]\!]\rho = (\mathcal{C}[\![H \triangleright M : s \to t]\!]\rho)(\mathcal{C}[\![H \triangleright N : s]\!]\rho)$

The semantics of the other constructs must now be explained. The semantic clauses can be viewed either as following the grammar for PCF or as following the typing rules in Table 4.1. Let us make a simplifying abuse of notation by omitting the type context H and type t unless there is a reason to emphasize the types of the free variables of an expression or the type of the expression itself; so long as the environment being used in the interpretation respects the types of the free variables as described by H, aspects of H such as its order will make no difference in the environment model interpretation of the term. The basic constants have the expected interpretations in the base types:

- Zero: $\mathcal{C}[\![\mathbf{0}]\!]\rho = 0$
- True: $\mathcal{C}[\![\mathbf{true}]\!]\rho = \mathsf{true}$

- False: $C[\![\mathbf{false}]\!]\rho = \mathsf{false}$

To emphasize the intended relationship between operational and denotational interpretations of the remaining constructs, I will attempt to provide an operational intuition for each of the semantic equations. First of all, the successor of an expression M is obtained by evaluating M and adding 1 to the result. If the evaluation of M diverges (that is, the meaning of M is equal to $\perp$), then so does the evaluation of the successor:

- Successor: $C[\![\mathbf{succ}(M)]\!]\rho = \begin{cases} C[\![M]\!]\rho + 1 & \text{if } C[\![M]\!]\rho \neq \perp \\ \perp & \text{if } C[\![M]\!]\rho = \perp. \end{cases}$

The predecessor of M is 0 if M evaluates to 0, and it is the value of M minus 1 if it evaluates to some other value. If the evaluation of M diverges, then so does the evaluation of the predecessor of M:

- Predecessor: $C[\![\mathbf{pred}(M)]\!]\rho = \begin{cases} 0 & \text{if } C[\![M]\!]\rho = 0 \\ C[\![M]\!]\rho - 1 & \text{if } C[\![M]\!]\rho \neq \perp, 0 \\ \perp & \text{if } C[\![M]\!]\rho = \perp. \end{cases}$

To test whether M is equal to zero, evaluate it and see if the result of a convergent evaluation is zero or not. If the evaluation of M diverges, then so will the evaluation of the test:

- Zero test: $C[\![\mathbf{zero?}(M)]\!]\rho = \begin{cases} \mathsf{true} & \text{if } C[\![M]\!]\rho = 0 \\ \mathsf{false} & \text{if } C[\![M]\!]\rho \neq \perp, 0 \\ \perp & \text{if } C[\![M]\!]\rho = \perp. \end{cases}$

To get the value of a conditional, begin by evaluating the test. If this evaluates to true, then evaluate the first branch and return the result of that computation. If it is false, then evaluate the second branch and return the result of *that* computation. If the test diverges, then so does the evaluation of the conditional:

- Conditional: $C[\![\mathbf{if}\ L\ \mathbf{then}\ M\ \mathbf{else}\ N]\!]\rho = \begin{cases} C[\![M]\!]\rho & \text{if } C[\![L]\!]\rho = \mathsf{true} \\ C[\![N]\!]\rho & \text{if } C[\![L]\!]\rho = \mathsf{false} \\ \perp & \text{if } C[\![L]\!]\rho = \perp. \end{cases}$

Finally, we come to the case of recursion. We interpret it along the lines explored at the beginning of the previous section, but we use the Fixed-Point Theorem as a tool for proving that the definition makes sense:

- Recursion: $C[\![H \rhd \mu x : t.\ M : t]\!]\rho = \mathsf{fix}(d \mapsto C[\![H,\ x : t \rhd M : t]\!]\rho[x \mapsto d])$.

To gain a computational intuition for this definition, recall how the fixed point is defined in the proof of the Fixed-Point Theorem 4.11. In the specific case of the recursion as defined above,

$$\mathcal{C}[\![H \rhd \mu x : t.\ M : t]\!]\rho = \bigsqcup_{n \in \omega} d_n$$

where

$$d_0 = \perp_{[\![t]\!]}$$
$$d_n = \mathcal{C}[\![H,\ x : t \rhd M : t]\!]\rho[x \mapsto d_{n-1}].$$

In effect, each d_n represents the approximation to the recursive definition obtained by allowing it to be unwound n times. This will be made more precise below.

Now, we must show that the definition offered above makes sense. The only potential problem is the possibility that some of the functions defined by the semantics may not be elements of the appropriate spaces. In particular, we must show that the functions used in the definition of abstraction are *continuous*. This is summarized as the following lemma:

4.19 Lemma. *If $H' = H, x : s$ is a type assignment such that $H' \vdash M : t$, then the function*

$$d \mapsto \mathcal{C}[\![H, x : s \rhd M : t]\!]\rho[x \mapsto d]$$

is continuous for any H'-environment ρ.

Proof: The proof is by induction on the structure of M. The lemma is obvious when M is a constant, since any constant function is continuous. Suppose the lemma is known for subterms of M. There are several cases for M; I will do the ones for predecessor and recursion and leave others as an exercise. Suppose $e \sqsubseteq e'$ for $e, e' \in \mathcal{C}[\![s]\!]$ and let $\rho' = \rho[x \mapsto \bigsqcup P]$ where P is a directed subset of $\mathcal{C}[\![s]\!]$.

Case $M \equiv \mathbf{pred}(N)$ and $t \equiv \mathbf{num}$. To show monotonicity,

$$d_0 = \mathcal{C}[\![M]\!]\rho[x \mapsto e] \sqsubseteq \mathcal{C}[\![M]\!]\rho[x \mapsto e'] = d_0', \tag{4.18}$$

we must consider the various cases for the value of N. By the induction hypothesis,

$$d_1 = \mathcal{C}[\![N]\!]\rho[x \mapsto e] \sqsubseteq \mathcal{C}[\![N]\!]\rho[x \mapsto e'] = d_1'.$$

If $d_1 = \perp$, then $d_0 = \perp$ too, so 4.18 follows immediately. If $d_1 = n \neq 0, \perp$, then $d_1' = n$ too since the ordering on the naturals is flat. Hence $d_0 = d_1 - 1 = d_1' - 1 = d_0'$ and 4.18

therefore follows. If $d_1 = 0$, then d'_1, d_0, and d'_0 must all be equal to zero as well and again 4.18 is satisfied. Now, for continuity, we need to show

$$\mathcal{C}[\![M]\!]\rho[x \mapsto \bigsqcup P] = \bigsqcup_{d \in P} \mathcal{C}[\![M]\!]\rho[x \mapsto d].$$

We again consider each of the three cases. If $\mathcal{C}[\![N]\!]\rho' = \bot$, then $\mathcal{C}[\![N]\!]\rho[x \mapsto d] = \bot$ for each $d \in P$, so

$$\mathcal{C}[\![\mathbf{pred}(N)]\!]\rho' = \bot = \bigsqcup_{d \in P} \bot = \bigsqcup_{d \in P} \mathcal{C}[\![\mathbf{pred}(N)]\!]\rho[x \mapsto d].$$

If $\mathcal{C}[\![N]\!]\rho' = n \neq 0$, then there is some $d_0 \in P$ such that $\mathcal{C}[\![N]\!]\rho[x \mapsto d_0] = n$, so

$$\mathcal{C}[\![\mathbf{pred}(N)]\!]\rho' = n - 1$$
$$= \mathcal{C}[\![N]\!]\rho[x \mapsto d_0] - 1$$
$$= \bigsqcup_{d \in P} \mathcal{C}[\![N]\!]\rho[x \mapsto d] - 1$$
$$= \bigsqcup_{d \in P} \mathcal{C}[\![\mathbf{pred}(N)]\!]\rho[x \mapsto d].$$

If $\mathcal{C}[\![N]\!]\rho' = 0$, then there is some $d_0 \in P$ such that $\mathcal{C}[\![N]\!]\rho[x \mapsto d_0] = 0$, so

$$\mathcal{C}[\![\mathbf{pred}(N)]\!]\rho' = 0$$
$$= \mathcal{C}[\![N]\!]\rho[x \mapsto d_0]$$
$$= \bigsqcup_{d \in P} \mathcal{C}[\![N]\!]\rho[x \mapsto d]$$
$$= \bigsqcup_{d \in P} \mathcal{C}[\![\mathbf{pred}(N)]\!]\rho[x \mapsto d].$$

Case $M \equiv \mu y : t.\ M'$. Let $d_0 = \bot$ and $d_{n+1} = \mathcal{C}[\![M']\!]\rho'[y \mapsto d_n]$ for $n \in \omega$. If $e \sqsubseteq e'$, then, by the inductive hypothesis, $\mathcal{C}[\![M']\!]\rho[y \mapsto d_n][x \mapsto e] \sqsubseteq \mathcal{C}[\![M']\!]\rho[y \mapsto d_n][x \mapsto e']$ for each d_n. Thus

$$\mathcal{C}[\![\mu y : t.\ M']\!]\rho[x \mapsto e] = \bigsqcup_{n \in \omega} \mathcal{C}[\![M']\!]\rho[y \mapsto d_n][x \mapsto e]$$
$$\sqsubseteq \bigsqcup_{n \in \omega} \mathcal{C}[\![M']\!]\rho[y \mapsto d_n][x \mapsto e']$$
$$= \mathcal{C}[\![\mu y : t.\ M']\!]\rho[x \mapsto e'].$$

For the proof of continuity, we calculate

$$\mathcal{C}[\![\mu y : t.\ M']\!]\rho' = \bigsqcup_{n \in \omega} \mathcal{C}[\![M']\!]\rho'[y \mapsto d_n]$$

$$= \bigsqcup_{n \in \omega} \mathcal{C}[\![M']\!]\rho[x \mapsto \bigsqcup P][y \mapsto d_n]$$

$$= \bigsqcup_{n \in \omega} \bigsqcup_{d \in P} \mathcal{C}[\![M']\!]\rho[x \mapsto d][y \mapsto d_n] \tag{4.19}$$

$$= \bigsqcup_{d \in P} \bigsqcup_{n \in \omega} \mathcal{C}[\![M']\!]\rho[x \mapsto d][y \mapsto d_n] \tag{4.20}$$

$$= \bigsqcup_{d \in P} \mathcal{C}[\![\mu y : t.\ M']\!]\rho[x \mapsto d]$$

where 4.19 follows from the inductive hypothesis and 4.20 from the Exchange Lemma. $\square$

The following will be central to our study of the relationship between the operational and fixed-point semantics of PCF:

4.20 Proposition. *If V is a value of gound type, then $\mathcal{C}[\![V]\!]\rho \neq \bot$.*

Proof: The result is obvious for the boolean constants and for **0**. It is easily proved for numerals $\underline{n}$ by induction on n, noting that the successor of a number is a number (not $\bot$). $\square$

Now, finally, we arrive at the analog to the Soundness Theorem for the Full Type Frame in Chapter 2 (Theorem 2.10, that is):

4.21 Theorem (Soundness). *If $\vdash (H \rhd M = N : t)$, then*

$$\mathcal{C}[\![H \rhd M : t]\!] = \mathcal{C}[\![H \rhd N : t]\!]. \tag{4.21}$$

Proof: The proof is by induction on the height of the derivation of $\vdash (H \rhd M = N : t)$. In other words, one checks that the rules in Tables 2.2 and 4.2 are all sound in the model. I will omit most of the cases since they are similar to those in the proof of Theorem 2.10. Let us look only at the test for zero and μ-rules. That $\mathcal{C}[\![\mathbf{zero?}(\mathbf{0})]\!] = \mathcal{C}[\![\mathbf{true}]\!]$ is immediate so {ZeroIsZero} is sound. To see that

$$\{\text{SuccIsNotZero}\} \qquad \vdash (H \rhd \mathbf{zero?}(\mathbf{succ}(V)) = \mathbf{false} : \mathbf{bool})$$

is also sound, let ρ be any H-environment and note that Lemma 4.20 says $\mathcal{C}[\![V]\!]\rho = n \neq \bot$. Hence $\mathcal{C}[\![\mathbf{succ}(V)]\!] = n + 1$, and therefore $\mathcal{C}[\![\mathbf{zero?}(\mathbf{succ}(V))]\!] = \mathbf{false}$. Now, to see that

$$\{\mu\} \qquad \frac{H, x : t \vdash M : t}{\vdash (H \rhd \mu x : t.\ M = [\mu x : t.\ M/x]M : t)}$$

is sound, let $f : d \mapsto \mathcal{C}[\![H, \; x : t \rhd M : t]\!]\rho[x \mapsto d]$. Then

$$
\begin{aligned}
\mathcal{C}[\![H \rhd \mu x : t. \; M]\!]\rho &= \mathsf{fix}(f) \\
&= f(\mathsf{fix}(f)) \\
&= \mathcal{C}[\![H, \; x : t \rhd M : t]\!]\rho[x \mapsto \mathcal{C}[\![H \vdash \mu x : t. \; M : t]\!]\rho] \\
&= \mathcal{C}[\![H \rhd [\mu x : t. \; M/x]M : t]\!]\rho
\end{aligned}
$$

where the last equality follows from the analog for PCF of the Substitution Lemma 2.12 (which must also be proved in order to establish soundness of the β-rule for PCF). $\quad\square$

From this, together with Theorem 4.4, we can conclude that the transition relation preserves the meanings assigned by the fixed-point semantics:

4.22 Corollary. *If $M \rightarrow N$, then $\mathcal{C}[\![M]\!] = \mathcal{C}[\![N]\!]$.* $\quad\square$

It also follows from this corollary and Theorem 4.6 that soundness holds for the natural semantics of PCF with respect to the fixed-point semantics. Despite the redundancy, I will sketch a direct proof of this fact from the soundness of the equational theory.

4.23 Proposition (Soundness). *If $M \Downarrow V$, then $\mathcal{C}[\![M]\!] = \mathcal{C}[\![V]\!]$.*

Proof: The proof is by induction on the height of the derivation of $M \Downarrow V$. The result is immediate for axioms (that is, for constants and abstraction). Suppose the result is known for derivations of height n and $M \Downarrow V$ has a derivation of height $n+1$. The result is proved by examining each of the possibilities for the last step of the proof. I treat only the application and recursion cases here.

Case $M \equiv L(N)$. If $M \Downarrow V$, then $L \Downarrow \lambda x : s. \; L'$ and $[N/x]L' \Downarrow V$ by the evaluation rules for application. By the inductive hypothesis, $\mathcal{C}[\![L]\!] = \mathcal{C}[\![\lambda x : s. \; L']\!]$ and $\mathcal{C}[\![[N/x]L']\!] = \mathcal{C}[\![V]\!]$. By the soundness of the β-rule,

$$
\mathcal{C}[\![(\lambda x : s. \; L')(N)]\!] = \mathcal{C}[\![[N/x]L']\!].
$$

Since $\mathcal{C}[\![L(N)]\!]$ is equal to the left-hand side of this equation and $\mathcal{C}[\![V]\!]$ is equal to its right-hand side, the desired conclusion follows.

Case $M \equiv \mu x : t. \; M'$. If $M \Downarrow V$, then $[M/x]M' \Downarrow V$ has a shorter proof (takes fewer steps to evaluate) so $\mathcal{C}[\![V]\!] = \mathcal{C}[\![[M/x]M']\!] =_\mu \mathcal{C}[\![\mu x : t. \; M]\!]$. $\quad\square$

Note, in particular, that a proof by structural induction on M would fail for the recursion case! It is typical for proofs of properties of programs under a natural semantics to proceed by induction on height of derivation.

As a brief digression, note that if M is a closed expression of type t, then $C[\![M]\!]$ is a constant function on environments. In particular, if M and N are closed and $C[\![M]\!]\rho = C[\![N]\!]\rho$ for *some* environment ρ, then $C[\![M]\!] = C[\![N]\!]$. To use this as a proof technique, it is sometimes convenient to appeal to the 'arid' or empty environment $\emptyset$, which makes no assignments. I will write $[x \mapsto d]$ for the updated empty environment $\emptyset[x \mapsto d]$. It will also be convenient to write $C[\![M]\!] = \bot$ if $C[\![M]\!]\emptyset = \bot$.

We have proved that evaluation respects the equality of programs under the fixed-point interpretation, but is there some converse? For instance, if $C[\![M]\!] = C[\![V]\!]$, for a value V, is it the case that $M \Downarrow V$? In fact, this is too much to expect for higher types: expressions $\lambda x : \textbf{num. } 0$ and $\lambda x : \textbf{num. succ}(\textbf{pred}(0))$ have the same meaning under the fixed-point semantics, but they are distinct expressions. However, at ground types **num** and **bool**, this strong relationship does hold. The purpose of the remainder of this section is to prove this property, which is known as *computational adequacy*. The desired result is stated as Theorem 4.24 below. To motivate the techniques need to prove this theorem, let me begin by attempting a straightforward proof by induction.

4.24 Theorem (Adequacy). *If M is a closed term of ground type and $C[\![M]\!] = C[\![V]\!]$ for a value V, then $M \Downarrow V$.*

Proof Attempt: I will attempt to prove the theorem by induction on the structure of M for closed terms M of ground type. If M is a constant, 0, **true**, or **false**, then the result is immediate. Suppose, for example, that M has the form $\textbf{pred}(N)$ where N is a closed term of type **num** to which our inductive hypothesis applies. If $C[\![\textbf{pred}(N)]\!] = C[\![V]\!] \neq 0$, then $C[\![N]\!]\emptyset - 1 = C[\![V]\!]\emptyset$ so $C[\![N]\!] = C[\![\textbf{succ}(V)]\!]$. By the inductive hypothesis, $N \Downarrow \textbf{succ}(V)$ so $\textbf{pred}(N) \Downarrow V$ by the evaluation rule for predecessors. If $C[\![\textbf{pred}(N)]\!] = 0$ a similar argument yields the desired conclusion so we can handle the predecessor case. So far, so good! Now, suppose $M \equiv L(N)$. If $C[\![M]\!] = C[\![V]\!]$, then $(C[\![L]\!]\emptyset)(C[\![N]\!]\emptyset) = C[\![V]\!]\emptyset$ but what next? There is no hypothesis about L because it is not of ground type! $\qquad\Box$

Our problem is that we have no hypothesis that applies to higher types. There are at least two approaches to repairing this problem. One method, drawn from ideas used to demonstrate related results in proof theory, uses a property of PCF terms known as 'computability'. This proof technique is fairly succinct given a basic syntactic fact called the 'Unwinding Theorem' that concerns the evaluation of PCF recursion terms. A second proof technique that can be used to prove the Adequacy Theorem integrates syntactic and semantic properties very tightly using a relation between terms and elements of semantic domains interpreting their types. This method requires proving a number of facts about this relation, but it is not necessary to rely on any non-trivial syntactic properties of PCF as in the computability proof. In fact, the Unwinding Theorem can then be obtained as a consequence of the Adequacy Theorem itself. I will provide the computability proof now assuming the needed syntactic property that one can obtain from the Unwinding Theorem. That theorem is then proved in the final section of this chapter by purely syntactic means. In Chapter 6 I will describe the proof technique using a relation and describe how the Unwinding Theorem can be proved by semantic means rather than syntactic ones. This will provide a characteristic example of the common tradeoff between syntactic and semantic approaches to proving properties about programming languages.

Our proof of the Adequacy Theorem is based on the following key concept:

Definition: The *computable terms* of PCF form the least set of terms such that

1. If M is a closed term of ground type, it is computable if $C[\![M]\!] = C[\![V]\!]$ implies $M \Downarrow V$.
2. If $\vdash M : s \to t$, then M is computable if $M(N)$ is computable for every closed computable term N of type s.
3. If $x_1 : t_1, \ldots, x_n : t_n \vdash M : t$, then M is computable if

$$[M_1, \ldots, M_n/x_1, \ldots, x_n]M$$

   is computable for any closed computable terms M_i such that $\vdash M_i : t_i$. □

By applying the three parts of the definition, it is possible to see that a term M is computable if, and only if, whenever σ is a substitution that instantiates the free variables of M by closed computable terms and $M_1, \ldots, M_n$ is a sequence of closed computable terms such that $(\sigma M)M_1 \cdots M_n$ is a closed term of ground type, then $(\sigma M)M_1 \cdots M_n$ is computable.

In particular, Theorem 4.24 is an immediate consequence of the following lemma, whose proof will be given in two parts:

4.25 Lemma. *Every term M of PCF is computable.*

Proof of Lemma 4.25, Part I of II: The proof is by structural induction on M. Let σ be a substitution of closed computable terms for the free variables in M. We must show that σM is computable.

Case $M \equiv x$ is trivial.

Case $M \equiv 0$ and $M \equiv \textbf{true}$ and $M \equiv \textbf{false}$ are also trivial.

Case $M \equiv \textbf{pred}(M')$ and $M \equiv \textbf{succ}(M')$ and $M \equiv \textbf{zero?}(M')$ are all quite similar to the proof for predecessors in the earlier proof attempt. I omit the proofs for these cases.

Case $M \equiv \textbf{if } M_0 \textbf{ then } M_1 \textbf{ else } M_2$. Suppose $N_1, \ldots, N_n$ are closed computable terms such that $N' \equiv (\sigma M)N_1 \cdots N_n$ is of ground type. Suppose $C[\![N']\!] = C[\![V]\!]$. By

Proposition 4.20 we must have $\mathcal{C}[\![N']\!] \neq \bot$ so $\mathcal{C}[\![\sigma M]\!] \neq \bot$ so $\mathcal{C}[\![\sigma M_0]\!] \neq \bot$. Since σM_0 is of boolean type, this means that $\mathcal{C}[\![\sigma M_0]\!] = \mathcal{C}[\![\textbf{true}]\!]$ or $\mathcal{C}[\![\sigma M_0]\!] = \mathcal{C}[\![\textbf{false}]\!]$. Assume that the former holds. Then $\mathcal{C}[\![N']\!] = \mathcal{C}[\![(\sigma M_1)N_1 \cdots N_n]\!]$ so, by the inductive hypothesis, $(\sigma M_1)N_1 \cdots N_n \Downarrow V$. By the inductive hypothesis on M_0, $\sigma M_0 \Downarrow \textbf{true}$. Hence $N' \Downarrow V$ too by the evaluation rules for application and branching. The argument for $\mathcal{C}[\![\sigma M_0]\!] = \mathcal{C}[\![\textbf{false}]\!]$ is similar.

Case $M \equiv L(N)$. Since L and N are computable by inductive hypothesis, so are σL and σN. Hence $\sigma M \equiv \sigma L(\sigma N)$ is also computable.

Case $M \equiv \lambda x : s.\ M'$. We must show that $N \equiv (\lambda x : s.\ \sigma M')N_1 \cdots N_n$ is computable if $M_1, \ldots M_n$ are closed computable terms and the application has ground type. If $\mathcal{C}[\![N]\!] = \mathcal{C}[\![V]\!]$, then $\mathcal{C}[\![([N_1/x](\sigma M'))N_2 \cdots N_n]\!] = \mathcal{C}[\![V]\!]$. But $[N_1/x](\sigma M') \equiv (\sigma[N_1/x])M'$ is computable, by the inductive hypothesis, so $([N_1/x](\sigma M'))N_2 \cdots N_n \Downarrow V$. By the evaluation rule for application, $N \Downarrow V$ too.

Case $M \equiv \mu x : t.\ M'$. We must show that $N \equiv (\mu x : t.\ \sigma M')N_1 \cdots N_n$ is computable if $M_1, \ldots M_n$ are closed computable terms and the application has ground type. If $\mathcal{C}[\![N]\!] = \mathcal{C}[\![V]\!]$, then $(\text{fix}(d \mapsto \mathcal{C}[\![\sigma M']\!][x \mapsto d]))(\mathcal{C}[\![N_1]\!]) \cdots (\mathcal{C}[\![N_n]\!]) = \mathcal{C}[\![V]\!]$. But how does computability enable us to deal with this fixed point? $\square$

The idea for completing this proof is to work with syntactic approximations to a recursion $\mu x : t.\ M'$ obtained by unwinding the recursion. The key fact is the following:

4.26 Lemma. *Let $M \equiv \mu x : t.\ M'$ be a well-typed term and define*

$$M^0 \equiv \mu x : t.\ x$$
$$M^{k+1} \equiv (\lambda x : t.\ M')(M^k).$$

Then

1. *$\mathcal{C}[\![M]\!] = \bigsqcup_{k \in \omega} \mathcal{C}[\![M^k]\!]$, and*
2. *if $N \equiv M^k N_1 \cdots N_n \Downarrow V$ for some V and M is of ground type, then*

$$MN_1 \cdots N_n \Downarrow V.$$
                                                                                                                $\square$

Proof: To see (1), recall that $\mathcal{C}[\![H \triangleright \mu x : t.\ M : t]\!]\rho = \bigsqcup_{k \in \omega} d_k$ where

$$d_0 = \bot_{\mathcal{C}[\![t]\!]}$$
$$d_{k+1} = \mathcal{C}[\![H,\ x : t \triangleright M : t]\!]\rho[x \mapsto d_k].$$

It is easy to show, by an induction on k, that $d_k = \mathcal{C}[\![M^k]\!]\rho$. I will delay the proof of (2) since some syntactic results are required and these are best organized in a section by themselves. The desired result is a corollary of the Unwinding Theorem, which is Theorem 4.34 below. $\square$

Let us return now to the proof of adequacy:

Proof of Lemma 4.25, Part II of II: To complete the proof, we must show that the lemma holds for the case $M \equiv \mu x : t.\ M'$. To do this we first show that M^k is computable for each k where

$$M^0 \equiv \mu x : t.\ x$$
$$M^{k+1} \equiv (\lambda x : t.\ \sigma M')(M^k).$$

Now M^0 has a meaning of $\bot$ since that is the meaning of $\mu x : t.\ x$. By Propositions 4.23 and 4.20, there is no value to which it evaluates, and hence it must be computable. Suppose $k > 0$ and the result is known for values less than k. Then

$$M^k \equiv (\lambda x : t.\ \sigma M')(M^{k-1}) =_\beta [M^{k-1}/x](\sigma M') \equiv (\sigma[x \mapsto M^{k-1}])M'$$

is computable by the inductive hypotheses on k and M'.

Now, suppose $M_1, \ldots, M_n$ are closed, computable and $L \equiv (\sigma M)N_1 \cdots N_n$ has ground type. If $\mathcal{C}[\![L]\!] = \mathcal{C}[\![V]\!]$, then by Lemma 4.26(1),

$$\bigsqcup_{k \in \omega} \mathcal{C}[\![M^k N_1 \cdots N_n]\!]\emptyset = \mathcal{C}[\![V]\!]\emptyset.$$

Since ground types are flat, there is some k such that

$$\mathcal{C}[\![M^k N_1 \cdots N_n]\!] = \mathcal{C}[\![V]\!].$$

Since M^k is computable, $M^k N_1 \cdots N_n \Downarrow V$. By Lemma 4.26(2), $L \Downarrow V$ so M is computable. □

Returning now to the relationship between evaluation and the equational theory, we can note the following theorem as a corollary of adequacy:

4.27 Theorem. *If t is a ground type and $\vdash M = V$, then $M \Downarrow V$.*

Proof: Since the equations for PCF are sound for the interpretation $\mathcal{C}[\![\cdot]\!]$, we know that $\mathcal{C}[\![M]\!] = \mathcal{C}[\![V]\!]$. Thus the desired conclusion follows immediately from the Adequacy Theorem for PCF. □

4.4 Bounded Recursion

In this section some aspects of evaluation and techniques for inductive proof on evaluation trees are considered. The primary objective is to prove a result called the *Unwinding Theorem* that relates the evaluation of unwindings of a recursively defined program to the evaluation of the recursive program itself. The result is very intuitive and has Lemma 4.26 as a corollary. In this section the result is proved syntactically by studying evaluation trees; later a contrasting semantic approach to the proof will be considered. Our discussion here is based on an extension of PCF, called *bounded PCF*. In addition to the constructs of PCF, the language bounded PCF includes a version of the recursion operator that carries with it a bound on the number of times it may be unwound. The terms P of bounded PCF are generated by the following grammar:

$$P \quad ::= \quad \mathbf{0} \mid \mathbf{true} \mid \mathbf{false} \mid$$
$$\mathbf{succ}(P) \mid \mathbf{pred}(P) \mid \mathbf{zero?}(P) \mid \mathbf{if}\ P\ \mathbf{then}\ P\ \mathbf{else}\ P \mid$$
$$x \mid \lambda x : t.\ P \mid P(P) \mid \mu x : t.\ P \mid \mu^n x : t.\ P$$

where n is a number that is greater than or equal to zero. A term of the form $\mu^n x : t.\ P$ is called a *bounded recursion* Bounded recursion terms have the same binding and parsing conventions as unbounded recursions (terms of the form $\mu x : t.\ P$ that is). Types for the extended language are the types of pure PCF. There are typing and operational rules for the bounded recursion:

$$\frac{H,\ x : t \vdash P : t}{H \vdash \mu^n x : t.\ P : t} \qquad \frac{[\mu^{n-1} x : t.\ P/x]P \Downarrow V}{\mu^n x : t.\ P \Downarrow V}.$$

Note that the second rule only makes sense when $n > 0$; in particular, there is no derivation with the conclusion $\mu^0 x : t.\ P \Downarrow V$. I will treat PCF as a subset of bounded PCF but continue to use L, M, N to represent terms that are in pure PCF. Letters P, Q, R are used for terms in bounded PCF that may not be terms of pure PCF.

Definition: The *bound sum* of a term P of bounded PCF is the sum of the bounds on bounded recursions in P (or zero if there are no bounded recursions in P). $\qquad\qquad\square$

The *unwinding P^** of P is the term of pure PCF defined by induction on the structure and bound sum of P. For the base cases, the unwinding is just the identity:

$$\mathbf{0}^* \equiv \mathbf{0} \qquad \mathbf{true}^* \equiv \mathbf{true} \qquad \mathbf{false}^* \equiv \mathbf{false} \qquad x^* \equiv x$$

Suppose now that we know how to define $(\cdot)^*$ for subterms of P, then the following equations define P^* for possible forms of P:

$$(\mathbf{succ}(Q))^* \equiv \mathbf{succ}(Q^*) \qquad (\mathbf{zero?}(Q))^* \equiv \mathbf{zero?}(Q^*)$$
$$(\mathbf{pred}(Q))^* \equiv \mathbf{pred}(Q^*) \qquad (P(Q))^* \equiv P^*(Q^*)$$
$$(\lambda x : t.\ Q)^* \equiv \lambda x : t.\ Q^* \qquad (\mu x : t.\ Q)^* \equiv \mu x : t.\ Q^*$$
$$(\mathbf{if}\ P_0\ \mathbf{then}\ P_1\ \mathbf{else}\ P_2)^* \equiv \mathbf{if}\ P_0^*\ \mathbf{then}\ P_1^*\ \mathbf{else}\ P_2^*$$

If P is a bounded recursion, then the definition is inductive on the structure of P and its bound sum:

$$(\mu^0 x : t.\ Q)^* \equiv \mu x : t.\ x$$
$$(\mu^n x : t.\ Q)^* \equiv (\lambda x : t.\ Q^*)(\mu^{n-1} x : t.\ Q)^*$$

The primary technical fact about unwinding that will be needed concerns its relationship to substitution. Proving the following lemma is left as an exercise:

4.28 Lemma. *For every pair of bounded PCF terms P and Q, $([P/x]Q)^* \equiv [P^*/x]Q^*$.* $\Box$

4.29 Theorem. *Let P be a term in bounded PCF. If there is a bounded PCF value U such that $P \Downarrow U$, then $P^* \Downarrow U^*$.*

Proof: The proof is by induction on the height of the derivation of $P \Downarrow U$. The axiom cases are all immediate and the remaining cases are routine given Lemma 4.28. To see at least one of the cases, suppose that the final step in the derivation of $P \Downarrow U$ is an instance of the rule,

$$\frac{[\mu^{n-1} x : t.\ Q/x]Q \Downarrow U}{\mu^n x : t.\ Q \Downarrow U}.$$

Then $P \equiv \mu^n x : t.\ Q$, and hence $P^* \equiv (\mu^n x : t.\ Q)^* \equiv (\lambda x : t.Q^*)(\mu^{n-1} x : t.\ Q)^*$. Since the derivation of $[\mu^{n-1} x : t.\ Q/x]Q \Downarrow U$ is strictly shorter than that for P, by the inductive hypothesis $([\mu^{n-1} x : t.\ Q/x]Q)^* \Downarrow U^*$. By Lemma 4.28, we therefore have the hypotheses of the following instance of the evaluation rule for application:

$$\frac{\lambda x : t.\ Q^* \Downarrow \lambda x : t.\ Q^* \qquad ([(\mu^{n-1} x : t.\ Q^*)/x]Q^*) \Downarrow U^*}{(\lambda x : t.\ Q^*)(\mu^{n-1} x : t.\ Q)^* \Downarrow U^*}$$

The relation below the line is the desired conclusion. $\Box$

4.30 Theorem. *Let P be term in bounded PCF. If there exists a value V in pure PCF such that $P^* \Downarrow V$, then there exists a value U in bounded PCF such that $P \Downarrow U$.*

Proof: The proof is by induction on the height of the derivation of $P^* \Downarrow V$. In the axiom cases, P^* is $\mathbf{0}$, **true**, **false**, or $\lambda x : t.\ M$ and P is correspondingly $\mathbf{0}$, **true**, **false**, or $\lambda x.\ Q$ for some Q with $Q^* \equiv M$. In each of these cases, $P \Downarrow P$. Fix P and V such that $P^* \Downarrow V$ by a derivation of height greater than one. Assume that, for all Q and W where $Q^* \Downarrow W$ by a shorter derivation, there exists a value Z such that $Q \Downarrow Z$. We must treat each of the possible cases for the last step of the derivation.

Suppose the last step in the derivation of $P^* \Downarrow V$ is an instance of the rule:

$$\frac{M \Downarrow \mathbf{0}}{\mathbf{pred}(M) \Downarrow \mathbf{0}}.$$

Then there exists a term Q such that $P \equiv \mathbf{pred}(Q)$ and hence such that $Q^* \equiv M$. Since $Q^* \equiv M \Downarrow \mathbf{0}$ by a shorter derivation the inductive hypothesis says there exists a value Z such that $Q \Downarrow Z$. Since $Z^* \equiv \mathbf{0}$, we have that $Z \equiv \mathbf{0}$. By the rules for evaluation in bounded PCF, $P \equiv \mathbf{pred}(Q) \Downarrow 0$. The cases for derivations ending in other the rule for **pred** as well as the rules for successor, zero test, and conditional are very similar.

Suppose that the last step in the derivation of $P^* \Downarrow V$ is an instance of the rule:

$$\frac{[\mu x : t.\ M/x]M \Downarrow V}{\mu x : t.\ M \Downarrow V}.$$

Then there exists a term Q such that $P \equiv \mu x : t.\ Q$ and $Q^* \equiv M$ and thus $[\mu x : t.\ Q^*/x]Q^* \Downarrow V$ by a shorter derivation than that for $P^* \Downarrow V$. Since

$$[\mu x : t.\ Q^*/x]Q^* \equiv ([\mu x : t.\ Q/x]Q)^*$$

the inductive hypothesis says there exists a value U such that $[\mu x : t.\ Q/x]Q \Downarrow U$. By the rule for evaluation of (unbounded) recursion in bounded PCF, $\mu x : t.\ Q \equiv P \Downarrow U$.

Suppose that the last step in the derivation of $P^* \Downarrow V$ is an instance of the rule:

$$\frac{M \Downarrow \lambda x : t.\ M_0 \qquad [N/x]M_0 \Downarrow V}{M(N) \Downarrow V}.$$

There are two possibilities for the form of P. Either it has the form $Q(R)$ or the form $\mu^n x : t.\ Q$. Assume the first of these two cases holds with $Q^* \equiv M$ and $R^* \equiv N$. The derivation of $Q^* \equiv M \Downarrow \lambda x : t.\ M_0$ is strictly shorter than that of $P^* \Downarrow V$. Therefore, by the inductive hypothesis, there exists a value Z such that $Q \Downarrow Z$. By Theorem 4.29, $Z^* \equiv \lambda x : t.\ M_0$. Since Z is a value, there exists Q_0 such that $Z \equiv \lambda x : t.\ Q_0$ and $Q_0^* \equiv M_0$. Now, $[N/x]M_0 \equiv [R^*/x]Q_0^* \equiv ([R/x]Q_0)^*$ and $[N/x]M_0 \Downarrow V$ by a strictly shorter derivation than that of $P^* \Downarrow V$. Therefore, once again by the inductive hypothesis, there exists a value U such that $[R/x]Q_0 \Downarrow U$. Since $Q \Downarrow \lambda x : t.\ Q_0$ and $[R/x]Q_0 \Downarrow U$, by the rule for evaluation of an application in bounded PCF, we have $P \Downarrow U$. Now, suppose the

form of P is $\mu^n x : t.\ Q$ so that $M \equiv \lambda x : t.\ Q^*$ and $N \equiv (\mu^{n-1} x : t.\ Q)^*$. Hence we must
have $[N/x]Q^* \Downarrow V$ and, therefore, $([\mu^{n-1} x : t.\ Q/x]Q)^* \Downarrow V$. Since this derivation is
shorter than that for P we can employ the inductive hypothesis to conclude that there is a
value U such that $[\mu^{n-1} x : t.\ Q/x]Q \Downarrow U$. This means that $(\lambda x : t.\ Q)(\mu^{n-1} x : t.\ Q) \Downarrow U$
too. But $P^* \equiv ((\lambda x : t.\ Q)(\mu^{n-1} x : t.\ Q))^*$ by definition, so we have obtained the desired
conclusion. $\Box$

If V is a value of ground type in bounded PCF, then $V^* \equiv V$. By the Lemma and
Theorem 4.29 we therefore obtain the following:

4.31 Corollary. *If P is of ground type in bounded PCF, then $P \Downarrow V$ iff $P^* \Downarrow V$.* $\Box$

After these technical lemmas we are now ready to describe a precise relationship between pure PCF terms and the unwindings of terms in bounded PCF.

Definition: If P is a term of PCF, the *bound erasure* $P^\dagger$ is the PCF term resulting
from erasing the bounds on the quantifiers μ^n in P. $\Box$

In particular, $(\mu^n x : t.\ P)^\dagger$ is $\mu x : t.\ P^\dagger$. It is easy to see that $([P/x]Q)^\dagger \equiv [P^\dagger/x]Q^\dagger$.
The primary observation about the relationship between P and $P^\dagger$ is the following:

4.32 Lemma. *For every P in bounded PCF, if $P \Downarrow V$, then $P^\dagger \Downarrow V^\dagger$.*

Proof: The proof is by induction on the height of evaluation. The base cases are given
by the axioms, and the desired result is immediate for these. Suppose that the lemma is
known for proofs of height less than k and $P \Downarrow V$ is the conclusion of a proof of height k.
The only case of interest is that for bounded recursion. If $P \equiv \mu^n x : t.\ Q$, then it must
be the case that $[\mu^{n-1} x : t.\ Q/x]Q \Downarrow V$ too since this is the only hypothesis that can be
used to derive $P \Downarrow V$. But the height of the derivation of the hypothesis is $k - 1$ so we
must have $([\mu^{n-1} x : t.\ Q/x]Q)^\dagger \Downarrow V^\dagger$ and therefore $[\mu x : t.\ Q^\dagger/x]Q^\dagger \Downarrow V^\dagger$. By the rule
for evaluating recursions, we therefore have $P^\dagger \Downarrow V^\dagger$ as well. $\Box$

Suppose we are given a term P of bounded PCF such that $P^* \Downarrow U$ for some value U.
We would like to make a conclusion about the evaluation of the PCF term $P^\dagger$. It is not
true that $P^\dagger \Downarrow U$, but one can find a suitable value for which this relation does hold.

4.33 Lemma. *Let M be a term in pure PCF. If there is a term P in bounded PCF such
that $P^* \Downarrow U$ and $P^\dagger \equiv M$, then there is a value V in bounded PCF such that $V^* \equiv U$
and $M \Downarrow V^\dagger$.*

Proof: If $P^* \Downarrow U$, then there is a value V such that $P \Downarrow V$ by Theorem 4.30. By Theorem 4.29, this means that $P^* \Downarrow V^*$ so by Lemma 4.5, we must have $V^* \equiv U$. By Lemma 4.32, we must also have $M \Downarrow V^\dagger$. $\square$

4.34 Theorem (Unwinding). *Let M be a pure PCF term of ground type. If there is a term P in bounded PCF such that $P^* \Downarrow U$ and $P^\dagger \equiv M$, then $M \Downarrow U$.*

Proof: By the lemma, there is a value V such that $V^* \equiv U$ and $M \Downarrow V^\dagger$. But M has ground type, so V also has ground type by the Subject Reduction Theorem 4.7. Hence, $V^\dagger \equiv V$ and $V^* \equiv V$. $\square$

To see why Lemma 4.26(2) is a corollary of the Unwinding Theorem, note first that each term M^k in the lemma is equivalent to the unwinding $(\mu^k x : t.\ M')^*$ of a corresponding term in bounded PCF. That

$$N \equiv M^k M_1 \cdots M_n \Downarrow V$$

therefore means that

$$((\mu^k x : t.\ M)M_1 \cdots M_n)^* \Downarrow V.$$

By the Unwinding Theorem, this implies that

$$M \equiv ((\mu^k x : t.\ M')M_1 \cdots M_n)^\dagger \Downarrow V,$$

the desired conclusion.

Exercises

4.24 Outline a proof for Lemma 4.28 by doing some representative steps of the needed induction, including the case for the bounded recursion.

4.25 Give an example of a term P of bounded PCF such that $P^* \Downarrow U$ for some value U and yet it is not the case that $P^\dagger \Downarrow U$.

4.5   Notes

The language PCF itself was introduced by Scott in what is probably the most well-known unpublished manuscript [221] in Programming Language Theory. This work was a precursor to the discovery of models of the untyped λ-calculus and the subsequent evolution of what Stoy [252] called the 'Scott-Strachey Approach to Denotational Semantics' [230] and what this book terms as 'fixed-point semantics'. The version of PCF introduced in this chapter is taken from [38]; it is one of many essentially equivalent formulations. PCF is often described using constants for operations such as successor and even the conditional rather than constructors as presented here. An advantage to using constants would be, for instance, the potential direct applicability of results on the simply-typed λ-calculus with constants from Chapter 3. This might eliminate the need to consider some cases in the proof of a result like Lemma 4.19 by obtaining them as instances of general results. Also, the use of constants and abstractions (such as the constant **Y** of Exercise 4.9) can eliminate the need for introducing scope and parsing conventions for new binding operators and the need to define substitution in each language extension. On the other hand, constants produce a false appearance of uniformity by overloading the application operation. This is reflected in proofs of theorems for such a formulation in the way that the cases break down with application divided into many subcases. Moreover, the introduction of special forms using 'mix-fix' notation (such as the conditional) makes expressions more readable, a fact recognized in the syntax of most programming languages. On the other hand, the definition of substitution for language extensions is usually obvious and does not require repetitive explanations, although it is still essential to carefully describe parsing and scope conventions.

The proof of the Adequacy Theorem given in this chapter is partly based on an adaptation by Plotkin [196] of a proof technique of Tait [255]. The argument was originally used for a different result about evaluation for the simply-typed λ-calculus concerning a property known as *strong normalization*. This involves the evaluation of terms by repeated uses of a directed form of the β-rule until the directed rule no longer applies. This form of non-deterministic reduction is rarely used in programming languages, but facts about it provide an applicable general theory. A good explanation of Tait's argument can be found in an appendix of the book on λ-calculus by Hindley and Seldin [114]. Proof of the Unwinding Theorem can be obtained from syntactic arguments using labeled reductions. The reader can consult Barendregt [21] and the citations there for more details. Proofs that apply specifically to PCF can be found in the doctoral dissertation of Smith [235] and in a paper by Howard and Mitchell [117]. The former proof is similar to the one in Section 4.4; the latter uses logical relations.

This chapter described one fixed-point model for PCF using cpo's and continuous functions. This can be viewed as a standard model for the language, but other models can also provide useful information about programs. In particular, finite models of languages can be useful for detecting certain computational properties that can be calculated automatically at compiletime. A finite model can be obtained by abstracting away from properties and allowing programs that are computationally inequivalent in some ways to be identified because of their similarity in other ways. For this reason, the technique is generally known as *abstract interpretation*. One extensively studied example of such an analysis seeks to use abstract interpretation to detect when the meaning of a program is strict. In a language like PCF, this property is not decidable, but it is possible to derive a sound test that will detect many instances of strictness. The method has potential practical significance since a static determination of strictness can enable a compiler to perform a helpful optimization. Discussions of strictness analysis can be found in the paper by Burn, Hankin, and Abramsky [41] mentioned earlier as an application of logical relations and in a paper of Young and Hudak [123]. Other forms of analysis are considered in the collection of papers on abstract interpretation [7] and in the book of Launchbury [150].

Although *directed*-complete posets were used in the discussion in this chapter (and will be thoughout most of the remainder of this book), it is also possible to formulate fixed-point semantics using ω-completeness since a version of the Fixed-Point Theorem (Theorem 4.12 to be precise) holds under this condition. Completeness with respect to chains vs. directed subsets is treated in papers of Markowsky [156; 157] in the mid-1970's. The use of directed-completeness in this book enables a simpler treatment of the theory of finite approximation, the subject of Chapter 5.

The Fixed-Point Theorem is also useful in describing semantics for logic programming. Articles of Apt and van Emden [13] and Apt [12] discuss this topic. A treatment of the denotational and operational semantics of Prolog appears in articles of Debray and Mishra [72] and de Vink [71]. Further references can be found in these articles.

5 Two Theories of Finite Approximation

Although the Fixed-Point Theorem provides a basis for the use of cpo's as semantic domains, there is more that we need to know about our semantic domains than we get from the axioms for cpo's alone. In particular, we shall need to make use of the fact that a program's meaning can be viewed as the limit of a sequence of 'finite approximations'. Fortunately, an abstract mathematical definition of the notion of finite approximation that we want is familiar from the study of ordered structures. An *algebraic* lattice is a lattice whose elements are limits of elements that can be viewed as abstractly 'finite'. This idea can be generalized from the setting of algebraic lattices to the kinds of cpo's that arise in the semantics of programming languages. It is the purpose of this chapter to describe two such theories. The first of these has a weak condition for finiteness that leaves open the possibility that a finite element may have infinitely many proper approximations. Nevertheless, the conditions we do impose will be sufficient for an important application of the concept described in the next chapter. A somewhat stronger definition of what it means to be a finite approximation—one in which a finite approximation is itself only approximated by finitely many elements—is also possible; one such theory is described in the second section of this chapter.

Before beginning the detailed discussion of finite approximation, let us look for a moment at complete partial orders, which were introduced in the previous chapter. It is easy to see that the identity function is continuous and that the ordinary composition of two continuous functions is continuous, so cpo's and continuous functions form a category **Cpo**. Examples of objects of the category are $\mathbb{N}_\perp$ with the flat domain ordering or $\mathcal{P}(S)$ ordered by subset inclusion. Examples of arrows are the strict factorial function from $\mathbb{N}_\perp$ to $\mathbb{N}_\perp$ and the extension $\mathcal{P}(f) : \mathcal{P}(S) \to \mathcal{P}(T)$ of a function $f : S \to T$. If D and E are cpo's, then Proposition 4.8 asserts that $D \times E$ is also a cpo. In fact, this is a product in **Cpo** because the projections $\mathsf{fst} : D \times E \to D$ and $\mathsf{snd} : D \times E \to E$ onto the first and second coordinates respectively are continuous functions and there is a unique function completing the following diagram

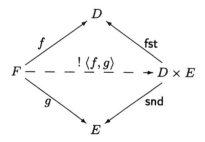

for any pair of continuous functions f, g having the indicated types. The unique function that completes the diagram

$$\langle f, g \rangle(x) = (f(x), g(x))$$

in the category of sets and functions is clearly continuous. Moreover, the poset $\mathbb{U}$ that consists of a unique element u is a terminal object, so **Cpo** is a category with finite products. **Cpo** is also well-pointed: if $f, g : D \to E$ are continuous functions such that $f \circ p = g \circ p$ for every point $p : \mathbb{U} \to D$, then $f(x) = g(x)$ for every $x \in D$, since $f \circ (\mathsf{u} \mapsto x) = g \circ (\mathsf{u} \mapsto x)$.

The category of cpo's and continuous functions can, in fact, be given the structure of a cartesian closed category. The exponential for the category is the continuous function space $[D \to E]$ ordered pointwise, together with continuous functions apply and curry defined as follows. For application, take

$$\mathsf{apply} : [D \to E] \times D \to E$$

by $\mathsf{apply}(f, x) = f(x)$ and, given $f : D \times E \to F$, we define $\mathsf{curry}(f)(x)(y) = f(x, y)$. It must be shown that these operations satisfy the right continuity requirements. We encountered the continuity of application in its first argument earlier in the proof of Proposition 4.10 where it was shown that

$$\mathsf{apply}(\bigsqcup M, x) = \bigsqcup_{f \in M} \mathsf{apply}(f, x)$$

for any directed subset $M \subseteq [D \to E]$. Proof for the other argument is easy, given that the functions considered are required to be continuous themselves. It is easy to see that $\mathsf{curry}(f)$ is monotone when f is. To see that $\mathsf{curry}(f)$ is a continuous function, suppose M is a directed subset of D. Let $y \in E$, then

$$\mathsf{curry}(f)(\bigsqcup M)(y) = f(\bigsqcup M, y) = \bigsqcup_{x \in M} f(x, y) = (\bigsqcup_{x \in M} \mathsf{curry}(f)(x))(y).$$

Thus $\mathsf{curry}(f)(\bigsqcup M) = \bigsqcup_{x \in M} \mathsf{curry}(f)(x)$. From these demonstrations that the operators in question do lie among the arrows of **Cpo** it is only a short distance to the conclusion that products and the cpo of continuous functions provide the structure of a cartesian closed category. The fact that $\mathsf{curry}(f)$ is the unique arrow such that

$$\mathsf{apply} \circ (\mathsf{curry}(f) \times \mathsf{id}) = f$$

follows from this fact for the category of sets and functions. In summary:

5.1 Theorem. *Complete partial orders and continuous functions with* $\times$, $[\cdot \to \cdot]$ *and* $1 = \mathbb{U}$ *form a cartesian closed category* **Cpo**. $\square$

5.1   Bc-Domains

Other than cpo's, the most widely used class of structures of the fixed-point semantics of programming languages are the *bc-domains*. They are sometimes simply called 'domains' or 'Scott domains', and they are one of the simplest cartesian closed categories of cpo's that have a basis of elements that can serve as a theory of finite approximation. The bc-domains are the intersection of two other categories of cpo's: the cartesian closed category of *bounded-complete* cpo's and the (non-ccc) of algebraic cpo's. The cpo's that lie in this intersection inherit a ccc structure from the cpo's. Our discussion focuses first on algebraicity, then on bounded completeness and the bc-domains.

Algebraic cpo's.

In our discussions throughout the rest of this book it will often be crucial to look at a subset of a semantic domain that can be viewed as a basic family of approximations to the values in the domain as a whole. We will be especially interested in elements that are 'primitive' in the sense that they cannot be non-trivially approximated by other elements of the domain. To see the idea in an illustrative example, consider the cpo of partial functions $[\mathbb{N} \rightsquigarrow \mathbb{N}]$ on the natural numbers. In this cpo, the notion of approximation is given by inclusion between the graphs of functions (that is, between the functions viewed as sets of pairs). The totally *undefined* function is the empty set, and a totally *defined* function f has a graph such that, for each $m \in \mathbb{N}$, there is some $n \in \mathbb{N}$ such that $(n, m) \in f$. Consider the special case of a partial function with a finite domain of definition. If it is expressed as the union (lub) of a directed collection of its subsets (approximations), then it must itself be an element of that directed collection. On the other hand, any total function f can be expressed as a union of the functions f_n where $f_n = \{(k, l) \in f \mid k \le n\}$, but it is not equal to any of these approximations. The fundamental idea in this case seems related to *finiteness*. If the graph of a function is finite and it is the lub of a directed family of approximations, then it must equal one of the approximations. The definition also makes sense for the cpo $\mathcal{P}(\mathbb{N})$ of subsets of the naturals: a set $u \subseteq \mathbb{N}$ is finite iff, whenever $M \subseteq \mathcal{P}(\mathbb{N})$ is directed and $u = \bigcup M$, we have $u \in M$. Now, if we have an arbitrary cpo D, then there is no *a priori* notion of finiteness for D in the way we had it for $[\mathbb{N} \rightsquigarrow \mathbb{N}]$ and $\mathcal{P}(\mathbb{N})$. This is because cpo's are abstractly defined: nothing says that a cpo is a collection of sets ordered by subset inclusion. So, if we want to capture finiteness for elements of an arbitrary cpo, we need a definition that makes sense abstractly. One approach to this is to use the property we just noted for $[\mathbb{N} \rightsquigarrow \mathbb{N}]$ and $\mathcal{P}(\mathbb{N})$ and say that an element x of D is 'finite' iff every directed set of approximations to x contains x.

This definition allows some possibly unexpected instances of finiteness. Consider another example, such as the cpo D of submonoids of a monoid G (a subset $H \subseteq G$ is a *submonoid* if it contains the unit and it is a monoid relative to the monoid operation of G). What is a 'finite' element of D? Interestingly, under our abstract idea of 'finiteness', the 'finite' elements of D may be infinite! To see why, consider the monoid of natural numbers with the binary operation of addition. The even numbers are a submonoid G_2, but any directed collection M of submonoids of $(\mathbb{N}, +)$ whose union (lub) is equal to G_2 must itself include the submonoid of even numbers as a member. This is because any submonoid that contains 0 and 2 must also be the submonoid of even numbers. In particular, if $2 \in H \in M$, then $H = G_2$. Since the union of M is G_2, it follows that $G_2 \in M$ since some element of M must contain 2. Thus the even numbers are a 'finite' element of D from our abstract perspective. The notion captured here is what algebraists call a finitely-generated submonoid: A submonoid H is said to be *finitely generated* if there is a (truly) finite subset $u \subseteq H$ such that H is the smallest submonoid of G that contains u. Finitely-generated submonoids are the 'finite' elements of D, the cpo of all submonoids of a monoid G. To see why, suppose $M \subseteq D$ is a directed collection and $\bigcup M = H$ where H is the smallest monoid that contains a finite set u. For each $x \in u$, there is some submonoid $H_x \in M$ with $x \in H_x$. Since M is directed, there is some $H' \in M$ that contains H_x for each $x \in u$. Since H is the *least* submonoid that contains u, it follows that $H = H' \in M$. In summary, 'finite' may mean 'essentially' finite rather than actually finite. In the next section we will return to this distinction, but for now, let us proceed with a rigorous definition of the intuitions I have been bandying about.

To avoid potential overuse of the word 'finite' the word 'compact' is used in the formal definition:

Definition: Let D be a cpo. An element $x \in D$ is *compact* if, for every directed collection M such that $x \sqsubseteq \bigsqcup M$, there is some $y \in M$ such that $x \sqsubseteq y$. We define $\mathsf{K}(D)$ to be the set of compact elements of D. $\qquad\square$

A cpo in which every element is a least upper bound of a directed collection of compact approximations is said to be algebraic:

Definition: A cpo D is *algebraic* if, for every $x \in D$, the set $M = \{a \in \mathsf{K}(D) \mid a \sqsubseteq x\}$ is directed and $\bigsqcup M = x$. $\qquad\square$

In the literature the term 'domain' is generally used to refer to the class of structures being used for the semantics in the application in question. It is common to locally 'bind' the term to a specific class of structures for the sake of precision. For the purposes of this book I will use *domain* as a synonym for 'algebraic cpo' in those instances where a precise usage is required. Particular kinds of algebraic cpo's are usually described by adjectives.

The most important of these for the semantics of programming languages are bounded-complete domains (abbreviated as 'bc-domains'), distributive domains with property I (abbreviated as 'dI-domains'), and bifinite domains. Bc-domains and dI-domains are discussed in this chapter, bifinite domains in Chapter 10.

Given a cpo D, a set D_0 of compact elements of D *forms a basis* if, for every $x \in D$, the set $M = \{a \in D_0 \mid a \sqsubseteq x\}$ is directed and $\bigsqcup M = x$. The following proposition is often a convenient way to show that a cpo is algebraic:

5.2 Proposition. *If D_0 forms a basis of D, then D is algebraic and $\mathsf{K}(D) = D_0$.*

Proof: If $x \in \mathsf{K}(D)$, then $\bigsqcup M = x$ where $M = \{a \in D_0 \mid a \sqsubseteq x\}$. Since x is compact, $x \sqsubseteq b$ for some $b \in M$. But then $x = b$ so $x \in D_0$. Thus $D_0 = \mathsf{K}(D)$ and it follows immediately that D is algebraic. $\qquad\square$

To see a few examples of algebraic cpo's, note first that any finite poset is algebraic because all of its elements are compact. Indeed, any poset that satisfies the ascending chain condition is algebraic. The cpo of partial functions $[\mathbb{N} \rightsquigarrow \mathbb{N}]$ is algebraic and the compact elements are the partial functions with finite graphs. Moreover, given a set S, the set $\mathcal{P}(S)$ of subsets of S is an algebraic cpo under the ordering by subset inclusion $\subseteq$. A subset of S is compact in this order if, and only if, it is finite. The poset of submonoids of a monoid is also algebraic, and the finitely generated submonoids are the compact elements. This is true of any cpo of subalgebras (subgroups of a group, subrings of a ring, and so on); indeed, this is where the term 'algebraic' originates.

Algebraic cpo's are closed under products. If D and E are algebraic, then so is $D \times E$, and $\mathsf{K}(D \times E) = \mathsf{K}(D) \times \mathsf{K}(E)$. Since $\mathbb{U}$ is obviously algebraic and is a terminal object in the category **Alg** of algebraic cpo's and continuous function, this category has finite products.

For our purposes, a serious problem with the category of algebraic cpo's is the fact that $[D \rightarrow E]$ may *not* be algebraic for algebraic cpo's D and E. To see an example that illustrates this, consider the poset ω^{op}, which is defined as the opposite of the poset ω. Say $\omega^{op} = \{0, -1, -2, \ldots\}$ is the set of negative numbers with their usual ordering. Since this poset satisfies the acc, it is an algebraic cpo. Suppose $f : \omega^{op} \rightarrow \omega^{op}$ is continuous. Define continuous functions $f_k : \omega^{op} \rightarrow \omega^{op}$ where $k \in \omega$ by taking

$$f_k(n) = \begin{cases} f(n) & \text{if } n \geq -k \\ f(n) - 1 & \text{otherwise} \end{cases}$$

It is not hard to see that $\bigsqcup_{k \in \omega} f_k = f$ although $f_k \neq f$ for any k. Thus $[\omega^{op} \rightarrow \omega^{op}]$ has no compact elements at all! It certainly cannot be algebraic.

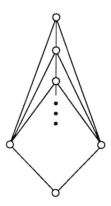

Figure 5.1
A Pointed Algebraic Cpo with Non-algebraic Function Space

Bounded completeness.

Since algebraic cpo's fail to be closed under the continuous function space operation, we must search for additional conditions on our semantic domains that are preserved under the essential operators. The goal is to impose a condition on domains that will rule out problematic examples like the one above without ruling out the domains we need for the semantics of programming languages. Finding the right condition is non-trivial, and early approaches to the theory of semantic domains sometimes complicated matters by not using an appropriate condition. At first one might think the problem above is trivial. For example, a false start would be thinking that the problem above could be solved simply by adding a requirement that domains be *pointed*. For example, if we let $(\omega^{op})_\perp$ be the cpo obtained by adding a bottom element to the cpo ω^{op}, then the problem above disappears. It will follow from results that we prove below that the cpo of continuous functions $[(\omega^{op})_\perp \to (\omega^{op})_\perp]$ is indeed algebraic, and least upper bounds of finite sets of functions of the form

$$(n \searrow m)(k) = \begin{cases} m & \text{if } k \geq n \\ \perp & \text{otherwise} \end{cases}$$

where $n, m \in (\omega^{op})_\perp$ can be used to generate a basis of compact elements. However, this does not solve the problem in general, since it occurs again in the cpo D in Figure 5.1 The proof that $[D \to D]$ fails to be algebraic is left as an exercise for the reader.

A poset is a *complete lattice* if every subset of M has a least upper bound. Obviously any complete lattice is a cpo, but there are cpo's that are not complete lattices. For example, the cpo of partial functions $[\mathbb{N} \rightsquigarrow \mathbb{N}]$ is a cpo, but it is not a complete lattice because the set of *all* partial functions does not have a least upper bound. Of course, this collection is not directed since, for example, the constant function yielding 0 and the constant function yielding 1 have no common bound. Let P be a poset. Recall that a subset M of P is said to be *bounded* or *consistent* if there is an element x such that $y \sqsubseteq x$ for each $y \in M$. Although $[\mathbb{N} \rightsquigarrow \mathbb{N}]$ is not a complete lattice, it does have the property that every *bounded* subset M has a least upper bound. To see this, simply note that a subset $M \subseteq [\mathbb{N} \rightsquigarrow \mathbb{N}]$ has a bound if, and only if, the union $\bigcup M$ is a partial function. This consistency property is so important that we often restrict our investigations to domains that satisfy it:

Definition: A non-empty cpo D is *bounded-complete* if every bounded subset $M \subseteq D$ has a least upper bound $\bigsqcup M$ in D. □

Since a bounded-complete cpo is assumed to be non-empty, the empty set is bounded so it has a least upper bound $\bot$. Hence bounded complete cpo's are pointed. Notationally, it would be uniform to refer to a poset as *complete* if it has least upper bounds for arbitrary subsets, to refer to it as *directed complete* if it has least upper bounds for directed subsets, and to refer to it as *bounded complete* if it has least upper bounds for bounded subsets. However, since we shall almost always be interested in directed-complete posets, I have chosen to refer to these simply as cpo's. Since we shall never be interested in bounded-complete posets that are not directed complete, read 'D is bounded complete' as 'D is a bounded-complete cpo' or, equivalently, 'D is a pointed poset with least upper bounds for collections that are bounded or directed'.

The category of bounded-complete cpo's has good closure properties. In particular,

5.3 Proposition. *If D and E are bounded complete, then so is the cpo $[D \to E]$ of continuous functions between D and E.*

Proof: Suppose $M \subseteq [D \to E]$ and f is a bound for M. Given $x \in D$, the set $\{g(x) \mid g \in M\}$ is bounded by $f(x)$. Since E is bounded complete, it has a least upper bound. Define $f'(x) = \bigsqcup \{g(x) \mid g \in M\}$ for each x. This function is continuous by the Exchange Lemma, and it is therefore obviously the least upper bound for M. □

There is a way to use this closure result to conclude that the bounded-complete cpo's can be given the structure of a ccc. We use the following categorical concept:

Definition: Let $\mathbf{C}$ and $\mathbf{C}'$ be categories such that $\mathrm{Ob}(\mathbf{C}') \subseteq \mathrm{Ob}(\mathbf{C})$. Then $\mathbf{C}'$ is said to be a *full subcategory* of $\mathbf{C}$ if $\mathbf{C}'(A, B) = \mathbf{C}(A, B)$ for any $A, B \in \mathrm{Ob}(\mathbf{C}')$. □

5.4 Lemma. *Let $\mathbf{C}$ be a category and suppose $\Rightarrow$, $\times$, and 1 give $\mathbf{C}$ a cartesian closed structure. If $\mathbf{C}'$ is a full subcategory of $\mathbf{C}$ such that 1 is an object of $\mathbf{C}'$ and $A \Rightarrow B$,*

$A \times B$ are objects of $\mathbf{C}'$ for any objects $A, B \in \mathrm{Ob}(\mathbf{C}')$, then $\Rightarrow$, $\times$, 1 also forms a cartesian closed category structure on $\mathbf{C}'$.

Proof: This is immediate since application and currying can be inherited from $\mathbf{C}$ and any equational property satisfied in $\mathbf{C}$ is also satisfied in $\mathbf{C}'$. $\square$

Since $\mathbf{Cpo}$ is a cartesian closed category, Propostion 5.3 and Lemma 5.4 imply the following:

5.5 Theorem. *The category of bounded complete cpo's is cartesian closed.* $\square$

It is understood here that the ccc structure is that which is inherited from $\mathbf{Cpo}$.

To show that a cpo is bounded complete, it is convenient to use the following lemma:

5.6 Lemma. *A pointed cpo D is bounded complete if, and only if, every consistent pair $x, y \in D$ has a least upper bound $x \sqcup y$.* $\square$

The proof is left as an exercise. The lemma makes it possible to check bounded completeness simply by checking pairs. Since we will often use the condition that a pair of elements y, z is consistent, it is handy to write $y \uparrow z$ to indicate this. In a bc-domain, $y \sqcup z$ exists if, and only if, $y \uparrow z$.

Our primary focus of attention will be on algebraic cpo's that are bounded complete.

Definition: A *bc-domain* is a bounded-complete algebraic cpo.

5.7 Lemma. *If D is bounded complete and a, b are consistent compact elements of D, then $a \sqcup b$ is compact in D.*

Proof: Suppose $M \subseteq D$ is directed and $a \sqcup b \sqsubseteq \bigsqcup M$. Then $a \sqsubseteq M$ and $b \sqsubseteq M$ and, since these are both compact elements, there are elements $x, y \in M$ with $a \sqsubseteq x$ and $b \sqsubseteq y$. Since M is directed there is some some $z \in M$ with $x, y \sqsubseteq z$ and hence $a, b \sqsubseteq z$ too. $\square$

This lemma is handy for showing that a bounded-complete cpo D is algebraic by proving that each element is a lub of compact elements. For if each element has this property, then the compact elements of D form a basis because, by Lemma 5.7, the set $M = \{a \in \mathsf{K}(D) \mid a \sqsubseteq x\}$ is directed for any x. Let us use it to prove that the category $\mathbf{Bcdom}$ of bc-domains and continuous functions has closure property we want.

5.8 Theorem. *If D and E are bc-domains, then so is $[D \to E]$.*

Proof: We have already noted that if D and E are bounded complete and pointed, then so is $[D \to E]$. We must show that $[D \to E]$ is algebraic. For any compact $a \in \mathsf{K}(D)$ and $b \in \mathsf{K}(E)$, define a function $a \searrow b : D \to E$ by

$$(a \searrow b)(x) = \begin{cases} b & \text{if } x \sqsupseteq a \\ \bot_E & \text{otherwise.} \end{cases} \tag{5.1}$$

Let us show that such maps are continuous and compact in $[D \to E]$. To see continuity, suppose $M \subseteq D$. If $\bigsqcup M \sqsupseteq a$, then $x \sqsupseteq a$ for some $x \in M$ since a is compact. Hence

$$(a \searrow b)(\bigsqcup M) = b = (a \searrow b)(x) = \bigsqcup((a \searrow b)(M)).$$

If $\bigsqcup M \not\sqsupseteq a$, then no element of M is greater than a, so $(a \searrow b)(\bigsqcup M) = \bot_E = \bigsqcup((a \searrow b)(M))$. Now, to show that $a \searrow b$ is compact, suppose $N \subseteq [D \to E]$ is directed and $a \searrow b \sqsubseteq \bigsqcup N$. Then $b = (a \searrow b)(a) \sqsubseteq (\bigsqcup N)(a) = \bigsqcup_{f \in N} f(a)$. Since b is compact, $b \sqsubseteq f(a)$ for some $f \in N$. Hence $a \searrow b \sqsubseteq f$.

To see that $[D \to E]$ is algebraic, suppose $f : D \to E$ is continuous. It suffices to show that $f = \bigsqcup M$ where $M = \{a \searrow b \mid f(a) \sqsupseteq b\}$. Since M is bounded by f, we know that $\bigsqcup M$ exists. Let $x \in D$ and suppose $b' \sqsubseteq f(x)$ for $b' \in \mathsf{K}(E)$. Then

$$b' \sqsubseteq f(\bigsqcup\{a' \in \mathsf{K}(D) \mid a' \sqsubseteq x\}) = \bigsqcup f(\{a' \in \mathsf{K}(D) \mid a' \sqsubseteq x\})$$

so $b' \sqsubseteq f(a')$ for some compact $a' \sqsubseteq x$. Since $a' \searrow b'$ is therefore in M, we must have $b' \sqsubseteq (\bigsqcup M)(x)$. This shows that every compact $b \sqsubseteq f(x)$ satisfies $b \sqsubseteq (\bigsqcup M)(x)$. Thus $f(x) \sqsubseteq (\bigsqcup M)(x)$. Since x was arbitrary, $f \sqsubseteq \bigsqcup M$. Since $\bigsqcup M \sqsubseteq f$ too, we are done. $\square$

Given algebraic cpo's D, E compact elements $a \in D$ and $b \in E$, functions of the form $a \searrow b$ as defined in Equation 5.1 are called *step functions*.

5.9 Lemma. *If D is a bounded-complete cpo, then any non-empty subset $S \subseteq D$ has a greatest lower bound*

Proof: The set $M = \{x \mid x \sqsubseteq y \text{ for each } y \in S\}$ of lower bounds of S is bounded since S is non-empty. By bounded completeness $\bigsqcup M$ exits, and it must be the greatest element of M. $\square$

Notation: If P is a poset and $x \in P$, then the *principal ideal generated by x* is the set

$$\downarrow x = \{y \in P \mid y \sqsubseteq x\}. \qquad \square$$

Let D be a bounded complete cpo. Let us write $x \sqcap y$ for the greatest lower bound (glb[1]) of x and y. The following fact about bc-domains will be needed in the next section:

---

[1] Pronounced 'glub'.

5.10 Lemma. *In a bc-domain, the binary operator $\sqcap$ is continuous.*

Proof: Let D be a bc-domain with basis of compact elements $\mathsf{K}(D)$. Suppose $x \in D$ and $M \subseteq D$ directed. Clearly, $x \sqcap (\bigsqcup M) \sqsupseteq \bigsqcup_{y \in M} x \sqcap y$. To prove that $x \sqcap (\bigsqcup M) \sqsubseteq \bigsqcup_{y \in M} x \sqcap y$ too, suppose $a \in \mathsf{K}(D)$ and $a \sqsubseteq x \sqcap (\bigsqcup M)$. Then $a \sqsubseteq \bigsqcup M$ so $a \sqsubseteq y_0$ for some $y_0 \in M$. Hence $a \sqsubseteq x \sqcap y_0 \sqsubseteq \bigsqcup_{y \in M} x \sqcap y$. Since D is algebraic,

$$x \sqcap \bigsqcup M = \bigsqcup (\mathsf{K}(D) \cap \downarrow(x \sqcap \bigsqcup M)) \sqsubseteq \bigsqcup_{y \in M} x \sqcap y.$$

Continuity in the other argument follows from the fact that $x \sqcap y = y \sqcap x$. $\qquad\square$

Exercises.

5.1 Let G be a group and suppose D is the poset of subgroups of G ordered by inclusion. Show that D is an algebraic lattice whose compact elements are the finitely generated subgroups of G.

5.2 Let D and E be algebraic cpo's. Show that the product $D \times E$ under the coordinatewise order is also algebraic.

5.3* Could it be the case that the class of *pointed* algebraic cpo's is closed under continuous function spaces? Show that the answer is *no* by demonstrating that $[D \to D]$ is not algebraic if D is the poset in Figure 5.1.

5.4 The proof of Proposition 5.3 did not use all of its hypotheses. Sharpen the statement to eliminate an unused assumption.

5.5 Prove Lemma 5.6.

5.6 Give an example of a pointed poset with five elements that is not bounded complete.

5.7 Let D and E be bc-domains. Show that $[D \multimap E]$ is also a bc-domain. (Recall that $[D \multimap E]$ is a pointed cpo by Exercise 4.13.)

5.8 Let D and E be bc-domains, and suppose $a, a' \in \mathsf{K}(D)$ and $b, b' \in \mathsf{K}(E)$. Show that $(a \searrow b) \sqcup (a' \searrow b')$ exists in $[D \to E]$ iff either

- $a \sqcup a'$ does not exist; or
- $a \sqcup a'$ and $b \sqcup b'$ exist.

5.9 Let D and E be bc-domains, and suppose $a \in \mathsf{K}(D)$ and $b, b' \in \mathsf{K}(E)$. Suppose also that $(a \searrow (b \sqcup b'))$ and $(a \searrow b) \sqcup (a \searrow b')$ exist in $[D \to E]$. Prove that

$$(a \searrow (b \sqcup b')) = (a \searrow b) \sqcup (a \searrow b')$$

5.10 Show that a pointed algebraic cpo D is bounded complete if, and only if, every consistent pair $a, b \in \mathsf{K}(D)$ has a least upper bound $a \sqcup b$.

5.11 Suppose that D is a bc-domain. Prove that a is compact if, and only if, whenever $a \sqsubseteq \bigsqcup X$ for some $X \subseteq D$, then $a \sqsubseteq \bigsqcup X_0$ for some finite subset $X_0 \subseteq X$.

Definition: An *algebraic lattice* is an algebraic cpo that is a lattice. $\square$

5.12 Prove that the category of algebraic lattices and continuous functions is cartesian closed.

Definition: A subset $u \subseteq P$ of a poset P is said to be *pairwise bounded* if each pair of elements in u has an an upper bound. A poset P is said to be *coherent* if every pairwise bounded subset of P has a least upper bound. $\square$

5.13 Given an example of a bounded-complete poset that is not coherent.

5.14 Prove that coherent cpo's and continuous functions form a ccc.

5.15 Could the assumption that S is non-empty be dropped from the hypothesis of Lemma 5.9?

5.16 Give an example of a bounded complete cpo for which $\sqcap$ is not a continuous function.

5.17 Let D be a bc-domain. Prove that $\mathsf{K}(D)$ is downward closed if, and only if, $\downarrow x$ has the acc for every $x \in \mathsf{K}(D)$.

5.2   Stable Functions and DI-Domains

In the discussion at the beginning of the previous section a theory of 'finite' elements was proposed in which a 'finite' element could have an infinite collection of distinct approximations. Although this will suffice for some of the technical applications we consider, one is led to wonder whether it is possible to develop a simpler theory of 'finite' elements in which a finite element has only finitely many approximations. More technically, what we seek is a category of algebraic cpo's having a special property:

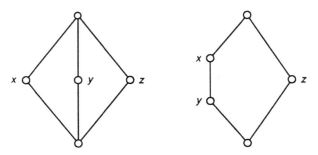

Figure 5.2
Examples of Lattices That Are Not Distributive

Definition: An algebraic cpo D *has property I* if $\downarrow a$ is finite for each $a \in \mathsf{K}(D)$. □

Ideally, perhaps, we would like to find that the bc-domains with property I are themselves a ccc. However, there are bc-domains D and E with property I such that $[D \to E]$ does not have property I (demonstrating two such cpo's is left as an exercise for the reader). Thus it is not possible to find a ccc directly through an application of Lemma 5.4 as we did for bc-domains. Instead we pursue a quite different path leading to a ccc that is *not* a full subcategory of **Cpo**.

To define the class we need one further definition:

Definition: A bc-domain is said to be *distributive* if $x \sqcap (y \sqcup z) = (x \sqcap y) \sqcup (x \sqcap z)$ whenever $y \uparrow z$. □

Some examples of bc-domains (in fact, lattices) that are *not* distributive appear in Figure 5.2; in each of the examples, $x \sqcap (y \sqcup z) \neq (x \sqcap y) \sqcup (x \sqcap z)$. The statement of distributivity above asserts that glb's distribute over lub's. There is an equivalent dual statement whose proof is left as an exercise:

5.11 Lemma. *Let D be a bc-domain. The following are equivalent:*

1. *D is distributive*
2. *$x \sqcup (y \sqcap z) = (x \sqcup y) \sqcap (x \sqcup z)$ whenever $x \uparrow y$ and $x \uparrow z$.* □

The class of domains with which we will be concerned are those that satisfy the properties in the previous pair of definitions.

Definition: A *dI-domain* is a distributive bc-domain that has property I. □

The goal of this section is to show that dI-domains can be given the structure of a cartesian closed category through an appropriate choice of arrows, exponentials, products, and terminal object. It is not difficult to show that the category of dI-domains and continuous functions has finite products, but there is a problem in showing that this category has exponentials. The right solution requires a new idea for the arrows of the category:

Definition: A continuous function $f : D \to E$ between dI-domains D and E is *stable* if $f(x \sqcap y) = f(x) \sqcap f(y)$ whenever $x \uparrow y$. $\quad\square$

With this, it is possible to obtain the desired result:

5.12 Theorem (Berry). *The category of dI-domains and stable maps can be given the structure of a cartesian closed category.* $\quad\square$

Stability of application.

One thing that makes the proof of Theorem 5.12 especially interesting is the fact that it is not possible to prove the theorem simply by checking that the stable functions from D to E form a dI-domain whenever D and E are dI-domains. A new idea is essential. Let D and E be dI-domains and let F be the set of stable maps from D to E under the pointwise order. Assuming for the moment that F is, in fact, a dI-domain, consider the application function $\mathsf{apply} : F \times D \to E$. We must show that this is stable. Suppose the pair $(f, x), (g, y) \in F \times D$ is consistent. Then

$$\mathsf{apply}((f, x) \sqcap (g, y)) = \mathsf{apply}(f \sqcap g, x \sqcap y) = (f \sqcap g)(x \sqcap y)$$
$$= (f \sqcap g)(x) \sqcap (f \sqcap g)(y) = f(x) \sqcap g(x) \sqcap f(y) \sqcap g(y).$$

Is this equal to $\mathsf{apply}(f, x) \sqcap \mathsf{apply}(g, y) = f(x) \sqcap g(y)$? In fact, this may fail in specific examples. Consider the poset $\mathbb{O}$ that has two distinct elements $\top$ and $\bot$ with $\bot \sqsubseteq \top$ and let $\mathsf{id} : \mathbb{O} \to \mathbb{O}$ and $t : \mathbb{O} \to \mathbb{O}$ be the identity map and the function that maps its arguments constantly to $\top$, respectively. Then $\mathsf{apply}(\mathsf{id} \sqcap t, \top \sqcap \bot) = \mathsf{id}(\bot) = \bot$, but $\mathsf{apply}(\mathsf{id}, \top) \sqcap \mathsf{apply}(t, \bot) = \top \sqcap \top = \top$. What is wrong here? These calculations made a number of apparently harmless assumptions. Have we proved that dI-domains cannot have a ccc structure? No: we have not shown that there is *no* choice of $\Rightarrow$, $\times$, and 1 that makes dI-domains into a ccc, we have only shown that the ones we used above could not be the ones. In fact, the problem *must* lie with our choice of exponential $\Rightarrow$, since $\times$ and 1 are certainly a product and a terminal object respectively. Note that we needed to show that if $f \uparrow g$ and $x \uparrow y$, then

$$f(x) \sqcap g(x) \sqcap f(y) \sqcap g(y) = f(x) \sqcap g(y).$$

But a different choice of how to match f and g with x and y would have forced us to show:

$$f(x) \sqcap g(x) \sqcap f(y) \sqcap g(y) = f(y) \sqcap g(x).$$

In particular, it seems that we need to have $f(x) \sqcap g(y) = f(y) \sqcap g(x)$!

The key to solving this dilemma is the choice of the correct ordering on the space of stable functions between two dI-domains.

Definition: Suppose D, E are dI-domains and $f, g : D \to E$ are stable. Then f is below g in the *stable ordering* and we write $f \sqsubseteq_s g$ if

$$x \sqsubseteq y \text{ implies } f(x) = f(y) \sqcap g(x)$$

for each $x, y \in D$. $\Box$

The condition for the stable ordering says that the smaller function applied to the smaller argument is the glb of the larger function applied to the smaller argument and the smaller function applied to the larger argument. Although its relevance may not seem clear at first, this is precisely what we need to solve the problem that we had with the application function above. Let $D \to_s E$ be the set of stable functions from D into E under the stable ordering. I will write $f : D \to_s E$ to indicate that f is a stable function from D to E. Note that $f \sqsubseteq_s g$ implies $f \sqsubseteq g$. But the converse fails.

Example: Function spaces under stable and extensional orderings appear in Figure 5.3. Any monotone function from Sierpinski space (upper left) into the four element lattice pictured on the upper right is also a stable map. The lower figures illustrate the difference in how they are ordered by the extensional and stable orders. The function spaces are clearly not isomorphic; indeed, the monotone functions do not even form a lattice under the stable order. $\Box$

The relevance of the stable ordering to the problem of the stability of application is clarified by a pair of lemmas of Berry.

5.13 Lemma (Berry). *Let D, E be dI-domains and suppose $f, g : D \to_s E$ such that $f \sqsubseteq g$ (pointwise order). Then the following are equivalent:*

1. *If $x \sqsubseteq y$ then $f(x) = f(y) \sqcap g(x)$ (that is, $f \sqsubseteq_s g$).*
2. *If $x \uparrow y$, then $f(x) \sqcap g(y) = f(y) \sqcap g(x)$.*

Proof: Suppose that (1) holds and $x, y \sqsubseteq z$. Then

$$f(x) \sqcap g(y) = (g(x) \sqcap f(z)) \sqcap g(y) = g(x) \sqcap (f(z) \sqcap g(y)) = g(x) \sqcap f(y).$$

Suppose that (2) holds and $x \sqsubseteq y$. Then $f(x) \sqsupseteq f(x) \sqcap g(y) = f(y) \sqcap g(x)$ and $f(x) = f(x) \sqcap g(x) \sqsubseteq f(y) \sqcap g(x)$. $\Box$

Let us write $f \uparrow_s g$ if the pair f, g is consistent in the stable ordering.

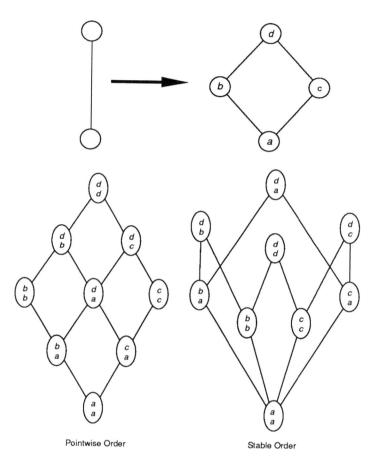

Figure 5.3
Extensional and Stable Orderings

5.14 Lemma (Berry). *If $f, g : D \to_s E$ and $f \uparrow_s g$, then $x \uparrow y$ implies*

$$f(x) \sqcap g(y) = f(y) \sqcap g(x).$$

Proof: Suppose $x \uparrow y$ and $f, g \sqsubseteq_s h$. Then

$$f(x) \sqcap g(y) = f(x) \sqcap h(y) \sqcap g(y) \tag{5.2}$$
$$= f(y) \sqcap h(x) \sqcap g(y) \tag{5.3}$$
$$= f(y) \sqcap h(y) \sqcap g(x) \tag{5.4}$$
$$= f(y) \sqcap g(x) \tag{5.5}$$

where Equation 5.3 and 5.4 both follow from Lemma 5.13. Equations 5.2 and 5.4 follow from the facts that $g \sqsubseteq_s h$ and $f \sqsubseteq_s h$ respectively. $\Box$

It is not difficult to see that the stable function space between two dI-domains is a cpo.

5.15 Lemma. *If D, E are dI-domains, then $D \to_s E$ is a cpo.*

Proof: Suppose $M \subseteq D \to_s E$ is directed. Since $f(x) \sqsubseteq g(x)$ for each $f, g \in M$ such that $f \sqsubseteq_s g$, we can define $\phi(x) = \bigsqcup_{f \in M} f(x)$. I will show that ϕ is the least upper bound of M in the stable order. We know already that ϕ is continuous. To see that it is stable, suppose x, y are consistent. Then

$$\phi(x \sqcap y) = \bigsqcup_{f \in M} f(x \sqcap y)$$
$$= \bigsqcup_{f \in M} f(x) \sqcap f(y)$$
$$= (\bigsqcup_{f \in M} f(x)) \sqcap (\bigsqcup_{f \in M} f(y))$$
$$= \phi(x) \sqcap \phi(y)$$

where Equation 5.6 follows from the continuity of the meet operation on bc-domains (Lemma 5.10). Hence ϕ is stable. Now, suppose $x \sqsubseteq y$ and $f \in M$. Then

$$f(y) \sqcap \phi(x) = f(y) \sqcap \bigsqcup_{g \in M} g(x) = \bigsqcup_{g \in M} f(y) \sqcap g(x) = f(x)$$

so $f \sqsubseteq_s \phi$ for each $f \in M$. It is clear that ϕ must be the least such upper bound for M. $\Box$

In particular, the proof of the lemma shows that application is a continuous function on the stable function space. It remains to be seen that it is actually stable. First we need a basic fact about glb's of stable functions.

5.16 Lemma. *Let D and E be dI-domains. If f and g are consistent elements of $D \rightarrow_s E$, then the pointwise glb $\phi(x) = f(x) \sqcap g(x)$ is the glb $f \sqcap g$ in $D \rightarrow_s E$.*

Proof: It is clear that ϕ is stable. To see that $\phi \sqsubseteq_s f$, suppose $x \sqsubseteq y$ and calculate

$$
\begin{aligned}
\phi(y) \sqcap f(x) &= f(y) \sqcap g(y) \sqcap f(x) \\
&= f(y) \sqcap f(x) \sqcap g(y) \sqcap f(x) \\
&= f(y) \sqcap f(y) \sqcap g(x) \sqcap f(x) & (5.6) \\
&= f(y) \sqcap g(x) \sqcap f(x) \\
&= f(x) \sqcap g(x) & (5.7) \\
&= \phi(x) & (5.8)
\end{aligned}
$$

where Equation 5.6 follows from Lemma 5.14 and Equation 5.7 from the fact that $x \sqsubseteq y$. Proof that $\phi \sqsubseteq_s g$ is similar. It is easy to check that $h \sqsubseteq_s f, g$ implies that $h \sqsubseteq_s \phi$. Thus ϕ is the glb of f and g.   □

Suppose now that $f \uparrow_s g$ and $x \uparrow y$. We can calculate as follows:

$$
\begin{aligned}
\mathsf{apply}((f,x) \sqcap (g,y)) &= \mathsf{apply}(f \sqcap g, x \sqcap y) \\
&= (f \sqcap g)(x \sqcap y) \\
&= (f \sqcap g)(x) \sqcap (f \sqcap g)(y) \\
&= (f(x) \sqcap g(x)) \sqcap (f(y) \sqcap g(y)) & (5.9) \\
&= f(x) \sqcap (g(x) \sqcap f(y)) \sqcap g(y) \\
&= f(x) \sqcap (g(y) \sqcap f(x)) \sqcap g(y) & (5.10) \\
&= \mathsf{apply}(f,x) \sqcap \mathsf{apply}(g,y)
\end{aligned}
$$

where Equation 5.9 follows from Lemma 5.16 and Equation 5.10 follows from Lemma 5.14.

Stable function spaces.

Now the key to completing the proof that dI-domains with stable functions form a ccc with exponential given by the stable function space under the stable ordering is the demonstration that the stable function space *is* a dI-domain. This requires two somewhat technical arguments. The first of these shows that joins in the stable function space can be calculated pointwise; from this it can easily be shown that the stable function space is bounded complete and distributive. The second proves that the stable function space between the stable function space is an algebraic cpo with property I. Some readers may find it helpful to skip the proofs of Lemma 5.17 and Theorem 5.21 on first reading.

5.17 Lemma. *Let D and E be dI-domains. If f and g are consistent elements of $D \to_s E$, then the pointwise least upper bound $\phi(x) = f(x) \sqcup g(x)$ is the least upper bound $f \sqcup g$ in $D \to_s E$.*

Proof: It is easy to see that ϕ is continuous. To see that it is also stable, suppose x and y are consistent. Let

$$u = (f(y) \sqcup g(x)) \sqcap (f(x) \sqcup g(y)). \tag{5.11}$$

We can calculate as follows:

$$\begin{aligned}
\phi(x \sqcap y) &= f(x \sqcap y) \sqcup g(x \sqcap y) \\
&= (f(x) \sqcap f(y)) \sqcup (g(x) \sqcap g(y)) \\
&= (f(x) \sqcup g(x)) \sqcap u \sqcap (f(y) \sqcup g(y)) \tag{5.12} \\
&= (f(x) \sqcup g(x)) \sqcap (f(y) \sqcup g(y)) \tag{5.13} \\
&= \phi(x) \sqcap \phi(y)
\end{aligned}$$

where Equation 5.12 follows from distributivity. To see that Equation 5.13 holds, it suffices to show that

$$(f(x) \sqcup g(x)) \sqcap (f(y) \sqcup g(y)) \sqsubseteq u.$$

This is equivalent to showing that $v \sqsubseteq u$ where

$$v = (f(x) \sqcap f(y)) \sqcup (f(x) \sqcap g(y)) \sqcup (g(x) \sqcap f(y)) \sqcup (g(x) \sqcap g(y))$$

is obtained from an application of the distributivity axiom. To prove this, it suffices to show that $v \sqsubseteq f(y) \sqcup g(x)$ and $v \sqsubseteq f(x) \sqcup g(y)$. To prove the former, consider each of the terms of which v is the lub. The first, third, and fourth terms are obviously below $f(y) \sqcup g(x)$. Moreover,

$$f(x) \sqcap g(y) = f(y) \sqcap g(x) \sqsubseteq f(y) \sqcup g(x)$$

by Lemma 5.14. A proof that $v \sqsubseteq f(x) \sqcup g(y)$ is similar.

To see that ϕ is actually the least upper bound in the stable order, suppose $x \sqsubseteq y$. Then

$$\begin{aligned}
\phi(x) \sqcap f(y) &= (f(x) \sqcup g(x)) \sqcap f(y) = (f(x) \sqcap f(y)) \sqcup (g(x) \sqcap f(y)) \\
&= f(x) \sqcup (g(y) \sqcap f(x)) = f(x)
\end{aligned}$$

so $f \sqsubseteq_s \phi$. The proof that $g \sqsubseteq_s \phi$ is similar so ϕ is an upper bound for f and g in the stable order. To see that it is the *least* one, suppose $f \sqsubseteq_s h$ and $g \sqsubseteq_s h$. If $x \sqsubseteq y$, then

$$\phi(y) \sqcap h(x) = (f(y) \sqcup g(y)) \sqcap h(x) = (f(y) \sqcap h(x)) \sqcup (g(y) \sqcap h(x))$$
$$= f(x) \sqcup g(x) = \phi(x).$$

Hence $\phi \sqsubseteq_s h$. □

5.18 Corollary. *If D, E are dI-domains, then $D \to_s E$ is bounded complete.* □

5.19 Lemma. *Let D be a bc-domain. If $\downarrow x$ is a distributive lattice for every $x \in D$, then D is a distributive bc-domain.*

Proof: Suppose we have $y \uparrow z$ for $y, z \in D$ and $x \in D$. Let $w = x \sqcap (y \sqcup z)$. We would like to say that $w = (x \sqcap y) \sqcup (x \sqcap z)$, but this does not follow instantly since x may not be consistent with y and z (that is, there may not be a principal ideal in which x, y, z all lie). However, we *do* know that w, y, and z are bounded by $y \sqcup z$. Since $\downarrow(y \sqcup z)$ is distributive, we can calculate as follows: $w = w \sqcap (y \sqcup z) = (w \sqcap y) \sqcup (w \sqcap z) = (x \sqcap y) \sqcup (x \sqcap z)$. □

5.20 Lemma. *If D, E are dI-domains, then $D \to_s E$ is distributive.*

Proof: Now, to show that $D \to_s E$ is distributive, suppose we are given

$$f, g, h : D \to_s E$$

such that $f \uparrow g$. By Lemma 5.19, we may also assume that $f \sqcup g \uparrow h$. Distributivity now follows immediately from the fact that E is distributive and the lub and glb can be computed pointwise. □

Now, for bc-domains D and E, it is possible to show that the cpo F of continuous functions from D to E under the pointwise order is algebraic by demonstrating a basis of 'step functions'. The step functions used in the proof of Theorem 5.8 do not approximate functions in the same way in the stable order that they did in the pointwise order. The reader may wish to demonstrate as an exercise a stable function f and a pair of compact elements a, b such that $b \sqsubseteq f(a)$ where it is *not* the case that $(a \searrow b) \sqsubseteq_s f$. However, with a suitable modification, a comparable class of functions can be made to do the job.

5.21 Theorem. *If D and E are dI-domains, then so is $D \to_s E$.*

Proof: Given the lemmas that we have proved above, we know that $D \to_s E$ is a distributive, bounded-complete cpo. We must show that it is a domain with property I.

$D \rightarrow_s E$ *is a domain.* We begin by showing that $D \rightarrow_s E$ has a basis consisting of functions $f_{ab}(x) = f(x \sqcap a) \sqcap b$ where $f : D \rightarrow_s E$ and $a \in \mathsf{K}(D)$ and $b \in \mathsf{K}(E)$ such that $b \sqsubseteq f(a)$. Since f_{ab} is defined from a composition of stable functions, it must be stable. To see that $f_{ab} \sqsubseteq_s f$, suppose $x \sqsubseteq y$. Then

$$
\begin{aligned}
f_{ab}(y) \sqcap f(x) &= (f(y \sqcap a) \sqcap b) \sqcap f(x) \\
&= (f(y \sqcap a) \sqcap f(x)) \sqcap b \\
&= f((y \sqcap a) \sqcap x) \sqcap b \qquad\qquad (5.14) \\
&= f_{ab}(x)
\end{aligned}
$$

where Equation 5.14 follows from the fact that $y \sqcap a$ and x are bounded by y and f is stable. The proof that

$$
f = \bigsqcup \{ f_{ab} \mid a \in \mathsf{K}(D) \text{ and } b \in \mathsf{K}(E) \text{ and } b \sqsubseteq f(a) \} \qquad\qquad (5.15)
$$

is essentially the same as for bc-domains.

To show that f_{ab} is compact, suppose $f_{ab} \sqsubseteq_s \bigsqcup_{g \in M} g$ for $M \subseteq D \rightarrow_s E$ directed. For each $x \sqsubseteq a$, let h_x be an element of M such that $b \sqcap h_x(x)$ is the largest element of $\{ b \sqcap g(x) \mid g \in M \}$. Such a largest element exists because M is directed and $\downarrow b$ is finite by property I for E. Now, since M is directed and $\downarrow a$ is finite by property I for D, there is a stable function $h \in M$ that is an upper bound for $\{ h_x \mid x \in \downarrow a \}$. If $x \sqsubseteq y$, then

$$
\begin{aligned}
f_{ab}(y) \sqcap h(x) &= f_{ab}(y \sqcap a) \sqcap h(x) \\
&= f_{ab}(x) \sqcap h(y \sqcap a) \\
&= f(x \sqcap a) \sqcap b \sqcap h(y \sqcap a) \\
&= f(x \sqcap a) \sqcap \bigsqcup_{g \in M} b \sqcap g(y \sqcap a) \qquad\qquad (5.16) \\
&= f(x \sqcap a) \sqcap b \sqcap (\bigsqcup M)(y \sqcap a) \\
&= f_{ab}(x) \sqcap (\bigsqcup M)(y \sqcap a) \\
&= f_{ab}(y \sqcap a) \sqcap (\bigsqcup M)(x) \\
&= f_{ab}(y) \sqcap (\bigsqcup M)(x) \\
&= f_{ab}(x)
\end{aligned}
$$

so $f_{ab} \sqsubseteq_s h$. That $\sqsubseteq$ holds in Equation 5.16 is clear. To see that $\sqsupseteq$ also holds, suppose $g \in M$, then $b \sqcap g(y \sqcap a) \sqsubseteq b \sqcap h_{y \sqcap a}(y \sqcap a) \sqsubseteq b \sqcap h(y \sqcap a)$.

$D \rightarrow_s E$ *is a domain.* Suppose f is a compact element of the stable function space and let

$$
M = \{ \bigsqcup \{ f_{ab} \mid (a, b) \in J, \ b \sqsubseteq f(a) \} \mid J \subseteq \mathsf{K}(D) \times \mathsf{K}(E), \ J \text{ finite} \}
$$

This is a directed collection of compact elements, and $\bigsqcup M = f$. Since f is compact, it follows that $f = f_{a_1,b_1} \sqcup \cdots \sqcup f_{a_n,b_n}$ for some set of a_i's and b_i's. We make use of this to show that property I holds. To keep down the number of indices, let us pretend that $f = f_{ab} \sqcup f_{cd}$ for some a, b, c, d (the proof with all of the indices is basically the same anyway). Now, suppose that $g \sqsubseteq_s f$. Let $x \in D$ be given and consider the element $z = (x \sqcap a) \sqcup (x \sqcap c)$. It is easy to see that $z \sqcap a = x \sqcap a$ and $z \sqcap c = x \sqcap c$. Since $z \sqsubseteq x$ we must therefore have

$$
\begin{aligned}
g(z) &= g(x) \sqcap (f_{ab}(z) \sqcup f_{cd}(z)) \\
&= g(x) \sqcap ((f(z \sqcap a) \sqcap b) \sqcup (f(z \sqcap c) \sqcap d)) \\
&= g(x) \sqcap ((f(x \sqcap a) \sqcap b) \sqcup (f(x \sqcap c) \sqcap d)) \\
&= g(x) \sqcap (f_{ab}(x) \sqcup f_{cd}(x)) \\
&= g(x).
\end{aligned}
$$

Reading these equations from bottom to top, g is uniquely determined by its values on arguments z such that $z = a' \sqcup c'$ where $a' \sqsubseteq a$ and $c' \sqsubseteq c$. By property I for D, there are only finitely many such arguments. Moreover, the values of $g(x)$ must satisfy $g(x) \sqsubseteq b \sqcup d$. By property I for E, there are only finitely many such values. Hence there can be only finitely many distinct functions $g \sqsubseteq_s f_{ab} \sqcup f_{cd}$.   □

I leave for the reader the completion of the proof of Theorem 5.12, noting the earlier argument that application is stable.

A fixed-point semantics for PCF.

The dI-domains can be used to give a semantics $\mathcal{D}[\![\cdot]\!]$ for PCF in the same way that we used cpo's to give a semantics $\mathcal{C}[\![\cdot]\!]$ in Section 4.3. One must prove the analog of Lemma 4.19.

5.22 Lemma. *If $H, x : s \vdash M : t$, then the function*

$$d \mapsto \mathcal{D}[\![H, x : s \triangleright M : t]\!]\rho[x \mapsto d]$$

is stable.

Proof: As with Lemma 4.19, the proof can be carried out by structural induction on M. The interesting cases are application and fixed points. The case of application follows from the proof that dI-domains form a ccc. The case of recursion is left for the reader. □

The computational properties of this model are similar to those for the interpretation $\mathcal{C}[\![\cdot]\!]$. Here is a summary of the basic facts:

5.23 Theorem. *Suppose M and V are well-typed closed terms where V is a value.*

1. If V has ground (boolean or number) type, then $\mathcal{D}[\![V]\!] \neq \bot$.
2. If $M \Downarrow V$, then $\mathcal{D}[\![M]\!] = \mathcal{D}[\![V]\!]$.
3. If M has ground type and $\mathcal{D}[\![M]\!] = \mathcal{D}[\![V]\!]$, then $M \Downarrow V$.   □

A deeper study of the connection between operational and denotational semantics for $\mathcal{C}[\![\cdot]\!]$ and $\mathcal{D}[\![\cdot]\!]$ will be carried out in the next chapter.

Exercises.

5.18 Give an example of a cpo D and an element $x \in D$ such that $\downarrow x$ is finite but x is not compact.

5.19 Demonstrate dI-domains D, E such that the space of continuous functions $[D \to E]$ under the pointwise order does not satisfy property I.

5.20 Prove Lemma 5.11.

5.21 Suppose that D is a bc-domain. Prove that the following conditions are equivalent

  a. D is distributive,
  b. $\downarrow x$ is distributive lattice for every $x \in \mathsf{K}(D)$,
  c. $x \sqcap (y \sqcup z) = (x \sqcap y) \sqcup (x \sqcap z)$ for any $x, y, z \in \mathsf{K}(D)$ such that $y \uparrow z$.

5.22 Give an example of dI-domains D, E, a stable function $f : D \to E$, and a pair of compact elements $a, b \in D$ such that $b \sqsubseteq f(a)$ and $a \searrow b \not\sqsubseteq_s f$.

5.23 Provide the proof that Equation 5.15 holds.

5.24 Complete the proof of Theorem 5.12.

5.25 Let D, E be dI-domains.

  a. Prove that a continuous function $f : D \to E$ is stable if, and only if, for each $a \in \mathsf{K}D$, the minimal elements of $f^{-1}(\uparrow a)$ are inconsistent.
  b. Prove that stable functions $f, g : D \to E$ satisfy $f \sqsubseteq_s g$ if, and only if, for each $a \in \mathsf{K}(E)$, the minimal elements in $f^{-1}(\uparrow a)$ are a subset of the minimal elements in $g^{-1}(\uparrow a)$

5.26 Prove the case for recursion in Lemma 5.22 by showing that if

$$d \mapsto \mathcal{D}[\![H, y : t \rhd M' : t]\!]\rho[y \mapsto d]$$

is stable for any H-environment ρ, then

$$e \mapsto \mathcal{D}[\![H \rhd \mu y : t.\ M' : t]\!]\rho[x \mapsto e]$$

is also stable for any such ρ and $x \in H$.

5.3   Equivalences between Categories

In working with virtually any category of structures, and certainly with domains, it is helpful to make use of different characterizations of the category under study. It is therefore helpful to develop a notion of structure-preserving maps between categories. The most important class of such maps is that of *functors*. Functors will be used throughout much of the rest of this book, but the proximate cause for their introduction here is their use in describing when two categories should be viewed as 'essentially' the same. The categorical analog of an isomorphism is easy to state once the idea of an identity functor is introduced. However, this definition of an equivalence between categories is usually stronger that what one really has or wants.

To begin this development, let us consider an extremely useful relationship between posets and domains. To define a continuous function from a domain D to a cpo E, it is only necessary to define a monotone function from the *basis* of D into E. This function will have a unique extension to a continuous function on all of D. This technique often simplifies the description of a function on a domain. It is expressed formally by the following lemma:

5.24 Lemma. *Let D be an algebraic cpo and E any cpo. If $f : \mathsf{K}(D) \to E$ is monotone, then there is a unique continuous function f' that completes the following diagram*

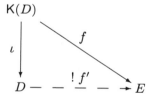

where ι is the inclusion map. In particular, a continuous function $f : D \to E$ between algebraic cpo's D and E is uniquely determined by its restriction to $\mathsf{K}(D)$.

Proof: If there *is* such a continuous function f', then

$$
\begin{aligned}
f'(x) &= f'(\bigsqcup(\downarrow x \cap \mathsf{K}(D))) \\
&= \bigsqcup\{f'(a) \mid a \in \downarrow x \cap \mathsf{K}(D)\} \\
&= \bigsqcup\{f(a) \mid a \in \downarrow x \cap \mathsf{K}(D)\}.
\end{aligned}
$$

Since this last expression depends only on the given function f, the final equation defines the unique function f' that could complete the diagram. To finish the proof we must demonstrate that the function so defined is actually continuous. To see that f' is monotone, note that if $x \sqsubseteq y$, then

$$\{f(a) \mid a \in \downarrow x \cap \mathsf{K}(D)\} \subseteq \{f(a) \mid a \in \downarrow y \cap \mathsf{K}(D)\}$$

so clearly $f(x) \sqsubseteq f(y)$. Suppose that $M \subseteq D$ is directed. Then

$$
\begin{aligned}
f'(\bigsqcup M) &= \bigsqcup \{f(a) \mid a \sqsubseteq \bigsqcup M \text{ and } a \text{ is compact}\} \\
&= \bigsqcup \{f(a) \mid a \leq x \text{ for some } x \in M \text{ and } a \text{ is compact}\} \\
&= \bigsqcup_{x \in M} \bigsqcup \{f(a) \mid a \leq x \text{ and } a \text{ is compact}\} \\
&= \bigsqcup_{x \in M} f'(x). \qquad \qquad \qquad \qquad \qquad \qquad \qquad \Box
\end{aligned}
$$

It is almost always possible to represent operations on algebraic cpo's through operations on their posets of compact elements. Indeed, there is a basic, underlying phenomenon here that is best understood through a categorical formulation.

Definition: Let $\mathbf{C}$ and $\mathbf{D}$ be categories. A *functor* $F : \mathbf{C} \to \mathbf{D}$ is an operator that associates with each object A of $\mathbf{C}$ an object $F(A)$ of $\mathbf{D}$ and with each arrow $f \in \mathbf{C}(A, B)$ an arrow $F(f) \in \mathbf{D}(F(A), F(B))$. It is required to have two preservation properties:

1. $F(\mathsf{id}_A) = \mathsf{id}_{F(A)}$ for each object A, and
2. if $g \in \mathbf{C}(A, B)$ and $f \in \mathbf{C}(B, C)$, then $F(f \circ g) = F(f) \circ F(g)$.

Given categories $\mathbf{C}, \mathbf{D}, \mathbf{E}$ and functors

$$
\mathbf{C} \xrightarrow{F} \mathbf{D} \xrightarrow{G} \mathbf{E},
$$

their *composition* $G \circ F$ is defined by taking $(G \circ F)(A) = G(F(A))$ and $(G \circ F)(f) = G(F(f))$. $\qquad \Box$

Examples of functors are extremely abundant. For instance, the powerset operation $\mathcal{P} : \mathbf{Set} \to \mathbf{Set}$ is a functor from sets to sets because $\mathcal{P}(\mathsf{id}_S) = \mathsf{id}_{\mathcal{P}(S)}$ and $\mathcal{P}(g \circ f) = \mathcal{P}(g) \circ \mathcal{P}(f)$. Functors are like arrows between categories; it is easy to check that composition of functors is associative and that there is an identity functor defined as the identity on both objects and arrows.

Example: If $\mathbf{C}$ and $\mathbf{D}$ are categories, then the *product category* $\mathbf{C} \times \mathbf{D}$ has, as its objects, pairs (C, D) where C is an object of $\mathbf{C}$ and D is an object of $\mathbf{D}$. The arrows of the product category are pairs $(f, g) : (C, D) \to (C', D')$ where $f : C \to C'$ is an arrow in $\mathbf{C}$ and $g : D \to D'$ is an arrow in $\mathbf{D}$. Composition of such arrows is defined by $(f, g) \circ (f', g') = (f \circ f', g \circ g')$. There are also functors

$$
\mathsf{fst} : \mathbf{C} \times \mathbf{D} \to \mathbf{C} \text{ and } \mathsf{snd} : \mathbf{C} \times \mathbf{D} \to \mathbf{C}
$$

where $\mathsf{fst}(C, D) = C$ and $\mathsf{fst}(f, g) = f$ and $\mathsf{snd}(C, D) = D$ and $\mathsf{snd}(f, g) = g$. If $\times$ is a product on a category $\mathbf{C}$, then it is a functor from $\mathbf{C} \times \mathbf{C}$ to $\mathbf{C}$ with an action on arrows that was defined earlier when binary products were introduced. A similar fact holds for coproducts. □

Functors can be viewed as a generalization of monotone functions between posets. To see why, let us begin by introducing a useful generalization of posets:

Definition: A *pre-order* is a set A together with a binary relation $\sqsubseteq_A$ on A that is reflexive and transitive. That is, for each $a, b, c \in A$,

1. $a \sqsubseteq_A a$, and
2. if $a \sqsubseteq_A b$ and $b \sqsubseteq_A c$, then $a \sqsubseteq_A c$. □

A pre-order is a relation that that is missing one of the axioms needed to be a poset. In a pre-order, there can be distinct elements a and b such that $a \sqsubseteq b$ and $b \sqsubseteq a$. One of the most typical examples is the pre-order of propositional formulas under the relation $\rightarrow$ of provable implication with equality taken to mean syntactic identity. The universe of the pre-order consists of propositions ϕ. The binary relation $\phi \rightarrow \psi$ holds if, and only if, there is a proof that ϕ implies ψ. Of course $\phi \rightarrow \phi$ holds for any proposition ϕ. Moreover, if $\phi \rightarrow \psi$ and $\psi \rightarrow \theta$ are both provable, then so is $\phi \rightarrow \theta$. However, we may have distinct propositions ϕ and ψ where $\phi \rightarrow \psi$ and $\psi \rightarrow \phi$. An easy example of such a pair are the propositions $A \wedge B$ and $B \wedge A$; they are logically equivalent but not syntactically equal. To obtain a partial order, one could take equivalence classes of propositions and order these by provable implication. This idea of taking equivalence classes to make a partial order out of a pre-order is the reason *pre*-orders are so named. Returning now to the relationship between functors and pre-orders/posets, the key result is that a pre-order $(A, \sqsubseteq)$ is a special kind of category $\mathbf{A}$ whose objects are the elements of A. For the arrows, if $a, b \in A$, then $\mathbf{A}(a, b)$ has a unique element if $a \sqsubseteq b$, and it is empty otherwise. Given this, the definitions of identity maps and composition are uniquely determined and the fact that we have a category is exactly what the reflexivity and transitivity conditions for a pre-order assert. Now, given pre-orders A and B considered as categories $\mathbf{A}$ and $\mathbf{B}$, a functor $F : \mathbf{A} \rightarrow \mathbf{B}$ is a map from A to B with the property that it preserves identity maps and composition. This just means that, whenever $a \sqsubseteq b$, we have $F(a) \sqsubseteq F(b)$. In other words, functors between pre-orders are functions that preserve the pre-order relation—an obvious generalization of monotone functions on partial orders.

Pre-orders and algebraic cpo's.

Now, the primary reason for introducing functors and pre-orders at this point is to study the relationship between pre-orders and algebraic cpo's. For pre-orders, it is conventional to think of a as 'larger' than b if $b \sqsubseteq a$. We will be especially interested in subsets of pre-orders that are directed and downward closed:

Definition: An *ideal* over a pre-order $(A, \sqsubseteq)$ is a subset $x \subseteq A$ such that

1. If $u \subseteq x$ is finite, then there is an $a \in x$ such that $b \sqsubseteq a$ for each $b \in u$ (that is, x is *directed*).
2. If $a \in x$, then $\downarrow a = \{b \mid b \sqsubseteq a\} \subseteq x$, (that is, x is *downward closed*).   □

We write $\mathsf{Idl}(A, \sqsubseteq)$ for the set of ideals over the pre-order $(A, \sqsubseteq)$.

As for posets, the set $\downarrow a = \{b \mid b \sqsubseteq a\}$ is called the *principal* ideal generated by a. We say that the *poset induced by A* is the set of principal ideals $\downarrow a$ ordered by set inclusion. There is a correspondence between algebraic cpo's and pre-orders that can be expressed formally by the following:

5.25 Lemma.   *1. For any pre-order A, the set of ideals, $\mathsf{Idl}(A)$, forms an algebraic cpo under the ordering by subset inclusion. The compact elements of $\mathsf{Idl}(A)$ are the principal ideals of A.*

2. If D is an algebraic cpo, then $D \cong \mathsf{Idl}(\mathsf{K}(D))$.

Proof: We prove only part (1) and leave (2) as an exercise. Clearly, the ideals of A form a poset under set inclusion, say $D = \mathsf{Idl}(A)$. To see that D is complete, suppose that $M \subseteq D$ is directed and let $x = \bigcup M$. If we can show that x is an ideal, then it is certainly the least upper bound of M in D. To this end, suppose $u \subseteq x$ is finite. Since each element of u must be contained in some element of M, there is a finite collection of ideals $s \subseteq M$ such that $u \subseteq \bigcup s$. Since M is directed, there is an element $y \in M$ such that $z \subseteq y$ for each $z \in s$. Thus $u \subseteq y$, and since y is an ideal, there is an element $a \in y$ such that $b \sqsubseteq a$ for each $b \in u$. But $a \in y \subseteq x$, so it follows that x is an ideal.

To see that D is algebraic, we show that the set of principal ideals is a basis. Suppose $M \subseteq D$ is directed and $\downarrow a \subseteq \bigcup M$ for some $a \in A$. Then $a \in x$ for some $x \in M$, so $\downarrow a \subseteq x$. Hence $\downarrow a$ is compact in D. Now suppose $x \in D$ and $u \subseteq A$ is a finite collection of elements of A such that $\downarrow a \subseteq x$ for each $a \in u$. Then $u \subseteq x$ and since x is an ideal, there is an element $b \in x$ with $a \sqsubseteq b$ for each $a \in u$. Thus $\downarrow a \subseteq \downarrow b$ for each $a \in u$, and it follows that the principal ideals below x form a directed collection. It is obvious that the least upper bound (that is, union) of that collection is x.   □

Note that the ideal completion of a pre-order has a least element if, and only if, the pre-order does. That is, pointed pre-orders correspond to pointed algebraic cpo's.

Definition: Let $F : \mathbf{C} \to \mathbf{D}$ be a functor. It is said to be *dense* if, for each object D of $\mathbf{D}$, there is an object C of $\mathbf{C}$ such that $F(C) \cong D$. It is said to be *full* if, for any pair of objects A and B of $\mathbf{C}$, the functor action on arrows defines a surjection from $\mathbf{C}(A, B)$ onto $\mathbf{D}(F(A), F(B))$. It is said to be *faithful* if this map is a injection. A functor that is dense, full, and faithful is called an *equivalence*. If there is an equivalence $F : \mathbf{C} \to \mathbf{D}$, then $\mathbf{C}$ and $\mathbf{D}$ are said to be *equivalent categories*. □

Note that the definition of equivalence did *not* require that the action of an equivalence F on objects be an injection; it is also not required to be a surjection—just a surjection 'up to isomorphism'. Incidentally, a 'full subcategory' is a subcategory for which the inclusion functor is full. My goal now is to demonstrate a notion of arrow between pre-orders that will yield a category equivalent to the category **Alg** of algebraic cpo's and continuous maps.

Definition: Suppose $(A, \subseteq_A)$ and $(B, \subseteq_B)$ are pre-orders. A relation $f \subseteq A \times B$ is *approximable* if it satisfies the following conditions:

- For every $a \in A$, there is a $b \in B$ such that $a \ f \ b$ (that is, $(a, b) \in f$).
- If $a \ f \ b$ and $a \ f \ b'$, then there is some b'' such that $b \subseteq_B b''$ and $b' \subseteq_B b''$ and $a \ f \ b''$.
- If $a' \subseteq_A a$ and $a' \ f \ b'$ and $b \subseteq_B b'$, then $a \ f \ b$.

If $g \subseteq A \times B$ and $f \subseteq B \times C$ are approximable relations, relation $f \circ g \subseteq A \times C$ is defined by relating a and c if, and only if, there is some $b \in B$ such that $a \ g \ b$ and $b \ f \ c$. □

I will leave for the reader the demonstration that pre-orders and approximable relations form a category. To prove that this category is actually equivalent to **Alg**, it is possible to define a functor action for the operation K that maps algebraic cpo's to posets. Given a continuous function $f : D \to E$ in **Alg**, define an approximable relation $\mathsf{K}(f) \subseteq \mathsf{K}(D) \times \mathsf{K}(E)$ to be the set of pairs (a, b) such that $b \sqsubseteq f(a)$. The proof that K is dense is left as an exercise. To see that it is also full and faithful we must demonstrate a bijection between approximable relations $g \subseteq \mathsf{K}(D) \times \mathsf{K}(E)$ and continuous functions $f : D \to E$. Given such an approximable relation g, define $\phi(g)$ to be the function given by taking

$$\phi(g)(x) = \bigsqcup \{ b \in \mathsf{K}(E) \mid a \ g \ b \text{ for some compact } a \sqsubseteq x \} \tag{5.17}$$

and, given a continuous function $f : D \to E$, define

$$a \ (\psi(f)) \ b \quad \text{iff} \quad b \sqsubseteq f(a). \tag{5.18}$$

It is left for the reader to complete the equivalence proof by showing that ϕ and ψ are inverse to one another.

Information systems.

In the case that the category in which we are interested is that of bc-domains, then the equivalence between pre-orders and algebraic cpo's cuts down to one between a class of bounded-complete, non-empty pre-orders and the category of bc-domains. It is possible to mimic the product and exponential operators on bc-domains by defining corresponding operations on this restricted class of pre-orders. This is advantageous because it makes it possible to work with structures that are not required to satisfy so many axioms; I think most readers will agree that it is easier to explain pre-orders and approximable relations than algebraic cpo's and continuous functions. Of course, we must still deal with the axiom of bounded completeness for pre-orders if we wish to work with those pre-orders that correspond to bc-domains. In fact, it is possible to use structures that eliminate a direct need for this axiom while, at the same time, providing a representation that stresses a philosophy of compact domain elements as pieces of information about elements they approximate. A class of such structures is defined as follows.

Definition: An *information system* is a tuple $(A, \Delta, Con, \vdash)$ where A is a set called the *universe of finite data objects*, Δ is an element of A called the *least informative* data object, Con is a set of finite subsets of A called the *consistent finite sets of objects*, and $\vdash$ is a relation between members of Con and members of A. The following axioms concerning Con must be satisfied for each pair u, v of finite subsets of A and data object $a \in A$:

- if $u \subseteq v$ and $v \in Con$ then $u \in Con$,
- $\{a\} \in Con$,
- if $u \vdash a$, then $u \cup \{a\} \in Con$,

and the following axioms concerning $\vdash$ must hold for all $u, v \in Con$ and $a \in D$:

- $u \vdash \Delta$
- if $a \in u$, then $u \vdash a$
- if $v \vdash b$ for all $b \in u$ and $u \vdash a$, then $v \vdash a$.

A set $x \subseteq A$ of finite data objects is said to be *consistent* if $u \in Con$ for each finite subset $u \subseteq x$.   □

It is convenient to write $u \vdash v$ for finite consistent sets u, v if $u \vdash a$ for each $a \in u$. The reader can verify as an exercise that the following facts hold for this relation:

5.26 Lemma. *For all* $u, v, u', v' \in Con$,

1. $\emptyset \vdash \{\Delta\}$,

2. $\vdash$ is a pre-order on Con,

3. if $u \subseteq u'$ and $u \vdash v$ and $v' \subseteq v$, then $u' \vdash v'$, and

4. if $u \vdash v$ and $u \vdash v'$, then $u \vdash v \cup v'$. $\Box$

Definition: Given an information system A, a consistent subset $x \subseteq A$ is said to be *downward closed* if $u \vdash v$ and $u \subseteq x$ implies $v \subseteq x$ whenever $u, v \in Con$. $\Box$

To define the notion of an arrow between information systems, it is convenient to have a notation for information systems similar to the one we used for posets. Let us write A for an information system $(A, \Delta_A, Con_A, \vdash_A)$ and B for a possibly different system $(B, \Delta_B, Con_B, \vdash_B)$.

Definition: Let A and B be information systems. An *approximable relation* between them is a subset $f \subseteq Con_A \times Con_B$ such that

- $\emptyset \, f \, \emptyset$,
- if $u \, f \, v$ and $u \, f \, v'$, then $u \, f \, (v \cup v')$, and
- if $u' \vdash_A u$ and $u \, f \, v$ and $v \vdash_B v'$, then $u' \, f \, v'$. $\Box$

Given information systems A, B, C and approximable relations $f \subseteq Con_A \times Con_B$ and $g \subseteq Con_B \times Con_C$, the *composition* of f and g is a subset of $Con_A \times Con_C$ defined by taking $u \, (g \circ f) \, w$ if, and only if, there is a consistent set $v \in Con_B$ such that $u \, f \, v$ and $v \, g \, w$. Of course, this is the definition of composition of relations on pre-orders defined above, and, as with pre-orders, information systems with this composition form a category **Infsys**. Also, there is a faithful functor F from **Infsys** into the category of cpo's and continuous functions. On objects, this functor is defined by taking $F(A)$ to be the poset of consistent, downward-closed subsets of A ordered by subset inclusion. For arrows $f : A \to B$ it is possible to show that

$$F(f)(x) = \bigcup \{v \in Con_B \mid u \, f \, v \text{ for some } u \subseteq x\}$$

defines a continuous function between the posets $F(A)$ and $F(B)$. It is possible to show that, for any information system A, the consistent sets $\bar{v} = \{a \in A \mid v \vdash a\}$ for $v \in Con$ form a basis for $F(A)$ and therefore the functor F goes from information systems into **Alg**. The functor is not full for this category because of the following:

5.27 Lemma. *The functor F defined above defines an equivalence between* **Infsys** *and* **Bcdom**. $\Box$

Now, given that F is a dense functor, if A, B are information systems, there must be information systems $A \times B$ and $A \Rightarrow B$ such that $F(A \times B)$ and $F(A \Rightarrow B)$ are isomorphic to product and exponential for $F(A)$ and $F(B)$ in the category of bc-domains. I will leave the discovery of a good definition for the product of information systems as an exercise for the reader. Define the exponential $A \Rightarrow B$ for information systems A and B as follows.

- $A \Rightarrow B$ is the set of pairs (u, v) such that $u \in Con_A$ and $v \in Con_B$,
- $\Delta = (\emptyset, \emptyset)$.

To define consistency and $\vdash$ for $A \Rightarrow B$, suppose $w = \{(u_1, v_1), \ldots, (u_n, v_n)\} \subseteq A \Rightarrow B$. Then

- $w \in Con$ iff, for each subset $I \subseteq \{1, \ldots, n\}$, $\bigcup\{u_i \mid i \in I\} \in Con_A$ implies $\bigcup\{v_i \mid i \in I\} \in Con_B$.
- $w \vdash (u, v)$ iff $\bigcup\{v_i \mid u \vdash_A u_i\} \vdash_B v$, for all $u \in Con_A$ and $v \in Con_B$.

To see that $F(A \Rightarrow B)$ is isomorphic to the continuous function space $[F(A) \rightarrow F(B)]$, suppose first that $f \in F(A \Rightarrow B)$. Then f is a set of pairs (u, v), and we can define a function $\phi(f)$ by

$$\phi(f)(x) = \bigcup\{v' \mid v \vdash_B v' \text{ for some } (u, v) \in f \text{ such that } u \subseteq x\}.$$

Suppose, on the other hand, that $g : F(A) \rightarrow F(B)$ is continuous. Let

$$\psi(g) = \{(u, v) \mid \bar{v} \subseteq g(\bar{u}) \text{ where } u \in Con(A) \text{ and } v \in Con_B\}.$$

These two maps define the desired isomorphism. On the other hand, a simpler way to view the exponential for information systems is to appreciate it as an information system whose data elements are the finite approximations of approximable relations. Given an approximable relation $f \subseteq Con_A \times Con_B$, a finite approximation to f can be viewed as a finite subset $w \subseteq f$. Indeed the approximable relations between A and B are exactly the elements of $F(A \Rightarrow B)$.

Exercises.

5.27 Prove the second part of Lemma 5.25.

5.28   a. Given a continuous function $f : D \rightarrow E$ in **Alg**. Prove that $\mathsf{K}(f)$ is an approximable relation and that K satisfies the axioms for being a functor.
    b. Prove that pre-orders and approximable relations form a category.
    c. Demonstrate that the maps ϕ and ψ defined by 5.17 and 5.18 define a bijection between approximable relations $f \subseteq \mathsf{K}(D) \times \mathsf{K}(E)$ and continuous functions

$$g : D \rightarrow E.$$

5.29 Given a pre-order A, prove that A is isomorphic to its ideal completion in the category of approximable relations and pre-orders. Prove, moreover, that the functor K is dense.

5.30 Prove Lemma 5.26.

5.31 Fill in the details proving that the category of information systems is equivalent to that of bc-domains. (Hint: given a domain D, define an information system that has the compact elements of D as its finite data objects.)

5.32 Propose a definition for products in **Infsys**.

5.4   Notes

The two theories of finite approximation are primarily due to Dana Scott [102; 223; 226; 227; 228] and Gerard Berry [25; 26; 30]. For this reason, the terms 'Scott domain' and 'Berry domain' are sometimes used for bc-domains and dI-domains respectively. Several of the lemmas here (such as Lemma 5.13 and Lemma 5.14) were drawn from [26]. There are many variations on the themes of bc-domains and dI-domains. Examples of the former can be found in work of Plotkin [197] and much of the early literature on the semantics of programming languages [222; 230; 252] where algebraic lattices were used. Examples of the latter can be found in work of Girard [88; 89; 90] who has studied several sub-categories of the dI-domains. Several categories that generalize the bc-domains have been studied. The best known of these are continuous cpo's, of which the continuous lattices [86] and the bounded complete cpo's are special cases. Another well-known category that generalizes bc-domains will be studied in some detail in Chapter 10. A more recent subject of investigation is the category of L-domains discovered by Jung [130] and Coquand [57]; these generalize the bc-domains by requiring only that least upper bounds exist in principal ideals. A closely related category was discovered by Gunter [96; 100]. There has been a great deal of work on dI-domains and their generalizations as well, including work by Taylor [256; 258] and Droste [77] on the stable analog of L-domains. Berardi [24] modified an argument of Girard [88] to provide a representational proof that dI-domains form a ccc. A formulation using information systems was given by Zhang [274], and an abstract proof can be obtained from the literature on L-domains.

One topic of some importance on which this chapter did not touch is the use of a theory of finite approximation to develop a theory of computability on domains. Some examples of work in this direction include several of the papers of Scott mentioned before, together with papers by Kamimura and Tang [132], by Smyth [236], and by Spreen [243]. A detailed discussion of computability for domains considered intuitionistically is provided in the dissertation of McCarty [159]; this line of investigation is now a topic of substantial interest. An investigation of computability in the context of stable functions has been given by Asperti [15] and computability for information systems by Larsen and Winskel.

6 Relating Interpretations

What is the bottom-line criterion for saying that program M has the same meaning as program N? Obviously this question can only be answered relative to a particular semantics, but this also suggests that the answer is related to the question of when two semantics should be viewed as being the same. A first attempt at an answer might be 'the results of their evaluation are the same'. This makes some sense if the programs are closed terms of ground type (surely we should have $M \Downarrow \underline{3}$ iff $N \Downarrow \underline{3}$), but it seems less meaningful at higher types. For example, the PCF programs $\lambda x : \textbf{num}. \ \textbf{0}$ and $\lambda x : \textbf{num}. \ (\lambda y : \textbf{num}. \ y)\textbf{0}$ should surely be viewed as having the same meaning, but the results of their evaluations are different (for the trivial reason that $\lambda x : t. \ M \Downarrow \lambda x : t. \ M$). These terms are equal by the β- and ξ-rules, so perhaps a better criterion would be to say that two programs have the same meaning if they can be proved equal in the equational theory. This is surely a mistake, however, since the equational theory in Table 4.2 is very weak and many intuitively equivalent programs will not be provably equal. So, a third idea is to take two programs to have the same meaning if they are identified by the fixed-point semantics of the language. This is a widely used criterion in programming languages, and it has often been taken that fixed-point semantics defines *the* notion of program equivalence. Nevertheless, a programmer might use a fourth criterion: two programs M and N are equivalent if, given a larger program P of which one is a part, the result of replacing M by N does not affect the outcome of evaluating the program. To be a bit more precise, this can be interpreted as saying that the answer P provides or the actions it appears to perform are unchanged by the substitution. What it means to be 'unchanged' is relative to what one can (or chooses to) observe, so this criterion makes sense only when a notion of *observability* is assumed. For example, we might only be able to observe the value obtained by evaluating a program of ground type. This means, for example, that we are unable (or choose not) to observe other aspects of the program's evaluation, such as how many steps are involved or what intermediate states may arise. In most cases these things cannot be ignored, but it will be useful to separate concerns so that one aspect of program behavior can be considered in isolation from others. How, then, do we relate these third and fourth views of the equivalence of programs? Might they be the same?

This chapter discusses how denotational and operational semantics can be related through extensions of the Computational Adequacy Theorem for PCF. There are several forms of extension. One of these, discussed in the first section below, involves demonstrating a closer relationship between PCF and its semantics. A relationship known as 'full abstraction' is described as a response to the questions of the previous paragraph. Unfortunately the operational and denotational semantics for PCF given earlier do not satisfy this strong condition. The first section of this chapter discusses a way to expand

PCF so that the relationship *is* satisfied. In the second section of the chapter another way
to prove adequacy is discussed, and this technique is employed to demonstrate adequacy
for a language with a call-by-value operation rule for application and observability of divergence at higher types. In the final section, the operational and fixed-point semantics
of product and sum types are studied.

6.1   Full Abstraction

Let us fix a language and provide some precise definitions. We have been discussing PCF,
so this is a convenient language to use here—but virtually any other language would have
a similar theory. What does it mean for PCF program M to be a part of a larger program
N? This could mean that the concrete syntax of M can be found as a substring of the
concrete syntax of N, but a more useful criterion would be the occurrence of M as a
subterm of N. In other words, N has the form $\{M/x\}N$ where the variable x has a free
occurrence in N. We might say that N and x define the *context* in which M occurs.
Recall though the difference between substitution on terms and substitution on term
trees. For example, consider the term

$$S \equiv \lambda x : \mathbf{o} \to (\mathbf{o} \to \mathbf{o}).\ \lambda y : \mathbf{o} \to \mathbf{o}.\ \lambda z : \mathbf{o}.\ (xz)(yz).$$

If we take S' and w to be a context where S' is the term tree

$$\lambda x : \mathbf{o} \to (\mathbf{o} \to \mathbf{o}).\ \lambda y : \mathbf{o} \to \mathbf{o}.\ \lambda z : \mathbf{o}.\ w(yz).$$

then $\{xz/w\}S' \equiv S$, which is quite different from

$$[xz/w]\lambda x : \mathbf{o} \to (\mathbf{o} \to \mathbf{o}).\ \lambda y : \mathbf{o} \to \mathbf{o}.\ \lambda z : \mathbf{o}.\ w(yz)$$
$$\equiv \lambda x' : \mathbf{o} \to (\mathbf{o} \to \mathbf{o}).\ \lambda y : \mathbf{o} \to \mathbf{o}.\ \lambda z' : \mathbf{o}.\ (xz)(yz').$$

Notation: The idea of a context, which should be viewed as a term tree with a missing
subterm, is so useful that it is sometimes convenient to have a special notation writing
contexts succinctly. We might write something like $\bar{\lambda}x : s.\ N$ with the idea that there is a
kind of β-reduction in which the free variables of M can become bound in the reduction:
$(\bar{\lambda}x : s.\ N)M \equiv \{M/x\}N$. This level of generality is not ordinarily required, so one might
instead fix the variable x and provide a special notation for a term with a distinguished
variable representing a program context. The most common notation in the literature
treats a pair of square brackets $[\ ]$ as a place holder for a missing subterm. A context
is then written in the form $C[\ ]$ where a new syntax class is introduced to emphasize
the distinction between context substitution, which is an operation on term trees, and
general substitution, which is an operation on terms. If the instances of $[\ ]$ in a context

$C[\ ]$ are replaced by a new variable x, then one obtains a term M and $C[N]$ is written for $\{N/x\}M$. This notation is less flexible than the one for term tree substitution that I will use in this book, but it can reduce the need for new variable names and make expressions easier to read. □

Using contexts, we define the key notion of operational equivalence as follows. Suppose M and N are terms of type t. Say M is an operational approximation of N and write $M \sqsubseteq_o N$ if, for every term L and variable x such that $\{M/x\}L$ and $\{N/x\}L$ are closed terms of ground type,

$$\{N/x\}L \Downarrow V \text{ implies } \{N/x\}L \Downarrow V.$$

It is possible to prove that $\sqsubseteq_o$ is a pre-order; terms M, N are *operationally equivalent*, and we write $M \approx N$ if $M \sqsubseteq_o N$ and $N \sqsubseteq_o M$. Now, suppose we are given a semantics $[\![\cdot]\!]$ for PCF that interprets types by posets. The interpretation $[\![\cdot]\!]$ is said to be *fully abstract* if the operational and denotational orderings coincide, that is, for every pair M, N of well-typed terms, $[\![M]\!] \sqsubseteq [\![N]\!]$ if, and only if, $M \sqsubseteq_o N$.

The standard model is not fully abstract.

One of the first interesting observations one can make about full abstraction as a criterion for correspondence between operational and denotational semantics is the fact that the semantics $C[\![\cdot]\!]$ defined in Chapter 4 *fails* to satisfy it! One aspect of the relationship is preserved, another not. To see what *is* true, note first the following:

6.1 Lemma. *Suppose $\{M/x\}L$ and $\{N/x\}L$ are well-typed terms. If $C[\![M]\!] \sqsubseteq C[\![N]\!]$ then $C[\![\{M/x\}L]\!] \sqsubseteq C[\![\{N/x\}L]\!]$.* □

The proof is a straightforward induction.

6.2 Proposition. *If $C[\![M]\!] \sqsubseteq C[\![N]\!]$, then $M \sqsubseteq_o N$.*

Proof: Suppose $P \equiv \{M/x\}L$ and $Q \equiv \{N/x\}L$ are well-typed, closed terms of ground type and $P \Downarrow V$. Then $C[\![V]\!] = C[\![P]\!] \sqsubseteq C[\![Q]\!]$ by Lemma 6.1. Since $C[\![V]\!] \neq \bot$ and Q has ground type, $C[\![Q]\!] = C[\![V]\!]$ so $Q \Downarrow V$ by adequacy (Theorem 4.24). □

This proposition shows that it is *sound* to prove that two programs have the same result of evaluation in all ground contexts by showing that they have the same meaning in the standard model $C[\![\cdot]\!]$. However, it does not mean that every pair of programs that should be viewed as equivalent relative to the operational ordering will have the same meaning in $C[\![\cdot]\!]$. So, if we are relying on $C[\![\cdot]\!]$ as our way to show that two programs are equivalent, is it possible that the semantics will let us down by failing to give the same meaning to

Table 6.1
Operationally Equivalent Programs with Different Denotations

$T \equiv \lambda f : \mathbf{bool} \rightarrow (\mathbf{bool} \rightarrow \mathbf{bool}).$
  if $f(\mathbf{true})(\Omega)$ then
    if $f(\Omega)(\mathbf{true})$ then
      if $f(\mathbf{false})(\mathbf{false})$ then Ω
    else true
  else Ω
else Ω

$F \equiv \lambda f : \mathbf{bool} \rightarrow (\mathbf{bool} \rightarrow \mathbf{bool}).$
  if $f(\mathbf{true})(\Omega)$ then
    if $f(\Omega)(\mathbf{true})$ then
      if $f(\mathbf{false})(\mathbf{false})$ then Ω
    else false
  else Ω
else Ω

$$
\begin{array}{cc}
f(\mathbf{true})(\Omega) & \\
\diagup \quad \diagdown & \\
f(\Omega)(\mathbf{true}) \quad \Omega & \\
\diagup \quad \diagdown & \\
f(\mathbf{false})(\mathbf{false}) \quad \Omega & \\
\diagup \quad \diagdown & \\
\Omega \quad \mathbf{true} &
\end{array}
\qquad
\begin{array}{cc}
f(\mathbf{true})(\Omega) & \\
\diagup \quad \diagdown & \\
f(\Omega)(\mathbf{true}) \quad \Omega & \\
\diagup \quad \diagdown & \\
f(\mathbf{false})(\mathbf{false}) \quad \Omega & \\
\diagup \quad \diagdown & \\
\Omega \quad \mathbf{false} &
\end{array}
$$

a pair of programs that cannot be distinguished operationally in any ground context? Viewed in this way, it is possible to see full abstraction as a *completeness* property of the model relative to the operational semantics.

There are several ways to show that this completeness fails for $\mathcal{C}[\![\cdot]\!]$. Since the machinery is already available to us, let us consider a semantic proof using the 'non-standard' interpretation $\mathcal{D}[\![\cdot]\!]$ in dI-domains. Using the methods appropriate for $\mathcal{D}[\![\cdot]\!]$, it is possible to obtain the analog for dI-domains of Proposition 6.2:

6.3 Proposition. *If M is a closed, well-typed term of PCF and $\mathcal{D}[\![M]\!] \sqsubseteq \mathcal{D}[\![N]\!]$, then $M \sqsubseteq_o N$.*   □

To prove that full abstraction fails for $\mathcal{C}[\![\cdot]\!]$, we need to demonstrate two terms that have the same operational behavior in all ground contexts but fail to be equal in the model. To this end, let

$$T, F : (\mathbf{bool} \rightarrow (\mathbf{bool} \rightarrow \mathbf{bool})) \rightarrow \mathbf{bool}$$

be the PCF terms given in Table 6.1. The term F is the same as T except for yielding a value of **false** in the fifth line. It may make it a bit easier to understand the code for

Table 6.2
Truth Tables for Parallel and Sequential Disjunction

por	true	false	$\perp$
true	true	true	true
false	true	false	$\perp$
$\perp$	true	$\perp$	$\perp$

or	true	false	$\perp$
true	true	true	true
false	true	false	$\perp$
$\perp$	$\perp$	$\perp$	$\perp$

T and F by looking at tree representations that indicate the results of the boolean tests involved in the clauses. These are given below the respective programs with the idea that the left branch represents the result of a boolean test that is **true**, and a right branch, one that is **false**.

Now, the programs T and F have the same operational behavior in all ground contexts. To see this, it suffices, by Proposition 6.3 to show that $\mathcal{D}[\![T]\!] = \mathcal{D}[\![F]\!]$. We show, in fact, that $\mathcal{D}[\![T]\!](\emptyset) = \mathcal{D}[\![F]\!](\emptyset) : f \mapsto \perp$, where $\emptyset$ is the arid environment (which makes no assignments). To this end, suppose $\mathcal{D}[\![T]\!](\emptyset)(f) \neq \perp$. This can only happen if $\mathcal{D}[\![T]\!](\emptyset)(f) = \textbf{true}$. If $f'(x, y) = f(x)(y)$ is the 'uncurrying' of f, then

$$f(\perp)(\perp) = f'(\perp, \perp) = f'((\textbf{true}, \perp) \sqcap (\perp, \textbf{true})) = f'(\textbf{true}, \perp) \sqcap f'(\perp, \textbf{true}) = \textbf{true}$$

since f' is stable. On the other hand, $f(\textbf{false})(\textbf{false}) = f'(\textbf{false}, \textbf{false}) = \textbf{false}$, and this contradicts the monotonicity of f! A similar argument applies to F so we can conclude that the terms T and F have the same operational behavior. Indeed, they both have the same operational behavior as $\lambda x. \Omega$. Switching now to the interpretations of these terms in the cpo semantics, we can show that $\mathcal{C}[\![T]\!] \neq \mathcal{C}[\![F]\!]$. To do this, consider a function $\textsf{por} : \mathbb{T} \to [\mathbb{T} \to \mathbb{T}]$, called the *parallel or*, defined by the left truth table in Table 6.2 where the values in the left column are those of the first argument and the values in the top row are those of the second argument. This can be contrasted with the truth table for the (left-to-right) sequential or defined by

$$\textsf{or} = \mathcal{C}[\![\lambda x : \textbf{bool}. \, \lambda y : \textbf{bool}. \, \textbf{if } x \textbf{ then true else } y]\!](\emptyset).$$

Note the difference in the value of $\textsf{or}(\perp)(\textbf{true})$ in the truth table for **or** given in Table 6.2. Now, the function **por** is monotone and therefore continuous, so it is an element of the interpretation $\mathcal{C}[\![\textbf{bool} \to (\textbf{bool} \to \textbf{bool})]\!]$. Hence

$$\mathcal{C}[\![T]\!](\emptyset)(\textsf{por}) = \textbf{true} \neq \textbf{false} = \mathcal{C}[\![F]\!](\emptyset)(\textsf{por})$$

so $\mathcal{C}[\![T]\!] \neq \mathcal{C}[\![F]\!]$, and $\mathcal{C}[\![\cdot]\!]$ is therefore not fully abstract.

Extending the language.

What is the problem here? There are two ways to view it: either our interpretation of the types by $\mathcal{C}[\![\cdot]\!]$ has 'too many elements', causing operationally indistinguishable programs to be given different meanings, or our programming language has too few contexts for distinguishing program behaviors. For the specific case of the programs T, F we have been discussing, the problem is related to the absence in PCF of a program whose meaning is the function **por**. It is not hard to see how one might add such a function as a new primitive **por** which could be written as an infix with the following operational rules:

$$\frac{M \Downarrow \textbf{true}}{M \textbf{ por } N \Downarrow \textbf{true}} \qquad \frac{N \Downarrow \textbf{true}}{M \textbf{ por } N \Downarrow \textbf{true}} \qquad \frac{M \Downarrow \textbf{false} \quad N \Downarrow \textbf{false}}{M \textbf{ por } N \Downarrow \textbf{false}}$$

Note that or cannot be the interpretation of **por** since this would violate the soundness of the second operational rule. The rules make clearer my use of term 'parallel or' since there are *two* rules for the evaluation of M **por** N. Intuitively, evaluation could proceed as follows: to evaluate M **por** N, assign a processor the task of evaluating M and assign another processor the task of evaluating N. If one of the processors terminates its evaluation with a value of **true**, then the result of evaluating M **por** N is **true**. If both processors terminate with a value of **false**, then the result of evaluating M **por** N is **false**. Of course, the outcome of the evaluation is deterministic even though the evaluation is intuitively parallel.

Our goal now is to show how $\mathcal{C}[\![\cdot]\!]$ can be made a fully abstract semantics for an expansion of the language PCF. Although this can be done simply by adding the construct **por** defined above, it is more convenient, for technical reasons, to use another form of parallel construct known as the *parallel conditional*. The new language PCF+**pif** is obtained by expanding the grammar of PCF to permit expressions of the form **pif** L **then** M **else** N. The calculus PCF+**pif** is the extension of PCF obtained by adding the parallel conditional construct together with its typing and operational rules as given in Table 6.3. The two rules at the top are the typing rules, and the three remaining rules are the additional operational rules. In the typing rules note that branches of the parallel conditional must have ground type. Let us refer to these as the parallel conditional *for booleans* and the parallel conditional *for numbers*. Note the last rule, which distinguishes the parallel conditional from the sequential conditional in PCF. A corresponding fixed-point interpretation of the parallel conditional can be given as follows:

$$\mathcal{C}[\![\textbf{pif } L \textbf{ then } M \textbf{ else } N]\!]\rho = \begin{cases} [\![M]\!]\rho & \text{if } [\![L]\!]\rho = \textsf{true} \\ [\![N]\!]\rho & \text{if } [\![L]\!]\rho = \textsf{false} \\ [\![N]\!]\rho & \text{if } [\![L]\!]\rho = \bot \text{ and } [\![M]\!]\rho = [\![N]\!]\rho \\ \bot & \text{otherwise} \end{cases}$$

Table 6.3
Typing and Operational Rules for the Parallel Conditional

$$\frac{H \vdash L : \textbf{bool} \qquad H \vdash M : \textbf{bool} \qquad H \vdash N : \textbf{bool}}{H \vdash \textbf{pif } L \textbf{ then } M \textbf{ else } N : \textbf{bool}}$$

$$\frac{H \vdash L : \textbf{bool} \qquad H \vdash M : \textbf{num} \qquad H \vdash N : \textbf{num}}{H \vdash \textbf{pif } L \textbf{ then } M \textbf{ else } N : \textbf{num}}$$

$$\frac{L \Downarrow \textbf{true} \qquad M \Downarrow V}{\textbf{pif } L \textbf{ then } M \textbf{ else } N \Downarrow V} \qquad\qquad \frac{L \Downarrow \textbf{false} \qquad N \Downarrow V}{\textbf{pif } L \textbf{ then } M \textbf{ else } N \Downarrow V}$$

$$\frac{M \Downarrow V \qquad N \Downarrow V}{\textbf{pif } L \textbf{ then } M \textbf{ else } N \Downarrow V}$$

This semantic equation makes sense for the parallel conditional on both numbers and booleans. It is possible to show that the parallel conditional on numbers can be used to define the one on booleans. This and the proof that the parallel conditional can be used to define the parallel or are left as exercises. To complete the demonstration that parallel or, parallel conditional for booleans, and parallel conditional for numbers are all definable in terms of one another, it therefore only remains to prove that the last can be defined in terms of the first. To see how we might define the parallel conditional

$$\textbf{pif } x \textbf{ then } y \textbf{ else } z \tag{6.1}$$

as a function of a boolean x and numbers y, z, note first that there are three circumstances in which the value of 6.1 is a number n. This can happen if

1. x is **true** and y is n, or
2. x is **false** and z is n, or
3. y and z are equal to n

This suggests that 6.1 could be defined using a function that checks these conditions for each number n, returning n in case any of them is found to be satisfied. Define

not $\equiv \lambda x : \textbf{bool. if } x \textbf{ then false else true}$

to be the PCF syntax for negation. If we also define disjunction by

or $\equiv \lambda x : \textbf{bool. } \lambda y : \textbf{bool. if } x \textbf{ then true else (if } y \textbf{ then true else false)},$

then conjunction can be defined by

$$\textbf{and} \equiv \lambda x : \textbf{bool}. \ \lambda y : \textbf{bool}. \ \textbf{not}(\textbf{or}(\textbf{not}(x))(\textbf{not}(y))).$$

Let $=$ be the equality predicate (its definition in PCF was an exercise). We might use these operators in an attempt to render the desired condition for x, y, z, n using the predicate

$$P \equiv (x \ \textbf{and} \ (y = n)) \ \textbf{or} \ (\textbf{not}(x) \ \textbf{and} \ (z = n)) \ \textbf{or} \ ((y = n) \ \textbf{and} \ (z = n)).$$

The reader may see already that something is wrong here. If, for example, y and z are equal to n, then this predicate may still not have a value of **true** since it is possible that $x = \bot$ and then the value of P is $\bot$. This is where the parallel or is needed. To get the right predicate, it is necessary to use the parallel versions of the logical connectives. Say

$$\textbf{pand} \equiv \lambda x : \textbf{bool}. \ \lambda y : \textbf{bool}. \ \textbf{not}(\textbf{por}(\textbf{not}(x))(\textbf{not}(y)))$$

and define

$$Q \equiv (x \ \textbf{pand} \ (y = n)) \ \textbf{por} \ (\textbf{not}(x) \ \textbf{pand} \ (z = n)) \ \textbf{por} \ ((y = n) \ \textbf{pand} \ (z = n)).$$

Now we can determine the value of 6.1 by testing whether it is equal to n for each number n and returning the lucky number if there is one. Putting this more denotationally, we can define 6.1 as the least upper bound of a chain of values d_k such that d_k is the meaning of the k'th unwinding of a conditional test. To be precise, define

$$F \equiv \mu f : \textbf{num} \to \textbf{num}. \ \lambda n : \textbf{num}. \ \textbf{if} \ Q \ \textbf{then} \ n \ \textbf{else} \ f(\textbf{succ}(n)).$$

Then we can define the parallel conditional by the program

$$\lambda x : \textbf{bool}. \ \lambda y : \textbf{num}. \ \lambda z : \textbf{num}. \ F(0).$$

By expanding the inductions needed to prove the necessary properties, it is possible to show that $\mathcal{C}[\![\cdot]\!]$ is a sound and adequate interpretation for PCF+**pif**. In order to prove that $\mathcal{C}[\![\cdot]\!]$ is, moreover, fully abstract for PCF+**pif**, we begin with the observation that $\mathcal{C}[\![t]\!]$ is a bc-domain for every type expression t. This follows immediately from Theorem 5.8 and the fact that $\mathbb{T}$ and $\mathbb{N}_\bot$ are bc-domains. The proof of full abstraction is based on two key lemmas. The first of these is the Adequacy Theorem and the second is a result called the *Definability Lemma*. If t is a type, an element $d \in \mathcal{C}[\![t]\!]$ is said to be *definable* (with respect to the semantics $\mathcal{C}[\![\cdot]\!]$) if there is a term M such that $\vdash M : t$ and $\mathcal{C}[\![M]\!](\emptyset) = d$. The Definability Lemma asserts that, for any type t, every compact element of $\mathcal{C}[\![t]\!]$ is definable. The Full Abstraction Theorem can then be proved using this and Adequacy.

The proof of the Definability Lemma is non-trivial. It is essential to develop a few basic facts about the form of a compact element of higher type in order to carry out the argument. Let us begin with a basic syntactic fact:

6.4 Lemma. *Any type of PCF has the form $t_1 \to t_2 \to \cdots t_n \to s$ where s is a ground type.* □

The proof of the lemma is left for the reader. Now, every compact element of the continuous function space between two bc-domains is a finite join of step functions $a \searrow b$ where a, b are compact (see the proof of Theorem 5.8, the definition is given in Equation 5.1). Moreover, $a \searrow (b \sqcup b')$ is equal to $(a \searrow b) \sqcup (a \searrow b')$ whenever the joins exist. From these observations it can be shown that each compact element of the interpretation $\mathcal{C}[\![t]\!]$ of a type expression t is a join of a finite set F of compact elements satisfying the following two conditions:

1. Each element of F has the form $(a_1 \searrow (a_2 \searrow (\cdots (a_n \searrow b) \cdots)))$ where $a_i \in \mathsf{KC}[\![t_i]\!]$ for each i and $b \neq \bot$.

2. If $(a_1 \searrow (a_2 \searrow \cdots (a_n \searrow b) \cdots))$ and $(a'_1 \searrow (a'_2 \searrow \cdots (a'_n \searrow b') \cdots))$ are in F and $a_i \uparrow a'_i$ for each i, then $b = b'$.

In fact, a set F satisfying the first of these conditions also satisfies the second one if, and only if, it is consistent. For the purposes of the proof of definability, let us say that a finite set of compact elements that satisfies (1) and (2) is *crisp*.

6.5 Lemma (Definability). *For every type t of PCF with the parallel conditional, the compact elements of $\mathcal{C}[\![t]\!]$ are definable.*

Proof: The proof is by structural induction on the type t, but it is necessary to work with a strengthened induction hypothesis. It is shown that, for each type expression t,

$$\forall a \in \mathsf{KC}[\![t]\!].\ a \text{ is definable.} \tag{6.2}$$

$$\forall a \in \mathsf{KC}[\![t]\!].\ a \searrow \mathsf{true} \text{ is definable.} \tag{6.3}$$

$$\forall a, a' \in \mathsf{KC}[\![t]\!].\ (a \searrow \mathsf{true}) \sqcup (a' \searrow \mathsf{false}) \text{ is definable if it exists.} \tag{6.4}$$

I will leave the base cases in which t is a ground type for the reader. Suppose t has the form $t_1 \to t_2 \to \cdots t_n \to s$ where s is a ground type and suppose that 6.2, 6.3, and 6.4 are all known for s and each type t_i for $i \leq n$. I will give a detailed proof of 6.2 and the key definition for each of the other two.

The element a is definable. The proof is by induction on the least number n such that there is a crisp set F with n elements such that $a = \bigsqcup F$. If a is a compact element for which this number is zero, then $F = \emptyset$, so $a = \bot$ and then a is definable by Ω_t. Suppose that an element $a' \in KC[\![t]\!]$ is definable if there is a crisp set F' with fewer than n elements such that $a' = \bigsqcup F'$. Suppose now that $a = \bigsqcup F$ where F is crisp and has n elements. We consider two cases.

First case. Suppose there are functions

$$f = (a_1 \searrow (a_2 \searrow \cdots (a_n \searrow b) \cdots)) \text{ and } f' = (a'_1 \searrow (a'_2 \searrow \cdots (a_n \searrow b') \cdots)) \in F$$

such that, for some i, the elements a_i and a'_i are inconsistent. Then $(a_i \searrow \text{true}) \sqcup (a'_i \searrow \text{false})$ exists, so, by the inductive hypothesis 6.4 on the structure of t, this function is definable by a term L. Now, the sets $F - \{f\}$ and $F - \{f'\}$ are crisp sets with fewer members than F so, by the inductive hypothesis on crisp sets, the elements $\bigsqcup F - \{f\}$ and $\bigsqcup F - \{f'\}$ are definable by terms N and N' respectively. Let

$$M \equiv \lambda x_1 : t_1 \ldots \lambda x_n : t_n.$$
$$\mathbf{pif}\ L(x_i)\ \mathbf{then}\ N'(x_1) \cdots (x_n)\ \mathbf{else}\ N(x_1) \cdots (x_n)$$

I claim that $\bigsqcup F$ is defined by M. To see this, let $d_j \in C[\![t_j]\!]$ for each $j \leq n$. There are three possibilities for d_i. If $d_i \sqsupseteq a_i$, then $C[\![L]\!](\emptyset)(d_i) = \text{true}$ and $f'(d_1) \cdots (d_n) = \bot$ so

$$(\bigsqcup F)(d_1) \cdots (d_n) = (\bigsqcup F - \{f'\})(d_1) \cdots (d_n)$$
$$= C[\![N']\!](\emptyset)(d_1) \cdots (d_n)$$
$$= C[\![M]\!](\emptyset)(d_1) \cdots (d_n).$$

A similar argument holds if $d_i \sqsupseteq a'_i$. These two possibilities are mutually exclusive since a_i and a'_i are inconsistent. Hence, the remaining possibility is that $d_i \not\sqsupseteq a_i$ and also $d_i \not\sqsupseteq a'_i$. In this case $f(d_1) \cdots (d_n) = f'(d_1) \cdots (d_n) = \bot$ so

$$(\bigsqcup F)(d_1) \cdots (d_n) = (\bigsqcup F - \{f\})(d_1) \cdots (d_n) = (\bigsqcup F - \{f'\})(d_1) \cdots (d_n).$$

It is now possible to appreciate the role of the parallel conditional. Since the values of the two branches of M are the same, the parallel conditional has the same value as each of the branches despite the fact that the test L has $\bot$ as its meaning. In particular, the sequential conditional would not work because the value of the conditional with L as its test would simply be $\bot$ (which might not be equal to $\bigsqcup F$). On the other hand, by the semantics for the parallel conditional, $C[\![M]\!](\emptyset)(d_1) \cdots (d_n) = (\bigsqcup F)(d_1) \cdots (d_n)$.

Second case. Suppose $a_i \uparrow a'_i$ for every a_i, a'_i such that there are functions

$$(a_1 \searrow (a_2 \searrow \cdots (a_n \searrow b) \cdots)) \text{ and } (a'_1 \searrow (a'_2 \searrow \cdots (a'_n \searrow b') \cdots)) \in F.$$

In this case $b = b'$. By the inductive hypothesis for 6.3 there are terms M_i defining $(a_i \searrow \text{true})$ for each $i \leq n$ and, by the structural inductive hypothesis for 6.2, there is a term M that defines b. Moreover, by the inductive hypothesis on crisp sets, there is a term N that defines $\bigsqcup F - \{f\}$. Finally, then, the following expression defines $\bigsqcup F$:

$$\lambda x_1 : t_1 \ldots \lambda x_n : t_n.$$
$$\textbf{pif } (M_1(x_1) \textbf{ and } \cdots \textbf{ and } M_n(x_n)) \textbf{ then } M \textbf{ else } N(x_1) \cdots (x_n)$$

where **and** is written as an infix to make the term more readable.

The function $a \searrow \text{true} : t \to \textbf{bool}$ *is definable.* Again, the proof is by induction on the least number n such that there is a crisp set F with n elements such that $a = \bigsqcup F$. If this number is zero, then $a \searrow \text{true}$ is defined by $\lambda x : t. \textbf{ true}$. Suppose that $a' \searrow \text{true}$ is known to be definable whenever there is a crisp set F' with fewer than n elements such that $a' = \bigsqcup F'$. Say $a = \bigsqcup F$ where F has n elements, and no crisp set with fewer elements has a as a least upper bound. Let $F' = F - \{f\}$ where

$$f = (a_1 \searrow (a_2 \searrow \cdots (a_n \searrow b) \cdots) \in F.$$

Now F' has fewer elements than F so, by the inductive hypothesis on crisp sets, there is a term N that defines $(\bigsqcup F') \searrow \text{true}$. By the structural inductive hypothesis on types for 6.3, there is also a term M that defines $b \searrow \text{true}$ and, by the structural inductive hypothesis for 6.2, there is a term M_i that defines a_i for each $i \leq n$. The term

$$\lambda x : t. \textbf{ if } M(x(M_1) \cdots (M_n)) \textbf{ then } N(x) \textbf{ else } \Omega_{\textbf{bool}}$$

then defines $a \searrow \text{true}$.

The function $(a \searrow \text{true}) \sqcup (a' \searrow \text{false}) : t \to \textbf{bool}$ *is definable if it exists.* Say $a = \bigsqcup F$ and $a' = \bigsqcup F'$ for crisp sets F and F'. If $(a \searrow \text{true}) \sqcup (a' \searrow \text{false})$ exists, then a and a' are inconsistent, so there are

$$(a_1 \searrow (a_2 \searrow \cdots (a_n \searrow b) \cdots)) \in F \text{ and } (a'_1 \searrow (a'_2 \searrow \cdots (a_n \searrow b') \cdots)) \in F'$$

such that $a_i \uparrow a'_i$ for each i, but $b \neq b'$. By 6.2 there are terms M_i that define $a_i \sqcup a'_i$ for each $i \leq n$. By the inductive hypothesis on types for 6.4, there is a term M' that defines $(b \searrow \text{true}) \sqcup (b' \searrow \text{false})$. By 6.3 (which we established for type t in the proceeding paragraph) there is a term N that defines $a \searrow \text{true}$ and a term N' that defines $a' \searrow \text{true}$. Then the following term

$$\lambda x : t. \textbf{ if } M'(x(M_1) \cdots (M_n)) \textbf{ then } N(x) \textbf{ else } \textbf{not}(N'(x))$$

defines $(a \searrow \text{true}) \sqcup (a' \searrow \text{false})$. $\square$

The readers who have made their way through the proof of the Definability Lemma above are due some special reward for their diligence. For those who have not worked through the proof, it will still be easy to appreciate how the lemma can be used to establish full abstraction (although said readers will not appreciate the use of the parallel conditional!).

6.6 Theorem (Full Abstraction). $\mathcal{C}[\![\cdot]\!]$ *is fully abstract for PCF+***pif***.*

Proof: Suppose M and N are PCF+**pif** terms such that $H \vdash M : t$ and $H \vdash N : t$. Assume first that the type assignment H is empty and M, N are closed terms such that $M \sqsubseteq_o N$ but $\mathcal{C}[\![M]\!] \not\sqsubseteq \mathcal{C}[\![N]\!]$. Then there are domain elements $a_1, \ldots, a_n$ such that $a = \mathcal{C}[\![M]\!](\emptyset)(a_1) \cdots (a_n)$ and $a' = \mathcal{C}[\![N]\!](\emptyset)(a_1) \cdots (a_n)$ are of ground type, $a \neq \bot$, and $a \neq a'$. Since ground types satisfy the acc, we may assume, moreover, that $a_1, \ldots, a_n$ are compact. By the Definability Lemma, there are terms $M_1, \ldots, M_n$ of PCF+**pif** such that $\mathcal{C}[\![M_i]\!](\emptyset) = a_i$ for each $i \leq n$. Since $a \neq \bot$, by adequacy there is a value V such that $M(M_1) \cdots (M_n) \Downarrow V$. Since $M \sqsubseteq_o N$, we must also have $N(M_1) \cdots (M_n) \Downarrow V$. But $a \neq a'$, so this contradicts the fact that evaluation preserves meaning. Hence we must have $\mathcal{C}[\![M]\!] \sqsubseteq \mathcal{C}[\![N]\!]$. Now, to prove the general case, suppose $H \equiv x_1 : t_1, \ldots, x_n : t_n$. Then

$$\vdash \lambda x_1 : t_1 \ldots \lambda x_n : t_n. \, M : t_1 \to (t_2 \to \cdots (t_n \to t) \cdots) \qquad \text{and}$$
$$\vdash \lambda x_1 : t_1 \ldots \lambda x_n : t_n. \, N : t_1 \to (t_2 \to \cdots (t_n \to t) \cdots).$$

Since $M \sqsubseteq_o N$ we must have

$$\lambda x_1 : t_1 \ldots \lambda x_n : t_n. \, M \sqsubseteq_o \lambda x_1 : t_1 \ldots \lambda x_n : t_n. \, N$$

as well, so $\mathcal{C}[\![\lambda x_1 \ldots \lambda x_n. \, M]\!] \sqsubseteq \mathcal{C}[\![\lambda x_1 \ldots \lambda x_n. \, N]\!]$. Hence $\mathcal{C}[\![M]\!] \sqsubseteq \mathcal{C}[\![N]\!]$ as desired. $\square$

One corollary of this result is the following: a term M of higher type is operationally equivalent to another term N of that type if, and only if, they have the same operational behavior in all applicative contexts of ground type. That is, for every sequence $P_1, \ldots, P_n$ such that $M' \equiv M(P_1) \cdots (P_n)$ and $N' \equiv N(P_1) \cdots (P_n)$ are of ground type, $M' \Downarrow V$ if, and only if, $N' \Downarrow V$. A more general statement of this property is given by the following:

6.7 Lemma (Context). *Let M and N be terms of type $s \to t$. $M \sqsubseteq_o N$ if, and only if, for every term P of type s, $M(P) \sqsubseteq_o N(P)$.* $\square$

Proof of the lemma is left as an exercise.

Exercises.

6.1 Prove that $\sqsubseteq_o$ is a pre-order.

6.2 Suppose L and M are well-typed PCF terms with the same type (using type assignment H). Show that $L \sqsubseteq_o M$ if, and only if, for any variable x and term tree N such that $\{L/x\}N$ and $\{M/x\}N$ are closed, well-typed terms of type **num**,

$$\{L/x\}N \Downarrow \mathbf{0} \text{ implies } \{M/x\}N \Downarrow \mathbf{0}.$$

(In other words, observing $\mathbf{0}$ alone yields the same operational approximation relation.)

6.3 Show that $\mathcal{C}[\![\cdot]\!]$ is a sound and adequate interpretation for PCF+**pif** by explaining how to extend the inductions used to prove that PCF is sound and adequate. (Assume that an appropriate generalization of Lemma 4.26 holds.)

6.4 Complete the proof that the three parallel constructs can all be defined in terms of one another by showing that

 a. parallel or can be defined using the parallel conditional for booleans, and
 b. the parallel conditional for booleans can be defined using the one for numbers.

6.5 Prove Lemma 6.4 and show that each compact element of the interpretation $\mathcal{C}[\![t]\!]$ of a type expression t of PCF is equal to the lub of a crisp set of compact elements of $\mathcal{C}[\![t]\!]$.

6.6 Carry out the base case of the induction in the proof of the Definability Lemma.

6.7 Prove the Context Lemma (that is, Lemma 6.7).

6.8 Find transition rules for the parallel or and parallel conditional to extend the transition semantics given for PCF in Table 4.3 so that it includes these constructs.

6.9* Although it was shown that continuous functions are not a fully abstract model for PCF (without parallel conditional), the question of whether dI-domains might be a fully abstract model was not answered. In fact, they are not a fully abstract model. To prove that this is the case, it is possible to turn around the trick with dI-domains that was used to show that the continuous model is not fully abstract and instead to use the continuous model to demonstrate that dI-domains are not fully abstract! The continuous model can be used to show that two terms with different meanings in the dI-domains model have the same operational behavior. To this end, define monotone functions p, q on the truth value poset by taking $p : x \mapsto$ **true** and taking q to be the function

$$q(x) = \begin{cases} \bot & \text{if } x = \bot \\ \text{true} & \text{otherwise.} \end{cases}$$

a. Prove that the following function is an element of $\mathcal{D}[\![(\textbf{bool} \rightarrow \textbf{bool}) \rightarrow \textbf{bool}]\!]$:

$$r(x) = \begin{cases} \textsf{true} & \text{if } x = p \\ \textsf{false} & \text{if } x = q \\ \bot & \text{otherwise.} \end{cases}$$

b. Demonstrate programs M and N such that $\mathcal{D}[\![M]\!](r) \neq \mathcal{D}[\![N]\!](r)$ but $\mathcal{C}[\![M]\!] = \mathcal{C}[\![N]\!]$.

c. Conclude that dI-domains are not a fully abstract model.

6.10 Suppose M, M' are closed PCF terms of type $\textbf{num} \rightarrow \textbf{num}$ and N, N' are closed PCF terms of type $\textbf{num}$ such that

- $\mathcal{D}[\![M]\!] \sqsubseteq_s \mathcal{D}[\![M']\!]$,
- $\mathcal{D}[\![N]\!] \sqsubseteq \mathcal{D}[\![N']\!]$, and
- $M(N')$ and $M'(N)$ both converge (that is, there are values U, V such that $M(N') \Downarrow U$ and $M'(N) \Downarrow V$).

Prove that $M(N)$ converges.

6.11* Show that the result in Exercise 6.10 fails for the continuous functions model. That is, demonstrate closed PCF terms M, M' of type $\textbf{num} \rightarrow \textbf{num}$ and N, N' of type $\textbf{num}$ such that

- $\mathcal{C}[\![M]\!] \sqsubseteq \mathcal{C}[\![M']\!]$,
- $\mathcal{C}[\![N]\!] \sqsubseteq \mathcal{C}[\![N']\!]$, and
- $M(N')$ and $M'(N)$ both converge.

but $M(N)$ diverges.

6.2   Extensions of Adequacy Results

After soundness, adequacy is the most basic property for relating fixed-point and operational semantics of a language. As such, it is a property that needs to be established for many languages and it is therefore worthwhile to have a good proof technique for it. It would be nice to have a lemma saying that if a simple property holds for fixed-point and operational semantics then adequacy follows, but it is too much to hope that a proof of adequacy for a given language will always be easy. Although the proof of the Adequacy Theorem (that is, Theorem 4.24) given in Section 4.3 is an intuitive one that draws on proof-theoretic ideas in a straightforward way, it is possible to prove this result in a more succinct way using the concept of an *inclusive subset*. An inclusive subset is a downwards closed subset of a cpo that is closed under limits of ω-chains. The proof technique to be introduced in this section uses a family of inclusive subsets determined by well-typed closed terms to organize the induction needed to establish adequacy.

Rather than simply reprove the result for PCF given in Theorem 4.24, it is more interesting to move on to an examination of the relationship between two interpretations of another language.

Adequacy at higher types.

Consider the following:

Conjecture: Suppose M is a term of PCF that has type t. Then $\mathcal{C}[\![M]\!] \neq \bot$ if, and only if, $M \Downarrow V$ for some V.

One direction of the conjecture holds: if $\mathcal{C}[\![M]\!] \neq \bot$, then there is a V such that $M \Downarrow V$. The converse also holds for the ground types, but there is a problem for higher types. For example,

$$\mathcal{C}[\![\lambda x : \textbf{bool}.\ \Omega_{\textbf{bool}}]\!] = \mathcal{C}[\![\Omega_{\textbf{bool}\rightarrow\textbf{bool}}]\!] = \bot$$

but

$$\lambda x : \textbf{bool}.\ \Omega \Downarrow \lambda x : \textbf{bool}.\ \Omega.$$

To make the conjecture work, we must change either the operational semantics or the fixed-point semantics for the abstractions. Both approaches are of interest, but I will only discuss the possibility of altering the fixed-point semantics since the operational semantics we have given matches the one used in the vast majority of higher-order functional programming languages. The problem with our denotational semantics is related to the concept of *delay* that one sees in functional languages. An abstraction introduces a degree of laziness in the evaluation of a program. For instance, we distinguish between the program $\lambda x.\ \Omega$, which diverges whenever it is applied, and the program Ω, which simply diverges. In short, the abstraction 'protects' the body from immediate evaluation. To model this concept in a domain, there is an extremely useful operation known as 'lifting', which we now define.

Given a cpo D, we define the *lift* of D to be the set $D_\bot = (D \times \{0\}) \cup \{\bot\}$, where $\bot$ is a new element that is not a pair, together with an partial ordering $\sqsubseteq$ given by stipulating that

$$(x, 0) \sqsubseteq (y, 0) \text{ if } x \sqsubseteq y$$

and

$$\bot \sqsubseteq z \text{ for every } z \in D_\bot.$$

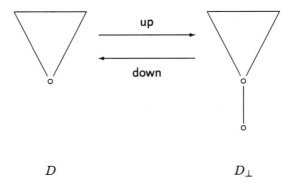

$$D \qquad\qquad\qquad\qquad D_\perp$$

Figure 6.1
The Lift of a Cpo

In short, $D_\perp$ is the poset obtained by adding a new bottom to D (see Figure 6.1). It is easy to show that $D_\perp$ is a cpo if D is. Define a strict continuous function $\mathsf{down} : D_\perp \multimap D$ by

$$\mathsf{down}(z) = \begin{cases} x & \text{if } z = (x,0) \\ \perp_D & \text{otherwise} \end{cases}$$

and a (non-strict) continuous function $\mathsf{up} : D \to D_\perp$ given by $\mathsf{up} : x \mapsto (x,0)$. These functions are related by

$$\mathsf{down} \circ \mathsf{up} = \mathsf{id}_D$$
$$\mathsf{up} \circ \mathsf{down} \sqsupseteq \mathsf{id}_{D_\perp}$$

which can both be proved by considering the cases for their arguments. To see the inequation for instance, note that

$$(\mathsf{up} \circ \mathsf{down})(x,0) = \mathsf{up}(x) = (x,0)$$
$$(\mathsf{up} \circ \mathsf{down})(\perp_{D_\perp}) = \mathsf{up}(\perp_D) = (\perp_D, 0) \sqsupseteq \perp_{D_\perp}.$$

The basic equational characterization of the lifting operation is described by the following:

6.8 Lemma. *Given cpo's D and E and continuous function $f : D \to E$, there is a unique strict continuous function $f^\dagger$ that completes the following diagram:*

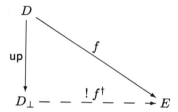

Proof: The desired properties hold for $f^\dagger = f \circ \mathsf{down}$. $\square$

Note that the uniqueness property of the arrow completing the diagram in the lemma implies that the following equation

$$g = (g \circ \mathsf{up})^\dagger \tag{6.5}$$

holds for each function $g : D_\perp \to E$. In fact, Equation 6.5 is equivalent to the uniqueness condition. To see why, suppose that 6.5 holds and $f = g \circ \mathsf{up}$ (that is, g completes the diagram in the lemma), then $f^\dagger = (g \circ \mathsf{up})^\dagger = g$. It is also possible to define a lifting functor; its action on objects (cpo's) is as already given, and, for each function $g : D \to E$,

$$g_\perp = (\mathsf{up} \circ g)^\dagger.$$

defines the action on arrows.

Returning now to the issue of adequacy at higher types for **PCF**, let us modify the semantics of PCF by altering the interpretation of higher type expressions and the interpretations for application and abstraction. The new semantics will account for the idea that an abstraction does not diverge. Let us call the new semantic function $\hat{\mathcal{C}}[\![\cdot]\!]$. For ground types, the interpretation is the same as for $\mathcal{C}[\![\cdot]\!]$ but for higher types we take:

$$\hat{\mathcal{C}}[\![s \to t]\!] = [\hat{\mathcal{C}}[\![s]\!] \to \hat{\mathcal{C}}[\![t]\!]]_\perp$$

and accordingly the definitions of abstraction and application are defined using the needed ups and downs:

$$\hat{\mathcal{C}}[\![H \rhd \lambda x.\, M : s \to t]\!]\rho = \mathsf{up}(\lambda d \in [\![s]\!].\, \hat{\mathcal{C}}[\![H, x : s \rhd M : t]\!]\rho[x \mapsto d])$$
$$\hat{\mathcal{C}}[\![H \rhd M(N) : t]\!]\rho = \mathsf{down}(\hat{\mathcal{C}}[\![H \rhd M : t]\!]\rho)(\hat{\mathcal{C}}[\![H \rhd N : t]\!]\rho)$$

The semantic clauses for the other constructs remain the same as before. With this adjusted semantics, it is possible to get the desired conclusion:

6.9 Theorem. *Suppose M is a term of PCF that has type t. Then $\hat{\mathcal{C}}[\![M]\!] \neq \bot$ if, and only if, $M \Downarrow V$ for some V.*   □

In particular the meaning of $\lambda x : t.\ \Omega_s$ is $\mathsf{up}(d \mapsto \bot)$, which is not equal to $\bot_{\mathcal{C}[\![s \to t]\!]}$.

I will not work through the proof of the theorem here because it is quite similar to the proof of Theorem 6.12 below. However, let us assume for the moment that a proof can be given without the using the Unwinding Theorem and complete a promise made on page 135 to show that this syntactic result can be obtained from the Adequacy Theorem. That is, let us prove Theorem 4.34 as a corollary of Theorem 6.9. Let M be a pure PCF term of ground type and suppose there is a term P in bounded PCF such that $P^* \Downarrow U$ and $P^\dagger \equiv M$. The goal is to show that $M \Downarrow U$. First of all, a straight-forward induction will show that $\hat{\mathcal{C}}[\![P^*]\!] \sqsubseteq \hat{\mathcal{C}}[\![P^\dagger]\!]$ for any term P of bounded PCF. If $P^* \Downarrow U$, then $[\![P^*]\!]\emptyset \neq \bot$ so $[\![M]\!]\emptyset \neq \bot$ and therefore, by Theorem 6.9, $M \Downarrow V$ for some value V. But $\hat{\mathcal{C}}[\![U]\!] \sqsubseteq \hat{\mathcal{C}}[\![V]\!]$ and this can only be the case for non-bottom terms of ground type if $U \equiv V$. Hence $M \Downarrow U$ as desired.

Call-by-value.

Recall that the operational rule for the evaluation of an application was given as follows:

$$\frac{M \Downarrow \lambda x : t.\ L \qquad [N/x]L \Downarrow V}{M(N) \Downarrow V}$$

In this rule the unevaluated argument N of the application is substituted for the bound variable of the abstraction in its body. In fact, most programming languages do not evaluate an application in this way. Instead, the argument of the call is evaluated before substituting for the variable in the body of the operator. As mentioned earlier, evaluation using the rule above is termed *call-by-name*; by contrast, using a strategy that evaluates the argument before substitution is termed *call-by-value*. Call-by-value PCF has the same operational rules as those given for PCF in Table 4.4 except for the evaluation rule for application, which is replaced by the following rule:

$$\frac{M \Downarrow \lambda x : s.\ L \qquad N \Downarrow U \qquad [U/x]L \Downarrow V}{M(N) \Downarrow V}$$

Although it may not be obvious at first glance, the evaluation relations defined by these two sets of rules are *not* the same! To see why, consider the difference between the two relations on

$$M \equiv (\lambda x : \mathbf{num}.\ \mathbf{0})\Omega$$

under the two different forms of evaluation. In the case of call-by-name, $M \Downarrow \mathbf{0}$ because $[\Omega/x]\mathbf{0} \Downarrow \mathbf{0}$. However, in call-by-value we must find a value U such that $\Omega \Downarrow U$ before

Table 6.4
Natural Rules for Call-by-Value Evaluation of PCF

$$\mathbf{0} \Downarrow^\circ \mathbf{0} \qquad\qquad \mathbf{true} \Downarrow^\circ \mathbf{true} \qquad\qquad \mathbf{false} \Downarrow^\circ \mathbf{false}$$

$$\frac{M \Downarrow^\circ \mathbf{0}}{\mathbf{pred}(M) \Downarrow^\circ \mathbf{0}} \qquad \frac{M \Downarrow^\circ \mathbf{succ}(V)}{\mathbf{pred}(M) \Downarrow^\circ V} \qquad \frac{M \Downarrow^\circ V}{\mathbf{succ}(M) \Downarrow^\circ \mathbf{succ}(V)}$$

$$\frac{M \Downarrow^\circ \mathbf{0}}{\mathbf{zero?}(M) \Downarrow^\circ \mathbf{true}} \qquad \frac{M \Downarrow^\circ \mathbf{succ}(V)}{\mathbf{zero?}(M) \Downarrow^\circ \mathbf{false}}$$

$$\lambda x : s.\ M \Downarrow^\circ \lambda x : s.\ M \qquad \frac{M \Downarrow^\circ \lambda x : s.\ L \qquad N \Downarrow^\circ U \qquad [U/x]L \Downarrow^\circ V}{M(N) \Downarrow^\circ V}$$

$$\frac{M_1 \Downarrow^\circ \mathbf{true} \qquad M_2 \Downarrow^\circ V}{\mathbf{if}\ M_1\ \mathbf{then}\ M_2\ \mathbf{else}\ M_3 \Downarrow^\circ V} \qquad \frac{M_1 \Downarrow^\circ \mathbf{false} \qquad M_3 \Downarrow^\circ V}{\mathbf{if}\ M_1\ \mathbf{then}\ M_2\ \mathbf{else}\ M_3 \Downarrow^\circ V}$$

$$\frac{[\mu x : t.\ M/x]M \Downarrow^\circ V}{\mu x : t.\ M \Downarrow^\circ V}$$

---

we can press on with noting that $[U/x]\mathbf{0} \Downarrow \mathbf{0}$. But the call-by-value rule for recursion is no different from the one for call-by-name, and we are therefore faced with the fact that there is *no* value U that satisfies $\Omega \Downarrow U$. Hence, there is no value V such that $M \Downarrow V$, and, in particular, it is not the case that $M \Downarrow \mathbf{0}$. Because of this difference, it is essential to distinguish between the evaluation relations for call-by-name and call-by-value. For the former let us write $\Downarrow$ as before, but for the latter a small circle is placed as a superscript on the downward pointing arrow as a reminder of the different rule for application. The remaining rules are the same as those in Table 4.4, but the call-by-name rule for application is omitted and the symbol $\Downarrow$ replaced by $\Downarrow^\circ$. For complete clarity, the full set of rules is given in Table 6.4.

Unsurprisingly, the semantics $\mathcal{C}[\![\cdot]\!]$ is not adequate for the operational semantics defined by $\Downarrow^\circ$. For example,

$$\mathcal{C}[\![(\lambda x : \mathbf{num.}\ \mathbf{0})(\Omega)]\!]\emptyset = \mathcal{C}[\![\mathbf{0}]\!][x \mapsto \bot]\emptyset = \mathbf{0},$$

but it is *not* the case that

$$(\lambda x : \mathbf{num.}\ \mathbf{0})(\Omega) \Downarrow^\circ \mathbf{0}$$

because Ω must be evaluated before it is substituted into the body of the abstraction. What is wrong here? Since the application of a term to a divergent term is divergent, the meanings of the terms of higher type must be *strict* functions. This is the problem with the interpretation of $\lambda x : \mathbf{num}.\ \mathbf{0}$. Under a call-by-value semantics this term should not be interpreted as a constant function. A move to the semantics $\hat{C}[\![\cdot]\!]$ does not improve the situation as the reader can check in the case of $\lambda x : \mathbf{num}.\ \mathbf{0}$. To rectify the problem, we must modify our functions to deal properly with the case in which the argument is divergent. To this end, given a pair of cpo's D and E and a continuous function $f : D \to E$, define a continuous function $\mathsf{strict}(f) : D \to E$ as follows:

$$\mathsf{strict}(f)(x) = \left\{ \begin{array}{ll} f(x) & \text{if } x \neq \bot \\ \bot & \text{if } x = \bot \end{array} \right.$$

and define a new semantics for PCF by interpreting the higher type expressions and the applications and abstractions as follows:

$$C^{\circ}[\![s \to t]\!] = [C^{\circ}[\![s]\!] \multimap C^{\circ}[\![t]\!]]_{\bot}$$
$$C^{\circ}[\![H \triangleright \lambda x : s.\ M : s \to t]\!]\rho = \mathsf{up}(\mathsf{strict}(d \mapsto C^{\circ}[\![H, x : s \triangleright M : t]\!]\rho[x \mapsto d]))$$
$$C^{\circ}[\![H \triangleright M(N) : t]\!]\rho = \mathsf{down}(C^{\circ}[\![H \triangleright M : s \to t]\!]\rho)(C^{\circ}[\![H \triangleright N : s]\!]\rho)$$

The other constructs of the language are interpreted using the same semantic equations as before.

Many of the basic properties of call-by-name and call-by-value are similar. It is possible to show that whenever $M \Downarrow^{\circ} V$ and M has type t, then V also has type t. I leave for the reader the demonstrations that values are interpreted by non-bottom elements and evaluation preserves meaning with respect to $C^{\circ}[\![\cdot]\!]$. It is also possible to take a similar approach to the proof of adequacy for the semantics with respect to the evaluation relation. However, there is another way to prove adequacy that I will illustrate for the call-by-value calculus; the technique can also be used for call-by-name. A new concept is the key:

Definition: Let D be a cpo. A subset $U \subseteq D$ is said to be *inclusive* if it is downward closed and, for every ω-chain $(d)_{n \in \omega} \subseteq U$, the least upper bound $\bigsqcup_{n \in \omega} d_n$ is an element of U.   □

The idea is to define a family of inclusive subsets and use them to establish the necessary results relating syntax and semantics.

Definition: Define a family of relations $\lesssim_t$ between elements of $C^{\circ}[\![t]\!]$ on the left and closed terms of type t on the right as follows. For any $d \in C^{\circ}[\![t]\!]$ and term M of type t, define $d \lesssim_t M$ if

1. $d = \bot$, or
2. $M \Downarrow^{\circ} V$ for some V and $d \lesssim_t V$ where

- $f \precsim_{u \to v} \lambda x : u. \ N$ if, for each $d \in \mathcal{C}^\circ[\![u]\!]$ and value $U : u$,

$$d \precsim_u U \text{ implies } \mathsf{down}(f)(d) \precsim_v (\lambda x : u. \ N)(U).$$

- $\mathsf{true} \precsim_{\mathbf{bool}} \mathbf{true}$ and $\mathsf{false} \precsim_{\mathbf{bool}} \mathbf{false}$.

- $n \precsim_{\mathbf{num}} \underline{n}$. $\hfill \square$

As an immediate consequence of the definition, note that if $d \precsim_t M$ and $M \Downarrow V$, then $d \precsim_t V$.

6.10 Lemma. *For each type t and closed term M of type t, the set of elements $d \in \mathcal{C}^\circ[\![t]\!]$ such that $d \precsim_t M$ is inclusive. In other words,*

1. *If $d \sqsubseteq e \precsim_t M$, then $d \precsim_t M$.*
2. *If $(d_n)_{n \in \omega}$ is an ω-chain and $d_n \precsim_t M$ for each $n \in \omega$, then $\bigsqcup_{n \in \omega} d_n \precsim_t M$.*

Proof: The proof of each part is by induction on the structure of t. The base cases are straightforward. Suppose $t \equiv u \to v$ and $g \sqsubseteq f \precsim_{u \to v} M$. If $g = \bot$, then there is nothing to prove, so suppose $g \neq \bot$. In this case $f \neq \bot$ too, so $M \Downarrow^\circ \lambda x : u. \ M'$ for some M'. Following now the definition of $\precsim_t$ for higher types, suppose $d \in \mathcal{C}^\circ[\![u]\!]$ and $d \precsim_u U$ for some value U of type u. Then $g(d) \sqsubseteq f(d) \precsim_v (\lambda x : u. \ M')(U)$ so, by the inductive hypothesis on types, $g(d) \precsim_v (\lambda x : u. \ M')(U)$ as desired. Moving on now to the proof of the second part of the lemma for higher types, suppose $(f_n)_{n \in \omega}$ is an ω-chain of continuous functions and $f_n \precsim_t M$ for each n. If each of the functions f_n is equal to $\bot$, then $f = \bigsqcup_{n \in \omega} f_n$ is equal to $\bot$ too and $f \precsim_t M$ is then immediate. Suppose, on the other hand, that $f_n \neq \bot$ for some n. In this case $M \Downarrow^\circ \lambda x : u. \ M'$ for some M' so the goal is to show that $f \precsim_{u \to v} \lambda x : u. \ M'$. Suppose $d \in \mathcal{C}^\circ[\![u]\!]$ and U is a value such that $d \precsim_u U$. By our assumption on f_n, for each n,

$$\mathsf{down}(f_n)(d) \precsim_v (\lambda x : u. \ M')(U),$$

and therefore by continuity and the inductive hypothesis on v,

$$\mathsf{down}(f)(d) = \bigsqcup_{n \in \omega} \mathsf{down}(f_n)(d) \precsim_v (\lambda x : u. \ M')(U),$$

which, by the definition of $\precsim_{u \to v}$, means that $f \precsim_t M$. $\hfill \square$

The proof of the desired adequacy result is based upon the following key technical lemma:

6.11 Lemma. *Suppose $H = x_1 : t_1 \ldots x_n : t_n$ and $H \vdash M : t$ is derivable. If $d_i \in [\![t_i]\!]$ and $d_i \precsim_{t_i} M_i$ for $i = 1, \ldots, k$, then*

$$\mathcal{C}^\circ[\![H \rhd M : t]\!][x_1, \ldots, x_k \mapsto d_1, \ldots, d_k] \precsim_t [M_1, \ldots, M_k/x_1, \ldots, x_k]M.$$

Proof: The proof proceeds by induction on the structure of M. Let σ be the substitution $[M_1, \ldots, M_n/x_1, \ldots, x_n]$ and let ρ be the environment $[x_1, \ldots, x_k \mapsto d_1, \ldots, d_k]$. I will do four illustrative cases.

Case $M \equiv x_i$. Then $\mathcal{C}^\circ[\![M]\!]\rho = d_i \lesssim_{t_i} M_i \equiv \sigma M$.

Case $M \equiv \lambda x : u.\ M' : u \to v$. Let

$$f' = \mathsf{strict}(d' \mapsto \mathcal{C}^\circ[\![H,\ x : u \rhd M' : v]\!]\rho[x \mapsto d'])$$

so that $f = \mathcal{C}^\circ[\![M]\!]\rho = \mathsf{up}(f')$. We must show that

$$\mathsf{down}(f)(d) \lesssim_v (\sigma\lambda x : u.\ M')(U). \tag{6.6}$$

If $\mathsf{down}(f)(d) = \bot$, then we are done, so suppose otherwise. Then

$$\mathsf{down}(f)(d) = \mathsf{down}(\mathsf{up}(f'))(d) = f'(d).$$

Since f' is strict and this value is not equal to bottom, it must be that $d \neq \bot$. Thus, by the inductive hypothesis on M',

$$f'(d) = \mathcal{C}^\circ[\![H,\ x : u \rhd M' : v]\!]\rho[x \mapsto d] \lesssim_v (\sigma[U/x])M' \equiv [U/x](\sigma M').$$

Thus $\mathsf{down}(f)(d) \lesssim_v [U/x](\sigma M')$. Since $\mathsf{down}(f)(d) \neq \bot$, there is a value V such that $[U/x](\sigma M') \Downarrow^\circ V$ and $\mathsf{down}(f)(d) \lesssim_v V$. But then, by the operational rules for abstraction and application, $(\sigma M)(U) \Downarrow^\circ V$ too, so $\mathsf{down}(f)(d) \lesssim_v (\sigma M)(U)$. This proves that 6.6 holds.

Case $M \equiv L(N)$. Suppose that $L : s \to t$ and $N : s$. If $\mathcal{C}^\circ[\![L(N)]\!]\rho = \bot$, then there the desired conclusion is immediate, so suppose $\mathcal{C}^\circ[\![L(N)]\!]\rho \neq \bot$. In this case, $\mathcal{C}^\circ[\![L]\!]\rho \neq \bot$ and, since elements of $\mathcal{C}^\circ[\![s \to t]\!]$ are (lifted) strict functions, $\mathcal{C}^\circ[\![N]\!]\rho \neq \bot$. By the structural inductive hypothesis,

$$\sigma L \Downarrow^\circ \lambda x : s.\ L' \tag{6.7}$$

where $\mathcal{C}^\circ[\![L]\!]\rho \lesssim_{s \to t} \lambda x : s.\ L'$. Also, by the inductive hypothesis,

$$\sigma N \Downarrow^\circ U \tag{6.8}$$

where $\mathcal{C}^\circ[\![N]\!]\rho \lesssim_s U$. By the definition of $\lesssim$ for functions,

$$\mathcal{C}^\circ[\![L(N)]\!]\rho = \mathsf{down}(\mathcal{C}^\circ[\![L]\!]\rho)(\mathcal{C}^\circ[\![N]\!]\rho) \lesssim_t (\lambda x : s.\ L')(U),$$

and therefore, by the evaluation rule for application, there is a value V such that

$$[U/x]L' \Downarrow^\circ V \tag{6.9}$$

where $\mathcal{C}^\circ[\![L(N)]\!]\rho \precsim_t V$. By 6.7, 6.8, and 6.9, we know that $(\sigma L)(\sigma N) \Downarrow^\circ V$ too, so $\mathcal{C}^\circ[\![L(N)]\!]\rho \precsim_t \sigma(L(N))$ as desired.

Case $M \equiv \mu x : t.\ M'$. Let $e_0 = \bot$ and $e_{i+1} = \mathcal{C}^\circ[\![H,\ x : t \triangleright M' : t]\!]\rho[x \mapsto e_i]$. That $e_0 \precsim_t \sigma\mu x : t.\ M'$ is immediate; suppose that $e_i \precsim_t \sigma\mu x : t.\ M'$. By our induction hypothesis on M, we have

$$
\begin{aligned}
e_{i+1} &= \mathcal{C}^\circ[\![H,\ x : t \triangleright M' : t]\!]\rho[x \mapsto e_i] \\
&\precsim_t (\sigma[\sigma\mu x : t.\ M'/x])M' \\
&\equiv [\mu x : t.\ \sigma M'/x](\sigma M').
\end{aligned}
$$

If $e_{i+1} \neq \bot$, then $[\mu x : t.\ \sigma M'/x](\sigma M') \Downarrow^\circ V$ such that $e_{i+1} \precsim_t V$. But then $\sigma M \Downarrow^\circ V$ too so $e_{i+1} \precsim_t \sigma M$. By Lemma 6.10, we conclude that $\mathcal{C}^\circ[\![\mu x : t.\ M']\!]\rho = \bigsqcup_{i \in \omega} e_i \precsim_t \sigma M$. $\square$

6.12 Theorem. *Suppose M is a closed term of PCF of type t. Then $\mathcal{C}^\circ[\![M]\!] \neq \bot$ if, and only if, $M \Downarrow^\circ V$ for some V.*

Proof: Since M is a closed term, Lemma 6.11 says that $\mathcal{C}^\circ[\![M : t]\!] \precsim_t M$. So, if $\mathcal{C}^\circ[\![M]\!] \neq \bot$, then, by the definition of $\precsim_t$, there is a value V such that $M \Downarrow^\circ V$. Proof of the converse of the theorem is left as an exercise. $\square$

Exercises.

6.12 Provide the proof of the converse of Theorem 6.12 by showing:

    a. $\mathcal{C}^\circ[\![V]\!](\emptyset) \neq \bot$ for any well-typed value V, and

    b. $M \Downarrow V$ implies $\mathcal{C}^\circ[\![M]\!] = \mathcal{C}^\circ[\![V]\!]$ for any well-typed term M.

6.3   Products and Sums

Product and sum types and their associated equational theories have been discussed earlier. As with abstraction and application for higher types, the terms that introduce and eliminate elements of these types can be evaluated in several ways. Since most languages include some form of product and sum datatype constructors, it is worthwhile to consider in detail the various ways in which the meanings of these types can be explained. To this end, let us start with a basic extension of PCF that includes two additional type constructors. The grammar of the new language is given as follows:

$$
\begin{array}{rcl}
t & ::= & \mathbf{num} \mid \mathbf{bool} \mid t \rightarrow t \mid t \times t \mid t + t \\
M & ::= & \mathbf{0} \mid \mathbf{succ}(M) \mid \mathbf{pred}(M) \mid \mathbf{true} \mid \mathbf{false} \mid \mathbf{zero?}(M) \mid \\
& & x \mid \lambda x : t.\ M \mid M(M) \mid \mu x : t.\ M \mid \mathbf{if}\ M\ \mathbf{then}\ M\ \mathbf{else}\ M \mid \\
& & (M, M) \mid \mathbf{fst}(M) \mid \mathbf{snd}(M) \mid \\
& & \mathbf{inl}[t + t](M) \mid \mathbf{inr}[t + t](M) \mid \\
& & \mathbf{case}\ M\ \mathbf{of}\ \mathbf{inl}(x) \Rightarrow M\ \mathbf{or}\ \mathbf{inr}(x) \Rightarrow M
\end{array}
$$

This is essentially the same as the syntax used to add products and sums to the simply-typed λ-calculus as described earlier, but here the boolean and arithmetic constructs of PCF are also included. The tags on the injections are needed to ensure that every well-typed expression has a unique type. I will usually fail to write them unless the types are in question; this can ordinarily be inferred from context. The typing rules for products are the last three rules in Table 3.1 (the rule for constants in that table is irrelevant in the current context). The typing rules for sums appear in Table 3.3. These rules, together with those for PCF, describe a system called PCF *with products and sums*.

Operational semantics.

Let us begin by looking at the operational semantics of products and sums. As with application, there is more than one possible option for how to carry out the evaluation. For example, suppose we are given a pair (M, N) and we are to evaluate $\mathbf{fst}(M, N)$. An obvious approach is to evaluate M and, if V is the result, then we say that $\mathbf{fst}(M, N)$ evaluates to V. How should (M, N) itself be evaluated? If we adopt the philosophy that this need only be evaluated when one of its coordinates is needed, then no evaluation is required before the application of one of the projections. When a projection is applied, then we evaluate only the required coordinate. Rules formalizing this approach appear in Table 6.5; the rule for call-by-name evaluation of application is also given there in the table as a kind of template. These rules should be viewed as an extension of rules for $\Downarrow$ given previously in Table 4.4, but some care must be taken in understanding the role of *values* for the expanded language. The rules should be read with the assumption that U, V range over arbitrary terms of the syntax of PCF with products and sums. It can then be shown by an induction that the terms V such that $M \Downarrow V$ for some term M can be described by the following grammar:

$$
\begin{array}{rcl}
V & ::= & \mathbf{0} \mid \mathbf{true} \mid \mathbf{false} \mid \mathbf{succ}(V) \mid \lambda x : t.\ M \mid \\
& & (M, M) \mid \mathbf{inl}(M) \mid \mathbf{inr}(M).
\end{array}
$$

which extends the grammar 4.12 for the core of PCF. Values can also be characterized as those terms M such that $M \Downarrow M$. Here are some comments on the rules in the table.

Table 6.5
Call-by-Name Evaluation of Products and Sums

$$\frac{M \Downarrow \lambda x : t.\ L \qquad [N/x]L \Downarrow V}{M(N) \Downarrow V}$$

$$(M, N) \Downarrow (M, N) \qquad \frac{M \Downarrow (L, N) \qquad L \Downarrow V}{\mathbf{fst}(M) \Downarrow V} \qquad \frac{M \Downarrow (L, N) \qquad N \Downarrow V}{\mathbf{snd}(M) \Downarrow V}$$

$$\mathbf{inl}(M) \Downarrow \mathbf{inl}(M) \qquad \frac{L \Downarrow \mathbf{inl}(L') \qquad [L'/x]M \Downarrow V}{\mathbf{case}\ L\ \mathbf{of}\ \mathbf{inl}(x) \Rightarrow M\ \mathbf{or}\ \mathbf{inr}(y) \Rightarrow N \Downarrow V}$$

$$\mathbf{inr}(M) \Downarrow \mathbf{inr}(M) \qquad \frac{L \Downarrow \mathbf{inr}(L') \qquad [L'/y]N \Downarrow V}{\mathbf{case}\ L\ \mathbf{of}\ \mathbf{inl}(x) \Rightarrow M\ \mathbf{or}\ \mathbf{inr}(y) \Rightarrow N \Downarrow V}$$

- Pairs (M, N) are values; neither component is further evaluated until a projection is applied.

- To evaluate a projection, first evaluate its argument, then evaluate the appropriate coordinate of the resulting pair. The result of this evaluation is the result of evaluating the projection.

- Injections $\mathbf{inl}(M)$ and $\mathbf{inr}(M)$ are values; the injected term is not further evaluated until it is involved in a case statement.

- To evaluate $\mathbf{case}\ L\ \mathbf{of}\ \mathbf{inl}(x) \Rightarrow M\ \mathbf{or}\ \mathbf{inr}(y) \Rightarrow N$, begin by evaluating L. If the result is an expression of the form $\mathbf{inl}(L')$, then substitute the expression L' (*not* the result of the evaluation of L') for the variable x in the expression M. If the term resulting from this substitution evaluates to a value V, then this is the outcome of the evaluation of the case statment. If, on the other hand, L evaluates to $\mathbf{inr}(L')$, then the evaluation uses y and N rather than x and M.

The rules for call-by-value for products and sums are given in Table 6.6 where the evaluation rule for application is also given as a template. These rules extend the rules in Table 6.4. As before, the rules should be read with the assumption that U, V range over arbitrary terms of the syntax of PCF with products and sums. The terms V such that $M \Downarrow^\circ V$ for some term M can be described by the following grammar:

$$V ::= \mathbf{0} \mid \mathbf{true} \mid \mathbf{false} \mid \mathbf{succ}(V) \mid \lambda x : t.\ M \mid (V, V) \mid \mathbf{inl}(V) \mid \mathbf{inr}(V)$$

Table 6.6
Call-by-Value Evaluation of Products and Sums

$$\frac{M \Downarrow^\circ \lambda x : t.\, L \quad N \Downarrow^\circ U \quad [U/x]L \Downarrow^\circ V}{M(N) \Downarrow^\circ V}$$

$$\frac{M \Downarrow^\circ U \quad N \Downarrow^\circ V}{(M, N) \Downarrow^\circ (U, V)} \qquad \frac{M \Downarrow^\circ (U, V)}{\mathbf{fst}(M) \Downarrow^\circ U} \qquad \frac{M \Downarrow^\circ (U, V)}{\mathbf{snd}(M) \Downarrow^\circ V}$$

$$\frac{M \Downarrow^\circ V}{\mathbf{inl}(M) \Downarrow^\circ \mathbf{inl}(V)} \qquad \frac{L \Downarrow^\circ \mathbf{inl}(U) \quad [U/x]M \Downarrow^\circ V}{\mathbf{case}\ L\ \mathbf{of}\ \mathbf{inl}(x) \Rightarrow M\ \mathbf{or}\ \mathbf{inr}(y) \Rightarrow N \Downarrow^\circ V}$$

$$\frac{M \Downarrow^\circ V}{\mathbf{inr}(M) \Downarrow^\circ \mathbf{inr}(V)} \qquad \frac{L \Downarrow^\circ \mathbf{inr}(U) \quad [U/y]N \Downarrow^\circ V}{\mathbf{case}\ L\ \mathbf{of}\ \mathbf{inl}(x) \Rightarrow M\ \mathbf{or}\ \mathbf{inr}(y) \Rightarrow N \Downarrow^\circ V}$$

Note, in particular, that a pair (M, N) is not a value unless M and N are values, and injections $\mathbf{inl}(M), \mathbf{inr}(M)$ are not values unless M is. Here are some remarks about the rules.

- Under a call-by-value evaluation strategy, the arguments of an application are evaluated regardless of whether they are needed. Hence, we evaluate (M, N) by evaluating M and N. If the results of these evaluations are U and V respectively, then (U, V) is the result of evaluating the pair.

- To evaluate a projection, first evaluate its argument and then select the appropriate coordinate of the resulting pair.

- The treatment of evaluation of an injection into a sum is similar to that for a pair: to evaluate $\mathbf{inl}(M)$, evaluate M, and, if this results in a value V, then $\mathbf{inl}(V)$ is the result of evaluating the injected term.

- To evaluate $\mathbf{case}\ L\ \mathbf{of}\ \mathbf{inl}(x) \Rightarrow M\ \mathbf{or}\ \mathbf{inr}(y) \Rightarrow N$, begin by evaluating L. If the result is a value $\mathbf{inl}(U)$ then substitute U for the variable x in the expression M. If the term resulting from this substitution evaluates to a value V, then this is the outcome of the evaluation of the case statement. If the result of evaluating L has the form $\mathbf{inl}(U)$, the procedure is similar, but uses y and U in place of x and M.

Smash product.

Now, to provide a fixed-point semantics for products and sums, it is necessary to introduce some new operators on domains. We have already discussed the product $D \times E$ of cpo's. In the product $D \times E$ of cpo's D and E, there are elements of the form $(x, \bot)$

and $(\bot, y)$. If $x \neq \bot$ or $y \neq \bot$, then these will be *distinct* members of $D \times E$. If we take the meaning of a term (M, N) to be of the meaning of M paired with that of N, then adequacy will not hold for this semantics relative to call-by-value. The problem occurs when one of the terms has $\bot$ as its meaning (that is, it diverges) but the other does not. Then the pair diverges in call-by-value so its meaning should be $\bot$. In short, for call-by-value semantics it is necessary to *identify* the pairs $(x, \bot)$ and $(\bot, y)$. For this purpose, there is a collapsed version of the product called the *smash product*. For cpo's D and E, the smash product $D \otimes E$ is the set

$$\{(x, y) \in D \times E \mid x \neq \bot \text{ and } y \neq \bot\} \cup \{\bot_{D \otimes E}\}$$

where $\bot_{D \otimes E}$ is some new element that is not a pair. The ordering on pairs is coordinatewise, and we stipulate that $\bot_{D \otimes E} \sqsubseteq z$ for every $z \in D \otimes E$. There is a continuous surjection $\mathsf{smash} : D \times E \to D \otimes E$ given by taking

$$\mathsf{smash}(x, y) = \begin{cases} (x, y) & x \neq \bot \text{ and } y \neq \bot \\ \bot_{D \otimes E} & \text{otherwise} \end{cases}$$

This function establishes a useful relationship between $D \times E$ and $D \otimes E$. Let us say that a function $f : D \times E \to F$ is *bistrict* if $f(x, y) = \bot$ whenever $x = \bot$ or $y = \bot$. The following describes the basic equational property:

6.13 Lemma. *If $f : D \times E \to F$ is bistrict and continuous, then there is a unique strict continuous function $f^\bullet$ that completes the following diagram:*

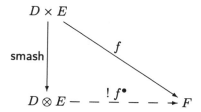

Proof: For each $z \in D \otimes E$, define

$$f^\bullet(z) = \begin{cases} f(x, y) & \text{if } z = (x, y) \text{ is a pair} \\ \bot & \text{if } z = \bot_{D \otimes E} \end{cases}$$

Clearly this map is strict and continuous. To see that it completes the diagram, suppose $(x, y) \in D \times E$ and $x, y \neq \bot$. Then $f^\bullet(\mathsf{smash}(z)) = f^\bullet(x, y) = f(x, y)$. If, on the other hand, either x or y is bottom, then $f^\bullet(\mathsf{smash}(z)) = f^\bullet(\bot) = \bot$, and this is equal to $f(x, y)$ because f is assumed to be bistrict. It is straightforward to check that $f^\bullet$ is the only function that could make the diagram commute. $\qquad\qquad\square$

The function $f^\bullet$ can also be expressed in terms of a function $\mathsf{unsmash} : D \otimes E \to D \times E$ which can be viewed intuitively as an inclusion map. More precisely, if we define

$$\mathsf{unsmash}(z) = \begin{cases} z & \text{if } z = (x, y) \text{ is a pair} \\ (\bot_D, \bot_E) & \text{if } z = \bot_{D \otimes E}, \end{cases}$$

then $f^\bullet = f \circ \mathsf{unsmash}$. If $f : D \to D'$ and $g : E \to E'$ are strict continuous functions, then, by the lemma, the function

$$f \otimes g = \mathsf{smash} \circ (f \times g) \circ \mathsf{unsmash} = (\mathsf{smash} \circ (f \times g))^\bullet$$

is the unique strict, continuous function that completes the following diagram:

$$
\begin{array}{ccc}
D \times E & \xrightarrow{\;\; f \times g \;\;} & D' \times E' \\
{\scriptstyle \mathsf{smash}}\big\downarrow & & \big\downarrow{\scriptstyle \mathsf{smash}} \\
D \otimes E & \xdashrightarrow{\;\; !\, f \otimes g \;\;} & D' \otimes E'
\end{array}
$$

It is straightforward to prove that this defines a functor action for $\otimes$.

Coalesced and separated sums.

To interpret sums, it is essential to have the correct corresponding semantic construction. For call-by-value, if M diverges, then $\mathbf{inl}(M)$ and $\mathbf{inr}(M)$ also diverge, so their meanings must be equal to bottom. Hence the interpretation of $s + t$ cannot simply be the disjoint sum of the meanings of s and t.

Given cpo's D and E, the *coalesced sum* $D \oplus E$ is defined to be the set

$$\Big((D - \{\bot_D\}) \times \{1\} \Big) \cup \Big((E - \{\bot_E\}) \times \{2\} \Big) \cup \{\bot_{D \oplus E}\}$$

where $D - \{\bot_D\}$ and $E - \{\bot_E\}$ are the sets D and E with their respective bottom elements removed and $\bot_{D \oplus E}$ is a new element that is not a pair. It is ordered by taking $\bot_{D \oplus E} \sqsubseteq z$ for all $z \in D \oplus E$ and taking $(x, m) \sqsubseteq (y, n)$ if, and only if, $m = n$ and $x \sqsubseteq y$. There are strict continuous functions $\mathsf{inl} : D \multimap (D \oplus E)$ and $\mathsf{inr} : E \multimap (D \oplus E)$ given by taking

$$\mathsf{inl}(x) = \begin{cases} (x, 1) & \text{if } x \neq \bot \\ \bot_{D \oplus E} & \text{if } x = \bot \end{cases}$$

and

$$\text{inr}(x) = \begin{cases} (x, 2) & \text{if } x \neq \bot \\ \bot_{D \oplus E} & \text{if } x = \bot. \end{cases}$$

The coalesced sum with these maps is a coproduct in the category $\mathbf{Cpo}^\circ$ of cpo's and strict maps. That is, if $f : D \multimap F$ and $g : E \multimap F$ are strict continuous functions, then there is a unique strict continuous function $[f, g]$ that completes the following diagram:

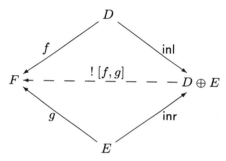

The function $[f, g]$ is given by

$$[f, g](z) = \begin{cases} f(x) & \text{if } z = (x, 1) \\ g(y) & \text{if } z = (y, 2) \\ \bot & \text{if } z = \bot. \end{cases}$$

Given continuous functions $f : D \multimap D'$ and $g : E \multimap E'$, a functor action can be defined by

$$f \oplus g = [\text{inl} \circ f, \text{inr} \circ g] : D \oplus E \multimap D' \oplus E'.$$

Moreover, as with the product, it is also useful to have a tuple notation for the coalesced sum. Recalling that $\mathbb{U} = \{u\}$ is (a representative instance of) the one element poset, define

$$\oplus() = \mathbb{U}$$
$$\oplus(D_1, \ldots, D_n) = \oplus(D_1, \ldots, D_{n-1}) \oplus D_n$$

and

$$\text{in}_i = \text{inr} \circ \text{inl}^{n-i}.$$

One may also define $[f_1, \ldots, f_n]$ and prove a universal property.

Let D and E be cpo's, the *separated sum* $D + E$ is defined to be the cpo $D_\bot \oplus E_\bot$. Some care must be taken in asserting the categorical properties of this operation. Given (possibly non-strict) continuous functions f, g, there is a unique *strict* continuous function that completes the following diagram:

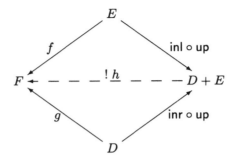

A function that completes the diagram is $h = [f^\dagger, g^\dagger]$ (recalling that $f^\dagger = f \circ \text{down}$ and $g^\dagger \circ \text{down}$) since then $h \circ \text{inl} \circ \text{up} = f^\dagger \circ \text{up} = f$ and a similar fact holds for g. That this is the *only* strict function with this property follows from the fact that if h completes the diagram above, then it also completes the following diagram:

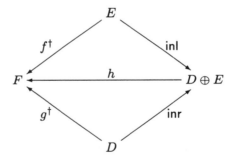

To see why, note that $f = h \circ \text{inl} \circ up$ implies $f^\dagger = (h \circ \text{inl} \circ up)^\dagger = h \circ \text{inl}$, and a similar argument proves the commutativity of the lower triangle of the diagram.

However, h may not be the only *continuous* function that completes the diagram. Given continuous functions $f : D \to D'$ and $g : E \to E'$, we define

$$f + g = f_\perp \oplus g_\perp : D + E \to D' + E'$$

where the reader may recall that $f_\perp = (\text{up} \circ f)^\dagger$ and $g_\perp = (\text{up} \circ g)^\dagger$.

Fixed-point semantics.

With these domain-theoretic preparations it is now possible to describe the fixed-point semantics of products and sums. I begin with a discussion of the call-by-value case; a sketch of call-by-name follows with the details left as an exercise.

For the semantics of call-by-value, the ground and higher types are interpreted as before:

$$\mathcal{C}^\circ[\![\mathbf{num}]\!] = \mathbb{N}_\perp$$
$$\mathcal{C}^\circ[\![\mathbf{bool}]\!] = \mathbb{T}$$
$$\mathcal{C}^\circ[\![s \rightarrow t]\!] = [\mathcal{C}^\circ[\![s]\!] \multimap \mathcal{C}^\circ[\![t]\!]]_\perp$$

The new product and sum operators are interpreted with the smash product and coalesced sum respectively:

$$\mathcal{C}^\circ[\![s \times t]\!] = \mathcal{C}^\circ[\![s]\!] \otimes \mathcal{C}^\circ[\![t]\!]$$
$$\mathcal{C}^\circ[\![s + t]\!] = \mathcal{C}^\circ[\![s]\!] \oplus \mathcal{C}^\circ[\![t]\!]$$

The terms are interpreted as follows:

$$\mathcal{C}^\circ[\![(M, N)]\!]\rho = \mathsf{smash}(\mathcal{C}^\circ[\![M]\!]\rho, \mathcal{C}^\circ[\![N]\!]\rho)$$
$$\mathcal{C}^\circ[\![\mathbf{fst}(M)]\!]\rho = \mathsf{fst}(\mathsf{unsmash}(\mathcal{C}^\circ[\![M]\!]\rho))$$
$$\mathcal{C}^\circ[\![\mathbf{snd}(M)]\!]\rho = \mathsf{snd}(\mathsf{unsmash}(\mathcal{C}^\circ[\![M]\!]\rho))$$

$$\mathcal{C}^\circ[\![\mathbf{inl}(M)]\!]\rho = \mathsf{inl}(\mathcal{C}^\circ[\![M]\!]\rho)$$
$$\mathcal{C}^\circ[\![\mathbf{inr}(M)]\!]\rho = \mathsf{inr}(\mathcal{C}^\circ[\![M]\!]\rho)$$
$$\mathcal{C}^\circ[\![\mathbf{case}\ L\ \mathbf{of}\ \mathbf{inl}(x) \Rightarrow M\ \mathbf{or}\ \mathbf{inr}(y) \Rightarrow N]\!]\rho = [\mathsf{strict}(f), \mathsf{strict}(g)](\mathcal{C}^\circ[\![L]\!]\rho)$$

where $f : d \mapsto \mathcal{C}^\circ[\![M]\!]\rho[x \mapsto d]$ and $g : d \mapsto \mathcal{C}^\circ[\![N]\!]\rho[y \mapsto d]$. That is,

$$\mathcal{C}^\circ[\![\mathbf{case}\ L\ \mathbf{of}\ \mathbf{inl}(x) \Rightarrow M\ \mathbf{or}\ \mathbf{inr}(y) \Rightarrow N]\!]\rho$$
$$= \begin{cases} \mathcal{C}^\circ[\![M]\!]\rho[x \mapsto d] & \text{if } \mathcal{C}^\circ[\![L]\!]\rho = \mathsf{inl}(d) \neq \perp \\ \mathcal{C}^\circ[\![N]\!]\rho[y \mapsto d] & \text{if } \mathcal{C}^\circ[\![L]\!]\rho = \mathsf{inr}(d) \neq \perp \\ \perp & \text{if } \mathcal{C}^\circ[\![L]\!]\rho = \perp. \end{cases}$$

The definitions are most easily appreciated through the proof of the adequacy theorem for the system since it is there that one sees why the handling of the bottom element in the smash product and coalesced sum properly reflects the operational behavior of the language. It is not difficult to prove that the interpretation is sound in the sense that $M \Downarrow^\circ V$ implies $\mathcal{C}^\circ[\![M]\!] = \mathcal{C}^\circ[\![V]\!]$. It is also easy to see that the meaning of a value is never bottom. From this we can conclude that if a term M evaluates to a value, then the meaning of M is not $\perp$. Proof of the converse requires more effort. A full proof must expand the induction used for the language in the previous section. I will describe the family of inclusive subsets needed for the desired result and the new steps required for the proof of an expanded version of Lemma 6.11. Other clauses for the inclusive subsets and the remaining steps of the induction remain as they were before.

Definition: For PCF with products and sums we define a family of relations $\lesssim_t$ between elements of $\mathcal{C}^\circ[\![t]\!]$ on the left and closed terms of type t on the right as follows. For any $d \in \mathcal{C}^\circ[\![t]\!]$ and term M of type t, define $d \lesssim_t M$ if

1. $d = \bot$, or
2. $M \Downarrow^\circ V$ for some V and $d \lesssim_t V$ where

   - $f \lesssim_{u \to v} \lambda x : u. \ N$ if, and only if, for each $d \in [\![u]\!]$ and value $U : u$,

     $$d \lesssim_u U \text{ implies } \mathsf{down}(f)(d) \lesssim_v (\lambda x : u. \ N)(U).$$

   - $\mathsf{true} \lesssim_{\mathbf{bool}} \mathbf{true}$ and $\mathsf{false} \lesssim_{\mathbf{bool}} \mathbf{false}$.

   - $n \lesssim_{\mathbf{num}} \underline{n}$.

   - $d \lesssim_{u \times v} (U, V)$ if, and only if, $d = \mathsf{smash}(d_1, d_2)$ where $d_1 \lesssim_u U$ and $d_2 \lesssim_v V$.

   - $d \lesssim_{u+v} V$ if, and only if, either $d = \mathsf{inl}(d')$ and $V \equiv \mathbf{inl}[s+t](V')$ where $d' \lesssim_u V'$ or $d = \mathsf{inr}(d')$ and $V \equiv \mathbf{inr}[s+t](V')$ where $d' \lesssim_v V'$. $\qquad \square$

It is left as an exercise to show that this does define a family of inclusive subsets. The key technical result is the following:

6.14 Lemma. *Suppose $H = x_1 : t_1 \ldots x_n : t_n$ and $H \vdash M : t$ is derivable for a term M of PCF with products and sums. If $d_i \in \mathcal{C}^\circ[\![t_i]\!]$ and $d_i \lesssim_{t_i} M_i$ for $i = 1, \ldots, k$, then*

$$\mathcal{C}^\circ[\![H \rhd M : t]\!][x_1, \ldots, x_k \mapsto d_1, \ldots, d_k] \lesssim_s [M_1, \ldots, M_k/x_1, \ldots, x_k]M.$$

Proof: The proof proceeds by induction on the structure of M. Let σ be the substitution $[M_1, \ldots, M_n/x_1, \ldots, x_n]$ and let ρ be the environment $[x_1, \ldots, x_k \mapsto d_1, \ldots, d_k]$. The inductive steps are the same as in the proof of Lemma 6.11 for cases other than products and sums, so I will only discuss the cases in which M is related to one of these new types. If $\mathcal{C}^\circ[\![M]\!]\rho = \bot$, then we are done, so let us assume that this is not the case.

Case $M \equiv (L, N)$. Suppose $t \equiv u \times v$. Since $\mathcal{C}^\circ[\![M]\!]\rho \neq \bot$, it must also be the case that $d = \mathcal{C}^\circ[\![L]\!]\rho \neq \bot$ and $e = \mathcal{C}^\circ[\![N]\!]\rho \neq \bot$. By the inductive hypothesis, this means that there are values U, V such that $\sigma L \Downarrow^\circ U$ and $\sigma N \Downarrow^\circ V$ and, moreover, $d \lesssim_u U$ and $e \lesssim_v V$. By the operational rule for products we know that $M \Downarrow^\circ (U, V)$. Thus, by the definition of $\lesssim_{u \times v}$, we must also have $\mathcal{C}^\circ[\![M]\!]\rho = \mathsf{smash}(d, e) \lesssim_{u \times v} M$.

Case $M \equiv \mathbf{fst}(M')$ where M' has type $t \times s$ in the assignment H. Since $\mathcal{C}^\circ[\![M]\!]\rho \neq \bot$, we must also have $\mathcal{C}^\circ[\![M']\!]\rho \neq \bot$ so there exist $\bot \neq d \in \mathcal{C}^\circ[\![t]\!]$ and $\bot \neq e \in \mathcal{C}^\circ[\![s]\!]$ with $\mathcal{C}^\circ[\![M']\!]\rho = \mathsf{smash}(d, e)$. Hence

$$\mathcal{C}^\circ[\![M]\!]\rho = \mathsf{fst}(\mathsf{unsmash}(\mathsf{smash}(d, e))) = d.$$

Now, by the inductive hypothesis, there is a value (U, V) such that $\sigma M' \Downarrow^\circ (U, V)$ and also $\mathsf{smash}(d, e) \lesssim_{t \times s} (U, V)$. By the definition of the inclusive subset, this means that $d \lesssim_t U$. Since $\sigma M \Downarrow^\circ U$ too by the operational rule for this projection, it follows that $d \lesssim_t M$, which is the desired conclusion. The proof for the case in which $M \equiv \mathbf{snd}(N)$ is similar.

Case $M \equiv \mathbf{inl}(N)$. Say $t \equiv u + v$. Since the meaning of M is not bottom in environment ρ, it must be the case that $d = \mathcal{C}^\circ[\![N]\!]\rho \neq \bot$, so, by the inductive hypothesis, there is a value V such that $\sigma N \Downarrow^\circ V$ and $d \lesssim_u V$. Then $\sigma M \Downarrow \mathsf{inl}(V)$ by the operational rules and $\mathsf{inl}(d) \lesssim_t \mathsf{inl}(V)$ by the definition of this relation. It follows then that $\mathsf{inl}(d) \lesssim_t \sigma M$, which is the desired conclusion. The proof for the case in which $M \equiv \mathbf{inr}(N)$ is similar.

Case $M \equiv \mathbf{case}\ P\ \mathbf{of}\ \mathbf{inl}(x) \Rightarrow Q\ \mathbf{or}\ \mathbf{inr}(y) \Rightarrow R$. Suppose that $H \vdash P : u + v$ and that $H, x : u \vdash Q : t$ and $H, y : v \vdash R : t$. If the meaning of M is not bottom, then the meaning of P is either $\mathsf{inl}(d)$ for some non-bottom $d \in \mathcal{C}^\circ[\![u]\!]$ or $\mathsf{inr}(e)$ for some non-bottom $e \in \mathcal{C}^\circ[\![v]\!]$. Assume that it is the former. Since the meaning of M is non-bottom, it must be the case that $d' = \mathcal{C}^\circ[\![Q]\!]\rho[x \mapsto d] \neq \bot$ since that is the meaning of M in this case. By the inductive hypothesis for P, there is a value such that $\sigma P \Downarrow^\circ \mathsf{inl}(U)$ and $\mathsf{inl}(d) \lesssim_{u+v} \mathsf{inl}(U)$. From the definition of $\lesssim_{u+v}$, this means that $d \lesssim_u U$. Therefore, by the inductive hypothesis for Q now, $d' \lesssim_t (\sigma[U/x])Q$, so the fact that $d' \neq \bot$ means there is a value V such that $d' \lesssim_t V$. By the operational rule for the case statement, $M \Downarrow^\circ V$ too, and this yields the desired conclusion. The other case, in which the meaning of P is $\mathsf{inr}(e)$ for some non-bottom $e \in \mathcal{C}^\circ[\![v]\!]$, has a similar proof. $\square$

This has the following corollary:

6.15 Theorem. *Suppose M is a term of PCF with products and sums such that $\vdash M : t$. Then $\mathcal{C}^\circ[\![M]\!] \neq \bot$ if, and only if, $M \Downarrow^\circ V$ for some V.* $\square$

For the semantics of PCF with products and sums for the call-by-name semantics, types are interpreted as follows:

$$\mathcal{C}[\![\mathbf{num}]\!] = \mathbb{N}_\bot$$
$$\mathcal{C}[\![\mathbf{bool}]\!] = \mathbb{T}$$
$$\mathcal{C}[\![s \to t]\!] = [\mathcal{C}[\![s]\!] \to \mathcal{C}[\![t]\!]]_\bot$$
$$\mathcal{C}[\![s \times t]\!] = (\mathcal{C}[\![s]\!] \times \mathcal{C}[\![t]\!])_\bot$$
$$\mathcal{C}[\![s + t]\!] = \mathcal{C}[\![s]\!] + \mathcal{C}[\![t]\!]$$

A pair is interpreted in the the lifted product:

$$\mathcal{C}[\![(M, N)]\!]\rho = \mathsf{up}(\mathcal{C}[\![M]\!]\rho, \mathcal{C}[\![N]\!]\rho)$$
$$\mathcal{C}[\![\mathbf{fst}(M)]\!]\rho = \mathsf{fst}(\mathsf{down}(\mathcal{C}[\![M]\!]\rho))$$
$$\mathcal{C}[\![\mathbf{snd}(M)]\!]\rho = \mathsf{snd}(\mathsf{down}(\mathcal{C}[\![M]\!]\rho))$$

Injections of elements into the sum type send lifted elements to the respective components:

$$\mathcal{C}[\![\mathbf{inl}(M)]\!]\rho = \mathsf{inl}(\mathsf{up}(\mathcal{C}[\![M]\!]\rho))$$
$$\mathcal{C}[\![\mathbf{inr}(M)]\!]\rho = \mathsf{inr}(\mathsf{up}(\mathcal{C}[\![M]\!]\rho))$$
$$\mathcal{C}[\![\mathbf{case}\ L\ \mathbf{of}\ \mathbf{inl}(x) \Rightarrow M\ \mathbf{or}\ \mathbf{inr}(y) \Rightarrow N]\!]\rho = [f^\dagger, g^\dagger](\mathcal{C}[\![L]\!]\rho)$$

where $f : d \mapsto \mathcal{C}[\![M]\!]\rho[x \mapsto d]$ and $g : e \mapsto \mathcal{C}[\![N]\!]\rho[y \mapsto e]$. In particular,

$$[f^\dagger, g^\dagger](\mathcal{C}[\![L]\!]\rho) = \begin{cases} \mathcal{C}[\![M]\!]\rho[x \mapsto d] & \text{if } \mathcal{C}[\![L]\!]\rho = \mathsf{inl}(\mathsf{up}(d)) \\ \mathcal{C}[\![N]\!]\rho[y \mapsto e] & \text{if } \mathcal{C}[\![L]\!]\rho = \mathsf{inr}(\mathsf{up}(e)) \\ \bot & \text{if } \mathcal{C}[\![L]\!]\rho = \bot. \end{cases}$$

Note that, if $\mathcal{C}[\![M]\!]\rho = \mathsf{inl}(\mathsf{up}(\bot))$, then

$$\mathcal{C}[\![\mathbf{case}\ L\ \mathbf{of}\ \mathbf{inl}(x) \Rightarrow M\ \mathbf{or}\ \mathbf{inr}(y) \Rightarrow N]\!]\rho = \mathcal{C}[\![M]\!]\rho[x \mapsto \bot].$$

6.16 Theorem. *Suppose M is a term of PCF with products and sums such that $\vdash M : t$. Then $\mathcal{C}[\![M]\!] \neq \bot$ if, and only if, $M \Downarrow V$ for some V.* $\qquad\Box$

Exercises.

6.13 Prove that $\mathbb{U} \oplus D \cong D$ and $\mathbb{O} \otimes D \cong D$ for any pointed cpo D.

6.14 As with the product $\times$ and function space $\to$, there is a relationship between the smash product $\otimes$ and the strict function space $\multimap$. Given cpo's D, E, F and a strict function $f : D \otimes E \multimap F$, show that there is a unique strict continuous function f' such that the following diagram commutes:

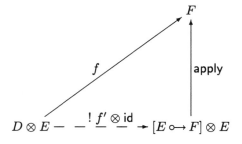

6.15 It was argued that there is a unique *strict* continuous function that completes the
following diagram

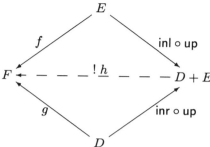

for any continuous functions f and g. Give examples of cpo's D, E and continuous
functions f, g such that there may be *more* than one *non*-strict function that completes
this diagram. This proves that $D + E$ and the maps inl ∘ up and inr ∘ up do not determine
a coproduct.

6.16 Show how to expand the induction in Lemma 6.10 to obtain a proof that the pred-
icates used for call-by-value evaluation of PCF with products and sums are inclusive.

6.17 Provide a complete proof for Theorem 6.16.

6.18* The rules given for the call-by-name evaluation of products and sums had the
property that the constructors that build elements of these types, $(\cdot, \cdot)$, inl$(\cdot)$, inr$(\cdot)$,
'protect' their arguments from immediate evaluation. However, this principle seems to
be violated by the interpretation of numbers where we used the rules

$$\mathbf{0} \Downarrow \mathbf{0} \qquad \frac{M \Downarrow V}{\mathbf{succ}(M) \Downarrow \mathbf{succ}(V)}.$$

To bring this into line with the evaluation of other constructors we might substitute the
rules

$$\mathbf{0} \Downarrow \mathbf{0} \qquad \mathbf{succ}(M) \Downarrow \mathbf{succ}(M).$$

Provide an adequate semantics for PCF with this new rule of evaluation. Hint: Figure 6.2.

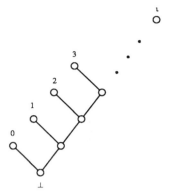

Figure 6.2
The Lazy Numbers

6.4 Notes

The term 'full abstraction' was coined by Milner [167]. The proof of full abstraction
for an appropriate extension of PCF was independently given by Plotkin [196] and by
Sazonov [216]. Plotkin's paper also contains some interesting results on computability
and PCF that were not discussed in this chapter. The discussion of PCF in [221] ends
with the question of the definability of the parallel or settled in the subsequent work by
Plotkin. Plotkin uses a syntactic method to prove that PCF is not fully abstract that
involves a fine analysis of the nature of PCF evaluation in what he calls the 'Activity
Lemma'. The proof given in this chapter uses a non-standard model approach that could
properly be credited to Berry, who introduced the dI-domains. Berry [26] also noted that
dI-domains were not fully abstract for PCF and studied further categories that might
provide the desired correspondence with the operational semantics of the language. Proof
of the failure of full abstraction for dI-domains can also be found in Curien [62], and
Exercise 6.9 appears as an example in a recent paper by Jim and Meyer [127]. That PCF
with parallel or is fully abstract for the bc-domain model was first noted by Abramsky
and Curien. The fact that the parallel conditional for numbers can be defined using the
parallel or was proved by Stoughton [251].Exercises 6.10 and 6.11 are due to Stoughton.

Shortly after the work of Sazonov and Plotkin, Milner [168] demonstrated that PCF
actually *has* a unique fully abstract model of a certain kind. The model was presented
syntactically, however, and the problem of finding a semantically-described fully abstract
model for PCF and for other languages is still an active topic of investigation as I am
writing these notes. A survey by Berry, Curien, and Levy [30] provides an update on the

understanding of the full abstraction problem as of 1982. A more up-to-date discussion is given by Meyer and Cosmadakis [163].

A book by Curien [62] contains a summary of work on full abstraction and studies the problem for another semantics called 'sequential algorithms on concrete data structures'. Further discussions can be found in joint papers with Berry [28; 29]. The book of Mulmuley [182] demonstrates that a certain kind of retraction can be used to obtain a fully abstract model. The book by Stoughton [250] contains a general discussion of the problem of finding fully abstract models; the discussion there includes some results about when it is *not* possible to find a fully abstract model. Jim and Meyer [127] have demonstrated further negative results for the dI-domains model.

The idea of using ω-chain complete subsets to prove relationships between different semantics for a language originated in the 1970's in work of Plotkin [194], Milne [166], and Reynolds [202]. Stemming from this work, the term 'inclusive predicate' is sometimes used to refer to a relation between cpo's that is ω-chain complete or, in some cases, directed complete (as a subset of a product of cpo's). Occasionally it is also assumed that bottom elements of pointed cpo's are related by an inclusive predicate. The terminology 'inclusive subset' used in this book deviates from these usages in imposing the additional condition of downward closure. Recent examples of techniques for proving adequacy results can be found in papers by Abramsky [4], and Mosses and Plotkin [181]. These papers focus on the untyped case, but the methods can be adapted to the typed one as discussed in the chapter here.

Although it is possible to prove the Context Lemma (Lemma 6.7) for PCF with the parallel conditional by using the Full Abstraction Theorem, this method of proof will not work for the system without parallel conditional since the less expressive system does not satisfy full abstraction. The theorem was proved for this system using syntactic means by Milner [168]. There are other papers discussing the Context Lemma by Bloom [31] (where the result is called 'operational extensionality') and by Jim and Meyer [127]. The Context Lemma is exploited as a basic tool for reasoning about programs through operational semantics in work of Mason and Talcott [158] and Smith [235].

Although one can begin with an operational semantics for a programming language and seek a fully abstract fixed-point semantics, it is dually possible to start with a fixed-point semantics and look for an operational semantics that makes it fully abstract. Meyer and Cosmadakis [163] discuss the search for such an operational semantics that corresponds to a fixed-point semantics in which Ω has the same meaning as $\lambda x.\ \Omega$ and it is possible to observe convergence at higher types. Bloom [31] considers how this might be done if complete lattices are used as a model (as they were in earlier work on the semantics of programming languages).

Full abstraction for call-by-name where convergence at higher types is observable is considered by Bloom and Riecke [32]. To obtain the desired result, it is necessary to add a 'convergence tester' to the language. Sieber [233] has given a proof of full abstraction for call-by-value PCF. In proving this result, some care must be taken about the definition of equality in the system. It is not possible to distinguish x from $\lambda y.\ xy$ operationally in call-by-value, but if x is allowed to have value $\bot$ in an environment, then these terms will have different meanings in the fixed-point semantics.

There has been considerable study of categorical aspects of strict or partial functions and call-by-value evaluation including work by Moggi [176; 177], by Curien and Obtulowicz [64], and by Robinson and Rosolini [211].Categorically, the property described in Exercise 6.14 is called *moniodal closure*. The category $\mathbf{Cpo}^\circ$ of cpo's and strict continuous functions is not cartesian closed because the smash product is not actually a product. The category does have a product, but it does not have the relationship with the function space operator that is required for cartesian closure. On the other hand, the category $\mathbf{Cpo}$ of cpo's and continuous functions is a ccc, but Exercise 6.15 shows that the operator $+$ is not a coproduct in this category; it can be shown, moreover, that there is *no* coproduct in $\mathbf{Cpo}$. This suggests a question about whether there is some conflict between coproducts and cartesian closure for categories like the ones considered here for modeling PCF. In fact, it can be shown that a ccc with coproducts and (a suitable categorical formulation of) fixed points is trivial. Details of this and several similar properties about the combination of categorical constructions with fixed points are summarized in a paper by Huwig and Poigné [124], which provides further references to literature on the subject.

A substantial body of work on the fixed-point and operational semantics of programming languages has focused on the interpretation of control flow constructs. The focus of this work has been on *continuations* and the form of semantics known as *continuation passing style* (CPS). Examples of the use of CPS for fixed-point semantics can be found in the standard books on denotational semantics such as those of Gordon [95], Schmidt [220], and Stoy [252]. CPS has also been studied for use in intermediate code in the compilation of functional programming languages. The book of Appel [11] provides a discussion of how this has been done for ML and cites other work on the use of CPS in compilation. A seminal paper of Plotkin [195] on the relationship between call-by-name and call-by-value evaluation orders used CPS to demonstrate how each can be simulated using the other. A full abstraction result for a language with continuations as a construct has recently been demonstrated by Sitaram and Felleisen [234]. The search for further results of this kind is now an active area of investigation.

Finding a good definition of the operational equivalence of two program fragments in a sequential language is relatively easy compared to finding a suitable definition for languages with concurrent constructs. One of the best-known ideas in that context is a relation called *bisimulation*. The idea is to define an equivalence relation from a transition semantics for processes based on the actions that a process is able to perform. Bisimulation is one of many theories of program equivalence that have been studied for process algebras. There is a book [170] and a handbook article [171] of Milner on his algebra CCS (**C**alculus of **C**ommunicating **S**ystems) that discusses several of these theories. Hennessy has developed a theory of equivalences between processes based on the idea of 'testing processes'; an exposition can be found in his book [110]. Hennessy's book also describes fully abstract denotational semantics for the the languages he studies.

7 Types and Evaluation

In the twentieth century, there have been at least two lines of development of the notion of a *type*. One of these seeks to use types to conquer problems in the foundations of mathematics. For example, type distinctions can resolve troubling paradoxes that lead to inconsistent systems. On the other hand, a more recent line of investigation into types pursues their application in programming languages. Although computer architectures themselves suggest few type distinctions, it is now common to program a computer indirectly through the use of 'higher-level' programming languages. In such languages a discipline of types can be introduced to serve a variety of different purposes. One of the earliest uses of types in programming languages such as Fortran was the enhancement of efficiency. For example, if a variable is declared to be an array of integers having a given number of entries, then it is possible to provide good space management for the variable in computer memory. A programmer's indication of the type of a datum might also save pointless testing in a running program. This use of types has remained a basic motivation for their presence in many modern languages and will remain an important application.

A second motivation for the use of types was appreciated by the end of the 1960's. This was their role as a programming *discipline*. Types could be used to enforce restrictions on the shape of well-formed programs. One key benefit in doing this was the possibility of detecting flaws in programs in the form of compiletime type errors. If a mistake in a program can be detected at the point that the program is submitted for compilation into machine code, then this mistake can be corrected promptly rather than being discovered later in a run of the program on data. Although the software engineering gains in this possibility are widely recognized, a price is also paid for them. First, by constraining the programmer with a type system, some apparently reasonable programs will be rejected even though their runtime behavior would be acceptable. Second, the typing system may demand extensive programmer annotations, which can be time-consuming to write and tedious to read. Reducing the impact of these two drawbacks is the central objective of much of the work on types in programming languages.

A third motivation for types in programming languages is the one most recently understood: their role in supporting data abstraction and modularity. Although these cornerstones of software engineering principle can be achieved to some extent without types, many programming languages employ a type system that enforces the hiding of data type representations and supports the specification of modules. For example, several languages support a separation between a package specification, which consists of a collection of type declarations, and the body of the package, which provides programs implementing the procedures, *etc.* that appear in the specification. These units are automatically analyzed to determine their type-correctness before code is generated by compilation.

The primary purpose of this chapter is to investigate the ideas and methods that have been generated by work on the second of these motivations. I will begin with a general description of the forces that drive work on types in programming languages toward calculi that are more expressive while pointing out the reasons that type constraints are more an aid than a hindrance when the right type discipline is imposed. After looking at the motives for achieving additional expressiveness, the techniques for proving properties about the benefits of the type system are discussed. Remaining sections of the chapter present some of the most important ideas in the design of type disciplines for programming languages with an emphasis on the operational semantics of the constructs introduced. The chapter ends with a discussion of the form of polymorphism used in the ML programming language.

7.1 Expressiveness

In this section I will walk through a series of programming examples intended to illustrate the motivations for various type structures. A handy pair of languages for making a comparison is Scheme, which can be viewed as based on the *untyped* λ-calculus, and ML, which can be viewed as based on the *typed* λ-calculus. Both languages have specifications that are at least as clear as one finds for most languages, so it is (usually) not difficult to tell what the meaning of a program in the language is actually specified to be. While both were designed with semantic clarity as a key objective, the designs are also sensitive to efficiency issues, and both have good compilers that are widely used. Finally, the functional fragments of Scheme and ML employ a call-by-value evaluation strategy so the chance of confusing operational differences with differences in the type system philosophy are reduced.

Higher types.

One of the first discoveries of researchers investigating the mathematical semantics of programming languages in the late 1960's was the usefulness of *higher-order* functions in describing the denotations of programs. The use of higher-order in *programming* was understood even earlier and incorporated in the constructs and programming methodology of Lisp and ALGOL 60. Programmers using the languages Scheme and ML employ higher-order functions as a tool for writing clear, succinct code by capturing good abstractions. On the other hand, the use of higher-order functions does have its costs, and it is therefore worthwhile to discuss some of the ways in which such functions can be useful. Their usefulness as a tool in the semantics of programming languages is adequately argued by books and articles that employ them extensively in semantic descriptions (many such references are listed in the bibliography at the end of this book). Rather than review the subject from that perspective, let me instead touch briefly on why they are useful in programming.

Consider a familiar mathematical operation: taking the derivative of a continuous real valued function. The derivative of a function f is the function f' where

$$f'(x) = \frac{f(x + dx) - f(x)}{dx}$$

for an infinitesimal dx. For purposes of an estimate, it will simplify our discussion to bind dx to a small number (say .0001). Of course, it could passed as a parameter, but this is not necessary for the point below. A Scheme program for computing the derivative can be coded as follows:

```
(define (deriv f)
  (/ (- (f (+ x dx)) (f x))
     dx))
```

Here the derivative is higher-order, since it takes a function as a parameter, but it is coded as returning a numerical value on a given argument, rather than returning a new function as is the case for the mathematical derivative. This can lead to problems if the distinction is not properly observed. For example, the program (deriv (deriv f 1)), which might be mistakenly intended to compute the second derivative of f at 1, will yield a *runtime type error* complaining that deriv has the wrong number of arguments. Of course, the second derivative at 1 could be successfully calculated using an explicit abstraction,

```
(deriv (lambda (x) (deriv f x)) 1).
```

and the 'lambda' could be eliminated by making a local definition if this intrusion of higher-order is considered undesirable. However, these approaches generalize poorly to the case where what I want is the third derivative or the fourth derivative, and so on. To accommodate these cases, it would be possible to include a parameter n for the n'th iteration of differentiation in the definition of deriv, but it is more elegant and understandable to quit fighting against the mathematical usage in the programming, and to start coding it instead. The derivative takes a function as an argument and produces a function as a value:

```
(define (deriv f)
  (lambda (x)
    (/ (- (f (+ x dx)) (f x))
       dx)))
```

The second derivative at 1 is now properly coded as ((deriv (deriv f)) 1) as in the mathematical notation $f''(1)$ where the primes denote an operation on a function. To calculate n'th derivatives, it is possible to write another function that takes a function g and a number n as arguments and produces the function $g^n = g \circ g \circ \cdots \circ g$ (n copies) as its value. This is a powerful abstraction since there are many other ways this function might be used; the key idea here, the composition exponential, can be used modularly with the derivative rather than being mixed up in the code for the n'th derivative function.

Where do types come into this? Lying at the heart of the distinction just discussed is the notion of 'currying' that has appeared so often in previous chapters. Fortunately, programmers manage to use currying without necessarily understanding cartesian closed categories; the concepts involved can be appreciated at a quite basic level in practice. In the first case above, the derivative function was coded as a function taking as its arguments a real-valued function f and a real number x. When coded in ML, it looks like this:

```
fun deriv (f:real -> real, x:real):real =  (f(x+dx) - f(x))/dx.
```

and the ML type-checker indicates its type as ((real -> real) * real) -> real. The way to read this is to think of it as the definition of a function deriv on a product type with the abstraction described using pattern matching. The second (curried) way to program this function is

```
fun deriv f = fn x:real => ((f(x+dx) - f(x))/dx):real
```

where, you may recall, the ML syntax for λ is fn and an arrow => is employed in place of a dot. For this term, the type is (real -> real) -> real -> real.

Another example of the usefulness of higher-order functions is the powerful programming technique that one obtains by combining them with references and assignments. A characteristic example drawn from a popular textbook that propounds Scheme programming appears in Table 7.1. The procedure make-account takes a starting balance as an argument and produces an 'account object' as a value. The account object is itself a higher-order function, returned as dispatch, that has its own local state given by the contents of the 'instance variable' balance, which contains the current balance of the object. The arguments taken by the object include the 'messages' represented by atoms 'withdraw and 'deposit and the arguments of the 'message sends', which appear in the formal parameters amount in the 'method definitions' of withdraw and deposit. Although the object-oriented jargon is a bit thick here, the programming technique is flexible and elegant. To create an account, the balance of the object must be initialized by applying make-account to the number that will be the starting value of its instance variable. For example, if Dan is defined as the value of (make-account 50) and George

Table 7.1
Using Local Variables and Higher-Order Functions in Scheme

```
(define (make-account balance)
  (define (withdraw amount)
    (if (>= balance amount)
        (sequence (set! balance
                        (- balance amount))
                  balance)
        "Insufficient funds"))
  (define (deposit amount)
    (set! balance (+ balance amount))
    balance)
  (define (dispatch m)
    (cond ((eq? m 'withdraw) withdraw)
          ((eq? m 'deposit) deposit)
          (else (error "Unknown request"
                       m))))
  dispatch)
```

is defined as the value of (make-account 100), then the account objects will correctly maintain their separate balance levels though a sequence of 'messages sends' describing the financial history of the objects.

Examples such as the ones given above are very common. It is possible to program around them in a first-order way, but useful abstractions may then be lost.

Recursive types.

Consider the following pair of programs:

```
(define (cbvY f)
  ((lambda (x) (lambda (y) (f (x x) y)))
   (lambda (x) (lambda (y) (f (x x) y)))))

(define (badadd x) (+ x "astring")).
```

Both of them are compiled without comment by Scheme. They illustrate a trade-off in the type-checking of programs. The first program cbvY is the *call-by-value fixed-point combinator.* It is an interesting program that can be used to make recursive definitions without using explicit recursive equations. The second program `badadd` contains a 'semantic' error in the form of a bad addition. Many of the actual bugs encountered in programs are like this one—despite how silly it looks in this simple example. Both of these programs can be executed in Scheme although the second program will probably cause a runtime type error. These two examples could be rendered in ML as follows:

```
fun cbvY f =
  ((fn x => (fn y => f (x x) y))
   (fn x => (fn y => f (x x) y)))


fun badadd x = x + "astring".
```

but the ML type-checker will reject both of them as having type errors. In the second case the rejection will occur because there is an expression that purports to add something to a string—an operation that is not allowed. The first program is rejected because it has an application `x x` of a variable to itself and no type can be inferred for this by the ML type-checker. From the viewpoint of a programmer, one might see the type-checking as a useful diagnostic for the second program and a hindrance for the first one.

A programming language is said to have *static* type-checking if the type-correctness of the program is established before the program is compiled. Scheme does not carry out such a check, but ML does. Of course, type-correctness is relative to the typing discipline, so this is a language design issue. In a language that allows most or all programs to be accepted as type-correct at compiletime, it will be necessary to carry out various runtime type checks, and some errors that might have been caught by a type-checker may not be detected as quickly as one would desire. At an alternate extreme, a way to ensure that there are no runtime type errors is to reject all programs as having type errors at compiletime. Of course, no programming language has a typing discipline as strict as that, but many languages are more restrictive than seems reasonable. The right balance in a language will discipline programming in order to provide useful diagnostic testing for errors while not ruling out programs that capture useful abstractions or efficient algorithms.

For example, languages that check the types of programs before compiling them can compensate for the problem with `cbvY` just mentioned by employing a more general type inference system than that of ML or by allowing the programmer to use explicit recursive types such as the ones discussed in the previous chapter. The ML version of the call-by-value fixed-point combinator is given in Table 7.2. If you find this program difficult to read (even if it is partly because you do not know ML syntax!) then you are probably in good company. To get a start on understanding it, think of this as an annotation of

Table 7.2
ML Version of the Call-by-Value Fixed-Point Combinator

```
local
  datatype 'a fix = FUN of 'a fix -> 'a
  fun NUF (FUN x) = x
in
  fun cbvY f =
    (fn x => (fn y => f((NUF x) x)y))
      (FUN(fn x => (fn y => f((NUF x) x)y)))
end
```

the earlier program with coercions that make the types of subterms explicit. In fact, the type of the ML program is

$$((a \rightarrow b) \rightarrow (a \rightarrow b)) \rightarrow (a \rightarrow b)$$

rather than $(c \rightarrow c) \rightarrow c$ as one might have hoped, but rather than carry out a detailed analysis of the program, let me just draw attention to a couple of points about it. First of all, the definition of the procedure cbvY itself in the three lines of code between **in** and **end** is *not* recursive since cbvY appears only on the left-hand side of the defining equation. The recursion lies instead in the **datatype** declaration in the local bindings where a unary operator **fix** (written in postfix notation) is defined by a recursive equation. In that expression, the symbol **'a** represents a *type variable*. A more mathematical way of writing the datatype declaration would be to indicate that $fix(a) \cong fix(a) \rightarrow a$ where

$$FUN : (fix(a) \rightarrow a) \rightarrow fix(a)$$

defines the isomorphism. The inverse of the isomorphism is the function

$$NUF : fix(a) \rightarrow (fix(a) \rightarrow a)$$

defined in the third line of the program. If we remove the declaration of the type and the isomorphisms from this ML program, we obtain the definition of cbvY that was rejected as having type errors.

Parametric polymorphism.

Although recursive types are a powerful tool for recovering the losses incurred by imposing a type discipline, there is another subtle concept to be found in the way certain

abstractions can be formed in the untyped language. Here is a Scheme program that
appends two lists of elements:

```
(define (append headlist taillist)
  (if (null? headlist)
      taillist
      (cons (car headlist)
            (append (cdr headlist) taillist))))
```

Scheme programmers never need to concern themselves about the *types* of the elements
in the lists being appended, since this program will work equally well on any pair of
arguments so long as they are *lists*. In some languages where programmers must declare
their types, it might be impossible to obtain this level of abstraction. Instead, it might
be necessary to write a program that appends lists of integers and another program that
appends lists of string arrays, and so on.

To avoid losing abstractions, languages with static type-checking deal with this problem by using *polymorphism*. The word 'polymorphism' means having many forms; in
typed programming languages it ordinarily refers to the idea that a symbol may have
many types. In one of its simplest forms, polymorphism arises from the use of a variable that specifies an indeterminate or parameterized type for an expression. This is
called *parametric polymorphism*. In its simplest form it can be seen as a kind of macro
expansion. For example, the Ada programming language has a construct known as a
generic that serves this purpose. A procedure declared with a generic in Ada is explicitly
instantiated with a type before it is used, but the abstraction can make it unnecessary to
rewrite a piece of code that would work equally well for two different types. For example,
the function that appends lists takes a pair of lists of elements of type t as an argument
and returns a list of elements of type t as a result. Here the particular type t is unimportant, so it is replaced by a variable a and the type is indicated as $\text{list}(a) \to \text{list}(a)$. To
see another example, consider the function that takes two reference cells and exchanges
their contents. Obviously, this operation is independent of the types of elements in the
reference cells; it is a 'polymorphic swapping' function. In ML it can be coded as follows:

```
fun swap (x,y) =
  let val temp = ! x
  in  x := ! y ; y := temp
  end
```

where the exclamation marks are the dereferencing operation: for example, !x denotes
the contents of the reference cell x. An interesting innovation introduced by ML is an
inference algorithm that can *infer* a polymorphic type for this program without the need
for programmer annotations. Specifically, using ML syntax, the type is inferred to be

```
swap : ('a ref * 'a ref) -> unit.
```

Let me offer a brief explanation of the notation in this type. Since **swap** works with a side effect (change of memory), its output is simply the unique value of the type **unit**. The type of **swap** indicates that the references have the same type since the type variable **'a** is used for *both* arguments. This means that it is type-correct to swap the contents of two integer references or swap the contents of two string references, but a program that might swap the contents of an integer reference with that of a string reference will be rejected with a type error before being compiled.

Let us anticipate the precise definition of ML polymorphism with some discussion of what its limitations are in programming. Although type inference is an excellent tool for cutting the tedium of providing type annotations for programs, there is a great deal of abstraction that is lost in the compromises of the ML polymorphic types. Consider, for example, the following Scheme program:

```
(define applyto
    (lambda (f) (cons (f 3) (f "hi"))))
```
(7.1)

It defines a procedure **applyto** which takes a function as an argument and forms a cons cell from the results of applying it to the number 3 and the string "hi". While it should not be difficult to think up many interesting things that can be applied to both 3 and "hi", let us keep things simple and consider

```
(applyto (lambda (x) x))
```

which evaluates to the cell (3 . "hi"). All this seems very simple and natural, but the ML type inference algorithm is unwilling to see this program as type-correct. In particular, the program

```
fn f => ( f(3), f("hi") )
```

will be rejected with an indication that the function **f** cannot take both 3 *and* "hi" as arguments since they have different types. This seems a bit dull-witted in light of the Scheme example, which evidently shows that there are perfectly good programs that *can* take both of these as arguments. ML has a construct that allows some level of such polymorphism. The program

```
let fun I x = x in (I(3), I("hi")) end
```

is type-correct but clearly fails to achieve the abstraction of the Scheme program since it only makes sense for a *given* value of **f** (in this case, **f** is **I**). To obtain a program as abstract as the one written in Scheme, it is necessary to introduce a more expressive type system than the one ML has. Such a system will be described in Chapter 11.

7.2   Security

What properties are expected for the evaluation of a type-correct program beyond those that may hold of an arbitrary one? To appreciate the significance of the types, look again at the operational rules in Table 4.4. Take a typical rule such as the one for application in call-by-name:

$$\frac{M \Downarrow \lambda x : t.\ M' \qquad [N/x]M' \Downarrow V}{M(N) \Downarrow V}$$

This is the only rule whose conclusion describes how to derive a value for an application, so any attempt to prove that $M(N)$ has value V must use it. The rule requires that two hypotheses be established. Let us focus on the first. We noted in Lemma 4.5 that if $M \Downarrow U$ for some value U, then U is the unique value that satisfies this relationship. Hence there are three possibilities that could result from the attempt to find a value for M:

1. there is no value U such that $M \Downarrow U$, or

2. there is a term N such that $M \Downarrow \lambda x : t.\ N$, or

3. there is a term U such that $M \Downarrow U$, but U does not have the form $\lambda x : t.\ N$.

The first of these might occur because of divergence, or perhaps for some other reason. The second is the conclusion we must reach to find a value for $M(N)$. The third case arises in an 'abnormal' situation in which something other than an abstraction is being applied to an argument. For example, this would happen if we attempted to evaluate the application $\mathbf{0}(\mathbf{0})$ of the number $\mathbf{0}$ to itself. Here is what the type-correctness of $M(N)$ ensures: the third possibility above never occurs. In the example $\mathbf{0}(\mathbf{0})$, this is clear, since $\mathbf{0}$ has type **num** rather than type **num** $\to t$ as it would be required to have if it is to be applied to a number.

Although the first and third cases above both mean that $M(N)$ does not have a value, there is an important difference in the way this failure occurs. In particular, if it is found that $M \Downarrow U$ but U does not have the desired form, then it is possible to report immediately that the attempt to find a value for $M(N)$ has *failed*. This will not always be possible for the first case, since the failure to find a value for M may be due to an infinite regression of attempts to apply operational rules (for example, try to find a value for $\mu x : \mathbf{num}.\ x$). Any attempt to determine whether this is the case through an effective procedure will fail, because this is tantamount to solving the halting problem. Hence, the last case is special.

For some guidance, let us consider the difference between these possibilities in a familiar programming language. Here is an example of a Scheme program that will diverge when applied to an argument:

```
(define (f x) (f x))
```

Evaluating (f 0) in the read-eval-print loop will be a boring and unfulfilling activity that will probably be ended by an interruption by the programmer. This program diverges and therefore does not have a value. On the other hand, what happens if we attempt to evaluate the program (0 0) in the read-eval-print loop? There is no value for this expression, but we receive an instant warning of this limitation that may look like this:

```
Application of inapplicable object 0
There is no environment available;
using the current REPL environment
```

The difference between these two outcomes arises from the distinction between *divergence* and a *runtime type error*. While divergence is generally undetectable, the runtime type error is unavoidable and is best reported when it arises.

Our next step is to bring out the special nature of a runtime type error by including operational rules for its detection. In each of the rules in Table 4.4 there are assumptions about the shape or pattern of the value resulting from evaluating a particular expression. If the expression does have a value and this pattern is not satisfied, then the rule is not applicable. To deal with runtime errors, we augment the rules by including additional rules that cover anomalous cases for the evaluation result. In these undesirable cases, the result of an expression's evaluation will be a special term **tyerr** which signals a type error. For example, in addition to the rule for application given in Table 4.4, where the rule applies only when the evaluation of the operator yields an abstraction, we include an additional rule that covers the other cases:

$$\frac{M \Downarrow V \qquad V \notin \text{Lambda}}{M(N) \Downarrow \textbf{tyerr}}$$

where Lambda is the syntactic class of expressions of the form $\lambda x : t.\ M$ where x, t, M are any variable, type, or term respectively.

PCF with type errors.

To study these ideas rigorously, let us focus on a specific language. The following grammar defines the syntax of *type expressions t* and *terms M* of a calculus called PCF *with*

Table 7.3
Call-by-Value Evaluation with Type Errors

$$\textbf{tyerr} \Downarrow^\circ \textbf{tyerr} \qquad \frac{L \Downarrow^\circ V \qquad V \notin \text{Boolean}}{\textbf{if } L \textbf{ then } M \textbf{ else } N \Downarrow^\circ \textbf{tyerr}}$$

$$\frac{M \Downarrow^\circ V \qquad V \notin \text{Number}}{\textbf{pred}(M) \Downarrow^\circ \textbf{tyerr}} \qquad \frac{M \Downarrow^\circ V \qquad V \notin \text{Number}}{\textbf{succ}(M) \Downarrow^\circ \textbf{tyerr}} \qquad \frac{M \Downarrow^\circ V \qquad V \notin \text{Number}}{\textbf{zero?}(M) \Downarrow^\circ \textbf{tyerr}}$$

$$\frac{M \Downarrow^\circ V \qquad V \notin \text{Lambda}}{M(N) \Downarrow^\circ \textbf{tyerr}} \qquad \frac{M \Downarrow^\circ \lambda x : t.\ M' \qquad N \Downarrow^\circ \textbf{tyerr}}{M(N) \Downarrow^\circ \textbf{tyerr}}$$

type errors. The extended calculus is the same as PCF except for the inclusion of a new constant called **tyerr**. Here is the expanded grammar:

$$
\begin{aligned}
t \quad &::= \quad \textbf{num} \mid \textbf{bool} \mid t \to t \\
M \quad &::= \quad \textbf{tyerr} \mid \textbf{0} \mid \textbf{succ}(M) \mid \textbf{pred}(M) \mid \textbf{true} \mid \textbf{false} \mid \textbf{zero?}(M) \mid \\
&\qquad x \mid \lambda x : t.\ M \mid M M \mid \mu x : t.\ M \mid \textbf{if } M \textbf{ then } M \textbf{ else } M
\end{aligned}
$$

The typing rules for extended PCF are the same as those for PCF itself. Note, in particular, that the relation $H \vdash \textbf{tyerr} : t$ fails for each H and t since there is no typing rule for proving such a relation.

The operational rules for *call-by-value* PCF with type errors are more interesting than the ones for call-by-name because of the form of the application rules. The rules for a natural operational semantics are those given earlier in Table 6.4 together with the 'error' rules given in Table 7.3. Values in the new language are those of PCF together with the term **tyerr** for a type error. The rules in the table are defined using syntactic judgements such as $V \notin$ Boolean where Boolean represents the values of boolean type. In the rules, Number is the set of values of numerical type (that is, numerals) and Lambda those of higher type (that is, abstractions). The expanded set of rules has properties similar to those of the system without explicit error elements. For example, the relation $\Downarrow^\circ$ for the full language is still a partial function, that is, if $M \Downarrow^\circ U$ and $M \Downarrow^\circ V$, then $U \equiv V$. What differentiates this system from the previous one is the fact that the hypotheses of the rules now cover all possible patterns for the outcome of an evaluation. If the evaluation of a term calls for the evaluation of other terms, then the error rules indicate what is to be done if the result of evaluating these subgoals is a type error or yields a conclusion having the wrong form. The interest of the claim we aim to establish—that the evaluation of a well-typed program does not yield a type error—depends entirely on the nature of these error rules so it is important to examine them closely to see that they do indeed encode all of the circumstances under which one would expect a type error to be reported. Consider closely, for example, the error rules for application. There are two of these: The first asserts that if there is a value such that $M \Downarrow^\circ V$ and yet V is not an abstraction, then evaluation of $M(N)$ results in a type error. The second asserts that if M does indeed evaluate to an abstraction but N evaluates to a type error, then $M(N)$ does so as well. In other words, type errors are percolated through the evaluation. Are there other possibilities? The answer seems to be 'yes'. Consider, for example, the possibility that there is *no* value V such that $M \Downarrow V$ and yet the evaluation of N results in a type error. Should a type error be recorded in this case? If that is desired, then the second of the two rules for application could be replaced by the following rule:

$$\frac{N \Downarrow^\circ \textbf{tyerr}}{M(N) \Downarrow^\circ \textbf{tyerr}} \tag{7.2}$$

The reader can easily supply an example showing that the result of this replacement is a different evaluation system in which a type error is more likely to occur. If we are still able to prove a stronger result about well-typed programs running without type errors, then this will be a stronger result for the latter system than it was for the former. The basic point is this: the significance of security from runtime type errors depends on the definition of a runtime type error. Not a stunning conclusion perhaps, but an important one all the same.

Now, we would like to prove a theorem that says that the evaluation of a well-typed term does not produce a type error. Here is a more precise statement:

7.1 Theorem. *If $H \vdash M : t$ then it is not the case that $M \Downarrow^\circ$ **tyerr**.* $\qquad\square$

The result we need to show absence of runtime type errors is a form of subject reduction. We have encountered this kind of result before, Theorem 4.4 expresses subject reduction for PCF relative to a transition semantics for instance. Here it must be proved relative to the typing system for PCF and the evaluation relation $\Downarrow^\circ$ described in Tables 6.4 and 7.3.

7.2 Theorem (Subject Reduction). *Let M be a term in extended* **PCF**. *If $M \Downarrow^\circ V$ and $H \vdash M : t$, then $H \vdash V : t$.*

Proof: The proof is by induction on the height of the evaluation $M \Downarrow^\circ V$. I will do only the cases for predecessor, application, and recursion.

Case $M \equiv \textbf{pred}(M')$. There are three possibilities for the last step in the derivation of $M \Downarrow^\circ V$. If $M' \Downarrow^\circ V'$, then we employ the induction hypothesis to conclude that

$H \vdash V' : \textbf{num}$. In particular, this means that $V' \in \text{Number}$ so $V' \equiv \mathbf{0}$ or the last step of the derivation must be an application of the rule

$$\frac{M \Downarrow^\circ \textbf{succ}(V) \qquad V \in \text{Number}}{\textbf{pred}(M) \Downarrow^\circ V}$$

where $V' \equiv \textbf{succ}(V)$. If $V' \equiv \mathbf{0}$, then the desired conclusion is immediate, since $H \vdash \mathbf{0} : \textbf{num}$. On the other hand, the only way to have $H \vdash \textbf{succ}(V) : \textbf{num}$ is if $H \vdash V : \textbf{num}$, so this possibility also leads to the desired conclusion.

Case $M \equiv L(N)$. Say $H \vdash L : r \rightarrow s$ and $H \vdash N : r$. There are two operational rules that may apply to the evaluation of an application. However, if $M \Downarrow^\circ V$ and $V \notin \text{Lambda}$, then we cannot have $H \vdash V : r$ since canonical forms of higher type are in Lambda. Hence the last step in the evaluation of M must have the following form:

$$\frac{L \Downarrow^\circ \lambda x : r.\ L' \qquad [N/x]L' \Downarrow^\circ V}{M(M') \Downarrow^\circ V}$$

Now, by the induction hypothesis, $H \vdash \lambda x : r.\ L' : r \rightarrow s$ so it must be that $H,\ x : r \vdash L' : s$. Hence, by Lemma 4.1(2), $H \vdash [N/x]L' : s$, and it therefore follows from the induction hypothesis that $H \vdash V : t$.

Case $M \equiv \mu x : t.\ M'$. In this case, $[\mu x : t.\ M'/x]M' \Downarrow^\circ V$. By Lemma 4.1, $H \vdash [\mu x : t.\ M'/x]M' : t$ so $H \vdash V : t$ by the induction hypothesis.

Theorem 7.1 now follows immediately, since **tyerr** does not have a type.

Exercises

7.1 If the rule 7.2 replaces the last rule in Table 7.3, is it still the case that well-typed programs do not have runtime type errors?

7.3   Reference Types

Almost all of the programming languages in widespread use include constructs for assignment and mutable data structures such as arrays. The techniques for modeling state and memory were a primary focus of research in the semantics of programming languages in the 1970's, and there is an extensive literature on the subject. Since such constructs are in widespread use, it is worthwhile to discuss types and assignment in the current context from the viewpoint of operational semantics.

The addition of assignments to our language PCF has a very significant effect on its semantics. First of all, it is not possible to describe the new semantics simply by extending the old one with a few rules for the additional constructs. Moreover, the nuances of references have an impact on language design decisions. To see why, it is necessary to think more about how the evaluation of programs will actually be carried out. Consider the call-by-name evaluation rule for application

$$\frac{M \Downarrow \lambda x : t.\ M' \qquad [N/x]M' \Downarrow V}{M(N) \Downarrow V}$$

from the perspective of its implementation. In the case that the bound variable (formal parameter) x in the abstraction does not appear in the body of the abstraction, we are spared the needless calculation of the value of N since the substitution simply discards this term. On the other hand, if there are many occurrences of x in M', it is possible that the term N will be re-evaluated many times in the course of finding a value for $[N/x]M'$. The typical optimization for dealing with this is to create a reference cell and put N into it. When a value for x is needed, this cell is consulted. The first time such a consultation occurs, the value of N is calculated and stored in the reference cell in anticipation of a future need for the value. In this way, the value of N is calculated at most once, and, if it is not needed, it is never calculated at all. Except for performance, the difference between actually substituting N for x versus holding a suspension in a reference cell is invisible to the programmer in the language as it currently stands. But this invisibility disappears when the language includes constructs that access and alter a store since the point *when* such an expression is evaluated makes a difference. Although there are languages that use call-by-name evaluation and assignments, most languages similar to PCF use a *call-by-value* evaluation when assignments are included in the language. For this reason, the language PCF$_{:=}$ that I describe below uses a call-by-value evaluation order.

The syntax of PCF$_{:=}$ is given as follows:

$$
\begin{aligned}
t \quad &::= \quad \textbf{num} \mid \textbf{bool} \mid t \rightarrow t \mid \textbf{ref}(t) \\
M \quad &::= \quad \textbf{0} \mid \textbf{succ}(M) \mid \textbf{pred}(M) \mid \textbf{true} \mid \textbf{false} \mid \textbf{zero?}(M) \mid \\
&\qquad x \mid \lambda x : t.\ M \mid MM \mid \mu x : t.\ M \mid \textbf{if}\ M\ \textbf{then}\ M\ \textbf{else}\ M \\
&\qquad \textbf{ref}(M) \mid\ !\ M \mid M := M \mid M; M
\end{aligned}
$$

The typing rules for the calculus are the same as those for PCF together with the rules in Table 7.4. The new constructs include new types $\textbf{ref}(t)$ of references to values of type t. If M is a term of type t, then $\textbf{ref}(M)$ is a location of type $\textbf{ref}(t)$ holding the value of M. In many programming languages, the position in which an identifier appears will determine whether the variable is referring to the location it is bound to or to the contents of that location. For example, in the expression $x := x + 1$, the occurrence of x on the left of the assignment connective denotes a *location*, called the *L-value* of x, into

Table 7.4
Typing for References

[Ref]	$$\dfrac{H \vdash M : t}{H \vdash \mathbf{ref}(M) : \mathbf{ref}(t)}$$
[Deref]	$$\dfrac{H \vdash M : \mathbf{ref}(t)}{H \vdash \,!M : t}$$
[Seq]	$$\dfrac{H \vdash M : s \qquad H \vdash N : t}{H \vdash M; N : t}$$
[Assign]	$$\dfrac{H \vdash M : \mathbf{ref}(t) \qquad H \vdash N : t}{H \vdash M := N : t}$$

which a numerical value is to be put. The occurrence of x on the right of the assignment connective denotes the *number,* called the *R-value* of x. After the assignment, the new contents of the L-value of x will be the previous R-value plus one. To keep this distinction clear, $\mathbf{PCF}_{:=}$ makes a rigid distinction on this point. A reference in the language always refers to a location and never to the contents of the location (regardless of the position of the expression relative to an assignment connective). So the command for incrementing the contents of a reference x is $x := \mathbf{succ}(!x)$. The typing rule says that $!x$ has type t if x has type $\mathbf{ref}(t)$. The assignment command itself requires a reference of type $\mathbf{ref}(t)$ on the left of $:=$ and a term of type t on the right. Finally, any two terms $M : s$ and $N : t$ can be composed by the sequencing connective, but $M; N$ has the type t of N.

Now, as I said before, the semantics of the new language must be substantially different from that of PCF without references. In particular, the semantics must include a notion of the *state* of a variable that cannot be modeled merely by substitution as in the semantics of Table 4.4. This means that evaluation must be carried out with respect to a model of *memory* in which values are associated with locations. This model of memory must account for the possibility that two references may refer to the *same* location, a phenomenon known as *aliasing*. To see it in a simple example using an intuitive semantics, consider the program

$$(\lambda x : \mathbf{ref}(\mathbf{num}). \, [\lambda y : \mathbf{ref}(\mathbf{num}). \, (y := \mathbf{0}); (!x)] \, x) \, \mathbf{ref}(\mathbf{succ}(\mathbf{0})) \qquad (7.3)$$

where two kinds of brackets are used to help emphasize the parsing. What is its value upon evaluation? The first step of evaluation will put the number one into a location denoted by the variable x of number reference type. The term $\lambda y \ldots$ will then be applied to this location binding the variable y of number reference type to it. Then the number zero is put into the location indicated by y. Finally, the value of the expression is given as the contents of the location denoted by x. Since this is the same location as that denoted by y, this value must be zero (not one).

It should be clear from this example that a semantics for this language will include not only the notion of the memory in which a term is evaluated but also a notion of *location* that a term of reference type denotes. There is a way to simplify the description of this relationship by describing the operational semantics of the language using an expanded language obtained by adding a syntax of locations to the language defined above. Let Location be a new primitive syntax class and consider the following grammar:

$$l \quad \in \quad \text{Location}$$
$$M \quad ::= \quad \mathbf{0} \mid \mathbf{succ}(M) \mid \mathbf{pred}(M) \mid \mathbf{true} \mid \mathbf{false} \mid \mathbf{zero?}(M) \mid$$
$$x \mid \lambda x : t.\ M \mid MM \mid \mu x : t.\ M \mid \mathbf{if}\ M\ \mathbf{then}\ M\ \mathbf{else}\ M$$
$$l \mid \mathbf{ref}(M) \mid !\ M \mid M := M \mid M; M$$

Values are given by the following grammar:

$$V \quad ::= \quad \mathbf{0} \mid \mathbf{succ}(V) \mid \mathbf{true} \mid \mathbf{false} \mid \lambda x : t.\ M \mid l$$

Let Value be the collection of values V. To define the operational semantics for $\text{PCF}_{:=}$, we need a model of memory; define $\mathbb{M}$ to be the set of partial functions $\pi : \text{Variable} \rightsquigarrow \text{Value}$ such that the domain of definition of π is finite. The semantics of $\text{PCF}_{:=}$ will be given relative to a function

$$\text{new} : \mathbb{M} \rightarrow \text{Location}$$

that associates with each memory π a location $\text{new}(\pi)$ that is not in the domain of definition of π—that is, a 'new' location. The operational semantics of this language is given by the rules in Table 7.5.

- A location is a value; it evaluates to itself without altering the memory. To evaluate a reference $\mathbf{ref}(M)$ in a memory π, begin by evaluating M to obtain a value V and a new memory θ. The result of the evaluation of the reference is then a pair consisting of a location not in the domain of definition of θ as its first coordinate and θ itself as its second coordinate.

- To evaluate the deferencing of M in a memory π, first evaluate M in π to obtain a location l and a memory θ. The result of the evaluation is the value associated with l in θ together with the memory θ.

- To evaluate an assignment $M := N$ in a memory π, begin by evaluating M to obtain a location l in a memory π'. Then N is evaluated in this memory to obtain a value V and a memory θ. The result of evaluating the assignment is the value V together with a memory $\theta[l \mapsto V]$ in which V is the value associated with l.

Table 7.5
Operational Rules for PCF with References

$$(l, \pi) \Downarrow (l, \pi) \qquad \frac{(M, \pi) \Downarrow (V, \theta)}{(\mathbf{ref}(M), \pi) \Downarrow (\mathrm{new}(\theta),\ \theta[\mathrm{new}(\theta) \mapsto V]])} \qquad \frac{(M, \pi) \Downarrow (l, \theta)}{(!M, \pi) \Downarrow (\theta(l), \theta)}$$

$$\frac{(M, \pi) \Downarrow (l, \pi') \qquad (N, \pi') \Downarrow (V, \theta)}{(M := N, \pi) \Downarrow (V, \theta[l \mapsto V])} \qquad \frac{(M, \pi) \Downarrow (U, \pi') \qquad (N, \pi') \Downarrow (V, \theta)}{(M; N, \pi) \Downarrow (V, \theta)}$$

$$(\lambda x : t.\ M, \pi) \Downarrow (\lambda x : t.\ M, \pi)$$

$$\frac{(M, \pi) \Downarrow (\lambda x : t.M', \pi') \qquad (N, \pi') \Downarrow (U, \pi'') \qquad ([U/x]M', \pi'') \Downarrow (V, \theta)}{(M(N), \pi) \Downarrow (V, \theta)}$$

$$(\mathbf{0}, \pi) \Downarrow (\mathbf{0}, \pi) \qquad (\mathbf{true}, \pi) \Downarrow (\mathbf{true}, \pi) \qquad (\mathbf{false}, \pi) \Downarrow (\mathbf{false}, \pi)$$

$$\frac{(M, \pi) \Downarrow (\mathbf{0}, \theta)}{(\mathbf{pred}(M), \pi) \Downarrow (\mathbf{0}, \theta)} \qquad \frac{(M, \pi) \Downarrow (\mathbf{succ}(V), \theta)}{(\mathbf{pred}(M), \pi) \Downarrow (V, \theta)}$$

$$\frac{(M, \pi) \Downarrow (V, \theta)}{(\mathbf{succ}(M), \pi) \Downarrow (\mathbf{succ}(V), \theta)}$$

$$\frac{(M, \pi) \Downarrow (\mathbf{0}, \theta)}{(\mathbf{zero?}(M), \pi) \Downarrow (\mathbf{true}, \theta)} \qquad \frac{(M, \pi) \Downarrow (\mathbf{succ}(V), \theta)}{(\mathbf{zero?}(M), \pi) \Downarrow (\mathbf{false}, \theta)}$$

$$\frac{(M_1, \pi) \Downarrow (\mathbf{true}, \pi') \quad (M_2, \pi') \Downarrow (V, \theta)}{(\mathbf{if}\ M_1\ \mathbf{then}\ M_2\ \mathbf{else}\ M_3, \pi) \Downarrow (V, \theta)} \qquad \frac{(M_1, \pi) \Downarrow (\mathbf{false}, \pi') \quad (M_3, \pi') \Downarrow (V, \theta)}{(\mathbf{if}\ M_1\ \mathbf{then}\ M_2\ \mathbf{else}\ M_3, \pi) \Downarrow (V, \theta)}$$

$$\frac{([\mu x : t.\ M/x]M, \pi) \Downarrow (V, \theta)}{(\mu x : t.\ M, \pi) \Downarrow (V, \theta)}$$

- A sequence $M; N$ is evaluated by evaluating M and then evaluating N in the memory obtained from the evaluation of M. The result of evaluating the sequence is the result of this evaluation of N. In particular, the value of M is 'lost', so the only reason for evaluating M in this way would concern how it changes the memory.

- The evaluation rules of other constructs of PCF are similar to the ones in Table 4.4 except for the presence of the memory in each rule. It is important to note, for example, that in an application, the argument of the application is evaluated in the memory resulting from the evaluation of the operator. Moreover, the substitution $[U/x]M'$ of the value of the operand into the body of the abstraction obtained from evaluating the operator is evaluated in the memory yielded by the evaluation of the operand. The memory resulting from *this* is the one obtained from the evaluation of the application. Intuitively, therefore, the evaluation proceeds from left to right, with each evaluation being done with respect to the memory obtained from the previous one.

Exercises

7.2 Write out the steps for the evaluation of Program 7.3.

7.3* Formulate and prove a theorem about runtime type errors for the well-typed programs of $PCF_{:=}$. (Hint: extend the typing system to include a rule for locations.)

7.4 Recursive Types

It was mentioned before how recursive types can be used to make a statically typed language more expressive. Recursively defined types are very common in programming; to provide a rigorous discussion of their semantics, let us focus on a particular system called the **F**ixed **P**oint **C**alculus, FPC, whose purpose is to do for recursive definitions of types what PCF did for recursive definitions of functions. The grammar of FPC requires two syntax classes of variables: one called Variable for *term* variables, and another called

Table 7.6
Typing Rules for Recursively Defined Types in FPC

[Unit]   **unity : unit**

$$[\text{Intro}] \qquad \frac{H \vdash M : [\mu a.t/a]t}{H \vdash \mathbf{intro}[\mu a.\ t]M : \mu a.\ t}$$

$$[\text{Elim}] \qquad \frac{H \vdash M : \mu a.\ t}{H \vdash \mathbf{elim}[\mu a.\ t]M : [\mu a.t/a]t}$$

TypeVariable for *type* variables. The syntax of the language is given as follows:

$$
\begin{array}{rcl}
x & \in & \text{Variable} \\
a & \in & \text{TypeVariable} \\
t & ::= & \mathbf{unit} \mid t \to t \mid t \times t \mid t + t \mid a \mid \mu a.\ t \\
M & ::= & x \mid \lambda x : t.\ M \mid MM \mid \\
  &   & \mathbf{unity} \mid (M, M) \mid \mathbf{fst}(M) \mid \mathbf{snd}(M) \mid \\
  &   & \mathbf{inl}[t + t](M) \mid \mathbf{inr}[t + t](M) \mid \\
  &   & \mathbf{case}\ M\ \mathbf{of}\ \mathbf{inl}(x) \Rightarrow M\ \mathbf{or}\ \mathbf{inr}(x) \Rightarrow M \mid \\
  &   & \mathbf{intro}[\mu a.\ t]M \mid \mathbf{elim}[\mu a.\ t]M
\end{array}
$$

Aside from the familiar function space, product, and sum operators on types, FPC has a constant type **unit**. A type variable is also a type, and a *recursive type* has the form $\mu a.\ t$. This expression is intentionally reminiscent of the notation $\mu x : t.\ M$ for recursive functions in PCF. Note, however, that terms $\mu x : t.\ M$ are not part of the FPC syntax: we shall see that recursive functions can be defined using recursive types. Free occurrences of a in t are bound by the μ-binding in $\mu a.\ t$, and the usual conventions about type trees and trees up to α-equivalence are to be assumed. FPC includes constructs of the λ-calculus with products and sums together with a new constant **unity** and two new forms of expression related to the recursive types. An expression of the form $\mathbf{intro}[\mu a.\ t]M$ is called an *introduction,* and one of the form $\mathbf{elim}[\mu a.\ t]M$ an *elimination.* Both operators consist of a (introduced or eliminated) term M together with a type tag $\mu a.\ t$.

The typing rules for FPC include those of the simply-typed λ-calculus as given in Table 2.1, the rules for products and sums in Tables 3.1 and 3.3, and the three new rules in Table 7.6. The term **unity** simply has type **unit**. If a term M has type $[\mu a.t/a]t$ in an assignment H, then $\mathbf{intro}[\mu a.\ t]M$ has type $\mu a.\ t$. On the other hand, if M has type $\mu a.t$ in assignment H, then $\mathbf{elim}[\mu a.\ t]M$ has type $[\mu a.t/a]t$. Unlike the system of types axiomatized in Table 7.8 for the implicit typing discipline, the terms of FPC, like those of PCF, are uniquely determined if a term has a type at all. The tags on the introduction are essential for proving the following:

7.3 Lemma. *For any type assignment H, term M, and type expressions s, t, if $H \vdash M : s$ and $H \vdash M : t$, then $s \equiv t$.*

The tag on the elimination operator is not actually needed for this, but it is sometimes handy to have it present as a reminder of the type; it can be dropped from an expression if economy of ink is desired. Indeed I will usually drop the tag on the introduction as well when it is clear from context or unimportant.

I will later come to a full discussion of the fixed-point semantics of FPC. For the moment, let us work with an intuitive semantics for the strict (call-by-value) interpretation of the language. Types are interpreted as pointed cpo's with the bottom element representing the interpretation of the divergent program of that type (assuming that there is a divergent program for the type). The constant type **unit** is interpreted by the two element lattice $\mathbb{O}$; the bottom element interprets divergence for this type and the non-bottom element interprets the constant **unity**. The interpretations of function, sum, and product types are similar to those described for call-by-value PCF in Chapter 6: the type $s \to t$ denotes the lift of the cpo of strict continuous functions from the cpo interpreting s to the cpo interpreting t, the type $s \times t$ denotes the smash product of the interpretations of s and t, and the type $s + t$ denotes the coalesced sum of the interpretations of s and t. A type variable a must be interpreted relative to an environment that binds such variables to cpo's; I will describe this precisely when the formal machinery to interpret recursive types has been developed adequately. Intuitively, a recursive type $\mu a.\ t$ is a union of the interpretations of the unwindings of the recursion. If we take $\mu^0 a.\ t \equiv \mu a.\ a$ and $\mu^{n+1} a.\ t \equiv [\mu^n a.\ t/a]t$, then the interpretation of $\mu a.\ t$ can be viewed as a kind of 'limit' of a chain

$$\llbracket \mu^0 a.\ t \rrbracket \subseteq \llbracket \mu^1 a.\ t \rrbracket \subseteq \cdots \subseteq \llbracket \mu^n a.\ t \rrbracket \subseteq \cdots \qquad (7.4)$$

Again, this will be made precise a bit later, but a better intuition can be gained from looking at some examples first. Most of the terms of the language can be interpreted using roughly the semantic equations for the function space, sum, and product constructs from Chapter 6. The constant **unity** is interpreted as the top element of $\mathbb{O}$. The 'limit' of Chain 7.4 can be viewed as a kind of least fixed point of the operator that t defines as a function of the type variable a. In particular, there are functions

$$\Phi : \llbracket \mu a.\ t \rrbracket \to \llbracket [\mu a.\ t\ /\ a]t \rrbracket$$
$$\Psi : \llbracket [\mu a.\ t\ a]t \rrbracket \to \llbracket \mu a.\ t \rrbracket$$

Table 7.7
Operational Rules for FPC

$$\textbf{unity } \Downarrow^{\circ} \textbf{ unity} \qquad \frac{M \Downarrow^{\circ} V}{\textbf{intro}(M) \Downarrow^{\circ} \textbf{intro}(V)} \qquad \frac{M \Downarrow^{\circ} \textbf{intro}(V)}{\textbf{elim}(M) \Downarrow^{\circ} V}$$

such that Φ and Ψ define an isomorphism: $[\![\mu a.\ t]\!] \cong [\![\mu a.\ t\ /\ a]t]\!]$. The interpretation then of a term $\textbf{intro}[\mu a.\ t]M$ is $\Psi(d)$ where d is the interpretation of M as an element of $[\![\mu a.t/a]t]\!]$. On the other hand, the interpretation of a term $\textbf{elim}[\mu a.\ t]N$ is $\Phi(e)$ if e is the interpretation of N as an element of $[\![\mu a.\ t]\!]$.

Let us now consider how the terms of FPC can be evaluated. As with other calculi, there is more than one choice for the evaluation order of expressions: this can be done call-by-value or call-by-name. Operational rules for call-by-value evaluation for recursive types can be found in Table 7.7. For the call-by-name case, the introduction construct restrains evaluation of the introduced term whereas, in the call-by-value case, this term is evaluated. The notion of a value in the two systems differs as well, of course. The terms M such that $M \Downarrow^{\circ} M$ can be characterized by the following grammar:

$$V ::= \textbf{unity} \mid \lambda x : t.\ M \mid (V, V) \mid \textbf{inl}(V) \mid \textbf{inr}(V) \mid \textbf{intro}[\mu a.\ t](V)$$

Finding a similar grammar for the values of the call-by-name calculus is left as an exercise for the reader. Both of these operational semantics are partial functions on well-typed terms and satisfy the subject reduction theorem.

The syntax of FPC appears rather sparse since it has no ground type other than **unit**. On the other hand, the ability to define types recursively is a powerful tool. Indeed, even **unit** is unnecessary since it can be defined in terms of the other operators! Perhaps the simplest datatype in FPC is the recursive type $\mu a.\ a$ because there are no values of this type. To see why, suppose V is a value such that the derivation of $\vdash V : \mu a.\ a$ is at least as short as that of any other value of this type. Now, V must be of the form $\textbf{intro}(U)$ for some value U and if $\vdash V : \mu a.\ a$, then, by the [Intro] typing rule, it must also be the case that $\vdash U : \mu a.\ a$. However, the derivation of this fact must be shorter than the derivation of the corresponding fact for V, which contradicts the assumption about the derivation of $\vdash V : \mu a.\ a$. Since $\mu a.\ a$ has no values, it is sometimes called the *void* type and written as **void**. In the fixed-point interpretation that we describe in the next chapter, the interpretation of **void** is the one point domain $\mathbb{U}$. Although **void** has no values, it can be combined with the function space operator to get a type $\textbf{void} \rightarrow \textbf{void}$ that does have values. Given the interpretations of **void** and $\rightarrow$, the interpretation of $\textbf{void} \rightarrow \textbf{void}$

is $\mathbb{O}$ and its non-bottom element is the interpretation of the value $\lambda x : \textbf{void}.\ x$, which could be used in place of $\textbf{unity}$.

The types $\textbf{void}$ and $\textbf{unit}$ represent the analogs for the FPC operations $+$ and $\times$ of the arithmetic operations of addition and multiplication. In the case of $\textbf{void}$, the values of type $\textbf{void} + t$ for any type t are of the form $\text{inr}(V)$ where V is a value of type t; this is because there are no values of the from $\text{inl}(U)$ having type $\textbf{void} + t$. On the other hand, $\textbf{unit} \times t$ has values of the form $(\textbf{unity}, V)$ where V is a value of type t since the only value of type $\textbf{unit}$ is $\textbf{unity}$. These facts are reflected in the cpo semantics of these types by the observations that $\mathbb{U}$ and $\mathbb{O}$ satisfy the isomorphisms $\mathbb{U} \oplus D \cong D$ and $\mathbb{O} \otimes D \cong D$.

In general, the type $\textbf{unit}$ is handy for adjoining a new element to an existing type. The interpretation of type $t + \textbf{unit}$ is the same as that of t except there is a new element adjoined alongside of t that is related only to the bottom element of the domain. In programming, this is sometimes called a t-$option$ since it can be used for the value which is ordinarily an element of t but may occasionally fail to be one. A typical example arises in programming association lists. An $association\ list$ is a list of pairs (k, d) where k is a key and d is a $datum$. For example, let us suppose that keys are variable names and a 'frame' is list of pairs consisting of variable names and associated values of a type t. We will want to define lookup function l which takes a key and finds its value in the association list. A possible type for l is $k \rightarrow (list(k \times t) \rightarrow t)$ where k is the type of keys (variable names), but this could be awkward if l is applied to an association list and a key where the association list does not have an element associated with that key. In this case, it is probably wrong to let the value of this application be some arbitrary value of t (since the fact that the key was not found probably needs some special response) and possibly bad programming practice to use some drastic measure like an exception (since the program may need to react to the absent key in a relatively normal manner, perhaps by applying the search to another frame). In a typed language like FPC, the proper implementation uses the option type $l : k \rightarrow (list(k \times t) \rightarrow (t + \textbf{unit}))$.

This brings us to the more general question of how one might code a program such as this given that there is no explicit syntax for recursive definitions of functions in the language. Indeed, it is not clear from the discussion so far that FPC has any significant computational power. To illustrate further the way recursive definitions of types can be used, let us now consider how constructs of PCF can be encoded in FPC, beginning with an encoding of the PCF types. $Enumeration\ types$ in FPC are sums of $\textbf{unit}$ types. The most familiar enumeration type is that of booleans: $\textbf{bool} = \textbf{unit} + \textbf{unit}$. We define $\textbf{true}$ and $\textbf{false}$ to be the values $\text{inl}(\textbf{unity})$ and $\text{inr}(\textbf{unity})$ respectively. The conditional expression $\textbf{if}\ L\ \textbf{then}\ M\ \textbf{else}\ N$ can now be defined as syntactic sugar for the expression $\textbf{case}\ L\ \textbf{of}\ \text{inl}(x) \Rightarrow M\ \textbf{or}\ \text{inr}(y) \Rightarrow N$. It is important to note, though, that there is $no\ function\ f$ such that $f(L)(M)(N)$ always has the same value as $\textbf{if}\ L\ \textbf{then}\ M\ \textbf{else}\ N$

since the former expression must be strict in all of its arguments whereas the the latter expression evaluates only one of M or N but never both.

Of course, it is also possible to define an enumeration type **unit + unit + unit + unit + unit + unit + unit** for modeling the days of the week—if we assume that association is to the right, then Tuesday is **inr(inr(inl(unity))))**. But what about the infinite type **unit + unit +** $\cdots$ of natural numbers? Here is where recursive types come in. The meaning of the recursive type **num** $\equiv \mu a.$ **unit** $+ a$ is the limit of an infinite chain of enumeration types in which each unwinding of the recursion adds a new number. The first number is zero: **0** $\equiv$ **intro(inl(unity))**, and successive numbers can be obtained by introduction into the right component of the body of the recursion: **succ**$(M) \equiv$ **intro[num](inr[unit, num]**(M)**)**. Predecessors can be calculated using the case statement:

$$
\begin{aligned}
\mathbf{pred}(M) \quad \equiv \quad &\mathbf{case} \quad \mathbf{elim[num]}(M) \\
&\mathbf{of} \quad \mathbf{inl}(x) \Rightarrow \mathbf{0} \\
&\mathbf{or} \quad \mathbf{inr}(y) \Rightarrow y.
\end{aligned}
$$

The test for zero is similar:

$$
\begin{aligned}
\mathbf{zero?}(M) \quad \equiv \quad &\mathbf{case} \quad \mathbf{elim[num]}(M) \\
&\mathbf{of} \quad \mathbf{inl}(x) \Rightarrow \mathbf{true} \\
&\mathbf{or} \quad \mathbf{inr}(y) \Rightarrow \mathbf{false}.
\end{aligned}
$$

But how, for example, can we calculate the addition function? Well, this can be expressed in PCF by the term

$$
\mu \text{ add. } \lambda x : \mathbf{num}. \ \lambda y : \mathbf{num}.
$$
$$
\mathbf{if} \ \mathbf{zero?}(x) \ \mathbf{then} \ y \ \mathbf{else} \ \text{add}(\mathbf{pred}(x))(\mathbf{succ}(y))
$$

so we must use recursive definitions for types to obtain recursive definitions for terms. The idea is to devise a recursive type that will allow us to type a fixed-point combinator. Let us first consider something that will not work. The best known fixed-point combinator for the *untyped* λ-calculus is

$$
Y \equiv \lambda f. \ (\lambda x. \ f(xx))(\lambda x. \ f(xx)).
$$

We can render this as a well-typed term of FPC having type $(t \to t) \to t$ for any given type t, by a use of the recursive type $s \equiv \mu a. \ a \to t$ as follows:

$$
\begin{aligned}
Y \quad \equiv \quad &\lambda f : t \to t. \\
&(\lambda x : s. \ f(\mathbf{elim[s]}(x)(x))) \\
&(\mathbf{intro[s]}(\lambda x : s. \ f(\mathbf{elim[s]}(x)(x)))).
\end{aligned}
$$

One can conjecture that, in the fixed-point semantics, $[\![Y(f)]\!] = [\![f(Y(f))]\!]$ for each function f. Indeed this is the case, but both of these programs diverge! To see why, consider how $Y(f)$ is evaluated. Suppose, for the sake of argument, that there is a value V such that $Y(f) \Downarrow^\circ V$. The last three steps in the derivation of this relation must look like this, where $W \equiv \lambda x : s.\ f(\mathbf{elim}[s](x)(x))$:

$$\frac{\vdots \atop f(\mathbf{elim}(\mathbf{intro}(W))(\mathbf{intro}(W))) \Downarrow^\circ V}{\dfrac{W(\mathbf{intro}(W)) \Downarrow^\circ V}{Y(f) \Downarrow^\circ V}}$$

Suppose the the total height of the derivation is n. Then the height of the derivation of $f(\mathbf{elim}(\mathbf{intro}(W))(\mathbf{intro}(W))) \Downarrow^\circ V$ is $n - 2$. Now, this relation holds only if there is a value U such that $\mathbf{elim}(\mathbf{intro}(W))(\mathbf{intro}(W)) \Downarrow^\circ U$ where the derivation of this has at most $n - 3$ steps. However, this relationship is only possible if $f(\mathbf{elim}(\mathbf{intro}(W))(\mathbf{intro}(W))) \Downarrow^\circ U$ with a derivation having height at most $n - 4$. But this contradicts the claim that $f(W(\mathbf{intro}(W)) \Downarrow^\circ V$ has a derivation with $n - 2$ steps, since such a derivation is uniquely determined by $f(W(\mathbf{intro}(W)))$. We therefore conclude that there is no V such that $Y(f) \Downarrow^\circ V$, and hence, by the Adequacy Theorem, $Y(f) = \bot$.

The trick to salvaging this problem and finding our fixed-point combinator is to use a form of the η-rule. If the term $\lambda x : s.\ f(\mathbf{elim}[s](x)(x))$ leads us to divergence when it is applied, perhaps we can replace it with the term $\lambda x : s.\ \lambda y : \mathbf{num}.\ f(\mathbf{elim}[s](x)(x))y)$, which will always converge when applied to a convergent argument. This changes the type, though, since the type on which the recursion is being defined must be a higher type. The desired term is

$$F \equiv \lambda f : (\mathbf{num} \to \mathbf{num}) \to (\mathbf{num} \to \mathbf{num}).$$
$$(\lambda x : s.\ \lambda y : \mathbf{num}.\ f(\mathbf{elim}[s](x)(x))y)$$
$$(\mathbf{intro}[s](\lambda x : s.\ \lambda y : \mathbf{num}.\ f(\mathbf{elim}[s](x)(x))y))$$

when the type t is $\mathbf{num}$. Although this combinator only works on higher types, this is enough for our example since

$$F\lambda\ \mathrm{add}.\ \lambda x : \mathbf{num}.\ \lambda y : \mathbf{num}.$$
$$\mathbf{if\ zero?}(x)\ \mathbf{then}\ y\ \mathbf{else}\ \mathrm{add}(\mathbf{pred}(x))(\mathbf{succ}(y))$$

defines the addition function. A rigorous proof that this is the case is most easily done using a suitable fixed-point semantics.

Let me turn now to a discussion of some other types that one can define in the type system of FPC. *Lists* are a very familiar example of a recursively defined type. For instance the type of lists of numbers is a solution of the equation

numlist = **unit** + (**num** * numlist),

which we denote by the type expression

μ numlist. **unit** + (**num** * numlist).

The term

intro[numlist](**inl**[**unit** + (**num** * numlist)](**unity**))

is most commonly called nil and represents the empty list, whereas a term

intro[numlist](**inr**[**unit** + (**num** * numlist)](M, L)

seems more familiar as cons(M, L). The language FPC is expressive enough that it is possible to write all of the expected functional programs for manipulating lists such as mapping, filtering, accumulating, and so on. These are what one might call *eager* lists; to get *lazy* lists one uses abstraction to delay evaluation. Among other things this idea makes it possible to work with recursive definitions of 'infinite' lists. To see this for FPC, consider the recursive type

lazynumlist = **unit** + (**num** $\times$ (**unit** $\rightarrow$ lazynumlist)),

which, unlike numlist, delays the evaluation of the tail of a list. Omitting type tags, the term

$M \equiv \mu f.\ \lambda n.\ \mathbf{inr}(n, \lambda u.\ f(\mathbf{succ}(n)))$: **num** $\rightarrow$ lazylist

can be used to define the list of all numbers as the application

$M(\mathbf{0})$.

In general, the type **unit** $\rightarrow t$ is isomorphic denotationally to the lift of t.

Exercises

7.4 Provide a grammar characterizing the values of the call-by-name operational interpretation of FPC.

7.5 Provide a proof for Lemma 7.3.

Table 7.8
Implicitly-Typed λ-Calculus

$$[\text{Proj}] \quad \frac{x \in H}{H \vdash x : H(x)}$$

$$[\text{Abs}]^- \quad \frac{H, \, x : s \vdash M : t}{H \vdash \lambda x. \, M : s \rightarrow t}$$

$$[\text{Appl}] \quad \frac{H \vdash M : s \rightarrow t \qquad H \vdash N : s}{H \vdash M(N) : t}$$

7.6 Provide a set of rules analogous to those in Table 7.7 that could be used for *call-by-name* evaluation of the recursion constructs.

7.7 Prove the claim that the conditional expression **if** L **then** M **else** N can now be defined as syntactic sugar for the expression **case** L **of** $\mathbf{inl}(x) \Rightarrow M$ **or** $\mathbf{inr}(y) \Rightarrow N$ by demonstrating that the operational rules for the **if** L **then** M **else** N,

$$\frac{M_1 \Downarrow \mathbf{true} \qquad M_2 \Downarrow V}{\mathbf{if} \ M_1 \ \mathbf{then} \ M_2 \ \mathbf{else} \ M_3 \Downarrow V} \qquad \frac{M_1 \Downarrow \mathbf{false} \qquad M_3 \Downarrow V}{\mathbf{if} \ M_1 \ \mathbf{then} \ M_2 \ \mathbf{else} \ M_3 \Downarrow V},$$

are properly represented by this encoding.

7.5   ML Polymorphism and Type Inference

Up to this point our discussion has been focused entirely on languages for which the type of a term, if it has one, is uniquely determined. Recall that the type tags in abstraction were introduced to make it possible to prove this fact. Let us now consider the λ-calculus *without* the type tags. Since the tags gave the types explicitly before, the new system is called the *implicitly*-typed (simply-typed) calculus. The syntax for the language is simply

$$M \ ::= \ x \mid \lambda x. \, M \mid MM$$

and the various syntactic conventions are exactly the ones used for earlier for the simply-typed λ-calculus with type tags. The typing rules for the implicit system are almost the same as those for the explicit calculus, but the abstraction rule now has different properties. The rules are given in Table 7.8. Consider now how one could find a type for a term M. If M has the form $L(N)$, then types need to be found for L and N. If M has the form $\lambda x.\ M'$, then a type needs to be found for M' assuming that x has *some* type s. Now, in the case that we are looking for the type of a term like $\lambda x.\ x$, then, for *any* type s, we can find a type with the following instances of the projection and application rule:

$$\frac{x : s \vdash x : s}{\vdash \lambda x.\ x : s \rightarrow s}$$

The choice of s here is arbitrary, but each of the types for $\lambda x.\ x$ must have the form $s \rightarrow s$. Indeed this form precisely characterizes what types *can* be the type of $\lambda x.\ x$. Let us now consider a slightly more interesting example; let

$$M \equiv \lambda x.\ \lambda f.\ f(x).$$

In a typing derivation ending with a type for M, the last two steps must have the following form:

$$\frac{\dfrac{x : t_1, f : t_2 \vdash f(x) : t_3}{x : t_1 \vdash \lambda f.\ f(x) : t_2 \rightarrow t_3}}{\vdash M : t_1 \rightarrow (t_2 \rightarrow t_3)}$$

Letting H be the assignment $x : t_1, f : t_2$, the derivation of the hypothesis at the top must have the form

$$\frac{H \vdash x : t_1 \qquad H \vdash f : t_2}{x : t_1, f : t_2 \vdash f(x) : t_3}$$

where, to match the application rule, it must be the case that t_2 have the form $t_1 \rightarrow t_3$. It is not hard to see that *any* choice of t_1, t_2, t_3 satisfying this one condition will be derivable as a type for M. In short, the types that M can have are exactly characterized as those of the form

$$r \rightarrow (r \rightarrow s) \rightarrow s. \tag{7.5}$$

This suggests that there may be a way to reconstruct a general form for the type of a term in the implicit calculus. If the types r and s could be viewed as variables in the type 7.5, then we could say that a type t satisfies $M : t$ just in case t is a substitution instance of 7.5. What is most important though is the prospect that a type for a term could be determined even though the type tags are missing. For a calculus like PCF, this might make it possible to omit type tags and still ensure the kind of security asserted for the well-typed terms of the language in Theorem 7.1.

Of course, there are terms that cannot be given a type because they 'make no sense'. This is easy to see in PCF where there are constants: a term such as $\mathbf{0}(\mathbf{0})$ is clearly meaningless. In the λ-calculus by itself, however, there is a gray area between what is and what is not a sensible term. The implicit system of Table 7.8 judges that $\vdash M : t$ if, and only if, there is a term of the *explicitly*-typed λ-calculus of Table 2.1 from which M can be obtained by erasing the tags. For example, it is impossible to find a type for $\lambda f.\ f(f)$ with the implicit typing system. To see this, suppose on the contrary that this term does have a type. The derivation of the type must end with an instance of $[\text{Abs}]^-$:

$$\frac{f : s \vdash f(f) : t}{\vdash \lambda f.\ f(f) : s \to t}$$

The proof of the hypothesis must be an instance of $[\text{Appl}]$:

$$\frac{f : s \vdash f : u \to t \qquad f : s \vdash f : u}{f : s \vdash f(f) : t},$$

which, by the axiom $[\text{Proj}]$, means that $u \to t \equiv s \equiv u$. However, there is no type that has this property since the type u cannot have itself as a proper subterm. But, as we touched upon earlier in our discussion of expressiveness, there are contexts in which this term seems to make some sense. For example, it might be argued that the term $(\lambda x.\ x(x))(\lambda y.\ y)$ is harmless, since the x in the first abstraction is bound to an argument in the application that can indeed be applied to itself.

The calculus ML_0 has a type system that can be viewed as a compromise between the implicit type discipline of Table 7.8 (which is essentially the simply-typed λ-calculus) and the *untyped* λ-calculus for which no typing system is used. ML_0 is a core representation of the system of the ML programming language.[1] The goal is to provide some level of additional flexibility to the implicit typing discipline while maintaining a close link to the simply-typed λ-calculus. The key idea in the system is the inclusion of a syntax class of what are known as *type schemes*. The full grammar for the language is given as follows:

$$
\begin{array}{rcl}
x & \in & \text{TermVariable} \\
a & \in & \text{TypeVariable} \\
t & ::= & a \mid t \to t \\
T & ::= & t \mid \Pi a.\ T \\
M & ::= & x \mid \lambda x.\ M \mid MM \mid \textbf{let } x = M \textbf{ in } M
\end{array}
$$

In addition to the primitive syntax class of term variables x, a new syntax class of *type* variables a has been added as we did for FPC in the previous section. A type scheme T has the form $\Pi a_1.\ \Pi a_2. \ldots . \Pi a_n.\ t$ where the type variables $a_1, \ldots, a_n$ bind any occurrences of these variables in the type t. The usual rules for substitution apply to type schemes;

---

[1] The actual Standard ML programming language includes many additional constructs. Some of these additional constructs can easily be incorporated in the treatment given in the rest of this section; others require important new ideas.

trees obtained from the grammar should be taken as given up to α-equivalence, and a substitution should not result in any free variable of the substituted type becoming bound after the substitution. In other words, for any substitution σ,

$$\sigma(\Pi a_1. \ldots \Pi a_n.\ t) \equiv \Pi a_1. \ldots \Pi a_n.\ \sigma(t)$$

where it is implicitly assumed by the Bound Variable Convention that no a_i is in the support of σ and none has a free occurrence in $\sigma(b)$ for any b in the support of σ. I will write $\mathrm{Ftv}(T)$ for the free type variables of a scheme T. The language includes one new construct for terms called a *let*. The term **let** $x = N$ **in** M is very similar to the construct $(\lambda x.\ M)N$ and can be thought of as an abbreviation for the latter expression as far as the evaluation of terms is concerned. The difference between the two lies entirely in the way they are treated in the typing system. In $L \equiv$ **let** $x = N$ **in** M, the x is a binding and all free occurrences of x in M are bound to it. Free occurrences of x that may appear in N are free in L.

The typing rules for ML_0 will include a generalization of the projection rule in the implicit system that allows the type of a variable to be any type obtained by instantiating the Π-bound variables of a scheme associated with it in a type assignment.

Definition: A type s is said to be an *instance* of a type scheme $T \equiv \Pi a_1. \ldots \Pi a_n.\ t$ if there is a substitution σ with its support contained in $\{a_1, \ldots, a_n\}$ such that $\sigma(t) = s$. If s is an instance of T then we write $s \leq T$. ☐

Assignments in ML_0 are defined similarly to assignments for simple types, but an ML_0 type assignment associates type *schemes* to term variables. Specifically, an *assignment* is a list H of pairs $x : T$ where x is a term variable and T is a type scheme. The set of free type variables $\mathrm{Ftv}(H)$ in an assignment H is the union of the sets $\mathrm{Ftv}(H(x))$ where $x \in H$. To give the typing rules for the system it is necessary to define a notion of the *closure* of a type relative to an assignment. This is a function on assignments H and types t such that

$$\mathrm{close}(H;\ t) = \Pi a_1. \ldots \Pi a_n.\ t$$

where $\{a_1, \ldots, a_n\} = \mathrm{Ftv}(t) - \mathrm{Ftv}(H)$. It is assumed that the function close chooses some particular order for the Π bindings here; it does not actually matter what this order is, but we can simply assume that our typing judgements are defined relative to a particular choice of the function close. A typing judgement is a triple $H \Vdash M : t$ where H is an assignment, M a term, and t a type. The typing rules for the system appear in Table 7.9. The symbol $\Vdash$ has been used in place of $\Vdash$ for this system to distinguish it from the implicit system of Table 7.8 and from another system to which it will be

Table 7.9
Typing Rules for ML_0

$$[\text{Proj}] \qquad \frac{x : T \in H \qquad t \leq T}{H \Vdash x : t}$$

$$[\text{Abs}]^{-} \qquad \frac{H,\, x : s \Vdash M : t}{H \Vdash \lambda x.\, M : s \to t}$$

$$[\text{Appl}] \qquad \frac{H \Vdash M : s \to t \qquad H \Vdash N : s}{H \Vdash M(N) : t}$$

$$[\text{Let}] \qquad \frac{H \Vdash M : s \qquad H, x : \text{close}(H;\, s) \Vdash N : t}{H \Vdash \mathbf{let}\ x = M\ \mathbf{in}\ N : t}$$

compared in Chapter 11 (the system described in Table 11.1 to be precise). The rules for abstraction and application are the same as for the implicit typing system. The rule [Proj] for variables is different though because the type of a variable x can be any instance of the type scheme $H(x)$. The rule [Let] for the let construct gives the type of the let as that of N in an assignment where the type associated with x is the closure of the type of M. Note that there is a rule for each clause for a term in the grammar of the language, and the hypotheses of each rule are judgements about subterms of that term. This is a *compositional* set of rules for typing judgements; later (Table 11.1) we will consider another way to describe the typing judgements for this system.

A basic property of the type variables and substitution in the system is given by the following:

7.4 Lemma. *If $H \Vdash M : t$, then $[s/a]H \Vdash M : [s/a]t$.* $\qquad\qquad\qquad\qquad$ □

In particular, if $a \notin \text{Ftv}(H)$, then $[s/a]H \equiv H$, so $H \Vdash M : t$ implies $H \Vdash M : [s/a]t$. The proof of the lemma is left as an exercise.

As in the implicit simply-typed system, ML_0 does not have a type for the term $\lambda f.\, f(f)$. However, if f is let-bound to an appropriate value M, then the term

$$N \equiv \mathbf{let}\ f = M\ \mathbf{in}\ f(f)$$

can have a type. To see this in a specific example, take M to be the identity combinator $\lambda x.\, x$. Let a be a type variable, let us show that N has type $a \to a$. First of all,

$$\frac{x : a \Vdash x : a}{\Vdash \lambda x.\, x : a \to a}$$

follows from [Proj] and [Abs]$^-$. Now, by [Proj], we must also have the hypotheses of the following instance of [Abs]$^-$:

$$\frac{f : \Pi a.\ a \to a \Vdash f : a \to a \qquad f : \Pi a.\ a \to a \Vdash f : (a \to a) \to (a \to a)}{f : \Pi a.\ a \to a \Vdash f(f) : a \to a}$$

Note, in particular, that it is possible to instantiate the Π-bound variable a as the type $a \to a$ in one hypothesis and simply as a in the other. From the derivations above, we now have both hypotheses of this instance of the [Let] rule:

$$\frac{\Vdash \lambda x.\ x : a \to a \qquad f : \Pi a.\ a \to a \Vdash f(f) : a \to a}{\Vdash \textbf{let } \lambda x.\ x = f \textbf{ in } f(f) : a \to a}$$

One of the most important characteristics of this typing system is the fact that we can determine whether a term has a type in a given assignment. Given an assignment H and a substitution σ, let $\sigma(H)$ be the assignment that associates $\sigma(H(x))$ to each $x \in H$. That is, if $H \equiv x_1 : T_1, \ldots, x_n : T_n$, then

$$\sigma(H) \equiv x_1 : \sigma(T_1), \ldots, x_n : \sigma(T_n).$$

Given assignment H and term M, define $\mathcal{S}(H, M)$ to be the set of all pairs (σ, t) such that σ is a substitution, t is a type, and $\sigma(H) \Vdash M : t$. There is an algorithm that, given H and M, provides an element of $\mathcal{S}(H, M)$ if the algorithm succeeds. To describe the algorithm, some background on substitutions is required.

Let σ and τ be substitutions. Then σ is said to be *more general* then τ if there is a substitution σ' such that $\sigma' \circ \sigma = \tau$. Given types s and t, a *unifier* for s, t is a substitution σ such that $\sigma(s) = \sigma(t)$. A *most general unifier* for s, t is a unifier σ that is more general than any other unifier for these types.

7.5 Theorem. *If there is a unifier for a pair of types, then there is also a most general unifier for them.* $\qquad\qquad\qquad\qquad\qquad\qquad\qquad\qquad\qquad\qquad\qquad\qquad\qquad\qquad$ □

Indeed, there is an algorithm for determining whether a pair of types can be unified and, if they can be unified, calculating their most general unifier. I will not describe the algorithm or the proof of the theorem here since it leads us too far from the purpose of the discussion at hand (but see the references in the notes for more details). This purpose is to describe an algorithm, called *algorithm* $\mathcal{W}$. It is given by induction on the structure of M by the following cases:

- Case $M \equiv x$. If $x \in H$, then the value is the identity substitution paired with the instantiation of the scheme $H(x)$ by a collection of fresh type variables. In other words, if $H(x) \equiv \Pi a_1.\ldots.\Pi a_n.\ s$ where $a_1, \ldots, a_n$ are new type variables, then

$$\mathcal{W}(H;\ x) = (\text{id},\ s).$$

If $x \notin H$, then the value of $\mathcal{W}(H; \; M)$ is failure.

- Case $M \equiv \lambda x. \; M'$. Suppose a is a new type variable and $(\sigma, t) = \mathcal{W}(H, x : a; \; M')$. Then

$$\mathcal{W}(H; \; \lambda x. \; M') = (\sigma, \; \sigma(a) \rightarrow t).$$

If, on the other hand, the value of $\mathcal{W}(H, x : a; \; M')$ is failure, then so is $\mathcal{W}(H; \; M)$.

- Case $M \equiv L(N)$. Suppose $(\sigma_1, t_1) = \mathcal{W}(H; \; L)$ and $(\sigma_2, t_2) = \mathcal{W}(\sigma_1(H); \; N)$. Let a be a new type variable. If there is a most general unifier σ for $\sigma_2(t_1)$ and $t_2 \rightarrow a$, then

$$\mathcal{W}(H; \; L(N)) = (\sigma \circ \sigma_2 \circ \sigma_1, \; \sigma a).$$

In the event that there is no such unifier or if the value of $\mathcal{W}(H; \; L)$ or $\mathcal{W}(\sigma_1(H); \; N)$ is failure, then this is also the value of $\mathcal{W}(H; \; M)$.

- Case $M \equiv$ let $x = L$ in N. Suppose $(\sigma_1, s_1) = \mathcal{W}(H; \; L)$ and $H' \equiv \sigma_1(H)$, $x : \text{close}(\sigma_1(H); \; s_1))$. If $(\sigma_2, s_2) = \mathcal{W}(H'; \; N)$, then

$$\mathcal{W}(H; \; M) = (\sigma_2 \circ \sigma_1, \; s_2).$$

If, on the other hand, the value of $\mathcal{W}(H; \; L)$ or $\mathcal{W}(H'; \; N)$ is failure, then that is also the value of $\mathcal{W}(H; \; M)$.

To prove that algorithm $\mathcal{W}$ is sound, it helps to have the following:

7.6 Lemma. *If $H, x : \Pi a_1. \dots . \Pi a_n. \; s \Vdash M : t$, then $H, \text{close}(H; \; s) \Vdash M : t$.* $\square$

To understand this, note that the Bound Variable Convention insists that the variables a_i that appear in s are not in $\text{Ftv}(H)$. The desired soundness property can be stated precisely as follows:

7.7 Theorem. *If $\mathcal{W}(H; \; M)$ exists, then it is an element of $\mathcal{S}(H; \; M)$.*

Proof: Suppose $\mathcal{W}(H; \; M)$ exists; we must show that $\sigma(H) \Vdash M : t$. The proof is by induction on the structure of M. If $M \equiv x$ is a variable, then t is an instantiation of $H(x)$. This means $H \Vdash x : t$ by the typing rule for variables.

Case $M \equiv \lambda x. \; M'$. If $(\sigma, t) = \mathcal{W}(H, x : a; \; M')$, then $\sigma(H, x : a) \Vdash M' : t$ by the inductive hypothesis. Thus $\sigma(H), x : \sigma(a) \Vdash M' : t$ so $\sigma(H) \Vdash \lambda x. \; M' : \sigma(a) \rightarrow t$ by the typing rule for abstraction. This means $\mathcal{W}(H; \; M) = (\sigma(H), \sigma(a) \rightarrow t) \in \mathcal{S}(H; \; M)$.

Case $M \equiv L(N)$. If $(\sigma_1, t_1) = \mathcal{W}(H; \ L)$ and $(\sigma_2, t_2) = \mathcal{W}(\sigma_1(H); \ N)$, then, by the inductive hypothesis, $\sigma_1(H) \Vdash L : t_1$ and $\sigma_2(\sigma_1(H)) \Vdash N : t_2$. Since $\mathcal{W}(H; \ M)$ exists, there is a substitution σ such that $\sigma(\sigma_2(t_1)) \equiv \sigma(t_2 \to a) \equiv \sigma(t_2) \to \sigma(a)$. By Lemma 7.4, $\sigma \circ \sigma_2 \circ \sigma_1(H) \Vdash L : \sigma \circ \sigma_2(t_1)$ so

$$\sigma \circ \sigma_2 \circ \sigma_1(H) \Vdash L : \sigma(t_2) \to \sigma(a).$$

Also by the inductive hypothesis,

$$\sigma \circ \sigma_2 \circ \sigma_1(H) \Vdash N : \sigma(t_2).$$

Combining these facts with the rule for the typing of applications, we can conclude that

$$\sigma \circ \sigma_2 \circ \sigma_1(H) \Vdash L(N) : \sigma(a),$$

which means that $\mathcal{W}(H; \ M) \in \mathcal{S}(H; \ M)$.

Case $M \equiv$ **let** $x = L$ **in** N. If $(\sigma_1, s_1) = \mathcal{W}(H; \ L)$ and $(\sigma_2, s_2) = \mathcal{W}(H'; \ N)$ where $H' = \sigma_1(H), x : \mathrm{close}(\sigma_1(H), s_1)$, then, by the inductive hypothesis, $\sigma_1(H) \Vdash L : s_1$ and $\sigma_2(H') \Vdash N : s_2$. By Lemma 7.4,

$$\sigma_2 \circ \sigma_1(H) \Vdash L : \sigma_2(s_1).$$

If $\Pi a_1. \ldots . \Pi a_n. \ s_1 \equiv \mathrm{close}(\sigma_1(H), s_1)$, then

$$\sigma_2 \circ \sigma_1(H), x : \Pi a_1. \ldots . \Pi a_n. \ \sigma_2(s_1) \Vdash N : s_2$$

so, by Lemma 7.6,

$$\sigma_2 \circ \sigma_1(H), x : \mathrm{close}(\sigma_2 \circ \sigma_1(H); \ \sigma_2(s_1) \Vdash N : s_2.$$

By the rule for typing lets, this says that $\mathcal{W}(H; \ M) = (\sigma_2 \circ \sigma_1, s_2) \in \mathcal{S}(H; \ M)$. $\qquad\square$

In the description of the algorithm above there is some vagueness about what a 'new' type variable is and how one obtains new variables. Intuitively, there is a list of type variables used so far, and new ones should be selected from those not in that list. In an actual implementation, issuing new variables might be done by using a reference that maintains a counter; a 'new' variable is obtained by using the current value of the counter as a tag and incrementing the counter as a side effect when a variable tag is obtained in this way. To give a rigorous description of algorithm $\mathcal{W}$ that does not explicitly use a global memory, we can treat this process of issuing new variables as we treated the provision of new memory locations in Section 7.3. Just as memory was included as a parameter in the semantic clauses there, a used variable list can be included in the clauses of the operational rules here. With this added level of rigor it is then possible to describe

Table 7.10
Rules for ML_0 Type Inference

$$\frac{x \in H}{(H;\ x;\ \Sigma) \Downarrow (\text{id};\ \text{inst}(\Sigma,\ H(x));\ \text{used}(\Sigma,\ H(x)))}$$

$$\frac{a = \text{new}(\Sigma) \qquad (H, x : a;\ M;\ \Sigma \cup \{a\}) \Downarrow (\sigma;\ s;\ \Sigma')}{(H;\ \lambda x.\ M;\ \Sigma) \Downarrow (\sigma;\ \sigma(a) \to s;\ \Sigma')}$$

$$\frac{\left\{ \begin{array}{l} (H;\ M;\ \Sigma) \Downarrow (\sigma_1;\ s_1;\ \Sigma_1) \\ (\sigma_1(H);\ N;\ \Sigma_1) \Downarrow (\sigma_2;\ s_2;\ \Sigma_2) \\ a = \text{new}(\Sigma_2) \\ \sigma\ \text{MGU}\ (\sigma_2(s_1),\ s_2 \to a) \end{array} \right\}}{(H;\ M(N);\ \Sigma) \Downarrow (\sigma \circ \sigma_2 \circ \sigma_1;\ \sigma(a);\ \Sigma_2 \cup \{a\})}$$

$$\frac{\left\{ \begin{array}{l} (H;\ M;\ \Sigma) \Downarrow (\sigma_1;\ s_1;\ \Sigma_1) \\ (H, x : \text{close}(\sigma_1(H);\ s_1);\ N;\ \Sigma_1) \Downarrow (\sigma_2;\ s_2;\ \Sigma_2) \end{array} \right\}}{(H;\ \textbf{let}\ x = M\ \textbf{in}\ N;\ \Sigma) \Downarrow (\sigma_2 \circ \sigma_1;\ s_2;\ \Sigma_2)}$$

the definition given above as a system of rules for deducing that a pair (σ, t) is a principal type of $(H;\ M)$. To this end, we define a relation $\Downarrow$ between triples

$$(H;\ M;\ \Sigma) \Downarrow (\sigma;\ t;\ \Sigma')$$

where H is an assignment, M is a term, σ is a substitution, t is a type, and Σ, Σ' are sets of type variables. Writing $\sigma\ \text{MGU}\ (\sigma_1, \sigma_2)$ if σ is the most general unifier of σ_1 and σ_2, the relation is defined to be the least set of such triples that satisfies the rules in Table 7.10. The sets Σ and Σ' should be viewed as the sets of variables used so far. These rules are based on a collection of operations that can be viewed as allocating from 'free list' of unused type variables; their role is precisely analogous to the operation new for generating fresh locations for reference cells. Indeed, assume we are given three functions—inst, used, and new—with the following properties. Given a set of type variables Σ, new(Σ) is a type variable not in Σ. Given a type scheme $T \equiv \Pi a_1 \ldots \Pi_n a_n.\ t$ and a set Σ of type variables, inst(Σ, T) is the type $[b_1, \ldots, b_n / a_1, \ldots, a_n]t$ where $\{b_1, \ldots, b_n\}$ is a set of type variables that are not in Σ and used(Σ, T) is defined as $\Sigma \cup \{b_1, \ldots, b_n\}$.

Exercises

7.8 Prove Lemma 7.4.

7.9 Prove Lemma 7.6.

7.10 Let $T \equiv \Pi a_1 \ldots \Pi a_n.\ t$ be a type scheme and suppose $s \leq T$. If σ and τ are substitutions such that $\sigma(t) \equiv s \equiv \tau(t)$ and $a \in \text{Ftv}(s)$, then $\sigma(a) \equiv \tau(a)$.

7.6 Notes

An IEEE standard for Scheme is currently under development based on the groundwork provided by various generations of the Scheme Report [199]. The Scheme example in Table 7.1 is drawn from the textbook by Abelson and Sussman [2]. ML has a formal definition using a natural semantics developed by Milner, Tofte, and Harper [173]. This official definition is supplemented by a commentary [172]. Some of the earliest study of the potential use of higher-order functions and the typed λ-calculus in programming was done by Peter Landin [147]. Although it does not explicitly use a λ-notation, ALGOL 60 has the typed λ-calculus as a sublanguage. Unlike Scheme and ML, ALGOL 60 employs a call-by-name evaluation order. The best-known recent languages based on a call-by-name evaluation for the typed λ-calculus are Miranda [264] and Haskell [122]. These latter languages use an ML-like type system and do not include constructs for mutable structures such as references. There has been a long-standing question of the best combination of language features, type systems, and orders of evaluation illustrated by Scheme, ML, ALGOL 60, Miranda, and Haskell. The first two of these use call-by-value and the last three use call-by-name. The first three include references and the last two do not. Of the five languages, only ALGOL 60 combines assignments with call-by-name. Scheme is an untyped language while each of the other four is typed; of the typed languages, all employ a polymorphic type system except for ALGOL 60. A new language called *Forsythe* developed by Reynolds [208] preserves much of the essence of ALGOL 60 (including, for instance, call-by-name, static typing, and references) in a language with a sophisticated polymorphic type system. A well-known paper on the virtues of pure higher-order functional programming was written by Backus [17]. This paper introduced a language based on combinators called *FP*. A recent discussion of an evolved form of the language appears in an article by Bakus, Williams, and Wimmers [18] and it has been implemented [19]. A paper by Goguen [94] argues a case for first-order programming.

An interesting technique for obtaining some of the advantages within a strongly typed frame work are provided by a typing mechanism known as a *dynamic type*. A theory of type security for dynamic types has been described by Abadi, Cardelli, Pierce, and Plotkin [1].

The program `applyto` in 7.1 is a simple, but by no means unique, example of the challenges faced by languages in which types are inferred for programs that have few or no type annotations. Other examples of the challenges involved in inferring types can be found in the work of Kfoury, Tiuryn, and Urzyczyn [137; 138], which focuses on the problem of inferring types for polymorphic mutually recursive definitions, and in work of C. Gunter, E. Gunter, and MacQueen [99], which considers the problem of inferring cases in which equality can be computed for the terms of a given type. One combination of language features that offers serious pitfalls arises in the use of references in a language with ML polymorphism and type inference. A recent proposal has been made by Tofte [263] using numbered variables called 'weak type variables'. Some of the newest languages that draw deeply from ideas in type theory such as Forsythe and the language Quest [46] of Cardelli require that some type annotations are given by the programmer and use inference algorithms to keep such requirements to a minimum.

As already mentioned, there is a substantial body of literature on fixed-point semantics for state. A detailed discussion of the techniques for modeling state appears in the book of Gordon [95], and up-to-date presentations are given by Schmidt [220] and by Tennent [261]. Unfortunately some of the most challenging questions in this area have never been settled; a sampling of some of the problems with providing a fixed-point semantics for block structure and higher-order functions is given by Meyer and Sieber [164]. A study of assignments from an operational perspective was carried out by Mason and Talcott [158].

The existence of a most general unifier as described in Theorem 7.5 and an algorithm for calculating it are due to Robinson[212]. The idea of reconstructing typed terms from untyped ones originated with Hindley [115] and Milner [169]. The 'let' construct appears in the latter work. Research of Milner and Damas [66] led to the formulation of a theorem describing the sense in which the type inferred by algorithm $\mathcal{W}$ is the 'best' type possible. To be precise,

Definition: A *principal type* for H and M is a pair $(\sigma, s) \in \mathcal{S}(H, M)$ such that, for any other pair $(\tau, t) \in \mathcal{S}(H, M)$, there is a substitution σ' such that

- $\tau(H) = \sigma' \circ \sigma(H)$ and
- t is an instance of $\sigma'(\text{close}(\sigma(H); s))$. $\qquad\qquad\Box$

In the case that H is the empty assignment, this boils down to saying that if a closed term M has a type at all, then there is a type s such that M has type s and, for any other type t, M has type t only if $t = \tau s$ for some substitution τ. Damas and Milner state the following:

7.8 Theorem. *If there is a type t such that $H \Vdash M : t$, then $\mathcal{W}(H; M)$ is a principal type scheme for H and M.* $\qquad\qquad\Box$

Its proof appears in the thesis of Damas [65]. In practice there are many optimizations that can be done to provide a more efficient implementation of principle type scheme inference. One discussion of implementation has appears in an article of Cardelli [43]. Most books on ML include some discussion of ML type inference; for instance, the book of Sokolowski [241] provides code for unification and inference using the Standard ML module system.

8 Universal Domains

In the previous chapters we have modeled types using objects drawn from a category of spaces. Each closed, well-typed term denotes a value in the space that interprets its type. In this chapter we consider a slightly different perspective on types in which a type is viewed as a subset of what is generally called a *universal domain*. In this approach, the meaning $[\![M]\!]$ of a closed, well-typed term M is a member of the universal domain, and $[\![M]\!]$ lies in the subset of the universal domain that interprets the type of M. There are several ways to view these subsets, resulting in different models. Our discussion begins with an examination of the interpretation of the *untyped* λ-calculus using a model of the simply-typed calculus that satisfies a special equation. We then consider how a model of the untyped calculus can be viewed as a model of the typed one by the use of a universal domain. Other approaches are described in the second half of the chapter using the idea that a type corresponds to the image of a map from the universal domain into itself. This model allows us to interpret recursively defined types using the Fixed Point Theorem by representing operators on domains as continuous functions on a domain of types.

8.1 Untyped λ-Calculus

The *untyped* λ-calculus is essentially the calculus obtained by removing the type system from the simply-typed calculus. The terms of the untyped calculus are generated by the following grammar:

$$M \;::=\; x \mid MM \mid \lambda x.\, M$$

where the abstraction of the variable x over a term M binds the free variable occurrences of x in M. (These are the same terms used for the implicitly-typed system in the previous chapter.) Expressions such as $M', N, N_1, \ldots$ are used to range over untyped λ-terms as well as typed terms—context must determine which class of terms is intended. For discussions below relating typed and untyped calculi, I will use P, Q, R for terms with type tags and L, M, N for those without such tags. Untyped λ-terms are subject to the same conventions about bound variables as we applied earlier to terms with type tags on bound variables. In particular, terms are considered equivalent if they are the same up to the renaming of bound variables (where no such renaming leads to capture of a renamed variable by a new binding). The equational rules for the untyped $\lambda\beta$-*calculus* are given in Table 8.1. They are very similar to those of the typed calculus. The untyped $\lambda\beta\eta$-*calculus* is obtained by including the untyped version of the η-rule,

$$\{\eta\} \qquad \lambda x.\, M(x) = M,$$

Table 8.1
Equational Rules for Untyped $\lambda\beta$-Calculus

$$\{\text{Refl}\} \qquad\qquad x = x$$

$$\{\text{Sym}\} \qquad\qquad \frac{M = N}{N = M}$$

$$\{\text{Trans}\} \qquad\qquad \frac{L = M \qquad M = N}{L = N}$$

$$\{\text{Cong}\} \qquad\qquad \frac{M = M' \qquad N = N'}{H \vdash M(N) = M'(N')}$$

$$\{\xi\} \qquad\qquad \frac{M = M'}{\lambda x.\ M = \lambda x.\ M'}$$

$$\{\beta\} \qquad\qquad (\lambda x : s.\ M)(N) = [N/x]M$$

---

where, as before, the variable x does not appear free in the expression M. It is not hard to see that every term of the simply-typed λ-calculus gives rise to a term of the untyped calculus obtained by 'erasing' the type tags on its free variables. More precisely, we define the *erasure* erase(P) of a term P of the simply-typed calculus by induction as follows:

$$\text{erase}(x) \equiv x$$
$$\text{erase}(P(Q)) \equiv (\text{erase}(P))(\text{erase}(Q))$$
$$\text{erase}(\lambda x : t.\ P) \equiv \lambda x.\ \text{erase}(P).$$

Although every term of the untyped calculus can be obtained as the erasure of a tagged one, it is not the case that every untyped term can be obtained as the erasure of a *well-typed* tagged term. For example, if erase$(P) \equiv \lambda x.\ x(x)$, then there is no context H and type expression t such that $H \vdash P : t$. Of course, distinct well-typed terms may have the same erasure if they differ only in the tags on their bound variables:

$$\text{erase}(\lambda x : \mathbf{o}.\ x) \equiv \lambda x.\ x \equiv \text{erase}(\lambda x : \mathbf{o} \to \mathbf{o}.\ x).$$

What is a model of the untyped λ-calculus?

It is possible to describe a semantics for the untyped λ-calculus using the simply-typed calculus. Such an interpretation must deal with the concept of self application such as we see in the term $\lambda x.\ x(x)$, so some care must be applied in explaining how an untyped term can be interpreted in a typed setting where this operation is not type-correct. The approach we use is to view the application as entailing an *implicit coercion* that converts an application instance of a value into a corresponding function. More precisely, assume we are given constants

$$\Phi : \mathbf{o} \rightarrow (\mathbf{o} \rightarrow \mathbf{o})$$
$$\Psi : (\mathbf{o} \rightarrow \mathbf{o}) \rightarrow \mathbf{o}$$

and an equational theory with one equation

$$\Phi \circ \Psi = \lambda x : \mathbf{o} \rightarrow \mathbf{o}.\ x. \tag{8.1}$$

Let us call this *theory U^β*. A model of theory U^β is a tuple

$$(\mathcal{A}, A, \Phi, \Psi)$$

where $(\mathcal{A}, A)$ is a type frame and $\Phi \in D^{\mathbf{o} \rightarrow (\mathbf{o} \rightarrow \mathbf{o})}$ and $\Psi \in D^{(\mathbf{o} \rightarrow \mathbf{o}) \rightarrow \mathbf{o}}$ satisfy 8.1. (To simplify the notation, let us make no distinction between Φ and Ψ as constant symbols in the calculus and their interpretations in the model.) We may use a model of theory U^β to interpret the untyped $\lambda\beta$-calculus in the following way. First, we define a *syntactic translation* that converts an untyped term into a term with type tags by induction as follows:

$$x^* \equiv x$$
$$(\lambda x.\ M)^* \equiv \Psi(\lambda x : \mathbf{o}.\ M^*)$$
$$(M(N))^* \equiv \Phi(M^*)(N^*)$$

For example, Y and Y^* are as follows:

$$Y \equiv \lambda f.\ (\lambda x.\ f(xx))(\lambda x.\ f(xx))$$
$$Y^* \equiv \Psi(\lambda f : \mathbf{o}.\ \Phi(\Psi(\lambda x : \mathbf{o}.\ \Phi(f)(\Phi(x)(x))))(\Psi(\lambda x : \mathbf{o}.\ \Phi(f)(\Phi(x)(x))))).$$

We must establish the following basic fact about the translation:

8.1 Proposition. *Let M be an untyped term. If $H \equiv x_1 : \mathbf{o}, \ldots, x_n : \mathbf{o}$ is a type context that includes all of the free variables of M, then $H \vdash M^* : \mathbf{o}$.*

Proof: The proof is by induction on the structure of M.

Case $M \equiv x$. The result is immediate.

Case $M \equiv \lambda x.\ N$. Then $M^* \equiv \Psi(\lambda x : \mathbf{o}.\ N^*)$ and $H, x : \mathbf{o} \vdash N^* : \mathbf{o}$. Hence $H \vdash (\lambda x : \mathbf{o}.\ N^*) : \mathbf{o} \rightarrow \mathbf{o}$. Since $\Psi : (\mathbf{o} \rightarrow \mathbf{o}) \rightarrow \mathbf{o}$, we conclude that $H \vdash M^* : \mathbf{o}$.

Case $M \equiv L(N)$. We have $H \vdash L^* : \mathbf{o}$ so $H \vdash \Phi(L^*) : \mathbf{o} \rightarrow \mathbf{o}$. Hence $H \vdash \Phi(L^*)(N^*) : \mathbf{o}$, that is, $H \vdash M^* : \mathbf{o}$. $\qquad\square$

With this translation, it is possible to assign a meaning to an untyped term M by taking $\mathcal{A}_u[\![M]\!] = \mathcal{A}[\![M^*]\!] \in D^{\mathbf{o}}$. To see that this respects the equational rules given in Table 8.1, note first the following:

8.2 Lemma. $[N^*/x]M^* \equiv ([N/x]M)^*$. $\qquad\qquad\qquad\qquad\qquad\qquad\qquad\qquad$ □

We then prove the β-rule for the untyped calculus by a calculation in the typed one:

$$
\begin{aligned}
((\lambda x.\ M)(N))^* &= \Phi((\lambda x.\ M)^*)(N^*) \\
&= \Phi(\Psi(\lambda x : \mathbf{o}.\ M^*))(N^*) \\
&= (\lambda x : \mathbf{o}.\ M^*)(N^*) \\
&= [N^*/x]M^* \\
&= ([N/x]M)^*
\end{aligned}
$$

so

$$
\mathcal{A}_u[\![(\lambda x.\ M)(N)]\!] = \mathcal{A}[\![((\lambda x.\ M)(N))^*]\!] = \mathcal{A}[\![([N/x]M)^*]\!] = \mathcal{A}_u[\![[N/x]M]\!].
$$

The other axioms and rules are not difficult.

Now, let *theory* $U^{\beta\eta}$ be theory U^β together with the equation

$$
\Psi \circ \Phi = \lambda f : \mathbf{o}.\ f, \tag{8.2}
$$

which asserts, in effect, that Φ is an isomorphism between the ground type $D^{\mathbf{o}}$ and the functions in $D^{\mathbf{o}\to\mathbf{o}}$. If a model $\mathcal{A}$ of theory U^β is also a model of theory $U^{\beta\eta}$, then $\mathcal{A}_u$ satisfies the η-rule as well as the β-rule. To see this, suppose the variable x does not appear free in the term M, then

$$
\begin{aligned}
(\lambda x.\ M(x))^* &= \Psi(\lambda x : \mathbf{o}.\ (M(x))^*) \\
&= \Psi(\lambda x : \mathbf{o}.\ \Phi(M^*)(x)) \\
&= \Psi(\Phi(M^*)) \\
&= M^*
\end{aligned}
$$

so $\mathcal{A}_u[\![\lambda x.\ M(x)]\!] = \mathcal{A}[\![(\lambda x.\ M(x))^*]\!] = \mathcal{A}[\![M^*]\!] = \mathcal{A}_u[\![M]\!]$. In summary, we have the following result.

8.3 Theorem. *If $\mathcal{A}$ is a model of U^β, then $\mathcal{A}_u$ is a model of the untyped $\lambda\beta$-calculus. If, moreover, $\mathcal{A}$ is a model of $U^{\beta\eta}$, then it is a model of the untyped $\lambda\beta\eta$-calculus.* $\qquad$ □

What models of the untyped λ-calculus are there?

Having established that models of theories of U^β and $U^{\beta\eta}$ provide models of the untyped $\lambda\beta$ and $\lambda\beta\eta$ calculi respectively, it is tempting to conclude that we have almost completed our quest for models of the untyped calculus. In fact, we have only done the *easy* part. We did not yet show that any models of theories U^β and $U^{\beta\eta}$ actually *exist*. To see why this might be a problem, consider the full type frame $\mathcal{F}_X$ over a set X. If we can find functions

$$\Phi : X \to (X^X)$$
$$\Psi : (X^X) \to X$$

satisfying Equation 8.1, then we have produced the desired model. But Equation 8.1 implies that the function Φ is a *surjection* from X onto the set of functions $f : X \to X$. Such a surjection exists only if X has exactly one point![1] This means that the full type frame can only yield a trivial model for the untyped calculus through a choice of Φ and Ψ. The problem lies in the fact that the interpretation of $o \to o$ in the full type frame has *too many functions*. To find a model of the untyped calculus, we must therefore look for a type frame that has a more parsimonious interpretation of the higher types.

To this end, let us use what we know about algebraic lattices and continuous functions. Given a set X, let $\mathcal{P}_f(X)$ be the set of all finite subsets of X. Define an operation G by

$$G(X) = \{(u, x) \mid u \in \mathcal{P}_f(X) \text{ and } x \in X\}.$$

Starting with any set X, let $X_0 = X$ and $X_{n+1} = G(X_n)$. Take D_X to be the set $\mathcal{P}(\bigcup_{n\in\omega} X_n)$ of all subsets of the union of the X_n's. Ordered by set inclusion, this is an algebraic lattice whose compact elements are the finite sets. To see how it can be viewed as a model of the untyped λ-calculus, consider an element $(u, x) \in G(X_n)$. This pair can be viewed as a piece of a function f, which has x in its output whenever u is a subset of its input. Suppose that $d \in D_X$. Following this intuition, we define a function $\Phi(d) : D_X \to D_X$ by taking

$$\Phi(d)(e) = \{x \mid u \subseteq e \text{ for some } (u, x) \in d\} \tag{8.3}$$

for each $e \in D_X$. In other words, if we are to view d as a function with e as its argument, the result of applying d to e is the set of those elements x such that there is a 'piece' (element) (u, x) of d where u is a subset of the input e. Also, given a continuous function $f : D_X \to D_X$, define $\Psi(f) \in \mathcal{P}(\bigcup_{n\in\omega} X_n)$ by

$$\Psi(f) = \{(u, x) \mid x \in f(u)\}. \tag{8.4}$$

---

[1]This is obvious when the set X is required to be finite. That it also holds when X is infinite is a result known as *Cantor's Theorem*, which is basic to modern set theory.

This says that f is to be represented by recording the pairs (u, x) such that x will be part of the result of applying f to an element that contains u.

Since D_X is an algebraic lattice, it generates a type frame in the cartesian closed category of algebraic cpo's and continuous functions. I will leave the proof that Φ and Ψ are continuous to the reader. Suppose that $f : D_X \to D_X$ is continuous. Then

$$
\begin{aligned}
\Phi(\Psi(f))(d) &= \{x \mid (u, x) \in \Psi(f) \text{ for some } u \subseteq d\} \\
&= \{x \mid x \in f(u) \text{ for some } u \subseteq d\} \\
&= \bigcup\{f(u) \mid u \subseteq d\} \\
&= f(d)
\end{aligned}
$$

where the last step follows from the fact that a continuous function on an algebraic cpo is determined by its action on compact elements (Lemma 5.24). It follows from this calculation that the continuous type frame generated by D_X, together with the continuous functions Φ and Ψ, is a model of the untyped $\lambda\beta$-calculus. It is obviously non-trivial if X has at least two distinct elements.

Could D_X also be a model of the untyped $\lambda\beta\eta$-calculus? Suppose $d \in D_X$, and let us attempt to calculate equation 8.2:

$$
\begin{aligned}
\Psi(\Phi(d)) &= \{(u, x) \mid x \in \Phi(d)(u)\} \\
&= \{(u, x) \mid v \subseteq u \text{ for some } (v, x) \in d\} \\
&\supseteq d.
\end{aligned}
$$

But since d could be an arbitrary subset of $\bigcup_n X_n$, it is clear that this superset relation may fail to be an *equality*. So we have not yet demonstrated a model for the $\lambda\beta\eta$-calculus! To do this using cpo's and continuous functions, what we need is a cpo D such that $D \cong [D \to D]$. This is our first example of what is usually called a *domain equation*. (It would be more accurate, of course, to refer to it as a 'domain isomorphism', but let us not concern ourselves with this notational quibble right now.) Certainly, the one point cpo $\mathbb{U}$ satisfies the equation $\mathbb{U} = [\mathbb{U} \to \mathbb{U}]$, but this is hardly an observation to get excited about. To demonstrate that $D \cong [D \to D]$ has a non-trivial solution is best done within the context of how one solves such equations *in general*, a topic addressed in the next section and again in the next chapter.

Using information systems to model the untyped calculus.

Some of the spirit of the previous example resembles that used in our understanding of *information systems* as defined in Section 5.3. Indeed information systems can be used to describe models of the untyped calculus. This is done indirectly using sets of finite data objects; a algebraic cpo model can then be derived from the equivalence between information systems and bc-domains.

Since the categories **Infsys** and **Bcdom** are equivalent, there is an operator $+$ on **Infsys** that is equivalent to the separated sum operator. As an illustration of the way a model of the untyped calculus can be given in **Infsys**, let A be any information system at all; the goal is to demonstrate an information system D that satisfies

$$D = A + (D \Rightarrow D) \tag{8.5}$$

where you may recall that $D \Rightarrow D$ is an exponential in the ccc of information systems and approximable relations.

Definition: *Separated sums.* First we need to define the separated sum operator in **Infsys**. Suppose we are given information systems A, B. Let Δ be some new element not in the universe of finite data objects of A or B.

- $A + B = \{(X, \Delta) \mid X \in A\} \cup \{(\Delta, Y) \mid Y \in B\} \cup \{(\Delta, \Delta)\}$.
- $\Delta_{A+B} = (\Delta, \Delta)$.

Let u be a finite subset of $A + B$. Suppose

$$u_1 = \{X \in A \mid (X, \Delta) \in u\} \text{ and } u_2 = \{Y \in B \mid (\Delta, Y) \in u\}.$$

- $u \in Con_{A+B}$ iff either $u_1 \in Con_A$ and $u_2 = \emptyset$ or $u_1 = \emptyset$ and $u_2 \in Con_B$.
- $u \vdash_{A+B} (X, \Delta)$ iff $u_1 \neq \emptyset$ and $u_1 \vdash_A X$.
- $u \vdash_{A+B} (\Delta, Y)$ iff $u_2 \neq \emptyset$ and $u_2 \vdash_B Y$.
- $u \vdash_{A+B} (\Delta, \Delta)$.   □

Now, to get the desired solution for Equation 8.5, let Δ be a new element not in the data objects of A. Let $\Delta_D = (\Delta, \Delta)$.

- $\Delta_D \in D$.
- $(X, \Delta) \in D$ for each $X \in A$.
- $(\Delta, (u, v)) \in D$ for each $u, v \in Con_D$.
- $\emptyset \in Con_D$.
- $u \cup \{\Delta\} \in Con_D$ for each $u \in Con_D$.
- $\{(X, \Delta) \mid X \in w\} \in Con_D$ for each $w \in Con_A$.
- $\{(\Delta, (u_1, v_1)), \ldots, (\Delta, (u_n, v_n))\} \in Con_D$ provided $u_i, v_i \in Con_D$ for each $i = 1, \ldots, n$, and whenever $I \subseteq \{1, \ldots, n\}$ satisfies $\bigcup\{u_i \mid i \in I\} \in Con_D$, then $\bigcup\{v_i \mid i \in I\} \in Con_D$.

Note that the data objects D and the set of consistent subsets are being defined mutually here. This definition makes sense for the much same reason that we were able to define D_X. To see this more precisely, let $D_0 = \{\Delta_D\}$ and $Con_0 = \{\emptyset\}$ and suppose D_n and $Con_n \subseteq \mathcal{P}_f(D_n)$ are given. Define

$$D_{n+1} = \{(X, \Delta) \mid X \in A\} \cup \{(\Delta, (u, v)) \mid u, v \in Con_n\}$$

$$
\begin{aligned}
Con_{n+1} = \quad & \{u \cup \{\Delta\} \mid u \in Con_n\} \cup \\
& \{\{(X, \Delta) \mid X \in w\} \mid w \in Con_n\} \cup \\
& \{\{(\Delta, (u_1, v_1)), \ldots, (\Delta, (u_m, v_m))\} \mid u_i, v_i \in Con_n \text{ for each } i = \\
& 1, \ldots, m \text{ and whenever } I \subseteq \{1, \ldots, m\} \text{ satisfies } \bigcup\{u_i \mid i \in I\} \in \\
& Con_n, \text{ then } \bigcup\{v_i \mid i \in I\} \in Con_n \}.
\end{aligned}
$$

Then it is possible to show that

$$D = \bigcup_{n \in \omega} D_n \text{ and } Con_D = \bigcup_{n \in \omega} Con_n. \tag{8.6}$$

The proof is left as an exercise. To complete the example we need to define $\vdash_D$:

- $u \vdash_D \Delta$.
- $u \cup \{\Delta_D\} \vdash_D Y$ if $u \vdash_D Y$.
- $\{(X, \Delta) \mid X \in w\} \vdash_D (W, \Delta)$ whenever $w \vdash_A W$.
- $\{(\Delta, (u_1, v_1)), \ldots, (\Delta, (u_n, v_n))\} \vdash_D (\Delta, (u', v'))\}$ whenever $w = \bigcup\{v_i \mid u' \vdash_D u_i\} \in Con_D$ and $w \vdash_D v'$.   □

That this information system satisfies Equation 8.5 is obvious based on the definitions of the operators involved. In summary:

8.4 Theorem. *For any information system A, there is an information system D that satisfies the equation $D = A + (D \Rightarrow D)$.*   □

Inclusive subsets as types.

Recall that a subset of a cpo is *inclusive* if it is downward closed and closed under lub's of ω-chains. Based on a universal domain, it is possible to use inclusive subsets to model types. Let X be any domain and suppose we are given a solution to the domain equation

$$D \cong X \oplus [D \to D]. \tag{8.7}$$

This is a model of the untyped λ-calculus: let $\Psi : [D \to D] \to D$ be the injection inr of the cpo of continuous functions from D to D into the right component of D (note that the function $x \mapsto \perp_D$ is being set to $\perp_D$) and let $\Phi : D \to [D \to D]$ be given by

$$\Phi(y) = \begin{cases} f & \text{if } y = \mathsf{inr}(f) \text{ for a continuous } f : D \to D \\ \perp_{[D \to D]} & \text{if } y = \mathsf{inl}(x) \text{ for some } x \in X. \end{cases}$$

It is easy to see that $\Phi \circ \Psi = \mathsf{id}$. To associate inclusive subsets on D with types of the simply-typed λ-calculus, define

$$[\![\mathbf{o}]\!] = \mathsf{inl}(X)$$
$$[\![s \to t]\!] = \{\Psi(f) \mid f \in [D \to D] \text{ and } f(x) \in [\![t]\!] \text{ whenever } x \in [\![s]\!]\}.$$

8.5 Lemma. *For each type t, the subset $[\![t]\!] \subseteq D$ is an inclusive subset.*

Proof: The proof is by induction on the structure of t. If this is $\mathbf{o}$, then the result is immediate since X is clearly inclusive. Suppose $t \equiv r \to s$ where $[\![r]\!]$ and $[\![s]\!]$ are inclusive.

First, suppose $x = \Psi(f) \in [\![r \to s]\!]$ and $y \sqsubseteq x$. Then y is in the image of Ψ (since this image is downward closed) so $y = \Psi(g)$ for some $g : D \to D$. Thus $g = \Phi(\Psi(g)) \sqsubseteq \Phi(\Psi(f)) = f$. Suppose that $z \in [\![r]\!]$. Then $g(x) \sqsubseteq f(z) \in [\![s]\!]$. But $[\![s]\!]$ is inclusive and therefore downward closed so $g(z) \in [\![s]\!]$ too. Hence $g([\![r]\!]) \subseteq [\![s]\!]$, so $\Psi(g) = y \in [\![r \to s]\!]$.

Now, suppose that $(x_n)_{n \in \omega}$ is an ω-chain in $[\![r \to s]\!]$. By definition, there are continuous functions $f_n : D \to D$ such that $f_n([\![r]\!]) \subseteq [\![s]\!]$ and $\Psi(f_n) = x_n$ for each $n \in \omega$. Since $\Psi(f_n) = x_n \sqsubseteq x_{n+1} = \Psi(f_{n+1})$, it must be the case that $f_n = \Phi(\Psi(f_n)) \sqsubseteq \Phi(\Psi(f_{n+1})) = f_{n+1}$. By continuity of Ψ, therefore, $\bigsqcup_{n \in \omega} x_n = \Psi(\bigsqcup_{n \in \omega} f_n)$. If $x \in [\![r]\!]$, then $(\bigsqcup_{n \in \omega} f_n)(x) = \bigsqcup_{n \in \omega} f_n(x) \in [\![s]\!]$ since $[\![s]\!]$ is inclusive. Thus $\bigsqcup_{n \in \omega} x_n \in [\![r \to s]\!]$. $\square$

Given a type assignment H, an H-environment ρ is defined to be a function from variables into D such that $\rho(x) \in [\![H(x)]\!]$ for each $x \in H$. If $H \vdash M : t$, then the interpretation of M is given by induction on the structure of M relative to an H-environment ρ as follows:

$$[\![x]\!]\rho = \rho(x)$$
$$[\![L(N)]\!]\rho = \Phi([\![L]\!]\rho)([\![N]\!]\rho)$$
$$[\![\lambda x : s. \, M']\!]\rho = \Psi(d \mapsto [\![M']\!]\rho[x \mapsto d])$$

The key result relating this interpretation to the interpretations of types is the following theorem:

8.6 Theorem. *If $H \vdash M : t$ and ρ is an H-environment, then $[\![M]\!]\rho \in [\![t]\!]$.* $\square$

The proof is left for the reader; part of the proof of a similar result is given below for PCF.

There is a problem with interpreting types in this way, however: the equational rules are not all satisfied. To see why this is the case, suppose that the domain X in Equation 8.7 has at least one element other than $\perp_X$. Define two terms

$$M \equiv \lambda y : s \to t.\ \lambda x : s.\ y(x)$$
$$N \equiv \lambda y : s \to t.\ y.$$

The meaning of M can be calculated as

$$
\begin{aligned}
[\![M]\!]\emptyset &= \Psi(e \mapsto [\![\lambda x : s.\ y(x)]\!][y \mapsto e]) \\
&= \Psi(e \mapsto \Psi(d \mapsto [\![y(x)]\!][y, x \mapsto e, d])) \\
&= \Psi(e \mapsto \Psi(d \mapsto \Phi([\![y]\!][y, x \mapsto e, d])([\![x]\!][y, x \mapsto e, d]))) \\
&= \Psi(e \mapsto \Psi(d \mapsto \Phi(e)(d)))
\end{aligned}
$$

and the value of N by

$$[\![N]\!]\emptyset = \Psi(d \mapsto [\![y]\!][y \mapsto d]) = \Psi(d \mapsto d).$$

Suppose $\perp \neq a \in [\![o]\!]$. Then $[\![M]\!] \neq [\![N]\!]$ because $\Phi[\![M]\!]\emptyset(a) \neq \Phi[\![N]\!]\emptyset(a)$. To see why, first calculate

$$
\begin{aligned}
\Phi([\![M]\!]\emptyset)(a) &= \Phi(\Psi(e \mapsto \Psi(d \mapsto \Phi(e)(d))))(a) \\
&= \Psi(d \mapsto \Phi(a)(d)) \\
&= \Psi(d \mapsto (e \mapsto \perp)(d)) \\
&= \Psi(d \mapsto \perp) \\
&= \perp
\end{aligned}
$$

whereas

$$\Phi([\![N]\!]\emptyset)(a) = \Phi(\Psi(d \mapsto d))(a) = a \neq \perp.$$

But these two terms are provably equal in the equational theory. Let $r \equiv s \to t$, then by projection

$$\vdash (y : r \rhd y = y : r)$$

so, by the η-rule,

$$\vdash (y : r \rhd \lambda x : s.\ y(x) = y : r)$$

Table 8.2
Call-by-Name Evaluation with Type Errors

$$\textbf{tyerr} \Downarrow \textbf{tyerr} \qquad \frac{L \Downarrow V \qquad V \notin \text{Boolean}}{\textbf{if } L \textbf{ then } M \textbf{ else } N \Downarrow \textbf{tyerr}}$$

$$\frac{M \Downarrow V \qquad V \notin \text{Number}}{\textbf{pred}(M) \Downarrow \textbf{tyerr}} \qquad \frac{M \Downarrow V \qquad V \notin \text{Number}}{\textbf{succ}(M) \Downarrow \textbf{tyerr}} \qquad \frac{M \Downarrow V \qquad V \notin \text{Number}}{\textbf{zero?}(M) \Downarrow \textbf{tyerr}}$$

$$\frac{M \Downarrow V \qquad V \notin \text{Lambda}}{M(N) \Downarrow \textbf{tyerr}}$$

Hence, by the ξ-rule,

$$\vdash (\triangleright \lambda y : r. \ \lambda x : s. \ y(x) = \lambda y : r. \ y : r \to r).$$

This is the equation $M = N$ that is not satisfied by the model. Where does the problem lie here? It is not the η-rule as one might orginally suspect: the η-rule is satisfied by the interpretation. The problem is the soundness of the ξ-rule: the terms M and N denote functions, but if they are applied (in the model) to elements of the 'wrong type', then the values may differ.

I will present a construction that solves this problem shortly. But what is the use of a model that does not satisfy the equational theory? The reason for looking at this interpretation of types is its usefulness in a proof that does not actually demand a model of the equational theory. Inclusive subsets as types can be used to carry out semantic proofs of results such as Theorem 7.1. To see this in an example, let us look at the analog of that theorem for call-by-name PCF. We expand the grammar of PCF to include a new expression **tyerr** that does not have a type and expand the operational rules in Table 4.4 to include rules for type errors as given in Table 8.2. To give a fixed-point model of the calculus, we use a domain U for which there is an isomorphism

$$U \cong \mathbb{T} \oplus \mathbb{N}_\perp \oplus [U \to U]_\perp \oplus \mathbb{O}. \tag{8.8}$$

To save some tedious numbering for the injections into this sum, let us just write $d : D$ for the injection of element d into the D component of the sum. For example, $n : \mathbb{N}_\perp$ is the injection of $n \in \mathbb{N}_\perp$ into the second component of U. Now, as usual, the semantics of a term M such that $H \vdash M : t$ is relative to an H-environment ρ.

- $\mathcal{I}[\![x]\!]\rho = \rho(x)$,

- $\mathcal{I}[\![\lambda x : t.\ M']\!]\rho = \mathsf{up}(f) : [U \to U]_\perp$ where

$$f(d) = \begin{cases} \mathsf{tyerr} & \text{if } d = \mathsf{tyerr} \\ \mathcal{I}[\![M']\!]\rho[x \mapsto d] & \text{otherwise.} \end{cases}$$

- $\mathcal{I}[\![L(N)]\!]\rho = \begin{cases} \mathsf{down}(f)(\mathcal{I}[\![N]\!]\rho) & \text{if } \mathcal{I}[\![L]\!]\rho = f : [U \to U]_\perp \text{ for some } f \\ \mathsf{tyerr} & \text{otherwise.} \end{cases}$

- $\mathcal{I}[\![\mu x : t.\ M']\!]\rho = \mathsf{fix}(d \mapsto \mathcal{I}[\![M']\!]\rho[x \mapsto d])$.

- $\mathcal{I}[\![\mathbf{tyerr}]\!]\rho = \mathsf{tyerr}$

Providing semantic clauses for the remaining constructs of PCF is left for the reader. They must be chosen to make the following results true.

8.7 Lemma. *For each type t, $\mathcal{I}[\![t]\!]$ is an inclusive subset.*   □

8.8 Lemma. *If $H \vdash M : t$ and ρ is an H-environment, then $\mathcal{I}[\![M]\!]\rho \in \mathcal{I}[\![t]\!]$.*

Proof: The proof is by induction on the structure of M. I will consider only the base case and the case for recursions. If M is a variable, then the lemma holds by the assumption that ρ is an H environment. Suppose M is a recursion $\mu x : t.\ M'$. In this case,

$$\mathcal{I}[\![M]\!]\rho = \bigsqcup_{n \in \omega} d_n$$

where $d_0 = \perp$ and, for each $n \in \omega$, $d_{n+1} = \mathcal{I}[\![M']\!]\rho[x \mapsto d_n]$. Now, $d_0 \in \mathcal{I}[\![t]\!]$ and d_{n+1} is in $\mathcal{I}[\![t]\!]$ if d_n is by the inductive hypothesis on M'. Since $\mathcal{I}[\![t]\!]$ is inclusive, it therefore follows that the least upper bound of the chain $(d_n)_{n \in \omega}$ is in $\mathcal{I}[\![t]\!]$.   □

8.9 Theorem. *If $M : t$ and $M \Downarrow V$, then V is not **tyerr**.*

Proof: If $M \Downarrow V$, then $\mathcal{I}[\![M]\!] = \mathcal{I}[\![V]\!]$. Since $\mathcal{I}[\![M]\!]\emptyset \in \mathcal{I}[\![t]\!]$ and $\mathsf{tyerr} \notin \mathcal{I}[\![t]\!]$, it must be the case that $\mathcal{I}[\![V]\!]\emptyset \neq \mathbf{tyerr}$ so it cannot be the case that V is **tyerr**.   □

Partial equivalence relations.

There is a simple approach to solving the problem with the unsoundness of ξ-rule in the interpretation of types as inclusive subsets. The idea is to interpret types as *equivalence relations* on subsets of the universal domain and interpret terms as equivalence classes in their respective types.

Definition: Let A be a set. A *Partial Equivalence Relation (PER)* on A is a relation $R \subseteq A \times A$ that is transitive and symmetric. The *domain* of a partial equivalence relation R is the set $\mathrm{dom}(R) = \{a \in A \mid a\ R\ a\}$.   □

Note that if R is a PER on a set A and $a \; R \; b$ for any $a, b \in A$, then a and b are in the domain of A by the symmetry axiom.

Now, suppose we are given a model of the untyped λ-calculus. Say $\Phi : U \to [U \to U]$ and $\Psi : [U \to U] \to U$ satisfy $\Phi \circ \Psi = \mathsf{id}_{[U \to U]}$. Let X be any PER on U. Take $\mathcal{P}[\![\mathsf{o}]\!] = X$ and define PER interpretations for types by structural induction as follows. Suppose $\mathcal{P}[\![s]\!]$ and $\mathcal{P}[\![t]\!]$ are PER's, then

$$f \; \mathcal{P}[\![s \to t]\!] \; g \text{ iff, for each } d \text{ and } e, \; d \; \mathcal{P}[\![s]\!] \; e \text{ implies } \Phi(f)(d) \; \mathcal{P}[\![t]\!] \; \Phi(g)(e).$$

It is easy to check that each of these relations is a partial equivalence. To see how they interpret terms, we use a semantic function that gives untyped meaning to typed terms. Given a term M of the simply-typed λ-calculus, let $\mathcal{U}[\![M]\!]$ be the meaning of untyped λ-term erase(M) in U based on the pair Φ, Ψ. Given a PER R on U and an element $d \in \mathrm{dom}(R)$, let $[d]_R$ be the equivalence class of d relative to R, that is, $[d]_R = \{e \mid d \; R \; e\}$.

Let M be a term of the typed λ-calculus such that $H \vdash M : t$. The meaning of M is given relative to a function ρ from variables $x \in H$ into U such that $\rho(x)$ is in the domain of the relation $\mathcal{P}[\![H(x)]\!]$ for each $x \in H$. Such a function is called an H-environment for the PER interpretation. Now, the interpretation for the term M is quite simple:

$$\mathcal{P}[\![H \rhd M : t]\!]\rho = [\mathcal{U}[\![M]\!]\rho]_{\mathcal{P}[\![t]\!]}$$

There are two basic facts about to be proved about this interpretation. First, if M has type t then the interpretation of M is in the domain of the relation $\mathcal{P}[\![t]\!]$. Second, all of the equational rules of the typed λ-calculus are satisfied. Given H-environments ρ and θ, define $\rho \sim_H \theta$ if, for each $x \in H$, $\rho(x) \; \mathcal{P}[\![H(x)]\!] \; \theta(x)$.

8.10 Lemma. *Suppose $H \vdash M : t$. If ρ and θ are H-environments and $\rho \sim_H \theta$, then $(\mathcal{U}[\![M]\!]\rho) \; \mathcal{P}[\![t]\!] \; (\mathcal{U}[\![M]\!]\theta)$.*

Proof: The proof is by induction on the structure of M. If $M \equiv x$, then $x \in H$, $t \equiv H(x)$, and $\rho \sim \theta$ implies the desired conclusion.

Case $M \equiv \lambda x : u. \; M'$ where $t \equiv u \to v$. Suppose $d \; \mathcal{P}[\![u]\!] \; e$. Then

$$\Phi(\mathcal{U}[\![\lambda x : u. \; M']\!]\rho)(d) = \Phi(\Psi(d \mapsto \mathcal{U}[\![M']\!]\rho[x \mapsto d]))(d) = \mathcal{U}[\![M']\!]\rho[x \mapsto d],$$

and, similarly, $\Phi(\mathcal{U}[\![\lambda x : u. \; M']\!]\theta)(e) = \mathcal{U}[\![M']\!]\theta[x \mapsto e]$. Now,

$$(\mathcal{U}[\![M']\!]\rho[x \mapsto d]) \; \mathcal{P}[\![v]\!] \; (\mathcal{U}[\![\lambda x : u. \; M']\!]\theta[x \mapsto e])$$

by the inductive hypothesis. The desired conclusion therefore follows from the definition of $\mathcal{P}[\![t]\!]$.

Case $M \equiv L(N)$ where $H \vdash L : s \to t$ and $H \vdash N : s$. By the inductive hypothesis for N, $(\mathcal{U}[\![N]\!]\rho) \; \mathcal{P}[\![s]\!] \; (\mathcal{U}[\![N]\!]\theta)$. So, by the inductive hypothesis for L, $d \; \mathcal{P}[\![t]\!] \; e$ where $d = \Phi(\mathcal{U}[\![L]\!]\rho)(\mathcal{U}[\![N]\!]\rho) = \mathcal{U}[\![M]\!]\rho$ and $e = \Phi(\mathcal{U}[\![L]\!]\theta)(\mathcal{U}[\![N]\!]\theta) = \mathcal{U}[\![M]\!]\theta$. $\qquad \square$

8.11 Corollary. *If $H \vdash M : t$ and ρ is an H-environment, then $\mathcal{P}[\![H \rhd M : t]\!]\rho$ is in the domain of the relation $\mathcal{P}[\![t]\!]$.* □

8.12 Lemma. *If $\vdash (H \rhd M' = N' : t')$ and $\rho \sim_H \theta$ are H-environments, then*

$$\mathcal{P}[\![H \rhd M' : t']\!]\rho = \mathcal{P}[\![H \rhd N' : t']\!]\theta.$$

Proof: The proof is by induction on the height of the derivation of the judgement $\vdash (H \rhd M' = N' : t')$. I will do some of the interesting cases for the last step of the proof: the ξ-, η-, and β-rules.

Suppose the last step of the derivation is an instance of

$$\{\xi\} \quad \frac{T \vdash (H, \ x : s \rhd M = N : t)}{T \vdash (H \rhd \lambda x : s. \ M = \lambda x : s. \ N : s \to t)}$$

where $M' \equiv \lambda x : s. \ M$ and $N' \equiv \lambda x : s. \ N$ and $t' \equiv s \to t$. By the inductive hypothesis, $(\mathcal{U}[\![M]\!]\rho[x \mapsto d]) \ \mathcal{P}[\![t]\!] \ (\mathcal{U}[\![N]\!]\theta[x \mapsto e])$ whenever $e \ \mathcal{P}[\![s]\!] \ d$. Hence $(\mathcal{U}[\![\lambda x. \ M]\!]\rho) \ \mathcal{P}[\![s \to t]\!]$ $(\mathcal{U}[\![\lambda x. \ N]\!]\theta)$ by the definition of the PER $\mathcal{P}[\![s \to t]\!]$. Thus $\mathcal{P}[\![H \rhd \lambda x : s. \ M : s \to t]\!]\rho = \mathcal{P}[\![H \rhd \lambda x : s. \ N : s \to t]\!]\theta$.

Suppose the last step of the derivation is an instance of

$$\{\eta\} \quad \frac{H \vdash M : s \to t \qquad x \notin \mathrm{Fv}(M)}{T \vdash (H \rhd \lambda x : s. \ M(x) = M : s \to t)}.$$

Suppose that $d \ \mathcal{P}[\![s]\!] \ e$. Then

$$
\begin{aligned}
\Phi(\mathcal{U}[\![\lambda x : s. \ M(x)]\!]\rho)(d) &= \Phi(\Psi(d \mapsto \mathcal{U}[\![M(x)]\!]\rho[x \mapsto d]))(d) \\
&= \mathcal{U}[\![Mx]\!]\rho[x \mapsto d] \\
&= \Phi(\mathcal{U}[\![M]\!]\rho[x \mapsto d])(\mathcal{U}[\![x]\!]\rho[x \mapsto d]) \\
&= \Phi(\mathcal{U}[\![M]\!]\rho[x \mapsto d])(d) \\
&= \Phi(\mathcal{U}[\![M]\!]\rho)(d)
\end{aligned}
$$

where the last equality follows from the fact that x is not free in M. Now,

$$(\mathcal{U}[\![M]\!]\rho) \ \mathcal{P}[\![s \to t]\!] \ (\mathcal{U}[\![M]\!]\theta)$$

by Lemma 8.10, so

$$(\Phi(\mathcal{U}[\![M]\!]\rho)(d)) \ \mathcal{P}[\![t]\!] \ (\Phi(\mathcal{U}[\![M]\!]\theta)(e)).$$

Therefore

$$(\mathcal{U}[\![\lambda x : s. \ M(x)]\!]\rho) \ \mathcal{P}[\![s \to t]\!] \ (\mathcal{U}[\![M]\!]\theta),$$

and therefore $\mathcal{P}[\![H \triangleright \lambda x : s. \ M(x) : s \to t]\!]\rho = \mathcal{P}[\![H \triangleright M : s \to t]\!]\theta$.

Suppose the last step of the derivation is an instance of

$$\{\beta\} \qquad \frac{H, x : s \vdash M : t \qquad H \vdash N : s}{T \vdash (H \triangleright (\lambda x : s. \ M)(N) = [N/x]M : t)}.$$

In this case, the desired conclusion basically follows from the soundness of the β-rule for the untyped calculus. To be precise, let $\sim$ be the PER $\mathcal{P}[\![t]\!]$ and note that

$$\mathcal{U}[\![[N/x]M]\!]\rho = \mathcal{U}[\![M]\!]\rho[x \mapsto \mathcal{U}[\![N]\!]\rho] \sim \mathcal{U}[\![M]\!]\theta[x \mapsto \mathcal{U}[\![N]\!]\theta] = \mathcal{U}[\![[N/x]M]\!]\theta$$

by the inductive hypothesis. Thus

$$\begin{aligned}
\mathcal{P}[\![H \triangleright (\lambda x : s. \ M)(N) : t]\!]\rho &= [\,\mathcal{U}[\![(\lambda x : s. \ M)(N)]\!]\rho\,]_{\mathcal{P}[\![t]\!]} \\
&= [\,\mathcal{U}[\![[N/x]M]\!]\rho\,]_{\mathcal{P}[\![t]\!]} \\
&= [\,\mathcal{U}[\![[N/x]M]\!]\theta\,]_{\mathcal{P}[\![t]\!]} \\
&= \mathcal{P}[\![H \triangleright [N/x]M : t]\!]\theta. \qquad \square
\end{aligned}$$

8.13 Corollary. *If* $\vdash (H \triangleright M = N : t)$, *then* $\mathcal{P}[\![H \triangleright M : t]\!] = \mathcal{P}[\![H \triangleright N : t]\!]$. $\qquad \square$

Exercises.

8.1 Prove that if P is a term such that $\mathrm{erase}(P) \equiv \lambda x. \ x(x)$, then there is no context H and type expression t such that $H \vdash P : t$.

8.2 Prove Lemma 8.2.

8.3 Prove that the functions defined in Equations 8.3 and 8.4 are continuous.

8.4 Define the coalesced sum operation for information systems and use this definition to demonstrate how to solve Equation 8.7.

8.5 Prove the equations in 8.6.

8.6 Prove Theorem 8.6.

8.7 Prove that the η-rule is sound for the the interpretation of types as inclusive subsets.

8.8 Prove that an intersection of PER's is a PER.

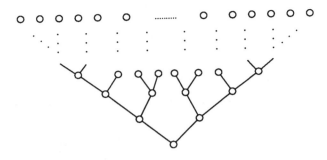

Figure 8.1
The Simple Binary Tree with Limit Points Added

8.2 Domain Equations

We have seen how information systems can be used to solve recursive domain equations. Let us now look at another way to solve such equations using universal domains and the Fixed-Point Theorem. Consider, for example, the equation $T \cong T + T$. How would we go about finding a domain and an isomorphism that solve this equation? Suppose we start with the one point domain $T_0 = \mathbb{U}$ as the first approximation to the desired solution. Taking the proof of the Fixed-Point Theorem as our guide, we build the domain $T_1 = T_0 + T_0 = \mathbb{U} + \mathbb{U}$ as the second approximation. Now, there is an embedding $e_0 : T_0 \to T_1$ that maps the one element of T_0 to the bottom element of T_1, so this gives a sense in which T_0 approximates T_1. The next approximation to our solution is the domain $T_2 = T_1 + T_1$, and again there is an embedding $e_1 = e_0 + e_0 : T_1 \to T_2$. If we continue along this path, we build a sequence

$$T_0 \xrightarrow{e_0} T_1 \xrightarrow{e_1} T_2 \xrightarrow{e_2} \cdots$$

of approximations to the full simple binary tree. To get a domain, we must add limits for each of the branches. The resulting domain—which is illustrated in Figure 8.1—is, indeed, a 'solution' of $T \cong T + T$. We can also be more precise about the structure pictured there and how it solves the domain equation. A simple way to describe the elements of solution to the domain equation is to view them as strings of 0's and 1's. An element of the poset $2^{<\omega} \cup 2^{\omega}$ of finite and infinite strings of 0's and 1's is either

- the empty string ϵ, or

- a finite string of 0's and 1's, or

- an infinite string of 0's and 1's.

It is ordered by the prefix ordering, that is: $s \sqsubseteq s'$ iff s is a prefix of s'. It is possible to show that this is bc-domain (but it is obviously not a lattice). Let $T = 2^{<\omega} \cup 2^{\omega}$. To see that $T \cong T + T$, define a function $f : T \to T + T$ as follows:

$$f(s) = \begin{cases} \mathsf{inl}(\mathsf{up}(s')) & \text{if } s = 0s' \\ \mathsf{inr}(\mathsf{up}(s')) & \text{if } s = 1s' \\ \bot_{T+T} & \text{if } s = \epsilon, \end{cases}$$

and define a function $g : T + T \to T$ by

$$g(x) = \begin{cases} 0s & \text{if } x = \mathsf{inl}(\mathsf{up}(s)) \\ 1s & \text{if } x = \mathsf{inr}(\mathsf{up}(s)) \\ \epsilon & \text{if } x = \bot_{T+T}. \end{cases}$$

It is easy to see that f and g are inverses defining the desired isomorphism.

How general is the technique we have just used? It seems that we might be able to use a similar strategy to solve an equation like $S \cong A + (S \times S)$ and a variety of other equations involving tree-like structures defined using constants and operators such as $+$ and $\times$. However, the situation becomes much more difficult when we move to the question of producing a solution to an equation like $D \cong A + [D \to D]$ and worse yet when we are confronted with an equation like $D \cong [D \to D]$, which never 'gets off the ground' when we employ this iteration technique.

The purpose of this section is to describe two techniques for using a universal domain to solve recursive equations. Both use idempotents as a way to represent types.

Solving domain equations with closures.

Definition: Let D and E be cpo's. A continuous function $r : D \to E$ is a *retraction* if there is a continuous function $s : E \to D$, called a *section for r*, such that $r \circ s = \mathsf{id}_E$. A retraction is called a *closure* if the inequation $s \circ r \sqsupseteq \mathsf{id}_D$ holds for some section s. □

One example of a closure that we encountered earlier was the function $\mathsf{down} : D_\bot \to D$ on cpo's; in this case a corresponding section is up. If there is a retraction $r : D \to E$, then E is said to be a *retract* of D. This term is sometimes also used for subsets of D that could be the image of a retraction because, if there are functions $r : D \to E$ and $s : E \to D$ such that $r \circ s = \mathsf{id}_E$, then $\mathsf{im}(s)$ is an isomorphic copy of E inside of D. To see why, let s' be the corestriction of s to its image (that is, s' is the map from E to $\mathsf{im}(s)$ given by taking $s'(x) = s(x)$). If r' is the restriction of r to $\mathsf{im}(s)$, and $s'(y) = x \in \mathsf{im}(s)$, then $(s' \circ r')(x) = s'(r'(s'(y))) = s'(y) = x$ so $s' \circ r' = \mathsf{id}_D$. Since $r' \circ s' = \mathsf{id}_E$, it follows that E and $\mathsf{im}(s)$ are isomorphic. The map $s \circ r$ from D into itself is therefore an idempotent whose image is isomorphic to E. Such idempotents will be our primary interest:

Definition: A function $r : D \to D$ is a *finitary closure* if $r \circ r = r \sqsupseteq \mathrm{id}$. $\qquad$ □

In the event that D is a domain, it is possible to show that the image of a finitary closure is also one:

8.14 Lemma. *If D is a domain and $r : D \to D$ satisfies the equation $r \circ r = r \sqsupseteq \mathrm{id}$, then $\mathrm{im}(r)$ is a domain.*

Proof: Proof that $\mathrm{im}(r)$ is a cpo is left as an exercise for the reader; I will show that $\{r(x) \mid x \in \mathsf{K}(D)\}$ forms a basis for $\mathrm{im}(r)$. Suppose $x \in \mathsf{K}(D)$ and $r(x) \sqsubseteq \bigsqcup M$ where $M \subseteq \mathrm{im}(r)$. Since $x \sqsubseteq r(x)$ and x is compact, there is some $y \in M$ such that $x \sqsubseteq y$. Hence $r(x) \sqsubseteq r(y) = y$, and it follows that $r(x) \in \mathsf{K}(\mathrm{im}(r))$. Now, if $x \in \mathrm{im}(r)$, then $M = \{y \in \mathsf{K}(D) \mid y \sqsubseteq x\}$ is directed and $x = \bigsqcup M$ so $x = r(x) = \bigsqcup r(M)$ and we are done. $\qquad$ □

A domain E is a *closure of D* if it is isomorphic to $\mathrm{im}(r)$ for some finitary closure r on D. We let $\mathsf{Fc}(D)$ be the poset of finitary closures $r : D \to D$ ordered pointwise, that is, $r \sqsubseteq r'$ iff $r(x) \sqsubseteq r'(x)$ for each $x \in D$.

8.15 Lemma. *If D is a domain, then $\mathsf{Fc}(D)$ is a cpo.* $\qquad$ □

Proof of the lemma is left as an exercise.

In using closures as a means for solving equations, the idea is to represent an operator on cpo's as operator on a cpo of closures.

Definition: An operator F on cpo's is *representable* over a cpo U if, and only if, there is a continuous function R_F that completes the following diagram (up to isomorphism):

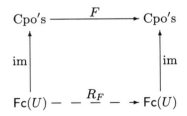

that is, $\mathrm{im}(R_F(r)) \cong F(\mathrm{im}(r))$ for every closure r. $\qquad$ □

This idea extends to operators on tuples as well. For example, the function space operator $[\cdot \to \cdot]$ is representable over a cpo U if there is a continuous function

$$R : \mathsf{Fc}(U) \times \mathsf{Fc}(U) \to \mathsf{Fc}(U)$$

such that, for any $r, s \in \mathsf{Fc}(U)$,

$$\mathrm{im}(R(r,s)) \cong [\mathrm{im}(r) \to \mathrm{im}(s)].$$

An operator $\langle F_1, \ldots, F_n \rangle$ is defined to be representable if each of the operators F_i is. The composition of representable operators is representable by the composition of their representations. It is possible to find a fixed point for a representable operator by using the Fixed-Point Theorem:

8.16 Theorem. *If an operator F is representable over a cpo U, then there is a domain D such that $D \cong F(D)$.*

Proof: Suppose R_F represents F. By the Fixed-Point Theorem, there is an $r \in \mathsf{Fc}(U)$ such that $r = R_F(r)$. Thus $\mathrm{im}(r) = \mathrm{im}(R_F(r)) \cong F(\mathrm{im}(r))$ so $\mathrm{im}(r)$ is the desired domain.
□

Now we have a general way to solve domain equations. For example, to solve $T \cong T + T$, we need to find a domain U and continuous function $f : U \to U$ that represents the operator $F(X) = X + X$. Of course, we are still left with the problem of finding a domain over which such operations can be represented! The next step is to look at a simple structure that can be used to represent several of the operations in which we are interested.

Given sets S and T, let T^S be the set of (all) functions from S into T. If T is a cpo, then T^S is also a cpo under the pointwise ordering. The domain equation $X \cong \mathbb{O} \times X$ (where $\mathbb{O}$ is the two point lattice) has, as one of its solutions, the cpo $\mathbb{O}^N$. To see why, define a map

$$\Phi : \mathbb{O}^N \to \mathbb{O} \times X$$

by taking $\Phi(f)$ to be the pair $(f(0), f')$ where $f' : n \mapsto f(n+1)$ and a map

$$\Psi : \mathbb{O} \times X \to \mathbb{O}^N$$

where

$$\Phi(d, f)(n) = \begin{cases} d & \text{if } n = 0 \\ f(n-1) & \text{if } n > 0. \end{cases}$$

It is easy to check that $\Phi \circ \Psi = \mathsf{id}$ and $\Psi \circ \Phi = \mathsf{id}$. In fact, these $\mathbb{O}^N$ is isomorphic to the algebraic cpo $\mathcal{P}(\mathbb{N})$ of subsets of $\mathbb{N}$. This solution to the domain equation $X \cong \mathbb{O} \times X$ can be used to solve many other domain equations as well:

8.17 Theorem. *For any (countably based) algebraic lattice L, there is a closure*

$$r : \mathcal{P}(\mathbb{N}) \to L.$$

Proof: Let $l_0, l_1, l_2, \ldots$ be an enumeration of the basis of L. Given $S \subseteq \mathbb{N}$, let $r(S) = \bigsqcup \{l_n \mid n \in S\}$. If $l \in L$, let $s(l) = \{n \mid l_n \sqsubseteq l\}$. We leave for the reader the (easy) demonstration that r, s are continuous with $r \circ s = \mathrm{id}$ and $s \circ r \sqsupseteq \mathrm{id}$. $\qquad\square$

Structures such as $\mathcal{P}(\mathbb{N})$ are often referred to as *universal domains* because they have a rich collection of domains as retracts. Unfortunately, there is no representation for the operator $F(X) = X + X$ over $\mathcal{P}(\mathbb{N})$. However, there are some quite interesting operators that *are* representable over $\mathcal{P}(\mathbb{N})$. In particular, we have the following lemma:

8.18 Lemma. *The function space operator is representable over $\mathcal{P}(\mathbb{N})$.*

Proof: Consider the algebraic lattice of functions $\mathcal{P}(\mathbb{N}) \to \mathcal{P}(\mathbb{N})$. By Theorem 8.17, we know that there are continuous functions

$$\Phi_\to : \mathcal{P}(\mathbb{N}) \to (\mathcal{P}(\mathbb{N}) \to \mathcal{P}(\mathbb{N}))$$
$$\Psi_\to : (\mathcal{P}(\mathbb{N}) \to \mathcal{P}(\mathbb{N})) \to \mathcal{P}(\mathbb{N})$$

such that $\Phi_\to \circ \Psi_\to = \mathrm{id}$ and $\Psi_\to \circ \Phi_\to \sqsupseteq \mathrm{id}$. Now, suppose $r, s \in \mathsf{Fc}(\mathcal{P}(\mathbb{N}))$ (that is, $r \circ r = r \sqsupseteq \mathrm{id}$ and $s \circ s = s \sqsupseteq \mathrm{id}$). Given a continuous function $f : \mathcal{P}\mathbb{N} \to \mathcal{P}\mathbb{N}$, let $\Theta(s, r)(f) = s \circ f \circ r$ and define

$$R_\to(r, s) = \Psi_\to \circ \Theta(s, r) \circ \Phi_\to.$$

To see that this function is a finitary closure, we take $x \in \mathcal{P}(\mathbb{N})$ and compute

$$
\begin{aligned}
(R_\to(r, s) \circ R_\to(r, s))(x) &= (\Psi_\to \circ \Theta(s, r) \circ \Phi_\to)(\Psi_\to(s \circ (\Phi_\to(x)) \circ r) \\
&= (\Psi_\to \circ \Theta(s, r) \circ \Phi_\to \circ \Psi_\to)(s \circ (\Phi_\to(x)) \circ r) \\
&= (\Psi_\to \circ \Theta(s, r))(s \circ (\Phi_\to(x)) \circ r) \\
&= \Psi_\to((s \circ s) \circ (\Phi_\to(x)) \circ (r \circ r)) \\
&= \Psi_\to(s \circ (\Phi_\to(x)) \circ r) \\
&= R_\to(r, s)(x)
\end{aligned}
$$

and $R_\to(r, s)(x) = \Psi_\to(s \circ (\Phi_\to(x)) \circ r) \sqsupseteq \Psi_\to(\Phi_\to(x)) \sqsupseteq x$. Thus we have defined a function

$$R_\to : \mathsf{Fc}(\mathcal{P}(\mathbb{N})) \times \mathsf{Fc}(\mathcal{P}(\mathbb{N})) \to \mathsf{Fc}(\mathcal{P}(\mathbb{N})),$$

which we now demonstrate to be a representation of the function space operator.

Given $r, s \in \mathsf{Fc}(\mathcal{P}(\mathbb{N}))$, we must show that there is an isomorphism

$$\mathrm{im}(R_\to(r,s)) \cong \mathrm{im}(r) \to \mathrm{im}(s)$$

for each $r, s \in \mathsf{Fc}(\mathcal{P}(\mathbb{N}))$. Now, there is an evident isomorphism between continuous functions $f : \mathrm{im}(r) \to \mathrm{im}(s)$ and set D of continuous functions $g : \mathcal{P}(\mathbb{N}) \to \mathcal{P}(\mathbb{N})$ such that $g = s \circ g \circ r$. We claim that $\Psi_\to$ cuts down to an isomorphism between such functions and the sets in the image E of $R_\to(r, s)$. First of all, if $g \in D$, then

$$\Psi(g) = \Psi(s \circ g \circ r) = (\Psi \circ \Theta(s, r) \circ \Phi(g) = R(r, s)$$

so Ψ maps D into E. On the other hand, if $x \in E$, then

$$\Phi(x) = \Phi(R(r, s)(x)) = \Phi(\Psi(s \circ \Psi(x) \circ r)) = s \circ \Phi(x) \circ r$$

so Φ maps E into D. Since $\Phi_\to \circ \Psi_\to = \mathrm{id}$, we need only show that $(\Psi_\to \circ \Phi_\to)(x) = x$ for each $x = R_\to(r, s)(x)$. If

$$x = \Psi_\to(s \circ (\Phi_\to(x)) \circ r),$$

then

$$\begin{aligned}
(\Psi_\to \circ \Phi_\to)(x) &= (\Psi_\to \circ \Phi_\to \circ \Psi_\to)(s \circ (\Phi_\to(x)) \circ r) \\
&= \Psi_\to(s \circ (\Phi_\to(x)) \circ r) \\
&= x.
\end{aligned}$$

Hence $\mathrm{im}(R_\to(r, s)) \cong \mathrm{im}(r) \to \mathrm{im}(s)$, and we may conclude that $R_\to$ represents $\to$ over $\mathcal{P}(\mathbb{N})$.

$\square$

A similar construction can be carried out for the product operator. Suppose

$$\Phi_\times : \mathcal{P}(\mathbb{N}) \to (\mathcal{P}(\mathbb{N}) \times \mathcal{P}(\mathbb{N}))$$
$$\Psi_\times : (\mathcal{P}(\mathbb{N}) \times \mathcal{P}(\mathbb{N})) \to \mathcal{P}(\mathbb{N})$$

such that $\Phi_\times \circ \Psi_\times = \mathrm{id}$ and $\Psi_\times \circ \Phi_\times \sqsupseteq \mathrm{id}$. For $r, s \in \mathsf{Fc}(\mathcal{P}(\mathbb{N}))$ define

$$R_\times(r, s) = \Psi_\times \circ (r \times s) \circ \Phi_\times.$$

We leave for the reader the demonstration that this makes sense and $R_\times$ represents the product operator.

Suppose that L is an algebraic lattice. Then there are continuous functions

$$\Phi_L : \mathcal{P}(\mathbb{N}) \to L$$
$$\Psi_L : L \to \mathcal{P}(\mathbb{N})$$

such that $\Phi_L \circ \Psi_L = \mathsf{id}_L$ and $\Psi_L \circ \Phi_L \sqsupseteq \mathsf{id}_{\mathcal{P}(\mathbb{N})}$. Then the function

$$R_L(r, s) = \Psi_L \circ \Phi_L$$

represents the constant operator $X \mapsto L$ because $\mathrm{im}(\Psi_L \circ \Phi_L) \cong L$. A similar argument can be used to show that a constant operator $X \mapsto D$ is representable over a domain U if, and only if, D is a closure of U.

Modeling the untyped $\lambda\beta\eta$-calculus.

It is tempting to try to solve the domain equation $D \cong D \to D$ by the methods just discussed. Unfortunately, the equation $\mathbb{U} \cong \mathbb{U} \to \mathbb{U}$ (corresponding to the fact that on a point set with only one point there is only one possible self-map) shows that there is no guarantee that the result will be at all interesting. There has to be a way to build in some nontrivial structure that is not wiped out by the fixed-point process.

8.19 Lemma. *Let U be a non-trivial cpo. If the product and function space operators can be represented over U, then there are non-trivial domains D and E such that $E \cong E \times E$ and $D \cong [D \to E]$.*

Proof: We can represent $F(X) = U \times X \times X$ over U, so there is a closure A of U such that $A \cong U \times A \times A$. Thus $U \times A \cong U \times (U \times A \times A) \cong (U \times A) \times (U \times A)$. So $E = U \times A$ is non-trivial and $E \cong E \times E$. Now, E is a closure of U so $G(X) = [X \to E]$ is representable over U. Hence there is a cpo $D \cong [D \to E]$. This cpo is non-trivial because E is. $\qquad\square$

8.20 Theorem. *If U is a non-trivial domain that represents products and function spaces, then there is a non-trivial domain D such that $D \cong D \times D \cong [D \to D]$ and D is the image of a closure on U.*

Proof: Let D and E be the domains given by Lemma 8.19. Then

$$D \times D \cong [D \to E] \times [D \to E] \cong [D \to E \times E] \cong [D \to E] \cong D$$

and

$$[D \to D] \cong [D \to [D \to E]] \cong [D \times D \to E] \cong [D \to E] \cong D. \qquad\square$$

Solving domain equations with projections.

As mentioned earlier, one bothersome drawback to $\mathcal{P}(\mathbb{N})$ as a domain for solving recursive domain equations is the fact that it cannot represent the sum operator $+$. One might try to overcome this problem by using as a substitute an operator $(\,\cdot\,+\,\cdot\,)^\top$, which takes the separated sum and adds a new top element. This *is* representable over $\mathcal{P}(\mathbb{N})$. However, the added top element seems unmotivated and gets in the way (both intuitively and technically). It is possible to find a cpo that will represent the operators $\times, \rightarrow, +$ using finitary closures. However, for the sake of variety, I will discuss a different method for solving domain equations using a notion dual to that of a finitary closure:

Definition: Let D and E be cpo's. A pair of continuous functions (e, p) such that $e : D \rightarrow E$ and $p : E \rightarrow D$ is called an *embedding-projection pair* if $p \circ e = \text{id}$ and $e \circ p \sqsubseteq \text{id}$. In this case e is said to be an *embedding* and p a *projection*. □

One example of an embedding-projection pair is given by the functions **unsmash** and **smash** defined in Section 6.3. If D and E are pointed cpo's, then the projections onto D and E are also projections in the sense of the definition. As with closures, the primary focus of attention in the discussion of this section is on the idempotent map $e \circ p$ rather than the embedding-projection pair itself.

Definition: A function $p : D \rightarrow D$ is a *finitary projection* if $p \circ p = p \sqsubseteq \text{id}$ and $\text{im}(p)$ is a domain. Given a domain D, define $\mathsf{Fp}(D)$ to be collection of finitary projections on D. □

8.21 Theorem. *If D is a domain, then*

1. *For every $p, q \in \mathsf{Fp}(D)$, $p \sqsubseteq q$ in the pointwise order if, and only if, the image of p is a subset of the image of q.*
2. *For each $p \in \mathsf{Fp}(D)$, the compact elements of the image of p are exactly the compact elements of D that are in the image, that is, $\mathsf{K}(\text{im}(p)) = \text{im}(p) \cap \mathsf{K}(D)$.*
3. *$\mathsf{Fp}(D)$ is a cpo and if D is pointed, so is $\mathsf{Fp}(D)$.*

Proof: To prove part 1, suppose first that $p \sqsubseteq q$ in the pointwise order. Since p is an idempotent, its fixed points are exactly its image. So, if x is in the image of p, then $q(x) \sqsubseteq x = p(x) \sqsubseteq q(x)$. Suppose, conversely, that the image of p is contained in that of q. Then $p(x) \sqsubseteq x$ implies $q(p(x)) \sqsubseteq q(x)$. But $q(p(x)) = p(x)$ so we are done.

To prove part 2, begin by noting that it is obvious that $\text{im}(p) \cap \mathsf{K}(D) \subseteq \mathsf{K}(\text{im}(p))$. To show the reverse inclusion, suppose x is compact in $\text{im}(p)$ and $M \subseteq D$ is directed with $x \sqsubseteq \bigsqcup M$. Then $x = p(x) \sqsubseteq p(\bigsqcup M) = \bigsqcup p(M)$. Since x is compact in the image of p, there is some $y \in M$ with $x \sqsubseteq p(y)$. But $p(y) \sqsubseteq y$ so x is compact in D.

For part 3, let $M \subseteq \mathsf{Fp}(D)$ be directed and let $q = \bigsqcup M$. The proof that $q \circ q = q \sqsubseteq id$ is left for the reader. We must show that $\mathrm{im}(q)$ is a domain. Suppose $q(x) = x$ and $a \sqsubseteq x$ is compact. Then $a \sqsubseteq p(x)$ for some $p \in M$. Since $\mathrm{im}(p)$ is a domain, $a \sqsubseteq \bigsqcup(\downarrow p(x) \cap \mathsf{K}(\mathrm{im}(p)))$. Since a is compact, there is some $b \in \downarrow p(x) \cap \mathsf{K}(\mathrm{im}(p))$ with $a \sqsubseteq b$. Now, $b \in \mathrm{im}(q)$ by 1 and it is compact by 2. Moreover, $b \sqsubseteq p(x) \sqsubseteq x$. This shows that for every compact element $a \sqsubseteq x$, there is a compact element b in the image of q such that $a \sqsubseteq b \sqsubseteq x$. Since D is a domain, it follows that x is the lub of its compact approximations in $\mathrm{im}(q)$. This set of compact approximations is directed since it is the union of the directed collections $\downarrow x \cap \mathrm{im}(p)$ such that $p \in M$. □

Let us say that an operator F on cpo's is *p-representable* over a cpo U if, and only if, there is a continuous function R_F that completes the following diagram (up to isomorphism):

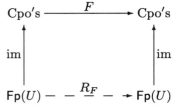

Since there will be no chance of confusion, let us just use the term 'representable' for 'p-representable' for the remainder of this section. Since $\mathsf{Fp}(U)$ is a cpo, we can solve domain equations in the same way we did before, *provided we can find domains over which the necessary operators can be represented.*

The construction of a suitable domain is somewhat more involved than was the case for $\mathcal{P}(\mathbb{N})$. I will describe a construction here but omit the proof of its universality since this would require a substantial effort and there will be a more general discussion of how to construct a universal domain Chapter 10. We begin by describing the basis of a domain U. Let S be the set of rational numbers of the form $n/2^m$ where $0 \le n < 2^m$ and $0 < m$. As the basis U_0 of our domain we take finite (non-empty) unions of half open intervals $[r, t) = \{s \in S \mid r \le s < t\}$. A typical element would look like this

We order these sets by superset so that the interval $[0, 1)$ is the *least* element. Note that there is no top element under this ordering. Here is the basic fact about U.

8.22 Theorem. *For any bounded complete domain D, there is a projection*

$$p : U \to D. \qquad\qquad\qquad\qquad\qquad\qquad □$$

We can now use this to see that an equation like $X \cong \mathbb{N}_\perp + (X \to X)$ has a solution. The proof that $\to$ is representable over U is almost identical to the proof we gave that it is representable over $\mathcal{P}(\mathbb{N})$. To get a representation for $+$, take a pair of continuous functions

$$\Phi_+ : U \to (U + U)$$
$$\Psi_+ : (U + U) \to U$$

such that $\Phi_+ \circ \Psi_+ = \mathrm{id}$ and $\Psi_+ \circ \Phi_+ \sqsubseteq \mathrm{id}$. Then take

$$R_+(r, s) = \Psi_+ \circ (r + s) \circ \Phi_+.$$

Also, there is a representation $R_{\mathbb{N}_\perp}$ for the constant operator $X \mapsto \mathbb{N}_\perp$. Hence the operator $X \mapsto \mathbb{N}_\perp + (X \to X)$ is represented over U by the function

$$p \mapsto R_+(R_{\mathbb{N}_\perp}(p), R_\to(p, p)).$$

We have, in fact, the following:

8.23 Lemma. *The following operators are representable over* U: $\to$, $\circ\!\!\to$, $\times$, $\otimes$, $+$, $\oplus$, $(\cdot)_\perp$. $\qquad\qquad\qquad\qquad\qquad\qquad\qquad\qquad\qquad\qquad\qquad\qquad\qquad\qquad\qquad$ $\Box$

This means that we have solutions over the bounded-complete domains for a quite substantial class of recursive equations.

Fixed-point semantics for FPC.

These techniques make it possible to provide a fixed-point interpretation for the types and terms of FPC, the Fixed-Point Calculus. Type variables are essential for recursive type definitions, but their existence forces us to use, at the level of *types*, some of the notations for the semantics of free variables at the level of *terms* for the simply-typed λ-calculus. In particular, a *type-value environment* is a function that assigns semantic domains to type variables. The meaning $\mathcal{R}[\![t]\!]\iota$ of a type t relative to type-value environment ι is a domain whose precise interpretation must be explained. In particular, we interpret $\mathcal{R}[\![a]\!]\iota = \iota(a)$. To interpret a type $\mu a.\, t$, one takes a 'fixed point' of the operator $F : D \mapsto \mathcal{R}[\![t]\!]\iota[D/a]$. To ensure that such fixed points exist, we can draw upon a universal domain construction such as the universal bc-domain described above.

Let H be an assignment and fix a type-value environment ι. An H, ι value environment ρ assigns to each variable $x \in H$ a value $\rho(x) \in \mathcal{R}[\![H(x)]\!]\iota$. If $H \vdash M : t$, then the interpretation $[\![H \rhd M : t]\!]\iota$ is a function from H, ι environments into $[\![t]\!]\iota$. This function is defined by induction on the height of a typing derivation of the term as follows.

Suppose we are given the following continuous functions from $\mathsf{Fp}(U) \times \mathsf{Fp}(U) \to \mathsf{Fp}(U)$:

- $R_\to$ represents the operator $(D, E) \mapsto [D \to E]_\bot$
- $R_\times$ represents the smash product
- R_+ represents the coalesced sum

then we define the semantics of types as follows:

- $\mathcal{R}[\![a]\!]\iota = \iota(a)$ where a is a type variable
- $\mathcal{R}[\![\mathbf{unit}]\!] = p$ where $p \in \mathsf{Fp}(U)$ and $\mathrm{im}(p)$ is isomorphic to $\mathbb{O}$, the two point lattice
- $\mathcal{R}[\![s \to t]\!]\iota = R_\to(\mathcal{R}[\![s]\!]\iota, \mathcal{R}[\![t]\!]\iota)$
- $\mathcal{R}[\![s \times t]\!]\iota = R_\times(\mathcal{R}[\![s]\!]\iota, \mathcal{R}[\![t]\!]\iota)$
- $\mathcal{R}[\![s + t]\!]\iota = R_+(\mathcal{R}[\![s]\!]\iota, \mathcal{R}[\![t]\!]\iota)$
- $\mathcal{R}[\![\mu a.\, t]\!]\iota = \mathsf{fix}(D \mapsto \mathcal{R}[\![t]\!]\iota[x \mapsto D])$

For a type t, define $\bar{\mathcal{R}}[\![t]\!]\iota = \mathrm{im}(\mathcal{R}[\![t]\!]\iota)$. A term M of type t is interpreted as an element of the domain $\bar{\mathcal{R}}[\![t]\!]\iota$. In particular, if ρ is an H, ι environment, then

$$\mathcal{R}[\![H \rhd x : H(x)]\!]\iota\rho = \rho(x) \in \bar{\mathcal{R}}[\![H(x)]\!]\iota.$$

For most of the other terms the interpretation is also very similar to the one given by the semantic function $\mathcal{C}^\circ[\![\cdot]\!]$ described in Chapter 6. Let us work though one example in detail. Suppose that $H \vdash \lambda x : s.\ M : s \to t$ is derivable in the typing system for FPC. The meaning function on terms is defined by induction on the structure of M or on the height of the derivation of the judgement $H \vdash \lambda x : s.\ M : s \to t$ in such a way that for each type-value environment ι, if $d \in \bar{\mathcal{R}}[\![s]\!]\iota$, then $\mathcal{R}[\![M]\!]\iota(\rho[x \mapsto d]) \in \bar{\mathcal{R}}[\![t]\!]\iota$. In particular, the function $f : \bar{\mathcal{R}}[\![s]\!]\iota \to \bar{\mathcal{R}}[\![t]\!]\iota$ given by

$$f : d \mapsto \mathcal{R}[\![M]\!]\iota(\rho[x \mapsto d])$$

is continuous. Now, there is an isomorphism

$$\phi : [\bar{\mathcal{R}}[\![s]\!]\iota \multimap \bar{\mathcal{R}}[\![t]\!]\iota]_\bot \cong \bar{\mathcal{R}}[\![s \to t]\!]\iota$$

because $R_\to$ represents the operator $(D, E) \mapsto [D \to E]_\bot$. We therefore define

$$\mathcal{R}[\![H \rhd \lambda x : s.\ M : s \to t]\!]\iota\rho = \phi(\mathsf{up}(\mathsf{strict}(f))) \in \bar{\mathcal{R}}[\![s \to t]\!]\iota.$$

If we are a bit imprecise and omit the isomorphisms that come from the fact that operators are being represented over finitary projections, then it becomes even simpler to write down the semantic equations. For example,

$$\mathcal{R}[\![H \rhd (M, N) : s \times t]\!]\iota\rho = \mathsf{smash}(\mathcal{R}[\![H \rhd M : s]\!]\iota\rho, \mathcal{R}[\![H \rhd N : t]\!]\iota\rho)$$

defines the semantics of pairs. For the semantics of terms from recursive types, suppose we are given $H \vdash \mathbf{intro}[\mu a.\ t](M) : \mu a.\ t$ and a type-value environment ι. Now,

$$\mathcal{R}[\![\mu a.\ t]\!]\iota = \mathcal{R}[\![t]\!]\iota[a \mapsto \mathcal{R}[\![\mu a.\ t]\!]\iota],$$

and therefore

$$\bar{\mathcal{R}}[\![\mu a.\ t]\!]\iota = \bar{\mathcal{R}}[\![t]\!]\iota[a \mapsto \mathcal{R}[\![\mu a.\ t]\!]].$$

So, if ρ is an H, ι environment, then we can take

$$\mathcal{R}[\ : \mu a.\ t]\!]\iota\rho = \mathcal{R}[\![H \rhd M : [\mu a.\ t/a]t]\!]\iota\rho$$

since it can be shown that $\bar{\mathcal{R}}[\![[\mu a.\ t/a]t]\!]\iota = \bar{\mathcal{R}}[\![t]\!]\iota[a \mapsto \mathcal{R}[\![\mu a.\ t]\!]\iota]$. Similarly, we define

$$\mathcal{R}[\ : [\mu a.\ t/a]t]\!]\iota\rho = \mathcal{R}[\![H \rhd M : \mu a.\ t]\!]\iota\rho.$$

Exercises.

8.9 Prove that the poset $2^{<\omega} \cup 2^{\omega}$ of finite or infinite strings of 0's and 1's is a bc-domain.

8.10 Prove Lemma 8.15.

8.11 Prove that a closure has a uniquely determined section. In other words, show that if $r \circ s = r \circ s' = \mathsf{id}$ and $s \circ r, s' \circ r \sqsupseteq \mathsf{id}$, then $s = s'$. Is this also true of retractions and sections generally?

8.12 Prove that if D and E are algebraic cpo's and $f : D \to E$ is an embedding with $d \in \mathsf{K}(D)$, then $f(d) \in \mathsf{K}(E)$.

8.3 Notes

The discovery of models of the untyped λ-calculus is due to Scott [222]. The book by Barendregt [21] is the encyclopedic reference on the untyped calculus for both its syntax and semantics. Categorical semantics of the untyped calculus was explored by Koymans [140]. The implicit coercion semantics for the untyped calculus was described in a paper by Meyer [165] which also discusses other ways in which a model can be defined and contains references to the literature on the topic.

There have been a number of papers on the universal domains for various classes of spaces. The idea of using a universal domain in general and the idea of using $\mathcal{P}(\mathbb{N})$ as a universal domain in particular are due to D. S. Scott [223]. Plotkin [197] demonstrated that the domain $\mathbb{T}^{\mathbb{N}}$ (that is, functions from $\mathbb{N}$ into $\mathbb{T}$ under the pointwise ordering) can also be used as a universal domain for coherent algebraic cpo's. The question of a universal domain for dI-domains is treated by Berardi [24] who demonstrates how retractions (rather than closures or projections) can be used to model a subtle type system. Universal domains and information systems were studied by Bracho [34] and by Droste and Göbel [79]. The universal bc-domain U described on page 278 is due to Scott [227; 228]. A proof that it is universal for the bc-domains was given using information systems by Bracho [34] (Theorem 2.11 on page 184).

The idea of using inclusive subsets as types to prove a lemma such as 8.9 originated with Milner [169] for the calculus $\mathrm{ML_0}$. The solution of recursive domain equations in this context has been addressed by MacQueen, Plotkin, and Sethi [155]. In both of these papers the term 'ideal' is used for an inclusive subset so the model of types as inclusive subsets is sometimes termed the 'ideal model'. The solution of domain equations for inclusive subsets is problematic because the approach one would try first—ordering the inclusive subsets by subset inclusion and using the Fixed-Point Theorem—does not work. The problem lies in the fact that $U \subseteq U'$ and $V \subseteq V'$ for inclusive subsets U, U', V, V' does *not* imply that

$$\{f : D \to D \mid f(U) \subseteq V\} \subseteq \{f : D \to D \mid f(U') \subseteq V'\}.$$

In fact, this relationship is only ensured in the event that $U' \subseteq U$ (not $U \subseteq U'$) and $V \subseteq V'$. As a result, there is no evident way to use the Fixed-Point Theorem here. The solution is to use another fixed-point existence theorem, known as the *Banach Contraction Theorem,* that works on certain kinds of metric spaces. The space of types as inclusive subsets and the operators of interest are then shown to satisfy the necessary conditions for the application of that theorem. For a variety of reasons, metric spaces have been useful in the providing semantics for programming languages, especially for languages with constructs for concurrent computation. A sample of such work and some references can be found in papers of America, de Bakker, Kok, and Rutten [10], de Bakker and Warmerdam [68], and, for real-time systems, in a paper of Reed and Roscoe. [198]

There are discussions of techniques for proving adequacy for the untyped calculus in papers of Abramsky [4] and Mosses and Plotkin [181]. The techniques needed to prove the results for these systems are closely connected to those required for proving adequacy for FPC. The difficulty lies in demonstrating the existence of the necessary relations on cpo's. A study of the techniques for proving this is given by Mulmuley [182] in his doctoral dissertation. A discussion of the typed case appears in [176] and an outline of a closely related proof appears in an appendix by Cosmodakis in [163].

Another class of structures called *filter domains* can be used to build models of the untyped λ-calculus. For example, a solution for $D \cong [D \to D]$ is given by Coppo, Dezani-Ciancaglini, and Zacchi in [55]. Their techniques provide a rich source of many interesting constructions; Cardone and Coppo have written a survey [49] that has a good bibiliography on the subject.

9 Subtype Polymorphism

The term 'polymorphism' comes from a Greek word that means 'having many forms'. It has a technical usage in biology and crystallography. In biology it refers to variation (other than sexual variation) in the forms of animals within a given species; the different castes of ants is an example. In crystallography it refers the appearance of a substance in more than one crystalline form; graphite and diamond, for instance, are two crystalline forms of carbon. In programming language theory, the term is used for instances in which an expression in a strongly-typed language is used to represent an operation for more than one type. Polymorphism in programming languages is classified into categories based on how this representation is done. The most obvious example is that of *overloading* or *coercion* in which a single symbol is used for two (possibly unrelated) operations. One of the best-known examples of this is the symbol $+$, which is used in most programming languages for binary addition on both the integers and the real numbers. Naturally these two operations are related from a mathematical perspective since addition on integers is a restriction of the addition on reals, of which the integers can be seen as a subset. Nevertheless, in computational terms, the algorithms for computing these two programs are very different, just as the internal representations of integers and reals are very different.

There is generally not much interest in the use of a single symbol to denote unrelated programs. Our interest will primarily lie in the instances where there is some relationship or uniformity connecting a program at one type to that at another. This state of affairs arises in the polymorphism evidenced by a program that can be used to reverse a list of integers and also to reverse a list of real numbers. In this case the internal representation of integers and reals is insignificant; it is the common idea of a list that matters and the algorithms for the two types of integer list and real list are intimately connected. The function r that takes a list as an argument and returns the reversal of that list as a value can be viewed as having the type $list(a) \rightarrow list(a)$ where a is a variable that ranges over types. In other words, the type of this program is 'parameterized' by a. This kind of polymorphism is therefore called *parametric polymorphism*. It will be discussed in detail in Chapter 11.

A third kind of programming language polymorphism that is being used in several modern languages is based on the notion of a *subtype*. This is a form of type polymorphism that arises from the classification of data according to collections of *attributes*. This perspective draws its inspiration from hierarchical systems of categories such as the taxonomy of the animal kingdom rather than from the variation of a parameter as in quantifiers of predicate logic.

To get some of the spirit of this kind of typing, let us begin with an informal example based on the kind of hierarchy that one might form in order to classify some of the indi-

viduals one finds at a university; let us call such individuals *academics*. Each academic
has an associated *university* and *department* within the university. At the university there
are *professors,* who teach courses, and *students,* who suffer through the courses taught
by the professors. Some of the students are *employees* of the university in a capacity as
teaching assistants (TA's) while others are *research assistants (RA's)* supported by the
research grants. Each of these various classes of individuals has associated attributes. For
instance, if we consider a typical semester, we can attribute to professors and teaching
assistants the courses they are teaching—their *teaching load*. In this capacity as teachers,
the professors and TA's are employees and therefore have a *salary* associated with them.
RA's have a *project* attribute for the research project on which they are working.

To bring some order to this assortment of groups and attributes, it is helpful to organize
a hierarchy of groups *classified by their defining attributes.* Let us begin to list each group
and its attributes. First of all, we could use a type of *persons,* whose members, which
include both academics and employees, have a *name* attribute. In addition to a name,
each academic has a university and each employee has a salary, a *social security number*
(for tax purposes), and an *employer.* In addition to attributes inherited from their
roles as academics, each student has an *advisor* and each professor has a teaching load
and a boolean *tenure* attribute. Professors are also employees, so they must possess the
attributes of employees as well as those of academics. We can now classify our assortment
by using common attributes to form the poset given in Figure 9.1. Each point in the
poset represents a *type* of individual based on attributes the individual must possess. If
a type s is below a type t in the poset, this means that each kind of attribute that an
individual of type of t possesses must also be had by each individual of type s. If we let
$\leq$ be the ordering for the poset, then if $s \leq t$, we say that s is a *subtype* of t. The fact
that a professor must have a social security number is something one can conclude by
the fact that the type of professors is a subtype of that of employees and the fact that
each employee has a social security number.

The purpose of this chapter is to develop a formal type system that supports some of
the intuitions behind subtyping in this example together with some further extensions of
these ideas to accommodate subtyping between other kinds of type constructors such as
sums and higher types. The language is an extension of PCF called PCF++ that supports
a simple form of subtyping. The semantics of PCF++ is described in two ways. The
first section of the chapter describes the calculus PCF++ and uses a universal domain
to interpret types as inclusive subsets. Under this interpretation subtypes can be viewed
as subsets. The second section looks at a quite different approach to the semantics of the
language in which no universal domain is employed. The approach views the subtyping
as indicating a kind of implicit coercion, much as we did in modeling the untyped λ-
calculus. This model challenges a basic identification that we have been using for calculi

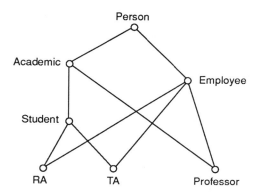

Figure 9.1
A Subtyping Hierarchy

considered before. In other calculi the model has been given by structural induction or *equivalently* by induction on the height of *the* proof of its type correctness. In the calculus with subtypes considered in this chapter, proofs are not uniquely determined by typing judgements and do not necessarily follow the structure of terms. An adequacy theorem for this semantics is proved at the end of the second section.

9.1 Subtypes as Subsets

Let us begin now to move toward a formalization and expansion of the idea of a subtype— again starting with intuitive examples, but using some formal notations. Each of the types in the example given above can be viewed as a kind of product where the components of a tuple having that type are its attributes. In programming languages these are generally called *records*, and the attributes are called the *fields* of the record. Records are usually written with curly brackets '{' and '}' rather than with parentheses as tuples are. Semantically they are very similar to tuples, but the field labels relieve the need to write the record fields in any particular order. A common record syntax is a sequence of pairs of the form $l = M$ where l is a *label* and M is the term associated with that label. The term M is generally called the *l-field* of the record. For example, the records

```
{Name = "Carl Gunter", University = "University of Pennsylvania"}
{University = "University of Pennsylvania", Name = "Carl Gunter"}
```

are considered equivalent, and the type of these records is given by the following equivalent pair of record type expressions:

```
{Name : String, University : String}
{University : String, Name : String}.
```

Ordinarily it is simplest to impose this equivalence on the syntax of records just as we use α-equivalence to identify term trees modulo renaming of bound variables.

Now, we would like to mix records such as these with the dual notion of a *variant*. A variant is a generalization of a binary sum in which the injections **inl** and **inr** are replaced by elements of a class of labels. As with sums, they make it possible to express a type as a 'union' of other types. Variants are ordinarily written with square (as opposed to curly) brackets '[' and ']'. For instance, a biological classification system might include a declaration such as

```
type ReproductiveSystem = [Male : MaleSystem,
                           Female : FemaleSystem]
```

defining a familiar partition of the collection of reproductive systems. In this expression, **Male** and **Female** are labels for the fields of the variant; the types of these fields must be **MaleSystem** and **FemaleSystem** respectively. The order in which the fields are written is insignificant. A classification system for vehicles might have a type

```
type Vehicle = [Air : AirVehicle,
                Land : LandVehicle,
                Water : WaterVehicle]
```

in which vehicles are classified according to their preferred milieu. A term of this type would come from one of the three possible components. For example,

```
[Air = SouthernCross]
```

is a term of type **Vehicle** if **SouthernCross** is a term of type **AirVehicle**. And

```
[Water = QueenMary]
```

is also a term of type `Vehicle` if `QueenMary` is a term of type `WaterVehicle`. To see a little more detail for these types, consider the following declarations:

```
type Thing = {Age : Int}
type Machine = Thing + {Fuel : String}
type MovingMachine = Machine + {MaxSpeed : Int}
type AirVehicle =
  MovingMachine + {MaxAltitude : Int, MaxPassengers : Int}
type LandVehicle =
  MovingMachine + {Surface : String, MaxPassengers : Int}
type WaterVehicle =
  MovingMachine + {Tonnage : Int, MaxPassengers : Int}
```

Here each of the defined types is a record type. To make the notation more succinct, a plus sign is written to indicate, for instance, that a `Machine` is a record having a field `Fuel` together with all of the fields had by a `Thing` (namely an `Age` field). (Our formal language below does not include any notation like this, but it could easily be added without affecting the semantics significantly.) Consider what a subtype of type `Vehicle` might be. In the case of records, a subtype has more fields than a supertype. In a variant, the dual holds. For instance,

```
type WheeledVehicle = [Air : WheeledAirVehicle,
                       Land : WheeledLandVehicle]
```

is a subtype of `Vehicle` where

```
type WheeledLandVehicle = LandVehicle + {WheelsNumber : Int}
type WheeledAirVehicle = AirVehicle + {WheelsNumber : Int}.
```

Intuitively, a wheeled vehicle is either an air vehicle with wheels or a land vehicle with wheels. If we forget about the wheels, then a wheeled vehicle can be viewed simply as a vehicle. This example also illustrates that it is not just the fact that there are fewer fields that matters for variants, but that the types of the fields that exist are subtypes of the corresponding fields from the supertype. Looking at this from the point of view of a term of type `WheeledVehicle`, note that

```
value MyCar = [Land = {Age = 3, Fuel = "Gasoline", MaxSpeed = 100,
                       Surface = "Roadway", MaxPassengers = 5,
                       WheelsNumber = 4}]
```

has the type `Vehicle` if the last field, which indicates the number of wheels, is omitted.

This provides some intuition about the subtyping relation between records and between variants, but there is still one more type constructor to which we would like to generalize the idea: the function space operator. Suppose, for instance, that we need a function

```
Using : String -> Machine
```

which, given a kind of fuel (described by a string), returns an example of a **Machine** that uses that fuel. In any context where such a function is needed, we could just as easily use a function

```
WaterVehicleUsing : String -> WaterVehicle,
```

which, given a kind of fuel (described by a string), returns an example of a **WaterVehicle** that uses that fuel. This suffices because a **WaterVehicle** is a kind of machine.

Suppose now that we need a function having the type

```
HowSoon : {Start : Place, Finish : Place, Mode : AirVehicle} -> Int
```

where the type **Place** is a record consisting of a latitude and a longitude and the function calculates a lower bound on how soon the given mode of transport could make it from **Start** to **Finish**. Suppose we have on hand a function

```
MovingMachineHowSoon : {Start : Place, Finish : Place,
                        Mode : MovingMachine} -> Int
```

which calculates a value from its arguments in the obvious way using the distance between the two places and the maximum speed of a **MovingMachine** as an argument. This can be used to serve the purpose of **HowSoon** since an **AirVehicle** is a special kind of **MovingMachine**. The method used to calculate **HowSoon** on an instance of the latter type also applies to an instance of the former.

These examples suggest that we should take **String -> Machine** to be a subtype of **String -> WaterVehicle** and take

```
{Start : Place, Finish : Place, Mode : AirVehicle} -> Int
```

to be a subtype of

```
{Start : Place, Finish : Place, Mode : MovingMachine} -> Int.
```

In the general case we will want to generalize this by taking $s \to t$ to be a subtype of $s' \to t'$ just in case t is a subtype of t' and s' is a subtype of s. Note the 'contravariance' in the first argument.

PCF++.

It is now time to turn to a more formal treatment using a fixed syntax. The calculus we study is obtained by extending PCF to a language that includes records and variants; this extension is called *PCF+* or 'PCF plus records and variants'. The syntax extends that of PCF. To define its term trees, we require a primitive syntax class of *labels* $l \in$ Label. The syntax of the language is defined in several stages because of a context-sensitive restriction that is imposed on the term trees. We begin with the following grammar:

$$
\begin{array}{rcl}
x & \in & \text{Variable} \\
l & \in & \text{Label} \\
t & ::= & \textbf{num} \mid \textbf{bool} \mid t \rightarrow t \mid \{l : t, \ldots, l : t\} \mid [l : t, \ldots, l : t] \\
M & ::= & \textbf{0} \mid \textbf{true} \mid \textbf{false} \mid \\
& & \textbf{succ}(M) \mid \textbf{pred}(M) \mid \textbf{zero?}(M) \mid \textbf{if } M \textbf{ then } M \textbf{ else } M \mid \\
& & x \mid \lambda x : t.\ M \mid MM \mid \mu x : t.\ M \mid \\
& & \{l = M, \ldots, l = M\} \mid M.l \mid \\
& & [l = M, l : t, \ldots, l : t] \mid \textbf{case } M \textbf{ of } l \Rightarrow M, \ldots, l \Rightarrow M
\end{array}
$$

where ellipsis (the notation with three dots) is used to indicate lists of pairs in records and variants. The type trees and term trees of PCF+ are of trees generated by this grammar for which there are no repeated labels in the lists of label/type and label/term pairs.

- If $t_1, \ldots, t_n$ are type trees and $l_1, \ldots, l_n$ are *distinct* labels, then

  $$\{l_1 : t_1, \ldots, l_n : t_n\}$$

  is a type called a *record type (tree)*.

- If $t_1, \ldots, t_n$ are types and $l_1, \ldots, l_n$ are distinct labels, then

  $$[l_1 : t_1, \ldots, l_n : t_n]$$

  is a type called a *variant type (tree)*.

- If $M_1, \ldots, M_n$ are term trees and $l_1, \ldots, l_n$ are distinct labels, then

  $$\{l_1 = M, \ldots, l_n = M\}$$

  is a term tree called a *record (term tree)*.

- If M is a term tree, then $M.l$ is a term tree called a *field selection*.

Table 9.1
Typing Rules for Records and Variants

[RecIntro]
$$\frac{H \vdash M_1 : t_1 \quad \cdots \quad H \vdash M_n : t_n}{H \vdash \{l_1 = M_1, \ldots, l_n = M_n\} : \{l_1 : t_1, \ldots, l_n : t_n\}}$$

[RecElim]
$$\frac{H \vdash M : \{l_1 : t_1, \ldots, l_n : t_n\}}{H \vdash M.l_i : t_i}$$

[VarIntro]
$$\frac{H \vdash M : t}{H \vdash [l = M, l_1 : t_1, \ldots, l_n : t_n] : [l : t, l_1 : t_1, \ldots, l_n : t_n]}$$

[VarElim]
$$\frac{H \vdash M : [l_1 : t_1, \ldots, l_n : t_n] \quad H \vdash M_1 : t_1 \to t \quad \cdots \quad H \vdash M_n : t_n \to t}{H \vdash \mathbf{case}\ M\ \mathbf{of}\ l_1 \Rightarrow M_1 \cdots l_n \Rightarrow M_n : t}$$

- If M is a term tree, $t_1, \ldots, t_n$ are types, and $l, l_1, \ldots, l_n$ are distinct labels, then

$$[l = M, l_1 : t_1, \ldots l_n : t_n]$$

  is a term tree called an *injection*.

- If M and $M_1, \ldots, M_n$ are term trees and $l_1, \ldots, l_n$ are distinct labels, then

$$\mathbf{case}\ M\ \mathbf{of}\ l_1 \Rightarrow M_1, \ldots, l_n \Rightarrow M_n$$

  is a term tree called a *case*.

The *terms* of PCF+ are equivalence classes of term trees modulo α-conversion (renaming of bound variables) and the order in which the pairs in records and variants are written. A similar equivalence is assumed for record and variant type trees. A *record type* is an equivalence class of type trees represented by a record type tree; a similar nomenclature applies to the other forms of types and terms.

The typing rules for PCF+ are those for PCF in Tables 2.1 and 4.1, together with rules for records and variants given in Table 9.1. They are quite similar to the rules for products and sums. As with the sum, it is essential to label the variations to ensure that a variant has a unique type. In general we have the following:

9.1 Theorem. *If $H \vdash M : s$ and $H \vdash M : t$, then $s \equiv t$.* $\square$

Table 9.2
Rules for Subtyping

$$\textbf{num} \leq \textbf{num} \qquad \frac{s' \leq s \qquad t \leq t'}{s \to t \leq s' \to t'}$$
$$\textbf{bool} \leq \textbf{bool}$$

$$\frac{s_1 \leq t_1 \quad \cdots \quad s_n \leq t_n}{\{l_1 : s_1, \ldots, l_n : s_n, \ldots, l_m : s_m\} \leq \{l_1 : t_1, \ldots, l_n : t_n\}}$$

$$\frac{s_1 \leq t_1 \quad \cdots \quad s_n \leq t_n}{[l_1 : s_1, \ldots, l_n : s_n] \leq [l_1 : t_1, \ldots, l_n : t_n, \ldots, l_m : t_m]}$$

This will not be true of the calculus PCF++ we now define. PCF++ is the extension of PCF+ in which we allow the use of a subtyping relation between types. The binary relation $s \leq t$ of subtyping between type expressions s and t is defined by the rules in Table 9.2. It is possible to show that $\leq$ is a poset on type expressions. The calculus PCF++ is the same as PCF+ but with the typing rules of PCF+ extended by the addition of the *subsumption rule*. Since a type can be derived for a term using subsumption that could not be derived without it, it will be essential to distinguish between typing judgements for PCF++ and those of PCF+. Let us write $\vdash_{\text{sub}}$ for the least relation that contains the relation $\vdash$ of PCF+ and satisfies

$$[\text{Subsump}] \qquad \frac{H \vdash_{\text{sub}} M : s \qquad s \leq t}{H \vdash_{\text{sub}} M : t}.$$

To see an example of how the subsumption rule affects the derivability of typing judgements, consider the following pair of PCF++ terms:

$$G \equiv \lambda f : \{l : \textbf{num}\} \to \textbf{num}.$$
$$\{k_1 = f(\{l = \underline{3}, l_1 = \underline{5}\}), k_2 = f(\{l = \underline{6}, l_2 = \textbf{false}\})\} \qquad (9.1)$$
$$F \equiv \lambda x : \{l : \textbf{num}\}. \, x.l$$

The program $G(F)$ does not have a type in PCF+ because G does not have one. It *does* have a type in PCF++ because the subsumption rule makes it possible to use the following subtyping relations:

$$r_1 \equiv_{\text{def}} \{l : \textbf{num}, l_1 : \textbf{num}\} \leq \{l = \textbf{num}\}$$
$$\qquad \qquad \qquad \qquad \qquad \qquad \qquad \qquad \qquad \qquad \qquad \qquad (9.2)$$
$$r_2 \equiv_{\text{def}} \{l : \textbf{num}, l_2 : \textbf{bool}\} \leq \{l = \textbf{num}\}$$

To see where this comes up in a typing derivation for $G(F)$, let us work backwards. Say we want to establish the hypotheses of the following instance of the application rule:

$$\frac{\vdash_{\text{sub}} G : (r \to \textbf{num}) \to t \qquad \vdash_{\text{sub}} F : r \to \textbf{num}}{\vdash_{\text{sub}} G(F) : t}$$

where $t \equiv \{k_1 : \mathbf{num},\ k_2 : \mathbf{num}\}$ and $r \equiv \{l : \mathbf{num}\}$. Let

$$M \equiv \{k_1 = f(\{l = \underline{3},\ l_1 = \underline{5}\}),\ k_2 = f(\{l = \underline{6},\ l_2 = \mathbf{false}\})\}$$

and $H \equiv f : r \rightarrow \mathbf{num}$. That F has the type in question is easy to see. To prove the desired result for G, we can establish the hypothesis of the following instance of abstraction:

$$\frac{H \vdash_{\mathrm{sub}} M : t}{\vdash_{\mathrm{sub}} G : (r \rightarrow \mathbf{num}) \rightarrow t}.$$

For this we can establish the hypotheses of the following instance of record introduction:

$$\frac{H \vdash_{\mathrm{sub}} f(\{l = \underline{3},\ l_1 = \underline{5}\}) : \mathbf{num} \qquad H \vdash_{\mathrm{sub}} f(\{l = \underline{6},\ l_1 = \mathbf{false}\}) : \mathbf{num}}{H \vdash_{\mathrm{sub}} M : t}. \tag{9.3}$$

Let us look at what proof there might be for the second hypothesis of this rule instance. It can be proved from the following instance of application:

$$\frac{H \vdash_{\mathrm{sub}} f : r \rightarrow \mathbf{num} \qquad \{l = \underline{6},\ l_2 = \mathbf{false}\} : r}{H \vdash_{\mathrm{sub}} f(\{l = \underline{6},\ l_1 = \mathbf{false}\}) : \mathbf{num}}. \tag{9.4}$$

The first hypothesis of 9.4 is easily established using the rules for abstraction and field selection. The second hypothesis of 9.4 can be established using the following instance of the subsumption rule:

$$\frac{\{l = \underline{6},\ l_2 = \mathbf{false}\} : r_2 \qquad r_2 \leq r}{\{l = \underline{6},\ l_2 = \mathbf{false}\} : r}. \tag{9.5}$$

A similar approach makes it possible to establish the other hypothesis of 9.3.

Typing derivations in PCF++ are not uniquely determined by their conclusions. For example, note that the conclusion of 9.4 could also be obtained with the following instance of application:

$$\frac{H \vdash f : r_2 \rightarrow \mathbf{num} \qquad \{l = \underline{6},\ l_2 = \mathbf{false}\} : r_2}{H \vdash_{\mathrm{sub}} f(\{l = \underline{6},\ l_1 = \mathbf{false}\}) : \mathbf{num}}$$

where the first hypothesis is established by the following instance of subsumption:

$$\frac{H \vdash f : r \rightarrow \mathbf{num} \qquad r \rightarrow \mathbf{num} \leq r_1 \rightarrow \mathbf{num}}{H \vdash f : r_2 \rightarrow \mathbf{num}}. \tag{9.6}$$

Inclusive subsets as a model for subtyping.

It is possible to build an intuitive model of PCF++ and its typing system by using inclusive subsets to model types. We looked at the use of inclusive subsets as a model of PCF types earlier; a model of PCF++ can be given by extending the interpretation used in Section 8.1. To this end we need an expanded version of the universal domain in Equation 8.8 (see page 265). Let us define

$$U \cong \mathbb{T} \oplus \mathbb{N}_\perp \oplus [U \to U]_\perp \oplus [\text{Label} \to U]_\perp \oplus (\text{Label} \times U)_\perp \oplus \mathbb{O}. \qquad (9.7)$$

As was the case for the semantics of PCF, it will spare us some tedious numbering for the injections into this sum if we write $d : D$ for the injection of element d into the D component of the sum. For example, $\mathsf{up}(f) : [U \to U]_\perp$ is the injection of a continuous function $f : U \to U$ into the third component of U. The semantics of types is defined as follows:

- $\mathcal{I}[\![\{l_1 : t_1, \ldots, l_n : t_n\}]\!] = \{r : [\text{Label} \to U]_\perp \mid \mathsf{down}(r)(l_i) \in \mathcal{I}[\![t_i]\!] \text{ for each } i = 1, \ldots, n\}$

- $\mathcal{I}[\![[l_1 : t_1, \ldots, l_n : t_n]]\!] = \{e : (\text{Label} \times U)_\perp \mid e = \perp, \text{ or } \mathsf{down}(e) = (l_i, d) \text{ and } d \in \mathcal{I}[\![t_i]\!]\}$

- $\mathcal{I}[\![s \to t]\!] = \{f : [U \to U]_\perp \mid \mathsf{down}(f)(d) \in \mathcal{I}[\![t]\!] \text{ for each } d \in \mathcal{I}[\![s]\!]\}$

The semantics of a term M such that $H \vdash_{\mathrm{sub}} M : t$ is relative to an H-environment ρ.

- $\mathcal{I}[\![\{l_1 = M_1, \ldots, l_n = M_n\}]\!]\rho = \mathsf{up}(r) : [\text{Label} \to U]_\perp$ where

$$r(l) = \begin{cases} \mathcal{I}[\![M_i]\!]\rho & \text{if } l = l_i \\ \mathbf{tyerr} & \text{otherwise} \end{cases}$$

- $\mathcal{I}[\![M.l]\!]\rho = \begin{cases} \mathsf{down}(f)(l) & \text{if } \mathcal{I}[\![M]\!]\rho = f : [\text{Label} \to U]_\perp \\ \mathbf{tyerr} & \text{otherwise} \end{cases}$

- $\mathcal{I}[\![[l = M, l_1 : t_1, \ldots, l_n : t_n]]\!]\rho = \mathsf{up}(l, \mathcal{I}[\![M]\!]\rho) : (\text{Label} \times U)_\perp$

- $\mathcal{I}[\![\mathbf{case} \; M \; \mathbf{of} \; l_1 \Rightarrow M_1 \cdots l_n \Rightarrow M_n]\!]\rho = d$ where

  - $d = \mathsf{down}(f_i)(e)$ if $\mathcal{I}[\![M]\!]\rho = \mathsf{up}(l_i, e) : (\text{Label} \times U)_\perp$ and $\mathcal{I}[\![M_i]\!]\rho = f_i : [U \to U]_\perp$

  - $d = \perp$ if $\mathcal{I}[\![M]\!]\rho = \perp$

  - $d = \mathbf{tyerr}$ otherwise

It is not difficult to check the following property of the interpretation:

9.2 Lemma. *For each type t the subset $\mathcal{I}[\![t]\!]\rho$ inclusive.* $\square$

Given a suitable choice of the definitions for arithmetic expressions, it is possible to arrange it to be the case that **tyerr** $\notin \mathcal{I}[\![t]\!]$ for each of the types t of PCF+. The interpretation also allows us the intuitive liberty of thinking of $s \leq t$ as meaning that the meaning of s is a *subset* of the meaning of t:

9.3 Theorem. *If $s \leq t$, then $\mathcal{I}[\![s]\!] \subseteq \mathcal{I}[\![t]\!]$.*

Proof: The proof is by induction on the height of the proof that $s \leq t$. The base cases are trivial.

If $s \equiv s_1 \rightarrow s_2$, then $t \equiv t_1 \rightarrow t_2$ where $t_1 \leq s_1$ and $s_2 \leq t_2$. By the inductive hypothesis this means that $\mathcal{I}[\![t_1]\!] \subseteq \mathcal{I}[\![s_1]\!]$ and $\mathcal{I}[\![s_2]\!] \subseteq \mathcal{I}[\![t_2]\!]$. If $f : [U \rightarrow U]_\perp \in \mathcal{I}[\![s]\!]$, then

$$\mathsf{down}(f)(\mathcal{I}[\![t_1]\!]) \subseteq \mathsf{down}(f)(\mathcal{I}[\![s_1]\!]) \subseteq \mathcal{I}[\![s_2]\!] \subseteq \mathcal{I}[\![t_2]\!]$$

so $f \in \mathcal{I}[\![t]\!]$.

If s has the form $\{l_1 : s_1, \ldots, l_n : s_n, \ldots, l_m : s_m\}$, then $s \leq t$ means that t has the form $\{l_1 : t_1, \ldots, l_n : t_n\}$ where $s_i \leq t_i$ for each $i \leq n$. Now, if $r \in \mathcal{I}[\![t]\!]$ and $i \leq n$, then $\mathsf{down}(r)(l_i) \in \mathcal{I}[\![s_i]\!]$, but this is a subset of $\mathcal{I}[\![t_i]\!]$ by the inductive hypothesis. Thus $r \in \mathcal{I}[\![t_i]\!]$ for each $i \leq n$, so $r \in \mathcal{I}[\![t]\!]$.

If s has the form $[l_1 : s_1, \ldots, l_n : s_n]$, then $t \equiv [l_1 : t_1, \ldots, l_n : s_n, \ldots, l_m : t_m]$ where $s_i \leq t_i$ for each $i \leq n$. By the induction hypothesis, this means that $\mathcal{I}[\![s_i]\!] \subseteq \mathcal{I}[\![t_i]\!]$ for each $i \leq n$. Now, if $d \in \mathcal{I}[\![s]\!]$ and $d = \perp$, then $d \in \mathcal{I}[\![t]\!]$ too. If $d \neq \perp$, then $d = \mathsf{up}(l_i, e) : (\text{Label} \times U)_\perp$ for some $i \leq n$ where $e \in \mathcal{I}[\![s_i]\!]$. But then $e \in \mathcal{I}[\![t_i]\!]$ too, so $d \in \mathcal{I}[\![t]\!]$. $\square$

The converse of the theorem also holds, given some basic assumptions about the solution to Equation 9.7.

9.4 Theorem. *If $H \vdash M : t$ and ρ is an H-environment, then $\mathcal{I}[\![H \rhd M : t]\!]\rho \in \mathcal{I}[\![t]\!]$.*

Proof: The proof is by induction on the height of the derivation of $H \vdash M : t$. I cover some of the cases for the last step of this derivation.

Suppose the last step of the derivation is an instance of the subsumption rule:

$$\frac{H \vdash M : s \qquad s \leq t}{H \vdash M : t}$$

By the inductive hypothesis, $\mathcal{I}[\![H \rhd M : s]\!]\rho \in \mathcal{I}[\![s]\!]$. By Theorem 9.3, $\mathcal{I}[\![s]\!] \subseteq \mathcal{I}[\![t]\!]$, so $\mathcal{I}[\![H \rhd M : t]\!]\rho \in \mathcal{I}[\![t]\!]$.

Suppose the last step of the derivation has the form

$$\frac{H \vdash M_1 : t_1 \quad \cdots \quad H \vdash M_n : t_n}{H \vdash \{l_1 = M_1, \ldots, l_n = M_n\} : \{l_1 : t_1, \ldots, l_n : t_n\}}.$$

By the inductive hypothesis, $\mathcal{I}[\![H \rhd M_i : t_i]\!]\rho \in \mathcal{I}[\![t_i]\!]$ for each $i \leq n$. Hence,

$$r(l) = \begin{cases} \mathcal{I}[\![M_i]\!]\rho & \text{if } l = l_i \\ \mathbf{tyerr} & \text{otherwise} \end{cases}$$

satisfies $r(l_i) \in \mathcal{I}[\![t_i]\!]$ for each $i \leq n$. This implies that

$$\mathcal{I}[\![H \rhd M : t]\!]\rho = \mathsf{up}(r) : [\text{Label} \rightarrow U]_\perp \in \mathcal{I}[\![t]\!].$$

Suppose the last step of the derivation has the form

$$\frac{H \vdash N : s}{H \vdash N.l_i : t_i}$$

where $s \equiv \{l_1 : t_1, \ldots, l_n : t_n\}$. By the inductive hypothesis, $\mathcal{I}[\![H \rhd N : s]\!]\rho \in \mathcal{I}[\![s]\!]$. If this value is $r : [\text{Label} \rightarrow U]_\perp$, then $\mathcal{I}[\![H \rhd N_i : s]\!]\rho = \mathsf{down}(r)(l_i) \in \mathcal{I}[\![t_i]\!]$ by the definition of record types.

Suppose the last step of the derivation has the form

$$\frac{H \vdash N : s}{H \vdash [l = N, l_1 : t_1, \ldots, l_n : t_n] : [l : s, l_1 : t_1, \ldots, l_n : t_n]}.$$

By the induction hypothesis, $\mathcal{I}[\![H \rhd N : s]\!]\rho \in \mathcal{I}[\![s]\!]$. Now $\mathcal{I}[\![H \rhd M : t]\!]\rho = \mathsf{up}(l, \mathcal{I}[\![N]\!]\rho) : (\text{Label} \times U)_\perp$, and, by the definition of the meaning of the variant type, this value is an element of $\mathcal{I}[\![t]\!]$.

Suppose the last step of the derivation has the form

$$\frac{H \vdash N : [l_1 : t_1, \ldots, l_n : t_n] \quad H \vdash M_1 : t_1 \rightarrow t \quad \cdots \quad H \vdash M_n : t_n \rightarrow t}{H \vdash \mathbf{case}\ N\ \mathbf{of}\ l_1 \Rightarrow M_1 \cdots l_n \Rightarrow M_n : t}.$$

If the meaning e of N is $\perp$, then the desired property is satisfied. It is not equal to $\mathbf{tyerr}$, because the inductive hypothesis ensures that $e \in \mathcal{I}[\![[l_1 : t_1, \ldots, l_n : t_n]]\!]$ and $\mathbf{tyerr}$ is not an element of this type. Also by the inductive hypothesis, $\mathcal{I}[\![M_i]\!]\rho = f_i : [U \rightarrow U]_\perp$ for each $i \leq n$ where each f_i is a function mapping elements of $\mathcal{I}[\![t_i]\!]$ into $\mathcal{I}[\![t]\!]$. Thus, for some $i \leq n$, $\mathcal{I}[\![M]\!]\rho = \mathsf{down}(f_i)(e)$ and this is an element of $\mathcal{I}[\![t]\!]$. □

Exercises.

9.1 Prove that the subsumption relation $\leq$ defines a poset over the types of PCF++.

9.2 If $H, x : s \vdash M : t$ and $s' \leq s$, then prove that $H, x : s' \vdash M : t$.

9.3* Prove that the converse of Theorem 9.3 also holds. Assume that the solution to Equation 9.7 is an algebraic cpo with a countable basis.

9.2   Subsumption as Implicit Coercion

Is it possible to provide a semantics for PCF++ *without* using a universal domain? In this section we explore a different approach that is reminiscent of the way we modeled the untyped λ-calculus using the typed λ-calculus. The idea is to see a term of PCF++ as a 'shorthand' for a term of PCF+. Recall that a term of the untyped λ-calculus can be interpreted by translating the term to a term of the typed λ-calculus and then interpreting this translated term in a model of a particular theory of the typed calculus. By analogy, a term of PCF++ can be viewed as a term of PCF+ from which certain tedious 'coercion' terms have been dropped. In particular, a term of PCF++ can be translated into a term of PCF+ in which the 'implicit coercions' in the PCF++ term are made explicit. These implicit coercions arise from the use of the subsumption rule in type-checking a PCF++ term, and so it is from the use of this rule that the coercions for the translation are constructed.

Before carrying out the general development, let us consider the terms F, G of Example 9.1 and how the term $F(G)$ might translate to a term of PCF+ in which implicit coercions are made explicit. The term G does not have a type in PCF+ because of the different types of arguments to which its formal parameter f is being applied in its body. To 'make the term $G(F)$ type-correct', we can alter G by inserting some 'coercions' to bring these types into line. For instance, one possibility is the term

$$G' \equiv \lambda f : \{l : \mathbf{num}\} \rightarrow \mathbf{num}.$$
$$\{k_1 = f(\xi_1(\{l = \underline{3},\ l_1 = \underline{5}\})),\ k_2 = f(\xi_2(\{l = \underline{6},\ l_2 = \mathbf{false}\}))\}$$

where ξ_1 and ξ_2 are the following 'coercion terms':

$$\xi_1 \equiv \lambda x_1 : \{l : \mathbf{num}, l_1 : \mathbf{num}\}.\ \{l = x_1.l\}$$
$$\xi_2 \equiv \lambda x_2 : \{l : \mathbf{num}, l_2 : \mathbf{bool}\}.\ \{l = x_2.l\}.$$

The term $G'(F)$ is type-correct in PCF+, and (intuitively) its meaning, which is $\{k_1 = \underline{3},\ k_2 = \underline{6}\}$, is the same as that of $G(F)$. The key point here is to see how G' can be obtained from a proof, in the PCF++ typing system, of the type-correctness of $G(F)$. At the basis of this relationship between between $G(F)$ and $G'(F)$ are the instances of subsumption that rely on the subtyping relations 9.2. The terms ξ_1 and ξ_2 can be viewed as explanations of how a term having the type on the left in these relations can also be viewed as having the type $r \equiv \{l = \mathbf{num}\}$ on the right.

Now, to translate $G(F)$ into a term of PCF+ using a derivation of a type in PCF++, we can replace the instance 9.5 of the subsumption rule by the following:

$$\frac{\{l = \underline{6},\ l_2 = \mathbf{false}\} : r_2 \qquad \xi_2 : r_2 \rightarrow r}{\xi_2(\{l = \underline{6},\ l_2 = \mathbf{false}\}) : r}.$$

This is an instance of the application rule of PCF+ rather than the subsumption rule of PCF++. From this it is possible to continue to a derivation of $\vdash G'(F) : t$ as follows. By the application rule,

$$\frac{H \vdash f : r \rightarrow \mathbf{num} \qquad \xi_2(\{l = \underline{6},\ l_2 = \mathbf{false}\}) : r}{H \vdash f(\xi_2(\{l = \underline{6},\ l_1 = \mathbf{false}\}) : \mathbf{num}}),$$

and we then have

$$\frac{H \vdash f(\xi_1(\{l = \underline{3},\ l_1 = \underline{5}\})) : \mathbf{num} \qquad H \vdash f(\xi_2(\{l = \underline{6},\ l_1 = \mathbf{false}\})) : \mathbf{num}}{H \vdash M' : t}$$

where

$$M' \equiv \{k_1 = f(\xi_1(\{l = \underline{3},\ l_1 = \underline{5}\})),\ k_2 = f(\xi_2(\{l = \underline{6},\ l_2 = \mathbf{false}\}))\}.$$

Thus

$$\frac{H \vdash M' : t}{\vdash G' : (r \rightarrow \mathbf{num}) \rightarrow t}$$

and finally

$$\frac{\vdash G' : (r \rightarrow \mathbf{num}) \rightarrow t \qquad \vdash F : r \rightarrow \mathbf{num}}{\vdash G'(F) : t}$$

So, could we take the meaning of $G(F)$ simply to be the same as the meaning of $G'(F)$ according to a semantics of PCF+? This would allow us to interpret subsumption indirectly using a language in which there is no subtyping. There is a problem though. In the example above, a derivation in PCF++ of a type for $G(F)$ was translated to a derivation of $G'(F)$. The translation seems to tell us what G' needs to be, assuming we know what coercion term was to be used for the subsumptions. But, as demonstrated earlier, a judgement of PCF++ does not necessarily have a unique derivation. If we follow the strategy mentioned above but using the second typing derivation for $G(F)$ given in the previous section, then the resulting translation is slightly different. To translate the instance 9.6 of subsumption used in that derivation, we could use the following term:

$$\zeta_2 \equiv \lambda f_2 : \{l : \mathbf{num}\} \rightarrow \mathbf{num}.\ \lambda x_2 : \{l = \mathbf{num}, l_2 = \mathbf{bool}\}.\ f_2(\xi_2(x_2))$$

We then have

$$\frac{H \vdash f : r \rightarrow \mathbf{num} \qquad \zeta_2 : (r \rightarrow \mathbf{num}) \rightarrow (r_2 \rightarrow \mathbf{num})}{H \vdash \zeta_2(f) : r_2 \rightarrow \mathbf{num}}.$$

So another possible translation for $G(F)$ is $G''(F)$ where

$$G'' \equiv \lambda f : \{l : \mathbf{num}\} \rightarrow \mathbf{num}.$$
$$\{k_1 = \zeta_1(f)(\{l = \underline{3}, l_1 = \underline{5}\}),\ k_2 = \zeta_2(f)(\{l = \underline{6}, l_2 = \mathbf{false}\})\}$$

and

$$\zeta_1 \equiv \lambda f_1 : \{l : \mathbf{num}\} \rightarrow \mathbf{num}. \ \lambda x_1 : \{l = \mathbf{num}, l_1 = \mathbf{num}\}. \ f_1(\xi_1(x_1)).$$

This presents a dilemma as far as giving a semantics is concerned. Before discussing the issues further, let us rigorously define the idea for translation that these examples suggest.

Translating PCF++ derivations into PCF+ derivations.

Let us now consider how to translate the derivations of typing judgements of PCF++ into derivations of PCF+. The translation is defined by induction on the structure of the derivation trees. To do this, we provide for each rule of PCF++ a corresponding rule of PCF+. Given an instance of a rule of PCF++, the corresponding PCF+ rule is an instance of a rule of PCF+, so this defines a translation from a derivation in PCF++ to a derivation in PCF+. To define this, we begin by defining a collection of 'coercion' terms that will be used in translating the subsumption rule. If M is a term of type $s \rightarrow t$ and N is a term of type $r \rightarrow s$, then $M \circ N$ is defined to be the term $\lambda x : r. \ M(N(x))$.

Definition: Given types s and t such that $s \leq t$ is provable, define a PCF+ term $\Theta[s \leq t]$ by induction on the proof of $s \leq t$ as follows:

- $\Theta[\mathbf{bool} \leq \mathbf{bool}] \equiv \lambda x : \mathbf{bool}. \ x$ and $\Theta[\mathbf{num} \leq \mathbf{num}] \equiv \lambda x : \mathbf{num}. \ x$.
- $\Theta[s \rightarrow t \leq s' \rightarrow t'] \equiv \lambda f : s \rightarrow t. \ \Theta[t \leq t'] \circ f \circ \Theta[s' \leq s]$
- If $s \equiv \{l_1 : s_1, \ldots, l_n : s_n, \ldots, l_m : s_m\}$ and $t \equiv \{l_1 : t_1, \ldots, l_n : t_n\}$ and $s \leq t$, then

$$\Theta[s \leq t] \equiv \lambda x : s. \ \{l_1 = \Theta[s_1 \leq t_1](x.l_1), \ldots l_n = \Theta[s_n \leq t_n](x.l_n)\}$$

- Say $s \equiv [l_1 : s_1, \ldots, l_n : s_n]$ and $t \equiv [l_1 : t_1, \ldots, l_n : t_n, \ldots, l_m : t_m]$ and $s \leq t$, then

$$\Theta[s \leq t] \equiv \lambda x : s. \ \mathbf{case} \ x \ \mathbf{of} \ l_1 \Rightarrow M_1, \ldots, l_n \Rightarrow M_n$$

  where $M_i \equiv \lambda y : s_i. \ [l_i = \Theta[s_i \leq t_i](y), \ldots]$ for each $i = 1, \ldots, n$. $\qquad\square$

It is not difficult to establish the following property of these terms:

9.5 Lemma. *If* $\vdash s \leq t$, *then* $\vdash \Theta[s \leq t] : s \rightarrow t$. $\qquad\square$

A PCF++ derivation Δ yielding a judgement $H \vdash_{\mathrm{sub}} M : t$ is translated to a derivation $T(\Delta)$ of a PCF+ judgement. This yields a translation $T^*(\Delta)$ of the form $H \vdash M^* : t$ for the original PCF++ judgement where $T^*(\Delta)$ is the conclusion of the derivation $T(\Delta)$.

All of the rules of PCF++ except the subsumption rule are translated 'without change'. For example, the axiom $\mathbf{0} : \mathbf{num}$ is translated as itself, and the rule

$$\frac{H \vdash_{\text{sub}} M : \mathbf{num}}{H \vdash_{\text{sub}} \mathbf{succ}(M) : \mathbf{num}}$$

is translated as

$$\frac{H \vdash M^* : \mathbf{num}}{H \vdash \mathbf{succ}(M^*) : \mathbf{num}}$$

where $H \vdash M^* : \mathbf{num}$ is the conclusion of the translation of the derivation of $H \vdash M : \mathbf{num}$. Only the subsumption rule is altered by the translation. In particular, the rule

$$\frac{H \vdash_{\text{sub}} M : s \qquad s \leq t}{H \vdash_{\text{sub}} M : t}$$

is translated by the rule

$$\frac{H \vdash M^* : s \qquad \Theta[s \leq t] : s \to t}{H \vdash \Theta[s \leq t](M^*) : t}$$

which 'makes the implicit coercion explicit' as an instance of application using the coercion $\Theta[s \leq t]$.

Semantics of PCF+.

Let us now define a fixed-point semantics for PCF+. In contrast with the previous section, let us do the semantics with an eager evaluation order in mind; this will then be related to a specific operational semantics for the language. The interpretation of types from PCF is the same as the one on page 196 where higher types are interpreted using the lifted space of strict functions. Thus we need concern ourselves only with records and variants. These need to generalize the interpretations of the smash product and coalesced sum respectively.

- $[\![\{l_1 : t_1, \ldots, l_n : t_n\}]\!]$ consists of a bottom element $\perp$, together with the set of pairs $\{l_1 = d_1, \ldots, l_n = d_n\}$ where each d_i is a non-bottom element of $[\![t_i]\!]$. The ordering is defined by

$$\{l_1 = d_1, \ldots, l_n = d_n\} \sqsubseteq \{l_1 = d'_1, \ldots, l_n = d'_n\}$$

  iff $d_i \sqsubseteq d'_i$ for each $i = 1, \ldots, n$ and $\perp \sqsubseteq d$ for each record d.

- $[\![[l_1 : t_1, \ldots, l_n : t_n]]\!]$ consists of a bottom element $\perp$, together with the set of pairs $[l_i = d_i]$ such that d_i is a non-bottom element of $[\![t_i]\!]$. For two such pairs, $[l_i = d] \sqsubseteq [l_j = d']$ iff $i = j$ and $d \sqsubseteq d'$.

Table 9.3
Rules for Call-by-Value Evaluation of Records and Variants

$$\frac{M_1 \Downarrow^\circ V_1 \quad \cdots \quad M_n \Downarrow^\circ V_n}{\{l_1 = M_1, \ldots, l_n = M_n\} \Downarrow^\circ \{l_1 = V_1, \ldots, l_n = V_n\}} \qquad \frac{M \Downarrow^\circ \{l_1 = V_1, \ldots, l_n = V_n\}}{M.l_i \Downarrow^\circ V_i}$$

$$\frac{M \Downarrow^\circ V}{[l = M, \ldots] \Downarrow^\circ [l = V, \ldots]} \qquad \frac{M \Downarrow^\circ [l_i = U, \ldots] \quad f_i(U) \Downarrow^\circ V}{\mathbf{case}\ M\ \mathbf{of}\ l_1 \Rightarrow f_1, \ldots, l_i \Rightarrow f_i, \ldots, l_n \Rightarrow f_n \Downarrow^\circ V}$$

It is clear that these interpretations do yield cpo's. Suppose M is a term of PCF+ such that $H \vdash M : t$ and suppose ρ is an H-environment.

- $[\![\{l_1 = M_1, \ldots, l_n = M_n\}]\!]\rho = d$ where
    - $d = \{l_1 = [\![M_1]\!]\rho, \ldots, l_n = [\![M_n]\!]\rho\}$ if $[\![M_i]\!]\rho \neq \bot$ for each $i \leq n$ and
    - $d = \bot$ otherwise
- $[\![M.l]\!]\rho = \begin{cases} d & \text{if } [\![M]\!]\rho \text{ is } [l = d] \\ \bot & \text{otherwise} \end{cases}$
- $[\![[l = M, l_1 : t_1, \ldots, l_n : t_n]]\!]\rho = \begin{cases} [l = d] & \text{if } d = [\![M]\!]\rho \neq \bot \\ \bot & \text{otherwise} \end{cases}$
- $[\![\mathbf{case}\ M\ \mathbf{of}\ l_1 \Rightarrow M_1 \cdots l_n \Rightarrow M_n]\!]\rho = d$ where
    - $d = \mathbf{down}(f_i)(e)$ if $[\![M]\!]\rho = \mathbf{up}(l_i, e)$ and $[\![M_i]\!]\rho = f_i$
    - $d = \bot$ if $[\![M]\!]\rho = \bot$

The remaining semantic clauses are basically the same as those given for the fixed-point semantics of call-by-value PCF.

The operational semantics of the closed terms of PCF+ is given by the least relation $\Downarrow^\circ$ between terms that satisfies the rules and axioms in Table 6.4 and those in Table 9.3. Ellipsis has been used to make the rules a little easier to read by eliminating some inessential information in the first rule for variants. It can be shown that a value V for this operational semantics is a term that can be obtained from the following grammar:

$$V \quad ::= \quad \mathbf{0} \mid \mathbf{true} \mid \mathbf{false} \mid \mathbf{succ}(V) \mid \mathbf{pred}(V) \mid \lambda x : t.\ M \mid$$
$$\{l = V, \ldots, l = V\} \mid [l = V, l : t, \ldots, l : t]$$

It is straightforward to check the following fact:

9.6 Lemma. *On PCF+ terms, the relation $\Downarrow^{\circ}$ is a partial function, that is, if $M \Downarrow U$ and $M \Downarrow V$, then $U \equiv V$.*

Coherence.

Let us return now to the question of how this translation can be used to provide a semantics for PCF++. The key problem is that the translation between PCF++ and PCF+ does not provide a unique translation for a given term. If $H \vdash_{\text{sub}} M : t$ and Δ is a derivation tree with this as its root (conclusion), then we could take $[\![H \rhd T^*(\Delta) : t]\!]$ as the meaning of the judgement as an element of $[\![t]\!]$. However, if Γ is another derivation of the judgement $H \vdash_{\text{sub}} M : t$, then $[\![H \rhd T^*(\Gamma) : t]\!]$ could also serve be used as the interpretation. There are several ways to approach this problem. Since we would ultimately like a well-defined meaning function mapping judgements and environments into the appropriate types, the problem might be solved by choosing somehow a *canonical* way to derive a given typing judgement. The meaning of the judgement would then be taken as the meaning of the judgement of PCF+ obtained by translating its canonical derivation. Another approach would be to assume that the semantics itself is determined by the choice of derivation. In other words, given a function Δ such that $\Delta(H \rhd M : t)$ is a derivation of a derivable judgement $H \vdash M : t$, there is a semantic interpretation $\Delta[\![\cdot]\!]$ that it determines.

Neither of the approaches above works well in practice, however. In previous chapters, we often relied on the idea that properties of well-typed terms could be proved by induction on the structure of the term or by induction on the height of the typing derivation for the term. These two proof techniques were equivalent because the typing rules were given inductively in the structure of the terms. For the two semantics described above, this coincidence fails and we will be forced to choose between the two inductive measures. In effect, the translation semantics of PCF++ defines the meaning of a term by induction on the height of typing derivation; as a result, most properties of the semantics must be proved by induction on the height of a typing derivation rather than on the structure of a term. This is a particular problem for the second of the two approaches mentioned above, since there is no *a priori* relationship between how a derivation is translated and how the subderivations (that is, the subtrees of the derivation tree) are translated. This will lead to difficulties in using an induction on the height of a derivation.

It is possible that this problem could be repaired by a judicious choice of a canonical derivation or by imposing some uniformity restriction on the derivation selection function. However, such patches are unnecessary because of a deep fact about the translation, a fact that resolves the apparent failure of the translation to provide a well-defined semantic function. In considering the example described at the beginning of the section, one is easily led to a conjecture that the distinction between different derivations of the same typing judgement is, in fact, superficial. For instance, the coercions ζ_i in the examples are hardly any different from coercions ξ_i; the term G' is obtained from G'' simply by applying the β-rule to the subterms $\zeta_i(f)$ for $i = 1, 2$. In particular, the meanings of G' are G'' as PCF+ terms are exactly the same under the interpretation we have assumed. The basic fact is this: *the meanings in PCF+ of all translations of a given judgement of PCF++ are exactly the same.* To be precise, we have the following theorem:

9.7 Theorem (Coherence). *If Γ and Δ are PCF++ derivations of a judgement $H \vdash_{\text{sub}} M : t$, then $\llbracket H \rhd T^*(\Gamma) : t \rrbracket = \llbracket H \rhd T^*(\Delta) : t \rrbracket$.* $\Box$

The term 'coherence' comes from category theory, where it is used as a property of a category asserting that each member of a specified class of diagrams commutes. The theorem above could be formulated categorically so that it is a special instance of this property by setting up a correspondence between derivations and arrows. The Coherence Theorem has a lengthy and technical proof that will not be included here; see the notes at the end of the chapter for further comments.

The semantic function for PCF++ is now defined as follows:

$$\llbracket H \rhd M : t \rrbracket^{++} \rho = \llbracket H \rhd M^* : t \rrbracket^+ \rho$$

where $H \vdash M^* : t$ is any translation of $H \vdash M : t$ and the superscripts are used to emphasize the distinction between the semantics of PCF++ and that of PCF+ (as already defined). In light of the Coherence Theorem, this yields a well-defined meaning for each derivable typing judgement of PCF++. This is called an *implicit coercion* semantics for the language.

Now, if we note that any PCF+ derivation *is* a PCF++ derivation, then we get the following corollary:

9.8 Corollary. *If $H \vdash M : t$, then $\llbracket H \rhd M : t \rrbracket^+ \rho = \llbracket H \rhd M : t \rrbracket^{++} \rho$ for any H-environment ρ.* $\Box$

This corollary makes it possible to obtain adequacy for PCF+ from adequacy for PCF++. In light of the corollary, it is harmless to omit the tags on the semantic brackets for typing judgements. I will nevertheless continue to write $\llbracket H \rhd M : t \rrbracket^{++} \rho$ for judgements $H \vdash_{\text{sub}} M : t$ of PCF++ to emphasize that the meaning of the term must be obtained through a translation of a typing derivation. If, in fact, $H \vdash M : t$, then that translation can be chosen as the unique PCF+ derivation of the judgement.

We now wish to show that the implicit coercion semantics for PCF++ just defined is closely related to its operational semantics. A preliminary lemma is needed.

9.9 Lemma. *Let r, s, and t be types.*

If $r \leq s \leq t$, then

1. $\llbracket \Theta[r \leq t] : r \to t \rrbracket = \llbracket \Theta[s \leq t] : s \to t \rrbracket \circ \llbracket \Theta[r \leq s] : r \to s \rrbracket$.

2. *If $s \leq t$, then $\llbracket \Theta[s \leq t] : s \to t \rrbracket(d) = \bot$ iff $d = \bot$.*   □

Proof of the lemma is left for the reader. It allows us to conclude the following:

9.10 Corollary. *If $\vdash_{\mathrm{sub}} V : t$, then $\llbracket V : t \rrbracket^{++} \neq \bot$.*   □

If $\vdash M : t$ and $M \Downarrow^\circ V$, then it is easy to show that $\vdash V : t$ too. This also holds for PCF++ and $\vdash_{\mathrm{sub}}$.

9.11 Lemma (Subject Reduction). *Suppose $\vdash_{\mathrm{sub}} M : t$ and $M \Downarrow V$, then $\vdash_{\mathrm{sub}} V : t$.*   □

Proof: For each of the systems we have considered before, it was possible to prove subject reduction by an induction on the height of the derivation tree for $M \Downarrow V$ and then by cases on the structure of M, or (equivalently) by cases on the last step of the derivation of $\vdash_{\mathrm{sub}} M : t$. For PCF++, the proof requires a slightly more elaborate induction hypothesis. Let p be the *sum* of the heights of the derivations of $\vdash_{\mathrm{sub}} M : t$ and $M \Downarrow V$. The proof is carried out by induction on this sum. In the cases where M is a term of PCF and the last step of the derivation $\vdash_{\mathrm{sub}} M : t$ is not an instance of subsumption, the proof of this lemma is similar to that of Theorem 7.2 (note that it is also necessary to prove an analog to Theorem 4.1). Let us now consider the remaining possibilities for the last step in the typing derivation for M.

Suppose the last step is an instance of record introduction,

$$\frac{\vdash_{\mathrm{sub}} M_1 : t_1 \quad \cdots \quad \vdash_{\mathrm{sub}} M_n : t_n}{\vdash_{\mathrm{sub}} \{l_1 = M_1, \ldots, l_n = M_n\} : \{l_1 : t_1, \ldots, l_n : t_n\}}.$$

Then the operational rule for the evaluation must be of the form

$$\frac{M_1 \Downarrow^\circ V_1 \quad \cdots \quad M_n \Downarrow^\circ V_n}{\{l_1 = M_1, \ldots, l_n = M_n\} \Downarrow^\circ \{l_1 = V_1, \ldots, l_n = V_n\}}.$$

Now, for each i, the sum of the heights of the proofs of $\vdash_{\mathrm{sub}} M_i : t_i$ and $M_i \Downarrow^\circ V_i$ is less than p, so we can conclude from the inductive hypothesis that $\vdash_{\mathrm{sub}} V_i : t_i$. From this and the record introduction rule, it follows that

$$\vdash_{\mathrm{sub}} \{l_1 = V_1, \ldots, l_n = V_n\} : \{l_1 : t_1, \ldots, l_n : t_n\}.$$

Suppose the last step is an instance of field selection (record elimination),

$$\frac{\vdash_{\mathrm{sub}} N : \{l_1 : t_1, \ldots, l_n : t_n\}}{H \vdash_{\mathrm{sub}} N.l_i : t_i}$$

Then the last step of the evaluation of M must have the form

$$\frac{N \Downarrow^\circ \{l_1 = V_1, \ldots, l_n = V_n\}}{N.l_i \Downarrow^\circ V_i}.$$

By the inductive hypothesis,

$$\vdash_{\text{sub}} \{l_1 = V_1, \ldots, l_n = V_n\} : \{l_1 : t_1, \ldots, l_n : t_n\}.$$

It is possible to show that this implies that $\vdash_{\text{sub}} V_i : t_i$. Since $V \equiv V_i$ and $t \equiv t_i$, this is the desired conclusion.

Suppose the last step is an instance of variant introduction,

$$\frac{\vdash_{\text{sub}} N : s}{\vdash_{\text{sub}} [l = N, l_1 : t_1, \ldots, l_n : t_n] : [l : s, l_1 : t_1, \ldots, l_n : t_n]}.$$

Then the last step of the evaluation of M must have the form

$$\frac{N \Downarrow^\circ U}{[l = N, \ldots] \Downarrow^\circ [l = U, \ldots]}.$$

The inductive hypothesis implies that $\vdash_{\text{sub}} U : s$ and hence that

$$\vdash_{\text{sub}} [l = U, \ldots] : [l : s, \ldots].$$

Since $V \equiv [l = U, \ldots]$ and $t \equiv [l : s, l_1 : t_1, \ldots, l_n : t_n]$, this is the desired conclusion.

Suppose the last step is an instance of variant elimination.

$$\frac{\vdash_{\text{sub}} N : [l_1 : t_1, \ldots, l_n : t_n] \qquad \vdash_{\text{sub}} M_1 : t_1 \to t \quad \cdots \quad \vdash_{\text{sub}} M_n : t_n \to t}{\vdash_{\text{sub}} \textbf{case } N \textbf{ of } l_1 \Rightarrow M_1 \cdots l_n \Rightarrow M_n : t}.$$

Then the last step of the evaluation of M has the form

$$\frac{N \Downarrow^\circ [l_i = U, \ldots] \quad f_i(U) \Downarrow^\circ V}{\textbf{case } N \textbf{ of } l_1 \Rightarrow f_1, \ldots, l_i \Rightarrow f_i, \ldots, l_n \Rightarrow f_n \Downarrow^\circ V}.$$

The inductive hypothesis then implies that

$$[l_i = U, \ldots] : [l_1 : t_1, \ldots, l_n : t_n].$$

It can be shown that this implies that $U : t_i$. Hence, by the inductive hypothesis again, $f_i(U) : t$ implies that $V : t$. $\qquad\square$

The proof of the soundness of the fixed-point semantics relative to the operational semantics has a similar proof, which is left as an exercise for the reader.

9.12 Theorem (Soundness). *If* $\vdash_{\text{sub}} M : t$ *and* $M \Downarrow V$, *then* $[\![M : t]\!]^{++} = [\![V : t]\!]^{++}$. $\quad\square$

The final goal of this section is to prove that the fixed-point semantics is also adequate:

9.13 Theorem (Computational Adequacy). *Suppose $M : t$ is derivable in PCF++. If $[\![M : t]\!]^{++} \neq \bot$, then $M \Downarrow V$ for some value V.*

The strategy for proving the theorem is very similar to that used to demonstrate Theorem 6.12. We begin by developing some properties of inclusive subsets and prove an analog of Lemma 6.11.

Definition: Define a family of relations $\lesssim_t$ between elements of $\mathcal{C}°[\![t]\!]$ on the left and closed terms of type t on the right as follows. For any $d \in \mathcal{C}°[\![t]\!]$ and term M of type t, define $d \lesssim_t M$ if

1. $d = \bot$, or
2. $M \Downarrow° V$ for some V and $d \lesssim_t V$ where

   - $f \lesssim_{s \to t} \lambda x : s.\ M$ iff, for every d and V, $d \lesssim_s V$ implies $\mathsf{down}(f)(d) \lesssim_t [V/x]M$.

   - $\{l_1 = d_1, \ldots, l_n = d_n\} \lesssim_{\{l_1:t_1,\ldots,l_n:t_n\}} \{l_1 = V_1, \ldots, l_n = V_n, \ldots, l_m = V_m\}$ iff $d_i \lesssim_{t_i} V_i$ for $i = 1, \ldots, n$.

   - $[l_i = d, \ldots] \lesssim_{[l_1:t_1,\ldots,l_n:t_n]} [l_j = V, \ldots]$ iff $i = j$ and $d \lesssim_{t_i} V$.

   - $\mathsf{true} \lesssim_{\mathbf{bool}} \mathsf{true}$ and $\mathsf{false} \lesssim_{\mathbf{bool}} \mathsf{false}$.

   - $0 \lesssim_{\mathbf{num}} 0$ and if $n \lesssim_{\mathbf{num}} V$ for a number n, then $n + 1 \lesssim_{\mathbf{num}} \mathsf{succ}(V)$. $\qquad\square$

The analog of Lemma 6.10 holds for the well-typed terms of PCF++.

9.14 Lemma. *For each closed term M of type t, the set of $d \in [\![t]\!]$ such $d \lesssim_t M$ is an inclusive subset.* $\qquad\square$

The key to proving the adequacy result is the following technical lemma:

9.15 Lemma. *Suppose $H = x_1 : r_1 \ldots x_k : r_k$ and $H \vdash_{\mathrm{sub}} P : r$. If $d_i \in [\![r_i]\!]$ and $d_i \lesssim_{r_i} P_i$ for $i = 1, \ldots, k$, then*

$$[\![H \triangleright P : r]\!]^{++}[x_1, \ldots, x_k \mapsto d_1, \ldots, d_k] \lesssim_r [P_1, \ldots, P_k/x_1, \ldots, x_k]P.$$

Proof: Let

$$\rho = [x_1, \ldots, x_k \mapsto d_1, \ldots, d_k] \text{ and } \sigma = [P_1, \ldots, P_k/x_1, \ldots, x_k].$$

Let Δ be a PCF++ derivation of the typing judgement $H \vdash_{\mathrm{sub}} P : r$. We prove that $[\![H \triangleright P : r]\!]^{++}\rho \lesssim_r \sigma P$ by an induction on Δ. Assume that the theorem is known for proofs of lesser height. There are eleven possibilities for the last step of Δ. Most resemble the cases in the proof of Lemma 6.11. I will write out some of the cases; subsumption is the most interesting.

Suppose that Δ is an instance of projection: $H \vdash_{\mathsf{sub}} x_i : r_i$. In this case $P \equiv x_i$ and we have $\llbracket H \rhd x_i : r_i \rrbracket^{++} \rho = d_i \lesssim_{r_i} P_i \equiv \sigma x_i$ by assumption.

Suppose the last step of Δ is an instance of lambda abstraction:

$$\frac{H,\ x : s \vdash_{\mathsf{sub}} M : t}{H \vdash_{\mathsf{sub}} \lambda x : s.\ M : s \to t}$$

In particular, $P : r \equiv \lambda x : s.\ M : s \to t$. Let Δ' be the part of the proof Δ that proves $H,\ x : s \vdash_{\mathsf{sub}} M : t$ and suppose $H,\ x : s \vdash M^* : t$ is $T^* \Delta'$. Let

$$f = \llbracket H \rhd \lambda x : s.\ M : s \to t \rrbracket^{++} \rho = \llbracket H \rhd \lambda x : s.\ M^* : s \to t \rrbracket^{+} \rho$$

and suppose $d \lesssim_s V$. We must show that

$$d' = \mathsf{down}(f)(d) \lesssim_t (\sigma \lambda x : s.\ M)(V). \tag{9.8}$$

If $d' = \bot$, then there is no problem. Suppose $d' \neq \bot$, then $\mathsf{down}(f) \neq \bot$, so

$$
\begin{aligned}
d' &= \mathsf{down}(\mathsf{up}(\mathsf{strict}\lambda d'' \in \llbracket s \rrbracket.\ \llbracket H, x : s \vdash M^* : t \rrbracket^{+} \rho[x \mapsto d'']))(d) \\
&= (\mathsf{strict}\lambda d'' \in \llbracket s \rrbracket.\ \llbracket H, x : s \rhd M^* : t \rrbracket^{+} \rho[x \mapsto d''])(d)
\end{aligned}
$$

and there are two cases. If $d = \bot$, then $d' = \bot \lesssim_t \sigma[V/x]M$ as desired. However, if $d \neq \bot$, then

$$
\begin{aligned}
d' &= \llbracket H, x : s \rhd M^* : t \rrbracket^{+} \rho[x \mapsto d] \\
&= \llbracket H, x : s \rhd M : t \rrbracket^{++} \rho[x \mapsto d] \\
&\lesssim_t \sigma[V/x]M
\end{aligned}
$$

by the induction hypothesis. Since $d' \neq \bot$, there is a value U such that $\sigma[V/x]M \Downarrow U$ and $d' \lesssim_t U$. Since $[V/x]\sigma M \equiv \sigma[V/x]M$, we have $(\lambda x : s.\ \sigma M)(V) \equiv (\sigma \lambda x : s.\ M)(V)$ so it must be the case that $(\sigma \lambda x : s.\ M)(V) \Downarrow U$ too, so 9.8 holds.

Suppose the last step of Δ is an instance of application:

$$\frac{H \vdash_{\mathsf{sub}} M : s \to t \qquad H \vdash_{\mathsf{sub}} N : s}{H \vdash_{\mathsf{sub}} M(N) : t}$$

Let $H \vdash M^* : s \to t$ and $H \vdash N^* : s$ be translations dictated by Δ. If

$$d' = \llbracket H \rhd M(N) : t \rrbracket^{++} \rho = \llbracket H \rhd M^*(N^*) : t \rrbracket^{+} \rho \neq \bot,$$

then

$$f = [\![H \rhd M : s \to t]\!]^{++}\rho = [\![H \rhd M^* : s \to t]\!]^+\rho \neq \bot$$

and $d = [\![H \rhd N : s]\!]^{++}\rho = [\![H \rhd N^* : s]\!]^+\rho \neq \bot$ by strictness. By the induction hypothesis, $f \lesssim_{s \to t} \sigma M : s \to t$ and $d \lesssim_s \sigma N : s$, so there is a term M' and a value U such that

$$\sigma M \Downarrow \lambda x : s.\ M' \text{ and } f \lesssim_{s \to t} \lambda x : s.\ M'$$
$$\sigma N \Downarrow U \text{ and } d \lesssim_s U.$$

Now $d' = \mathsf{down}(f)(d) \lesssim_t [U/x]M'$ by the definition of $\lesssim_{s \to t}$, so there is a value V such that $[U/x]M' \Downarrow V$ and $d' \lesssim_t V$. But $[U/x]M' \Downarrow V$ means $(\sigma M)(\sigma N) \Downarrow V$. Since $(\sigma M)(\sigma N) \equiv \sigma(M(N))$, we have $d' \lesssim_t \sigma(M(N))$ as desired.

Suppose that the last step of Δ is an instance of recursion:

$$\frac{H,\ x : t \vdash_{\mathrm{sub}} M : t}{H \vdash_{\mathrm{sub}} \mu x : t.\ M : t}$$

Let $H,\ x : t \vdash M^* : t$ be the translation dictated by Δ. Let $d_0 = \bot$ and $d_{i+1} = [\![H, x : t \rhd M : t]\!]^{++}\rho[x \mapsto d_i] = [\![H, x : t \rhd M^* : t]\!]^+\rho[x \mapsto d_i]$. We show that $d_i \lesssim_t \sigma \mu x : t.\ M$ for each i. This is immediate for $d_0 = \bot$. Suppose $d_i \lesssim_t \sigma \mu x : t.\ M$. By induction hypothesis, $d_{i+1} = [\![H, x : t \rhd M : t]\!]^{++}\rho[x \mapsto d_i] \lesssim_t \sigma[\mu x : t.M/x]M$. If $d_{i+1} \neq \bot$, then $\sigma[\mu x : t.\ M/x]M \Downarrow V$ for some V such that $d_{i+1} \lesssim_t V$. Now $\sigma[\mu x : t.\ M/x]M \equiv [\sigma \mu x : t.\ M/x]\sigma M \equiv [\mu x : t.\ \sigma M/x]\sigma M$. Hence $\sigma \mu x : t.\ M \equiv \mu x : t.\ \sigma M \Downarrow V$ as well. Since $[\![H \rhd \mu x : t.\ M : t]\!]^{++}\rho = [\![H \rhd \mu x : t.\ M^* : t]\!]^+\rho = \bigsqcup_{i \in \omega} d_i$, the desired result follows.

Suppose that the last step of Δ is an instance of the subsumption rule:

$$\frac{H \vdash_{\mathrm{sub}} M : s \qquad s \leq t}{H \vdash_{\mathrm{sub}} M : t}$$

The proof for this case is by induction on the height of the proof that $s \leq t$. Assume that we know that the theorem holds for $H \vdash_{\mathrm{sub}} M : s$ and let $H \vdash M^* : s$ be any translation of this judgement to PCF+. There are four subcases for how the proof that $s \leq t$ could end.

- If s and t are ground types, then the result is immediate since the coercion is the identity map.
- Suppose the last step in the proof of $s \leq t$ is an instance of the subtyping rule for functions:

$$\frac{u' \leq u \qquad v \leq v'}{u \to v \leq u' \to v'}$$

Suppose $s \equiv u \to v$ and $t \equiv u' \to v'$. Let $\xi_1 = \mathsf{down}[\![\Theta[u' \leq u]\!]$ and $\xi_2 = \mathsf{down}[\![\Theta[v \leq v']\!]$. Then $\xi = \mathsf{down}[\![\Theta[u \to v \leq u' \to v']\!]$ satisfies $\xi(f) = \xi_2 \circ f \circ \xi_1$ for $f : [\![u]\!] \circ\!\!\!-\!\!\!\to [\![v]\!]$. Set $f = \mathsf{down}[\![H \rhd M : s]\!]^{++}\rho$. If $d \precsim_{u'} U$, then $\xi_1(d) \precsim_u U$ by induction hypothesis on $u' \leq u$. Thus $f(\xi_1(d)) \precsim_v (\sigma M)(U)$ by induction hypothesis on $H \vdash_{\mathsf{sub}} M : s$. We may now apply the induction hypothesis on $v \leq v'$ to conclude that $\xi(f) = \xi_2(f(\xi_1(d))) \precsim_{v'} (\sigma M)(U)$. Since $\xi(f) = [\![H \rhd M : t]\!]^{++}\rho$, we conclude that $[\![H \rhd M : t]\!]^{++}\rho \precsim_t \sigma M$.

- Suppose the last step in the proof of $s \leq t$ is an instance of the subsumption rule for records:

$$\frac{s_1 \leq t_1 \quad \cdots \quad s_n \leq t_n}{\{l_1 : s_1, \ldots, l_n : s_n, \ldots, l_m : s_m\} \leq \{l_1 : t_1, \ldots, l_n : t_n\}}$$

Let $\xi_i = \mathsf{down}[\![\Theta[s_i \leq t_i]\!]$ for $i = 1, \ldots n$ and let $\xi = \mathsf{down}[\![\Theta[s \leq t]\!]$. By induction hypothesis, we have $d = [\![H \rhd M : s]\!]^{++}\rho \precsim_s \sigma M$. If $d = \bot$, then $\xi(d) = [\![H \rhd M : t]\!]^{++}\rho = \bot$ and we are done. If $d \neq \bot$, then $d = \{l_1 = d_1, \ldots, l_m = d_m\}$ where $d_1, \ldots, d_m \neq \bot$ and $\sigma M \Downarrow V$ for some value V of the form $V \equiv \{l_1 = V_1, \ldots, l_j = V_j\}$ such that $j \geq m$ and $d_i \precsim_{s_i} V_i$ for $i = 1, \ldots m$. By the inductive hypothesis on subtyping judgements, we must therefore have $\xi_i(d_i) \precsim_{t_i} V_i$ for each $i = 1, \ldots, n$. Hence $\xi(d) = \{l_1 = \xi_1(d_1), \ldots, l_n = \xi_n(d_n)\} \precsim_t \{l_1 = V_1, \ldots, l_j = V_j\}$ by the definition of $\precsim_t$ and we are done.

- Suppose the last step in the proof of $s \leq t$ is an instance of the subsumption rule for variants:

$$\frac{s_1 \leq t_1 \quad \cdots \quad s_n \leq t_n}{[l_1 : s_1, \ldots, l_n : s_n] \leq [l_1 : t_1, \ldots, l_n : t_n, \ldots, l_m : t_m]}$$

Let $\xi_i = \mathsf{down}[\![\Theta[s_i \leq t_i]\!]$ for $i = 1, \ldots n$ and let $\xi = \mathsf{down}[\![\Theta[s \leq t]\!]$. By induction hypothesis, we have $d = [\![H \rhd M : s]\!]^{++}\rho \precsim_s \sigma M$. If $d = \bot$, then $\xi(d) = [\![H \rhd M : t]\!]^{++}\rho = \bot$ and we are done. If $d \neq \bot$, then $d = [l_i = d_i]$ where $d_i \neq \bot$ and $\sigma M \Downarrow V$ where $d \precsim_s V$. By the definition of $\precsim_s$, the term V has the form $[l_i = V_i]$ and $d_i \precsim_{s_i} V_i$. By induction hypothesis on $s_i \leq t_i$, we know that $\xi_i(d_i) \precsim_{t_i} V_i$ so $\xi(d) = [l_i = \xi_i(d)] \precsim_t [l_i = V_i]$.   □

We may now express the desired proof of Computational Adequacy for PCF++.

Proof: (of Theorem 9.13) By Lemma 9.15 we know that $[\![M : t]\!]^{++} \precsim_t M$. Since the value on the left is assumed to differ from $\bot$, the theorem follows immediately from the definition of $\precsim_t$.   □

The following theorem follows immediately from Soundness and Computational Adequacy for PCF++ together with Corollary 9.8 of the Semantic Coherence Theorem for PCF++.

9.16 Theorem. *(Soundness and Adequacy for PCF+) If $\vdash M : t$, then*

1. *(Soundness) $M \Downarrow V$ implies $[\![M : t]\!]^+ = [\![V : t]\!]^+$.*
2. *(Computational Adequacy) $[\![M : t]\!]^+ \neq \perp$ implies $M \Downarrow V$ for some value V.*   □

Exercises.

9.4 Prove Lemma 9.9.

9.5 Prove Lemma 9.5.

9.6 Prove that if $H, x : s \vdash_{\text{sub}} M : t$ and $s' \leq s$, then $H, x : s' \vdash_{\text{sub}} M : t$.

9.7 Prove the following facts about $\vdash_{\text{sub}}$.

a. If $H \vdash_{\text{sub}} \{l_1 = M_1, \ldots, l_n = M_n\} : \{l_1 : t_1, \ldots, l_n : t_n\}$, then $H \vdash_{\text{sub}} M_i : t_i$.
b. If $H \vdash_{\text{sub}} [l = M, \ldots] : [l : t, l_1 : t_1, \ldots, l_n : t_n]$, then $H \vdash_{\text{sub}} M : t$.
c. If $H \vdash_{\text{sub}} \lambda x : s'. M : s \rightarrow t$, then $H, x : s \vdash_{\text{sub}} M : t$.

9.8 Prove the Soundness Theorem for call-by-value PCF++ (Theorem 9.12).

9.3   Notes

The typing system of PCF++ is adapted from similar systems proposed by Reynolds [204] and Cardelli [44].   A naive approach to the semantics of this type system is described by Reynolds in [207]. The semantics based on inclusive subsets presented in Section 9.1 essentially appears in the papers of Cardelli (where his interpretation is intended for call-by-value rather than call-by-name). The implicit coercions semantics in Section 9.2 are drawn from work of Breazu-Tannen, C. Gunter, and Scedrov [38]. The idea of coherence has its origins in research on category theory where it refers to the uniqueness of certain canonical arrows (see, for example, papers of Kelly, Mac Lane, and Pare [136; 149]); its relevance to the semantics of types and the idea of interpreting subsumption as implicit coercion is due to Breazu-Tannen, Coquand, C. Gunter, and Scedrov [37]. A technique for proving a coherence theorem such as Theorem 9.7 is described there.   A seminal paper showing how to use PER's rather than inclusive subsets to model subtypes is that of Bruce and Longo [39].

There is a strong impetus to allow more flexible type systems for records in strongly-typed programming languages. A substantial body of effort directed toward achieving this has focused on extending ML polymorphism to infer types for a wider range of programs that include record operations. The seminal paper on this line of research is that of Wand [268; 269]. Such type systems have been extensively studied and are likely to be used in future programming language type systems. Some of this work is described in the doctoral dissertations of Rémy [200] and Ohori [188]. These approaches provide an alternative to the use of subtyping systems such as the one described in this chapter. In most instances the semantic techniques required to model such systems draw on the methods used for parametric polymorphism as described in Chapter 11.

The subtyping system of this chapter did not consider subtyping between primitive types such as integers and reals, an idea present in many programming languages. Studying this kind of relationship was, in fact, the primary focus of [204]. There is a body of research attempting to apply the idea of a *intersection* (or *conjunctive*) type to developing a typing system in which the relationship between types such as these can be handled effectively. Intersection types were introduced by Coppo, Dezani-Ciancaglini, and Venneri [53; 54]. The idea behind intersection types is to allow types of the form $s \wedge t$ together with a rule of the form

$$\frac{H \vdash M : s \qquad H \vdash M : t}{H \vdash M : s \wedge t}$$

for introducing terms of intersection type and rules

$$\frac{H \vdash M : s \wedge t}{H \vdash M : s} \qquad \frac{H \vdash M : s \wedge t}{H \vdash M : s}$$

for eliminating them. Note, in particular, that these rules imply that a term does not have a unique typing derivation. The filter domains mentioned in the notes at the end of Chapter 8 provide one technique for giving a semantics for intersection types. Reynolds has shown how this can be done using implicit coercions and has proved a coherence theorem for a system with intersection types [208]. The language Forsythe includes intersection types. Tennent [259] also examines the use of intersection types for the design of an Algol-like language. Principal type schemes for intersection types have been studied by Ronchi Della Rocca [213].

10 Domain Theory

There is much more that one can say about the mathematical structures needed for the fixed-point semantics than we have discussed in Chapter 5, Chapter 8, and elsewhere up to this point. Some of the fundamental themes have been put forward—the concept of finite approximation and the idea of modeling types using a universal domain—but there is another central theme that has not been brought out as much as it deserves to be. Almost all of the classes of spaces used so far for the foundations of fixed-point semantics can be viewed as classes of posets. So, recalling the observation in Section 5.3 that posets are a special kind of category in which there is at most one arrow between any two objects, we can also view semantic domains as categories. Now, many of the conditions placed on domains can be generalized to conditions on categories. The benefit in doing this arises from the fact that most of the conditions on domains were imposed for purposes that apply equally well to the classes of domains themselves. Perhaps the clearest example of this is the Fixed-Point Theorem where the requirement that a poset D is directed complete and pointed ensures that a continuous function $f : D \to D$ has a least fixed point. This result is used as a tool for providing a semantics for recursively defined functions. In the previous chapter a similar technique for interpreting recursively defined *types* was obtained by using points of a cpo (retracts on a universal domain) to mimic domains themselves and by using the Fixed-Point Theorem for this cpo of domains. Another approach to interpreting recursively defined types is to generalize the Fixed-Point Theorem itself so that it applies to *categories* that satisfy certain properties. If it can then be shown that the categories of domains in which we are interested satisfy these properties, then techniques applicable to finding a fixed point of a map from a domain to itself can be applied to finding a fixed point of a map from the *category* of domains to itself.

What then is the analog of the Fixed-Point Theorem at the level of domains? Is this analog satisfied by bc-domains, dI-domains, and so on? Some of the needed ideas have already been developed. For instance, the categorical analog of a monotone function between posets is a functor between categories, and the categorical analog of having a least element is having an initial object (recall that an initial object 0 in a category is the dual of a terminal object: for any object A, there is a unique arrow $i_A : 0 \to A$). We must now find categorical analogs for the poset notions of directed completeness (or ω-completeness) and continuity of functions. To formulate the directed or ω-completeness conditions we need an analog of a limit. A *continuous functor* can then be defined as one that preserves category-theoretic directed limits. The purpose of the first section of this chapter is to formulate these notions precisely and prove a generalization of the Fixed-Point Theorem for them. The remainder of the chapter explores other categorical topics in the foundations of fixed-point semantics with an emphasis on the idea of generalizing poset conditions on domains to categorical conditions and exploring how these categorical conditions can then be used to understand categories of domains themselves. The second section of the chapter discusses posets called *bifinite domains,* which are cpo's that are built up as limits of finite posets. It is shown that this category has a universal domain that can be used to obtain universal domains for other categories. The third section discusses a crucial categorical generalization of embedding-projection pairs called an *adjunction* and looks at the application of this notion in the study of operators called *powerdomains* that can be defined on bifinite domains and provide domain-theoretic analogs to the powerset operation.

10.1   Fixed Points of Functors

The best approach to obtaining a categorical analog of the Fixed-Point Theorem is to begin with a very simple technique for obtaining a fixed point using the idea of a *pre-fixed* point. We encountered the notion before in Theorem 4.12 without putting a specific name on it. Let P be a poset and suppose $f : P \to P$ is a monotone map on P. A *pre-fixed* point of f is an element $x \in P$ such that $f(x) \sqsubseteq x$. Suppose there is a *least* pre-fixed point $x \in P$, that is, if y is another pre-fixed point, then $x \sqsubseteq y$. Now, $f(x)$ is also a pre-fixed point of f because $f^2(x) \sqsubseteq f(x)$ by the monotonicity of f. Since x is the least pre-fixed point, this means that $x \sqsubseteq f(x)$. But this must mean that $x = f(x)$ since $f(x) \sqsubseteq x$ too. In other words, if there is one, the least pre-fixed point of a monotone function f on a poset is also a fixed point of f.

F-algebras.

What could be the categorical analog of a pre-fixed point? Since a poset is a category where $x \sqsubseteq y$ means there is an arrow between x and y, it seems natural to replace a pair $f(x) \sqsubseteq x$ by an arrow $f : F(A) \to A$ where F is a functor and A an object. More precisely, let $\mathbf{C}$ be a category and suppose $F : \mathbf{C} \to \mathbf{C}$ an endofunctor on $\mathbf{C}$. An *algebra over F* is an arrow $f : F(A) \to A$. A *homomorphism* between two algebras over F, $f : F(A) \to A$ and $g : F(B) \to B$, is an arrow h of $\mathbf{C}$ such that the following diagram commutes:

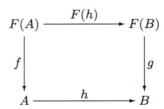

As an abbreviation, an algebra over a functor F is called an F-*algebra* and a homomorphism between two F-algebras is called an F-*homomorphism*. The reader can show as an exercise that F-algebras and F-algebra homomorphisms form a category. An *initial F-algebra* is an initial object in the category of F-algebras and F-algebra homomorphisms. Now, a categorical analog of the observation that the least pre-fixed point of a monotone function on a poset is also a fixed point is given in the following lemma:

10.1 Lemma. *If $f : F(A) \to A$ is an initial F-algebra, then f is an isomorphism.*

Proof: Since $F(f) : F^2(A) \to F(A)$ is an F-algebra and f is initial as an F-algebra, there is a unique F-homomorphism g from f to $F(f)$. In particular, the left rectangle of the following diagram commutes:

$$
\begin{array}{ccccc}
F(A) & \xrightarrow{\ F(g)\ } & F^2(A) & \xrightarrow{\ F(f)\ } & F(A) \\
{\scriptstyle f}\downarrow & & {\scriptstyle F(f)}\downarrow & & \downarrow{\scriptstyle f} \\
A & \xrightarrow{\ \ g\ \ } & F(A) & \xrightarrow{\ \ f\ \ } & A
\end{array}
$$

The right rectangle clearly also commutes, so the outer rectangle commutes too. This means that

$$f \circ g : A \to A$$

is an F-homomorphism. But

$$\mathrm{id}_A : A \to A$$

is also an F-homomorphism, so the fact that f is initial as an F-algebra means that $f \circ g = \mathrm{id}_A$. On the other hand, the commutativity of the left rectangle in the diagram above says

$$g \circ f = F(f) \circ F(g) = F(f \circ g) = F(\mathrm{id}_A) = \mathrm{id}_{F(A)}.$$

Thus f is an isomorphism.   □

Colimits.

Let us now attempt to generalize the idea of a directed set and a limit of a directed set to the level of categories. Given a poset D, we could view a directed subset of D as a monotone function $f : I \to D$ from a directed poset I into D. If we replace D by a category and stipulate that F is a functor, then we have achieved the desired generalization. In fact there is no need to restrict I only to posets that are directed:

Definition: Let I be a poset and $\mathbf{C}$ a category. A *diagram indexed by I over $\mathbf{C}$* is a functor $\Delta : I \to \mathbf{C}$. □

Let Δ be a diagram indexed by a poset I over a category $\mathbf{C}$. For each $i \in I$, Δ_i is an object, and if $i \sqsubseteq j$, then $\Delta(i \sqsubseteq j)$ is an arrow from Δ_i to Δ_j. To make the notation more convenient, it is helpful to take $D_i = \Delta_i$ and $f_{ij} = \Delta(i \sqsubseteq j)$ and say that the indexed family

$$\Delta = (D_i, f_{ij})_{i,j \in I}$$

is a diagram indexed by I. The fact that Δ is a functor means that if $i, j, k \in I$ with $i \sqsubseteq j \sqsubseteq k$, then $f_{ik} = f_{jk} \circ f_{ij}$. A *cone* over such a diagram Δ is a family of maps $\mu = (\mu_i)_{i \in I}$ indexed by I such that, for each $i \in I$, $\mu_i : D_i \to D$. A cone is required to satisfy the property that, for each $i, j \in I$ such that $i \sqsubseteq j$, the following diagram commutes:

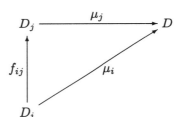

Given a diagram Δ indexed by I, write $\mu : \Delta \to D$ to indicate that μ is a cone over Δ where the maps μ_i have D as their (mutual) codomain. Given another cone $\nu : \Delta \to E$, an arrow $f : D \to E$ is said to be a *mediating arrow* between the cones if the following diagram

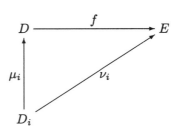

commutes for each $i \in I$. In this case we write $f : \mu \to \nu$. The cone μ is said to be *colimiting* (with respect to Δ) if, for any other cone $\nu : \Delta \to E$, there is a *unique* mediating arrow $f : \mu \to \nu$. In this case D is said to be a *colimit* of Δ.

Colimits are the categorical generalization of least upper bounds (lub's) in posets. To see this, suppose P is a poset and $M \subseteq P$. If x is the colimit of M with P considered as a category, then, for each $y \in M$, there is an arrow $y \sqsubseteq x$. In other words, x is an upper bound for M. Another upper bound x' for M determines a cone consisting of the arrows $y \sqsubseteq x'$ for each $y \in M$ so, for each such x', there is an arrow $x \sqsubseteq x'$. All uniqueness and commutativity requirements are trivial here since we are dealing with a poset, so these remarks prove that x is the least upper bound of M. A reversal of the steps of the argument provides a demonstration that if x is the least upper bound of M, then it is also the colimit of M. Now, it was noted when least upper bounds were first introduced that the least upper bound of a subset of a poset is uniquely determined. Does an analogous result hold for colimits? The answer is basically yes, but some care must be taken in finding the correct generalization. Recall that a pre-order is a set A with a binary relation $\sqsubseteq$ on A that is reflexive and transitive. A least upper bound can be defined in a pre-order just as it is in a poset but with the poset relation $\sqsubseteq$ replaced by the pre-order relation $\sqsubseteq$. The conclusion that every subset $M \subseteq A$ has a *unique* least upper bound no longer holds. Instead, it is possible to conclude that the lub is uniquely determined *up to equivalence*. That is, if a and b are lub's of M, then $a \sqsubseteq b$ and $b \sqsubseteq a$. Now, the categorical analog of this property is *isomorphism*. The desired generalization says that the colimit of a diagram is uniquely determined *up to isomorphism*:

10.2 Lemma. *Suppose Δ is a diagram. If $\mu : \Delta \to D$ and $\nu : \Delta \to E$ are both colimiting cones, then D and E are isomorphic. That is, the colimit of a diagram is unique up to isomorphism if it exists.*

Proof: If μ and ν are both colimiting, then there are mediating arrows $f : \mu \to \nu$ and $g : \nu \to \mu$. The fact that these arrows are mediating means that each of the inner triangles of the following diagram

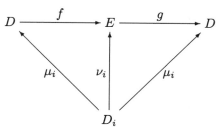

commutes for each $i \in I$ so it follows that the outer triangle does. This means that $g \circ f$ is a mediating arrow between μ and itself. Since μ is colimiting, there is at most one such arrow, and because the identity on D is clearly a mediating arrow between μ and μ, it must be the case that $g \circ f = \mathrm{id}_D$. A similar argument can be used to show that $f \circ g = \mathrm{id}_E$. Hence the mediating arrows define the desired isomorphism.   □

We will primarily be interested in the case in which the indexing poset I is directed and, most particularly, the case where it is the poset ω. A diagram indexed by ω over a category $\mathbf{C}$ is the categorical analog of an ω-chain and it is simply called an ω-*chain over* $\mathbf{C}$. An ω-chain can be given as an indexed family $(D_i, f_i)_{i \in \omega}$ where $f_i : D_i \to D_{i+1}$ for each $i \in \omega$. If $i \sqsubseteq j$, then an arrow $f_{ij} : D_i \to D_j$ can be defined as the composition $f_{j-1} \circ \cdots \circ f_i$ since the indexed family $(D_i, f_{ij})_{i,j \in I}$ then forms a directed diagram over ω. For such a cone the diagram

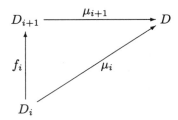

commutes for each i. If $\Delta = (D_i, f_i)_{i \in \omega}$ is an ω-chain, then there is an ω-chain Δ^- with $D_i^- = D_{i+1}$ and $f_i^- = f_{i+1}$ for each $i \in \omega$. Given a cone $\mu : \Delta \to D$, the cone $\mu^- : \Delta^- \to D$ is defined by taking $\mu_i^- = \mu_{i+1}$ for each $i \in \omega$. A categorical analog to the result about pre-fixed points can now be expressed as follows.

10.3 Theorem. *Let $\mathbf{C}$ be a category with an initial object 0 and suppose $F : \mathbf{C} \to \mathbf{C}$ is an endofunctor on $\mathbf{C}$. Let Δ be the ω-chain $(F^n(0), F^n(\mathsf{i}))_{n \in \omega}$ where $\mathsf{i} = \mathsf{i}_{F(0)}$ is the unique map from the initial object 0 to $F(0)$. If there is a colimiting cone $\mu : \Delta \to A$ and the cone $F(\mu) : F(\Delta) \to F(A)$ is also colimiting, then the mediating arrow $a : F(A) \to A$ between $F(\mu)$ and μ^- is an initial F-algebra.*

Proof: That a is mediating means

$$a \circ F(\mu_n) = \mu_{n+1}$$

for each $n \in \omega$. Suppose $b : F(B) \to B$ is an F-algebra. Define maps $\nu_n : F^n(0) \to B$ by induction on n by taking $\nu_0 = \mathsf{i}_B$ and $\nu_{n+1} = b \circ F(\nu_n)$. We show that $(\nu_n)_{n \in \omega}$ is a cone over Δ by showing that, for each $n \in \omega$,

$$\nu_{n+1} \circ F^n(\mathsf{i}) = \nu_n. \tag{10.1}$$

This is done by induction on n. If $n = 0$, then the result is immediate by the uniqueness property of the initial object. Suppose the result is known for n and calculate

$$\nu_{n+2} \circ F^{n+1}(\mathsf{i}) = b \circ F(\nu_{n+1}) \circ F^{n+1}(\mathsf{i}) = b \circ F(\nu_{n+1} \circ F^n(\mathsf{i}))$$
$$= b \circ F(\nu_n) = \nu_{n+1}.$$

Hence Equation 10.1 holds for all n. Since ν is a cone over Δ and μ is the colimiting cone, there is a mediating arrow $f : A \to B$ satisfying

$$f \circ \mu_n = \nu_n$$

for each $n \in \omega$. The next step is showing that f is an F-homomorphism, that is,

$$b \circ F(f) = f \circ a. \tag{10.2}$$

This is done by showing that both sides of this equation define mediating arrows between the cones $F(\mu)$ and ν^-. To this end, we calculate

$$(b \circ F(f)) \circ F(\mu_n) = b \circ F(f \circ \mu_n) = b \circ F(\nu_n) = \nu_{n+1}$$

and

$$(f \circ a) \circ F(\mu_n) = f \circ \mu_{n+1} = \nu_{n+1}.$$

By the uniqueness of the mediating arrow for a colimit, Equation 10.2 holds, and f is therefore an F-homomorphism. It remains to establish that this homomorphism is unique. To this end, suppose $g : A \to B$ satisfies

$$b \circ F(g) = g \circ a.$$

To prove that g is equal to f, it suffices to show that it is a mediating arrow between μ and ν by showing that, for all $n \in \omega$,

$$g \circ \mu_n = \nu_n.$$

This equation clearly holds when n is zero. Suppose it is known for n and calculate

$$g \circ \mu_{n+1} = g \circ a \circ F(\mu_n) = b \circ F(g) \circ F(\mu_n) = b \circ F(g \circ \mu_n) = b \circ F(\nu_n) = \nu_{n+1}.$$

Thus $f = g$, and f is therefore the unique F-homomorphism from A to B. $\quad\square$

Let us say that a category $\mathbf{C}$ is (directed) complete if every directed diagram Δ over $\mathbf{C}$ has a colimit. A functor $F : \mathbf{C} \to \mathbf{D}$ is said to be *continuous* if it preserves colimits of directed families. That is, if μ is a colimiting cone for a directed diagram Δ, then $F(\mu)$ is colimiting for $F(\Delta)$.

Fixed points and embedding-projection pairs.

To obtain the desired generalization of the Fixed-Point Theorem, we need to formulate a categorical analog of the orderings on domains. This ordering was one that we viewed as 'information theoretic' in the sense that $x \sqsubseteq y$ means that x is somehow less defined than y. In this case x is to be viewed as an approximation to y. What would be the corresponding relationship between cpo's? There is more than one reasonable choice for this. As a first guess one might take an approximation of D to E to be an isomorphism between D and a subposet of E, that is, an *order embedding*. This definition does not provide much to work with though; ideally we would like to find that the set of approximations in D of an element of E has good properties. The best idea for the desired relationship is one we have encountered before. Recall that an an embedding-projection pair (hearafter an 'ep-pair') is a pair (f, g) of continuous functions $f : D \to E$ and $g : E \to D$ between cpo's D, E such that

$$g \circ f = \mathsf{id}_D \tag{10.3}$$
$$f \circ g \sqsubseteq \mathsf{id}_E. \tag{10.4}$$

Following this approach we generalize the relationship $x \sqsubseteq y$ defining the information ordering on elements in a domain to an arrow for embedding a cpo D into a cpo E.

Actually it will be essential for us to go beyond the basic idea of an embedding between cpo's to an even more general categorical analog of this idea. The desired generalization is defined in terms of a special kind of category:

Definition: An *O-category* is a category **C** together with a cpo structure given on each set of arrows $\mathbf{C}(D, E)$ for objects D, E in **C**. In other words, for each pair of objects D, E of **C**, there is a (chosen) binary relation $\sqsubseteq$ on the arrows in $\mathbf{C}(D, E)$ such that $(\mathbf{C}(D, E), \sqsubseteq)$ is a complete partial order. It is required that the composition function is continuous with respect to this partial ordering on arrows. □

Several of the categories we have considered so far are O-categories. For instance, the category **Cpo** itself can be given the structure of an O-category by taking the point-wise ordering on continuous functions. Any full subcategory, such as the algebraic cpo's or the bc-domains, will also be an O-category. DI-domains are another example of an O-category where the arrows could be taken under the stable ordering. It is also possible to form new O-categories from old ones by taking a product category. If **C** is the product of O-categories $\mathbf{C}_1, \ldots, \mathbf{C}_n$, then the ordering on arrows

$$(f_1, \ldots, f_n), \ (g_1, \ldots, g_n) \in \mathbf{C}(\times(D_1, \ldots, D_n), \ \times(E_1, \ldots, E_n))$$

can simply be taken from the orderings of the coordinates in the O-categories $\mathbf{C}_i$. This last example is especially important for the applications; indeed, it is the primary reason for generalizing from cpo's to O-categories.

Now, given an O-category $\mathbf{C}$, an ep-pair in $\mathbf{C}$ is defined in exactly the same way it is defined in the category of cpo's using Equation 10.3 and Inequation 10.4, except that the ordering used in 10.4 now comes from the O-category structure on $\mathbf{C}$. Such pairs can be made the arrows of a category as follows. It helps to name the pair rather than naming its coordinates; given an ep-pair h, let h^e be the first coordinate of the pair (the embedding) and let h^p be the second component (the projection). Write $h : D \to E$ if $h^e : D \to E$. In other words, as an arrow, the embedding-projection pair points from the domain of the embedding to its range. The composition of ep-pairs $h = (h^e, h^p) : D \to E$ and $k = (k^e, k^p) : E \to F$ is defined by taking

$$k \circ h = (k^e \circ h^e, h^p \circ k^p) : D \to F.$$

To see that $f = k \circ h$ is indeed an ep-pair, calculate

$$f^p \circ f^e = (h^p \circ k^p) \circ (k^e \circ h^e) = h^p \circ (k^p \circ k^e) \circ h^e = h^p \circ h^e = \mathsf{id}_D$$

and

$$f^e \circ f^p = (k^e \circ h^e) \circ (h^p \circ k^p) = k^e \circ (h^e \circ h^p) \circ k^p \sqsubseteq k^e \circ k^p \sqsubseteq \mathsf{id}_F.$$

It is obvious that $(\mathsf{id}_D, \mathsf{id}_D)$ is an ep-pair for any object D, and this acts as an identity for ep-pairs. That composition of ep-pairs is associative follows easily from this property for the underlying category, thus ep-pairs form a category $\mathbf{C}^{ep}$ with the same objects as $\mathbf{C}$.

We will ordinarily be interested in continuous functors $F : \mathbf{C}^{ep} \to \mathbf{D}^{ep}$ between the categories of ep-pairs for O-categories $\mathbf{C}$ and $\mathbf{D}$. Because it is generally tedious to verify that a given cone is colimiting, it is tedious to verify that a functor $F : \mathbf{C}^{ep} \to \mathbf{D}^{ep}$ is continuous directly from the definition of functor continuity. The next theorem provides a powerful technique for demonstrating that a functor between O-categories is continuous by providing an easily verified condition for when a cone is actually a colimit.

10.4 Theorem (Colimit). *Let $\mathbf{C}$ be an O-category. If Δ is a diagram over $\mathbf{C}^{ep}$ indexed by a directed poset I and $\mu : \Delta \to D$ is a cone, then it is colimiting if*

$$\bigsqcup_{i \in I} \mu_i^e \circ \mu_i^p = \mathsf{id}_D.$$

Proof: First of all, note that the least upper bound in the lemma actually makes sense. Suppose $\Delta = (D_i, f_{ij})_{i,j \in I}$. If $i \sqsubseteq j$, then

$$\mu_i^e \circ \mu_i^p = (\mu_j \circ f_{ij})^e \circ (\mu_j \circ f_{ij})^p = \mu_j^e \circ f_{ij}^e \circ f_{ij}^p \circ \mu_j^p \sqsubseteq \mu_j^e \circ \mu_j^p$$

so the indexed family $(\mu_i^e \circ \mu_i^p)_{i \in I}$ is directed, and therefore its lub exists because $\mathbf{C}$ is an O-category.

Suppose $\nu : \Delta \to E$ is another cone. The goal is to demonstrate a unique mediating arrow $f : \mu \to \nu$. To prove that there is at most one such arrow (if any), suppose that one is given. Then

$$f^e = f^e \circ \mathrm{id}_D = f^e \circ (\bigsqcup_{i \in I} \mu_i^e \circ \mu_i^p) = \bigsqcup_{i \in I} f^e \circ \mu_i^e \circ \mu_i^p = \bigsqcup_{i \in I} \nu_i^e \circ \mu_i^p \tag{10.5}$$

and

$$f^p = \mathrm{id}_D \circ f^p = (\bigsqcup_{i \in I} \mu_i^e \circ \mu_i^p) \circ f^p = \bigsqcup_{i \in I} \mu_i^e \circ \mu_i^p \circ f^p = \bigsqcup_{i \in I} \mu_i^e \circ \nu_i^p \tag{10.6}$$

so, if there is a mediating arrow f, then its components must satisfy Equations 10.5 and 10.6 and these equations uniquely determine its value. Taking these equations as a definition now, the proof will be complete if it can be shown that $f = (f^e, f^p)$ is indeed a mediating arrow between μ and ν. First of all, f actually is an ep-pair,

$$f^e \circ f^p = (\bigsqcup_{i \in I} \nu_i^e \circ \mu_i^p) \circ (\bigsqcup_{i \in I} \mu_i^e \circ \nu_i^p) = \bigsqcup_{i \in I} \nu_i^e \circ \mu_i^p \circ \mu_i^e \circ \nu_i^p = \bigsqcup_{i \in I} \nu_i^e \circ \nu_i^p \sqsubseteq \mathrm{id}_E$$

and

$$f^p \circ f^e = (\bigsqcup_{i \in I} \mu_i^e \circ \nu_i^p) \circ (\bigsqcup_{i \in I} \nu_i^e \circ \mu_i^p) = \bigsqcup_{i \in I} \mu_i^e \circ \nu_i^p \circ \nu_i^e \circ \mu_i^p = \bigsqcup_{i \in I} \mu_i^e \circ \mu_i^p = \mathrm{id}_D.$$

To show that f is a mediating arrow, it remains to check that $f \circ \mu = \nu$, that is, $f \circ \mu_i = \nu_i$ for each $i \in I$. Let $i \in I$ and let $J = (\uparrow i) \cap I$. If $(x_j)_{j \in I}$ is a family indexed by I where $x_j \sqsubseteq x_k$ whenever $j \sqsubseteq k$, then $\bigsqcup_{j \in I} x_j = \bigsqcup_{j \in J} x_j$ because I is a directed poset. This allows us to replace the lub of a family indexed by I with one indexed by elements of I that are above i. Now, by the definition of composition for ep-pairs, we need to show

$$f^e \circ \mu_i^e = (\bigsqcup_{j \in J} \nu_j^e \circ \mu_j^p) \circ \mu_i^e = \bigsqcup_{j \in J} \nu_j^e \circ \mu_j^p \circ \mu_i^e = \bigsqcup_{j \in J} \nu_j^e \circ \mu_j^p \circ (\mu_j^e \circ f_{ij}^e)$$

$$= \bigsqcup_{j \in J} \nu_j^e \circ f_{ij}^e = \bigsqcup_{j \in J} \nu_i^e = \nu_i^e$$

and

$$\mu_i^p \circ f^p = \mu_i^p \circ (\bigsqcup_{j \in J} \mu_j^e \circ \nu_j^p) = \bigsqcup_{j \in J} \mu_i^p \circ \mu_j^e \circ \nu_j^p$$

$$= \bigsqcup_{j \in J} (f_{ij}^p \circ \mu_j^p) \circ \mu_j^e \circ \nu_j^p = \bigsqcup_{j \in J} f_{ij}^p \circ \nu_j^p$$

$$= \bigsqcup_{j \in I} \nu_i^p = \nu_i^p$$

so f is indeed a mediating arrow.   □

All of the O-categories that will be of interest to us also satisfy the converse of the Colimit Theorem.

Definition: An O-category $\mathbf{C}$ is said to have *locally determined colimits* if, for every diagram Δ over $\mathbf{C}^{ep}$ indexed by a directed poset I, the following are equivalent for every cone $\mu : \Delta \to D$:

1. μ is colimiting.
2. $\bigsqcup_{i \in I} \mu_i^e \circ \mu_i^p = \mathrm{id}_D$.   □

Of course, the Colimiting Theorem says that only the implication from (1) to (2) ever needs to be established. Let us consider the example of the O-category $\mathbf{Cpo}$. Let $\Delta = (D_i, f_{ij})_{i,j \in I}$ be a diagram over $\mathbf{Cpo}^{ep}$ indexed by a directed poset I. Define D to be the set of I-indexed families $(x_i)_{i \in I}$ such that

- $x_i \in D_i$ for each $i \in I$ and
- $x_i = f_{ij}^p(x_j)$ whenever $i \sqsubseteq j$.

The coordinatewise order on these families, which takes $(x_i)_{i \in I} \sqsubseteq (y_i)_{i \in I}$ just in case $x_i \sqsubseteq y_i$ for each i, is a cpo since the functions f_{ij}^p are continuous. For each $j \in I$, we define an ep-pair $\mu_j : D_j \to D$ as follows. Given $x = (x_i)_{i \in I} \in D$, let $\mu_j^p(x) = x_j \in D_j$. To define μ_j^e, suppose we are given $x \in D_j$; we must define a family $(y_i)_{i \in I} \in D$. Given $i \in I$, there is some $k \in I$ such that $i \sqsubseteq k$ and $j \sqsubseteq k$ since I is directed. Define $y_i = f_{ik}^p \circ f_{jk}^e(x)$. It can be shown that this value is independent of the choice of k. Taking $\mu_j^e(x) = (y_i)_{i \in I}$, we have the following lemma:

10.5 Lemma. *The maps μ_i defined above are all ep-pairs, and $\bigsqcup \mu_i^e \circ \mu_i^p = \mathrm{id}_D$.*   □

The proof is left as an exercise for the reader. Of course, the Colimit Theorem implies that μ is a colimiting cone. Suppose on the other hand that $\nu : (D_i, f_{ij}) \to E$ is another colimiting cone and $f : D \to E$ is the mediating isomorphism between them. Then

$$\bigsqcup_{i \in I} \nu_i^e \circ \nu_i^p = \bigsqcup_{i \in I} f^e \circ \mu_i^e \circ \mu_i^p \circ f^p = f^e \circ f^p = \mathrm{id}_E$$

where the last equality is a basic fact about isomorphisms in the category of cpo's and ep-pairs. This shows that, in the category $\mathbf{Cpo}^{ep}$, a cone ν is colimiting if, and only if, $\bigsqcup_i \nu_i^e \circ \nu_i^p = \mathsf{id}$, that is, $\mathbf{Cpo}$ has locally determined colimits.

One of the key advantages of O-categories that have locally determined colimits is the possibility of demonstrating that a functor between such categories is continuous by checking some facts about the functor's action on arrows. Suppose $F : \mathbf{C} \to \mathbf{D}$ is a functor between O-categories $\mathbf{C}$ and $\mathbf{D}$. Let us say that F is *locally monotone* if $f \sqsubseteq g$ implies $F(f) \sqsubseteq F(g)$. Given an ep-pair f, write $F^e(f)$ for $(F(f))^e$ and $F^p(f)$ for $(F(f))^p$. A functor $F : \mathbf{C}^{ep} \to \mathbf{D}^{ep}$ is locally monotone just in case F^e and F^p are locally monotone.

10.6 Lemma (Functor Continuity). *Suppose $\mathbf{C}$ and $\mathbf{D}$ are O-categories with locally determined colimits. Then a locally monotone functor $F : \mathbf{C}^{ep} \to \mathbf{D}^{ep}$ is continuous if, and only if, for every diagram Δ in $\mathbf{C}^{ep}$ indexed by a directed poset I and every cone $\mu : \Delta \to D$,*

$$\bigsqcup_{i \in I} \mu_i^e \circ \mu_i^p = \mathsf{id}_D \ \text{implies} \ \bigsqcup_{i \in I} F^e(\mu_i) \circ F^p(\mu_i) = \mathsf{id}_{F(D)}.$$

Proof: This follows immediately from the Colimit Theorem and the condition that $\mathbf{C}$ and $\mathbf{D}$ have locally determined colimits.   □

Given a functor $F : \mathbf{C} \to \mathbf{D}$ between categories with locally determined colimits, this lemma can be obtained from a slightly more general condition that is satisfied by almost all of the functors we have encountered so far. A locally monotone functor $F : \mathbf{C} \to \mathbf{D}$ induces a functor between $\mathbf{C}^{ep}$ and $\mathbf{D}^{ep}$, since $(F(f^e), F(f^p))$ is an ep-pair if f is. A locally monotone functor F is said to be *locally continuous* if $F(\bigsqcup M) = \bigsqcup F(M)$ for any directed set of arrows $M \subseteq \mathbf{C}(D, E)$. The following is an immediate corollary of the Functor Continuity Lemma:

10.7 Lemma. *If $F : \mathbf{C} \to \mathbf{D}$ is a locally continuous functor between O-categories with locally determined colimits, then the functor that F induces between $\mathbf{C}^{ep}$ and $\mathbf{D}^{ep}$ is continuous.*   □

To see how the lemma can be used, consider the product functor on cpos,

$$F : \mathbf{Cpo} \times \mathbf{Cpo} \to \mathbf{Cpo}$$

where $F(D, E) = D \times E$ and $F(f, g) = f \times g$. Let me leave the proof that this functor is locally monotone as an exercise and demonstrate that it is locally continuous. An object

D in $\mathbf{Cpo} \times \mathbf{Cpo}$ is a pair of cpo's (D_1, D_2). Let M be a directed subset of the arrows between objects D and E in $\mathbf{Cpo} \times \mathbf{Cpo}$. Define

$$P = \{f \mid (f, g) \in M \text{ for some } g\} \text{ and } Q = \{g \mid (f, g) \in M \text{ for some } f\}.$$

Then

$$\bigsqcup F(M) = \bigsqcup_{(f,g) \in M} f \times g = (\bigsqcup P) \times (\bigsqcup Q) = F(\bigsqcup P, \bigsqcup Q) = F(\bigsqcup M).$$

So, if we can show that the product $\mathbf{Cpo} \times \mathbf{Cpo}$ has locally determined colimits, then the continuity of the induced product functor from $\mathbf{Cpo}^{ep} \times \mathbf{Cpo}^{ep}$ to $\mathbf{Cpo}^{ep}$ follows from Lemma 10.7. That the product of any pair of O-categories with locally determined colimits also has locally determined colimits is left as an exercise for the reader.

Almost all of the functors on the category of cpo's and continuous functions or on the category of cpo's and strict continuous functions can be shown to be continuous by checking local continuity. However, there is one crucial operator that requires a direct application of the Functor Continuity Lemma. This is the continuous function space operator $F(X, Y) = [X \to Y]$. Now this can be viewed as an operator on pairs of cpo's, but its functor action is *contravariant* in the first argument. That is,

$$F : \mathbf{Cpo}^{op} \times \mathbf{Cpo} \to \mathbf{Cpo}$$

where $\mathbf{Cpo}^{op}$ is the category with the same objects as $\mathbf{Cpo}$, but with the arrows in $\mathbf{Cpo}^{op}(D, D')$ defined to be continuous functions $f : D' \to D$. To see what the functor action is, suppose (f, g) is an arrow in $\mathbf{Cpo}^{op} \times \mathbf{Cpo}$ with domain (D, E) and codomain (D', E'). Then $f : D' \to D$ and $g : E \to E'$. To get a continuous function between $F(D, E)$ and $F(D', E')$, suppose $h : D \to E$ is continuous and define

$$F(f, g)(h) = g \circ h \circ f : [D \to E] \to [D' \to E']. \tag{10.7}$$

The reader can verify as an exercise that this does make F into a functor. However, for the purpose of solving domain equations, this functor action on arrows is problematic since we cannot directly apply the categorical version of the Fixed-Point Theorem because of the contravariance in the first argument. This problem can be corrected through the use of ep-pairs as follows. Let us define a functor

$$[\cdot \to \cdot] : \mathbf{Cpo}^{ep} \times \mathbf{Cpo}^{ep} \to \mathbf{Cpo}^{ep}$$

called the *covariant function space functor*. On objects its action is that of the continuous function space operator. To define the action on arrows, suppose $f : D \to D'$ and $g : E \to E'$ are ep-pairs. For each continuous function $h : D \to E$, define

$$[f \to g]^e(h) = g^e \circ h \circ f^p,$$

and for each continuous function $k : D' \to E'$, define

$$[f \to g]^p(k) = g^p \circ k \circ f^e.$$

I leave the proof of local monotonicity of the functor as an exercise. To see that it is continuous, suppose we are given a colimiting cone over a directed diagram. In the product category, each of the arrows in the cone is a pair of arrows, so write (μ_i, ν_i) for the cone arrow between D and D_i where I is the indexing poset and $i \in I$. Then

$$(\bigsqcup_{i \in I} [\mu_i \to \nu_i]^e \circ [\mu_i \to \nu_i]^p)(h) = \bigsqcup_{i \in I} [\mu_i \to \nu_i]^e (\mu_i^p \circ h \circ \nu_i^e)$$

$$= \bigsqcup_{i \in I} \mu_i^e \circ \mu_i^p \circ h \circ \nu_i^e \circ \nu_i^p$$

$$= (\bigsqcup_{i \in I} \mu_i^e \circ \mu_i^p) \circ h \circ (\bigsqcup_{i \in I} \nu_i^e \circ \nu_i^p)$$

$$= h.$$

10.8 Theorem. *The category* $\mathbf{Alg}^{ep}$ *has colimits for directed systems.*

Proof: Let $\Delta = (D_i, f_{ij})_{i,j \in I}$ be a diagram over $\mathbf{Alg}^{ep}$ indexed by a directed poset I. Recall that the colimit of D is the set of I-indexed families $(x_i)_{i \in I}$ such that $x_i \in D_i$ for each $i \in I$ and $x_i = f_{ij}^p(x_j)$ whenever $i \sqsubseteq j$. Let μ be the colimiting cone described earlier. For each i, the elements $K_i = \mu_i^e(D_i)$ are compact in D since an embedding maps compact elements to compact elements (Exercise 8.12). To see that D is algebraic, it suffices to show that $\bigcup_{i \in I} K_i$ is a basis for D. Suppose $x \in D$. For each i, let $M_i = (\downarrow x) \cap \mu_i^p(x)$. Since D_i is algebraic for each $i \in I$, this collection is directed and its lub is $\mu_i^p(x)$. Now,

$$x = (\bigsqcup_{i \in I} \mu_i^e \circ \mu_i^p)(x) = \bigsqcup_{i \in I} \mu_i^e(\mu_i^p(x)) = \bigsqcup_{i \in I} \mu_i^e(\bigsqcup M_i) = \bigsqcup_{i \in I} \bigsqcup_{a \in M_i} \mu_i^e(a)$$

so x is the lub of a directed family of compact elements. From this it follows that the compact elements below x are a directed set with x as a least upper bound. □

10.9 Lemma. *Suppose* $e : D \to E$ *is an embedding and the pair* $x, y \in D$ *has a least upper bound* z *in* D. *Then the pair* $e(x), e(y)$ *has* $e(z)$ *as a least upper bound in* E.

Proof: Clearly $e(x), e(y) \sqsubseteq e(z)$ by monotonicity. Let $p : D \to E$ be the projection corresponding to e and suppose $e(x), e(y) \sqsubseteq z'$. Then $x, y \sqsubseteq p(z')$. This implies that $z \sqsubseteq p(z')$ since z is the lub of x, y. Thus $e(z) \sqsubseteq e(p(z')) \sqsubseteq z'$ so $e(z)$ is the lub. □

10.10 Theorem. *The category* **Bcdom**^{ep} *of bounded complete cpo's and ep-pairs has colimits for directed systems.*

Proof: Let $\Delta = (D_i, f_{ij})_{i \in I}$ be a directed system in **Bcdom**^{ep}. Suppose $\mu : \Delta \to D$ is a colimit and $x, y \in D$ such that $x, y \sqsubseteq z$ for some $z \in D$. To see that the pair x, y has a least upper bound, note that the Colimit Lemma implies that $x = \bigsqcup_{i \in I} \mu_i^e \circ \mu_i^p(x)$ and $y = \bigsqcup_{i \in I} \mu_i^e \circ \mu_i^p(y)$. For each $i \in I$, the pair $\mu_i^p(x), \mu_i^p(y)$ has $\mu_i^p(z)$ as an upper bound, so there is an lub $\mu_i^p(x) \sqcup \mu_i^p(y)$ of this pair in D_i. Now,

$$z' = \bigsqcup_{i \in I} \mu_i^e(\mu_i^p(x) \sqcup \mu_i^p(y)) = \bigsqcup_{i \in I} \mu_i^e \circ \mu_i^p(x) \sqcup \mu_i^e \circ \mu_i^p(y)$$

by Lemma 10.9 and z' is clearly an lub for x, y. The element $\mu_i^e(\perp)$ (for any $i \in I$) is a bottom element of D, so D is bounded complete. That D is algebraic follows from Theorem 10.8 □

Exercises.

10.1 Prove that F-algebras and F-algebra homomorphisms form a category.

10.2 Prove Lemma 10.5.

10.3 Prove that if f is an isomorphism in **Cpo**^{ep}, then $f^e \circ f^p = \mathrm{id}$.

10.4 Prove that the product functor is locally monotone.

10.5 If **C** and **D** are O-categories with locally determined colimits, show that $\mathbf{C} \times \mathbf{D}$ also has locally determined colimits.

10.6 Let $\mu : (D_i, f_{ij})_{i \in I} \to D$ be a cone over a directed diagram and suppose that $i, j \in I$. Suppose that $k, l \in I$ are upper bounds for $\{i, j\}$. Prove that $f_{jk}^p \circ f_{ik}^e = f_{jl}^p \circ f_{il}^e$.

10.7 Complete the demonstration that the function space operator can be extended to a functor between **Cpo**$^{op} \times$ **Cpo** and **Cpo** by the choice of functor action in Equation 10.7.

10.8 Give an example of a projection p and a pair of elements x, y of its domain such that x, y have a least upper bound z, but $p(z)$ is not the least upper bound of $p(x), p(y)$.

10.9 Suppose $p : E \to D$ is a projection and $x, y \in D$ have a greatest lower bound z in D. Show that the pair $p(x), p(y)$ has $p(z)$ as a greatest lower bound in D.

Definition: Suppose D, E are dI-domains and there are stable functions $e : D \to E$ and $p : E \to D$. The pair (e, p) is said to be a *stable embedding-projection pair* if $e \circ p = \mathrm{id}_E$ and $p \circ e \sqsubseteq_s \mathrm{id}_D$. □

10.10 Prove that $f = (f^e, f^p)$ is a stable ep-pair if, and only if, f is an ep-pair and the image of f^e is a downward closed subset. ☐

10.11 Prove that the category of dI-domains and stable ep-pairs has colimits for directed collections. ☐

10.2   Bifinite Domains

An algebraic cpo is a cpo that has a basis of 'finite' elements; that is, if D is an algebraic cpo, then every element $x \in D$ is the least upper bound of a directed family of 'finite' approximations. Is there an analog to this idea at the level of the categories? A relatively straightforward approach to the generalization in the case of cpo's is to consider a cpo to be 'finite' just in the case where it is indeed finite as a set. In this section we explore the class of cpo's that are directed colimits of finite posets in the category of cpo's and ep-pairs. This is the most important and useful of the classes of semantic domains we have not yet discussed.

Definition: A cpo D is *bifinite* if it is the colimit of a directed diagram of finite posets over the category $\mathbf{Cpo}^{ep}$ of cpo's and ep-pairs. ☐

This definition is somewhat indigestible from an order-theoretic perspective, but it is quite handy for categorical analysis. One thing that can be observed almost immediately is that the category **Bif** of bifinite cpo's and continuous functions is cartesian closed. To see why, first let $F : \mathbf{Cpo}^{ep} \to \mathbf{Cpo}^{ep}$ be any continuous functor. If F maps finite posets to finite posets, then it must also map bifinite cpo's to bifinite cpo's, for if D is the colimit of a directed diagram Δ of finite posets, then $F(D)$ is the colimit of $F(\Delta)$. This result extends immediately to functors such as the product and covariant function space that are defined on tuples of arguments. Since **Bif** is a full subcategory of **Cpo** and the terminal object is bifinite, this means that **Bif** is a ccc. A similar argument can be used to establish further closure properties:

10.11 Lemma. *If D and E are bifinite domains, then so are the following posets:* $[D \to E]$, $[D \multimap E]$, $D \times E$, $D \otimes E$, $D + E$, $D \oplus E$, $D_\perp$.

Let us now characterize the order-theoretic properties of bifinite cpo's. One of the ones to be established is the fact that a bifinite cpo is algebraic. A useful concept for thinking about the basis of a bifinite cpo is given in the following definition:

Definition: Let P be a poset. A subset $N \subseteq P$ is said to be *normal* in P and we write $N \lhd P$, if, for every $x \in P$, the set $(\downarrow x) \cap N$ of elements below x in N is directed. ☐

The primary significance of normal subsets comes from their relationship to finitary projections.

10.12 Theorem. *For any domain D there is an isomorphism between the cpo of normal subsets of $\mathsf{K}(D)$, ordered by subset inclusion, and the poset $\mathsf{Fp}(D)$ of finitary projections on D.* ☐

The following lemma asserts a useful property about a way in which a finite poset can be viewed as a 'compact' element from a categorical perspective:

10.13 Lemma. *Suppose $\mu : (D_i, f_{ij})_{i,j \in I} \to D$ is a colimiting cone in $\mathbf{Bif}^{ep}$. If E is a finite poset and there is an ep-pair $f : E \to D$, then there is an ep-pair $g : E \to D_i$ such that $f = \mu_i \circ g$.*

Proof: The image of f^e is a normal subposet $N \lhd \mathsf{K}(D)$ and is therefore in the image of a map μ_i^e. The pair $g = (\mu_i^p \circ f^e, f^p \circ \mu_i^e)$ therefore satisfies the desired properties. ☐

Bifinite domains can be characterized in terms of their bases using normal subsets or in terms of a family of finitary projections.

10.14 Theorem. *Suppose D is a cpo and M is the set of finitary projections $p \in \mathsf{Fp}(D)$ such that $\mathrm{im}(p)$ is a finite set. The following are equivalent:*

1. *D is bifinite.*
2. *M is directed and $\bigsqcup M = \mathrm{id}_D$.*
3. *D is an algebraic cpo and, for any finite set $u \subseteq \mathsf{K}(D)$, there is a finite set N such that $u \subseteq N \lhd \mathsf{K}(D)$.*

Proof: I prove that (1) and (2) are equivalent and leave the proof that (3) is equivalent to these as an exercise for the reader. That (2) implies (1) follows immediately from the fact that M defines a cone of which D is the colimit by the Colimit Theorem. To see that (1) implies (2), suppose that $\mu : (D_i, f_{ij})_{i,j \in I} \to D$ is a colimiting cone where each poset D_i is finite. Then $(\mu_i^e \circ \mu_i^p)_{i \in I}$ is a directed family of finitary projections whose lub is id. If p is a finitary projection with a finite image, then it is compact in the algebraic cpo of finitary projections so $p \sqsubseteq \mathrm{id}$ implies $p \sqsubseteq \mu_i^e \circ \mu_i^p$ for some i. If $p, q \in M$, then there are functions $p' = \mu_i^e \circ \mu_i^p$ and $q' = \mu_j^e \circ \mu_j^p$ such that $p \sqsubseteq p'$ and $q \sqsubseteq q'$. Since I is directed, there is some $k \in I$ with $p', q' \sqsubseteq \mu_k^e \circ \mu_k^p$. Since $\mu_k^e \circ \mu_k^p$ is also an element of M, it follows that M is directed. Since it is also the case that

$$\mathrm{id} = \bigsqcup_{i \in I} \mu_i^e \circ \mu_i^p \sqsubseteq \bigsqcup M \sqsubseteq \mathrm{id},$$

it must be the case that (2) holds. ☐

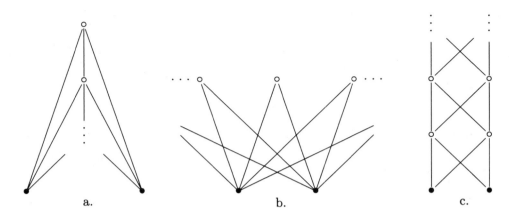

Figure 10.1
Bases for Domains That Are Not Bifinite

To get some idea what the basis of a bifinite domain looks like, it helps to have a definition. Given a poset A and a finite set $u \subseteq A$, an upper bound x for u is *minimal* if, for any upper bound y for u, $y \sqsubseteq x$ implies $y = x$. A set v of minimal upper bounds for u is said to be *complete* if, for every upper bound x for u, there is a $y \in v$ with $y \sqsubseteq x$. Now, let A be the basis of a bifinite domain and suppose $u \subseteq A$ is finite. Then there is a finite $N \lhd A$ with $u \subseteq N$. The set N must contain a complete set of minimal upper bounds for u. This shows the first fact about the basis of a bifinite domain: every finite subset has a complete set of minimal upper bounds. This rules out configurations like the one pictured in Figure 10.1a where the pair of points indicated by the black dots does not have such a complete set of minimal upper bounds. But the set N is *finite* so we have our second fact: every finite subset must have a *finite* complete set of minimal upper bounds. This rules out configurations like the one pictured in Figure 10.1b where the pair of points indicated by black dots has a complete set of minimal upper bounds but not a finite one. However, having finite complete sets of minimal upper bounds for finite subsets is not a sufficient condition for characterizing the bases of bifinite domains. To see why, let A be a poset that has finite complete sets of minimal upper bounds for finite subsets. If $u \subseteq A$ is finite, let

$$\mathcal{U}(u) = \{x \mid x \text{ is a minimal upper bound for some } v \subseteq u\}.$$

Now, if $u \subseteq N \lhd A$, then $\mathcal{U}(u) \subseteq N$. Hence, $\mathcal{U}^n(u) \subseteq N$ for each n. If N is finite, then there must be an n for which $\mathcal{U}^n(u) = \mathcal{U}^{n+1}(u)$. This is a third fact about the basis of bifinite domain: for each finite $u \subseteq A$, $\mathcal{U}^\infty(u) = \bigcup_n \mathcal{U}^n(u)$ is finite. To see what can go wrong, note that $\mathcal{U}^\infty(u)$ is infinite when u is the pair of points indicated by black dots in Figure 10.1c.

10.15 Lemma. Bif^{ep} *has colimits of directed collections.*

Proof: Suppose $\mu : \Delta \to D$ is a directed colimit of bifinite domains where Δ is indexed by I. This D is an algebraic cpo; suppose u is a finite subset of $\mathsf{K}(D)$. The basis of D is a directed union of the images $K_i = \mu_i(\mathsf{K}(D_i))$ of domains in Δ. Hence, there is some $i \in I$ such that $u \subseteq K_i$. Since D_i is bifinite, there is a finite subset $N \lhd K_i$ with $u \subseteq N$. Since $K_i \lhd \mathsf{K}(D)$ it must also be the case that $N \lhd \mathsf{K}(D)$ too. By Lemma 10.14, this shows that D is bifinite. $\qquad\qquad\Box$

10.16 Proposition. *A bounded complete domain is bifinite.*

Proof: Suppose D is bounded complete and $u \subseteq \mathsf{K}(D)$ is a finite subset of the basis of D. Let

$$N = \{x \mid x \text{ is the least upper bound of a finite subset of } u \}.$$

Note that N is finite; we claim that $N \lhd \mathsf{K}(D)$. Suppose x is the least upper bound of a finite set $v \subseteq \mathsf{K}(D)$. Since D is algebraic, there is a directed subset $M \subseteq \mathsf{K}(D)$ such that $x = \bigsqcup M$. But the elements of v are compact. Hence, for every $y \in v$, there is a $y' \in M$ with $y \sqsubseteq y'$. Since M is directed, there is some $z \in M$ that is an upper bound for v. Now, $z \sqsubseteq x$ so $x = z$ and x is therefore compact. This shows that $N \subseteq \mathsf{K}(D)$. Suppose $v \subseteq N$ is bounded, then the least upper bound of v is the same as the least upper bound of the set $\{x \in u \mid x \sqsubseteq y \text{ for some } y \in v\}$ so the least upper bound of v is in N. Now, if $x \in \mathsf{K}(D)$, then $S = (\downarrow x) \cap N$ is bounded. Since S has a least upper bound that lies in S, we conclude that S is directed. $\qquad\qquad\Box$

A universal bifinite domain.

In the previous chapter it was demonstrated that a universal domain can be a convenient tool for interpreting fixed points of operators. Let us now turn to the question of the existence of universal domains. An *ω-bifinite domain* is a bifinite domain with a countable basis; following the original notation, let us write **SFP** for the category of pointed ω-bifinite domain and continuous functions. The letters stand for **S**equence of **F**inite **P**osets; a name partly justified by the following fact:

10.17 Lemma. *A bifinite domain D has a countable basis if, and only if, it is the colimit of an ω-chain of finite posets.* $\qquad\qquad\Box$

The proof is left for the reader. As an immediate corollary of the lemma, note that **SFP** is a ccc since it must be closed under products and function spaces. Let us write **SFP**^{ep} for the category of pointed ω-bifinite domains and ep-pairs. For the purposes of this section, suppose that **C** is a non-trivial full subcategory of **SFP**^{ep} that satisfies the following two closure properties:

1. the colimit of an ω-chain of objects of **C** is an object of **C**, and

2. if there is an ep-pair $f : D \to E$ between two objects in **SFP**^{ep} and E is an object in **C**, then so is D. In other words, every ω-bifinite domain embedded in an object of **C** is also an object in **C**.

In particular, this property is satisfed by **SFP**^{ep} itself and by the category of bc-domains with countable bases. The goal is to demonstrate a method for finding a canonical domain U in **C** with the property that, for each object D of **C**, there is an ep-pair $f : D \to U$. Actually we do better than this and work with a stronger property that defines U up to isomorphism.

Definition: An object $U \in$ **C** is *saturated in* **C** if, for every pair of finite domains M, N and ep-pairs $f : M \to U$ and $g : M \to N$, there is a (not necessarily unique) ep-pair h that completes the following diagram:

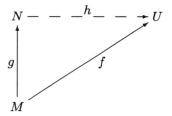

$\square$

A saturated domain has the property we seek:

10.18 Lemma. *If U is saturated in* **C***, then, for each object D of* **C***, there is an ep-pair* $f : D \to U$.

Proof: Let D be an object of **C**. Since D is ω-bifinite, there is an ω-chain $(D_n, f_n)_{n \in \omega}$ of which D is a colimit and such that each D_n is finite. We may assume that $D_0 = \mathbb{U}$ is the initial object of **C**. Since this is initial, there is an ep-pair $\mu_0 : D_0 \to U$. Suppose we are given an arrow $\mu_n : D_n \to U$. Because U is saturated, there is an arrow μ_{n+1} that makes the following diagram commute.

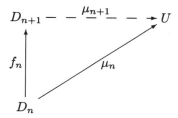

The maps $(\mu_n)_{n \in \omega}$ define a cone between $(D_n, f_n)_{n \in \omega}$ and U. Since D is colimiting, there is an ep-pair $f : D \to U$. □

Moreover, a saturated domain is *canonical* in the sense that it is uniquely determined up to isomorphism. To prove this we employ a technique for demonstrating an isomorphism that is known as a 'back-and-forth' argument. The idea is this: given two countable posets P and Q, we define a familiy of isomorphisms $f_n \colon P_n \cong Q_n$ where $n \in \omega$ such that each f_{n+1} extends f_n and P_n, Q_n are finite subposets of P, Q respectively. If these isomorphisms are constructed in such a way that the union of the subposets P_n is P and the union of the subposets Q_n is Q, then the union of these isomorphisms is an isomorphism between P and Q. This property is ensured by enumerating the elements of each of the two posets and passing 'back-and-forth' between the enumerations to build the needed subposets and finite isomorphisms.

10.19 Lemma. *If U is a saturated object in* **C***, then for every finite $M \triangleleft K(U)$ and ep-pair $f : M \to N$ into a finite poset N, there is a poset $N' \triangleleft K(U)$ such that $N \cong N'$.* □

10.20 Theorem. *If a category of domains has a saturated object, then it is unique up to isomorphism.*

Proof: Suppose that U and V are saturated objects of **C**. Let $u_0, u_1, \ldots$ and $v_0, v_1, \ldots$ be enumerations of the bases of U and V respectively. Assume that $u_0 = \perp_U$ and $v_0 = \perp_V$. Define an isomorphism $f_0 \colon \{u_0\} \cong \{v_0\}$. Suppose now that we have finite posets $L \triangleleft K(U)$ and $L' \triangleleft K(V)$ such that there is an isomorphism $f_{n-1} \colon L \cong L'$. Suppose further that $\{u_0, \ldots, u_{n-1}\} \subseteq L$ and $\{v_0, \ldots, v_{n-1}\} \subseteq L'$. We wish to extend the isormorphism f_{n-1} to an isomorphism $f_n \colon M \cong M'$ where $M \triangleleft K(U)$ and $M' \triangleleft K(V)$ are finite and $u_n \in M$ and $v_n \in M'$. Now, we know that there is a finite poset $N \triangleleft K(U)$ with $L \cup \{u_n\} \subseteq N$. From the inverse of the isomorphism f_{n-1} we can build an ep-pair $f : L' \to N$. Since V is saturated, there is a poset $N' \triangleleft K(V)$ and an isomorphism $g \colon N' \cong N$. To complete the argument, we add $\{v_n\}$ to N' and find a subset $M' \subseteq \mathsf{K}(V)$ such that $\{v_n\} \cup N' \subseteq M'$. Since U is saturated, we find an isomorphic copy M of M' inside U, containing L, such that the isomorphism $g^{-1}\colon N \cong N'$ is extended to an isomorphism $f_n\colon M \cong M'$. In this way we obtain a sequence $f_0, f_1, \ldots$ of isomorphisms whose union is an isomorphism between $\mathsf{K}(U)$ and $\mathsf{K}(V)$. This isomorphism extends to an isomorphism between U and V. $\qquad\square$

Having established these pleasing properties of saturated domains, there is still a question of when there *exists* such a domain. The next goal is to demonstrate a set of conditions under which such a domain can be constructed. A saturated domain can be constructed as the colimit of an ω-chain of finite domains. The trick is to build this up using the following notion:

Definition: An *increment* in $\mathbf{C}$ is an ep-pair $f : M \to M'$ between finite posets M, M' in $\mathbf{C}$ such that M' has exactly one more element than M. $\qquad\square$

Definition: A *finite saturation* in $\mathbf{C}$ is an ep-pair $s : D \to D^+$ such that, for every increment $f : M \to M'$ in $\mathbf{C}$ and embedding $g : M \to D$, there is a (not necessarily unique) ep-pair h that completes the following diagram:

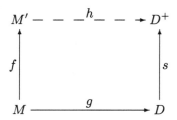

$\qquad\square$

10.21 Lemma. *If $f : M \to N$ is an ep-pair between finite posets M and N where N has at least one more element than M, then there is an increment $h : M \to M'$ and an ep-pair $g : M' \to N$ such that $f = g \circ h$.*

Proof: Consider the image $N' = f^e(M) \lhd N$. Choose a maximal element $x \in N - N'$ and let $M' = N' \cup \{x\}$. It is easy to see that $M' \lhd N$. Constructing the desired maps g and h from f is left as an exercise. $\qquad\square$

10.22 Theorem. *If, for every finite D in $\mathbf{C}$ there is a finite saturation $f : D \to D^+$ in $\mathbf{C}$, then there is a saturated domain in $\mathbf{C}$.*

Proof: Let $U_0 = \mathbb{U}$ and given U_n, let $f_n : U_n \to U_{n+1}$ be a finite saturation. Let $\mu : (U_n, f_n)_{n \in \omega} \to U$ be a colimiting cone. The colimit U is an object in $\mathbf{C}$ since $\mathbf{C}$ is closed under colimits of ω-chains. To show that it is saturated in $\mathbf{C}$, suppose $f : M \to U$ and $g : M \to N$ are ep-pairs where M, N are finite. We must demonstrate an ep-pair h to complete the following diagram:

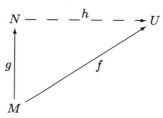

The demonstration that there is such an arrow goes by induction on the difference $k - l$ where k is the number of elements in N and l the number in M. If this number is 0, then g is an isomorphism and the ep-pair $f \circ g^{-1}$ will be satisfactory. Suppose the result is known for any p and M' if this number is less than j where j is bigger than 0. Now, by Lemma 10.21, there is an increment $g' : M \to M'$ and an ep-pair $p : M' \to N$ such that $g = p \circ g'$. By Lemma 10.13, there is an $n \in \omega$ and an ep-pair $k : M \to U_n$ such that $f = \mu_n \circ k$. Since f_n is a finite saturation, there is an ep-pair h' that completes the following diagram:

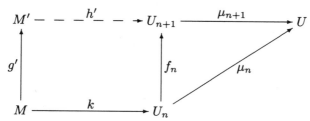

And, by the induction hypothesis, there is an arrow h such that

$$
\begin{array}{ccc}
N & \text{-- -- } \overset{h}{\text{-- --}} \text{ -- } & U \\
\uparrow p & \nearrow \mu_{n+1} \circ h' & \\
M' & &
\end{array}
$$

Chasing the diagrams we calculate

$$f = \mu_n \circ k = \mu_{n+1} \circ f_n \circ k = \mu_{n+1} \circ h' \circ g' = h \circ p \circ g' = h \circ g,$$

which is the desired conclusion.   ☐

Of course, we still have not demonstrated that there *are* finite saturations in **C**. Whether this is the case will depend entirely on what **C** is. There are two cases of primary interest to us here, although there are other important examples. Let me treat the case in which **C** is **SFP**^{ep} itself and leave for an exercise the case in which it is instead the category of bc-domains with countable bases.

Given a finite poset D, define $M(D)$ to be the set of pairs $(x, u) \in D \times \mathcal{P}_f(D)$ such that $x \sqsubseteq z$ for every $z \in u$. Define a pre-ordering on $M(D)$ by setting $(x, u) \subsetsim (y, v)$ if, and only if, there is a $z \in u$ such that $z \sqsubseteq y$. Now, take D^+ to be the (principal) ideals over $(M(D), \subsetsim)$ ordered by subset inclusion, and define $s' : D \to D^+$ by taking $s'(x)$ to be the principal ideal in $(M(D), \subsetsim)$ generated by the pair $(x, \{x\})$. This map is an embedding, so there is an ep-pair $s : D \to D^+$ with $s^e = s'$. In particular, s is a finite saturation in **SFP**^{ep}. To see why, suppose we are given an increment $f : M \to M'$ for a finite poset M and an ep-pair $g : M \to D$. To simplify the notation somewhat, assume that f^e and g^e are inclusions so that $M \lhd M'$ and $M \lhd D$. There is exactly one point $p \in M' - M$; to what element of D^+ does it correspond? In M there are the points greater than p and those less than p. The points less than p are a directed collection; since M is finite and $M \lhd M'$, this means that there is a largest element x in $M \cap {\downarrow}p$. If u is the set of points in M that are greater than p and we define $h' : M' \to D^+$ as follows:

$$h'(y) = \begin{cases} s'(y) & \text{if } y \in M \\ (x, u) & \text{if } x = p, \end{cases}$$

then h' is an embedding and there is an ep-pair h with $h^e = h'$ such that the following diagram commutes

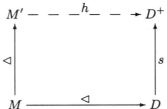

The construction of the saturated bifinite domain $\mathbb{V}$ is done by taking a colimit of finite saturations. It is possible to get a picture of the first few steps of this colimit. At the first step take the domain $\mathbb{U}$ containing only the single point $\perp$. At the second step, $\mathbb{U}^+$, there are elements $a = (\perp, \{\perp\})$ and $b = (\perp, \emptyset)$ with $a \subsetsim b$. At the third step there are five elements,

$$(a, \{a\}), \ (a, \{b\}), \ (b, \{b\}), \ (b, \emptyset), \ (a, \emptyset)$$

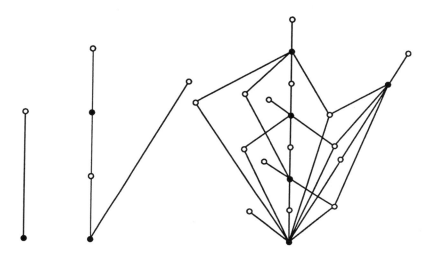

Figure 10.2
The Saturated SFP Domain

which form the partially ordered set $\mathbb{U}^{++}$ pictured in Figure 10.2. Note that there is another element $(a, \{a, b\}) \in M(\mathbb{U}^+)$, but this satisfies $(a, \{a, b\}) \sqsubseteq (a, \{a\})$ and $(a, \{a\}) \sqsubseteq (a, \{a, b\})$ so these elements are identified in the picture. The next step $\mathbb{U}^{+++}$ has 20 elements (up to equivalence in the sense just mentioned) and it is also pictured in Figure 10.2. It should be noted that each stage of the construction is *embedded* in the next one by the map $x \mapsto (x, \{x\})$. The closed circles in the figure are intended to give a hint of how this embedding looks.

Exercises.

10.12 Prove Theorem 10.12.

10.13 Prove that (2) and (3) are equivalent in Theorem 10.14.

Definition: An object A in a category $\mathbf{C}$ is *compact* if, whenever

1. $\mu : \Delta \to D$ is a colimit such that Δ is a diagram indexed by a directed poset I, and
2. there is an arrow $f : A \to D$,

then there is an $i \in I$ such that there is a unique arrow $g : A \to D_i$ satisfying $f = \mu_i \circ g$. □

10.14 Show that a finite poset in the category $\mathbf{Cpo}^{ep}$ is compact.

10.15 Complete the proof of Lemma 10.21 by providing explicit definitions of the ep-pairs g, h.

10.16 Let D be a bc-domain. Prove that there is a finitary projection $\wp$ from $[D \to D]$ onto $\mathsf{Fp}(D)$. (Hint: given a continuous function $f : D \to D$, define $S_f = \{x \in \mathsf{K}(D) \mid x \sqsubseteq f(x)\}$ and show that $f \mapsto S_f$ defines the desired finitary projection.)

10.17* Suppose D is a finite poset that is bounded complete. Define D^+ to be the set of pairs (x, u) such that

1. $u = \uparrow u$,
2. $x \sqsubseteq y$ for each $y \in u$, and
3. $\{x\} \cup u$ is closed under non-empty meets.

Define a relation on D^+ by taking

$$(x, u) \sqsubseteq_{\sim} (y, v) \text{ iff } y \in u \text{ or } u \subseteq v.$$

Prove that D^+ with this ordering is a poset and that the map $x \mapsto (x, \uparrow x)$ is a finite saturation in the category whose objects are bc-domains with a countable basis and whose arrows are ep-pairs. Conclude that there is a saturated object in that category.

10.3   Adjunctions and Powerdomains

One of the central motivating constructions of category theory is the notion of an *adjunction*. The construction was originally introduced to provide an abstraction that covered a wide range of familiar examples of mathematical constructions. This abstraction has been an especially useful tool in the semantics of programming languages as well. Characterizing an operator on semantic domains as an adjoint often draws one's attention to the most basic properties, allowing other properties to be derived from these basics. Experience has shown that the operators associated with an adjoint situation are often exactly the primitives needed for describing the semantics of a language in terms of the operator whose categorical definition is being given. Throughout this book new constructs have been given together with their characterizations as adjoints—although the terminology of adjoints has not yet been formally presented. So we can view ourselves as approaching the definition of the construction in much the same way as the pioneers of category theory did, with an eye to explaining what lies behind several different but somehow related phenomena.

We have often encounted isomorphisms such as $A \times (B \times C) \cong (A \times B) \times C$ whose proof required us to give a family of isomorphisms indexed by the objects A, B, C. Athough it was not emphasized, this choice of isomorphism was always given 'uniformly' in a sense because it did not depend on arbitrary choices or particular cases for the objects involved.

This uniformity is captured formally in the following concept, which can be viewed as the definition of an arrow between functors.

Definition: Suppose we are given functors $F, G : \mathbf{C} \to \mathbf{D}$ and an operator η that associates with each object A of $\mathbf{C}$ an arrow $\eta_A : F(A) \to G(A)$. The operator η is said to be a *natural transformation,* and we write $\eta : F \to G$ if the following diagram commutes for any pair of objects A, B of $\mathbf{C}$ and arrow $f : A \to B$:

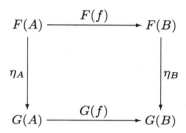

We have already encounted many examples of natural transformations. In most cases, the subscript on the η was suppressed to enhance readability. Consider, for example, the lift operation $D_\perp$ that adds a new bottom element to a cpo D. For each cpo D we defined a non-strict map up_D from D into $D_\perp$ that maps elements of D to their lifted counterparts. For each continuous function $f : D \to E$, a map $f_\perp$ was also defined in such a way that the diagram

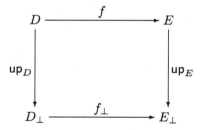

commutes. If we take $L(f)$ to be $f_\perp$ for each continuous function f and $L(D) = D_\perp$ for each cpo D, then this is a functor and up can be viewed as a natural transformation between the identity functor id and L.

We have captured an important categorical aspect of the arrows up and the lifting operation. But we have still not isolated the key idea implicit in Lemma 6.8, which appears to express a categorical property of lifting and up. Note for example that Lemma 6.8 says there is a unique strict continuous function that completes the diagram. This assertion seems to have nothing to do with the fact that **up** is a natural transformation. There is another central categorical concept lying at the bottom of this lemma. To draw out this idea clearly, let me begin by defining the key idea in categorical generality and then focusing on how the idea is related to Lemma 6.8 and the fact that $D \mapsto \mathbf{up}_D$ is a natural transformation.

Definition: Let $\mathbf{C}$ and $\mathbf{D}$ be categories and suppose $F : \mathbf{C} \to \mathbf{D}$ and $U : \mathbf{D} \to \mathbf{C}$ are functors. Then F is a *left adjoint* and U is a *right adjoint* if there is a natural transformation $\eta : \mathsf{id} \to U \circ F$ between the identity functor on $\mathbf{C}$ and the functor $U \circ F$ such that, for each object B and arrow $f : A \to U(B)$, there is a unique arrow f' such that the following diagram commutes:

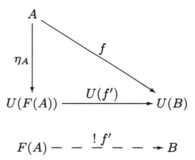

In this case we say that the triple (F, U, η) is an *adjunction*. The natural transformation η is called the *unit* of the adjunction. □

The current statement of Lemma 6.8 obscures the assertion of the adjoint property to some extent because it does not emphasize the distinction between the arrows in the category of strict continuous functions and the arrows coming from the category with all continuous functions as arrows. So, to provide a completely precise restatement, let $\mathbf{Cpo}^\circ$ be the category of cpo's and strict continuous functors, and let $U : \mathbf{Cpo}^\circ \to \mathbf{Cpo}$ be the inclusion functor from this category into the category of cpo's and continuous functions.

6.8* Lemma: Given cpo's D and E and continuous function $f : D \to U(E)$, there is a unique strict continuous function $f^\dagger$ that completes the following diagram:

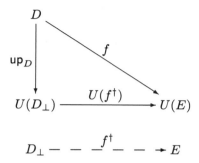

A more succinct way of saying this is the following lemma:

6.8** Lemma: The lift functor $(\cdot)_\perp$ is left adjoint to the inclusion functor from $\mathbf{Cpo}^\circ$ into $\mathbf{Cpo}$ with up as the unit of the adjunction.   ☐

Adjoints can be viewed as a generalization of the notions of embedding-projection pairs and closure-section pairs that we have studied before. Suppose P and Q are posets with monotone functions $f : P \to Q$ and $g : Q \to P$. Then (f, g) is said to be a *galois connection* when

$$f \circ g \sqsubseteq \mathrm{id}_Q \text{ and } g \circ f \sqsupseteq \mathrm{id}_P.$$

It is obvious that an embedding f and corresponding projection g satisfy this condition and that a closure f and corresponding section g will also satisfy it. It is only a little less obvious that this definition characterizes f and g as left and right adjoints when viewed as functors between categories P and Q. Suppose that (f, g, η) is an adjunction where η is a natural transformation between id_P and $g \circ f$. The fact that η is a natural transformation is equivalent to the inequality $g \circ f \sqsupseteq \mathrm{id}_P$. The adjoint condition says that if $x \sqsubseteq g(y)$ then $f(x) \sqsubseteq y$. Taking $x = g(y)$ then yields the conclusion that (f, g) is a galois connection. Conversely, to see the adjoint condition based on the assumption that (f, g) is a galois connection, suppose $x \sqsubseteq g(y)$. Then $f(x) \sqsubseteq f(g(y)) \sqsubseteq y$ by monotonicity and the assumption that $f \circ g \sqsubseteq \mathrm{id}$.

Powerdomains.

Let us now turn our attention to another collection of operators on domains. Just as we have defined a domain-theoretic analog to the *function space*, we will now define a domain-theoretic analog to the *powerset operation*. Actually, we will produce three such operators. In the domain theory literature these are called *powerdomains*. They were introduced as a tool for modeling the semantics of non-deterministic programs. Aside from a brief description of how they are related to this application I will focus my attention on using them as an illustration of categorical techniques for the semantics of programming languages. For any set S, let $\mathcal{P}_f^*(S)$ be the set of finite non-empty subsets of S.

Definition: Given a poset $(A, \sqsubseteq)$, define a pre-ordering $\sqsubseteq^\sharp$ on $\mathcal{P}_f^*(A)$ as follows,

$$u \precsim^\sharp v \text{ if and only if } (\forall y \in v)(\exists x \in u).\ x \sqsubseteq y.$$

Dually, define a pre-ordering $\sqsubseteq^\flat$ on $\mathcal{P}_f^*(A)$ by

$$u \precsim^\flat v \text{ if and only if } (\forall x \in u)(\exists y \in v).\ x \sqsubseteq y.$$

And define $\sqsubseteq^\natural$ on $\mathcal{P}_f^*(A)$ by

$$u \precsim^\natural v \text{ if and only if } u \precsim^\sharp v \text{ and } u \precsim^\flat v.$$

If D is a domain, then let $\mathsf{C}(D)$ be the domain of ideals over $(\mathcal{P}_f^*(\mathsf{K}(D)), \precsim^\natural)$. We call $\mathsf{C}(D)$ the *convex powerdomain* of D. Similarly, define the *upper powerdomain* $\mathsf{U}(D)$ and the *lower powerdomain* $\mathsf{L}(D)$ to be the domains of ideals over $(\mathcal{P}_f^*(\mathsf{K}(D)), \precsim^\sharp)$ and $(\mathcal{P}_f^*(\mathsf{K}(D)), \precsim^\flat))$ respectively. $\qquad\Box$

Example: *Lower Powerdomain of* $\mathbb{N}_\perp$. Since $\mathsf{K}(\mathbb{N}_\perp) = \mathbb{N}_\perp$, the lower powerdomain of $\mathbb{N}_\perp$ is the set of ideals over the pre-order $(\mathcal{P}_f^*(\mathbb{N}_\perp), \precsim^\flat)$. To see what such an ideal must look like, note first that $u \cup \{\perp\} \precsim^\flat u$ and $u \precsim^\flat u \cup \{\perp\}$ for any $u \in \mathcal{P}_f^*(\mathbb{N}_\perp)$. From this fact it is already possible to see why $\precsim^\flat$ is usually only a *pre-order* and not a poset. Now, if u and v both contain $\perp$, then $v \precsim^\flat u$ iff $v \supseteq u$. Hence we may identify an ideal $x \in \mathsf{L}(\mathbb{N}_\perp)$ with the union $\bigcup x$ of all the elements in x. Thus $\mathsf{L}(\mathbb{N}_\perp)$ is isomorphic to the domain $\mathcal{P}\mathbb{N}$ of all subsets of $\mathbb{N}$ under subset inclusion. $\qquad\Box$

Example: *Upper Powerdomain of* $\mathbb{N}_\perp$. Note that if u and v are finite non-empty subsets of $\mathbb{N}_\perp$ and $\perp \in v$, then $v \precsim^\sharp u$. In particular, any ideal x in $\mathsf{U}(\mathbb{N}_\perp)$ contains all of the finite subsets v of $\mathbb{N}_\perp$ with $\perp \in v$. So, let us say that a set $u \in \mathcal{P}_f^*(\mathbb{N}_\perp)$ is *non-trivial* if it does not contain $\perp$ and an ideal $x \in \mathsf{U}(\mathbb{N}_\perp)$ is non-trivial if there is a non-trivial $u \in x$. Now, if u and v are non-trivial, then $v \precsim^\sharp u$ iff $u \subseteq v$. Therefore, if an ideal x is non-trivial, then it is the principal ideal generated by the intersection of its non-trivial elements! The smaller this set is, the larger is the ideal x. Hence, the non-trivial ideals in the powerdomain (ordered by subset inclusion) correspond to finite subsets of $\mathbb{N}$ (ordered by superset inclusion). If we now throw in the unique trivial ideal, we can see that $\mathsf{U}(\mathbb{N}_\perp)$ is isomorphic to the domain of sets $\{\mathbb{N}\} \cup \mathcal{P}_f^*(\mathbb{N})$ ordered by superset inclusion. $\qquad\Box$

Example: *Convex Powerdomain of* $\mathbf{N}_\perp$. If $u, v \in \mathcal{P}_f^*(\mathbf{N}_\perp)$, then $v \mathrel{\underset{\sim}{\sqsubseteq}}^\natural u$ iff

1. $\perp \in v$ and $v \subseteq u \cup \{\perp\}$, or
2. $u = v$

Hence, if x is an ideal and there is a set $u \in x$ with $\perp \notin u$, then x is the principal ideal generated by u. No two distinct principal ideals like this will be comparable. On the other hand, if x is an ideal with $\perp \in u$ for each $u \in x$, then $x \subseteq y$ for an arbitrary ideal y iff $\bigcup x \subseteq \bigcup y$. Thus the convex powerdomain of $\mathbf{N}_\perp$ corresponds to the set of finite, non-empty subsets of $\mathbf{N}$ unioned with the set of arbitrary subsets of $\mathbf{N}_\perp$ that contain $\perp$. The ordering on these sets is like the pre-ordering $\underset{\sim}{\sqsubseteq}^\natural$ but extended to include infinite sets. □

If $f : D \to E$ is continuous, we can define a continuous function $\mathsf{C}(f)$ using Lemma 5.24 by defining a monotone function from the compact elements of $\mathsf{C}(D)$ into $\mathsf{C}(E)$. Let $s = \downarrow u$ be the principal ideal generated by a finite non-empty subset $u \subseteq \mathsf{K}(D)$. Let $f(u) = \{f(a) \mid a \in u\}$. Then

$$\mathsf{C}(f)(s) = \{v \in \mathcal{P}_f^*(\mathsf{K}(E)) \mid v \mathrel{\underset{\sim}{\sqsubseteq}}^\natural f(u) \text{ for some } u \in s\}.$$

Similar definitions can be given for the upper and lower powerdomains. If $s, t \in \mathsf{C}(D)$, then we define a binary operation

$$s \uplus t = \{w \mid w \mathrel{\underset{\sim}{\sqsubseteq}}^\natural u \cup v \text{ for some } u \in s \text{ and } v \in t\}.$$

This set is an ideal, and the function $\uplus : \mathsf{C}(D) \times \mathsf{C}(D) \to \mathsf{C}(D)$ is continuous. Similar facts apply when $\uplus$ is defined in an analogous way for $\mathsf{U}(D)$ and $\mathsf{L}(D)$. Now, if $x \in D$, define

$$\{\!\!|x|\!\!\} = \{u \in \mathcal{P}_f^*(\mathsf{K}(D)) \mid u \mathrel{\underset{\sim}{\sqsubseteq}}^\natural \{a\} \text{ for some compact } a \sqsubseteq x\}.$$

This forms an ideal, and $\{\!\!|\cdot|\!\!\} : D \to \mathsf{C}(D)$ is a continuous function called the *powerdomain singleton*. When one replaces $\underset{\sim}{\sqsubseteq}^\natural$ in this definition by $\underset{\sim}{\sqsubseteq}^\sharp$ or $\underset{\sim}{\sqsubseteq}^\flat$, then similar facts apply.

Given the operators $\uplus$ and $\{\!\!|\cdot|\!\!\}$, we may say that a point $x \in D$ for a domain D is an 'element' of a set s in a powerdomain of D if $\{\!\!|x|\!\!\} \uplus s = s$. If s and t lie in a powerdomain of D, then s is a 'subset' of t if $s \uplus t = t$. Care must be taken, however, not to confuse 'sets' in a powerdomain with sets in the usual sense. The relations of 'element' and 'subset' described above will have different properties in the three different powerdomains. Moreover, it may be the case that s is a 'subset' of t without it being the case that $s \subseteq t$!

To get some idea how non-deterministic programs are intrepreted in domains, let us discuss non-deterministic partial functions from $\mathbf{N}$ to $\mathbf{N}$. As we have noted before, there is a correspondence between partial functions from N to N and strict functions $f : \mathsf{N}_\perp \multimap \mathsf{N}_\perp$. These may be thought of as the meanings of 'deterministic' programs, because the output of a program is uniquely determined by its input (that is, the meaning is a partial *function*). Suppose, however, that we are dealing with programs that permit some *finite non-determinism*. Then we may wish to think of a program as having as its meaning a function $f : \mathsf{N}_\perp \to P(\mathsf{N}_\perp)$ where P is one of the powerdomains. For example, if a program may give a 1 or a 2 as an output when given a 0 as input, then we will want the meaning f of this program to satisfy $f(0) = \{\!\!\{1\}\!\!\} \cup \{\!\!\{2\}\!\!\} =_{\mathrm{def}} \{\!\!\{1,2\}\!\!\}$. The three different powerdomains reflect three different views of how to relate the various possible program behaviors in the case of divergence. The upper powerdomain identifies program behaviors that *may* diverge. For example, if program P_1 can give output 1 or diverge on any of its inputs, then it will be identified with the program Q that diverges everywhere, since $\{\!\!\{1, \perp\}\!\!\} = \perp = \{\!\!\{\perp\}\!\!\}$ in $\mathsf{U}(\mathsf{N}_\perp)$. However, program P_2, which always gives 1 as its output (on inputs other than $\perp$), will *not* have the same meaning as P_1 and $\lambda x.\,\perp$. On the other hand, if the lower powerdomain is used in the interpretation of these programs, then P_1 and P_2 will be given the same meaning since $\{\!\!\{1, \perp\}\!\!\} = \{\!\!\{1\}\!\!\}$ in $\mathsf{L}(\mathsf{N}_\perp)$. However, P_1 and P_2 will not have the same meaning as the always divergent program Q since $\{\!\!\{1, \perp\}\!\!\} \neq \perp$ in the lower powerdomain. Finally, in the convex powerdomain, *none* of the programs P_1, P_2, Q have the same meaning since $\{\!\!\{1, \perp\}\!\!\}$, $\{\!\!\{1\}\!\!\}$ and $\{\!\!\{\perp\}\!\!\}$ are all distinct in $\mathsf{C}(\mathsf{N}_\perp)$.

Powerdomains as adjunctions.

These three operators $\mathsf{U}(\cdot)$, $\mathsf{L}(\cdot)$ and $\mathsf{C}(\cdot)$, may not seem to be the most obvious choices for the computable analog of the powerset operator. But when one views the constructions categorically in terms of adjunctions they appear to be quite natural. The first step is to clarify the categories involved.

Definition: A *continuous semi-lattice* is a cpo D together with a continuous binary function $* : D \times D \to D$ that satisfies the following equations:

1. associativity: $(r * s) * t = r * (s * t)$
2. commutativity: $r * s = s * r$
3. idempotence: $s * s = s$.

A *homomorphism* between continuous semi-lattices D and E is a continuous function $f : D \to E$ such that $f(s * t) = f(s) * f(t)$ for all $s, t \in D$. A *semi-lattice domain* is a continuous semi-lattice $(D, *)$ where D is an algebraic cpo. $\square$

Continuous semi-lattices and continuous homomorphisms form a category of which the semi-lattice domains are a full subcategory. Let us write **Sld** for the category of semi-

lattice domains and continuous homomorphisms. The following fact about the powerdomains follows immediately from their definitions and facts about sets:

10.23 Lemma. *Let D be a domain. Each of the structures $(\mathsf{U}(D),\sqcup)$, $(\mathsf{L}(D),\sqcup)$, and $(\mathsf{C}(D),\sqcup)$ is a semi-lattice domain.*

Moreover, it can be shown that each of the operators $\mathsf{C},\mathsf{U},\mathsf{L}$ can be viewed as functors
from **Alg** to **Sld**. If we let U be the 'forgetful' functor from **Sld** to **Alg** that simply takes
the underlying domain of a semi-lattice domain (and has the identity action on arrows),
then we have the following:

10.24 Lemma. *For each of the powerdomain functors P, the continuous functions $\{\!\cdot\!\}$
define a natural transformation between the identity functor on **Alg** and the functor
$U \circ P$.*

Proof: Suppose $f : D \to E$ is a continuous function and $x \in D$. To save clutter, let u, v
range over finite non-empty sets of compact elements in the following calculation:

$$
\begin{aligned}
\mathsf{C}(f)(\{\!x\!\}) &= \{u \mid u \sqsubseteq^\natural f(v) \text{ for some } v \in \{\!x\!\}\} \\
&= \{u \mid u \sqsubseteq^\natural f(v) \text{ for some } v \text{ such that } a \sqsubseteq x \text{ for each } a \in v\} \\
&= \{u \mid a \sqsubseteq f(x) \text{ for each } a \in u\} \\
&= \{u \mid u \sqsubseteq^\natural \{a\} \text{ for some } a \sqsubseteq f(x)\} \\
&= \{\!f(x)\!\}
\end{aligned}
$$

$\square$

The key result then is the following:

10.25 Theorem. *The convex powerdomain functor is left adjoint to the forgetful functor
from **Sld** to **Alg** with the powerdomain singleton operation as the unit of the adjunction.
In other words, for any domain D and semi-lattice domain E, if $f : D \to U(E)$ is continuous, then there is a unique homomorphism f' such that*

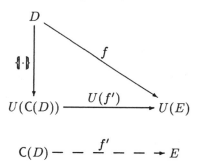

Proof: By Lemma 5.24, we need only find a monotone function from the basis of $C(D)$ into E in order to define f'. To see what this function might be, note that compact elements of $C(D)$ have the form of principal ideals $\downarrow u$ under the ordering $\sqsubseteq^{\natural}$ where $u = \{x_1, \ldots, x_n\} \subseteq K(D)$. Since f' is a homomorphism, we must have

$$f'(\downarrow u) = f'(\{x_1\} \sqcup \cdots \sqcup \{x_n\}) = f'(\{x_1\}) * \cdots * f'(\{x_n\}) = f(x_1) * \cdots * f(x_n)$$

where parentheses on expressions involving $*$ are dropped because of the associativity axiom and the order in which u is listed is irrelevant because of the commutativity axiom. The last expression in this sequence of equations is independent of f', so, if there is a function having the necessary properties, it must be defined as the unique continuous extension of this definition to all of $C(D)$. This proves the uniqueness of f' provided we are able to demonstrate that the equation above does indeed define a monotone function. The proof of existence depends on the semi-lattice axioms, of course. Given finite subsets $u, v \subseteq K(D)$, we must show that $f'(\downarrow u) \sqsubseteq f'(\downarrow v)$ if $\downarrow u \subseteq \downarrow v$. The latter inclusion holds just in the case where $u \sqsubseteq^{\natural} v$. Given $u = \{x_1, \ldots, x_n\}$ and $v = \{y_1, \ldots, y_m\}$, we must use this to show that

$$f(x_1) * \cdots * f(x_n) \sqsubseteq f(y_1) * \cdots * f(y_m). \tag{10.8}$$

Let us carry out this proof by induction on the size n of the finite set u. Suppose that $n = 1$. Since $\{x_1\} \sqsubseteq^{\natural} v$, each element of v is bigger than x_1. Hence

$$f(x_1) = \underbrace{f(x_1) * \cdots * f(x_1)}_{m \text{ copies}} \sqsubseteq f(y_1) * \cdots * f(y_m)$$

by the idempotence axiom for $*$ and the monotonicity of f and $*$. Suppose that 10.8 is known for sets with fewer than n elements where $n > 1$. Since $u \sqsubseteq^{\natural} v$, there is an element of v such that is bigger than x_1. For the sake of simplicity, assume that this element is y_1. There are two cases to consider. If y_1 is not bigger than any of the elements $x_2, \ldots, x_n$, then

$$f(x_2) * \cdots * f(x_n) \sqsubseteq f(y_2) * \cdots * f(y_n)$$

by the inductive hypothesis since $u - \{x_1\} \sqsubseteq^{\natural} v - \{y_1\}$. Hence 10.8 follows from the monotonicity of f and $*$. On the other hand, if y_1 *is* bigger than one of the elements $x_2, \ldots, x_n$, then

$$f(x_2) * \cdots * f(x_n) \sqsubseteq f(y_1) * f(y_2) * \cdots * f(y_n)$$

by the inductive hypothesis and the fact that $u - \{x_1\} \sqsubseteq^{\natural} v$. In either of these two cases, the monotonicity of f and $*$ allows us to conclude that 10.8 holds. $\qquad\square$

Closure properties.

Two of the powerdomains preserve the property of bounded completeness:

10.26 Lemma. *If D is a bounded-complete domain then so are $\mathsf{U}D$ and $\mathsf{L}D$.*

Proof: We leave for the reader the exercise of showing that a domain D is bounded complete if and only if every finite bounded subset of its basis has a least upper bound. To see that $\mathsf{L}D$ is bounded complete, just note that, for any pair of sets $u, v \in \mathcal{P}_f^*(\mathsf{K}(D))$, the ideal generated by their union $u \cup v$ is the least upper bound in $\mathsf{L}D$ for the ideals generated by u and v. To see that $\mathsf{U}D$ is bounded complete, suppose $u, v, w \in \mathcal{P}_f^*(\mathsf{K}(D))$ with $u \sqsubseteq^\sharp w$ and $v \sqsubseteq^\sharp w$. Let w' be the set of elements $z \in \mathsf{K}(D)$ such that there are elements $x \in u$ and $y \in v$ and z is the least upper bound of $\{x, y\}$. The set w' is non-empty because $\{u, v\}$ is bounded. Moreover, it is not hard to see that $w' \sqsubseteq^\sharp w$ and $u \sqsubseteq^\sharp w'$ and $v \sqsubseteq^\sharp w'$. Hence the ideal generated by w' is the least upper bound of the ideals generated by u and v. $\qquad\square$

However, of the operators that we have discussed so far, only the convex powerdomain $\mathsf{C}(\cdot)$ does not take bounded-complete domains to bounded-complete domains. To see this in a simple example, consider the finite poset $\mathbb{T} \times \mathbb{T}$ and the following elements of $\mathcal{P}_f^*(\mathbb{T} \times \mathbb{T})$:

$$
\begin{aligned}
u &= \{(\bot, \mathsf{true}),\ (\bot, \mathsf{false})\} \\
v &= \{(\mathsf{true}, \bot),\ (\mathsf{false}, \bot)\} \\
u' &= \{(\mathsf{true}, \mathsf{true}),\ (\mathsf{false}, \mathsf{false})\} \\
v' &= \{(\mathsf{true}, \mathsf{false}),\ (\mathsf{false}, \mathsf{true})\}
\end{aligned}
$$

It is not hard to see that u' and v' are *minimal* upper bounds for $\{u, v\}$ with respect to the ordering $\sqsubseteq^\natural$. Hence no *least* upper bound for $\{u, v\}$ exists, and $\mathsf{C}(\mathbb{T} \times \mathbb{T})$ is therefore not bounded complete.

10.27 Lemma. *Each of the powerdomains is locally continuous.* $\qquad\square$

10.28 Corollary. *If D is bifinite, then $\mathsf{C}(D)$ is bifinite.* $\qquad\square$

We have the following:

10.29 Lemma. *The following operators are p-representable over $\mathbb{V}$: $\rightarrow$, $\circ\!\!\rightarrow$, $\times$, $\otimes$, $+$, $\oplus$, $(\cdot)_\bot$, and the powerdomains, U, L, and C.* $\qquad\square$

The empty set.

It is sometimes handy to include in a powerdomain the analog of the empty set $\emptyset$. What would happen if we expanded our definitions of the powerdomains by using all of the finite subsets of the basis of the domain rather than just the non-empty ones? In the case of the upper powerdomain, the principal ideal generated by the empty set would be the set of all finite subsets of the basis of the domain since the condition

$$v \sqsubseteq^{\sharp} \emptyset \text{ iff } (\forall y \in \emptyset)(\exists x \in v). \, x \sqsubseteq y.$$

is vacuously true for any v. Thus the empty set is the *largest* element of the upper powerdomain. On the other hand, the principal ideal generated by the empty set in the lower powerdomain is the singleton consisting only of the empty set. Moreover, the condition

$$\emptyset \sqsubseteq^{\flat} u \text{ iff } (\forall x \in \emptyset)(\exists y \in u). \, x \sqsubseteq y.$$

is vacuously true for any u, so the empty set is the *least* element of the lower powerdomain. But in the convex powerdomain, the empty set is *incomparable* to any other element of the domain since $\emptyset \sqsubseteq^{\natural} u$ implies $u = \emptyset$ and also $u \sqsubseteq^{\natural} \emptyset$ implies $u = \emptyset$. This situation can be problematic when one would like to use the powerdomain with empty set, but the use of pointed domains would make it easier to employ the Fixed-Point Theorem. In applications of this kind, the empty set is sometimes adjoined to the convex powerdomain by taking $\mathbb{O} \oplus \mathsf{C}(D)$ where $\mathbb{O}$ is the two element lattice. In effect this provides an empty set as an element related only to the bottom element of the domain.

Following the categorical approach to the semantics of programming languages, it seems natural to ask if this construction can be motivated categorically or if another construction—based on sound categorical foundations—can be used instead. A categorical formulation of the equational property of the empty set is not difficult to provide. Let us say that a semi-lattice domain *with unit* is a triple $(D, *, e)$ where $(D, *)$ is a semi-lattice domain and $e \in D$ such that

$$e * x = x * e = x$$

for each $x \in D$. We are interested in the case where D is pointed (that is, D has a least element $\bot$). Let $\mathbf{Sld}'_{\bot}$ be the category of pointed semi-lattice domains with unit and let $\mathbf{Alg}_{\bot}$ be the category of pointed algebraic cpo's and continuous functions. The fact is, however, that there actually *is* no powerdomain that can be obtained from this categorical formulation. This result provides an example of how one might show that an adjoint construction does *not* exist.

10.30 Proposition. *There is no left adjoint to the forgetful functor from* $\mathbf{Sld}'_{\bot}$ *to* $\mathbf{Alg}_{\bot}$.

Proof: Let $U : \mathbf{Sld}'_\perp \to \mathbf{Alg}_\perp$ be the forgetful functor and suppose that there is an adjunction (F, U, η). Let $D = F(\mathbb{U})$ where $\mathbb{U}$ is the poset with one element u. Let $\mathbb{O}$ be the semi-lattice with unit that has two elements $\perp, e \in U(\mathbb{O})$ with $\perp \sqsubseteq e$ and $\perp * e = \perp$. Let f be the function from $\mathbb{U}$ to $U(\mathbb{O})$ that maps u to e. We demonstrate a contradiction by showing that there is more than one homomorphism f^+ that completes the following diagram:

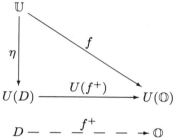

Let $T = (U(T), *, e)$ be the object of $\mathbf{Sld}'_\perp$ such that

- $U(T)$ is the poset with exactly three distinct elements $e, x, \perp$ such that $\perp \sqsubseteq e$ and $\perp \sqsubseteq x$.
- e is a unit for $*$ and $x * \perp = \perp$.

Let $g : \mathbb{U} \to U(T)$ be the function that sends u to x. By the conditions for an adjunction, there is a homomorphism $g^+ : D \to T$ such that $U(g^+)(\eta(\mathsf{u})) = x$. If e is the unit of D, then $g^+(e) = e$. Since $U(g^+)$ is monotone, this means $\eta(\mathsf{u})$ is incomparable to e in $U(D)$ and, consequently, $g^+(\perp) = \perp$. Now, consider the homomorphism $h : T \to \mathbb{O}$ that sends the elements of T constantly to e and the homomorphism $k : T \to \mathbb{O}$ that sends $\perp$ to $\perp$ and x to e. If $h' = h \circ g^+$ and $k' = k \circ g^+$, then

$$U(h') \circ \eta = f = U(k') \circ \eta.$$

But h' and k' are unequal, so this contradicts the assumption that (F, U, η) is an adjunction. ▯

Exercises.

Definition: Let $\mathbf{C}$ and $\mathbf{D}$ be categories and suppose $F : \mathbf{C} \to \mathbf{D}$ and $U : \mathbf{D} \to \mathbf{C}$ are functors such that (F, U, μ) is an *adjunction*. A *counit* of the adjunction is a natural transformation $\epsilon : F \circ U \to \mathsf{id}$ such that for each object B and arrow $f : F(B) \to A$, there is a unique arrow f' such that the following diagram commutes:

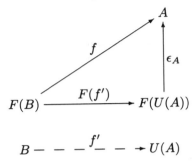

$$B - - - \xrightarrow{f'} U(A)$$

☐

10.18 Let (F, U, μ) be an adjunction. Prove that if ϵ and ϵ' are counits of this adjunction, then $\epsilon = \epsilon'$. In other words, the counit of an adjunction is uniquely determined if it exists.

10.19* Let (F, U, μ) be an adjunction. Given an object A, there is a unique arrow ϵ such that the following diagram commutes:

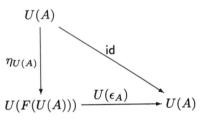

$$F(U(A)) - \xrightarrow{\epsilon_A} A$$

Prove that ϵ is a natural transformation and that it is the counit of the adjunction (F, U, μ).

10.20 Let **Usld** be the full subcategory of **Sld** whose objects $(A, *)$ satisfy the axiom

$s * t \sqsubseteq s.$

Let **Lsld** be the full subcategory of **Sld** whose objects $(A, *)$ satisfy

$s * t \sqsupseteq s.$

Prove that the upper and lower powerdomains are left adjoint to the forgetful functors from **Usld** and **Lsld** respectively to **Alg**.

10.4 Notes

Most of the categorical concepts in this chapter have their origins in mathematical investigations of the 1960's and can be found in standard category theory books such as those given in the notes for Chapter 3. The idea of applying category theory in computer science in general began in the 1970's; for domain theory in particular the idea of using categorical formulations of basic concepts was present at the start in the work of D. S. Scott [222; 224]. Much of the material in Section 10.1 is drawn from seminal papers by Wand [267] and by Smyth and Plotkin [240].

The category **SFP**, which is the full subcategory of the bifinite domains in which the objects are pointed and have a countable basis, was introduced by Plotkin [196] as a ccc of domains over which the convex powerdomain could be defined. The larger category of bifinite domains was studied by Gunter [96; 97], who used the term 'profinite' rather than bifinite. The term 'bifinite' used in this chapter was coined by Taylor [257] to avoid prejudicing between the category with projections as arrows and that with embeddings as arrows in building domains from limits or colimits of finite domains. The idea of using a categorical formulation of finiteness and ideal completion to produce a new category from an existing one was already familiar to categorists before the idea was exploited in domain theory. The book of Johnston [128] provides a good exposition of some of the mathematical results from which domain theory has drawn many of its most important ideas.

Properties of **SFP** and the bifinites have been a topic of continuing interest to the present time. Smyth [238] proved that **SFP** is the largest cartesian closed full subcategory of the pointed ω-algebraic cpo's. This result relied on the following key theorem:

10.31 Theorem (Smyth). *If D and $D \to D$ are pointed algebraic cpo's with countable bases, then D is an object of the category* **SFP**. $\Box$

The proof is carried out by analyzing each of the cases pictured in Figure 10.1 and showing that if $D \to D$ is not a domain, then D cannot be an object of **SFP**. Smyth's Theorem was generalized by Jung [129] who proved that it still holds if the condition that there be a least element is dropped. The big challenge was to find some generalization of Smyth's Theorem in which the assumption of a countable basis was dropped. This was done by Jung [130] in a thorough analysis that involved the discovery of the ccc of *L-domains*. He was able to classify the maximal cartesian closed full subcategories of **Bif**.

Another treatment of bifinite domains can be found in work of Abramsky [3; 6] who shows how to derive a logic for reasoning about programs from a denotational semantics for the language in which the programs are written. A treatment of similar topics has been given in a book by Zhang [274]. Both of these works focus on the relationships between order-theoretic and topological properties of domains. A more expository treatment of topology and domains can be found in the book by Vickers [265]. A categorical treatment is given in a book of Johnstone [128].

Research on the applications and mathematical properties of powerdomains was initiated by papers of Plotkin [196] and Smyth [237]. These investigations lead to the use of the terms 'Plotkin powerdomain' and 'Smyth powerdomain' for the upper and lower powerdomains respectively. The lower powerdomain is often called the 'Hoare' powerdomain because of Hoare's contributions to the study of partial correctness properties of programs and a close technical connection between the lower powerdomain and such properties. The names used for these operators in this chapter come from the concepts of upper and lower semi-continuity as described by Smyth [239]. The fact that powerdomains are left adjoints was proved by Hennessy and Plotkin in a paper [112] that also included a full abstraction theorem for a concurrent programming language. An interesting aspect of their work is the observation that the needed operators and properties of the powerdomain used there (the convex powerdomain, to be precise) could all be derived from the categorical treatment. The adjoint properties of the powerdomains are related to a more general theory of algebras with continuous operations. Basic elements of that theory have been described by Meseguer [161; 162], and an expository treatment is included in the book on process algebras by Hennessy [110]. A further discussion of the categorical and order-theoretic properties of powerdomains can be found in a pair of papers by Hrbacek [120; 121].

Powerdomains have been used extensively for the semantics of concurrency. An excellant example of their utility can be found in a semantic treatment by Abramsky [5] of the notion of bisimulation, an operational equivalence relation on process algebras. His model is based on a recursive domain equation involving the convex powerdomain.

There is a substantial body of literature on the specification of datatypes using sets of equations, an idea known as *algebraic specification*. This work is surveyed in a handbook article of Wirsing [272]. Goguen, Thatcher, and Wagner (the 'ADJ group') used *initial algebras* to provide interpretations [92; 93] while a dual perspective, using *final* (terminal) algebras has been examined by Wand [266] and Kamin [133].

The idea of building a universal domain using saturations is inspired by first-order model theory [50] where a similar technique is used to construct universal models. The saturated bifinite domain was introduced by C. Gunter [96; 97] using a model-theoretic proof technique and generalized generalized by C. Gunter and Jung [100] to a level of abstraction that could be used for other categories of domains such as bifinite L-domains and algebraic lattices. Another proof of the existence of a universal L-domain using a kind of retraction on the category of domains was given by E. Gunter [103]. Work on a general theory of universal domains and the application of model-theoretic techniques in domain theory has been extended significantly further through work of Droste and Göbel [78] and Droste [76].

11 Parametric Polymorphism

This chapter continues the discussion of parametric polymorphism begun in Section 7.5. The treatment is in two parts. In the first section of the chapter we consider three type systems for expressing parametric polymorphism and focus on the differences in their relative expressiveness. A key theme is the distinction between *predicative* and *impredicative* definitions of types. The system ML_0, which was introduced in Section 7.5, is an example of a predicative system; the first section below discusses the semantics of this system and introduces two impredicative systems, the Girard-Reynolds polymorphic λ-calculus and the Type:Type calculus. A standard model for ML_0 is given in the first section. Modeling the impredicativity of the other two calculi demands more subtlety; domain theory can be used to provide the needed structures by providing suitable concepts of indexed families. Three models are described in the second section of the chapter. The first of these uses partial equivalence relations (PER's) to model types in the polymorphic λ-calculus. The second uses a universal domain to model the Type:Type calculus. The fit between universal domains based on retractions and the Type:Type calculus is so close that the universal domains could be considered the standard class of models for Type:Type. The last model in the section uses domains continuously indexed over domains to provide a model for the polymorphic λ-calculus without a type of types or the use of a universal domain.

11.1 Calculi for Expressing Parametric Polymorphism

We considered a polymorphic typing system in Section 7.5 where ML_0 was introduced. This system is more expressive than the simply-typed λ-calculus and yet it has a useful type inference algorithm that can be used to compensate for the omission of type tags on bound variables. Let us go back now and consider its semantics. The goal is to provide a model for polymorphic types analogous to the full type frame for simple types. Recall the syntax of types, type schemes, and terms for the language:

$$
\begin{array}{lll}
x & \in & \mathrm{Term\,Variable} \\
a & \in & \mathrm{Type\,Variable} \\
t & ::= & a \mid t \to t \\
T & ::= & t \mid \Pi a.\, T \\
M & ::= & x \mid \lambda x.\, M \mid MM \mid \mathbf{let}\ x = M\ \mathbf{in}\ M
\end{array}
$$

As with FPC it will be necessary to have two forms of environment to model the language. Since types may contain variables, we will need the notion of a *type-value environment*, ι which is a function that maps types to semantic domains. An H, ι-*environment* is a mapping ρ that assigns to each $x \in H$ an element $\rho(x) \in [\![H(x)]\!]\iota$. In modeling FPC this map had finitary projections as its range. For ML_0 we use sets drawn from a collection obtained by constructing the full type frame.

Let X_0 be any non-empty set; it will serve as the analog of the interpretation of the ground type. Define $D_0 = \{X_0\}$ and $D_{n+1} = \{Y^X \mid X, Y \in D_n\} \cup D_n$. The *universe* of our interpetation is the set $U = \bigcup_{n \in \omega} D_n$. To model types of ML_0, we must interpret type schemes as well as types. Given an operator F such that $F(X)$ is a set for each $X \in U$, define the *dependent product determined by* F to be the set $\Pi_{X \in U} F(X)$ that consists of functions π such that $\pi(X) \in F(X)$ for each $X \in U$. To be more precise about the nature of such maps π, they can be taken as functions with domain U and range $\bigcup_{X \in U} F(X)$ satisfying the given constraint that $\pi(X) \in F(X)$. The interpretation of types and type schemes can now be given as follows:

- $[\![a]\!]\iota = \iota(a)$
- $[\![s \rightarrow t]\!]\iota = ([\![t]\!]\iota)^{[\![s]\!]\iota}$
- $[\![\Pi a.\ T]\!]\iota = \Pi_{X \in U}[\![T]\!]\iota[a \mapsto X]$

It is easy to see that $[\![t]\!]\iota$ is an element of U for each type t since the universe U is closed under exponentiation. Note, however, that $[\![\Pi a.\ T]\!]\iota$ need not be an element of U despite the fact that type variables a are mapped to elements of U. Implicitly we are therefore working with two universes. The first of these, U, is used for interpreting types, while the second contains sets that can be the interpretations of type schemes. To be more precise, let $U = U_0$ and, for each $n \in \omega$, define $V_{n+1} = (V_n)^U \cup V_n$. Then the meaning $[\![\Pi a.\ T]\!]\rho$ of a type scheme is an element of a second universe $V = \bigcup_{n \in \omega} V_n$.

The interpretation of the terms of ML_0 is more subtle than that of types. Let me write out the equations for the semantics in full and then consider whether they describe a well-defined function.

- Suppose $H \Vdash x : t$ and $t \leq H(x) \equiv \Pi a_1 \ldots . \Pi a_n.\ s$. Let σ be a substitution such that $\sigma(s) \equiv t$. Letting $X_i = [\![\sigma(a_i)]\!]\iota$ for each i, define $[\![H \rhd x : t]\!]\iota\rho = \rho(x)(X_1) \cdots (X_n)$.

- $[\![H \rhd \lambda x.\ M : s \rightarrow t]\!]\iota\rho$ is the function from $[\![s]\!]\iota$ to $[\![t]\!]\iota$ defined by $d \mapsto [\![H, \ x : s \rhd M : t]\!]\iota\rho[x \mapsto d]$.

- $[\![H \rhd M(N) : t]\!]\iota\rho = ([\![H \rhd M : s \rightarrow t]\!]\iota\rho)([\![H \rhd N : s]\!]\iota\rho)$.

- Suppose $\text{close}(H;\ s) = \Pi a_1 \ldots . \Pi a_n.\ s$ and $H \Vdash M : s$. Define $\pi \in [\![\text{close}(H;\ s)]\!]\iota$ by

$$\pi(X_1) \cdots (X_n) = [\![H \rhd M : s]\!](\iota[a_1, \ldots, a_n \mapsto X_1, \ldots, X_n])\rho.$$

  Then $[\![H \rhd \mathbf{let}\ x = M\ \mathbf{in}\ N : t]\!]\iota\rho = [\![H, x : \text{close}(H;\ s) \rhd N : t]\!]\iota\rho[x \mapsto \pi]$.

The primary question about the sense of this definition concerns whether the type-value environment $\iota' = \iota[a_1, \ldots, a_n \mapsto X_1, \ldots, X_n]$ in the semantic equation for the **let** construct is compatible with the environment ρ; that is, whether ρ is an H, ι'-environment. This question is resolved by recalling that none of the type variables a_i is in $\mathrm{Ftv}(H)$ and by noting the following:

11.1 Lemma. *If ρ is an H, ι-environment and $a \notin \mathrm{Ftv}(H)$, then it is also an $H, \iota[a \mapsto X]$-environment.*

Proof: This follows from the fact that $[\![t]\!]\iota[a \mapsto X] = [\![t]\!]\iota$ if a is not free in t. □

Another typing system for ML_0.

In light of the semantics we just gave, the type system we have been using for ML_0 appears to be slightly indirect in some ways. In the rule [Let], for instance, the meaning of the term M in **let** $x = M$ **in** N is calculated, and then a 'parameterized' version of its meaning is bound to x in the environment. Similarly, the meaning of a variable is drawn from the environment and then instantiated to the type assigned to x. Permitting judgements of the form $H \vdash M : T$, where T is a type scheme, together with rules for generalization and instantiation might lead a more elementary system. It is indeed possible to reformulate the typing system for ML_0 in this way. The rules for deriving such judgements appear in Table 11.1. The rules for abstraction and application remain unchanged, but the rules for projections and **let** constructs now reflect the more general form of judgement in this system. In the new system, the projection rule looks more or less the way it does in most of the systems we have considered rather than having the somewhat different form it has in Table 7.9. The 'close' operator is no longer used in the rule for **let** since the term M in the hypothesis may be given a type scheme rather than a type that must be generalized on variables not in H. But the real difference in the two systems lies in the presence of rules for introduction and elimination of Π bindings. One particular difference made by the addition of these rules is the fact that the derivation of a judgement $H \vdash M : T$ is not uniquely determined by H, M, T. There will, in fact, be many (superficially) distinct proofs of any such judgement obtained by alternating the application of rules $[\Pi\text{-Intro}]^-$ and $[\Pi\text{-Elim}]^-$. Nevertheless, it is possible to show that two systems are essentially the same on judgements of types.

11.2 Proposition. *Let H be a type assignment, M a term, and t a type.*

1. *If $H \Vdash M : t$, then $H \vdash M : t$.*
2. *If $H \vdash M : T$ and $t \leq T$, then $H \Vdash M : t$.*

Table 11.1
Typing Rules for ML_0 with Π Introduction and Elimination

$$[\text{Proj}] \qquad \frac{x : T \in H}{H \vdash x : T}$$

$$[\text{Abs}]^- \qquad \frac{H,\ x : s \vdash M : t}{H \vdash \lambda x.\ M : s \to t}$$

$$[\text{Appl}] \qquad \frac{H \vdash M : s \to t \qquad H \vdash N : s}{H \vdash M(N) : t}$$

$$[\text{Let}] \qquad \frac{H \vdash M : T \qquad H, x : T \vdash N : t}{H \vdash \textbf{let } x = M \textbf{ in } N : t}$$

$$[\Pi\text{-Intro}]^- \qquad \frac{H \vdash M : T \qquad a \notin \text{Ftv}(H)}{H \vdash M : \Pi a.\ T}$$

$$[\Pi\text{-Elim}]^- \qquad \frac{H \vdash M : \Pi a.\ T}{H \vdash M : [t/a]T}$$

Proof: To prove (1), suppose that $H \Vdash M : t$. The proof that $H \vdash M : t$ is by induction on the structure of M. If $M \equiv x$ is a variable, then it must be the case that $t \leq H(x)$. Since $H \vdash M : H(x)$, repeated applications of [Π-Elim] proves $H \vdash M : t$. Proofs for the case in which M is an application or an abstraction are trivial since the rules for these constructs are the same in both systems. Suppose M has the form **let** $x = L$ **in** N. Then $H \Vdash L : s$ and $H, x : \text{close}(H;\ s) \Vdash N : t$ for some type s. By the inductive hypothesis, therefore, $H \vdash L : s$ and $H, x : \text{close}(H;\ s) \vdash N : t$. By repeated applications of [Π-Intro]$^-$, it is possible to see that $H \vdash L : \text{close}(H;\ s)$ by noting that the operation close Π-abstracts variables $a \notin \text{Ftv}(H)$. Hence, by the [Let] rule, $H \vdash M : t$.

To prove (2), suppose $H \vdash M : T$ and $t \leq T$. The result is obtained by induction on the height of the proof that $H \vdash M : T$. There are six possible cases for the last step of the proof. If M is a variable x, then $t \leq H(x)$ so $H \Vdash x : t$ as desired. The cases for abstraction and application are immediate. If the last step of the derivation is an instance of [Let] for $\vdash$, then M has the form **let** $x = L$ **in** N and $H \vdash L : T$ for some type scheme T such that $H, x : T \vdash N : t$. If we instantiate the bound variables of T by fresh type variables to get a type s, then we have $H \Vdash L : s$ by the inductive hypothesis. Moreover, $H, x : \text{close}(H;\ s) \Vdash N : t$ by the inductive hypothesis and Lemma 7.6. Thus $H \Vdash M : t$. Now suppose that the last step of the proof of $H \vdash M : T$ is an instance of

[Π-Intro]$^-$ where $T \equiv \Pi a.\ T'$ and $a \notin \mathrm{Ftv}(H)$. Since $t \leq T$, there are types s and t' such that $t' \leq T'$ and $t \equiv [s/a]t'$. By the inductive hypothesis, $H \Vdash M : t'$ so, by Lemma 7.4, $H \Vdash M : t$. Suppose, finally, that the last step of the derivation of $H \vdash M : T$ is an instance of [Π-Elim]$^-$ where $T \equiv [s/a]T'$ and $H \vdash M : \Pi a.\ T'$. Then $t \leq \Pi a.\ T'$ too, so $H \Vdash M : t$ by the inductive hypothesis.   □

The polymorphic λ-calculus.

In many of the calculi we have considered, type annotations in terms were used to force each typeable term to have a unique type. The rules tagged with a superscript minus sign in the typing system for ML_0 described in Table 11.1 cause this property to fail. To recover it, we might place type tags on the λ-bound variables, but the rules [Π-Intro]$^-$, [Π-Elim]$^-$ would still pose a problem. In effect, terms must contain some indication about the generalization and instantiation of type variables if their types are to be uniquely determined. Let us now consider an important generalization of ML_0 that has explicit abstraction and application for type variables in terms. The system is sometimes called the *Girard-Reynolds* polymorphic λ-calculus, since the system was discovered independently by Girard (who was working on a proof-theoretic problem) and by Reynolds (who was interested in programming language design). With the possible exception of 'ML polymorphism', it is the best-known polymorphic type system, so it is most often simply called the *polymorphic λ-calculus*. The terms of the language are given as follows:

$$
\begin{array}{rcl}
x & \in & \mathrm{Term\,Variable} \\
a & \in & \mathrm{Type\,Variable} \\
t & ::= & t \rightarrow t \mid a \mid \Pi a.\ t \\
M & ::= & x \mid \lambda x : t.\ M \mid M(M) \mid \Lambda a.\ M \mid M\{t\}
\end{array}
$$

A term of the form $\Lambda a.\ M$ is called a *type abstraction*, and one of the form $M\{t\}$ is called a *type application*. Types of the form $\Pi a.\ t$ are called Π-*types*, and the type variable a is bound in $\Pi a.\ t$ by the Π-quantification. The following clauses define the free type variables for types and terms:

- $\mathrm{Ftv}(a) = a$
- $\mathrm{Ftv}(s \rightarrow t) = \mathrm{Ftv}(s) \cup \mathrm{Ftv}(t)$
- $\mathrm{Ftv}(\Pi a.\ t) = \mathrm{Ftv}(t) - \{a\}$
- $\mathrm{Ftv}(x) = \emptyset$
- $\mathrm{Ftv}(\lambda x : t.\ M) = \mathrm{Ftv}(t) \cup \mathrm{Ftv}(M)$
- $\mathrm{Ftv}(M(N)) = \mathrm{Ftv}(M) \cup \mathrm{Ftv}(N)$

Table 11.2
Typing Rules for the Polymorphic λ-Calculus

$$[\Pi\text{-Intro}] \qquad \frac{H \vdash M : s \qquad a \notin \text{Ftv}(H)}{H \vdash \Lambda a.\ M : \Pi a.\ s}$$

$$[\Pi\text{-Elim}] \qquad \frac{H \vdash M : \Pi a.\ s}{H \vdash M\{t\} : [t/a]s}$$

- $\text{Ftv}(\Lambda a.\ M) = \text{Ftv}(M) - \{a\}$
- $\text{Ftv}(M\{t\}) = \text{Ftv}(M) \cup \text{Ftv}(t)$

For an assignment H, the set of free type variables $\text{Ftv}(H)$ in H is the union of the free type variables in $H(x)$ for each $x \in H$. Substitution for both types and terms must respect bindings in the sense that no free variable of the term being substituted can be captured by a binding in the term into which the substitution is made. A precise formulation distinguishing between term trees and terms can be described in the way this was done for the simply-typed λ-calculus in Section 2.1.

As with the type system of ML_0 or the Fixed-Point Calculus, FPC, the types for terms of the polymorphic λ-calculus may be built using type variables. For example, $\lambda y : a.\ \lambda x : a \to b.\ x(y)$ is a well-typed term with type $a \to (a \to b) \to b$. However, unlike either of these other systems, the polymorphic λ-calculus allows type variables to be explicitly abstracted in terms. For example, the term

$$M \equiv \Lambda a.\ \Lambda b.\ \lambda y : a.\ \lambda x : a \to b.\ x(y)$$

has the type $\Pi a.\ \Pi b.\ a \to (a \to b) \to b$. It is possible to instantiate the abstracted type variables through a form of application. Given types s and t, for example, $M\{s\}\{t\}$ is equivalent to the term $\lambda y : s.\ \lambda x : s \to t.\ x(y)$. This latter term has the type $s \to (s \to t) \to t$.

The precise typing rules for the polymorphic λ-calculus are those in Table 2.1 together with the two rules that appear in Table 11.2. Of course, the rules in Table 2.1 must be understood as applying to all of the terms of the polymorphic calculus as given in the grammar for the language (and not just to the terms of the simply-typed calculus). As with earlier calculi, the type tags on the bound variables ensure the following:

11.3 Lemma. *For any type assignment H, term M, and type expressions s, t, if $H \vdash M : s$ and $H \vdash M : t$ then $s \equiv t$.* $\qquad\qquad\qquad\qquad\qquad\qquad\qquad\qquad$ $\square$

The virtue of the polymorphic λ-calculus is that it can be used to express general algorithms in a clear way. To see how this works, consider how one would write a program in FPC that takes a pair (x, y) to the pair (y, x). For example, we could write this function for specific types s, t,

$$\lambda z : \mathbf{num} \times \mathbf{bool}.\ (\mathbf{snd}(z), \mathbf{fst}(z))$$

or we could use type variables to write a program

$$L \equiv \lambda z : a \times b.\ (\mathbf{snd}(z), \mathbf{fst}(z)).$$

Despite the type variables, this program is not really polymorphic since its application to a term $(M, N) : s \times t$ is not type-correct in FPC. Indeed there is no way to write a 'general' pair-swapping function in FPC. To simplify the comparison of this to the situation in ML_0 or the polymorphic λ-calculus, let us consider the system obtained by augmenting each with a product construct; this is done by adding the syntax for pairs and projections and augmenting the typing systems with the rules from Table 3.1. The ML_0 term

$$L' \equiv \lambda z.\ (\mathbf{snd}(z), \mathbf{fst}(z))$$

obtained by removing the type tag on the binding occurrence in L can be considered polymorphic when it is used in a **let** construct. For instance, the term

let $f = L'$ **in** $f(f(M, N), f(N, M))$

is well-typed although each of the three instances of f in the body of the **let** is being applied to arguments with possibly different types. In the polymorphic λ-calculus, the polymorphism that is implicit in the type of L is made explicit:

$$\Lambda a.\ \Lambda b.\ \lambda z : a \times b.\ (\mathbf{snd}(z), \mathbf{fst}(z)).$$

This function can be used for swapping pairs of any type, provided the type is explicitly instantiated. For example, the program

$$(\Lambda a.\ \Lambda b.\ \lambda z : a \times b.\ (\mathbf{snd}(z), \mathbf{fst}(z)))\{s\}\{t\}(M, N)$$

is well-typed, and, given the needed axioms concerning pairs and projection, one can use the equational theory of the calculus to show that it is equal to (N, M). The polymorphism permitted in ML_0 is limited compared to that permitted in the polymorphic λ-calculus; for instance, the term L' must appear in a **let** construct if it is to be treated polymorphically in ML_0.

Table 11.3
Equational Rules for the Polymorphic λ-Calculus

$$\{\text{TypeCong}\} \qquad \frac{\vdash (H \rhd M = N : \Pi a.\ t)}{\vdash (H \rhd M\{s\} = N\{s\} : [s/a]t)}$$

$$\{\text{Type } \xi\} \qquad \frac{\vdash (H \rhd M = N : t)}{\vdash (H \rhd \Lambda a.\ M = \Lambda a.\ N : \Pi a.\ t)}$$

$$\{\text{Type } \beta\} \qquad \frac{H \vdash M : t}{\vdash (H \rhd (\Lambda a.\ M)\{s\} = [s/a]M : [s/a]t)}$$

$$\{\text{Type } \eta\} \qquad \frac{H \vdash M : \Pi a.\ t}{\vdash (H \rhd \Lambda a.\ M\{a\} = M : \Pi a.\ t)}$$

Restrictions:

- In $\{\text{Type } \xi\}$, there is no free occurrence of a in the type of a variable in H.
- In $\{\text{Type } \eta\}$, the type variable a does not appear free in H or M.

Returning to the problem illustrated earlier by Program 7.1 (on page 225), consider a function that takes a function as an argument and applies it to each of the components of a given pair, returning a pair as a result:

$$\lambda f : (\Pi a.\ a \rightarrow u).\ (f\{s\}(M), f\{t\}(N))$$

The types must be explicitly instantiated as part of the application, but the program is truly general, since it will work for any function f that can take a first argument of arbitrary type. More convincing programming examples can be given, but this shows that the phenomenon arises quite naturally.

The equational rules for the pure polymorphic λ-calculus are those in Table 2.2 together with the rules that appear in Table 11.3 modulo the theory T that appears on the left-hand sides of the turnstiles.[1] The new rules $\{\text{TypeCong}\}$ and $\{\text{Type } \xi\}$ assert that type application and type abstraction are congruences. The most fundamental new rules are the type-level analogs $\{\text{Type } \beta\}$ and $\{\text{Type } \eta\}$ of the β and η rules.

---

[1]We could also define the polymorphic λ-calculus more generally relative to a theory T, but the discussion of this chapter is based on using the empty theory.

A set-theoretic model of the polymorphic λ-calculus?

The interpretation of the polymorphic λ-calculus has been one of the most serious challenges in the semantics of programming languages. Of course, it is possible to construct a term model for the calculus as we did earlier for the simply-typed λ-calculus. But finding a model analogous to the full type frame is much harder. To appreciate the primary reason for this difficulty, let us attempt to provide such a model by partial analogy to the one we used for ML_0. We will need the notion of a *type-value environment* ι that maps type variables to semantic interpretations as sets. The interpretation $[\![t]\!]$ of a type t is a function that takes type assignments indicating the meanings of free variables of t into sets. As with the full type frame, we define $[\![s \to t]\!]\iota = [\![s]\!]\iota \to [\![t]\!]\iota$ where the arrow on the right is the full function space operator. The central question is, how do we interpret $\Pi a.\ t$? Let us naively take this to be a product of sets indexed over sets; an element of $[\![\Pi a.\ t]\!]\iota$ is a function that associates with each set X an element of the set $[\![t]\!]\iota[a \mapsto X]$. Such a function is called a *section* of the *indexed family* $X \mapsto [\![t]\!]\iota[a \mapsto X]$. It can improve the readability of expressions involving sections to write the application of a section to a set with the argument as a subscript. So, for example, if π is a section of $X \mapsto [\![t]\!]\iota[a \mapsto X]$, then $\pi_X \in [\![t]\!]\iota[a \mapsto X]$. To provide the semantic interpretation for terms, we will also want to know that a form of substitution lemma holds for types: $[\![[s/a]t]\!]\iota = [\![t]\!]\iota[a \mapsto [\![s]\!]\iota]$.

Given a type-value environment ι and a type assignment H, let us say that ρ is an ι, H-*environment* if $\rho(x) \in [\![H(x)]\!]\iota$ for each $x \in H$. If $H \vdash M : t$, then the interpretation $[\![H \rhd M : t]\!]$ is a function that takes a type-value environment ι and an ι, H-environment as an argument and returns a value in $[\![t]\!]\iota$. It sometimes helps to drop the type information in the interpreted expression and write $[\![M]\!]\iota\rho$ to save clutter when the types are clear enough from context.

The interpretation of terms is now defined by induction on their structure. The interpretation of an abstraction $[\![H \rhd \lambda x : s.\ M : s \to t]\!]\iota\rho$ over term variables is the function from $[\![s]\!]\iota$ to $[\![t]\!]\iota$ defined by $d \mapsto [\![H, x : s \rhd M : t]\!]\iota(\rho[x \mapsto d])$. On the other hand, the interpretation of the application of a term to a term is given by the usual application of a function to its argument: $[\![M(N)]\!]\iota\rho = ([\![M]\!]\iota\rho)([\![N]\!]\iota\rho)$. In considering the interpretation of the application of a term $M : \Pi a.\ s$ to a type t, recall that $[\![H \rhd M : \Pi a.\ s]\!]\iota\rho$ is a section of the indexed family $X \mapsto [\![s]\!]\iota[a \mapsto X]$. We take $[\![H \rhd M\{t\} : [t/a]s]\!]\iota\rho = ([\![H \rhd M : \Pi a.\ s]\!]\iota\rho)_X$ where $X = [\![t]\!]\iota$. This squares with the claim that $[\![[t/a]s]\!]\iota = [\![s]\!]\iota[a \mapsto [\![t]\!]\iota]$. Now, finally, the meaning of a type abstraction $[\![H \rhd \Lambda a.\ M : \Pi a.\ t]\!]\iota\rho$ is a section of the indexed family $X \mapsto [\![t]\!]\iota[a \mapsto X]$ given by $X \mapsto [\![H \rhd M : t]\!](\iota[a \mapsto X])\rho$. One must show that ρ is an $\iota[a \mapsto X], H$-value environment, but this follows from the restriction in [Π-Intro] that says the type variable a does not appear in H.

The semantics just sketched is sufficiently simple and convincing that something like it was actually used in early discussions of the semantics of the calculus. As it stands, however, there is a problem with the interpretation of types. A type is presumably a function from type-value environments to sets. But consider a type like $\Pi a.\ a$, which we have naively interpreted as the family of sections of the indexed family $X \mapsto X$. In other words, $[\![\Pi a.\ a]\!]\iota$ is the 'product' of all sets. We must assume that this product is itself a set, because this is needed to make our interpretation work. Consider, for instance, the term $M = (\Lambda a.\ \lambda x : a.\ x)(\Pi a.\ a)$. The term $\Lambda a.\ \lambda x : a.\ x$ is interpreted as a section over all sets and M is interpreted as the application of this section to the meaning of $\Pi a.\ a$.

Readers familiar only with 'naive set theory' may be curious about the attention being drawn here to the interpretation of $\Pi a.\ a$ as the product of all sets and my mysterious claim that this product must itself be a 'set'. This leads to a foundational question that must now be discussed. One of the crucial discoveries of logicians in the late nineteenth and early twentieth centuries was the fact that care must be taken in how collections of entities are formed if troubling paradoxes are to be avoided. Such paradoxes caused intricate and carefully constructed theories of the foundations of mathematics to crumble into rubble. Perhaps the best-known and most important of these paradoxes is *Russell's paradox,* which is named after the philosopher and logician Bertrand Russell. It can be described quite simply as follows. Let us assume that any property at all can be used to define a collection of entities. Define $\mathcal{X}$ to be the collection of all collections X having the property that X is not an element of X. This seems clear enough since we (think we) know what it means for an entity to be part of a collection. Let us therefore ask whether $\mathcal{X}$ is in $\mathcal{X}$ or not. Well, if it is, then it has the property common to all elements of $\mathcal{X}$, that of not being a member of itself. This is a contradiction, since we had postulated that $\mathcal{X}$ was a member of itself. Suppose, on the other hand, that $\mathcal{X}$ is *not* a member of itself. Then this is a contradiction as well, since we defined $\mathcal{X}$ to be those collections having exactly this property.

At first it was thought that minor adjustments in proposed foundational theories could deal with Russell's paradox, but the paradox arises in many different guises, and repairing the problem requires an approach that is now at the heart of the modern foundations of mathematics. The idea is to distinguish between two kinds of collections: those that inhabit a 'first universe' known as the universe of *sets* and those inhabiting a more general 'second universe' consisting of *proper classes.* In particular, a set is formed by collecting together members of the first universe according to rigorously formulated rules that exclude the troublesome collection $\mathcal{X}$ of Russell's paradox as well as other forms of the same problem. The idea is to limit the rule of *comprehension,* which says that a collection can be formed from a property of entities by allowing only certain kinds of properties to be used in comprehension if the collection being formed is to be a set. We have seen various examples of this distinction before, although explicit mention of the distinction has been suppressed because it did not arise as a problem. For example, a poset is a *set* with a certain binary relation on it, whereas the collection of all posets is a *proper class*. If, for instance, we stipulate that a poset P is less than a poset Q if P is a subposet of Q, then this defines a binary relation on posets that is transitive, reflexive, and anti-symmetric. However, the class of posets under this ordering is not a poset since it is not a set. Almost all of the categories we have discussed have a collection of objects that lies in the second universe. Some examples include **Set**, **Infsys**, **Monoid**, and most of the subcategories of **Poset** that have been used to provide semantic domains. An exception to this is the case in which a pre-order is viewed as a category in which there is at most one arrow between any pair of objects. The objects in this category form a set because the universe of a pre-order must be a set. I will not attempt to go further in developing the concepts of sets and classes since this would carry us far from the primary focus of this discussion, which is the semantics of the polymorphic λ-calculus. The reader interested in pursuing the matter beyond the intuitive remarks I have just made can consult references in the notes for this chapter.

Returning now to the polymorphic λ-calculus and our problem with its interpretation, we need to ask what led to the transgression into the domain of Russell's paradox. Technically the problem is that the restrictions placed on the formation of sets makes it impossible to view the product of all sets as itself a set. However, the underlying phenomenon here was recognized by Russell and by the mathematician and philosopher of science Henri Poincaré in a property he called 'impredicativity'. If a set $\mathcal{X}$ and an entity X are defined so that X is a member of $\mathcal{X}$ but is defined only by reference to $\mathcal{X}$, then the definition of $\mathcal{X}$ or X is said to be *impredicative*. Clearly this is the case for Russell's paradox, but it also applies to the class $\mathcal{X}$ of semantic domains that we are attempting to use for modeling the types of the polymorphic λ-calculus and the domain X that is to serve as the interpretation for $\Pi a.\ a$. To give a precise answer to this question, we need to develop further the mathematical tools at hand by studying the construction of indexed families in greater generality that we have done before.

The Type:Type calculus.

While the typing system of the polymorphic λ-calculus is, in a sense, more expressive than that of ML_0, it is possible to go further still beyond the polymorphic λ-calculus. There are many systems that do this; I will discuss one of these in which a new term **tp** is included in the grammar to denote the collection of types and an axiom of the form **tp** : **tp** is included in the typing rules. The new system is aptly called the *Type:Type calculus*. It originated as a false start on developing a foundations for mathematics based on type theory, but has subsequently been proposed as the basis for the type systems of several experimental programming languages. Our particular interest in this system here is its potential role as a calculus for denoting elements of a universal domain, which has a type of types in the form of its domain of finitary closures or projections. It can be shown that the polymorphic λ-calculus can be embedded into the Type:Type calculus in a certain sense, so this facilitates the demonstration of a model of the former when it is shown how to model the latter with a universal domain in the next section.

To appreciate the relationship between the polymorphic λ-calculus and this new system, let us now consider a reformulation of the polymorphic λ-calculus using explicit judgements about when an expression is a *type*. It is not strictly necessary to do this for the polymorphic λ-calculus, since types can be described with a context-free grammar for the calculus, but it will be useful to see the system in this more elaborate form to facilitate its comparison to the Type:Type calculus. The goal is to show that typing judgements in the polymorphic λ-calculus are embedded in those of the Type:Type calculus.

A type system that describes 'types' for the types of the system is called a 'three-level' type system. The types that are used for types are sometimes called *kinds,* so the three levels are those of terms, types, and kinds. As an example of the idea with this, recall some of the differences between various operators on types that have been presented. Product and function space are binary operations on types while lifting or the powerdomains are unary, and, for instance, we say that $s \to t$ *is a type* if s and t *are types.* Written as a rule with these assertions as judgements, this might take the following form:

$$\frac{s \text{ is a type} \qquad t \text{ is a type}}{s \to t \text{ is a type}}$$

Judgements like these are sometimes called *kinding* judgements to distinguish them from typing judgements, which assert that a term has a particular type. An idea for making the notation more succinct and uniform while still keeping a notational distinction between kinding judgements and typing judgements is to use a pair of colons and a symbol for types to indicate the desired property:

$$\frac{\vdash s :: \mathbf{tp} \qquad \vdash t :: \mathbf{tp}}{\vdash s \to t :: \mathbf{tp}}$$

To do this for the polymorphic λ-calculus, we need a notion for a type assignment H in which there are pairs of the form $a :: \mathbf{tp}$, which describe kindings, as well as ones of the form $x : t$, which describe typings. As with variables, we make the restriction that the pair $a :: \mathbf{tp}$ appears at most once in a type assignment. A set of such rules appears in

Table 11.4
Three-Level Typing Rules for the Polymorphic λ-Calculus

[Type Proj]	$H, a :: \mathbf{tp}, H' \vdash a :: \mathbf{tp}$

[$\rightarrow$ Formation]
$$\frac{H \vdash s :: \mathbf{tp} \qquad H \vdash t :: \mathbf{tp}}{H \vdash s \rightarrow t :: \mathbf{tp}}$$

[Π Formation]
$$\frac{H, a :: \mathbf{tp} \vdash t :: \mathbf{tp}}{H \vdash \Pi a.\, t :: \mathbf{tp}}$$

[Proj]
$$\frac{H \vdash t :: \mathbf{tp}}{H, x : t, H' \vdash x : t}$$

[Abs]
$$\frac{H \vdash s :: \mathbf{tp} \qquad H, x : s \vdash M : t \qquad H, x : s \vdash t :: \mathbf{tp}}{H \vdash \lambda x : s.\, M : s \rightarrow t}$$

[Appl]
$$\frac{\begin{array}{cc} H \vdash s :: \mathbf{tp} & H \vdash t :: \mathbf{tp} \\ H \vdash M : s \rightarrow t & H \vdash N : s \end{array}}{H \vdash M(N) : t}$$

[Π-Intro]
$$\frac{H, a ::\vdash_{\mathbf{tp:tp}} M : s \qquad H, a :: \mathbf{tp} \vdash s :: \mathbf{tp}}{H \vdash \Lambda a.\, M : \Pi a.\, s}$$

[Π-Elim]
$$\frac{H, a :: \mathbf{tp} \vdash s :: \mathbf{tp} \qquad H \vdash M : \Pi a.\, s \qquad H \vdash t :: \mathbf{tp}}{H \vdash M\{t\} : [t/a]s}$$

Table 11.4. The restriction on type assignments implies that the type variable a in the [Π-Intro] rule does not appear free in the assignment H. This makes it unnecessary to include this as a side condition. Given a derivation of a typing judgement using these rules, a derivation in the typing system of the polymorphic λ-calculus as described in Tables 2.1 and 11.2 can be obtained by omitting those parts of the proof that pertain to kinding judgements.

Now, the Type:Type calculus can be viewed as the system obtained by adding an axiom of the form $\mathbf{tp} : \mathbf{tp}$ and 'accepting the consequences' of this new axiom. In effect, the three levels of the hierarchy that distinguishes between terms, types, and kinds is collapsed (in the sense that it can be encoded) into a single level whose grammar is given as follows:

$$M ::= \mathbf{tp} \mid x \mid \Pi x : M.\ M \mid \lambda x : M.\ M \mid MM$$

In the Π- and λ-abstraction terms, the quantification binds the varible following Π or λ in the body of the abstraction, not in the tag. So, for instance, in a term $L \equiv \lambda x : M.\ N$, free occurences of x in M are also free in L while, as one expects, free occurences of x in N are bound to the occurence of x that follows the outermost λ.

Because of this collapsing the typing and equational rules are mingled in a single typing/equational rule system linked by a rule called [Type Equality]. This rule, together with the other rules that do not mention equality are given in in Table 11.5. In describing the rules, let us say that M *is a type* just in case $H \vdash M : \mathbf{tp}$.

- The [Type:Type] rule is the essence of the system. It asserts that the collection of all types can itself be viewed as a type.

- The rule [Π-Formation] describes the conditions for the formation of Π-types. It says that if M is a type and if N is a type given that the variable x has type M, then $\Pi x : M.\ N$ is also a type. This is analogous to the rules [Π Formation] and [$\rightarrow$ Formation] for the three-level description of the polymorphic λ-calculus given in Table 11.4.

- The rule [Proj] says that a variable x has type M if this is indicated in the type assignment *and* M is a type. Note that the hypothesis of the rule judges that M is a type based on the part of the type assignment from the conclusion that proceeds the typing $x : M$. This rule is analogous to [Type Proj] and [Proj] in the three-level description of the polymorphic λ-calculus.

- The rule [Π-Intro] says that an abstraction $\lambda x : M.\ N$ has type $\Pi x : M.\ L$ provided N has type L if the variable x has type M. This conclusion also requires that M is a type and that L is a type if x has type M. This rule is analogous to [Abs] and [Π-Intro] in three-level description of the polymorphic λ-calculus.

Table 11.5
Typing Rules for the Type:Type Calculus

[Type:Type] $H \vdash \mathbf{tp} : \mathbf{tp}$

[Π-Formation] $\dfrac{H \vdash M : \mathbf{tp} \qquad H, x : M \vdash N : \mathbf{tp}}{H \vdash \Pi x : M.\ N : \mathbf{tp}}$

[Proj] $\dfrac{H \vdash M : \mathbf{tp}}{H, x : M, H' \vdash x : M}$

[Π-Intro] $\dfrac{H \vdash M : \mathbf{tp} \qquad H, x : M \vdash L : \mathbf{tp} \qquad H, x : M \vdash N : L}{H \vdash \lambda x : M.\ N : \Pi x : M.\ L}$

[Π-Elim] $\dfrac{\begin{array}{cc} H \vdash L : \mathbf{tp} & H, x : L \vdash N : \mathbf{tp} \\ H \vdash M : \Pi x : L.\ N & H \vdash M' : L \end{array}}{H \vdash M(M') : [L/x]N}$

[Type Equality] $\dfrac{\begin{array}{cc} H \vdash L : \mathbf{tp} & H \vdash M : \mathbf{tp} \\ H \vdash N : M & H \vdash L = M : \mathbf{tp} \end{array}}{H \vdash N : L}$

- The rule [Π-Elim] says that $M(M')$ has type $[L/x]N$ provided M has type $\Pi x : L.\ N$ and M' has type L. It is also necessary that L be a type and that N be a type if x has type L. This rule is analogous to [Appl] and [Π-Elim] in the three-level description of the polymorphic λ-calculus.

- The rule connecting the typing and equational rules is [Type Equality], which says that if N has type M and L is equal to M, then N also has type L.

Aside from [Type Equality], the equational rules for the Type:Type calculus are very similar to those of the polymorphic λ-calculus. There are rules for equality asserting that it is an equivalence relation, rules asserting that abstraction and application are congruences, and the β- and η-rules. These last two rules are given in Table 11.6.

Many of the basic facts that held for other systems we have considered also hold for the Type:Type calculus. For instance, we have the following lemma:

11.4 Lemma. *Let L, M, N be terms, x a variable, and H a type assignment.*

Table 11.6
β- and η-Rules for the Type:Type Calculus

$$
\{\beta\} \qquad \frac{\begin{array}{cc} H \vdash M : \mathbf{tp} & H, x : M \vdash N : \mathbf{tp} \\ H \vdash M' : M & H, x : M \vdash N' : N \end{array}}{H \vdash (\lambda x : M.\ N')(M') = [M'/x]N' : N}
$$

$$
\{\eta\} \qquad \frac{H \vdash M : \mathbf{tp} \qquad H, x : M \vdash N : \mathbf{tp} \qquad H \vdash L : \Pi x : M.\ N}{H \vdash (\lambda x : M.\ L(x)) = L : \Pi x : M.\ N}
$$

---

1. *If $H \vdash M : N$, and x has no free occurrence in H, then $H, x : L \vdash M : N$.*
2. *If $H, x : L \vdash M : N$ and x has no free occurrence in M or N, then $H \vdash M : N$.* □

The goal now is to provide a translation relating terms of the polymorphic λ-calculus to those of the Type:Type calculus. This task is simplified by making no distinction under the translation between the syntax class of type variables and that of term variables. The translation t^* of a type t is defined by induction. If the type is a variable, then it is translated without change: $a^* \equiv a$. If it is a Π-abstraction, then the binding occurrence of the variable is tagged as a type, $(\Pi a.s)^* \equiv \Pi a : \mathbf{tp}.\ s^*$. If it is a function type, then it is translated though a vacuous quantification on a new variable: $(u \rightarrow v)^* \equiv \Pi x : u^*.\ v^*$ where x is not free in v (and is therefore not free in v^* either). The translation for terms is also defined inductively:

- $x^* \equiv x$,
- $(\lambda x : t.\ M)^* \equiv \lambda x : t^*.\ M^*$,
- $(M(N))^* \equiv M^*(N^*)$,
- $(\Lambda a.\ M)^* \equiv \lambda a : \mathbf{tp}.\ M^*$,
- $(M\{t\})^* \equiv M^*(t^*)$.

Given a type assignment H, the type assignment H^* is obtained by replacing each pair $x : t$ by $x : t^*$ and replacing each pair $a :: \mathbf{tp}$ by $a : \mathbf{tp}$. To state the desired result precisely, let us write $H \vdash_{\mathrm{poly}} M : t$ for the relation defined for the three-level description of the polymorphic λ-calculus given in Table 11.4 and $H \vdash_{\mathbf{tp:tp}} M : t$ for the relation defined for Table 11.5. Whether H, M, t are taken to range over the grammar for the (three-level) polymorphic λ-calculus or over that of the Type:Type calculus will be determined by context.

11.5 Theorem. *If $H \vdash_{\mathrm{poly}} M : t$ or $H \vdash_{\mathrm{poly}} M :: t$, then $H^* \vdash_{\mathbf{tp:tp}} M^* : t^*$.*

Proof: The proof is done by induction on the height of the derivation of $H \vdash_{\text{poly}} M : t$. The idea is to use the correspondence informally mentioned in the discussion of the rules for Type:Type.

- [Type Proj] and [Proj] in the polymorphic λ-calculus correspond to [Proj] in the Type:Type calculus.
- [$\rightarrow$ Formation] and [Π-Formation] in the polymorphic λ-calculus correspond to [Π-Formation] in the Type:Type calculus.
- [Abs] and [Π-Intro] in the polymorphic λ-calculus correspond to [Π-Intro] in the Type:Type calculus.
- [Appl] and [Π-Elim] in the polymorphic λ-calculus correspond to [Π-Elim] in the Type:Type calculus.

I will examine a few illustrative cases; the others can be given a similar treatment. Suppose the last step of the proof is an instance of the [Type Proj] rule (for the polymorphic λ-calculus), then the desired translation can be obtained using [Type] and [Proj] rules (for the Type:Type calculus). Specifically, we have

$$[\text{Proj}] \quad \frac{H_1^* \vdash_{\textbf{tp:tp}} \textbf{tp} : \textbf{tp}}{H_1^*, a : \textbf{tp}, H_2^* \vdash_{\textbf{tp:tp}} a : \textbf{tp}},$$

which yields the desired conclusion. Suppose the last step of the proof is an instance of

$$[\rightarrow \text{Formation}] \quad \frac{H \vdash_{\text{poly}} s :: \textbf{tp} \qquad H \vdash_{\text{poly}} t :: \textbf{tp}}{H \vdash_{\text{poly}} s \rightarrow t :: \textbf{tp}}.$$

Then, by the inductive hypothesis, we have $H^* \vdash_{\textbf{tp:tp}} s^* : \textbf{tp}$ and $H^* \vdash_{\textbf{tp:tp}} t^* : \textbf{tp}$. If x is a new variable, then we also have $H^*, x : s^* \vdash_{\textbf{tp:tp}} t^* : \textbf{tp}$ so we have an instance of the rule

$$[\Pi\text{-Formation}] \quad \frac{H^* \vdash_{\textbf{tp:tp}} s^* : \textbf{tp} \qquad H^*, x : s^* \vdash_{\textbf{tp:tp}} t^* : \textbf{tp}}{H^* \vdash_{\textbf{tp:tp}} \Pi x : s^*.\, t^* : \textbf{tp}}.$$

Since $(s \rightarrow t)^* \equiv \Pi x : s^*.\, t^*$, this is the desired conclusion. Suppose the last step in the proof is an instance of the rule

$$[\text{Appl}] \quad \frac{\begin{array}{cc} H \vdash_{\text{poly}} s :: \textbf{tp} & H \vdash_{\text{poly}} t :: \textbf{tp} \\ H \vdash_{\text{poly}} M : s \rightarrow t & H \vdash_{\text{poly}} N : s \end{array}}{H \vdash_{\text{poly}} M(N) : t}.$$

By our inductive hypothesis, we obtain the translations of each of the relations in the hypothesis of this rule. In particular, $H^* \vdash_{\textbf{tp:tp}} M^* : \Pi x : s^*.\, t^*$ where x is a new type variable. Since $H^* \vdash_{\mathbf{tp:tp}} t^* : \mathbf{tp}$ by the inductive hypothesis, this means that we also have $H^*, x : s^* \vdash_{\mathbf{tp:tp}} t^* : \mathbf{tp}$. Thus we have the following instance of

$$[\Pi\text{-Elim}] \quad \frac{\dfrac{H^* \vdash_{\mathbf{tp:tp}} s^* : \mathbf{tp} \qquad H, x : s^* \vdash_{\mathbf{tp:tp}} t^* : \mathbf{tp}}{H^* \vdash_{\mathbf{tp:tp}} M^* : \Pi x : s^*.\, t^* \qquad H^* \vdash_{\mathbf{tp:tp}} N^* : s^*}}{H^* \vdash_{\mathbf{tp:tp}} M^*(N^*) : [N^*/x]t^*}.$$

Since x does not appear in t, this means that $H^* \vdash_{\mathbf{tp:tp}} (M(N))^* : t^*$. $\qquad\qquad$ □

11.2   Indexed Families of Domains

The key to understanding the semantics of polymorphism can be found in the general mathematical theory of indexed families. We have encountered indexed families on several previous occasions. Perhaps the earliest example is that of an H-environment ρ for a type assignment H. Such a mapping associates with each variable $x \in H$ an element $\rho(x) \in [\![H(x)]\!]$. A more general idea, of which this is an instance, is that of a product $\Pi_{i \in I} X_i$ indexed over I. This product is defined as the set of indexed families $(x_i)_{i \in I}$ where $x_i \in X_i$ for each $i \in I$. To model polymorphism, we must somehow interpret $\Pi a.\, t$ so that it can be viewed as a kind of dependent product

$$\Pi_{D \in U} [\![t]\!]\iota[a \mapsto D]$$

where U is the universe of semantic domains interpreting types. There are several ways to do this; this section outlines two ways that involve a universal domain and one that works directly from the category of domains itself.

Partial equivalence relations.

Recall that a PER (Partial Equivalence Relation) on a set A is a relation $R \subseteq A \times A$ that is transitive and symmetric. We have already seen that if we are given a model (U, Φ, Ψ) of the untyped λ-calculus, then PER's over U can be used to interpret the types of the simply-typed λ-calculus. It is also possible to use PER's to interpret types of the polymorphic λ-calculus. To make this extension, we define the meaning of a type relative to a type-value environment that maps type variables to PER's. To interpret $\Pi a.\, t$ as an indexed family over PER's, let ι be a type-value environment that has all of the free type variables of $\Pi a.\, t$ in its domain. We want to define its meaning to be the 'product' of the relations $[\![t]\!]\iota[a \mapsto R]$ as R ranges over the PER's over U. Given $x, y \in U$, this says that x and y are related modulo $[\![t]\!]\iota[a \mapsto R]$ for each R. That is,

$$[\![\Pi a.\, t]\!]\iota = \bigcap_{R \in \mathrm{PER}} [\![t]\!]\iota[a \mapsto R]. \tag{11.1}$$

This defines a partial equivalence relation because the intersection of PER's is a PER. Notice the role of impredicativity in Equation 11.1 where the intersection ranges over the class of all PER's which must necessarily contain the PER that interprets $\Pi a.\ t$ itself. The interpretation of function spaces remains basically the same as for simple types:

$$f\ (\llbracket s \to t \rrbracket \iota)\ g \text{ iff, for each } d \text{ and } e,\ d\ (\llbracket s \rrbracket \iota)\ e \text{ implies } \Phi(f)(d)\ (\llbracket t \rrbracket \iota)\ \Phi(g)(e).$$

The *erasure* of a term of the polymorphic λ-calculus is defined by induction as follows:

- $\text{erase}(x) \equiv x$
- $\text{erase}(\lambda x : t.\ M) \equiv \lambda x.\ \text{erase}(M)$
- $\text{erase}(M(N)) \equiv (\text{erase}(M))(\text{erase}(N))$
- $\text{erase}(\Lambda a.\ M) \equiv \text{erase}(M)$
- $\text{erase}(M\{t\}) \equiv \text{erase}(M)$

The meaning of a term is defined using the meaning, as an untyped term, of its erasure. We assume that a retraction from U onto $[U \to U]$ is given and define $\mathcal{U}\llbracket M \rrbracket$ to be the meaning of untyped λ-term $\text{erase}(M)$ in U. As before, given a PER R on U and an element $d \in \text{dom}(R)$, let $[d]_R$ be the equivalence class of d relative to R, that is, $[d]_R = \{e \mid d\ R\ e\}$. Let M be a term of the polymorphic λ-calculus such that $H \vdash M : t$. The meaning of M is given relative to a type-value environment ι and a function ρ from variables $x \in H$ into U such that $\rho(x)$ is in the domain of the relation $\llbracket H(x) \rrbracket \iota$. The interpretation of the term M is given by

$$\mathcal{P}\llbracket M \rrbracket \iota \rho = [\ \mathcal{U}\llbracket M \rrbracket \rho\ ]_{\llbracket t \rrbracket \iota}.$$

To complete the demonstration that this defines a model, it must be shown that if a term M has type t, then the interpretation of M relative to an H, ι-environment is in the domain of the relation $\llbracket t \rrbracket \iota$, and that the equational rules of the polymorphic λ-calculus are satisfied. The treatment follows the general pattern of the argument for interpretation of simple types. I will state the necessary lemmas and describe the new steps in one of the proofs.

11.6 Lemma. $\llbracket [s/a]t \rrbracket \iota = \llbracket t \rrbracket \iota [a \mapsto \llbracket s \rrbracket \iota].$ $\qquad\qquad\qquad\qquad\qquad\qquad\qquad$ □

11.7 Lemma. *Suppose $H \vdash M : t$ and ρ, θ are H, ι-environments such that*

$$\rho(x)\ (\llbracket H(x) \rrbracket \iota)\ \theta(x)$$

for each $x \in H$. Then

$$(\mathcal{U}\llbracket M \rrbracket \rho)\ \llbracket t \rrbracket \iota\ (\mathcal{U}\llbracket M \rrbracket \theta).$$

Proof: The proof is by induction on the structure of M. Let us look at the cases for type abstraction and application. If $M \equiv \Lambda a.\ M' : \Pi a.\ t'$, then

$$(\mathcal{U}[\![M']\!]\rho)\ ([\![t']\!]\iota[a \mapsto R])\ (\mathcal{U}[\![M']\!]\theta)$$

for any PER R by the inductive hypothesis. Since $\mathrm{erase}(M') \equiv \mathrm{erase}(M)$ and the interpretation of $\Pi a.\ t'$ is the intersection of PER's of the form $[\![t']\!]\iota[a \mapsto R]$, we must have

$$(\mathcal{U}[\![M]\!]\rho)\ ([\![\Pi a.\ t']\!]\iota)\ (\mathcal{U}[\![M]\!]\theta).$$

Suppose now that $M \equiv M'\{s\}$. Then $H \vdash M' : \Pi a.\ t'$ and $t \equiv [s/a]t'$. Applying the inductive hypothesis to M', we have

$$(\mathcal{U}[\![M']\!]\rho)\ (\bigcap_{R \in PER} [\![t']\!]\iota[a \mapsto R])\ (\mathcal{U}[\![M']\!]\theta)$$

and therefore, in particular,

$$(\mathcal{U}[\![M']\!]\rho)\ ([\![t']\!]\iota[a \mapsto [\![s]\!]\iota])\ (\mathcal{U}[\![M']\!]\theta)$$

Now $\mathrm{erase}(M') \equiv \mathrm{erase}(M)$ so, by Lemma 11.6,

$$(\mathcal{U}[\![M]\!]\rho)\ ([\![[s/a]t']\!]\iota)\ (\mathcal{U}[\![M]\!]\theta). \qquad \Box$$

11.8 Corollary. If $H \vdash M : t$ and ρ is an H, ι-environment, then $\mathcal{U}[\![H \rhd M : t]\!]\iota\rho$ is in the domain of the relation $[\![t]\!]\iota$. $\qquad \Box$

11.9 Lemma. If $\vdash (H \rhd M' = N' : t')$ and ρ, θ are H, ι-environments such that $\rho(x)\ ([\![H(x)]\!]\iota)\ \theta(x)$ for each $x \in H$, then

$$\mathcal{P}[\![H \rhd M' : t']\!]\iota\rho = \mathcal{P}[\![H \rhd N' : t']\!]\iota\theta. \qquad \Box$$

11.10 Corollary. If $\vdash (H \rhd M = N : t)$, then $\mathcal{P}[\![H \rhd M : t]\!] = \mathcal{P}[\![H \rhd N : t]\!]$. $\qquad \Box$

Domains indexed over a domain.

Let us now change directions and look at how the Type:Type calculus can be modeled. For this we first develop some basic tools for describing indexed families of domains. Let D be a cpo and suppose $F : D \to \mathbf{Cpo}^{ep}$ is a continuous functor into the category of cpo's and ep-pairs. Given $x, y \in D$ such that $x \sqsubseteq y$, let us write $F(x, y)$ for the ep-pair that F associates to the arrow from x to y and write $F^e(x, y) : F(x) \to F(y)$ and $F^p(x, y) : F(y) \to F(x)$ for the embedding and projection respectively. We define the *dependent sum* ΣF to be the set of pairs (x, t_x) where $x \in D$ and $t_x \in F(x)$. A binary relation on such pairs is defined by taking

$$(x, t_x) \sqsubseteq (y, t_y) \text{ iff } x \sqsubseteq y \text{ and } F^e(x, y)(t_x) \sqsubseteq t_y.$$

It is easy to check this relation defines a poset. Moreover, we have the following:

11.11 Theorem. *If D is a cpo and $F : D \to \mathbf{Cpo}^{ep}$ is a continuous functor, then ΣF is a cpo.*

Proof: Suppose $M = \{(x_i, t_i) \mid i \in I\}$ is a directed subset of ΣF. Then $\{x_i \mid i \in I\}$ is a directed subset of D and therefore has a least upper bound $x = \bigsqcup_{i \in I} x_i$ in D. It is easy to see that $\{F^e(x_i, x)(t_i) \mid i \in I\}$ is directed. Let $t = \bigsqcup_{i \in I} F^e(x_i, x)(t_i)$. We show that that (x, t) is the least upper bound of M in ΣF. Clearly it is an upper bound for M. Suppose $(x_i, t_i) \sqsubseteq (x', t')$, for all $i \in I$. Then $x \sqsubseteq x'$ and $F^e(x_i, x')(t_i) \sqsubseteq t'$ for all $i \in I$. Hence

$$F^e(x, x')(t) = F^e(x, x')(\bigsqcup_{i \in I} F^e(x_i, x)(t_i)) = \bigsqcup_{i \in I}(F^e(x, x') \circ F^e(x_i, x))(t_i)$$

$$= \bigsqcup_{i \in I} F^e(x_i, x')(t_i) \sqsubseteq t'$$

so $(x, t) \sqsubseteq (x', t')$. $\qquad\square$

If D and $F(D)$ are pointed, then ΣF is also pointed with $(\bot_D, \bot_{F(\bot_D)})$ as the least element. Also, the projection on the first coordinate, $\mathsf{fst} : \Sigma F \to D$, is a continuous function between cpo's.

The dependent sum has other good closure properties. Proofs for these lemmas are left for the reader.

11.12 Lemma. *If D is a bounded-complete cpo and $F : D \to \mathbf{Cpo}^{ep}$ is a continuous functor such that $F(x)$ is bounded complete for each $x \in D$, then ΣF is also bounded complete.* $\qquad\square$

11.13 Lemma. *If D is a bc-domain and $F : D \to \mathbf{Bcdom}^{ep}$ is a continuous functor, then ΣF is a bc-domain.* $\qquad\square$

The dependent product for a continuous functor $F : D \to \mathbf{Cpo}^{ep}$ is defined from the dependent sum ΣF as follows. A *section* of F is a mapping $s : D \to \Sigma F$ such that $\mathsf{fst} \circ s = \mathsf{id}_D$. In other words, for each $x \in D$, $s(x)$ is a pair (x, t). Note that there is a correspondence between sections and indexed families $(t_x)_{x \in D}$ such that $t_x \in F(x)$ for each $x \in D$. Given a section s, one defines $t_x = \mathsf{snd}(s(x))$ and given a family $(t_x)_{x \in D}$ one defines $s(x) = (x, t_x)$. In this case, the following conditions are equivalent:

1. s is monotone.

2. For all $x, y \in D$, $x \sqsubseteq y$ implies $(x, t_x) \sqsubseteq (y, t_y)$.

3. For all $x, y \in D$, $x \sqsubseteq y$ implies $F^e(x, y)(t_x) \sqsubseteq t_y$.

A family $(t_x)_{x \in D}$ that satisfies this condition is said to be *monotone*. Continuous sections correspond to families that are monotone such that the condition

$$t_y = \bigsqcup_{x \in M} F^e(x, y)(t_x)$$

holds whenever $M \subseteq D$ is directed and $y = \bigsqcup M$. Such a family is said to be *continuous*. The *dependent product* ΠF is the set of continuous sections over F. This is a poset under the pointwise ordering. Like the dependent sum, it is itself a cpo.

11.14 Lemma. *If D is a cpo and $F : D \to \mathbf{Cpo}^{ep}$ is a continuous functor, then ΠF is a cpo.*

Proof: Suppose $\{t^{(i)} \mid i \in I\}$ is a directed set in ΠF and let $t = (\bigsqcup_{i \in I} t_x^{(i)})_{x \in D}$. This is a monotone section; to see that it is continuous, suppose M is a directed subset of D and $\bigsqcup M = y$. Then

$$t_y = \bigsqcup_{i \in I} t_y^{(i)} = \bigsqcup_{i \in I} \bigsqcup_{z \in M} F^e(z, y)(t_z^{(i)}) = \bigsqcup_{z \in M} \bigsqcup_{i \in I} F^e(z, y)(t_z^{(i)})$$

$$= \bigsqcup_{z \in M} F^e(z, y)(\bigsqcup_{i \in I} t_z^{(i)}) = \bigsqcup_{z \in M} F^e(z, y)(t_z).$$

Thus ΠF is a cpo.   □

11.15 Lemma. *If D is a bc-domain and $F : D \to \mathbf{Bcdom}^{ep}$ is a continuous functor, then ΠF is a bc-domain.*

Proof: The proof that ΠF is a bounded complete cpo is left as an exercise. To see that it is algebraic, we need to demonstrate a basis. Suppose $e \in \mathsf{K}(D)$ and $f \in \mathsf{K}(F(e))$. Define the family $(e \searrow f)$ to have component

$$(e \searrow f)_x = \begin{cases} F^e(e, x)(f) & \text{if } e \sqsubseteq x, \\ \bot_{F(x)} & \text{otherwise,} \end{cases}$$

for $x \in D$. It is easy to check $(e \searrow f)$ is a continuous family and that it is compact in the ordering on families in ΠF. A continuous family t is the least upper bound of the directed set of families $(e \searrow f)$ such that $f \sqsubseteq t_e$.   □

The tools just developed for understanding indexed families can be combined with the idea of a universal domain to yield a model of the Type:Type calculus. This provides a model of the polymorphic λ-calculus indirectly via the embedding defined by Theorem 11.5. To describe such a model, suppose we are given a bc-domain D together with an ep-pair $(\Psi, \Phi) : [D \to D] \to D$. The set of finitary projections $\mathsf{Fp}(D)$ on D is the image of a finitary projection $\wp$ on $[D \to D]$ (see Exercise 10.16). In our model of the Type:Type calculus, the terms and types of the calculus are interpreted as elements of D. The type of types $\mathbf{tp}$ is interpreted by the element $\Psi(\wp)$. In general, if $\vdash M : N$, then the interpretation M is an element of the image of $\Phi(d)$ where d is the interpretation of N. In particular, $\mathbf{tp} : \mathbf{tp}$ satisfies this property because $\Psi(\wp) \in \mathrm{im}(\wp) = \mathrm{im}(\Phi(\Psi(\wp)))$. Aside from the idea of using $\wp$ to interpret the type of types, the key idea in the model of the calculus is the choice of a canonical embedding from a dependent product of domains into the domain D. Let $p = \Phi(\llbracket H \triangleright M : \mathbf{tp} \rrbracket \rho)$ and suppose A is the image of this finitary projection. The meaning of $\Pi x : M.\ N$ is a representation as an element of D of a dependent product of domains indexed over A. To be precise, define a functor $F : A \to \mathbf{Bcdom}^{ep}$ by

$$F(a) = \mathrm{im}(\Phi(\llbracket H, x : M \triangleright N : \mathbf{tp} \rrbracket \rho[x \mapsto a]))$$

where $a \in A$. If $a \sqsubseteq b$, then $F(a, b)$ is the ep-pair determined by the inclusion between $F(a)$ and $F(b)$. To interpret $\Pi x : M.\ N$, we begin by defining an embedding of ΠF into D. To this end, suppose $t \in \Pi F$ and define

$$\alpha(t) = \Psi(f)$$

where $f : D \to D$ is defined by $d \mapsto t_{p(d)}$. Continuity of f follows from continuity of the section t. On the other hand, suppose $d \in D$ and define

$$\beta(d) = (a \mapsto q(\Phi(d)(a)))$$

where $a \in A$ and $q = \Phi(\llbracket H, x : M \triangleright N : \mathbf{tp} \rrbracket \rho[x \mapsto a])$. Let us now check that (α, β) is an ep-pair. Suppose $d \in D$, then

$$\alpha(\beta(d)) = \Psi(e \mapsto q(\Phi(d)(p(e)))) \sqsubseteq \Psi(e \mapsto \Phi(d)(e)) \sqsubseteq d$$

where the second equality follows from the fact that $p \sqsubseteq \mathrm{id}$. If $t \in \Pi F$ and $a \in A$, then

$$\beta(\alpha(t))(a) = q(\Phi(\Psi(e \mapsto t_{p(e)}))(a)) = q(t_a) = t_a$$

since $a \in \mathrm{im}(p)$ and $t_a \in \mathrm{im}(q)$. Hence (α, β) is an ep-pair and $\alpha \circ \beta$ is a finitary projection. We take

$$\llbracket H \triangleright \Pi x : M.\ N : \mathbf{tp} \rrbracket \rho = \Psi(\alpha \circ \beta).$$

The interpretations of application and abstraction are not difficult now. Suppose $H \vdash \lambda x : M.\ N : (\Pi x : M.L)$. Let $p = \Phi(\llbracket H \rhd M : \mathbf{tp} \rrbracket \rho)$. For each $a \in \mathrm{im}(p)$, define

$$t_a = \llbracket H, x : M \rhd N : L \rrbracket \rho[x \mapsto a].$$

Then

$$\llbracket H \rhd \lambda x : M.\ N : (\Pi x : M.\ L) \rrbracket \rho = \Psi(e \mapsto t_{p(e)}).$$

Suppose that $H \vdash M(M') : [M'/x]N$. Let $d = \llbracket H \rhd M : (\Pi x : L.\ N) \rrbracket \rho$ and $a = \llbracket H \rhd M' : L \rrbracket \rho$. Then

$$\llbracket H \rhd M(M') : [M'/x]N \rrbracket \rho = q(\Phi(d)(a))$$

where $q = \Phi(\llbracket H, x : L \rhd N : \mathbf{tp} \rrbracket \rho[x \mapsto a])$. It is possible to show that

$$\llbracket H, x : L \rhd N : \mathbf{tp} \rrbracket \rho[x \mapsto a] = \llbracket H \rhd [M'/x]N : \mathbf{tp} \rrbracket \rho$$

so the meaning of $M(M')$ is an element of the subdomain associated with the meaning of $[M'/x]N$.

Domains indexed over the category of domains.

Both of the models described so far in this section rely on some kind of universal domain. In the case of the Type:Type calculus, this seems quite reasonable since the contrast between $\mathbf{tp}$ as an element and $\mathbf{tp}$ as a type is naturally reflected by the contrast between $\mathbf{tp}$ as an element of the domain of finitary projections and the finitary projections themselves. In the case of the polymorphic λ-calculus, the use of a universal domain is less satisfying, however. While we have seen that a non-trivial model can be constructed by interpreting the underlying untyped terms and then taking equivalence classes modulo PER's interpreting the types of terms, it is natural to ask if a model can be given in the way we used cpo's to interpret PCF. To some extent this is done indirectly through the interpretation of the Type:Type calculus since this provides an interpretation of the polymorphic λ-calculus as well via the translation described at the end of Section 11.1. This interpretation seems excessive, however, since the model must contain a type of types while this concept is not explicitly present in the polymorphic λ-calculus itself. In short, is it possible to describe a model of the polymorphic λ-calculus without the explicit use of a universal domain or a type of types?

There is an interesting technique that provides an affirmative answer to this question. The construction is based on two central ideas, both of which are familiar from domain-theoretic ideas that have been discussed before. The objective is to make sense of the idea of a product indexed by all domains while taking foundational issues properly into account. The two ideas that make it possible for us to do this in a satisfactory way are *continuity* and *bifiniteness*. To interpret $\Pi a.\ t$ we build a product over a set $\mathfrak{S}$ of representatives of isomorphism classes of *finite* bc-domains. There are only countably many of these so no foundational problem arises. The application of a term $\Lambda a.\ M : \Pi a.\ t$ to a type s is then interpreted by describing the interpretation of s as a colimit of finite bc-domains (recall that bc-domains are bifinite, so this is possible) and using the value of M on finite domains to build its value in the interpretation of s as the lub of a directed collection. To make this model as simple as possible, it helps to think of $\Pi a.\ t$ as really having two meanings, an official one in which it is a countable product indexed over $\mathfrak{S}$ and an unofficial one in which it is indexed over all domains and its elements are *continuous* sections in a sense now to be rigorously defined.

We must replace the construction of ΠF, where $F : D \to \mathbf{Cpo}^{ep}$ is a continuous functor into the category of cpo's and ep-pairs, by a construction in which F is an endofunctor on $\mathbf{Bcdom}^{ep}$. In other words, F is an indexed family of bc-domains where the category of bc-domains is itself the indexing collection. As we have seen on many other occasions, a good guide to how this generalization can be done lies in passing to the appropriate categorical generality and then seeing the crucial construction as a specialization of the more general concept. To define the desired generalization, let $\mathbf{Cat}$ be the category whose objects are categories[2] and whose arrows are functors between categories.

Definition: Given a functor $F : \mathbf{C} \to \mathbf{Cat}$, define the *Grothendieck fibration*[3] of F to be the category ΣF such that

- An object of ΣF is a pair (X, t_X) where $X \in \mathbf{C}$ and t_X is an object in $F(X)$.
- An arrow between an object (X, t_X) and an object (Y, t_Y) is a pair (f, α) where $f : X \to Y$ in $\mathbf{C}$ and $\alpha : F(f)(t_X) \to t_Y$ in $F(Y)$.

The *composition* of arrows $(f, \alpha) : (X, t_X) \to (Y, t_Y)$ and $(g, \beta) : (Y, t_Y) \to (Z, t_Z)$ is given by $(g, \beta) \circ (f, \alpha) = (g \circ f, \beta \circ F(g)(\alpha))$. $\square$

The proof that ΣF is a category with $(\mathrm{id}_X, \mathrm{id}_{t_X})$ as the identity arrow on each object (X, t_X) is left as an exercise for the reader, an exercise that might help relieve some of the initial impression that the definition above is indigestibly abstract. The category of categories has been chosen as the target of the functor because of its generality. To see how it is specifically related to the indexing of domains over domains, note that a

---

[2]This is often restricted to categories that are sets ('small' categories) but this is not essential for the limited use we make of the concept.

[3]Strictly speaking, in category theory this construction is ordinarily defined using a functor $F : \mathbf{C}^{op} \to \mathbf{Cat}$ with the opposite category as its domain. This would be moderately inconvenient in the discussion here though.

category such as the bc-domains and ep-pairs is a subcategory of **Cat**. So, for instance, a functor $F : D \to \mathbf{Cpo}^{ep}$ where D is a poset can be viewed as indexing the domains in $\mathbf{Cpo}^{ep}$ (which are categories) by the poset (category) D. The arrow α in a poset is just an order relationship, so the existence of an arrow between objects (x, t_x) and (y, t_y) amounts to the condition that $x \sqsubseteq y$ and $F^e(x, y) \sqsubseteq y$. In other words, the Grothendieck fibration ΣF is exactly the dependent sum as it was defined earlier. Now, if D is itself replaced by $\mathbf{Cpo}^{ep}$, then we have a category built from domains indexed by domains. This can only help us for the semantics of the polymorphic λ-calculus if we are also able to generalize to the construction ΠF of continuous sections as we did before, but now using a functor $F : \mathbf{Cpo}^{ep} \to \mathbf{Cpo}^{ep}$.

Suppose now that $F : \mathbf{C} \to \mathbf{Cat}$ is a functor on a category $\mathbf{C}$ that has directed colimits. Define $\mathsf{fst} : \Sigma F \to \mathbf{C}$ to be the projection functor (using the same notation as projection for products) that takes $(f, \alpha) : (X, t_X) \to (Y, t_Y)$ to $f : X \to Y$. The category ΠF has continuous sections as objects: a *section* of ΣF is a functor $s : \mathbf{C} \to \Sigma F$ such that $\mathsf{fst} \circ s = \mathrm{id}_C$, and a section is continuous if it is continuous as a functor. An arrow of ΠF is a natural transformation $\mu : s \to s'$ such that the first component of μ_X is the identity function on X. It is easier to see what this means by thinking of a section as an indexed family as we did for the dependent product earlier. An object of ΠF can be viewed as a family $(t_X)_{X \in \mathbf{C}}$ where $t_X \in F(X)$ for each X. An arrow between $(t_X)_{X \in \mathbf{C}}$ and $(t'_X)_{X \in \mathbf{C}}$ is a family of arrows $\mu_X : t_X \to t'_X$ satisfying the naturality condition. If the categories $F(X)$ are actually posets, then this simply amounts to saying that t is below t' in the pointwise order.

For the purposes of our application of these categorical concepts to the interpretation of polymorphic λ-calculus, we can specialize the discussion to a category of domains. Let $F : \mathbf{Bcdom}^{ep} \to \mathbf{Bcdom}^{ep}$ be a continuous functor. A *section* t of F is a function on domains such that $t_D \in F(D)$ for each domain D. A section is *monotone* if, for every arrow ep-pair $f : D \to E$ between bc-domains, we have $f^e(t_D) \sqsubseteq t_E$. Now, to define continuity for sections, we could use the categorical definition as given for the general Grothendieck construction, but an equivalent condition derived from the Colimit Theorem is much easier to check. Let us say that a *directed decomposition* of a bc-domain D is a family of ep-pairs $f_i : D_i \to D$ indexed by a directed poset I, where each D_i is a bc-domain, and the following conditions hold:

1. for each $i, j \in I$, there is some $k \in I$ such that the images of f_i^e and f_j^e are contained in the image of f_k^e, and

2. $\bigsqcup_{i \in I} f_i^e \circ f_i^p = \mathrm{id}$.

This is really just another way of saying that D is the the colimit of a directed collection. A monotone section t of a continuous functor $F : \mathbf{Bcdom}^{ep} \to \mathbf{Bcdom}^{ep}$ is said to be *continuous* if $\bigsqcup_i f_i^e(t_{D_i}) = t_D$ whenever $\{f_i \in \mathbf{Bcdom}^{ep}(D_i, D)\}_{i \in I}$ is a directed decomposition of D. Let us write ΠF for the family of continuous sections of a continuous functor $F : \mathbf{Bcdom}^{ep} \to \mathbf{Bcdom}^{ep}$ under an ordering given by defining $t \sqsubseteq t'$ if $t_D \sqsubseteq t_D'$ for every domain D.

Now, the category ΠF could not be a domain because it is not a set; each section is a mapping over the proper class of all domains. To achieve the goal of producing a *domain* that can serve as the interpretation of a Π-type for the polymorphic λ-calculus, we must represent the category ΠF indirectly. As before, let $\Im$ be a set of finite posets containing exactly one representative of each isomorphism class of finite poset. Define $\Pi_\Im F$ to be the collection consisting of families $(t_X)_{X \in \Im}$ where $t_X \in F(X)$ that are monotone in the sense that for any ep-pair $f : X \to Y$, $F^e(f)(t_X) \sqsubseteq t_Y$. The product of countably many sets is a set; since $\Im$ is a countable set and each $F(X)$ is also a set, it follows that $\Pi_\Im F$ is a set that determines a poset under the pointwise ordering. By using continuity and the fact that each bc-domain can be given as a directed decomposition of finite posets, we can demonstrate a close relationship between ΠF and $\Pi_\Im F$ by showing how, given an element of one, an element of the other can be obtained in a canonical way. First of all, it is clear that any continuous section $t \in \Pi F$ determines, by restriction, an element $\check{t} \in \Pi_\Im F$. Conversely, any element $t \in \Pi_\Im F$ can be extended to a continuous section $\hat{t}$ by taking

$$\hat{t}_D = \bigsqcup \{F^e(f)(t_X) \mid X \in \Im \text{ and } f : X \to D\} \tag{11.2}$$

for any domain D. Of course, it must be shown that this is well-defined. The argument demonstrating the desired correspondence between ΠF and $\Pi_\Im F$ includes most of the ideas needed to complete the proof that the interpretation of the polymorphic λ-calculus we are about to offer makes sense. I will therefore provide some steps in the proof of this correspondence lemma and omit most of the remaining proofs needed to show that all necessary conditions are satisfied. The enterprising reader can fill in these details or consult the literature by following citations in the notes at the end of the chapter.

11.16 Lemma. $\Pi_\Im F$ *is a bc-domain. Moreover, the maps $t \mapsto \check{t}$ and $t \mapsto \hat{t}$ are order preserving and inverse to one another.*

Proof: Let us begin by showing that the definition in 11.2 really does make sense by proving that the set

$$M = \{F^e(f)(t_X) \mid X \in \Im \text{ and } f : X \to D\}$$

is directed if it is non-empty. To this end, suppose $y_0 = F^e(f_0)(t_{X_0})$ and $y_1 = F^e(f_1)(t_{X_1})$ are elements of this set arising from ep-pairs $f_0 : X_0 \to D$ and $f_1 : X_1 \to D$. Since X_0

and X_1 are finite, there is a finite domain X and ep-pairs $g : X \to D$, $g_0 : X_0 \to X$, and $g_1 : X_1 \to X$ with $f_0 = g \circ g_0$ and $f_1 = g \circ g_1$. Because t is monotone, $F^e(g_i)(t_{X_i}) \sqsubseteq t_X$, for each $i = 1, 2$ so

$$y_i = F^e(g)(F^e(g_i))(t_{X_i}) \sqsubseteq F^e(g)(t_X) \in M.$$

Hence M is directed and 11.2 does at least define a family. It remains to show that the family is continuous. To show that it is monotone, assume $g : D \to E$ is an ep-pair and calculate

$$\begin{aligned}
F^e(g)(\hat{t}_D) &= F^e(g) \bigsqcup \{F^e(f)(t_X) \mid X \in \Im \text{ and } f : X \to D\} \\
&= \bigsqcup \{F^e(g \circ f)(t_X) \mid X \in \Im \text{ and } f : X \to D\} \\
&\sqsubseteq \bigsqcup \{F^e(h)(t_X) \mid X \in \Im \text{ and } h : X \to E\} \\
&= \hat{t}_E.
\end{aligned}$$

Suppose now that $(f_i : D_i \to D)_{i \in I}$ is a directed decomposition of D. We must show that

$$\hat{t}_D = \bigsqcup_{i \in I} F^e(f_i)(\hat{t}_{D_i}). \tag{11.3}$$

The monotonicity of $\hat{t}$ immediately implies that $\sqsupseteq$ holds. Now, according to its definition, $\hat{t}_D$ is the least upper bound of elements $F^e(f)(t_X)$ for $X \in \Im$ and $f : X \to D$. Consider such an element t_X. Since X is finite, there is some $i \in I$ and an ep-pair $h : X \to D_i$ such that $f = f_i \circ h$, so

$$F^e(f)(t_X) = F^e(f_i \circ h)(t_X) = F^e(f_i)(F^e(h)(t_X)) \sqsubseteq F^e(f_i)(\hat{t}_{D_i}).$$

It follows that $\hat{t}_D \sqsubseteq \bigsqcup_{i \in I} F^e(f_i)(\hat{t}_{D_i})$, so Equation 11.3 follows.

It is easy to see that $t \mapsto \check{t}$ and $t \mapsto \hat{t}$ are order preserving. Suppose $t \in \Pi_\Im F$, and let $s = \hat{t}$. Clearly $t_Y \sqsubseteq s_Y$ for $Y \in \Im$. Given $Y \in \Im$, we have

$$\check{s}_Y = \bigsqcup \{F^e(f)(t_X) \mid X \in \Im \text{ and } f : X \to Y\} \sqsubseteq t_Y$$

by the monotonicity of t. Thus $\check{s} = t$. Suppose now that $s \in \Pi F$, and let $t = \check{s}$. If $X \in \Im$, then $s_X = t_X$, so

$$\hat{t}_D = \bigsqcup \{F^e(f)(t_X) \mid X \in \Im \text{ and } f : X \to D\} = s$$

for any domain D since the second equality follows from the fact that D is bifinite.

It is possible to prove that $\Pi_\Im F$ is a bounded-complete cpo using basically the techniques that worked for the dependent product earlier. To prove that it is an algebraic cpo, we need to demonstrate a basis of compact elements. To this end, suppose there is a monotone family t such that $t_X = e \in F(X)$ is finite for some $X \in \Im$. Define

$$(X \searrow e)_Y = \bigsqcup \{F^e(f)(e) \mid f : X \to Y\}.$$

This is well-defined since t_Y is a bound for the set whose join is being taken on the right. It is possible to show that it is a monotone family that does not depend on the choice of t. The proof that it is a basis is basically the same as that given for the basis of the dependent product. □

We are now almost ready to provide a domain-theoretic semantics for the polymorphic λ-calculus without the use of a universal domain. However, the operator Π for continuous sections clearly takes a *functor* as an argument rather than just an operator on types, so the interpretation of a type $[\![t]\!]$ cannot be given simply as a mapping from type-value environments to domains. We must place more structure on our interpretation. To this end, let us define the *category* $\mathbf{E}$ *of type-value environments* to have, as its objects, type-value environments ι. An arrow $f : \iota \to \kappa$ in $\mathbf{E}$ is a family of embedding-projection pairs such that $f(a) : \iota(a) \to \kappa(a)$ for each type variable a in the domain of ι. The interpretation of a type $[\![t]\!]$ is a functor from $\mathbf{E}$ to $\mathbf{Bcdom}^{ep}$ defined by structural induction on types as follows.

- First of all, the interpretation of a type variable is given by the type-value environment $[\![a]\!]\iota = \iota(a)$. The functor action is trivial: if $f \in \mathbf{E}(\iota, \kappa)$, then $[\![a]\!](f) = f(a)$.
- The function space is interpreted as the domain of all continuous functions: $[\![s \to t]\!]\iota = [\![s]\!]\iota \to [\![t]\!]\iota$. If $f : \iota \to \kappa$, then $[\![s \to t]\!](f)$ is an embedding-projection pair $h \in \mathbf{Bcdom}^{ep}([\![s \to t]\!]\iota, [\![s \to t]\!]\kappa)$ where

  $$h^e(k) = [\![t]\!]^e(f) \circ k \circ [\![s]\!]^p(f)$$
  $$h^p(k) = [\![t]\!]^p(f) \circ k \circ [\![s]\!]^e(f).$$

- The interpretation $[\![\Pi a.\ t]\!]\iota$ of a Π type is the domain ΠF of continuous sections of a functor $F : \mathbf{Bcdom}^{ep} \to \mathbf{Bcdom}^{ep}$ whose action on domains is given by $F(D) = [\![t]\!]\iota[a \mapsto D]$. If $f \in \mathbf{Bcdom}^{ep}(D, E)$, then $F(f) = [\![t]\!](f_1) : [\![t]\!]\iota[a \mapsto D] \to [\![t]\!]\iota[a \mapsto E]$ where

  $$f_1(b) = \begin{cases} f & \text{If } b \equiv a \\ \text{id} & \text{Otherwise.} \end{cases}$$

Now, suppose $g : \iota \mapsto \kappa$ is an arrow in $\mathbf{E}$, then we must define the functor action $[\![\Pi a.\ t]\!](g)$. Suppose $\pi \in [\![\Pi a.\ t]\!]\iota$ and D is a domain, then we define

$$([\![\Pi a.\ t]\!](f)(\pi))_D = [\![t]\!](f_2)(\pi_D)$$

where $f_2 : \iota \to \kappa$ is defined by

$$f_2(b) = \begin{cases} \text{id} & \text{If } b \equiv a \\ f(b) & \text{Otherwise.} \end{cases}$$

Now that we have succeeded in interpreting elements of Π types as sections and elements of higher types as functions, the semantics of the polymorphic λ-calculus is basically the one we gave earlier.

Exercises.

11.1 Outline the proof of Lemma 11.9 giving details for the equational rules in Table 11.3.

11.2 Prove Lemma 11.12.

11.3 Prove Lemma 11.13. (Hint: Let K be the set of pairs (e, f) such that $e \in \mathsf{K}(D)$ and $f \in \mathsf{K}(F(e))$ and show that K is a basis for ΣF.)

11.4 Suppose D is a bounded-complete cpo and $F : D \to \mathbf{Cpo}^{ep}$ is a continuous functor such that $F(x)$ is bounded-complete for each $x \in D$. Prove that ΠF is a bc-domain.

11.5 Let $F : \mathbf{C} \to \mathbf{Cat}$ be a functor from a category $\mathbf{C}$ into the category $\mathbf{Cat}$ of categories. Prove that ΠF, Grothendieck fibration of F, is a category.

11.3 Notes

For a general overview of the literature and research on the polymorphic λ-calculus the reader can consult the survey article by Scedrov [217] in the collection [186]. This collection has an excellent selection of articles on polymorphism.

The treatment of ML_0 and the polymorphic λ-calculus is due to Damas and Milner [65; 66], and the rules in Table 7.9 are sometimes known as the 'Damas-Milner rules'. The polymorphic λ-calculus was introduced by Girard [87], and the system was independently rediscovered by Reynolds [203]. An obvious approach toward patching the problem with the set-theoretic semantics of the polymorphic λ-calculus proposed in Section 11.1 is to give up on the assumption that $\Pi a.\ t$ is interpreted as the set of *all* sections of a family indexed over *all* sets. More generally put: is there *any* collection of sets that could serve as the interpretation of such types? The answer to this question is *no*. Reynolds [206] demonstrated that there is no choice of sets as interpretations for Π-types that would yield a non-trivial model. An expansion of this work in a joint paper with Plotkin [210] together with an introductory survey and history of work on the polymorphic λ-calculus is given in [209] (a further of [210] is also in press [201]). An interesting twist on this theme is given by Pitts [193], who showed that if one adopts a constructive approach to the foundations of mathematics, then a set-theoretic model is possible after all. A rigorous development of set theory as a foundations for mathematics can be found in a number of books on set theory; one such book is that of Kunen [141]. Readers interested in a study of the philosophical issues surrounding the 'limitation of size' may consult the book of Hallett [105].

The Type:Type calculus originated as a proposal of Martin-Löf for a logical foundations of constructive mathematics based on type theory. Girard demonstrated that this system was inconsistent in a result known as *Girard's paradox*. It is a type-theoretic version of what is known as the *Burali-Forti* paradox, which concerns the existence of certain kinds of relations. Recent discussions of Girard's paradox appear in papers of Coquand [56], which discusses how it can be obtained from ML-like polymorphism in some circumstances, and Howe [119], which discusses computational aspects of the paradox. Despite this inauspicious origin in logic, the Type:Type calculus has appealed to designers of programming languages for whom these foundational problems are not directly relevant. Efforts to develop a programming language in which types are values on the level of terms include work of Donahue and Demers [74] and the Pebble language of Lampson and Burstall [144]. Another discussion of Type:Type and programming languages is given in a techincal report of Luca Cardelli [42].

Whatever may be the virtues of Type:Type as itself being the foundation for the type system of a programming language, one theoretical advantage of the calculus is the sense in which it provides an extreme in the type-theoretic 'design space'. Besides ML_0 and the polymorphic λ-calculus, there are a number of other systems that can be viewed as polymorphic fragments of Type:Type. The best-known of these is Martin-Löf type theory, a predicative modification of Type:Type that avoids Girard's paradox. This is used as the foundation for the Nuprl theorem proving system [52]. A recent book on this and other topics in type theory has been written by Thompson [262], and further references can be found there. The polymorphic λ-calculus as it was presented here was called F_2 by Girard; it is one of a collection of calculi allowing increasing levels of complexity in the entities over which Π-abstractions can be formed. The calculus F_2 allows only quantification over types, but another step of generalization might permit quantification over operators mapping types to types, a system called F_3. Further generalization leads to a system called F_ω that allows arbitrarily high levels of such quantification. This calculus is part of the Quest programming language of Cardelli [45]; the semantics of which has been studied by Cardelli and Longo [47]. Another system that can be viewed as coming from a wedding of the predicative quantification in a system like Martin-Löf type theory and the impredicative quantification of F_ω is the *Calculus of Constructions* of Coquand and Huet [60]. Constructions forms the logical foundation for the Coq theorem proving system [75]. Other calculi using predicative quantification include LF [107] and the type systems of the Automath family of languages [69].

The first non-trivial model of the polymorphic λ-calculus was described by Girard [87] using partial equivalence relations using essentially the technique described in this chapter. An alternative approach using PER's has been given by Bainbridge, Freyd, Scedrov, and P. J. Scott [20]. A domain-theoretic model was described by McCracken [160] using retractions on a universal domain. D. S. Scott [228] noted that this construction applies to finitary projections as well. Berardi [24] demonstrated that retractions on dI-domains can also be used to model the polymorphic λ-calculus. Girard [88] showed how a domain-theoretic model can be constructed without recourse to a universal domain. His construction worked for a class of what he called *qualitative domains,* which are bc-domains where every principal ideal is isomorphic to $\mathcal{P}(S)$ for some set S (such posets are generally called 'boolean lattices'). Coquand, C. Gunter, and Winskel showed how to generalize this to dI-domains [58], and the model using Grothendeick fibrations described in Section 11.2 is taken from their work in [59]. Similar ideas in the context of universal domains were described by Taylor [257]. The question of whether the Grothendeick construction can be used for other categories has been considered as well. Jung [131] made the unexpected discovery that the cpo of continuous sections of a continuous functor on bifinite domains might *fail* to be a bifinite domain. This provided some counter-evidence to the conventional wisdom that the bifinite domains are the most robust category of domains with respect to closure properties. Modeling the calculus of constructions without the use of a universal domain required significant generalizations of the work in [59]. A model was demonstrated by Coquand [57] using what he called *categories of embeddings*. In the poset case his construction cut down to the ccc of L-domains. Another model for constructions was demonstrated by Hyland and Pitts [125]. A semantics for constructions using an extension of the PER semantics for the polymorphic λ-calculus was given by Scedrov [218].

As with the simply-typed λ-calculus, there are two primary approaches to providing a general description of what a model of the polymorphic λ-calculus *is*. An analog of type frames for polymorphic λ-calculus has been described by Bruce, Meyer, and Mitchell [40]. A more general categorical definition has been given by Seely [231]. Examples of models in the latter class that are not in the former include the qualitative domains model in [88] and the model using Grothendeick fibrations described at the end of Section 11.2. Another discussion of models of the calculus can be found in a paper by Jacobs [126].

One question that arises in looking at models of the polymorphic λ-calculus is how many undefinable elements they contain. For instance, there are no terms of type $\Pi a.\ a$, and, up to equality, there is exactly one term of type $\Pi a.\ a \to a$ (namely, the identity function). In the model at the end of Section 11.2, the interpretation of the type $\Pi a.\ a$ actually has one element, the section that is equal to $\bot$ for each bc-domain, and the interpretation of $\Pi a.\ a \to a$ has *infinitely* many elements. Another example is the type $\Pi a.\ a \to (a \to a)$, which is known as the type of *polymorphic booleans* because, up to equality, there are exactly two terms that have this type. An answer to the question of how to build a model in which the interpretation of this type has only two elements was given by Breazu-Tannen and Coquand [36] who use a collapsing method capable of yielding more parsimonious models of polymorphic types. The general idea of restricting the interpretations of the polymorphic types so that the elements of these interpretations have nice properties dates back to work of Reynolds [205] on a property of the interpretation of a polymorphic type known as *parametricity*. This is a formulation of the idea that the instantiations at various types of an element of a polymorphic type are related to one another in a unifom way. For instance, the monotonicity and continuity conditions on sections that were discussed in this chapter are examples of properties intended to ensure a certain level of uniformity. However, Reynold's uniformity condition is different from these. It was formulated in [205] for a set-theoretic model that was later shown not to exist, so a rigorous formulation for a general class of models had to wait, but it is now the topic of considerable investigation. A paper of Ma and Reynolds [154] has recent results on the problem.

The study of the operational semantics of languages with polymorphic type systems has begun only quite recently. Amadio [9] has described an adequacy result for the PER model while Sorensen and Clausen [242] have provided one for an information systems model of the polymorphic λ-calculus with recursive types based on the construction at the end of Section 11.2. As yet there are no results on full abstraction and polymorphism. It seems likely that full abstraction and parametricity are related properties.

There has been a great deal of effort focused on integrating subtype polymorphism with parametric polymorphism. One system that has received considerable attention is the calculus *Fun* of Cardelli and Wegner [48]. This system permits what is known as *bounded quantification* through a typing rule of the form

$$\frac{H,\; a \leq s \vdash M : t}{H \vdash \Lambda a \leq s.\; M : \Pi a \leq s.\; t}$$

for the introduction of a bounded quantification and

$$\frac{H \vdash M : \Pi a \leq s.\; t \qquad s' \leq s}{H \vdash [s'/a]M : [s'/a]t}$$

for its elimination. Note that the type assignments are generalized to include information about the bounds of type variables. In [48] a model using inclusive subsets is given. A semantics using PER's was subsequently given by Bruce and Longo [39], and a semantics using implicit coercions (including a coherence theorem) by Coquand, Breazu-Tannen, C. Gunter, and Scedrov [59].

An area of some importance for the future is the interpretation of abstract datatypes and modules. The semantics of abstract datatypes has been described by Mitchell and Plotkin [174]. The semantics of modules is more tentative, however, since there are many different module systems under investigation and no clear design 'front-runner'. A treatment of the module system of Standard ML has been given by Harper and Mitchell [108]. Categorical methods are likely to be especially useful in finding the fundamental issues and promoting the designs having the clearest mathematical significance. For instance, a paper of Moggi [178] provides an instance of how this categorical analysis can be carried out. Such analyses will need to be combined with the numerous engineering criteria stemming from the need to build large software systems in order to discover the most important structures.

List of Notations

Bibliography

[1] M. Abadi, L. Cardelli, B. Pierce, and G. D. Plotkin. Dynamic typing in a statically typed language. *Transactions on Programming Languages and Systems*, 13(2):237–268, April 1991. Preliminary version in Proceedings of the Sixteenth Annual ACM Symposium on Principles of Programming Languages (Austin, TX), January, 1989.

[2] H. Abelson and G. J. Sussman. *Structure and Interpretation of Computer Programs*. The MIT Press, 1985.

[3] S. Abramsky. *Domain Theory and the Logic of Observable Properties*. PhD thesis, University of London, 1987.

[4] S. Abramsky. The lazy λ-calculus. In D. A. Turner, editor, *Logical Foundations of Functional Programming*, pages 65–116. Addison-Wesley, 1990.

[5] S. Abramsky. A domain equation for bisimulation. *Information and Computation*, 92:161–217, 1991.

[6] S. Abramsky. Domain theory in logical form. *Annals of Pure and Applied Logic*, 51:1–77, 1991.

[7] S. Abramsky and C. Hankin, editors. *Abstract Interpretation of Declarative Languages*. Ellis Horwood, 1987.

[8] A. V. Aho, R. Sethi, and J. D. Ullman. *Compilers: Principles, Techniques, and Tools*. Addison-Wesley, 1985.

[9] R. Amadio. On the adequacy of per models. Technical Report CRIN 91-R-177, Centre de Recherche en Informatique de Nancy, 1991.

[10] P. America, J. de Bakker, J. N. Kok, and J. Rutten. Denotational semantics of a parallel object-oriented language. *Information and Computation*, 83:152–205, 1989.

[11] A. Appel. *Compiling with Continuations*. Cambridge University Press, 1992.

[12] K. R. Apt. Logic programming. In J. van Leeuwen, editor, *Handbook of Theoretical Computer Science*, pages 493–574. North-Holland, 1990.

[13] K. R. Apt and M. H. van Emden. Contributions to the theory of logic programming. *Journal of the ACM*, 29(3):841 – 862, 1982.

[14] M. Arbib and E. G. Manes. *Structures and Functors: the Categorical Imperative*. Academic Press, 1975.

[15] A. Asperti. Stability and computability in coherent domains. *Information and Computation*, 86:115–139, 1990.

[16] A. Asperti and G. Longo. *Categories, Types, and Structures: An Introduction to Category Theory for the Working Computer Scientist*. The MIT Press, 1991.

[17] J. Backus. Can programming be liberated from the von Neuman style? A functional style and its algebra of programs. *Communications of the ACM*, 21:613–641, 1978.

[18] J. Backus, J. H. Williams, and E. L. Wimmers. An introduction to the programming language FL. In David A. Turner, editor, *Research Topics in Functional Programming*, pages 219–247. Addison-Wesley, 1990.

[19] J. Backus, J. H. Williams, E. L. Wimmers, P. Lucas, and A. Aiken. The FL language manual parts 1 and 2. Technical Report RJ 7100 (67163), IBM, 1989.

[20] E. S. Bainbridge, P. J. Freyd, A. Scedrov, and P. J. Scott. Functorial polymorphism. In G. Huet, editor, *Logical Foundations of Functional Programming*, pages 315–330. Proceedings University of Texas Year of Programming, June 1987.

[21] H. Barendregt. *The Lambda Calculus: Its Syntax and Semantics*, volume 103 of *Studies in Logic and the Foundations of Mathematics*. Elsevier, revised edition, 1984.

[22] M. Barr and C. Wells. *Category Theory for Computing Science*. Prentice Hall, 1990.

[23] M. Ben-Or, D. Kozen, and J. Reif. The complexity of elementary algebra and geometry. *Journal of Computer Systems Science*, 32(2):251–264, 1986.

[24] S. Berardi. Retractions on dI-domains as a model for Type:Type. *Information and Computation*, 94:204–231, 1991.

[25] G. Berry. Stable models of typed λ-calculus. In *International Colloquium on Automata, Languages and Programs*, pages 72–89. *Lecture Notes in Computer Science vol. 62,* Springer, 1978.

[26] G. Berry. *Modèles Complètement Adéquats et Stables des Lambda-calculs Typés.* Thèse d'État, University of Paris VII, 1979.

[27] G. Berry. Some syntactic and categorical constructions of lambda-calculus models. Technical Report 80, Institut de Recherche en Informatique et en Automatique, 1981.

[28] G. Berry and P.-L. Curien. Sequential algorithms on concrete data structures. *Theoretical Computer Science*, 20:265–321, 1982.

[29] G. Berry and P.-L. Curien. Theory and practice of sequential algorithms: the kernal of the applicative language CDS. In M. Nivat and J. C. Reynolds, editors, *Algebraic Methods in Semantics*, pages 35–87. Cambridge University Press, 1985.

[30] G. Berry, P.-L. Curien, and J.-J. Levy. Full abstraction for sequential languages: the state of the art. In M. Nivat and J. C. Reynolds, editors, *Algebraic Methods in Semantics*, pages 89–132. Cambridge University Press, 1985.

[31] B. Bloom. Can lcf be topped? flat lattice models of typed λ-calculus. *Information and Computation*, 87:264–301, 1990.

[32] B. Bloom and J. G. Riecke. LCF should be lifted. In Teodor Rus, editor, *Algebraic Methodology and Software Technology*, pages 133–136. Department of Computer Science, University of Iowa, 1989.

[33] G. S. Boolos and R. C. Jeffrey. *Computability and Logic.* Cambridge University Press, second edition, 1980.

[34] F. Bracho. *Continuously Generated Fixed-Points.* PhD thesis, Oxford University, 1983.

[35] M. Bréal. *Semantics: Studies in the Science of Meaning.* Henry Holt and Company, 1900.

[36] V. Breazu-Tannen and T. Coquand. Extensional models for polymorphism. *Theoretical Computer Science*, 59:85–114, 1988.

[37] V. Breazu-Tannen, T. Coquand, C. A. Gunter, and A. Scedrov. Inheritance as implicit coercion. *Information and Computation*, 93:172–221, 1991.

[38] V. Breazu-Tannen, C. Gunter, and A. Scedrov. Computing with coercions. In M. Wand, editor, *Lisp and Functional Programming*, pages 44–60. ACM, 1990.

[39] K. B. Bruce and G. Longo. A modest model of records, inheritance, and bounded quantification. *Information and Computation*, 87:196–240, 1990.

[40] K. B. Bruce, A. R. Meyer, and J. C. Mitchell. The semantics of second-order lambda calculus. *Information and Computation*, 85:76–134, 1990.

[41] G. L. Burn, C. Hankin, and S. Abramsky. Strictness analysis for higher-order functions. *Science of Computer Programming*, 7:249–278, 1986.

[42] L. Cardelli. A polymorophic λ-calculus with Type:Type. Research Report 10, DEC Systems, Palo Alto, 1986.

[43] L. Cardelli. Basic polymorphic typechecking. *Science of Computer Programming*, 8:147–172, 1987.

[44] L. Cardelli. A semantics of multiple inheritance. *Information and Computation*, 76:138–164, 1988.

[45] L. Cardelli. The Quest language and system. Tracking draft, 1991.

[46] L. Cardelli. Typeful programming. In E. J. Neuhold and M. Paul, editors, *Formal Description of Programming Concepts*, IFIP State-of-the-Art Reports, pages 431–507. Springer, 1991.

[47] L. Cardelli and P. Longo. A semantic basis for Quest. *Journal of Functional Programming*, 1:417–458, 1991.

[48] L. Cardelli and P. Wegner. On understanding types, data abstraction and polymorphism. *ACM Computing Surveys*, 17(4):471–522, 1985.

[49] F. Cardone and M. Coppo. Two extensions of Curry's type inference system. In P. Odifreddi, editor, *Logic and Computer Science*, pages 19–76. Academic Press, 1990.

[50] C. C. Chang and H. J. Keisler. *Model Theory*, volume 73 of *Studies in Logica and the Foundations of Mathematics*. North-Holland, 1973.

[51] E. M. Clarke, S. M. German, and J. Y. Halpern. On effective axiomatizations of Hoare logics. *Journal of the ACM*, 30:612–636, 1983.

[52] R. L. Constable, S. F. Allen, H. M. Bromley, W. R. Cleaveland, J. F. Cremer, R. W. Harper, D. J. Howe, T. B. Knoblock, N. P. Mendler, P. Panangaden, J. T. Sasaki, and S. F. Smith. *Implementing Mathematics with the Nuprl Proof Development System*. Prentice-Hall, 1986.

[53] M. Coppo and M. Dezani-Ciancaglini. An extension of basic functionality theory for lambda-calculus. *Notre Dame Journal of Formal Logic*, 21:685–693, 1980.

[54] M. Coppo, M. Dezani-Ciancaglini, and B. Venneri. Functional characters of solvable terms. *Z. Math. Log. Grund. Math.*, 27:45–58, 1981.

[55] M. Coppo, M. Dezani-Ciancaglini, and M. Zacchi. Type theories, normal forms and d_∞-lambda models. *Information and Computation*, 72:85–116, 1987.

[56] T. Coquand. An analysis of Girard's paradox. In A. Meyer, editor, *Logic in Computer Science*, pages 227–236. IEEE Computer Society Press, 1986.

[57] T. Coquand. Categories of embeddings. *Theoretical Computer Science*, 68:221–237, 1989.

[58] T. Coquand, C. A. Gunter, and G. Winskel. DI-domains as a model of polymorphism. In M. Main, A. Melton, M. Mislove, and D. Schmidt, editors, *Mathematical Foundations of Programming Language Semantics*, pages 344–363. *Lecture Notes in Computer Science vol. 298,* Springer, April 1987.

[59] T. Coquand, C. A. Gunter, and G. Winskel. Domain theoretic models of polymorphism. *Information and Computation*, 81:123–167, 1989.

[60] T. Coquand and G. Huet. The calculus of constructions. *Information and Computation*, 76:95–120, 1988.

[61] P. Cousot. Methods and logics for proving programs. In J. van Leeuwen, editor, *Handbook of Theoretical Computer Science*, pages 841–994. North-Holland, 1990.

[62] P.-L. Curien. *Categorical Combinators, Sequential Algorithms and Functional Programming*. Pitman, 1986.

[63] P.-L. Curien, G. Cousineau, and M. Mauny. The categorical abstract machine. *Science of Computer Programming*, 8:173–202, 1987.

[64] P.-L. Curien and A. Obtulowicz. Partiality, cartesian closednes, and toposes. *Information and Computation*, 80:50–95, 1989.

[65] L. Damas. *Type Assignment in Programming Languages*. PhD thesis, Edinburgh University, 1985.

[66] L. Damas and R. Milner. Principal type-schemes for functional programs. In *Principles of Programming Languages*, pages 207–212. ACM, 1982.

[67] D. Davidson and G. Harman, editors. *Semantics of Natural Language*. Humanities Press, 1972.

[68] J. W. de Bakker and J. H. A. Warmerdam. Four domains for concurrency. *Theoretical Computer Science*, 90:127–149, 1991.

[69] D. G. de Bruijn. A survey of the project AUTOMATH. In J. P. Seldin and J. R. Hindley, editors, *To H. B. Curry: Essays on Combinatory Logic, Lambda Calculus and Formalism*, pages 579–606. Academic Press, 1980.

[70] R. A. De Millo, R. J. Lipton, and A. J. Perlis. Social processes and proofs of theorems and programs. *Communications of the ACM*, 22:271–280, 1979.

[71] E. P. de Vink. Comparative semantics for PROLOG with cut. *Science of Computer Programming*, 13:237–264, 1990.

[72] S. K. Debray and P. Mishra. Denotational and operational semantics for PROLOG. *Journal of Logic Programming*, pages 61–91, 1988.

[73] E. W. Dijkstra. *A Discipline of Programming*. Prentice-Hall, 1976.

[74] J. Donahue and A. Demers. Data types are values. *ACM Transactions on Programming Languages and Systems*, 7:426–445, 1985.

[75] G. Dowek, A. Felty, H. Herbelin, G. Huet, C. Paulin-Mohring, and B. Werner. The Coq proof assistant user's guide. Technical Report 134, INRIA, December 1991.

[76] M. Droste. Universal homogenous event structures and domains. *Information and Computation*, 94:48–61, 1991.

[77] M. Droste. On stable domains. *Theoretical Computer Science*. To appear.

[78] M. Droste and R. Göbel. Universal domains in the theory of denotational semantics of programming languages. In J. C. Mitchell, editor, *Logic in Computer Science*, pages 19–34. IEEE Computer Society, June 1990.

[79] M. Droste and R. Göbel. Universal information systems. *International Journal of Foundations of Computer Science*, 1:413–424, 1991.

[80] C. N. Fischer and R. J. LeBlanc. *Crafting a Compiler with C*. Benjamin/Cummings, 1991.

[81] G. Frege. *Die Grundlagen der Arithmetik: Enie logisch mathematische Untersuchung über den Begriff der Zahl*. Verlag von Wilhelm Koebner, 1884.

[82] G. Frege. *The Foundations of Arithmetic: A logico-mathematical enquiry into the concept of number*. Northwestern University Press, 1978.

[83] D. P. Friedman, M. Wand, and C. T. Haynes. *Essentials of Programming Languages*. The MIT Press, 1992.

[84] H. Friedman. Equality between functionals. In R. Parikh, editor, *Proceedings of the Logic Colloqium '73*, pages 22–37. *Lecture Notes in Mathematics vol. 453*, Springer, 1975.

[85] S. M. German, E. M. Clarke, and J. Y. Halpern. True relative completeness of an axiom system for the language L4. In A. Meyer, editor, *Logic in Computer Science*, pages 11–25. IEEE Computer Society, June 1986.

[86] G. Gierz, K. H. Hofmann, K. Keimel, J. D. Lawson, M. Mislove, and D. S. Scott. *A Compendium of Continuous Lattices*. Springer, 1980.

[87] J. Y. Girard. *Interprétation Fonctionelle et Élimination des Coupures de l'Arithmétique d'Ordre Supérieur*. Thèse d'État, University of Paris VII, 1972.

[88] J. Y. Girard. The system F of variable types: fifteen years later. *Theoretical Computer Science*, 45:159–192, 1986.

[89] J. Y. Girard. Linear logic. *Theoretical Computer Science*, 50:1–101, 1987.

[90] J. Y. Girard, Y. Lafont, and P. Taylor. *Proofs and Types*. Cambridge University Press, 1989.

[91] A. Goerdt. Hoare logic for lambda-terms as basis of Hoare logic for imperative languages. In D. Gries, editor, *Symposium on Logic in Computer Science*, pages 293–299, Ithaca, New York, June 1987. IEEE Computer Society Press.

[92] J. A. Goguen, J. W. Thatcher, and E. G. Wagner. Initial algebra semantics and continuous algebras. *Journal of the ACM*, 24(1):68–95, 1977.

[93] J. A. Goguen, J. W. Thatcher, and E. G. Wagner. An initial algebra approach to the specification, correctness, and implementation of abstract data types. In R. T. Yeh, editor, *Current Trends in Programming Methodology*, volume 4. Prentice-Hall, 1978.

[94] Joseph Goguen. Higher-order functions considered unnecessary for higher-order programming. In David Turner, editor, *Research Topics in Functional Programming*, pages 309–352. Addison-Wesley, 1990.

[95] M. J. C. Gordon. *The Denotational Description of Programming Languages*. Springer, 1979.

[96] C. A. Gunter. *Profinite Solutions for Recursive Domain Equations*. PhD thesis, University of Wisconsin at Madison, 1985.

[97] C. A. Gunter. Universal profinite domains. *Information and Computation*, 72:1–30, 1987.

[98] C. A. Gunter. Forms of semantic specification. *Bulletin of the European Association for Theoretical Computer Science*, 45:98–113, 1991.

[99] C. A. Gunter, E. L. Gunter, and D. B. MacQueen. Using abstract interpretation to compute ML equality kinds. *Information and Computation*. In press.

[100] C. A. Gunter and A. Jung. Coherence and consistency in domains. *Journal of Pure and Applied Algebra*, 63:49–66, 1990.

[101] C. A. Gunter and D. S. Scott. Semantic domains. In J. van Leeuwen, editor, *Handbook of Theoretical Computer Science*, pages 633–674. North-Holland, 1990.

[102] C. A. Gunter and D. S. Scott. Semantic domains. In J. van Leeuwen, editor, *Handbook of Theoretical Computer Science*, pages 633–674. North-Holland, 1990.

[103] E. L. Gunter. Pseudo-retract functors for local lattices and bifinite l-domains. In M. Main, A. Melton, M. Mislove, and D. Schmidt, editors, *Mathematical Foundations of Programming Semantics*, pages 351–363. *Lecture Notes in Computer Science vol. 442*, Springer, March 1989.

[104] Y. Gurevich. Logic and the challenge of computer science. In E. Börger, editor, *Trends in Theoretical Computer Science*, pages 1–57. Computer Science Press, 1988.

[105] M. Hallett. *Cantorian Set Theory and the Limitation of Size*. Oxford University Press, 1984.

[106] J. Hannan and D. Miller. From operational semantics to abstract machines. *Mathematical Structures in Computer Science*. In press for a special issue of papers selected from the 1990 Lisp and Functional Programming Conference.

[107] R. Harper, F. Honsell, and G. Plotkin. A framework for defining logics. In D. Gries, editor, *Symposium on Logic in Computer Science*, pages 194–204, Ithaca, New York, June 1987. IEEE Computer Society Press.

[108] R. Harper and J. C. Mitchell. On the type structure of Standard ML. *ACM Transactions on Programming Languages and Systems*. To appear.

[109] P. Henderson. *Functional Programming: Application and Implementation*. Prentice-Hall, 1980.

[110] M. Hennessy. *Algebraic Theory of Processes*. The MIT Press, 1988.

[111] M. Hennessy. *The Semantics of Programming Languages: An Elementary Introduction using Structural Operational Semantics*. Wiley Press, 1990.

[112] M. Hennessy and G. D. Plotkin. Full abstraction for a simple parallel programming language. In J. Bečvář, editor, *Mathematical Foundations of Computer Science*, pages 108–120. *Lecture Notes in Computer Science vol. 74*, Springer, 1979.

[113] H. Herrlich and G. E. Strecker. *Category Theory*. Allyn and Bacon, 1973.

[114] J. R. Hindley and J. P. Seldin. *Introduction to Combinators and λ-calculus*. Cambridge University Press, 1986.

[115] R. Hindley. The principal type-scheme of an object in combinatory logic. *Transactions of the American Mathematics Society*, 146:29–60, 1969.

[116] C. A. R. Hoare. An axiomatic basis for computer programming. *Communications of the ACM*, 12:567–580, 1969.

[117] B.T. Howard and J.C. Mitchell. Operational and axiomatic semantics of PCF. In *ACM Conference on LISP and Functional Programming*, pages 298–306, 1990.

[118] W. Howard. Hereditarily majorizable functionals of finite type. In A. S. Troelstra, editor, *Metamathematical Investigation of Intuitionistic Arithmetic and Analysis*, pages 454–461. *Lecture Notes in Mathematics vol 344*, Springer, 1973.

[119] D. Howe. The computational behavior of Girard's paradox. In D. Gries, editor, *Symposium on Logic in Computer Science*, pages 215–224, Ithaca, New York, June 1987. IEEE Computer Society Press.

[120] K. Hrbacek. Convex powerdomains I. *Information and Computation*, 74:198–225, 1987.

[121] K. Hrbacek. Convex powerdomains II. *Information and Computation*, 81:290–317, 1989.

[122] P. Hudak, S. Peyton Jones, and P. Wadler (editors). Report on the Programming Language Haskell, A Non-strict Purely Functional Language (Version 1.2). *ACM SIGPLAN Notices*, 27(5), May 1992.

[123] P. Hudak and J. Young. Collecting interpretations of expressions. *ACM Transactions on Programming Languages and Systems*, 13:269–290, 1991.

[124] H. Huwig and A. Poigné. A note on inconsistencies caused by fixpoints in a cartesian closed category. *Theoretical Computer Science*, 73:101–112, 1990.

[125] J. M. E. Hyland and A. Pitts. The theory of constructions: categorical semantics and topos-theoretic models. In J. W. Gray and A. Scedrov, editors, *Categories in Computer Science and Logic*, pages 137–199. ACM, 1989.

[126] B. Jacobs. Semantics of the second order lambda calculus. *Mathematical Structures in Computer Science*, pages 327–360, 1991.

[127] T. Jim and A. R. Meyer. Full abstraction and the context lemma. In T. Ito and A. R. Meyer, editors, *Theoretical Aspects of Computer Software*, volume 526 of *Lecture Notes in Computer Science*, pages 131–151. Springer-Verlag, September 1991.

[128] P. Johnstone. *Stone Spaces*, volume 3 of *Studies in Advanced Mathematics*. Cambridge University Press, 1982.

[129] A. Jung. New results on hierarchies of domains. In M. Main and A. Melton, editors, *Mathematical Foundations of Programming Language Semantics*, pages 303–311. *Lecture Notes in Computer Science vol. 298*, Springer, 1987.

[130] A. Jung. *Cartesian Closed Categories of Domains*. PhD thesis, Darmstadt Technische Hochschule, 1988.

[131] A. Jung. The dependent product construction in various categories of domains. *Theoretical Computer Science*, 79:359–363, 1991.

[132] T. Kamimura and A. Tang. Effectively given spaces. *Theoretical Computer Science*, 29:155–166, 1984.

[133] S. Kamin. Final data types and their specifications. *ACM Transactions on Programming Languages and Systems*, 5:97–123, 1983.

[134] S. Kamin. *Programming Languages: An Interpreter Based Approach*. Addison-Wesley, 1990.

[135] E. L. Keenan, editor. *Formal Semantics of Natural Language*. Cambridge University Press, 1975.

[136] G. M. Kelly and S. Mac Lane. Coherence in closed categories. *Journal of Pure and Applied Algebra*, 1:97–140, 1971. Erratum ibid. 2(1971), p. 219.

[137] A. J. Kfoury, J. Tiuryn, and P. Urzyczyn. On the computational power of universally polymorphic recursion. In Y. Gurevich, editor, *Logic in Computer Science*, pages 72–81. IEEE Computer Society, July 1988.

[138] A. J. Kfoury, J. Tiuryn, and P. Urzyczyn. Type-reconstruction in the presence of polymorphic recursion. *ACM Transactions on Programming Languages and Systems*. To appear.

[139] D. E. Knuth. The remaining troublespots in ALGOL 60. *Comm. ACM*, 10(10):611–617, 1967.

[140] C. Koymans. Models of the lambda calculus. *Information and Control*, 52:306–332, 1982.

[141] K. Kunen. *Set Theory: An Introduction to Independence Proofs*. North-Holland, 1980.

[142] J. Lambek. From λ-calculus to cartesian closed categories. In J. P. Seldin and J. R. Hindley, editors, *To H. B. Curry: Essays on Combinatory Logic, Lambda Calculus and Formalism*, pages 375–402. Academic Press, 1980.

[143] J. Lambek and P. J. Scott. *Introduction to Higher-Order Categorical Logic*, volume 7 of *Studies in Advanced Mathematics*. Cambridge University Press, 1986.

[144] B. Lampson and R. Burstall. Pebble, a kernal language for modules and abstract data types. *Information and Computation*, 76:278–346, 1988.

[145] J. Landin. An abstract machine for designers of computing languages. In *IFIP Congress*, pages 438–439. North-Holland, 1965.

[146] P. Landin. The mechanical evaluation of expressions. *Comput. J.*, 6:308–320, 1964.

[147] P. Landin. A correspondence between ALGOL 60 and Church's lambda notation. *Communications of the ACM*, 8:89–101, 1965.

[148] S. Mac Lane. *Categories for the Working Mathematician*. Springer, 1971.

[149] S. Mac Lane and R. Pare. Coherence for bicategories and indexed categories. *Journal of Pure and Applied Algebra*, 37:59–80, 1985.

[150] J. Launchbury. *Projection Factorizations in Partial Evaluation*. Cambridge University Press, 1992.

[151] P. Lee. *Realistic Compiler Generation*. Foundations of Computing. The MIT Press, 1989.

[152] H. R. Lewis and C. H. Papadimitriou. *Elements of the Theory of Computation*. Prentice-Hall, 1981.

[153] J. Lyons. *Semantics*. Cambridge University Press, 1977.

[154] Q. Ma and J. C. Reynolds. Types, abstraction, and parametric polymorphism, part 2. In Stephen Brookes, Michael Main, Austin Melton, Michael Mislove, and David A. Schmidt, editors, *Proceedings of the 1991 Mathematical Foundations of Programming Semantics Conference*, volume 598 of *Lecture Notes in Computer Science*, pages 1–40, Berlin, 1992. Springer-Verlag.

[155] D. B. MacQueen, G. D. Plotkin, and R. Sethi. An ideal model for recursive polymorphic types. *Information and Control*, 71:95–130, 1986.

[156] G. Markowsky. Chain-complete posets and directed sets with applications. *Algebra Universalis*, 6:53–68, 1976.

[157] G. Markowsky. Categories of chain-complete posets. *Theoretical Computer Science*, 4:125–135, 1977.

[158] I. Mason and C. Talcott. Equivalence in functional languages with effects. *Journal of Functional Programming*, 1:287–327, 1991.

[159] David C. McCarty. *Realizability and Recursive Mathematics*. PhD thesis, Oxford University, 1984.

[160] N. McCracken. *An Investigation of a Programming Language with a Polymorphic Type Structure*. PhD thesis, Syracuse University, 1979.

[161] J. Meseguer. Varieties of chain-complete algebras. *Journal of Pure and Applied Algebra*, 19:347–383, 1980.

[162] J. Meseguer. Order completion monads. *Algebra Universalis*, 16:63–82, 1983.

[163] A. Meyer and S. S. Cosmadakis. Semantical paradigms: Notes for an invited lecture. In Y. Gurevich, editor, *Logic in Computer Science*, pages 236–255. IEEE Computer Society, July 1988.

[164] A. Meyer and K. Sieber. Towards fully abstract semantics for local variables: preliminary report. In *Principles of Programming Languages*, pages 191–208. ACM, 1989.

[165] A. R. Meyer. What is a model of the lambda calculus? *Information and Control*, 52:87–122, 1982.

[166] R. Milne. *The Formal Semantics of Computer Languages and their Implementations*. Ph. d. dissertation, Oxford University, 1974. Report PRG-13 and Technical Microfiche TCF-2.

[167] R. Milner. Processes: a mathematical model of computing agents. In H. E. Rose and J. C. Schepherdson, editors, *Proceedings of the Logic Colloqium '73*. North-Holland, 1975.

[168] R. Milner. Fully abstract models of typed lambda-calculi. *Theoretical Computer Science*, 4:1–22, 1977.

[169] R. Milner. A theory of type polymorphism in programming. *Journal of Computer and System Sciences*, 17:348–375, 1978.

[170] R. Milner. *Communication and Concurrency*. Prentice Hall International, 1989.

[171] R. Milner. Operational and algebraic semantics of concurrent processes. In J. van Leeuwen, editor, *Handbook of Theoretical Computer Science*, pages 1201–1242. North-Holland, 1990.

[172] R. Milner and M. Tofte. *Commentary on Standard ML*. The MIT Press, 1991.

[173] R. Milner, M. Tofte, and R. Harper. *The Definition of Standard ML*. The MIT Press, 1990.

[174] J. Mitchell and G. Plotkin. Abstract types have existential type. *ACM Transactions on Programming Languages and Systems*, 10:470–502, 1988.

[175] J. C. Mitchell. Types systems for programming languages. In J. van Leeuwen, editor, *Handbook of Theoretical Computer Science*, pages 365–458. North-Holland, 1990.

[176] E. Moggi. *The Partial Lambda-Calculus*. PhD thesis, University of Edinburgh, 1988.

[177] E. Moggi. Partial morphisms in categories of effective objects. *Information and Computation*, 76:250–277, 1988.

[178] E. Moggi. A category-theoretic account of program modules. *Mathematical Structures in Computer Science*, 1:103–139, 1991.

[179] P. D. Mosses. Denotational semantics. In J. van Leeuwen, editor, *Handbook of Theoretical Computer Science*, pages 577–632. North-Holland, 1990.

[180] P. D. Mosses. *Action Semantics*, volume 26 of *Cambridge Tracts in Theoretical Computer Science*. Cambridge University Press, 1992.

[181] P. D. Mosses and G. D. Plotkin. On proving limiting completeness. *SIAM Journal of Computing*, 16:179–194, 1987.

[182] K. Mulmuley. *Full Abstraction and Semantic Equivalence*. The MIT Press, 1987.

[183] P. Naur (editor). Report on the algorithmic language ALGOL 60. *Communications of the ACM*, 6:299–314, 1960.

[184] P. Naur and M. Woodger (editors). Revised report on the algorithmic language ALGOL 60. *Communications of the ACM*, 6:1–20, 1963.

[185] H. R. Nielson and F. Nielson. *Semantics with Applications: A Formal Introduction for Computer Science*. Wiley Press.

[186] P. Odifreddi, editor. *Logic and Computer Science*. Academic Press, 1990.

[187] P. W. O'Hearn. *Semantics of Non-Interference: a Natural Approach*. Ph.D. thesis, Queen's University, Kingston, Canada, 1990.

[188] A. Ohori. *A Study of Types, Semantics and Languages for Databases and Object-oriented Programming*. PhD thesis, University of Pennsylvania, 1989.

[189] L. C. Paulson. *ML for the Working Computer Scientist*. Cambridge University Press, 1991.

[190] Benjamin Pierce. *Basic Category Theory for Computer Scientists*. The MIT Press, 1991.

[191] D. H. Pitt, editor. *Proceedings of the Conference on Category Theory and Computer Science. Lecture Notes in Computer Science*, Vol. 283, Springer-Verlag, 1987.

[192] D. H. Pitt, S. Abramsky, A. Poigné, and D. Rydeheard, editors. *Proceedings of the Conference on Category Theory and Computer Programming. Lecture Notes in Computer Science*, Vol. 240, Springer-Verlag, 1985.

[193] A. Pitts. Polymorphism is set-theoretic, constructively. In D. H. Pitt, A. Poigné, and David E. Rydeheard, editors, *Category Theory and Computer Science*, pages 12–39. *Lecture Notes in Computer Science vol. 283*, Springer, 1987.

[194] G. D. Plotkin. Lambda-definability and logical relations. Memorandum SAI-RM-4, University of Edinburgh, October 1973.

[195] G. D. Plotkin. Call-by-name, call-by-value and the lambda calculus. *Theoretical Computer Science*, 1:125–159, 1975.

[196] G. D. Plotkin. A powerdomain construction. *SIAM Journal of Computing*, 5:452–487, 1976.

[197] G. D. Plotkin. $\mathbb{T}^\omega$ as a universal domain. *Journal of Computer and System Sciences*, 17:209–236, 1978.

[198] G. M. Reed and A. W. Roscoe. Metric spaces as models for real-time concurrency. In M. Main and A. Melton, editors, *Mathematical Foundations of Programming Language Semantics*, pages 331–343. *Lecture Notes in Computer Science vol. 298*, Springer, 1987.

[199] J. Rees and W. Clinger (editors). The revised[3] report on the algorithmic language Scheme. *Sigplan Notices*, 21:37–79, 1986.

[200] D. Rémy. *Algèbres Touffues. Application au Typage Polymorphe des Objects Enregistrements dans les Langages Fonctionnels*. Thèse de doctorat, Université de Paris 7, 1990.

[201] J. Reynolds and G. D. Plotkin. On functors expressible in the polymorphic lambda calculus. *Information and Computation*. To appear.

[202] J. C. Reynolds. On the relation between direct and continuation semantics. In Jacques Loeckx, editor, *International Colloquium on Automata, Languages and Programming*, pages 141–156. *Lecture Notes in Computer Science vol. 14*, Springer, 1974.

[203] J. C. Reynolds. Towards a theory of type structure. In B. Robinet, editor, *Programming Symposium*, pages 408–425. *Lecture Notes in Computer Science vol. 19*, Springer, 1974.

[204] J. C. Reynolds. Using category theory to design implicit conversions and generic operators. In N. D. Jones, editor, *Semantics-Directed Compiler Generation*, pages 211–258. *Lecture Notes in Computer Science vol. 94*, Springer, 1980.

[205] J. C. Reynolds. Types, abstraction and parametric polymorphism. In R. E. A. Mason, editor, *Information Processing 83*, pages 513–523, Amsterdam, 1983. Elsevier Science Publishers B. V. (North-Holland).

[206] J. C. Reynolds. Polymorphism is not set-theoretic. In G. Kahn, D. B. MacQueen, and G. D. Plotkin, editors, *Semantics of Data Types*, pages 145–156. *Lecture Notes in Computer Science vol. 173,* Springer, 1984.

[207] J. C. Reynolds. Three approaches to type structure. In H. Ehrig, C. Floyd, M. Nivat, and J. Thatcher, editors, *Mathematical Foundations of Software Development*, pages 97–138. *Lecture Notes in Computer Science vol. 185,* Springer, 1985.

[208] J. C. Reynolds. Preliminary design of the programming language Forsythe. Technical Report CMU-CS-88-159, Carnegie-Mellon University, 1988.

[209] J. C. Reynolds. Introduction to part II, polymorphic lambda calculus. In Gérard Huet, editor, *Logical Foundations of Functional Programming*, University of Texas at Austin Year of Programming, pages 77–86. Addison-Wesley, Reading, Massachusetts, 1990.

[210] J. C. Reynolds and G. D. Plotkin. On functors expressible in the polymorphic typed lambda calculus. In Gérard Huet, editor, *Logical Foundations of Functional Programming*, University of Texas at Austin Year of Programming, pages 127–152. Addison-Wesley, Reading, Massachusetts, 1990.

[211] E. Robinson and G. Rosolini. Categories of partial maps. *Information and Computation*, 79:95–130, 1988.

[212] J. A. Robinson. A machine oriented logic based on the resolution principle. *Journal of the ACM*, 12:23–41, 1965.

[213] S. Ronchi Della Rocca. Principal type scheme and unification for intersection type discipline. *Theoretical Computer Science*, 59:181–209, 1988.

[214] J. F. Rosenberg and C. Travis, editors. *Readings in the Philosphy of Language*. Prentice-Hall, 1971.

[215] D. E. Rydeheard and R. M. Burstall. *Computational Category Theory*. Prentice Hall, 1988.

[216] V. Sazonov. Expressibility of functions in D. Scott's LCF language. *Algebra i Logika*, 15:308–330, 1976.

[217] A. Scedrov. A guide to polymorphic types. In P. Odifreddi, editor, *Logic and Computer Science*, pages 387–420. Academic Press, 1990.

[218] A. Scedrov. Recursive realizability semantics for calculus of constructions. In G. Huet, editor, *Logical Foundations of Functional Programming*, pages 419–430. Addison-Wesley, 1990.

[219] W. L. Scherlis and D. S. Scott. First steps toward inferential programming. *Information Processing*, 83:199–213, 1983.

[220] David Schmidt. *Denotational Semantics: A Methodology for Language Development*. Allyn and Bacon, 1986.

[221] D. S. Scott. A type theoretical alternative to CUCH, ISWIM, OWHY. Unpublished manuscript, 1969.

[222] D. S. Scott. Continuous lattices. In F. W. Lawvere, editor, *Toposes, Algebraic Geometry and Logic*, pages 97–136. *Lecture Notes in Mathematics vol. 274,* Springer, 1972.

[223] D. S. Scott. Data types as lattices. *SIAM Journal of Computing*, 5:522–587, 1976.

[224] D. S. Scott. Logic and programming languages. *Communications of the ACM*, 20:634–641, 1976.

[225] D. S. Scott. Relating theories of the lambda calculus. In J. P. Seldin and J. R. Hindley, editors, *To H. B. Curry: Essays on Combinatory Logic, Lambda Calculus and Formalism*, pages 403–450. Academic Press, 1980.

[226] D. S. Scott. Some ordered sets in computer science. In I. Rival, editor, *Ordered Sets*, pages 677–718. D. Reidel, 1981.

[227] D. S. Scott. Domains for denotational semantics. In M. Nielsen and E. M. Schmidt, editors, *International Colloquium on Automata, Languages and Programs*, pages 577–613. *Lecture Notes in Computer Science vol. 140*, Springer, 1982.

[228] D. S. Scott. Lectures on a mathematical theory of computation. In M. Broy and G. Schmidt, editors, *Theoretical Foundations of Programming Methodology*, pages 145–292. *NATO Advanced Study Institutes Series*, D. Reidel, 1982.

[229] D. S. Scott, D. C. McCarty, and J. F. Horty. Bibliography. In J. Barwise, editor, *Model-Theoretic Logics*, pages 793–891. Springer Verlag, 1985.

[230] D. S. Scott and C. Strachey. Towards a mathematical semantics for computer languages. In J. Fox, editor, *Computers and Automata*, pages 19–46. Polytechnic Institute of Brooklyn Press, 1971.

[231] R. A. G. Seely. Categorical semantics for higher-order polymorphic lambda calculus. *Journal of Symbolic Logic*, 52:969–989, 1987.

[232] R. Sethi. *Programming Languages: Concepts and Constructs*. Addison-Wesley, 1989.

[233] Kurt Sieber. Relating full abstraction results for different programming languages. In *Foundations of Software Technology and Theoretical Computer Science, Bangalore, India*, 1990.

[234] Dorai Sitaram and Matthias Felleisen. Reasoning with continuations II: full abstraction for models of control. In M. Wand, editor, *Lisp and Functional Programming*, pages 161–175. ACM, 1990.

[235] S. F. Smith. *Partial Objects in Type Theory*. PhD thesis, Cornell University, 1988.

[236] M. Smyth. Effectively given domains. *Theoretical Computer Science*, 5:257–274, 1977.

[237] M. Smyth. Power domains. *Journal of Computer System Sciences*, 16:23–36, 1978.

[238] M. Smyth. The largest cartesian closed category of domains. *Theoretical Computer Science*, 27:109–119, 1983.

[239] M. Smyth. Power domains and predicate transformers: a topological view. In J. Diaz, editor, *International Colloquium on Automata, Languages and Programs*, pages 662–676. *Lecture Notes in Computer Science vol. 154*, Springer, 1983.

[240] M. Smyth and G. D. Plotkin. The category-theoretic solution of recursive domain equations. *SIAM Journal of Computing*, 11:761–783, 1982.

[241] S. Sokolowksi. *Applicative High Order Programming: The standard ML perspective*. Chapman and Hall, 1991.

[242] B. B. Sørensen and C. Clausen. Adequacy results for a lazy functional language with recursive and polymorphic types. Unpublished manuscript.

[243] D. Spreen. Computable one-to-one enumerations of effective domains. *Information and Computation*, 84:26–46, 1990.

[244] R. Statman. Completeness, invariance and λ-definability. *Journal of Symbolic Logic*, 47:17–26, 1982.

[245] R. Statman. Equality between functionals. In *Harvey Friedman's Research on the Foundations of Mathematics*, pages 331–338. North-Holland, 1985.

[246] R. Statman. Logical relations and the typed λ-calculus. *Information and Control*, 65:85–97, 1985.

[247] R. Statman. On translating lambda terms into combinators: the basis problem. In A. Meyer, editor, *Symposium on Logic in Computer Science*, pages 378–382. ACM, 1986.

[248] D. D. Steinberg and L. A. Jakobovits, editors. *Semantics*. Cambridge University Press, 1971.

[249] L. Sterling and E. Shapiro. *The Art of Prolog*. The MIT Press, 1986.

[250] A. Stoughton. *Fully Abstract Models of Programming Languages*. Pitman, 1988.

[251] A. Stoughton. Interdefinability of parallel operations in PCF. *Theoretical Computer Science*, 79:357–358, 1991.

[252] J. E. Stoy. *Denotational Semantics: The Scott-Strachey Approach to Programming Language Semantics*. The MIT Press, 1977.

[253] G. J. Sussman and G. L. Steele. Scheme: an interpreter for extended lambda calculus. Technical Report AI Memo 349, MIT Laboratory for Computer Science, 1975.

[254] G. J. Sussman and G. L. Steele. The revised report on Scheme, a dialect of lisp. Technical Report AI Memo 452, MIT Laboratory for Computer Science, 1978.

[255] W. W. Tait. Intensional interpretation of functionals of finite type. *Journal of Symbolic Logic*, 32:198–212, 1967.

[256] P. Taylor. Trace factorization. Unpublished manuscript.

[257] P. Taylor. *Recursive Domains, Indexed Category Theory and Polymorphism*. PhD thesis, Cambridge University, 1987.

[258] P. Taylor. An algebraic approach to stable domains. *Journal of Pure and Applied Algebra*, 64:171–203, 1990.

[259] R. D. Tennent. Elementary data structures in Algol-like languages. *Science of Computer Programming*, 13:73–110, 1989.

[260] R. D. Tennent. Semantical analysis of specification logic. *Information and Computation*, 85(2):135–162, 1990.

[261] R. D. Tennent. *Semantics of Programming Languages*. Prentice-Hall, 1991.

[262] S. Thompson. *Type Theory and Functional Programming*. Addison-Wesley, 1991.

[263] M. Tofte. Type inference for polymorphic references. *Information and Computation*, 89:1–34, 1990.

[264] D. A. Turner. Miranda: a non-strict functional language with polymorphic types. In J. P. Jouannaud, editor, *Functional Programming Languages and Computer Architecture*, pages 1–16. *Lecture Notes in Computer Science vol. 201,* Springer, 1985.

[265] S. Vickers. *Topology via Logic*, volume 5 of *Tracts in Theoretical Computer Science*. Cambridge University Press, 1989.

[266] M. Wand. Final algebra semantics and data type extensions. *Journal of Computer and System Sciences*, 19:27–44, 1979.

[267] M. Wand. Fixed point constructions in order-enriched categories. *Theoretical Computer Science*, 8:13–30, 1979.

[268] M. Wand. Type inference for record concatenation and multiple inheritance. In *Proceedings of the Symposium on Logic in Computer Science*, pages 92–97. IEEE, June 1989.

[269] M. Wand. Type inference for record concatenation and multiple inheritance. *Information and Computation*, 93:1–15, 1991.

[270] P. Wegner. The Vienna Definition Language. *ACM Computing Surveys*, 1:5–63, 1972.

[271] J. Welsh, W. J. Sneeringer, and C. A. R. Hoare. Ambiguities and insecurities in pascal. *Software Practice and Experience*, pages 685–696, 1977.

[272] M. Wirsing. Algebraic specification. In J. van Leeuwen, editor, *Handbook of Theoretical Computer Science*, pages 675–788. North-Holland, 1990.

[273] F. Zabeeth, E. D. Klemke, and A. Jacobson, editors. *Readings in Semantics*. University of Illinois Press, 1974.

[274] G-Q. Zhang. *Logic of Domains*. Birkhauser, 1991.

Subject Index

The MIT Press, with Peter Denning as general consulting editor, publishes computer science books in the following series:

ACL-MIT Press Series in Natural Language Processing
Aravind K. Joshi, Karen Sparck Jones, and Mark Y. Liberman, editors

ACM Doctoral Dissertation Award and Distinguished Dissertation Series

Artificial Intelligence
Patrick Winston, founding editor
J. Michael Brady, Daniel G. Bobrow, and Randall Davis, editors

Charles Babbage Institute Reprint Series for the History of Computing
Martin Campbell-Kelly, editor

Computer Systems
Herb Schwetman, editor

Explorations with Logo
E. Paul Goldenberg, editor

Foundations of Computing
Michael Garey and Albert Meyer, editors

History of Computing
I. Bernard Cohen and William Aspray, editors

Logic Programming
Ehud Shapiro, editor; Fernando Pereira, Koichi Furukawa, Jean-Louis Lassez, and David H. D. Warren, associate editors

The MIT Press Electrical Engineering and Computer Science Series

Research Monographs in Parallel and Distributed Processing
Christopher Jesshope and David Klappholz, editors

Scientific and Engineering Computation
Janusz Kowalik, editor

Technical Communication and Information Systems
Edward Barrett, editor